CW01189181

THE PETLYAKOV Pe-2

Books on Dive-Bombers and dive-bombing by Peter C. Smith

Definitive Histories

Aichi D3A1/2 Val (Crowood)
Blackburn Skua (Pen & Sword)
Curtiss SB2C Helldiver (Crowood)
Douglas SBD Dauntless (Crowood)
Douglas AD Skyraider (Crowood)
Junkers Ju.87 Stuka (Crécy Publishing)
Straight Down! – the North American A-36 dive-bomber (Crécy Publishing)
Vengeance! – the Vultee Vengeance dive-bomber (Airlife)
Dauntless in Battle (Pen & Sword)
Vengeance in Battle (Pen & Sword)

General Histories

Dive Bomber! – an illustrated history (Moorland Press)
Dive Bombers in Action (Blandford Press)
Impact! – the dive-bomber pilots speak (William Kimber)
Into the Assault – famous dive bomber aces of World War II (John Murray)
Jungle Dive Bombers at War (John Murray)
Stuka at War (Ian Allan)
Stuka Squadron; St.G.77 the Luftwaffe's Fire Brigade (PSL)

Photo Histories

Stukas over the Mediterranean (Pen & Sword)
Stukas over the Steppe (Pen & Sword)
Stuka Spearhead (Pen & Sword)

For full details, see www.dive-bombers.co.uk

THE PETLYAKOV Pe-2

STALIN'S SUCCESSFUL RED AIR FORCE LIGHT BOMBER

PETER C. SMITH

AIR WORLD

THE PETLYAKOV Pe-2
Stalin's Successful Red Air Force Light Bomber

First published in Great Britain in 2020 by
Air World
An imprint of
Pen & Sword Books Ltd
Yorkshire – Philadelphia

Copyright © Peter C. Smith, 2020

ISBN 978 1 52675 930 6

The right of Peter C. Smith to be identified as Author of this work has been asserted by him in accordance with the Copyright, Designs and Patents Act 1988.

A CIP catalogue record for this book is available from the British Library.

All rights reserved. No part of this book may be reproduced or transmitted in any form or by any means, electronic or mechanical including photocopying, recording or by any information storage and retrieval system, without permission from the Publisher in writing.

Typeset by Aura Technology and Software Services, India.
Printed and bound in England by TJ International.

Pen & Sword Books Limited incorporates the imprints of Atlas, Archaeology, Aviation, Discovery, Family History, Fiction, History, Maritime, Military, Military Classics, Politics, Select, Transport, True Crime, Air World, Frontline Publishing, Leo Cooper, Remember When, Seaforth Publishing, The Praetorian Press, Wharncliffe Local History, Wharncliffe Transport, Wharncliffe True Crime and White Owl.

For a complete list of Pen & Sword titles please contact

PEN & SWORD BOOKS LIMITED
47 Church Street, Barnsley, South Yorkshire, S70 2AS, England
E-mail: enquiries@pen-and-sword.co.uk
Website: www.pen-and-sword.co.uk

Or
PEN AND SWORD BOOKS
1950 Lawrence Rd, Havertown, PA 19083, USA
E-mail: Uspen-and-sword@casematepublishers.com
Website: www.penandswordbooks.com

Contents

Introduction		xiv
About the Author		xvi
Dedication		xvii
Acknowledgements		xviii
Chapter 1	Inspiration Imprisoned	1
	The Dive-Bomber in the Soviet Air Force	2
	Tupolev Tu-2	4
	The I-16 SPB	5
	The OKB	10
	STO=100	10
	PESHKA MEN – Vladimir Mikhailovich Petlyakov	12
Chapter 2	Many Starts, Many Endings	15
	The Perceived Threat	15
	Design commences	16
	Modifications to Proposals	17
	First Flight Problems	19
	The Second Prototype destroyed	21
	Evaluation resumed	23
	May Day Fly-past	25
	Comparison with other types	25
	Change of requirement	26
Chapter 3	*Sotka* becomes *Peshka*	28
	Dive-Bombing	28
	The PB-100	28
	Pe-2	31
	Petlyakov restored to favour	36
	Shift to Kazan	36
	The death of Petlyakov	38

	Friction at Kazan	39
	Problems with 14-11	41
	Summons from Moscow	42
	Rushed decisions	43
	Disaster	44
	Verdict	45
Chapter 4	The Pe-2 Described	47
	Structure	48
	Diving brakes	48
	Engine installation	49
	Undercarriage	50
	Armament	50
	Bomb load	52
	Entry	53
	Crew positions and duties	53
	Cockpit layout	54
	Flying the *Peshka*	56
	Taxiing	56
	Take-off	56
	Climb	56
	Level flight	56
	Diving	57
	Single-engined performance	58
	Approach and landing	58
	View	58
	Emergency exits	59
	Technical data	59
	Statistical Data	59
Chapter 5	The Pe-3 fighter variant	67
	The One-Week Wonder!	67
	The Modifications	68
	Performance, Problems and Production	70
	The Flight Testing	70
	Combat experience modifications	71
	Night Fighter	72
	The Pe-3*bis*	73
	Specification	74
	Production Changes	75

CONTENTS

	Armament	75
	Pe-3 – Production Re-started	77
	False Dawn	78
	Front-line allocation	79
	Pe-2 Tow-tugs	79
	Korolev's Rocket proposals	80
	Experimental Fighter Projects	81
	The Pe-2I (1941)	82
	Pe-2VI (1941)	83
	Pe-2VI (1942)	84
Chapter 6	First Combat	86
	Early *Peshka* operations	90
	Operation TYPHOON	97
	Formation Leaders	101
	Other winter battles	102
Chapter 7	Counter-Attack	104
	Fresh German assaults	105
	Transfer to the Arctic Theatre of War	106
	Changes of organisation	106
	Navy Pe-2s	108
	Stalingrad's air defence re-organised	110
	Spanish Pe-2 pilot	110
	Polbin's command	111
	Penal Squadrons	115
Chapter 8	New Tactics, New Defences, New Confidence	117
	Polbin's Experiments	118
	Pe-2 and -3 Operations in Norway	119
	Strengths	125
	More Actions	131
	Southern Operations	133
	Northern Fleet combat	133
	Baltic operations	134
Chapter 9	Tilting the Scales – Stalingrad to the Donets	135
	New thinking	135
	Progress on other fronts	136
	Failure of the Kharkov offensive	137
	Kuban air fighting	137

	Peshka Men – Aleksei Fedorov	139
	Radar-equipped night fighters	140
	Pe-2 Tactics	141
	Bloodletting on the Western Front	143
	Photo-reconnaissance missions	145
Chapter 10	Heroines of the Skies	147
	Bombs fall on target	150
	July 1943, Western Front. The airfield of Ezovinia Yezovnia	151
	October 1943. Leomdovo airfield (near Elna)	154
	Still October 1943, Leomidovo airfield	155
	The Right Stuff	156
	Peshka Women – Colonel Nadezhda *(Nadya)* Nikifozovna Fedutenko	159
	Women Flyers – their place in history	162
	Peshka Women – Mariya Ivanovna Dolina-Mel'Nikova	163
Chapter 11	The Fighting Finns	169
	Finnish Test Pilots' reports	171
	Cockpit arrangement	171
	Electrical Systems	172
	Take-off Procedure	175
	Flying Characteristics	177
	Finnish Test Pilots view of the Pe-2	178
	Captured Pe-2s transferred by Germany to Finland	179
	Finnish Pe-3	182
	PESHKA MEN – Captain Aimo Olavi Pietarinen, FAF	184
Chapter 12	Production Line Progression	185
	Series Modifications History	188
	Front-Line Demand	190
	Air Cushion undercarriage	193
	Retractable skis	193
	Pe-2M (1941)	194
	Pe-2*Sh*	194
	Other Modifications	194
	Pe-2 fighter	194
	In-the-Field modifications	195
	Reconnaissance	195

CONTENTS

Chapter 13	The Great Offensive – June 1944	197
	The Campaign in White Russia	197
	The Bobruysk Cauldron	201
	Ukrainian Front	203
	Peshka Men: Abdiraim Izmailovich Reshidov	203
	Further actions	209
Chapter 14	On to Berlin!	211
	North Prussian Operations	212
	Peshka Men – Major General Ivan Semyonovich Polbin	215
	The fall of Berlin	222
Chapter 15	Action in the Far East	225
	Operation AUGUST STORM	225
	Ship Targets	228
	Soviet Navy Pe-2 missions	229
	Peshka Men – Major General Pavel Artem'evich Plotnikov	230
Chapter 16	Variations on a Theme	232
	Pe-2F	232
	Speed as defence	233
	Re-design and Mock-up	234
	Resumption of development	235
	Disappointing Results	236
	Pe-2D	237
	The saga of the M-107A	238
	NKAP alternatives	239
	19-78	240
	16-163	240
	2-187	240
	19-205	240
	The 'August Programme' of 1943	241
	The Pe-2A	242
	The Pe-2B	242
	Delays, delays and yet more delays	243
	The Pe-2V	245
	The Pe-4	245
	Radial-engined *Peshka*	245
	The Experimental 19-31	247
	Air trials	248
	Limited Production	250

	Combat Evaluation	251
	End of the Experiment	252
	The Pe-4A	252
	Pe-2VI. (1943)	252
	Pe-2 No. 19/223	253
	Pe-2 No. 14/226	253
	Pe-4 (1944)	256
	Pe-2R	257
	Pe-2P	257
	Pe-2K	257
	Pe-2 *Paravan*	257
	Rocket-powered *Peshka*	258
	Prototype 15-185 Built	259
	Propulsion method	260
	The trials	260
	Double-rocket proposal for the Pe-3 fighter	261
	Results	262
	RATOG	263
	Ejector-seat trials	263
	Pe-2 UT (UPe-2)	264
Chapter 17	Pe-2 Colour Schemes	265
	The Background	265
	The Reality	268
	The Scheme of Aircraft Camouflage Finishes – July 1943	269
	Interiors and Components	271
Chapter 18	The Final Developments	272
	Pe-2I	272
	Myasishchev's compromise – the Pe-2I	274
	The engine problem	275
	Armament	276
	Re-design	277
	Selyakov's memoirs	279
	Official vetting	279
	First air trials	279
	Second prototype	280
	Trials resumed	281
	Air-to-air combat simulation	283
	Conflicting Priorities	284

CONTENTS

	The Plans … and the Reality!	284
	Solutions … and yet more Problems	286
	Special Armament Recommendations	286
	Jet-propelled *Peshka*?	288
	The Pe-2M (1945)	288
	The Prototype	289
	The evaluation programme	289
	Termination	290
	DB-108	290
	Delays and Interruptions	291
	Disaster!	291
	DB-108 abandoned	292
	New long-ranger fighter and high-altitude bomber concepts	293
	The DIS (12) escort fighter	293
	The VB-109 high-altitude bomber	294
	PESHKA MEN – Vladimir Mikhailovich Myasishchev	298
Chapter 19	The *Peshka* in Foreign Service	301
	Polish *Peshkas*	301
	Bulgaria	306
	Czechoslovakia	307
	Hungary	311
	Yugoslavia	312
	France	314
	Red China	314
Chapter 20	The Survivors	315
	Russia	315
	Bulgaria	317
	Poland	317
	Yugoslavia	318
	Norway	318
	Preserved *Peshka* at Morino Air Museum	320
	Hungarian Site Reclamation Project	321
Appendix 1	Pe-2 Units	323
	Abbreviations	323
	Air Armies	324
	Bomber Aviation Army	325
	Bomber Air Corps (BAC)	325

		Bomber Air Division (BAD)	326
		Bomber Air Regiments (BAR)	328
		Long-Range Reconnaissance Regiments (DRAP)	342
		Reconnaissance Regiments (RAP)	343
		Naval Aviation units	344
		Polish Air Force	345
Appendix 2		Pe-2 Unit Commanders	347
Appendix 3		Pe-2 Pilot Biographies	354
Appendix 4		Glossary	410
Appendix 5		Some Pe-2 Aces	417
Appendix 6		Further reading	418
Notes			419

Map:

1	The Western Soviet Union 1941-45	46

Diagrams:

1:	Pe-2 General Layout	47
2:	Pe-2 Disposition of Gun Armament	50
3:	Pe-2 Disposition of fuel tanks and external bomb load	52
4:	Pe-2 Layout/Location of Fuel & Hydraulic fluid distribution	63
5:	Pe-2 Pilots control stick and transmission layout	60
6:	Pe-2 Undercarriage arrangements	62
7:	Pe-2 Electric Motor distribution and detail	64
8:	Pe-2 Engine-cooling system	65
9:	Pe-2 Hydraulic system	53
10:	Pe-2 Composition of Wing	61
11:	Pe-2 Wing Flaps and Access	57
12:	Pe-2 Remote control *Mozharovsky & Venevidov* (MN) mounting	66
13:	Pe-2 *Frontovoe Zadani* (FZ) mounting	66
14:	Belgorod-Kharkov battles -2nd Pe-2 attack 3 August 1943	238
15:	Belgorod-Kharkov battles - 3rd Phase Pe-2 attacks	238
16:	Belgorod-Kharkov Battles – 1st Pe-2 attack 3rd August 1943	144

CONTENTS

Tables:

1:	Development of the Pe-3	80
2:	Pe-2s in Service on 1 June 1941	90
3:	Northern Fleet *Peshka* strength July-December 1942	126
4:	Soviet Northern Fleet Pe-2 & Pe-3 Combat Sorties 1942-43	126
5:	Outstanding Women Pe-2 Pilots	150
6:	*Peshka* Data	165
7:	*Peshka* Strengths at various dates during the Second World War	167
8:	*Peshka* Supply at various dates in the Second World War	168
9:	*Peshka* Losses during the Second World War	168
10:	Finnish Pe-2s	179
11:	Production Figure Comparisons for *Peshka* by Plants	195
12:	Soviet Air Force units, Far Eastern Front, July 1945	227
13:	Comparisons of Proposed types, Pe2I/Pe-2M/DB-108/VB-109	296
14:	Polish Pe-2 allocations 1 May 1945	303
15:	Soviet serials of Pe-2s allocated to Polish Pe-2 units	304
16:	Soviet serials of UP-2s allocated to Polish UPe-2 units	304
17:	Pe-2/UP-2 Strength in Polish service	305
18:	Total numbers of Pe-2/UP-2 in Polish units	305
19:	25 Bomber Regiment, Czechoslovakian Air Force, Pe-2 serials	309

Introduction

The Petlyakov Pe-2, or *Peshka* (Chess pawn), was the principal Soviet dive- and light-bomber of the Second World War, and continued in service until the early 1950s with Warsaw Pact nations' air forces and Yugoslavia. Conceived by a team of top aircraft designers that Stalin had incarcerated in a prison camp on trumped-up political charges, the concept had originally been for a high-altitude, twin-engined fighter aircraft, but, due to circumstances, was quickly converted into a high-speed dive-bomber just in time for the Great Patriotic War.

Of twin-engined design, sleek, innovative and incorporating many radical features, new even to the West at that time, the Pe-2 proved to be as fast, or faster, than even the German Bf.109F fighter. The RAF had earlier announced this could not be done, but the Soviets did it, and did it convincingly, more than 11,000 of the type, including many variants, being built up to 1945. Although only a handful had reached front-line units by June 1941 when hostilities commenced with Germany, they soon became the main front-line dive-bomber in both VVS and Navy service. Mass production from factories hastily moved back from the front line, beyond the Urals, rapidly increased numbers and the Pe-2 became the mainstay of the Soviet counter-offensive that resulted in the fall of Berlin and also took part in the brief war against Japan in 1945.

Many of the most renowned Soviet bomber aces flew the *Peshka* in combat, new tactics were devised from the experience of war and new skills were honed in this outstanding aircraft. The biographies of both designers and dive-bomber aces are covered fully in this book, as well as in-depth descriptions of the design, construction, offensive and defensive armaments, combat records, colour schemes and the many variants that sprang from this design. Numerous tables cover production, combat losses, unit and mission details, commanding officers and other facets of the Pe-2. The only female dive-bomber unit of the Second World War is also featured.

Sections include both foreign nations' air forces uses of the *Peshka*, including wartime use of captured Pe-2s by the Finnish air force and the proposed French units. The complete post-war details of Bulgarian, Czechoslovakian, Hungarian, Polish and Yugoslavian usage also feature. The known preserved survivors are described in depth, along with the numerous re-construction projects currently underway in Finland, Norway and Hungary.

INTRODUCTION

Using official sources, including the official Pe-2 handbook, and numerous photographs made available to the author from official and private sources and collections, including both internal and external detailed views, diagrams and drawings, contemporary and historic, this book is the definitive record of the Pe-2 – dive-bomber supreme!

Ray Wagner, the highly-respected historian and former curator at the San Diego Aerospace Museum wrote that 'This is the best history of a Russian bomber in the English language that I have ever read.'

Long out of print, the original volume has commanded enormous prices on the second-hand book market but, thankfully, this new edition not only brings my book back into the range of most enthusiasts, it also enables me to update some of the data, make some corrections, and add new material including photographs and diagrams.

© Peter C. Smith, 2020

About the Author

Peter C. Smith was born in Norfolk, UK, in 1940. After living in London, Kent and Cambridge, he has resided in the small Bedfordshire village of Riseley since 1982. Peter has been both a book and a magazine editor for Colourmaster, Balfour Books, *Cape Sun* and *World War II Investigator* as well as Publications Co-ordinator for the RSPB.

Peter has been researching and writing books for more than five decades and his books have been published all over the world including Australia, China, Czech Republic, Germany, Italy, Japan, Malta, Russia, Sweden and the United States. In addition he has published a novel, many short stories and articles, contributes reviews to various specialist publications, and is a consultant on TV documentaries. Many of his works are considered to be the definitive publications on their subjects, which include aviation and maritime history. Peter also writes on English heritage including London and Thames bridges, and London ceremonies and traditions.

Peter is a member of the Society of Authors, London, and the Paternosters Society, London. When not researching, interviewing and writing, he and his wife, Pat, now divide their time between world and UK travel and walking. Details of all his books are on his web-site at *www.dive-bombers.co.uk*.

Dedication

To
George Mellinger & Nigel Eastaway

'With proper handling a Pawn advances to become a Queen.'

(Aleksei Fedorov)

Black Raven, Black Raven –
Why are you circling above me?
You will not get any luck, Black Raven.
I am young and not yet ready to die.

(Soviet dive-bomber crews' lament)

Acknowledgements

This book owes its completion to a great many very kind and generous people, mainly in Russia, but also in Poland, the Czech Republic, Slovakia, Croatia, England, France, Hungary, Finland, Switzerland, Canada and the United States. Experts in their field and with wide knowledge, they have unstintingly shared their information with me and been generous in their support of this difficult project. Having no Russian myself, I relied heavily on the generosity of my Russian friends for translation and explanations, but I would like to record here that any errors or mistakes in such interpretation are my own.

I give sincere and heartfelt thanks then to the following kind people:

In Russia – Victor Kulikov, Moscow; Andrei Alexandrov, St Petersburg; M. Maslov, Moscow; Yefim Gordon, Moscow; Gennadii F. Petrov, St Petersburg; Roman Larincew, Severodwinsk Arkhangelskaja Oblast; Dr Mikhail N. Souproun, Pomor State University, Faculty of History, Arkhangelsk; Vladimir A. Petrov, St Petersburg; Alex G. Bolnykh, Ekaterinburgh. *In Poland* – Robert Michulec, Gdynia; Piotr Butowski, Gdansk; Jarostaw Waligora, Rzeszow; Zbigniew Lalak, Warsaw; Mirek Wawrzynski, Pultusk; acknowledgements to the memory of the late Jan Krumbach for some fine photographs. *In the Czech Republic* – Martin Ferkl of Nová Paka for details of the Czech *Peshkas*; Milan Krajci for much information and photographs of the Czech Pe-2s; Stanislav Štepánek; Ladislav Hladik. *In Croatia* – Eng. Danijel Frka, Kraljevica; Boris Kolka, Zagreb. *In Finland* – Carl-Frederick Geust, Masala; Hannu Valtonen, Director of the Finnish Air Force Museum, Tikkakoski; Linda Knudsen, Defense Training Development Centre, Photographical Section, Helsinki; Pentti Manninen BA (Hist.), Finnish Aviation Historical Magazine, Helsinki. *In Norway* – Birger Larsen; special thanks to Major Ulf Larsstuvold, Bodø; Rune Rautio, Kirkenes; *In Serbia* – M.S. Ostric; M.B. Ciglic. *In Slovakia* – Milan Krajci: Jiri Rajlich. *In Switzerland* – M. Hans-Heiri Stapfer, Horgen. *In Germany* – Mario Isack, Am Dielenberg; Dr Zvonimir Freivogel, Coburg; Rene Greger; *In Yugoslavia:* Mr Zdenko Kinjerovac, Zagreb; Cedomir Janic; Henrik Krog; M. Bosanac. *In France* – Herbert Léonard, Barbizon. *In Hungary* – George Punka; Legrady Lajos; Ferenc Toth. *In Canada* – Dénes Bernád. *In the USA* – Erik Pilawski; George Mellinger, Richard S. Dann, Friendswood, Texas; Ray Wagner, San Diego Aerospace Museum, CA; James T. Parker II, Archival Research International, Woodbine, MD. *In England* – Nigel Eastaway, Takeley; Ian Carter, Photographic Archives, Imperial War Museum,

ACKNOWLEDGEMENTS

London; Stephen Walton, Archivist, Microfilm Records, Imperial War Museum, London: G. Clout, Department of Printed Books, Imperial War Museum, London; Simon Watson, The Aviation Bookshop, London; Angela M. Wootton, Department of Printed Books, Imperial War Museum, London; Ralph Gibson, Novosti Press Agency, London; The ever-helpful and reliable staff at Bedford Central Library, for obtaining for me direct from Moscow many rare Soviet books, including, in one case, the *only* existing known copy of Polbin's biography! Ivan Dzydzora, Bedford, for translation of many papers.

Peter C. Smith, February 2020.
Riseley, Bedfordshire, UK

Chapter One

Inspiration Imprisoned

To most people in the West who have been fortunate enough not to know at first-hand what it is like to live under a true dictatorship, it will appear incredible that one of a nation's leading aircraft designers, was, on the eve of the greatest and most bitter war in that country's history, callously incarcerated in a prison camp by his paranoid and demonic leader. Unfortunately for many thousands of perfectly innocent and dedicated Soviet citizens, this was standard treatment from Marshal Josef Stalin, probably the most evil and ruthless person thrown up by the twentieth century, in an age when such monsters have become commonplace and where contempt for human rights, indeed for human life, is almost routine. Even this nightmare existence was more than the fate suffered by millions more of the Russian people during those terrible years of misrule.[1]

Nonetheless, incredible or not, the man who designed one of the most successful, and certainly one of the fastest, dive-bombers of the Second World War, an aircraft that played a major part in 'The Great Patriotic War' and which continued to serve in the front line for the first post-war years of the 'Cold War' that followed, did much of his work behind barbed wire, and did it well enough to have his (totally unjustified) incarceration commuted just before his tragic death.

Vladimir Mikhailovich Petlyakov was a great Russian aircraft designer, and his work went back many years, but the *Peshka (*Chess Pawn*)* proved to be his masterpiece.[2] With this sleek and aerodynamically excellent twin-engined aircraft, he, without any previous experience in this field, proved that a dive-bomber did not have to be a slow aeroplane, and that precision bombing could be carried out without sacrificing speed and styling. This, unfortunately, was in direct opposition to the line that RAF experts had been stating for the previous ten years so that, when, later, British Hawker Hurricane fighters based in North Russia during the war, told of their great difficulty in keeping up with the Pe-2s they were supposed to be escorting,[3] there was disbelief at the Air Ministry. Reporting of the Pe-2's great success and magnificent war record was deliberately played down and muted in Britain, the emphasis being always on the exploits of the Ilyushin IL-2 *Shturmovik*, whose low-level methods were more in harmony with acceptable British practice. In fact, despite detailed reports on the *Peshka* by serving RAF officers being sent to Whitehall, the Air Ministry stated publicly that they had 'no information to indicate that its contribution is in any way outstanding'.[4]

THE PETLYAKOV Pe-2

The Dive-Bomber in the Soviet Air Force

The Soviet Air Force (*Voenno-vozdushnye sili* or VVS) came late to the dive-bomber, their name for which was *Pikiruyushchi Bombardirovochny*. Although communist 'historians' claimed that their nation invented everything from the tank to the jet engine, there was little or no interest in this form of attack until the late 1930s. The British had used dive bombing in actual combat as early as March 1918, and the American Air Force had experimented with it between 1919 and 1921 and the French Navy in 1920-21; the main exponents had become the United States Navy and Marine Corps, the German Luftwaffe and the Japanese Navy in the period 1925-35.[5]

The earliest Soviet experimentation with the dive-bomber type was the production of the VIT-1 and VIT-2 aircraft, experimental machines that were built and tested in the period 1933-38.[6] However, the chief thrust of their light bomber design in this period culminated in the twin-engined Tupolev SB.[7] Of standard construction, this did not fare so well in the pre-war clashes between the Soviet Union and the Japanese, during the July/August, 1938, clash at Lake Khasan, and the even more intense Nomonhan incident that began on 11 May 1939 and did not finally fade out until 16 September. Losses had been heavy and accuracy in bombing indifferent and plans were put in hand to produce a dive-bomber variant of the SB, following demands for such an aircraft from Stalin himself in 1939. This became the SB-RK, (also known as the Arkhangel'skii Ar-2 as A.A. Arkhangel'skii, who was Tupolev's young deputy, worked on the project), dive-bomber. The conversion took place during 1940-41 and was extremely basic; it was only intended as an

The pre-war scenario of Soviet battle tactics, with low-flying ground-attack biplanes supporting a tank advance. This was advanced thinking before Stalin's purges of the High Command turned the clock back. (Soviet Official)

INSPIRATION IMPRISONED

interim solution until proper dive-bombers could be designed from the ground up. Some 210 standard three-seater SBs, powered by the M105R engine, were fitted with dive brakes. They did not perform outstandingly in their new rôle, partly because the aircraft themselves were not designed for the job, and partly because only the haziest concepts of what dive-bombing involved were taught to their aircrews.

This latter was to be a recurring problem with all air forces that adopted dive-bombers or dive-bombing late, no matter what the merits of their aircraft. Thus the US Navy used the Douglas SBD Dauntless to enormous effect in the Pacific War, but the US Army Air Forces failed to do the same with their version of the same aircraft, the A-24 Banshee.[8] The highly-successful North American A-36A Apache dive-bomber was later used by the USAAF, but the correct and best way to use them had to be learnt the hard way, during actual combat, as teaching of the subject itself was rudimentary and, indeed, at first resulted in orders to wire their dive brakes shut. This order was very soon reversed when the aircraft got into action, but it reflected the same attitude and outlook.[9] Similarly the RAF squadrons that later used the Vultee A-36 Vengeance to such good effect at Kohima and Imphal during the Burma campaign, equally had to start almost from scratch in devising their own dive-bombing techniques, such had been the opposition to any use of such an obvious Army support weapon and method by the Air Ministry.[10]

Therefore, the SB-RK, although used during the early stages of the war with Germany in 1941-42, was *not* a success and no more SBs were produced. There were also problems with production and maintenance of the type. Other options were tried. Stalin put pressure on Andrei Nikolaevich Tupolev, the doyen of Soviet aircraft designers, but himself also imprisoned, to come up with a brand-new dive-bomber. This concept hoped to combine both dive-bombing and horizontal bombing capability in one twin-engined, three-crew monoplane that would have

The twin-engine Arkhangel'skii SB-RK (Ar-2) late 1930s fast bomber. Two hundred of these were fitted with dive-brakes in an attempt to turn them into dive-bombers, but this experiment was not a success. (Soviet Official)

a speed equal to front-line fighter aircraft, the Samolet-103. Tupolev's team of designers (also incarcerated in the TsKB-20 'Special Prison') came up with an aircraft that bore much superficial resemblance to the Pe-2, whose initial designation was the ANT-58.[11] Impetus to come up with a successful dive-bomber was given by practical demonstrations of their effectiveness taking place at the other end of Europe at this time.

With the advent of the Spanish Civil War (1936-39) there was considerable involvement by many of the great military powers. While Britain and France declared a policy of strict neutrality and 'Non-Intervention' the Germans and Italians were eager to support General Franco's Nationalist armies, while the Soviet Union was equally determined to back the Republican cause, increasingly dominated by the communists and fellow-travellers as it was. As the fighting spread, this support led to a more and more active involvement of their own forces, with the German 'Legion Kondor' using the war as a kind of combat dress rehearsal for their newly created Luftwaffe, and the Soviets trying out their latest aircraft designs also. Both sides learned valuable lessons, not only about the qualities and limitations of their own aircraft, but also of the potential of their most likely opponents' aircraft as well. One lesson the Soviet Air Force took on board from this involvement was the accuracy and potential of the dive-bomber, as ably demonstrated by the Junkers Ju. 87A and B models in this conflict.[12]

Tupolev Tu-2

So Tupolev's new design was eagerly awaited. Powered by two Mikulin AM-37 twelve-cylinder liquid-cooled engines, which developed 1,400hp and fitted with three-bladed variable-pitch propellers, this twin-tailed mid-wing cantilever monoplane, the ANT-58, could carry a crew of three, pilot, navigator/bomb-aimer and radio operator/gunner, along with 1,000kg (2,204lb) of internally carried bombs and a further 2,000kg (4,409lb) externally under the wings at speeds of up to 395mph (635km/h). Slatted, electrically-operated dive brakes were to be fitted on production models, beneath the outer wing panels.[13] This more than met the specification asked of it, and the first flight took place on 29 January 1941, with test pilot M.P. Vasyakin at the helm. Alterations in internal layout and crew accommodation were required, and the engines were far from reliable. This led to a considerable delay before the second prototype took to the air in May 1941, just a few weeks before the German invasion.

The type was progressively modified and improved with better (radial) engines and propellers, and finally entered service as the Tu-2 with three pre-production aircraft, in September 1942, but a full production model, the Tu-2S (S = *Seriinyi* – Series), did not join frontline combat squadrons until early 1944, and then was only very rarely employed for dive-bombing. This was, in part, due to its size, but also because the shift of the factories manufacturing it called for a great reduction in complexity of construction to get them into service and the dive brakes were among many features generally sacrificed. One unique variant appeared as late as 1947 in the dive-bomber configuration; this was the UTB-2P (P = *Pikiruyushchi*). The UTB was the Sukhoi-designed training version with two Ash-21 engines. This particular machine was fitted with 'Venetian Blind' type slatted dive brakes on the underside of the wings outboard of the engine nacelles but was only used for experimental purposes.

The I-16 SPB

A rather more bizarre approach to the dive-bomber solution was made by Vladimir S. Vakhmistrov, from the Soviet *Nauchno-ispytatel'ny* (Scientific Test Institute). As long ago as 1932, he had envisaged long-range heavy bombers toting into battle their very own defending fighters, which would be slung below them on underwing cradles. (The Americans were trying the same thing with fighters cradled beneath airships at this time.) Although this brainwave eventually came to naught, the idea was modified to give the normally short-range dive-bomber the extended range needed to hit distant targets, but with the dive-bomber's accuracy.

This concept was the I-16 SPB (*Skorostnyi Pikiruyushchii Bombardirovshcik*, or Fast Dive Bomber). The first suggestion for such an aircraft, based on work on the *Aviamatka PVO* (*Protivovozdushnaya Oborona* – Protective Air Defence Mother Plane, or AMPVO concept), was made on 14 August 1936.[14]

The actual dive bombers themselves were again conversions, this time from the standard Polikarpov I-16 *Ishak* (Donkey), a stubby little, radial-engined monoplane, which had seen combat in Spain but was by now outclassed in the air in its intended rôle. Two of these fighters had their main offensive armament of two cannon removed to save weight, and retained only a pair of machine guns for their own limited self-defence. They could carry a 550lb (250kg) FAB-550 (*Fugsasnaya AviaBomba*, or demolition bomb) bomb under each wing in their new configuration. This increased each fighter's payload by half-a-ton. They featured reinforced wing-spars for strength, reinforced ribs in the wing joints which carried overwing suspension spindles and underwing bomb racks. An extra fuel tank, to feed oil to the dive-bombers from the mother ship, was also a new feature.

The Soviet method was to carry out a very steep diving attack, 80 degrees, which was defined by the position of the edge of the cockpit top. The new aircraft proved very stable in such a dive, and reached a sustained dive speed of 403mph (650km/h). Recovery from the dive was at 6,500 feet (2000m) at 4G load, and did not exceed 2,000 feet (600m) with 6G. The target was shaped like a battleship and by the end of the range-bombing trials high accuracy was being achieved, with 'a staggering compactness of bomb hits – with sometimes less than 10ft (3 m) between them'.[15]

Despite these good results the political situation saw the suspension of further trials until 1939 when the first of twenty Z-SPBs, as the new Zveno composite mother plane and parasite were designated, started to join both the Air Force and the Navy. But the type aroused little enthusiasm in the upper command of the Air Force, they having already decided to switch to the more orthodox dive-bomber type.

THE PETLYAKOV Pe-2

Among the more unusual solutions to the dive-bomber requirement was the 'piggy-back' concept, by which a pair of adapted I-16 *Rata* fighters, converted to carry bombs, were carried to the target area slung below the wings of a long-range TB-3 bomber. The idea actually saw full combat deployment for a brief period over the Black Sea area. (Novosti Press Agency, London)

The actual carrier, the aircraft adapted to hoist a pair of these little dive-bombers under her own massive wings, was the giant Tupolev TB-3 bomber. This had great lifting power and a good range, although thus burdened was a sitting duck for any interceptor, so the idea was to use them at night. These aircraft had already been modified to carry two of the proposed specially adapted I-ZW as the Z-6 (*Zveno*) with a combination of pylon and trapeze under either massive wing. To give them added power to carry two of the new dive-bomber types the latest variant, fitted with the Mikulin AM-34FRN engine, was proposed.

The idea was for the TB-3 to haul its cargo to within striking distance of the target, release them and then turn back. Meantime the I-16 SPBs, having dropped free with engines running, would conduct the actual precision dive-bombing attack under their own power, before using their full fuel tanks to regain friendly territory.

Although the idea was scoffed at by some, and abandoned by the Air Force Command in June 1940, nonetheless it was actually carried out, with a total of twelve I-16SPBs and six parent TB-3s duly altered, all such Z-SPB conversions being delivered by Plant No. 207 that same June. Deliveries continued until late 1940 when all further production was terminated.

However, the Navy Air Command had a more enthusiastic viewpoint. The Deputy Commander, Major General G.F. Korobkov, and the chief of the Experimental

INSPIRATION IMPRISONED

Aircraft Manufacturing Board, Colonel J.K. Nikitenko, had a different philosophy. They reasoned the Navy would not receive even the first of the new land-based Pe-2 dive-bombers until 1941, and even then much training would be required to master the technique and the type. By contrast, the I-16SPB could be mastered by pilots in two weeks and would be immediately ready for combat. So, in effect, the Navy took over the project, financially and operationally, from that point.

The Junkers Ju.87 was daily proving what an effective anti-shipping weapon the dive-bomber was, and the proposed new versions of Vakhmistrov's I-16SPB would, if produced, be capable of carrying the BRAB-500 bomb of 1,100lb (500kg), which would be sufficient to inflict massive damage on all types of enemy warships. Even these plans were threatened when Admiral N.G. Kuznetsov, the Navy People's Commissar Minister of the Navy, issued Order No. 00155, which brought about the immediate cessation of experimental work by Vakhmistorv on the Zvenso/TB-3 concept. This stopped even flight testing of the I-16-SPB-BRAB-500.

Despite this, the idea somehow survived. The first composite was accepted into the NII-VVS by a group of flight and technical personnel detached from 32 FAR in August 1940. They ferried it to Evpatoria along with spare equipment for more conversions and thus 'Special Mission Squadron SPB' came, almost clandestinely, into being. Under the command of Major Evgeniy Razinko, this unit's true function remained unknown to its higher commanders, and even to Razinko himself, until the TB-3 arrived with her two 'parasite' aircraft. They were piloted respectively by Captain Vladimir Razumov, Lieutenant Boris Litvinchuk and Lieutenant Evgraf Ryzhov, to become the kernel of the Baltic force. More composite teams arrived in September and in November 1940, intended for the Black Sea and Pacific Fleets. However, the sum total of just four TB-3 aircrew and eight I-16-SPB pilots were all that finally arrived and they formed a unique unit.

The 92nd Fighter Regiment had trained sufficient pilots in the techniques and methods involved. The 92nd was based at Evpatoria air base in the Crimea and much training and flight evaluation was done, which proved that the idea was practical. Optimum range for these unique teams was 730 miles, a range at which no dive-bomber would be expected to operate and thus surprise could be achieved which might minimise the inherent risks involved.

The composites did not arouse much enthusiasm from the Baltic Sea Fleet Air Force under General V. Rusakov but, after appraisal tests conducted by Arseniy Shubikov, a demonstration of the accuracy and deadliness of the Zveno-SPB was arranged during which they performed the singular feat of not only hitting, but sinking the 'unsinkable' floating target at their first attempt. Naval gunnery had repeatedly failed to destroy this barge packed with logs, but two direct hits from the four FAB-250s delivered in a dive-bombing attack reduced it to 'firewood'. Impressed, further trials were conducted using a high-speed, radio-controlled motor torpedo boat as a moving target.

In spring 1941 the Navy's special unit was, in the event of conflict with their German ally, assigned to the task of attacking the main Romanian naval base at Constantza where an Axis military build-up had already been observed to be taking place. They were given facilities by the Army's 96th Detached Squadron, which was based at Ismail, near the river Danube, under the command of Major General Alexander Korobitsyn. When war broke out on 21 June the regimental commander, far from showing eagerness to use this specialised team, re-iterated the earlier order No. 000148, that the Special Squadron was to be de-activated immediately. Only the personal intervention of Arseniy Shubikov, at great personal risk, prevented the Army technicians from carrying out this order and the composites were left intact. In mid-July Shubikov took his plea to Army Commissar I.V. Rogov, the Navy's second-in-command. The latter, desperate for some way of halting the onrushing German hordes, asked him if his aircraft could strike at Chernavoda rail bridge, which also carried below it, the oil pipeline between the oilfields of Ploesti and Constantza, on which the invaders' fuel supplies depended. Repeated attacks by orthodox bombers had failed to hit this vital target, let alone destroy it.

Based at Evpatoria in the Crimea, the optimum range for these unique teams was 730 miles, a range at which no conventional dive-bomber would be expected to operate, and thus surprise could be achieved which might minimise the inherent risks involved. A precision strike could inflict a major blow to the Axis war effort in the east, but without fear of encountering too much in the way of aerial or anti-aircraft defences. With the co-opting of Romania into the Axis camp, this bridge was the ideal target. Vakhmistrov, himself specially released from prison, had flown down to Evpatoria, to personally oversee the operations and ensure the best use of his unique force. It was decided that this target met all the required criteria for a first mission.

And thus it was that, on 1 August 1941 (or 26 July, sources vary), the first attack was made on Constanza. Four I-16SPBs, piloted by Shubiokov, Filimonov, Litvnichuk and Samartsev, hit the oil tanks in vertical dives from 6,500 feet (2,000m), releasing their bombs at 2,600 feet (800m). Despite interception attempts by two Bf109s, all four made it back to base at Odessa, although one ran out fuel and had to crashland.[16]

This first raid was followed up on 10 August by a second combat mission, this time mounted against the strategically vital bridge across the Danube at Chernovoda as discussed earlier. Two TB-3s took off and their four SPBs, under the overall command of Captain A. Shubikov, and with Litvinchuk, Filimonov and Kaparov once more, made a night approach followed by a dawn attack. They were followed by six Pe-2s of the 40th BAR, commanded by Captain A.P. Tsurtsumiya, (shortly afterward to be posthumously awarded HSU) each also carrying two FAB-250 bombs, which had taken off from Odessa. Despite claims of three direct hits on the bridge, as well as on the trestles and refinery, the bridge still stood the next morning. Claims in the Soviet press that the target had been destroyed aroused Stalin's ire when they were found to be untrue and so a follow-up attack was launched on 13 August.

This time six of the dive-bombers took part, departing at 0330 in three flights, with the pilots of the composites being respectively (a) Gavrilov, Shubikov and Kasparov, (b) Ognev, Filimonov and Danilin, and (c) Trushin, Skrypnick and Kuzemenko. They flew from Evpatoria to Chernavoda, bombed and returned to Odessa, an all-round flight of 725 kilometres. They scored five direct hits on the bridge and two near misses. All returned safely from the mission. After photographic analysis of the target had been examined it was claimed that the dive-bombers had demolished a 15-yard section of the bridge, together with the equally vital oil pipeline which ran across it and supplied the frontline Axis armies.

With this success behind them, the TB-3/I-16 SPB 'piggy-back' combination was thrown against further such targets, notably the Ploesti oil refineries (attacked at such cost in losses to the bombers of the USAAF later in the war) and Axis supply ships unloading war materials in the docks at Constanza, one freighter being claimed as hit and sunk as a result of an attack on 17 August by two composites. On the latter mission two of the I-16SPBs, piloted by Skrypnik and Kuzmenko, were intercepted by German fighter aircraft from III/JG52, some twenty-four miles (40km) offshore north-east of Constanza, and destroyed.[17]

The German war machine was rolling remorselessly eastward in the greatest *Blitzkreig* of all time and, in September 1941, they had just about wiped out most of the Soviet southern armies in the Uman Pocket. In desperation, on 20 August, SPB dive-bombing attacks were made on the Dnieper rail bridges, another essential supply artery that was keeping the Wehmarcht supplied with fuel, ammunition and men with which to keep up the headlong momentum of the battle. Four pilots took part in the actual dive-bombing attack, Shubikov, Litvinchuk, Filimonov and Kaparov, and they dropped eight FAB-250 bombs, scoring five direct hits. Unfortunately, these bombs proved not powerful enough to do the job, for the bridge was a two-tier one, with the vital rail track on the upper part, and a road bridge on the lower. The latter part of this combination survived the demolition of the top part, and continued to function. Nonetheless the rail link was severed and not restored until autumn 1943. This led to all such traffic having to pass through the one remaining bottleneck of Dnepropetrovsk, a fact which the German General Erich von Manstein considered to be one of the main reasons for the Stalingrad disaster in 1942.[18] Thus did six small dive-bombers have enormous strategical impact on the whole course of the war on the Eastern Front.

Despite all the dire predictions, only two of the SPBs had been lost in all these attacks. However, this relative immunity did not last much longer. When the German army reached the critical Perekop Isthmus, the narrow strip of land that guarded the Crimea and the approaches to the fortress of Sevastopol, caution was thrown to the wind and the remaining four dive-bombers were committed totally in an attempt to stem the enemy advance. Losses were subsequently severe, Isaac Kasparov, Arseniy Shubikov and Boris Filimonov all being killed during this period. After this the few surviving TB-3s were withdrawn to airfields in the Caucasus to resume their normal long-range bombing activities, while the two or three surviving SPBs were likewise re-converted to fighters and expended in the defence of Sevastopol the following year, two of them being captured intact by the advancing German army.[19] Both remaining SPB pilots, Pavel Danilin and Alexander Samartsev, survived the war.

Thus, after twenty-nine combat sorties ended a unique experiment, but it did not solve the Soviet Union's need for their own fast and accurate dive-bomber.[20] All, then, rested upon Petlyakov and his team, by now transferred to the infamous Menzhinskii Factory No. 39, which, in 1941, had been evacuated to Kazan, on the Volga, hundreds of miles to the east of Moscow, and, it was hoped, far beyond the reach of the German army.

The OKB

Some background detail is required in order to fully understand the origins of the military aircraft design rationale of the Soviet Union prior to the outbreak of what they termed The Great Patriotic War.[21]

STO=100

The appointment of Vladimir Petlyakov to the post of Designer General at the *Zavod opytnil konstruktsii*, (ZOK – Experimental Design Plant) on 23 July 1937 had appeared to mark another high point in his career, a career that had commenced with his graduation, in 1920, from the Moscow Higher Technical School where he had studied under N.E. Zhukovskii. The latter had established, with the blessing of Lenin, the *Tsentral'nyy aero-gidrodinamicheskiy institut*, TsAGI (Central Institute for Aerodynamics and Hydrodynamics) two years earlier and, in 1919, had founded the Engineers' School for the Red Air Fleet, which later bore his name as the Zhukovskiy Military Air Academy.

In July 1936 the TsAGI underwent re-organisation. The entire *Osobyknh Konstruktorskoe Byuro* (OKB – Special Design Bureau) became fragmented and a whole series of special design teams split away, some devoted to specific aircraft projects like the A.A. Arkhangel'sky KB devoted to the SB, and the P.O. Sukhoi KB concerned with the ANT-51 and BB-1 (Su-2) project.

Formerly an integral part of this organisation, the experimental aircraft construction division was also split from it and became the autonomous Experimental Aircraft Works (ZOK). V.M. Petlyakov was appointed as chief of the design office and a first deputy director. His team consisted of P.O. Sukhoi, as deputy design office chief, I.F. Nezval as deputy design office chief for land-based aircraft, N.S. Nyekrasov and A.P. Golubkov, deputy design office chief for maritime aircraft, and A.M. Izakso, deputy chief for rotorcraft design.

Under the aegis of this appointment, Petlyakov built a strong team, which designed, among others, the TB-7 heavy bomber, later the Pe-8. This failed to save him from the fate that Stalin meted out to more than 450 of Russia's top designers and aircraft engineers. They were arrested on trumped-up and imaginary charges of being 'enemies of the people' by the *Narodnij Komissariat Vnutrennik Del*, NKVD

INSPIRATION IMPRISONED

(People's Commissariat for Internal Affairs) between 1936 and 1940, leaving just a rump of 300 or so who were forced to work in design bureaux closely scrutinised by the political police. The same wholesale purges also decimated the ranks of the VVS with equal intensity, the Soviet Air Force losing all its top commanders, Ya.I. Alksnis, Ya.V. Smushkevich and V.V. Khripin being summarily executed along with such talented experts on aerial matters as A.N. Lapchinskiy, A.C. Algazin and A.K. Mednis.[22]

When these late 1930s purges gathered up most of these people, those that survived with their lives were held at TsKB 29, which was attached to GAZ 156 at Moscow, under the control of NKVD Colonel G. Ya Kutyepov.[23] They were organised into various STOs (*SpetsTekhOdyel* – Special Technical Departments).

In Petlyakov's case, he was arrested in 1938 and, as no real guilt could be found, he escaped the firing squad and was instead sent to the TsKB-29 Special Prison located in Factory 156 near TsAGI.

The project assigned to this department was designing a new type of aircraft, a high-altitude interceptor, intended to be a single-seater, with a fully-pressurised cabin and incorporating all the latest advances in aeronautical technology. The aircraft was to be powered by twin M-105 engines. Petlyakov was named chief designer on this project, with Isakson as his immediate deputy. In March 1938, the draft project received official approval and preliminary project work commenced.[24]

By coincidence, the word *sto* in the Russian language stands for 'hundred'. Thus the STO project was re-named as the KB-100 project when the STO became the *Osoboe Tekhnicheskoe Byuro* (Special Technical Bureau) OTB, and Petlyakov was put in charge of one of the *Konstruktorskoe byuro* – KB – (Design Bureaux) working within it. These KBs were KB-100 under Petlyakov, KB-102 under V.M. Myasishchev and KB-103 under A.N. Tuoplev, to which KB-110 under D. Tomashevich was later added.[25] Within KB-100 what had become the kernel of the *Samoliot* (Aircraft) 100 concept later became the Pe-2.

Petlyakov's team in KB-100 consisted firstly of his number two or deputy, A.M. Izakson, who had also been among those arrested and jailed, and who had become one of Petlyakov's closest and most talented assistants. There was V.M. Myasishchev, who had originally headed up the wing-construction group, and who would later become head of KB-102. Others on the strength of KB-100 were Ye P. Shekunov, K.G. Nurov, I.K. Protsenko, S.M. Lemeshko, P.L. Otten, Yu T. Shatalov, N.I. Pogossky (who later moved over to KB-103), K.G. Rogov, S.M. Meyerson and N.I. Polonsky.

The KB-100 team also enlisted the help of other KBs, especially those headed by A.I. Mikoyan and M.I. Guryevich, P.O. Sukhoi and A.S. Yakovlev. Thus it is not surprising that work conducted on Project 100 could later be found in their own subsequent projects, like the Yak-1 and Lavochkin Garbanvov Gudkov LaGG-3 fighter aircraft, both of which had planned high-altitude variants.

PESHKA MEN – Vladimir Mikhailovich Petlyakov

Vladimir Mikhailovich Petlyakov, talented designer of the Pe-2, who was killed in an air crash in January 1942. (San Diego Aerospace Museum).

The designer of the Pe-2 was born on 15 (27 under the new calendar) June, 1891, at the small village of Sambek, near to Taganrog, on that north-eastern arm of the almost landlocked Sea of Azov known as the Gulf of Taganrog. After a normal boyhood, the bright young man graduated from the Taganrog Technical School, and, at the age of 19, enrolled as a student in the Mechanical Department of the MVTU, where he learnt the rudiments of aeronautics at the feet of the great Russian designer and innovator, N.E. Zhukovsky.

The impetus of the First World War, which began in summer 1914, and which was to have consequences so tragic for the Russian Empire, saw an impetus into aviation development everywhere and Petlyakov was in the thick of Russian developments, despite the overthrow of the Czar and the subsequent turmoil in the country as a whole, serving between 1917 and 1918 as a technician at the *Moskovskoe Vysshee Tekhnicheskoe Uchilishche* (Moscow Higher Technical School) MVTU's Aviation Calculations and Test Bureau. He graduated from the Higher Technical School in 1920, with high acclaim.

With the formation of the *Tsentral'nyi Aero-Gidrodinamicheskii Institut*, TsAGI, (Central Aero- and Hydrodynamic Institute), [26] Petlyakov became a laboratory technician in the Experimental Construction section of the new organisation. Among his early ground-breaking work was the development of the ANT-1 hydroplane, a surface-skimmer, being a planing high-speed boat, of great potential. He also worked on such diverse projects as airships and aero-sleighs in an organisation which was straining at the boundaries of what was possible in all matters appertaining to flight.

On being co-opted onto the design team of the famous A.N. Tupolev, joining a team charged with the special task of designing all-metal aircraft for the first time, Petlyakov's main area of expertise was with wing design and construction, working initially on the ANT-3. Between 1925 and 1926 he was Head of the First Design Brigade (Wings). He personally developed methods of calculating and testing wing parameters. He was also involved in studies into the best ways to achieve mass production and helped to organise well-publicised record-breaking flights by Soviet aircraft. During Tupolev's period of visiting American aircraft companies, it was Petlyakov that initiated the early studies into the ANT-20 *Maksim Gorkii* project.

After a decade of dedicated work, and at the very early age of 30, Petlyakov was appointed as Chief of the Heavy Aircraft Section in October 1931 and this was followed, between 1932 and 1934, as Head of the Second Brigade and Deputy Supervisor of the Experimental Construction Sector of the TsAGI's design bureau, where he headed up the multi-engined design team.

The ANT-6 (TB-3) four-engined heavy bomber and parachute-troop transport aircraft proved a great success and spurred further development along these lines, with the cry of bigger, further, faster. Already Petlyakov had undertaken a series of preliminary studies of an even larger aircraft, a six-engined machine, with a 55-metre wing-span, capable of carrying 10,000kg of bombs, which was almost five times as much ordnance as the TB-3 could tote. This became the ANT-16, which made her maiden flight on 3 July 1933. She had a unique engine configuration, with two M-34 engines mounted on the leading edges of each wing, with two more mounted back-to-back in tandem on great girders above the fuselage, and suffered from excessive vibration, but she paled into insignificance with the next design, the ANT-20, which was an eight-engined monster.[27]

The *Maksim Gorkii* was not built as a bomber, but purely as a propaganda aircraft, to demonstrate to the world the culmination of the achievements of Communist aeronautics, and was a one-off. She first flew on 17 June 1934 and became the flagship of the Propaganda Squadron. Another seven of her type were proposed, but when she crashed after a collision with a fighter plane on 18 May 1935, with the loss of fifty-six people, only a solitary modified six-engined aircraft was built, in 1938.

During the important development work on the Tupolev ANT-42 (TB-7) heavy bomber, as a replacement for the TB-3, in the period 1934 to 1936, Petlyakov worked as the great man's deputy and then, in July, 1936, became Head of the Construction Department and Deputy Director at the *Zavod Opytnii Konstruktsii*, ZOK (Experimental Design Plant) A year later and he was appointed as Designer General. In this period, his work included the further development of the TB-7 heavy bomber, his influence on its final design being acknowledged by the later re-designation of this aircraft as the Pe-8. It was the first Soviet aircraft to bomb Berlin, but only seventy-nine were built before construction was stopped in 1944.

His arrest on trumped-up and imaginary charges during the great purges followed, and his transfer to the NKVD's 29 TsKB, under the auspices of the STO (Special Technical Department) is related in these pages. His brilliant work on the VI-100 and PB-100 projects, resulting in the Pe-2, followed, along with his pardon and reinstatement. With the onset of the Great Patriotic War his immense organisational abilities ensured the smooth transfer of production facilities to the east, and new and improved designs, as well as improvements

THE PETLYAKOV Pe-2

to the Pe-2, were already under way from his fertile and gifted brain, when, as recorded, he was cut down in his prime when his aircraft crashed soon after taking off from *Gousudarstvenny Aviatsionny Zavod*, GAZ (State Aircraft Factory) No. 22 *en route* to Moscow in January, 1942.

Petlyakov, Stalin Prize winner, awarded the Order of Lenin twice and the Order of Red Star, had a monument erected to him on the central avenue of the Arsk cemetery at Kazan. His legacy was a series of fast, elegant and highly effective warplanes that helped turn the tide of the war on the Eastern Front and his name is still an honoured one in modern Russia's aeronautical establishment.[28]

Chapter Two

Many Starts, Many Endings

The *Sotka* was ultimately to turn into the *Peshka*, but it was a long and convoluted road before that remarkable volte-face came about.

The Perceived Threat

The *raison d'être* of the 100 Project could be traced back to a growing fear of the threat posed by extra-fast, high-flying bombers. The accelerating pace of technological development of military aircraft at the time was pushing the envelope more and more in favour of such bombers and it was known that Germany, in particular, had experiments in hand to develop such weapons. (For example the Junkers Ju-86 P, Ju-86R and HS-130 were under development as special high-altitude bomber-reconnaissance aircraft.)[1]

Gloomy forecasts were made on the future inability of Soviet fighter aircraft to intercept waves of such stratosphere-grazing intruders. Kombrig P.P. Ionov's tactical fighter development volume, published in 1940, reflected this perceived threat. He pointed out that the average ceiling of contemporary combat aircraft was about 9,000-10,000 metres and that it would soon reach 11,000. His message, drummed home to his RKKVF (*Raboche-Krest'yanski Krasny Vozdushny Flot* – Workers & Peasants Red Air Fleet) readership was 'the higher the enemy bombers fly, the longer is the distance from the front line that interception can take place.'[2]

The need for a high-speed, high-altitude fighter there seemed to be a high priority. Such an aircraft would be at the absolute edge of Soviet aviation's technical abilities, however, and radical solutions were required. Pressurised cabin for the crew, an aerodynamically sleek and projection-free shape, and engines capable of high performance at these new combat altitudes. To reduce weight, a single-seater aircraft was desirable, but this was quickly rejected as impracticable. Long-range interception, coupled with the multiple tasks of flying, navigating, evaluation of the combat situation, maintaining radio communications and engaging the enemy, was deemed too complex for one man to handle on his own. Therefore a navigator was a requirement, making the design a two-seater from the outset. This complicated the pressurised cabin requirement of course.

Petlyakov's team was assigned sub-assembly projects according to their special talents. Thus the fuselage was under direction of A.I. Putilov, the undercarriage design was headed up by T.P. Saprykin, N.M. Petrov concentrated his team on producing a workable pressurised cabin in time, while the complex electrical systems were tackled by A.A. Yengibariyan and I.M. Sklyansky's men.[3]

The base from which they worked was that the *Sotka* was to be a low-wing, all-metal cantilever monoplane. The wing was based on the two-spar system with pressed ribs and stringers with a 0.6 to 0.8mm gauge dural sheet skin. Along the trailing edge were the ailerons and Schrenk-type split flaps. Only the control surfaces were to be fabric covered.

Design commences

One of the main causes of concern as the design got underway at KB-100 at the end of 1939 was how to retain an adequate power reserve of the engine at the heights that the air fighting was envisaged. There were several possible solutions, but the one considered the best bet was providing the engine with an exhaust-gas-driven turbo-supercharger. Overall, speed was desirable but not as much as rate of climb and range. The parameters were for the new fighter to be capable of a speed of 630km/h at a height of 10,000 m, with an overall ceiling of 12,500m in order to gain an altitude advantage over the target. This had somehow to be coupled with a range of 1,400 km in normal condition and 2,400 km in overload condition.[4] The power plant selected was the M-105, designed by V.Ya. Klimov, boosted at altitude by centrifugal impellers, with each having a pair of TK-2 turbo-superchargers. The latter were still under development at the TsIAM (*Tsentral'nyi Institut Aviatsionnovo motorostroeniya* – Central Aero-engine Institute).

The principle behind these turbines was that they were propelled by the exhaust gases. In order to achieve an enormously enhanced compression ratio over that obtained by conventionally driven supercharging units, the higher revolution type under development did away with the need for multi-staging usually required at the higher altitudes. In order to obtain the optimum thermal conditions these turbines were to be positioned at the sides of the engine nacelles, below the leading edges of the wings. The coolant radiators were located inside the wings.[5] The engines' airscrews were of the VISh-42 automatic pitch type.

Envisaged wing area was 40.7m^2, while normal take-off weight was 7,200 kg, 8,000 kg in overload condition. The choice of BBS airflow sections was B at the root and BS at the wingtips.[6] Bearing in mind that the speed of sound is 13 per cent lower at 11,000m than at ground level, the airflow sections at low angles of attack had to be taken into consideration, and included TsGAGI 'V' sections. The actual diving attack from above the enemy formation would increase this Mach stress even further of course. By adopting such airflow sections a considerable reduction of wing torque would be achieved and stability maintained. However, such high-altitude considerations would naturally result in loss of lift at lower levels, which would reduce manoeuvrability, take-off and landing characteristics. These penalties were acceptable for the original concept, of course, but were to pose problems when the design was changed.

MANY STARTS, MANY ENDINGS

The *Samoliot* 100, or VI-100 (VI = *Vysotnyi Istrebitel* = High-Altitude Fighter) design was commenced in 1938 and pressed ahead with. The aircraft was full of advanced ideas for a Soviet aircraft, and featured a fully pressurised cabin for the two-man crew. The internal cabin pressure was maintained equal to that for 3,700m at an altitude of 10,000 m. This had been designed by another of the team, Doctor (Science) N.I. Petrov. To aid in this, Petrov's original design featured only small windows and visibility was poor.

Modifications to Proposals

However, this layout was modified before the completion of the first prototype as the original cabin was not ready, and instead an extended dorsal spine was built along the forward top of the slender fuselage which housed the pilot in his own cockpit at the fore end. The observer/rear gunner was located at the rear end, situated just above and behind the trailing edge of the wing. This change reflected the alteration of the requirement by the VVS, who now wanted a fast, high-altitude bomber, capable of penetrating enemy air space unescorted. This gave a much-improved outlook.

The VI-100 was a twin-engined cantilever, stressed-skin, monoplane, of all-metal construction, featuring a slender profile and cross-section for maximum speed, the wings being cantilever and of a mid-wing configuration, with twin fins and rudders, very much like the Tu-2 design. The initial power plant was two M-105R engines, developing 1,100 hp, fitted with the TK-3 turbo-supercharger, fed

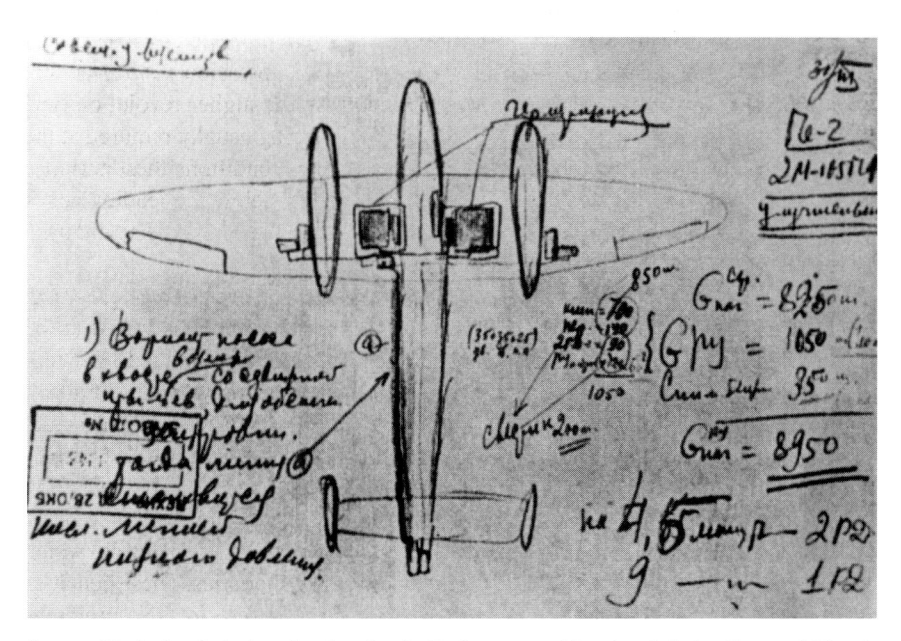

Some of Petlyakov's design sketches for the Pe-2 concept. (Russian Aviation Research Trust).

THE PETLYAKOV Pe-2

by the PTsN centrifugal feeding system, each of which drove the three-bladed VISh variable-pitch propellers, with wing-mounted radiators. The cockpit canopies were fixed and, in an emergency, the aircrew would have had to evacuate the aircraft via the ventral entry hatch.

For the first time in Soviet-designed aircraft, there was a widespread reliance on electrically-operated systems. This was largely dictated by the needs of pressurisation, because it was far easier to seal off an electric cable than conventional cable and lever linkage systems. Electric motors therefore operated the undercarriage, the wing flaps, the trimmers, the coolant radiator control flaps, indeed, almost everything. It was a quantum leap and leading edge technology for the time.[7]

The main fuel tanks were located between the two cabins at the centre of gravity.[8] The main undercarriage wheels retracted fully into the engine nacelles, and the aircraft had a semi-retractable tail-wheel. The main wheel suspension was fairly rigid leading to bounce or 'porpoising' of the aircraft on landings. The design team introduced dampers to try to reduce this effect, but, despite this, it was one rough edge that was to follow the aircraft through all its many stages and become its trademark.

Offensive armament comprised a pair of 7.62mm ShKAS machine guns, with 900rpg, and a pair of 20mm ShVAK cannon, 300rpg, with individual shell containers. These were all fixed, forward-firing weapons. In addition, there was a rearward-firing ShKAS, 700rpg, mounted in a remotely-operated barbette located in the fuselage tail section. Additional planned weaponry carried centrally included two cassettes. The K-76 contained forty-eight modified 76mm artillery shells, which were on pre-set timers to explode among close-knit enemy bomber formations. The shells were fired off in salvoes of four at a time, the distance tube settings causing them to detonate at intervals of 100 metres to spread the effect. Alternatively, a K-100 cassette containing ninety-six 2.5kg AO-2.5 anti-aircraft fragmentation bomblets could be embarked. These were to be used against the massed enemy bomber formations in order to break them up and, once dispersed, allow individual target selection with reduced defensive fire.[9]

A view of the V-100 prototype on a test airfield. (M Maslov)

MANY STARTS, MANY ENDINGS

On 7 May 1939 the blueprints were completed and the mock-up was inspected, and approved, by a GUAS (*Glavnoe Upravlenie Aviatsionnoi Sluzhba* – Chief Directorate of Aviation Service) commission, led by A.I. Filin, and project formally got underway. The former ZOK TsAGI, GAZ 156, built the machine, which was completed by November 1939. By December of that year, the prototype was ready for evaluation, and the first of some twenty-three test flights by the NII VVS,[10] omitting the Company Flight Development programme, took place on 22 December,[11] the aircraft being flown by test pilot P.M. Stefanovskii, with leading engineer I.V. Markov as observer.

First Flight Problems

The first flight was almost the last flight, for the starboard engine developed a terminal fault and an emergency landing had to be hastily made. The aircraft was put down on an area adjacent to the technical hangar and storage, which was strewn with working trestles. This might have proven fatal had not the aircraft 'bounced' heavily on touchdown, lifting her clear of the obstructions. The fault that saved her was found to be in the main wheel leg shock absorbers. Although a 'fix' was made, the legendary hard landing reputation of the *Peshka,* which was to follow her all her life, was thus firmly established from the very beginning.[12]

This part of the programme, with Stefanovskii as pilot, was concluded on 10 April 1940. These further trials went reasonably well. The aircraft fulfilled the specifications most satisfactorily, achieving a speed of 387 mph (623 km/h) at a height of 32,800 feet (10,000m) at a fully-laden weight of 13,227lb (6,050kg). Range was 1,800 km Rate of climb was 6.6 minutes to 5,000 metres. The normal M-105R supercharger could maintain adequate engine power, at lower altitudes. Incidents of wing flutter caused the drafting into the team of M.V. Keldysh, the Soviet Union's leading expert on this phenomenon, to affect a cure.

As the first stage of the evaluation continued, these engines had to be totally changed on two occasions, and numerous replacement parts had to be fitted in the interim, the oil pumps being particularly prone to failure. Above an altitude of 5,000 metres, oil temperatures soared, and at 6,000 metres the coolant temperature exceeded recommended safety limits. The fitting of far more efficient oil radiators was considered essential. At low and medium altitudes, the recorded parameters almost matched the predicted ones; above that performance was sadly lacking, with a maximum speed of 538km/h at 6,600 metres being the best recorded. A shortfall in the maximum speed at every level was about 10 to 20km/h. Speed of climb was 6.8 minutes to 4,000 metres. Despite this shortfall from expectation, it was nonetheless concluded that improved engine sub-assemblies would eventually give the *Sotka* a maximum speed of 600 to 620km/h at an altitude of 10,000 metres

There were successes; for example, the pressurised cabin maintained an even temperature of 7-8-degrees C at 8000 metres compared to the external temperature of minus 37 C, and this without full pressurisation. It had the bonus, as far as the crew was concerned, of cutting down the engine and airscrew noise levels considerably,

THE PETLYAKOV Pe-2

making for sustained comfortable conditions. Fully pressurising the cabin made the temperature inside positively uncomfortable, 30 C being recorded, and caused condensation. The cabin was, in some respects, too efficient, Stefanovskii reporting on the resulting human failing, in that it was difficult to 'sense' the flight attitude, and that might lead to loss of concentration and a drop in speed. He added that pressurisation made handling more complex, 'therefore the aircraft should be flown by a pilot of higher than intermediate proficiency level.'[13]

Alterations were made in the light of the first test flights. The modifications recommended at this stage included improvement to the cooling system and strengthening the undercarriage shock absorbers. Although the desired speed (where it could be ascertained) was 12km/h lower than hoped for, the general opinion of the NII VVS (*Nauchno-spytael'ny Institute - Voenno-vozdushnye sili* – Scientific Test Institute of the Air Force) was high. On 25 May Filin recommended continuation of development and further test flights continued, taking the grand total to seventy-three. However, the concept was not *now* a total success, for the VI-100 could not carry out its *new* primary function properly.

The State Acceptance Evaluation trials continued, with the same test pilot, between 11 April and 10 May 1940. Flying was conducted on eleven days, totalling twenty-three flights with less than seven full hours airborne. The results were less favourable, for, although the turbo-superchargers proved reliable at all altitudes and caused no problems, engine performance above 5,000 metres was mediocre. The prototype did not attain its planned ceiling and the engines did not develop the power planned. Flights were made at altitudes of 7,000-8,000 metres in the main.

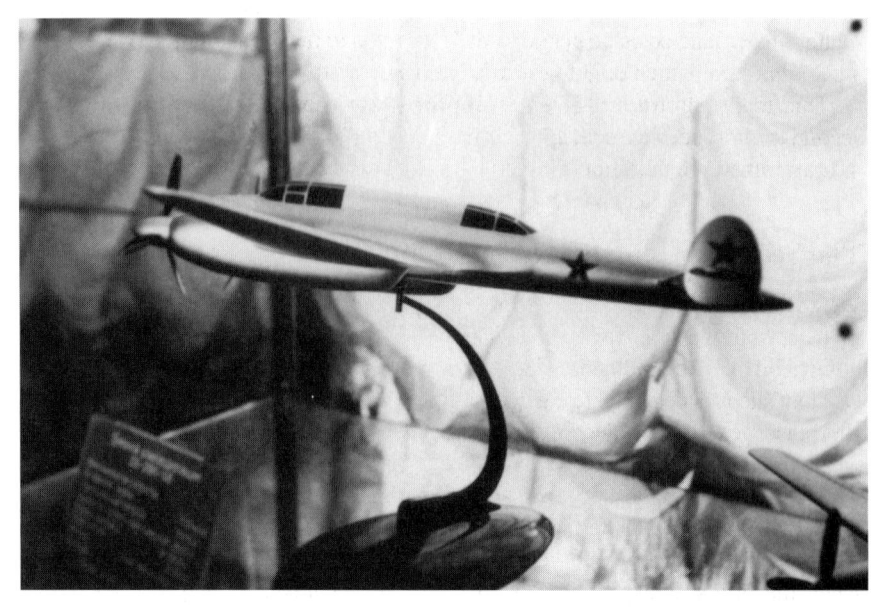

Display model of the VI-100 high-altitude fighter as originally conceived. (Russian Aviation Research Trust)

MANY STARTS, MANY ENDINGS

A view of the original high-altitude fighter concept, the Samolet-100 or VI-100. (Russian Aviation Research Trust)

The undercarriage also required a great deal of attention, and this took much longer to rectify. The VI-100 came down hard on landing, and was very prone to 'bounce' which made for uncomfortable touchdowns even on the most pristine of airfields; rough battle-front airstrips made this condition not just irritating but downright dangerous. Differing hydraulic solutions were tried repeatedly but the problem was never to be totally solved.

Both these aircraft failed; the first prototype was fitted with a ski undercarriage, part-and-parcel of any possible winter flying and fighter scenario at the northern and eastern extremities of the vast Soviet Union. Test pilot Stefanovksii was again at the controls when one leg of the undercarriage thus fitted refused to extend, no matter what manouvres he performed. The pilot had no choice, finally, but to make a belly landing, which effectively totalled the aircraft.

Due to the protracted delay caused by the earlier crash, construction of the second prototype was accelerated. In the spring of 1940 this almost identical aircraft joined the first, but only served to emphasise the earlier lessons.

The Second Prototype destroyed

Meanwhile a second prototype (the 'doubler') had been completed, being rolled out in the spring of 1940. Almost identical to the first, this aircraft featured an external bomb load of either 250kg or 500kg bombs totalling 1,000kg, but the main difference was that she was designed to carry 600kg of bombs internally instead of the artillery shell cassettes. It thus reflected the first shift in emphasis towards dive-bombing. This weapons bay could accommodate a range of small bombs, from 25kg up to 100kg.

This aircraft made a successful debut flight but, on its second outing, met a tragic fate. Flown by test pilot A.M. Khripkov for a routine test take off with navigator P.I. Perevalov aboard, the VI-100 had barely got to a reasonable height when the pilots' cockpit was enveloped in thick smoke, blotting out vision and threatening to fumigate both men. Khripkov, knowing that he did not have sufficient altitude to bale out, courageously tried to make a blind landing. Perevalov was less

THE PETLYAKOV Pe-2

The second prototype, with test pilot A M Khripkov at the controls, comes to grief after a fire in the cockpit shortly after take-off. (Russian Aviation Research Trust)

Wreckage of the second prototype Pe-2 after her on-board fire during trials in 1940. (Russian Aviation Research Trust)

affected by the smoke and directed the pilot towards a seemingly safe area, a gently undulating meadow. Following a line of electricity masts out of the corner of his eye, Khripkov headed for this area. He almost made it but, again having to guess his height and with the inevitable hard 'bounce' as she struck the ground, the aircraft ground-looped and ploughed into a bunch of children from the *KhimKombinat* kindergarten who were out walking with their young teacher, killing them all.

The aircraft then nosed over and came to rest at the edge of the meadow. Amazingly, Khripkov and his navigator, although both unconscious, survived this ordeal, and were rushed to hospital. There they were placed under arrest by the NKVD while the accident and the deaths of the children were fully investigated. The commission which looked into the incident reached the conclusion that it had been caused by negligence. A nut on one of the fuel pipes had not been properly tightened. Fuel therefore leaked out and entered the electrical switches and surrounding area. When the pilot activated the flaps sparks from these switches ignited this seeping fuel, which quickly spread to the insulation and the internal varnish. Both aircrew were, accordingly, cleared of any guilt. Amazingly, considering the emotive loss of young lives that had resulted from such carelessness, those held responsible, a mechanic and two service engineers, escaped with only reprimands.

However, this tragedy marked the end of the second VI-100, which was declared a complete write-off.[14]

Evaluation resumed

Trials continued with the repaired first prototype. A further thirty-four flights were subsequently carried out totalling 13 hours 25 minutes flight time. Other faults were revealed, principal of which was the lack of vertical tail area provided by the small twin oval-shaped fins. Trials naturally included flying on one engine in case of malfunction

The VI-100 was originally completed with small twin-fins inset of her tail plane, but these later had to be enlarged by one-third and a marked dihedral introduced to improved stability. (Russian Aviation Research Trust)

THE PETLYAKOV Pe-2

The VI-100 prototype is seen here during early trials. Note the elongated cockpit. (M Maslov)

Ground-testing of the VI-100 with undercarriage fully raised. (Russian Aviation Research Trust)

or battle damage, and in this condition it was found that the VI-100 lacked directional stability. This resulted in an increase in the total area of the fins, which mainly rectified this fault. To improve the directional stability, found wanting, the tail-fin area was increased in size from $0.77m^2$ to $1m^2$. The surface finish was cleaned up considerably, with the immediate bonus of a 14km/h improvement in speed.

Longitudinal stability also left much to be desired, leading for calls for the leading edge sweepback to be increased. Similarly take-off and landing difficulties had to be addressed. It was found that, with fully-deployed flaps, the elevator power did not ensure a smooth three-point touchdown. The incidence angle of the tail plane was therefore planned to be increased on production aircraft.

Compromise is always necessary in aircraft design, and the special wing airflow sections that gave optimum performance at high altitude had a trade off at low level and landing of reduced lift. This translated into long take-off-run distance and higher landing speeds, and these, coupled with the notorious 'bounce', made for difficult handling, out of reach of tyro pilots.

MANY STARTS, MANY ENDINGS

Close-up view of the VI-100 high-altitude fighter in April 1940, with the two pressurised cabins separated by a long dorsal spine. Also seen are the large trailing-edge flaps. (Russian Aviation Research Trust)

May Day Fly-past

The prototype was shown to the world during the May Day fly-past over Red Square when Stefanovskii lowered the aircraft's undercarriage and made a slow roll with the undercarriage down! Petlyakov and his team were permitted to watch their brainchild make her public debut from the wired exercise compound that had been built on the flat roof of the KOSOS building (known to the detainees as 'The Monkey Cage').[15]

Comparison with other types

Lest the above should lead to the impression that the *Sotka* was a failure, nothing could be further from the truth. The price for pushing the parameters would always be problems, but Petylakov had produced an outstanding aircraft almost straightaway. The new Soviet single-engined interceptor, also designed with high-altitude operations in mind, the I-200 (which would become the MiG-1), could not match the VI-100 for speed at altitudes above 8,000 metres. Nor was the single-engined machine equipped with either turbo-supercharger or pressurised cabin.

Against foreign contenders in this small class, like the French Potez 630, the British Bristol Beaufighter Mk I or the German Messerschmitt Bf110C, the VI-100 could show them all a clean pair of heels at both medium and high altitudes.

Her weakness in such competition lay in her offensive capability, which was less than the latter pair of twin-engined fighters.[16] The omens all appeared good. Then, almost overnight, everything changed.

Change of requirement

The outbreak of war between Germany on the one hand, and Poland, Great Britain and France on the other had taken place in September 1939. From the many surprises which the resulting combat had revealed, lessons, which affected the future role of the VI-100, were gradually assimilated, and, step-by-step, her rationale changed from one extreme to the other, an astounding volte face.

The success of the German Junkers Ju.87 in spearheading fast tank columns which carved through conventional armies, broke all resistance far behind the range of normal heavy artillery and contributed to the breaking of the morale of whole armies, was a revelation. Nations all over the world sat up and took notice. However, just as important as the new need for such an aircraft in every nation's armoury, were the other lessons absorbed. This was that it was tactical, rather than strategical, bombing which led to the progressive defeat of Poland, Norway, the Netherlands and France and drove the British from the Continent in a few brief weeks. No use was made of high-altitude, long-range bombers, and this threat, so dominant and all pervasive in 1939, seemed remote in 1940.

As (nominal) friends and allies for a period between September 1939 and June 1941, the aircraft factories of Germany were visited by Soviet experts. They came home secure in the knowledge that no large-scale development of the high-altitude bomber was underway, and that such a design was only in the earliest stage of experiment. Such threats as remained viable could, the specialists stated on their return to Moscow, easily be dealt with by a fighter like the single-engined MiG-3.

The need for the high-altitude fighter had gone away; the requirement for a high-speed accurate dive-bomber had arrived on the scene at the same time. The Defence Committee issued a directive in May 1940 to proceed with series production of two versions, an escort fighter at GAZ 39 and a dive-bomber at GAZ 22. On 25 May 1940 the NII VVS technical committee issued a report which said:

> With the aim of utilising the high aerodynamic characteristics of the '100' aircraft, a conversion of it without its pressurised cabin and superchargers into a dive bomber is to be carried out. The conversion and a (full-scale) mock-up should be presented by 1 June 1940. Once the mock-up is approved, a production of thirty aircraft for in-service evaluation will be authorised.[17]

The head of the UVVS, Ya Smushkevich, approved the report, and emphasised the change of direction with the statement that the *Sotka*, 'in the dive-bomber variant, is recognised as being expedient for series production.'

MANY STARTS, MANY ENDINGS

Vladimir Mikhailovich Petlyakov in his office with models of the most famous of his creations. (Russian Aviation Research Trust)

And what of the VI-100 herself? She languished for a year, and, in the summer of 1941, was allocated to Colonel G.I. Khatiashvili's 63 Aviation Brigade of the Black Sea Fleet VVS. She was reported as being on active service with that unit early in the war, presumably in her intended role, but the author has been unable to ascertain her ultimate fate.

Chapter Three

Sotka becomes *Peshka*

The sudden change of tack on the *Sotka*'s role could not have been more dramatic. Petlyakov was instructed to square the circle and convert one requirement into another. That he did so, and did so brilliantly, is to his everlasting credit. Later, many criticisms were made of the faults of the Pe-2; what is really remarkable, given her lineage, is that these were so few. Indeed at this time the RAF were vehement in their opposition to the dive-bomber, their experts even roundly declaring 'aircraft of clean aerodynamic design will reach too high a velocity to make recovery from 1,500 feet reasonable safe and certain... .'[1] The KB-100 team was about to show what utter nonsense that viewpoint really was.

Dive-Bombing

When the Russians came to conducting the actual bombing trials, with bombs released from the nominated operating altitude of 16,400 feet (5,000m), it was found, hardly surprisingly, that accuracy was mediocre from such a height. Once again, as with so many other nations, the Soviets found that it was pointless in building a bomber, which looked good, flew high, carried a good bomb load over a long distance, if, when it reached its target, it could not hit it! However excellent an aircraft it might have been from every other aspect, a bomber is useless if it is not accurate. Merely using a great deal of fuel to fly many miles to put holes in fields was pressed to its ultimate conclusion by RAF Bomber Command during the war.[2] The Soviets wisely abandoned that idea and, noting the high rate of accuracy being achieved by their arch-enemies the Luftwaffe with the Ju.87 in Poland gave them a new perspective. A visit made by a Soviet delegation to Germany in 1940 (the two countries were still nominally bound by their alliance) prompted a deeper study of German military aviation doctrine and altered the requirement yet again. Now the specification was changed to the PB-100 (*Pikiruyushchii Bombardirovshchik*) and Petlyakov was instructed to totally re-design the aircraft within the space of five months.

The PB-100

In order to fulfil the change from two-seater interceptor to three-seater dive-bomber in time to meet the one-and-a-half month deadline, Petlyakov's team was heavily supplemented with some 300 specialists. Included among these were experts from

SOTKA BECOMES PESHKA

the A.S. Yakovlev, S.V. Il'yushi and A.A. Arkhangel'sky OKBs. The technical drawings were sent to the production facilities as soon as they were drafted and work on series production was initiated on 23 June 1940. The need for a fresh prototype was done away with totally, and they relied on the sole remaining 100 prototype since the airframe remained basically the same. Thus the tight deadline was met, and Petlyakov later received the Stalin Prize in recognition of his achievement. (A fact which did not prevent his OKB being integrated into the NKAP design organisation on outbreak of war!)

The PB-100 had her crew of three housed in two separate pressurised cabins, with the pilot in front and the navigator below him. The navigator was provided with a second set of controls, with limited instrumentation, in the event of the pilot being put of out action.[3] The forward armament was a fixed battery of four ShKAS machine guns. The rear cabin, also pressurised was for the air gunner/wireless operator, who was responsible for the periscopic optical gunsight of the two flexibly-mounted ShKAS machine guns firing aft, both above and below the rear fuselage. There was an alternative armament layout, which comprised a battery of two ShVAK and two ShKAS guns under the fuselage, which could be depressed for the strafing of ground targets in the ground-attack configuration. Alternatively, a 1,000kg bomb load could be toted, with 400kg carried internally. This was destined to remain only a drawing-board concept.

The overriding need for an uninterrupted flow of series production was to dominate VVS-RKKA thinking throughout almost the whole life of the Pe-2 and this was the first manifestation of that thought. The pressurised cabins, however innovative and successful, were considered needless complications for a dive-bomber and the design was changed.

Although basically the same aircraft, there were obviously some changes to be made to fit an entirely different mission requirement. The most obvious ones were the fitting of a large glazed area on the lower nose of the aircraft, which was also re-designed, in order to give the pilot the maximum possible visibility during his dive attack. It was not just ventrally that pilot visibility was enormously enhanced, for, as there was no longer any requirement for a pressurised cabin, the whole cockpit was re-designed, being raised and extensively glazed, with the pilot and navigator's positions being once more merged under a single canopy with 360-degree vision. This was at first overdone, and the amount of window space was gradually reduced in later models in response to battlefield experience, both to reduce vulnerability to ground fire and to give less drag and thus improve aerodynamics for better performance at low level.

The same redundancy that saw the abandonment by the UVVS of the pressurised cabin applied equally to the power plant; there being no need for the turbo-superchargers, they were omitted. The twin power plant remained the M-105R, twelve-cylinder; vee liquid-cooled engine fitted with two-speed superchargers and these gave early models a maximum speed of 336mph (540 km/h) at 16,400 feet (5,000 m). Rate of climb was 6.8 minutes to 5000 metres. The improved superchargers raised the service ceiling to 12000 metres.[4]

THE PETLYAKOV Pe-2

The wing configuration shifted from mid- to low-wing, having a compound taper over most of its form. Of course, being now a dive-bomber, the fitting of electrically-operated, 'Venetian-Blind' type slatted brakes below each outer wing panel was standard and there were changes in armament requirement, from offensive back to defensive. This requirement necessitated stronger rear protection and the crew was increased to three by the addition of rear gunner accommodated in a separate, and somewhat cramped, compartment located in the rear fuselage.

This gunner, lying out flat on the floor, operated a ventrally mounted 7.62 ShKAS (*Shpitalny-Komaritski Aviatsionny Skorostrelnij* or *Shpitalny-Komaritski* rapid-fire) machine gun[5] fitted with a 120-degree periscope sight, which was swung down beneath the fuselage to cover stern attacks from below. It could be placed to fire out from either port or starboard gun ports. There were two more such weapons mounted in the nose, with a fourth on a flexible mount operated by the navigator to fend off stern attacks from above. (Some considerable experimentation with defensive guns took place, again because of battle experience and these will be covered in their turn.) There was also 9mm thick back and side armour plating fitted.

For offence the PB-100 could carry up to six 100kg bombs in an internal bomb bay in the central fuselage, with an additional two 100kg bombs in the rear of each engine nacelle and another four externally, two under each wing centre-section. Dive brakes of the slatted type were fitted under each wing.

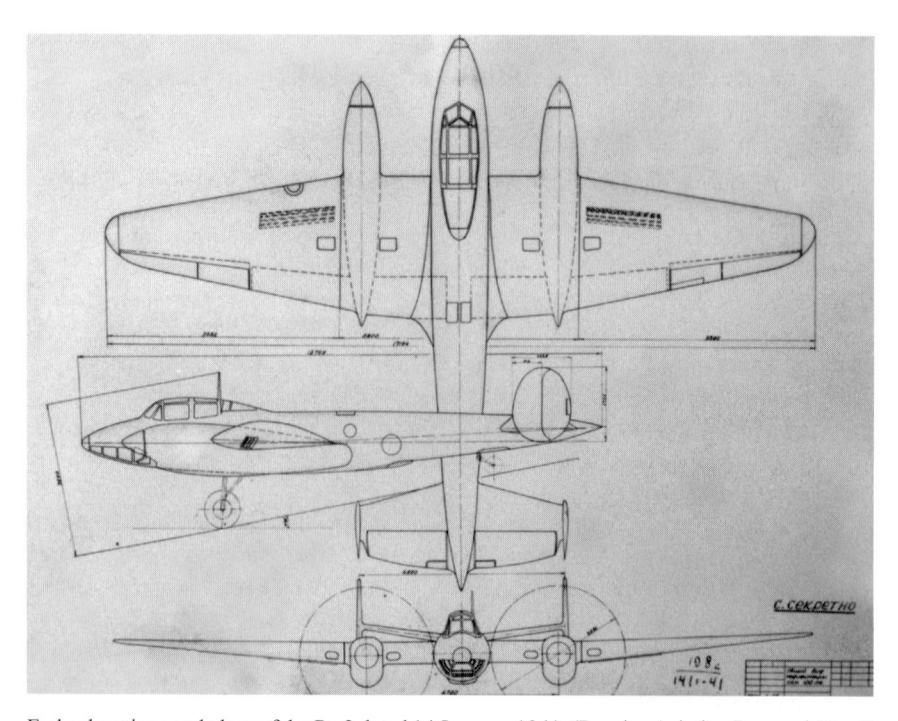

Early elevations and plans of the Pe-2 dated 14 January 1941. (Russian Aviation Research Trust)

SOTKA BECOMES PESHKA

Opportunity was also taken to enhance the inherently poor lateral stability of the aircraft; the tail-plane was given an 8-degree dihedral. The first of two production aircraft was completed to this specification in 1940 and trials commenced.

The Defence Committee of the Soviet People's Commissars issued their Order of 23 June 1940, which set the whole development in train, on the basis of the VI-100 high-altitude fighter. The new dive-bomber was assigned to factory No. 39 in Moscow. The outstanding performance of the German Junkers Ju.87 Stuka in the conquest of Poland had only emphasised the need for such an aircraft, and quickly.

One aspect of the change should be noted. The decision to proceed to serial production would have meant the end of detention for many of the team, and they were looking forward to it. The change in emphasis meant back to the drawing-board and continuation of their confinement, and was not welcomed for that reason if for no other!

Although self-deluded and blinded by the German-Soviet Pact of 1939, even Stalin could see that once Hitler had made an accommodation and peace (as most outsiders expected he would) with Great Britain, his military machine was primed and ready to settle old scores with the Kremlin. The pace of rearmament reached fever pitch as the Soviets tried to buy time.

The first flight of the PB-100 took place in the late autumn of 1940, by which time she was again re-designated as the Pe-2.

Pe-2

Testing of the new aircraft (for such it was) the Pe-2 2M-105, commenced in December 1940 with major flights taking place between January and February 1941, and was completed by June of that year. Some problems were encountered. For example, during on early flight the starboard engine failed, causing Stefanoskii

First production Pe-2 with national markings and standard colour scheme is displayed at Factory 39, Moscow, February 1941. (M Maslov)

THE PETLYAKOV Pe-2

to make an emergency landing on a maintenance apron, narrowly missing the roof of a nearby hangar and some trestles on the runway itself. He escaped unscathed.

So successful was the new design felt to be that she was immediately ordered into full and large-scale production. The initial design showed an empty weight of 5,673kg, a flight weight of 7,400kg, with wing loading of 183.5-193kg/sq.m. Airspeed at ground level was logged as 452km/h, with a maximum airspeed at 5,000 metres of 540km/h. The aircraft had a service ceiling of 8,800 metres and a range of 1,200 kilometres.

The official Soviet report on the tests stated that: 'Flight characteristics of Pe-2 airplane is higher than of native serial two-engined airplanes and at the same level as foreign ones.'

In fact, they were not doing justice to themselves for the Pe-2 was a dive-bomber that was faster than most contemporary fighters!

Meanwhile production lines had been established and quickly geared up to pump out the new dive-bomber. This series production was entrusted to Putilov. The 1100hp M-105R, equipped with centrifugal compressors and VIShP-61P variable-pitch airscrew, became the main powerplant. They were compressed-air started. Coolant radiators were mounted in the wings on both sides of the engine, with the oil radiators immediately below the engines. Expelling of the coolant air from the radiators was by means of upper wing surface apertures. Fuel tanks were protected with the inert gas extinguisher system, which included the main fuselage tank, a pair of tanks in the centre section and two outer wing panels cells abaft the engines.[6]

The aircraft was fitted with the new AP-1 automatic dive-control system, which automatically opened and closed the dive brakes. The slatted dive brakes themselves were built of steel tubing and hinged beneath the other wing panels in the traditional manner. The front cabin instrumentation included the ATP artificial horizon and the RPK-2 HF/DF (High Frequency/Direction Finder) receiver, but

Starboard profile of the first production Pe-2 at Factory 39, Moscow, in February 1941. (M Maslov)

had no autopilot. The pilot had an armoured backrest of 9mm thick armour plate; similar protection was later extended to the navigator with a side-shield of 6mm thick plating.

Considering the size of the Pe-2, the weight of ordnance she could deliver seemed rather puny, especially compared to the only other similar twin-engined dive-bomber of any merit, the Junkers Ju.88A-4. The German aircraft could carry a 3,000kg bomb load and was better defended and had a longer reach. The Pe-2 was faster by some 80km/h; in fact it equated to the speed of the Bf.109F fighter, the latest German type in 1941. But the Petlyakov could only deliver a maximum payload a mere one-third the size of its opposite number dive-bomber in the Luftwaffe. Much of this was due to the limitations of the Soviet aero-engine industry; the power plant was so much less efficient.

Whatever the reason the largest bomb capable of being carried into combat by the *Peshka* was a single FAB-500 or a pair of FAB-250 bombs, with wing loads of FAB-100 ordnance carried in special cassettes. The split of 600kg carried internally and 400kg externally placed loading complications on the Pe-2, especially as only the wing-mounted bombs could be released in the 70-degree dive, the maximum angle cleared for operations. The internally toted bombs had no special dive-release gear and had to be dropped in level flight. The old SB had provision for chemical spray gear, but no such equipment formed part of the Pe-2's capability.

Considering that this aircraft broke much new ground in Soviet aeronautical engineering, being the first to feature total electrically-operated equipment, with no less than fifty electric motors of five differing types, ranging from 30 to 17000 watts (these worked the hydraulic pump system, engine fuel pumps, hydraulic undercarriage, ailerons, elevator, rudder trim tabs, radiator flaps, wing flaps, dive-brakes, bomb doors; bomb rack release mechanism etc., etc.) this was no mean feat. In the first six months of 1941 no fewer than 458 Pe-2s had been completed, while by the second half of that same year this figure had almost tripled, to 1,405.[7]

Monocoque, when an aircraft fuselage takes the bulk of the stress on the outer casing, gave for simplicity of construction and this was the ideal at which Putilov aimed. He achieved it almost completely. The skin of between 1.5 to 2mm thick, was stretched taunt over bulkheads set at approximately 0.5m intervals, and there were no stringer supports to reinforce this. Only apertures in the fuselage, joints, hatches and glazed panels as well as the ventral gun position, were framed with attached longerons.

The same concept was applied to the wings. This was of twin-spar construction, and of a tapered planform. It was built in three sections, the centre section and two outer-wing panels. The skin of these wing sections varied in thickness between 0.6 to 0.8mm gauge, but was backed with a large number of much stronger and closely-set stringers. The spar beams were D16 dural steel flanges and both walls and ribs were perforated to save weight. The centre section was flat; the two outer sections had a 7-degree dihedral at their trailing edges.

The split flaps were the Schrenk four-section type, with a maximum deflection of -45 degrees. When these were extended the Pe-2 could achieve a 584metre

THE PETLYAKOV Pe-2

Wind-tunnel testing of the Pe-2 at Central Aerohydrodynamic Institute (TsAGI), Moscow. (Russian Aviation Research Trust)

TsAGI wind-tunnel tests on the Pe-2. Note fully lowered slatted dive brakes. (Russian Aviation Research Trust)

take-off distance. The ailerons were of twin-section design with internal compensation. Only the starboard aileron had a trimmer. The slatted type dive brakes were located on the lower surfaces of the outer wing panels and of welded steel tube construction. Activation was by means of the AP-1 automatic system.

SOTKA BECOMES *PESHKA*

This device activated the diving sequence on impulse from the sighting controls and also operated the automatic pullout on termination of the attack sequence. Operational units frequently removed these dive brakes when the occasion warranted it and it was not fitted at all to some serial production batches. With regard to the empennage, the tail plane had an 8-degree dihedral. The range of elevator movement was between +31 to -18 degrees while the twin rudders had 25-degree travel to each side.

The fuselage length was 12.6 metres. The nose section was heavily glazed on its lower level, which gave both pilot and navigator an enormous field of downward vision. Two fixed forward-firing ShKAS 12.7 machine guns were fired by the pilot. The navigator sat to the rear of the pilot and also worked the upper machine gun, initially on a flexible mounting, later in its own turret. Situated aft the mainplane were ventrally positioned apertures for a further ShKAS machine gun to fire to port or starboard. Set above these in the top of the fuselage was a further glazed observation panel, which doubled as an emergency exit, although comparatively small and later having to be enlarged. All these light machine guns were progressively upgraded as the war went on, being replaced by either ShVAK or UBT cannon.[8]

Armour protection was provided, but only on a limited scale. The pilot had 9mm thick backrest armour, and there were two 6mm thick armoured side panels to provide some protection to both pilot and navigator. The main weapons bay was located abaft the rear wing main spar. This could accommodate four single FAB-100 bombs. On occasion extra fuel tanks for long-range missions took their place. Externally four FAB-250 bombs could be carried on racks below the centre section and *only* these could be used for dive-bombing. The normal bomb load was therefore a miserly 600kg, although 1,000kg could be accommodated in overload condition for close-range missions. A further two single FAB-100 bombs could be carried in the undercarriage space at the back of the engine nacelles.

An early production Pe-2 with the pointed tail-cone. The outer wing trailing flap on the starboard side is also clearly seen. (Russian Aviation Research Trust)

THE PETLYAKOV Pe-2

The main undercarriage fully retracted backwards into the engine nacelles. They were fitted with 900 x 300mm tyres which had twin-legged shock absorbers, but were never fully up the job. The main wheel base was 4,730mm. The tail wheel was also retractable, into the fuselage tail section in front of the tail plane.

The engine coolant radiators were positioned in the centre section, with their oval air intakes let into the leading edge and the exhaust outlets located in the rear upper surface. The main fuel tanks varied from five to nine from version to version, the original total fuel capacity of 1,000 litres rising to 1,484 litres. In all versions the main fuselage tank held either 440 or 518 litres; the oil tanks set behind each engine were of 100-litre capacity, with fuel capacity at 1,200kg, and oil capacity of 150kg. The NG inert gas fire-extinguisher system was installed with two zone stages.

The Pe-2, as the PB-100 had become, made her public debut in May 1941. A newly-equipped squadron of these aircraft took part in the traditional display of military might and power at the annual May Day Parade in Red Square, Moscow, which might have given the German Air Attaché in the reviewing assembly some food for thought – indeed, it was intended to! If so, it was by now far too late for already the Wehmarcht stood ready to implement Hitler's much-cherished Operation BARBAROSSA which he had long foretold as the final settling of accounts between the totally opposing ideologies of Nazism and Communism.

Petlyakov restored to favour

For his part the complete success of the VI-100's conversion to the PB-100 earned Petlyakov a 'Pardon' for his (non-existent) misdeeds in July 1940, and the aircraft he had designed had already been re-designated as the Pe-2. Further worsening of the international situation, prompting the need for larger numbers of modern warplanes, very quickly led to many such reprieves at this time, even if they were sometimes abruptly rescinded later when things got better! Vladimir Petlyakov's rehabilitation went further, for in January 1941 he was awarded the State Prize for achievement.

However, when, on 22 June 1941, the German invasion of the Soviet Union erupted over their western borders and The Great Patriotic War began its bloody course his OKB (*Osoboe Konstructorskoe Buro*) was transferred into the NKAP (*Narodnij Kommissariat Tiazholoj Promyshlennosti* – People's Commissariat for Heavy Industry).

Shift to Kazan

The initial onrush of the German Blitzkrieg, coupled with the destruction of Soviet warplanes on their airfields during the first two days of the invasion, threatened to engulf even Moscow in short order. The Russian nation had always had three trump cards, however. These were (a) its mass of people, the surrender of a million soldiers, which would have finished any other nation, failing to shake her as they could be replaced by two million more; (b) her appalling winter weather; if the enemy could be delayed, by no matter what sacrifice, from reaching his target line,

SOTKA BECOMES *PESHKA*

then first General Mud and then General Winter with its sub-zero temperatures would come to their aid (and, in fact, did so by coming early and by being the most severe for decades); (c) her huge area – her abundance of space. Whereas Western European nations, reacting sluggishly to the new form of mobile warfare, were overrun before they could find time and space to re-organise, save of course, for the United Kingdom, which had twenty-two miles of salt water and the Royal Navy to give them the breather they required, the Soviet Union could withdraw 100 miles, 200 miles and even 300 miles, and still have a whole continent at her back.

It was this latter ace that the Soviet leadership played once the scale of the catastrophe that had initially overwhelmed them was realised. Early in July the State Defence Committee decided upon the mass evacuation of essential war industries to the east, even to beyond the Ural Mountains. No less than 1,500 such vital plants, and their 10 million skilled and unskilled workers, were included in this gigantic migration of resources and it says much for the Russian people that such an enormous undertaking was carried out, and carried out successfully, even while fighting was continuing along the whole 1,000-mile front.

Naturally, such an upheaval had a dire effect on the workers, which in a totalitarian state could be ignored, but also on actual output. Thus, by November 1941,

Assembly line at Factory No.39 in Kazan, Tartarstan, on the banks of the Volga. The hasty move of the entire plant eastward in the face of the German invasion resulted in rather primitive conditions, but by sheer dedication and hard work production rapidly increased, although the employing of fresh and largely undertrained labour did leave much to be desired in the early aircraft built there. However, this was a common problem in every combatant nation's aircraft factories with rapid wartime expansion. One result of such inexperience contributed to the death of Petlyakov himself. (Russian Aviation Research Trust)

THE PETLYAKOV Pe-2

aircraft production fell to only 500-600 per month,[9] and this at a time when the Germans were pressing hard for Moscow itself under Operation TYPHOON. Nonetheless, this hiatus was relatively quickly overcome and the brand-new plants had resumed production to 25,000 aircraft in 1942, a magnificent achievement.[10]

Thus, it was that, in October 1941, while still in the early stages of the Pe-2 production, the whole of the OKB organisation was uprooted and moved to Menzhinskii Factory No. 39, as previously related. Here, as chief designer at Kazan, Petlyakov oversaw the setting up of the new production line for the Pe-2. The *Peshka* was high on the list of the most urgently needed aircraft and was given priority. So hard and so well did the whole team work that mass production of the Pe-2 was back on stream by February 1942.

Vladimir Mikhailovich Petlyakov and his family. (Russian Aviation Research Trust)

Tragically, Petlyakov did not live to see the fruits of his final labour. On 12 January 1942 he and Izakson were summoned to attend a vital emergency meeting in Moscow. Groups of newly built Pe-2s were regularly flown from the factory airfield to front-line units, and the two designers were taken aboard two of them as passengers to get there quickly. *En route* there was a repeat of the second VI-100 disaster, the aircraft carrying Petlyakov catching fire, which rapidly engulfed both crew and passenger, killing them all. It was a disaster. Izakson's aircraft was not affected and he was immediately placed in temporary charge of the programme.

His death in such circumstances, and at such a vital time, roused the suspicions of the paranoid dictator in the Kremlin. Mourning the loss of a 'talented designer and patriot' whom he had jailed with no justification just a few years earlier, Stalin ordered a full and ruthless inquiry into the accident to determine if there had been sabotage or other treachery. No such case was proven, but Izakson was soon replaced as director of the bureau and the job given to A.I. Putilov. He in turn, having supervised the production and modification programme through to the summer of 1943, was replaced by V.M. Myasishchev, who remained in control until the closure of the OKB in 1946.

The death of Petlyakov

Just what did the inquiry into the accident unearth if not the sabotage that Stalin's acute paranoia saw everywhere? The team conducting the search for clues was extremely professional and their work makes fascinating reading.[11]

SOTKA BECOMES PESHKA

The investigators, including many 'voluntary assistants' (agents from the State Security Service), were thorough and meticulous; after all, their expertise had been well honed. They sifted through all the evidence, interviewed every witness who had even the remotest connection with the tragedy and analysed the wreckage of the aircraft. The story they expertly uncovered had all the hallmarks and horrible inevitability of a Greek tragedy. It began with an obsessive fear on the part of Petlyakov, which became so overwhelming that it overrode every other consideration. It continued through a succession of relatively minor faults, failures of routine and hastily taken decisions, and culminated in the needless death of one of the Soviet Union's major aircraft designers. Thanks to the work of the commission, under the chairmanship of Colonel Murzin, commander of a special purpose air regiment, we can follow each step of the process as it unfolded.

Friction at Kazan

The hastily arranged move of the Gorbunov aircraft factory (factory No. 22) to Kazan, undertaken in 1941 when the German advance on Moscow seemed irresistible, was, in itself, a magnificent achievement. Picking up such a complex organisation lock, stock and barrel, and shifting many hundreds of miles east was undertaken with the speed, vigour and ruthlessness only possible under a dictatorial regime, but it worked. There was an inevitable fall in production, but this was far less than might have been expected and soon the factory was running at a high capacity, far from the threat of even the most forward Panzer column.

However, of course, no matter how brilliantly it was carried out, there *was* a price to be paid for this, even though that price was not public knowledge. Production of the Pe-2 remained the priority for the factory but it was now forced to work in conjunction with the existing aircraft manufacturing plant already established in the same area, the Orzhonikidze factory (aircraft factory No. 124). The latter was turning out the TB-7 and Li-2 aircraft, both less advanced technological types with virtually nothing in common with the Pe-2. Nonetheless, the two factories were officially 'merged' for administrative convenience as aircraft factory No.22.

Despite the merger, in practice both factories continued their semi-autonomous existence, with each having their own directors as well as their own chief engineers. Thus, Petlyakov's high-spec OKB team continued carrying forward both improvements to the *Peshka* and developing the many spin-off designs arising from it, at the cutting edge of development. The rival team, headed by I.F. Nezval, continued to build the TB-7. There developed rivalry for some resources, for the increasingly rare skilled workers and even for new machinery and materials. The sudden descent of so many workers also led to a shortage of accommodation, and the situation between the old-timers and the new arrivals rapidly descended into acrimonious brawling and ill feeling. In such conditions rumour was rife and speculation high. Thus, when Moscow ordered the Pe-2 to take the higher priority, rumours rapidly spread that Nezval's team and workforce were to be shot down entirely! This talk soon took hold and relations between the two sites of the same plant deteriorated even more.

THE PETLYAKOV Pe-2

This tense situation at Kazan was exacerbated by the drafting to the front of many of the most skilled and experienced workers from the final assembly shop and flight-test station (LIS). This panic culling of the teams' most vital members led to a dramatic fall in the quality standard of the Pe-2 production and testing programme. The men taken away were replaced by men too old for military service and by cadres of very young and inexperienced youths from the factory technical school (FZU) with a predictable falling off of standards resulting. At this stage also, the factory had no system of senior inspectors with a specific remit to a particular aspect of the production line (this did not occur until 11 January 1942). *Any* inspector could be called upon to vet *any* part of the production line's output, and so the fall in standards on the line was not picked up and corrected as often as it should have been.

The drop in skill levels was even more marked in the powerplant of the Pe-2 itself at this time. A similar situation with regard to the M-105 engine output had taken place. In autumn 1941 aero-engine factory No. 16 had been moved from Voronezh and positioned with aero-engine factory No. 27 at Kazan, with similar difficulties being met because of the forced merger. The plants were again combined under the aegis of aero-engine factory No. 16 and, as both plants were building the same engine rather than different ones, this *should* have worked more harmoniously. However, once again the calling to the front of a large part of the skilled work force of both units, and their replacement with Asiatic Uzbeks from the south, proved disastrous. Many of these primitive peoples could not read, speak or write the Russian language and could not therefore follow anything but the most basic instructions, operate machinery or even count beyond ten. Such a hopeless workforce was set to work producing the VVS's main aero engine. Not surprisingly, problems mushroomed.

Over everyone at the plant loomed the absolute and overriding necessity to increase production week-on-week, month-on-month to the strict timetable and plan laid down from on high. The pressure was remorseless and the price of failure was not loss of bonus, or loss of job, but loss of liberty and of life itself. The director of the Kuzan aero-engine factory made it crystal clear to even the meanest intelligence that failure to meet output numbers would not be tolerated, stating, 'I will walk over corpses, but I will fulfil Comrade Stalin's plan.' These were not idle words spoken in the heat of the moment but a cool statement of intent! Hundreds of the drafted-in Uzbeks died of the cold and starvation in the winter of 1941/42 before their uselessness became obvious. The survivors were given less-demanding ancillary work and then shipped off home the following spring. But the damage this short-sighted policy had caused had already been lethal.

There began to be a succession of crashes of Pe-2s from factory No. 22 while flying under test conditions. Examination of the wreckage revealed that, in some instances, the engine fuel-ingestion pipes had shaken loose and parted company when the pilot opened the throttle fully! This was traced back to the assembly shop where the superchargers were fitted. The attachment clips had not been fitted correctly or tightened up, and indeed some cases where the workers had even failed to put the nuts on the clips at all. The inspection process had failed to pick up this shoddy workmanship. When this happened while the test aircraft were airborne and the retaining clips came away it caused the disconnection of the fuel pipe which led from the compressor to the rear carburettor. As a result there was insufficient combustion of the mix in the engine cylinders. The exhaust gases vented this overflow fuel into the exhaust manifold with resulting fire and loss of control.

Problems with 14-11

One of the many hundreds of Pe-2s on the line was factory number 14-11. She was one of a pair of standard Pe-2s, the other being No. 12-11, which had been selected for use as special long-range reconnaissance machines. They were allocated to 2 DRAP (Long-Range Reconnaissance Regiment). As well as being equipped with special cameras and associated equipment, they were converted to carry extra fuel tanks to give the additional range required.

She was the subject of fire testing near Arzamas and, in the early hours of 30 December 1941, was undergoing a fuel-system test for petrol tightness on the rig. Increased pressure during the tests ruptured five of her fuel tanks, and these were duly replaced. At 0315 14-11 was taken off the rig and moved to the next stage of testing. A senior shop inspector named Nurullin submitted the aircraft for inspection at Shop No. 8 where she was examined by an air force representative. The latter found no fewer than thirteen defects in the aircraft's electrical and navigation systems. Work was immediately put in hand to rectify these and, five-and-a-half hours later, twelve of the thirteen had been corrected satisfactorily.

The end of the year was imminent. Every last machine was needed to rack up the total for that part of the master plan and, so, another senior inspector, named Tutubalin, passed 14-11 as OK in this respect and she was moved on. The engine and associated airscrew were pronounced satisfactory that same evening and thus she beat the New Year's Day deadline and was finally accepted into the Air Force under the 1941 allocation.

On 9 January two aircrews from 2 DRAP, under the overall command of Senior Lieutenant F.A. Ovechkin, were assigned to collect their new mounts. His crewmembers for 14-11 were the navigator, Junior Lieutenant M. Gundorov, and radio operator/gunner, V. Skrebnev, along with a second-grade technician, N.M. Orekhov, to help with maintenance on both aircraft. Both assigned pilots were experienced aviators with combat experience, and Ovechkin had racked up more than 500 hours flying time on the Pe-2. The two new *Peshkas* were to be flown to Monino airfield near Moscow to carry out their first combat sorties against the advancing German armies. On collecting their two new machines, the aircrews carried out routine pre-flight checks and discovered new faults with both aircraft. Moreover, due to weather conditions, specially reinforced skis were fitted, but this had been carried out by inexperienced workers on the night shift, in a hasty and careless manner. Securing bolts had been knocked through with hammers, fracturing the skis, which split on arrival at the flight-test station. The flight to Morino was postponed until these new bugs were satisfactorily ironed out. Meanwhile other events had been taking place behind the scenes.

Summons from Moscow

In December 1941 rumour and wild stories had continued to permeate and sour the atmosphere at Kazan. It was catching, and Petlyakov was no less immune to its effect than the humblest worker on the production line. Among the persistent stories that reached the team at this time was that the new Tupolev dive-bomber was going into full production and would replace the Pe-2 being built at Gorbunov. In fact the Tu-2 was in competition for factory priority with the Yak-9 fighter plane at the Omsk plant. The respective designers of both aircraft, Tupolev and Yakovlev, had been engaged in a power struggle and were still duelling it out.[12]

It was hard to establish truth from fiction in such a feverish atmosphere. In all events Petlyakov feared the worst. He feared that in his absence it was the Pe-2 that would go by the board, and he became more-and-more tense and edgy. Eventually he despatched a ciphered telegram to Shakhurin, the head of the aircraft ministry in Moscow, requesting a personal interview to raise the matter. Shakhurin agreed to see him but no specific date was made at that time. The worrying increased as days passed without a word.

On the evening of 9 January 1942 a meeting to discuss further modifications to the *Peshka* was held in the chief designer's office. Present with Petlyakov were his deputy, A.M. Izakson, and the head of the OKO. Their discussion was abruptly interrupted at 2000 by a summons from Moscow and he rushed off to answer it. On his return he told his companions that Shakhurin at the ministry now wanted to see him as soon as possible about the new power plant for the Pe-2. The confirmation of the meeting, far from easing Petlyakov's agitation, only increased it. The test results had not yet been finalised, and all he could take to Moscow were the theoretical calculations. Petlyakov told his colleagues that he doubted that this in itself would be sufficient to save the Pe-2.

Next day the pressure increased with a second call came from Moscow. It proved to be Protasov, Shakhurin's secretary, with instructions from his chief that Petlyakov must report with whatever he had as soon as possible. Ready or not, he could not ignore such a summons and he grew even more excited. He informed the factory duty officer, Vaskevich, that he would have to fly to Moscow, despite the weather conditions. Vaskevich had to inform him that the factory transport aircraft, a twin-engined Douglas, was *en route* to Stalingrad and that no other machine was available to transport him until it returned to Kazan. Petlyakov retorted that, if that was the case, he could not wait and he would just have to fly to Moscow in a combat aircraft instead.

There was some dismay at this decision and a further meeting was held later on 10 January. Present were Petlyakov, Izakson, chief engineer S.M. Leshchencko and Kutuzov, the chief VVS representative at the plant. All his colleagues expressed opinions on the trip. Leshchencko, accepting that Petlyakov was fretting to get to Moscow as quickly as possible, suggested he fly as a passenger in a brand-new Pe-2, No. 905. This machine had passed all the tests without a single fault being reported. This suggestion was directly opposed by Kutuzov on the rather nebulous grounds that this particular aircraft had not yet had official VVS acceptance. The next alternative was the train, but Petlyakov curtly rejected that option out of hand as being too slow and unpredictable.[13]

Finally, as if to make amends for his earlier blocking decision, Kutuzov came up with the idea of Petlyakov and Izakson flying out in the two 2 DRAP reconnaissance Pe-2s, which were due to take off for Monino anyway once the new faults with the skis had been rectified. From that field a short hop in U-2 liaison aircraft could bring them to the central Moscow airport in short order. This seemed the best solution. Neither of the two designers could just leave the prison factory, even to answer a summons from Shakhurin himself, without the written permission of the local NKVD TASSR (Autonomous Tartar Republic). This even applied to the military aircrews themselves, let alone civilians. Further delay was inevitable and Petlyakov continued to chaff with impatience and frustration. Leshchencko continued to press Petlyakov to take the train; it was safer, but the latter would not hear of it.

Rushed decisions

By the early morning of 12 January, the two aircraft were repaired and again submitted to testing and evaluation. The mechanic in charge at this time, Pavlov, requested the controller of the flight-testing station, Esakov, to inspect and prepare 14-11 for the flight. Officially, this could only be done with the sanction of the head of the LIS's bureau for technical control. Esakov somehow got the impression that the two special Pe-2s were being flown, not the long distance to Morino, but merely ferried across to another Kazan airfield, just a short hop away. His inspection was therefore cursory to say the least. Crucially the upper inspection panel atop the engine nacelle was not opened up for close examination. Further flouting of the rules followed for, once the aircraft were pronounced fit to fly, the crew began to load their own equipment aboard in great haste, thus inviting damage to vulnerable parts and fittings. They were in an equal hurry to get away, having already been delayed, so much so that when Petlyakov himself, still awaiting his own NKVD clearance, phoned to ask them to delay their take off until 1100, he was told that it could not be done. 'Moscow cannot wait.' While he might fervently agree with these sentiments, such a refusal could have done nothing to calm Petlyakov down.

In the event bureaucracy worked for him as well as against him, for, when the two aircrews turned up at the airfield at 0800 they were refused entry as their own passes had not been prepared in time. Not until 1100 did the passes arrive, by which time the two designers had finally got their clearance to make the trip. It seemed as if fate had smiled on them at last and all was almost ready. Two hours prior to this Usmanov, the senior weatherman at the LIS, received the weather forecast along the flight route. At each end, Kazan and Moscow, the weather was clear and fine, but in the Arzamas area there was a low cloud base, right down to 200 metres. Again rules were brushed aside, for it was a standing requirement that permission for take off was only granted on production of a form with the weather forecast along with a permit from the head of the LIS. In the confusion and haste neither aircrew had requested such a form, but they went anyway.

In addition, 2 DRAP's groundman, N.M. Orekhov, should have made the standard pre-flight inspection of both Pe-2s; that, after all, was why he had been assigned to them. By 1300 he had completed the examination of 12-11 but had not yet commenced that of 14-11. The brief daylight hours were ticking on and neither aircraft carried night-flying equipment or instruments. It was now or never if they were to leave this day, and both aircrew and their impatient civilian passengers were in no mood for further tarrying. Accordingly, Ovechkin instructed them to prepare for immediate despatch. Orekhov hastened away to collect the flight orders. By the time he had got back with them both aircraft were stationary on the runway but ready to move.

By 1320 all was ready and the aircrew were standing by the two *Peshkas,* along with a group of VIPs. As well as Petlyakov, who was to take passage in 14-11, and Izaksonk, who was to fly in 12-11, there was a farewell party consisting of A.Kh. Kabakchiev, the head of the airfield group of the VVS representatives, along with another VVS officer, Colonel S. Shestakov.[14] Yet again, and for the last time, Kabakchiev requested Petlyakov not to fly in the untested Pe-2, but to wait one more day and make the journey in the Douglas with a factory ferry pilot. Again, and also for the last time, the frenzied designer refused to listen. Nor would he accept a parachute or a proper flying kit, stating firmly that he did not need it 'on my aircraft!' He boarded without further ado, taking Orekhov's place alongside the gunner in the rear crew position. In fairness, the whole flight was scheduled to be made at low level so a parachute would have only been a useless encumbrance.

Disaster

And so fate fell out. The two Pe-2s took off and vanished over the horizon in close formation. Just over half-an-hour into their journey, while some three kilometres from Kamkino railway station on the Kazan railway line, eyewitnesses on the ground saw one of the Pe-2s suddenly begin to trail smoke and lose height. As she crossed over the railway track at low altitude the *Peshka* was observed to veer radically off course, turning violently to port, through 160 to 200 degrees and then going into a steep 60-degree dive, as if in an attempt to make a crash-landing. The smoke had turned to flames at this point as the stricken aircraft was at a height of only some 50 to 100 metres, which left no room to manoeuvre. Within seconds 14-11, for such it was, hit the ground about one kilometre from the hamlet of Mameshevo and exploded. The wreckage was thrown over a 150 by 150-metre area as the fuel tanks ignited. There was no question of anyone aboard surviving.

SOTKA BECOMES *PESHKA*

Verdict

At first put down as just another Kazan Pe-2 flying accident, the discovery of four bodies, rather than the normal three, at first raised suspicions. Then, once word had reached Moscow, the special team descended on the crash site and painstakingly gathered together every atom of the wreckage and took it away for minute inspection. Despite the security blanket, rumours and tales began to spread, exciting Stalin's already paranoid suspicion of deliberate sabotage. The discovery that the pilot, F.A. Ovechkin, had a bullet in his stomach aroused the wildest assassination speculation. Ballistic laboratory analysis revealed that this bullet lacked gun-barrel markings and that it had just 'cooked off' in the heat of the fire. Forensic examination of the corpses of Ovechkin and Gundorov, the navigator, in the forward cabin, revealed that both had been badly burned while still alive, while still in the air in fact, and not just as a result of the crash. This gave the examiners the clue they needed. It had been an accident, *not* sabotage, *not* suicide, and *not* murder.

Evidence of the previous engine fires on Pe-2s was obtained from Agent Shakhov and the final verdict, transmitted to Marshal Stalin and Malenkov, was that 14-11 was destroyed by a fire, the seat of which was

> the inner surface of the starboard wing. Traces of fire were found on the starboard section of the centreplane (sic). The covering of the starboard aileron was badly burnt, as was the surface of the water radiator and the pipe attachments.

The likely cause was said to be 'a petrol leak in the area of the starboard engine nacelle'.

Strangely enough, in the circumstances, there was very little in the way of arrests and accusations, despite the less-than-commendable practices which had been uncovered at the factory. Considerable changes were put in place on the production and testing lines, senior examiners were made to specialise on different aspects of the whole process, but the use of untrained and unreliable aged, female and adolescent workers continued. In truth in the extremes the Soviet Union found itself in at the beginning of 1942 there was little option. Only when the immediate pressure on the front had been relieved somewhat did experienced men start to be released and trickle slowly back to the factories.

Of course a scapegoat of some sort had to be found, the case was too high profile not to have one. The senior VVS representative at the factory, Kabakchiev, the man who had refused Petlyakov the fully-tested Pe-2, but had suggested 14-11 as an alternative, was called back to Moscow. He did not return and vanished from history. Stalin praised Petlyakov and mourned him in public as 'This Great Patriot', but the war continued and so did the development of the Pe-2, which ironically (considering Petlyakov's fears that drove him to his premature demise) went on to become the principal Soviet attack bomber of the Second World War.[15]

THE PETLYAKOV Pe-2

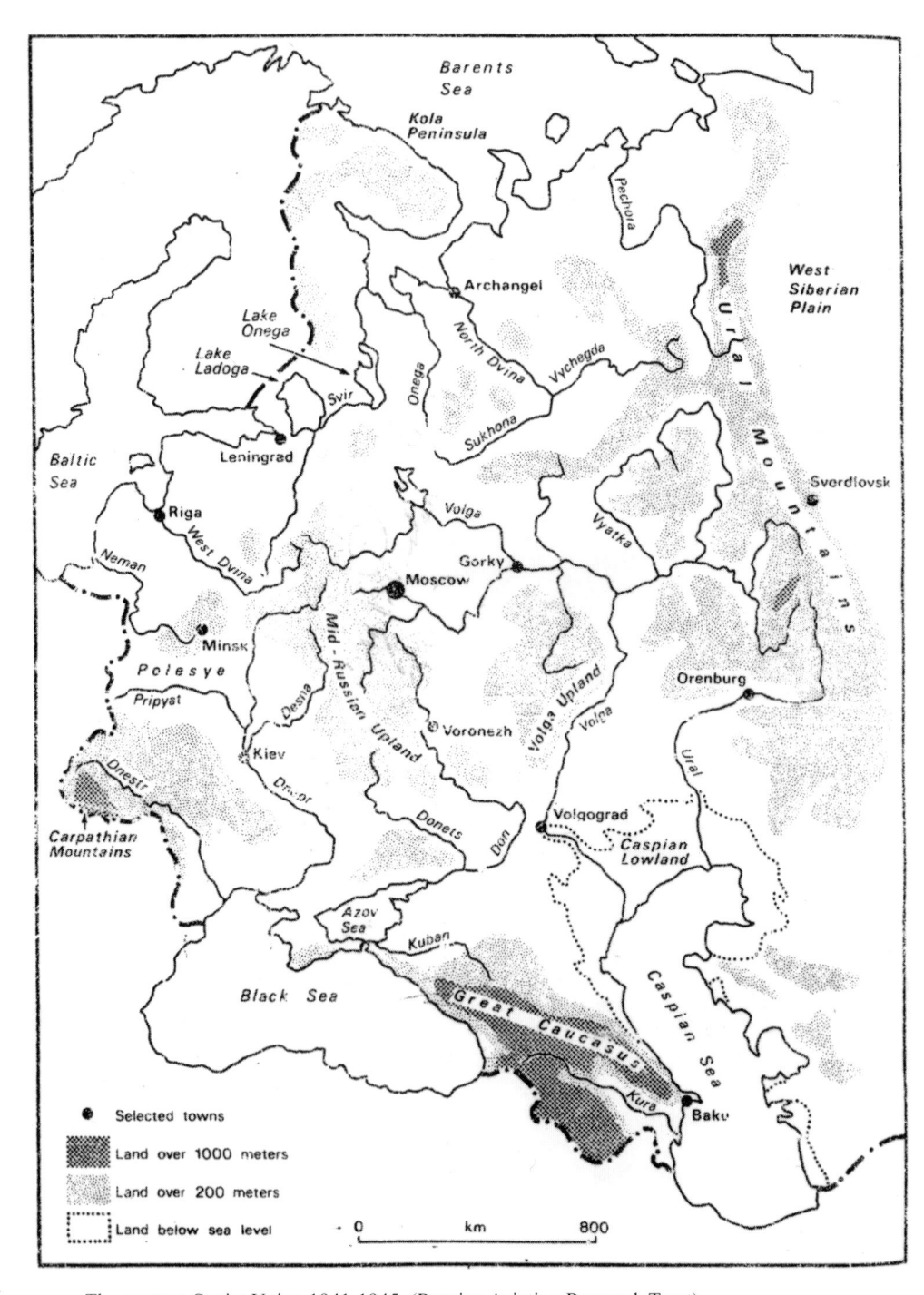

The western Soviet Union 1941-1945. (Russian Aviation Research Trust).

Chapter Four

The Pe-2 Described

Squadron Leader Lapraik recorded an excellent description of the Pe-2 for the Air Ministry as early as September 1941.[1] His description is herewith reproduced, supplemented by more detailed factual information from the author in brackets and italics.

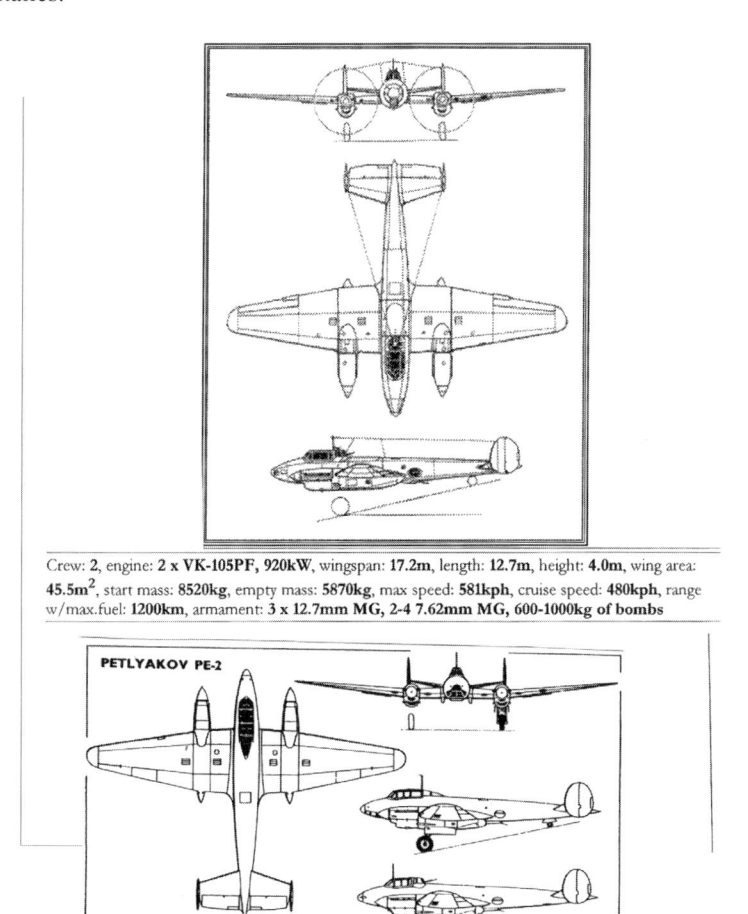

Crew: 2, engine: **2 x VK-105PF, 920kW**, wingspan: **17.2m**, length: **12.7m**, height: **4.0m**, wing area: **45.5m^2**, start mass: **8520kg**, empty mass: **5870kg**, max speed: **581kph**, cruise speed: **480kph**, range w/max.fuel: **1200km**, armament: **3 x 12.7mm MG, 2-4 7.62mm MG, 600-1000kg of bombs**

Diagram 1: General Layout of Pe-2. (Russian Aviation Research Trust)

THE PETLYAKOV Pe-2

Lapraik described the *Peshka* as 'One of the most notable aircraft produced in Russia ... a highly specialised dive-bomber and is a type with no counterpart in the RAF.' He continued by analysing the aircraft thus:

Structure

The Pe-2 was a twin-engined low-wing monoplane of metal construction. Details of the airframe construction were not available, although photographs suggested that this was of fairly conventional stressed-skin type. (*The structure was all-metal, with cloth on control surfaces and aileron skin. The fuselage was mainly cigar-shaped; round sectioned, 1.5m in diameter; from the middle to the tail tip it had a truncated cone shape for simplicity of construction, which was not noticeable to the casual observer; the fuselage structure was near to a monocoque, the length of fuselage being 12.6m. The main fuel tank in the fuselage had a capacity, which varied from 440 to 518 litres in volume, with 100-litre oil tanks located to the rear of the engines. Total fuel capacity was 1,200kg; oil capacity 1,509kg, with the tanks themselves fitted with both first and second zone inert gas protection systems.*)

The tail had twin fins and rudders and was remarkable for the pronounced dihedral on the tail-plane; this, however, was not so marked as on the Douglas Boston. (*The wing angle to the fuselage axis was 2^0, the tailplane angle $1^0\ 15'$, with the option of being turned down at an angle of $3^0\ 45'$. The tailplane dihedral angle - 8^0, the upward elevator angle - 31^0, the downward elevator angle - 18^0, and the rudder angle + 25^0.*)

All control surfaces were fabric-covered and aerodynamically balanced, the elevators by setback hinges and the rudder by a section of the surface, which encroached into the fin. Trimming tabs were fitted to all moveable surfaces except the port aileron, and all tabs were fabric-covered. An examination by British experts in Russia revealed no mass balancing. (*The wing was tapered, two-sparred, consisting of a centre wing section and outer panels. Thick triangular stringers strengthened a relatively thin (0.6-0.8mm) skin. The spar booms were steel T-beams, the walls and ribs were made of sheet with lightening holes, all built from D-16 duralumin. The centre wing section dihedral angle was 0^0, the other panel's angle - 7^0 on the trailing edge. Four Schrenk-type flaps could be deflected to 45^0 and at partial flaps the take-off run was 584m. The ailerons were internally balanced; the right one had a trim-tab, each divided in two.*)

Diving brakes

Diving brakes of the 'Venetian-blind' type were attached to the main spar and lay snug against the surface of the wing. Electrical operation was used. (*On the lower part of the outer panels there were steel tube welded deceleration lattice flaps, extended on the automatic dive-recovery control device command. A second automatic control device recovered the aircraft from the dive, and also entered it into the dive on the aiming command.*)

THE Pe-2 DESCRIBED

This head-on view of a *Peshka* landing with flaps fully down gives some idea of their size and shape. (Russian Aviation Research Trust)

The marked dihedral of the tail plane compared to the wings can be seen here. (Russian Aviation Research Trust)

Engine installation

Two M-105 (Hispano-Suiza type) 12-cylinder liquid-cooled engines, giving about 1,000hp at 12,000 feet, were fitted. The radiators were under the nacelles and the temperature of each engine was regulated by a flap at the rear of each radiator housing. Oil coolers were fitted in the wings immediately inboard of the nacelles.

THE PETLYAKOV Pe-2

Those coolers were of circular format and air was admitted to them through ducts in the leading edge.

Muffs, similar to those on Merlin installations on Beaufighter aircraft, were fitted over the exhaust pipes. *(The radiators were in the wing, with oval air intakes let into the leading edge, and air outlets vented upward through the upper wing surface.)*

Undercarriage

All three wheels of the undercarriage were retractable. *(The undercarriage had a tail wheel retracting into the fuselage in front of the horizontal tail. The main 900 x 300mm wheels had two shock-absorbed struts and were rearward retracted into the engine nacelles. Behind them were compartments for one FAB-100 bomb. The undercarriage track was 4,830mm.)*

Armament

Two fixed 7.62mm machine guns were installed in the nose and were fired by the pilot. The navigator had charge of a third 7.62mm gun on a 'rocking pillar', somewhat similar to the Fairey 'high-speed' mounting. Firing through the floor was a 12.7mm gun, which was fired by the radio operator. *(The navigator had a pivot, sometimes a turret, machine-gun mounting (on the latter series). Behind the wing there was a hatched, rear-ventral machine-gun mounting operated by*

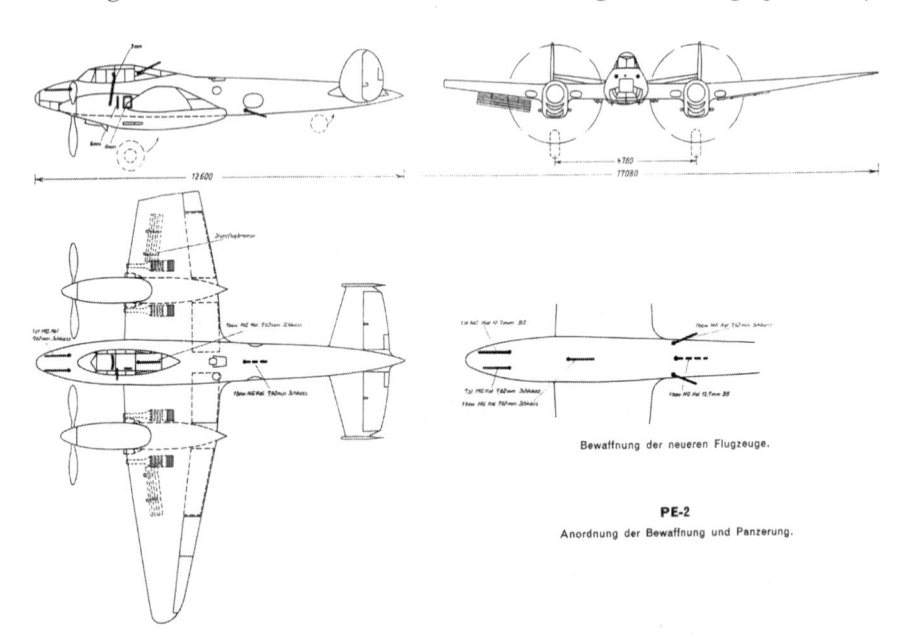

Diagram 2: Pe-2 Disposition of defensive gun armament. (E Jaakkola via Keski-Suomen Ilmailumuseo, Tikkakoski)

THE Pe-2 DESCRIBED

Details of the nose configuration and starboard nose-gun and sight of the *Peshka*. Notice the access hatch opened below. E Jaakkola via Keski-Suomen Ilmailumuseo, Tikkakoski)

Details of the cockpit and rear-gun mounting arrangement on the Pe-2FT, with radio mast (incorporating pitot tube) positioned forward of the cockpit. (Russian Aviation Research Trust)

THE PETLYAKOV Pe-2

the radio operator and a portable ShKAS, forward- firing with, over it, a hatch for aft hemisphere observation (if the navigator was killed or wounded) and for abandoning the aircraft. There were two stationary machine guns in front of the cockpit; initially these were ShKASs but, gradually, all ShKAS guns were replaced by heavier calibre UBTs and ShVAK 20mm cannon.)

Bomb load

Four 100kg bombs were stowed internally in the same fashion as on the Vickers Wellington. All heavy bombs were carried externally, alternative combinations being two bombs of 500kg, four bombs of 250kg, or four bombs of 100kg. Additional stowage was provided in the tails of the engine nacelles for two bombs

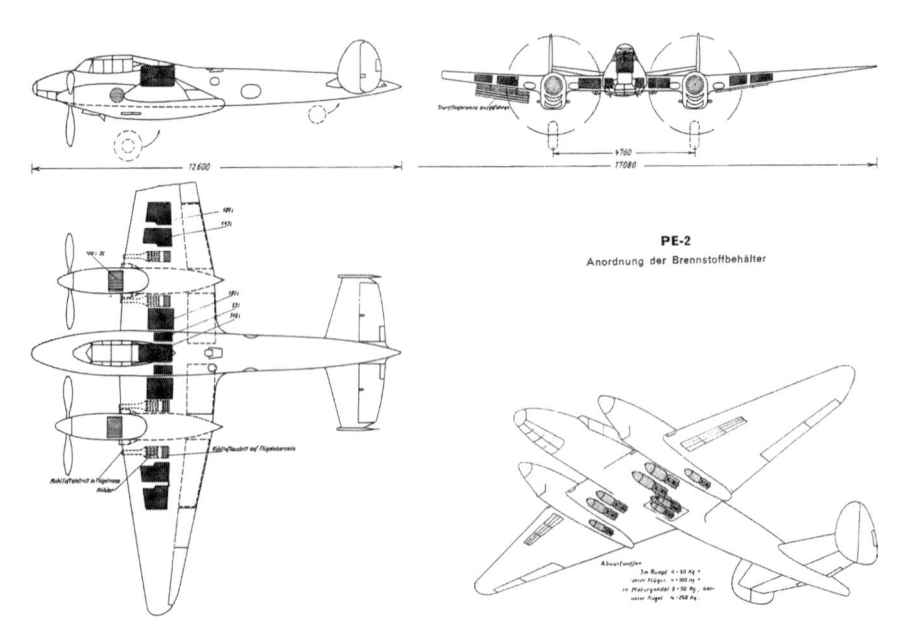

Diagram 3: Pe-2 disposition of fuel tanks and external bomb load. (Russian Aviation Research Trust)

The capacious central under-fuselage bomb-bay is revealed here, as are the two smaller bomb-bays under the engine nacelles. Also shown is some undercarriage detail. (Novosti Press Agency, Moscow)

THE Pe-2 DESCRIBED

of 100kg. (*In the fuselage there was a bomb bay behind the centre wing-section rear spar for four FAB-100 bombs, which sometimes housed a fuel tank in place of bombs. Beneath the centre wing section there were four externally carried FAB-100 bombs. The normal bomb load (clearly inadequate) was 600kg, but overloading over 1,000kg.*)

Entry

The pilot and the navigator entered the aircraft through a trap-door in the bottom of the fuselage. The pilot moved forward to his seat, which was on the port side of the fuselage, access being facilitated by the back of the seat hinging to the side of the fuselage.

Crew positions and duties

The pilot was well forward and was responsible for dropping the bombs. He also controlled, to a certain extent, the radio; this was done by means of a four-position switch by his left elbow. The positions of the switch were: intercommunication; intercommunication and radio; radio only; and radio compass for homing.

The navigator was just behind, and to the right of, the pilot. No drift sight or chart board was noted but it is stated that besides navigation this man not only operated the top rear gun but the emergency undercarriage system. This was of hydraulic type and was worked by a hand pump.

The radio operator, who was also the lower gunner, was completely shut off from the pilot and the navigator.

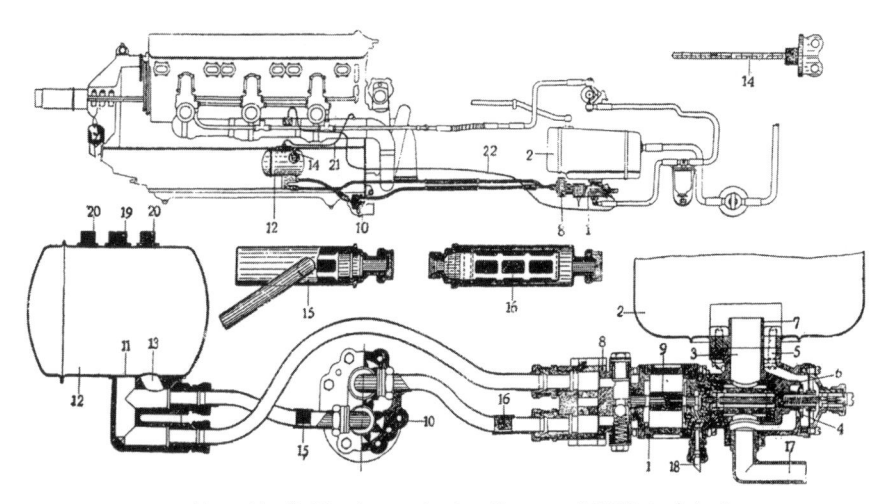

Kuva 23 - Polttoaineen hydraulinen syöttöjärjestelmä

Diagram 9: Pe-2 hydraulic system. (Russian Aviation Research Trust)

THE PETLYAKOV Pe-2

Cockpit layout

The test pilot thought the layout of the cockpit was 'good'. All controls were readily accessible and very clearly marked. A shelf along the left side of the cockpit carried all controls, which were frequently used. (*In the nose there was a lower transparent flat surface for the pilot's and navigator's downward view. The navigator sat behind the pilot, shifted to the right. The crew seats were armoured, the pilot's back armour plate was 9mm thick, and two 6mm armour plates protected the pilot and the navigator on the port side.*)

All services, including the trimming devices, were electric.

At the rear of the shelf mentioned was the radio selection switch and in front of that a switch for the electrically-operated two-speed superchargers. Beside this was a control for the windscreen de-icing spray. Further forward were the mixture controls and, alongside those, two switches, the tops of which were painted white, for controlling the constant-speed airscrew. These latter were spring-loaded to return to neutral; a forward movement increased rpm. In front of the mixture controls were the throttles and beside the throttles were the undercarriage and flap control switches, the former being painted red and having a safety catch. The flap switch was blue and was likewise spring-loaded so that the flaps could be lowered to any required angle up to the maximum of 50 degrees. If the flaps were lowered more than 30 degrees the tail trimmer was cut out by a switch and the machine became rather tail heavy though not uncomfortably so. The flap indicator was outboard of the throttle controls.

This view shows the close concentration in the cockpit area of the Pe-2 pilot (Lieutenant Sakarin) and his tail gunner (P S Sein). The radio mast is positioned aft on this aircraft. (H Valtonen via Keski-Suomen Ilmailumuseo, Tikkakoski)

THE Pe-2 DESCRIBED

In front of the throttles were two levers for operating the fire extinguishers and beside them the diving-brake switch. This was yellow in colour and had two positions. Next to it was the tail-trimmer switch, which was painted black and was spring-loaded to return it to neutral. A forward movement made the aircraft nose heavy and a rearward movement, tail heavy.

In front of the fire-extinguisher levers were the rudder and aileron trimmers, which were also painted black and spring-loaded; the inboard switch was the rudder trimmer.

Three small white lights, one beside each trimmer switch, showed when the trimmers were in the neutral position, the slightest movement from that position being enough to extinguish the lights.

At the bottom of the dashboard, just above the rudders and aileron-trimmer switches, were the undercarriage warning lights. While the undercarriage was up red lights were permanently illuminated; three green lights showed when undercarriage was locked down. A warning horn, which sounded when the throttle was more than half back, was also fitted.

The dashboard was in two parts. The left-hand side carried the flying instruments, which included an artificial horizon, directional gyro and turn-and-bank indicator, and on the right-hand side, where they were well grouped, were all the engine instruments. It was reported that these were rather difficult to read accurately, the pilot obtaining his information from noting the direction of the needles as the figures were obscured.

The right-hand side of the cockpit is taken up with the oxygen equipment and a panel carrying the petrol cocks, coolant radiator shutter switches and starting equipment. The three petrol cocks were operated pneumatically by pressing small buttons, green lights showing when the petrol was 'on' and red lights when it was 'off'.

The oil-cooler shutters are under the nacelles and were operated electrically by two brown switches near the petrol cocks. These switches were spring-loaded to return to neutral; a downward movement opened the shutters.

The radiator shutter switches were green and operated in the same manner as those for the oil cooler. The shutters themselves were halved, three louvres being outboard of the nacelle and three inboard. It was said that there was no change of trim when the shutters were operated in the air.

A hand-operated hydraulic pump for lowering the undercarriage in an emergency was mounted well below the radiator shutter switches.

To the rear of the hand pump was the fuel pressure balance cock, which had to be opened for take off, and closed for normal flying.

The compass was poorly positioned, being on the floor of the cockpit well away from the pilot.

Rudder controls were of the pedal type and made of some plastic material. They were adjustable fore and aft.

The control column was similar to that on the Airspeed Oxford, and the 'spectacles' carried the bomb-release switch and a thumb-operated brake lever.

THE PETLYAKOV Pe-2

In front of the pilot was a very neat reflector sight and, beside it, the radio compass.

The pilot's seat was adjustable vertically over a range of about 6 inches. Heavy armour plate and thick padding were fitted to the back.

Flying the *Peshka*

Squadron Leader Lapraik reported on a test flight conducted by a British pilot who took the Pe-2 up for a spin and this gave an invaluable description of how she handled.

Taxiing

Taxiing was considered very easy but rather uncomfortable, as the undercarriage was harsh. This harshness, however, was thought to be less noticeable with full load.

Take-off

With a light load the take-off was 'easy and straightforward' using 15-20-degrees of flap. There was no swing and the indicated take-off speed was 109mph. (175km/h). The undercarriage could be retracted in 12-14 seconds, resulting in a slight tail-heaviness. Trimmer settings were:

> Elevator: Very slight nose heavy.
> Aileron and Rudder: Neutral
> Throttles: Can be pushed fully forward.

The British test pilot was advised to raise the flaps in stages after retracting the undercarriage, as the sink was very pronounced if they were raised in one operation.

Climb

The best climbing speed was 167mph. (270km/h) indicated.

Level flight

Throughout the whole speed range, the controls were reasonably light and effective. Although longitudinally unstable, the aircraft was stable directionally and laterally.

Accurate trimming was most difficult as there was a very slight lag between the electric motor and the trimmer, which means that it was very easy to over-trim.

THE Pe-2 DESCRIBED

Two level speeds were made in 'M' blower with the following results:

Height	Indicated airspeed	RPM	Boost
1,250m (4,100ft)	400km/h (248mph)	2,500	91
2,000m (5,900ft)	390-395km/h (242-245mph)	2,500	91

The noise level was not considered unduly high.

Diving

A dive was made without the diving brakes to the limiting speed of 360mph (600km/h).[2] The aircraft handled well, there being no change in trim and no sign of vibration. Small movements were made with the controls but all seemed reasonably light, although they did get slightly stiffer as speed was gathered.

Recovery was easy, the aircraft regaining level flight in 820-985 feet (250-300m)

One of the more interesting aids to dive-bombing was an electrical device, which showed a red light if acceleration during recovery is above 7g.

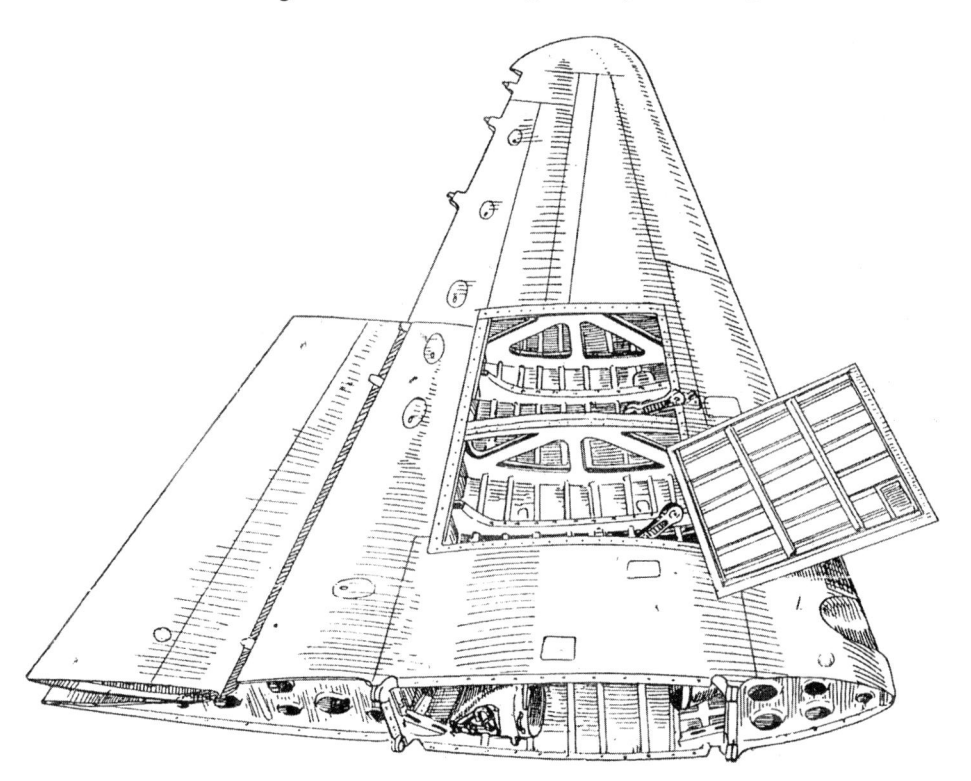

Diagram 11: Pe-2 wing flaps and access layout. (Russian Aviation Research Trust)

THE PETLYAKOV Pe-2

The test pilot had not used the diving brakes, as his passenger was not strapped in. The diving procedure, however, was fully explained to him as follows:

> The throttles are eased back and the diving brakes selected. The brakes extend fairly rapidly and as they extend they cut out the normal trimming device and trim the aircraft nose-heavy. On the release of the bombs, the trimmer is automatically returned to its original position and the aircraft recovers from its dive.
>
> For practice dives without bombs, the trimmer is returned to its original position by a small white push button on the shelf near the diving brake selector switch.
>
> There was *no* provision for level bombing.

Single-engined performance

With a light load, height could be maintained on one engine but it was not considered that this would be possible with a full load. Turns were possible, both with and against the working engine, and all foot loads could be relieved by the trimmer.

Approach and landing

After reducing speed to 300km/h (186mph) indicated, the undercarriage was lowered; this produced a slight nose-heaviness. The flaps were then lowered to 15 degrees and the circuit continued at an indicated speed of 250-260km/h (155-161mph). After the final turn, the flaps were lowered fully (50 degrees) and when they passed the 30-degree mark decided tail-heaviness was noticed. It was impossible to moderate this by trimming as lowering the flaps disengaged the tail trimmer.

The glide was reported to be 'rather flat' and the view good. At touchdown, the indicated speed was 170km/h (105mph). The shock-absorbing qualities of the undercarriage were not good and the machine was inclined to 'hop' along the ground. A slightly tail-up landing was advised by the Russians. The brakes were good.

View

The view was generally good but forward is reported as 'excellent' owing to the tapering nose and a large glass panel in the floor of the nose. This panel, incidentally, had a red line painted on it, which, it was presumed, was used to simplify the pilot's approach to the target.

No direct vision panels were fitted but two small windows, one on each side of the pilot, could be slid back during landing and take off.

THE Pe-2 DESCRIBED

Emergency exits

The navigator could make an exit through the normal entrance trap and the top of the pilot's and navigator's compartment could be readily jettisoned should it become necessary to abandon the aircraft.

Technical data

Accurate data were not at that time to hand but an approximate estimate, based on a span of 57 feet was that the maximum speed of the aircraft, without external bombs, would be of the order of 300mph at 14,000 to 15,000 feet.

Statistical Data

We can amplify Lapraik's reports further with details to which he was not privy to give the full picture.

Description:	Twin-engined, low-wing monoplane, all metal, stressed-skin construction with duralumin skin.
Power Plant:	Two M-105R (VK-105PF) twelve-cylinder vee liquid-cooled engines, each engine fitted with a pair of TK-2 two-speed turbo-superchargers (gear ratios 1:7.85 and 1:10). Each engine developed 1,100hp at 2,600rpm for take off. Rated power 1,100hp at 2,700rpm at 2,000m. and 1,050hp at 2,700rpm at 4,000m. Each engine enclosed in a slender, elongated nacelle, extending aft of the trailing edge of each wing, with long collector exhaust pipes. (These were progressively made shorter as time went on.) Each engine drove a three-bladed VISh-61 electrically-operated, constant-speed metal propeller, with reduction gearing (Ratio 1.694:1). Each wing had radiator air intakes located in tunnels in the leading edge, either side of nacelle, with exhaust via adjustable louvres on upper wing surface. Oil radiators were located beneath each engine.
Construction:	Circular-section monocoque structured fuselage, spaced 0.5m thick ribbing, with unsupported aluminum alloy skin (from 1.5 to 2.0mm thick), without stringers, built in three sections, forward, amidships and aft. Enforced framing to windows, cockpit and gun-turret openings only.
Wingspan:	56ft 3-1/4ins (17.16m)
Length:	41ft 6ins (12.66m)
Height:	13ft 11ins (4.0m)
Wing Area:	435.9 sq ft (40.5 sq m)
Weight:	Empty – 12,941lb (5,870kg) Normal – 17,130lb (7,770kg) Maximum – 18,783lb (8,520kg)

THE PETLYAKOV Pe-2

Wing Loading: 38.9 – 43lb/sq ft (190-210kg/sq. m)
Crew: 3. Pilot/Navigator-Bomb-aimer-dorsal rear gunner/Radio operator-ventral rear gunner. Latter was completely separated from rest of crew but had access to a dorsal hatch atop the fuselage in case navigator was incapacitated. Both pilot and navigator supplied with set of controls.

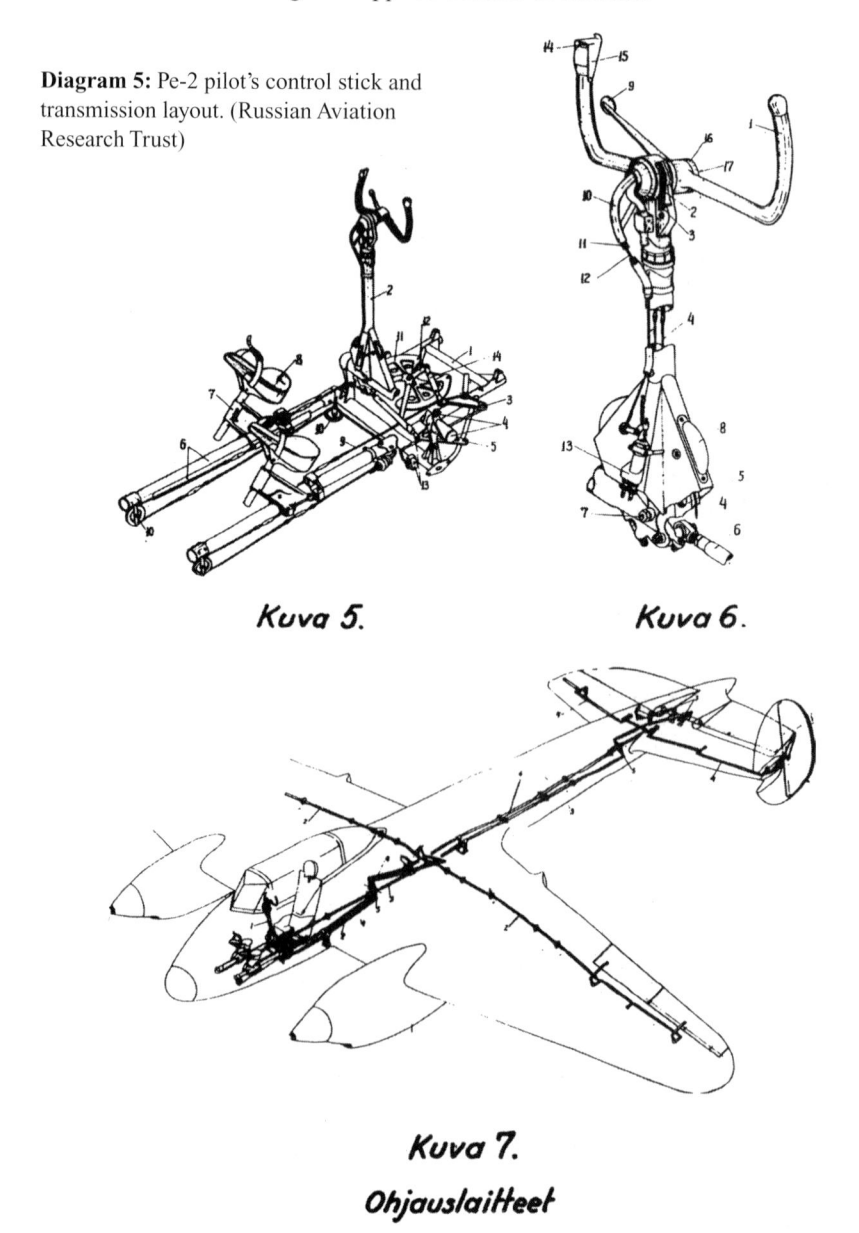

Diagram 5: Pe-2 pilot's control stick and transmission layout. (Russian Aviation Research Trust)

Kuva 5.   *Kuva 6.*

Kuva 7.

Ohjauslaitteet

THE Pe-2 DESCRIBED

Crew Protection: Both Pilot (fixed) and Navigator's (swivel) seats fitted with 9mm back armour. Two 6mm side panel armour shielded pilot's and navigator's positions.

Wings: Two-spar, constructed in three sections, centre section and two outer panels, the latter with a 5° dihedral. Thin skin (0.6 to 0.8mm) supported by multiple stringers. Compound taper wings, with the exception of the leading edge of the centre section. Divided, split trailing-edge flaps, which extended from the two-part, fabric-covered ailerons and the all-metal fuselage. Single, adjustable trim-tab (duralumin) only fitted to starboard aileron. Pair of electrically-operated (by the AP-1 automatic dive unit) 'Venetian blind' dive brakes made of steel tubing in rectangular grid form, under outer wing panels. A signal from the bombsight automatically triggered the AP-1 device to start the dive sequence and pulled the Pe-2 out of the dive at a pre-set altitude.

Diagram 10: Composition of the wing of the Pe-2. (Russian Aviation Research Trust)

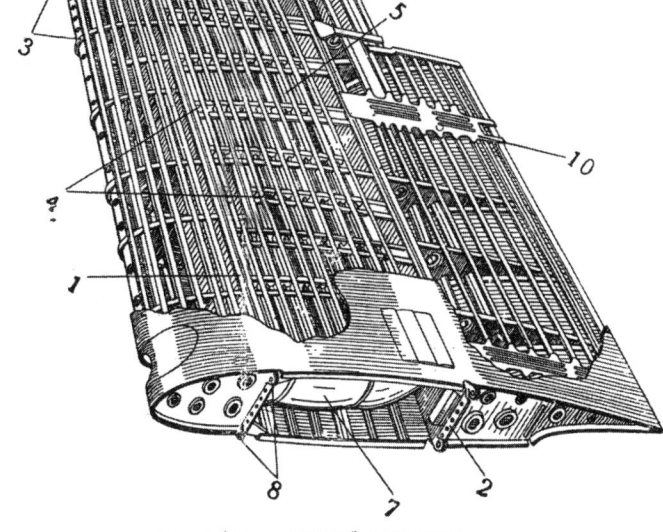

Фиг. 1. Каркас отъемной части крыла.

1—передний лонжерон; *2*—задний лонжерон; *3*—основные нервюры; *4*—скобы для бензобака; *5*—зетобразный стрингер; *6*—стрингер из бульб-уголков; *7*—туннель водорадиатора; *8*—стыковые узлы; *9*—кронштейны крепления элерона; *10*—нервюры крепления посадочного щитка.

THE PETLYAKOV Pe-2

Empennage: Trapezoidal tail plane with 8° dihedral, with oval-shaped twin fins and rudders either end to allow clear field of fire for dorsal rear gun. Control surfaces metal-framed and fabric-covered, and with duralumin trim tabs fitted.

Landing Gear: Twin-oleo leg main units, which were fully retractable folding aft into recesses. Fully retractable fork-leg tail wheel, aft retracting and also folding into recess.

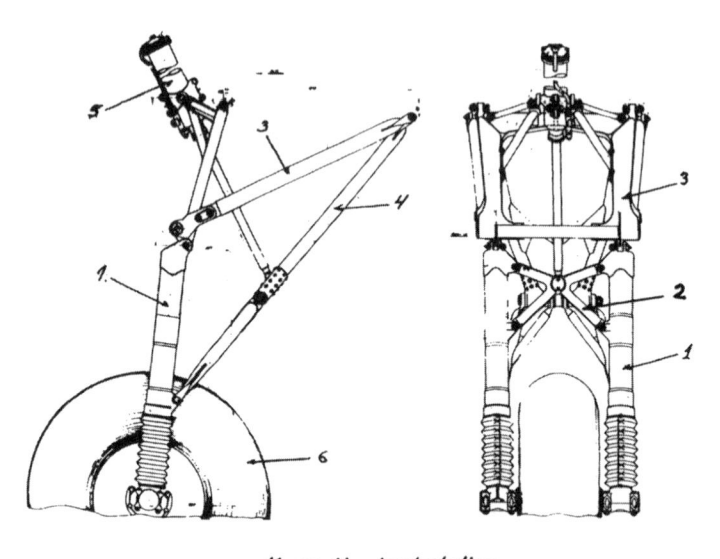

Kuva 11.- Laskuteline

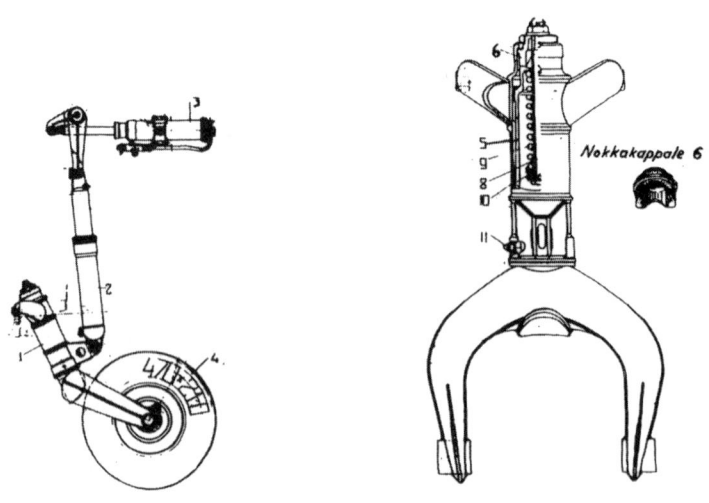

Kuva 12.- Kannus.

Diagram 6: Undercarriage arrangements. (Russian Aviation Research Trust)

THE Pe-2 DESCRIBED

Fuel Capacity: Fully self-sealing soft protected tanks. Later equipped with automatic external and internal nitrogen gas pumps which filled them as the fuel was used up. One main tank, mounted in central fuselage, with capacity 127 Imperial gallons (578 litres). Six wing tanks, three per side, located between the spars of the centre-section and the outer wing panels. Total combined capacity of 145 Imperial gallons (660 litres). From the 64th series, early 1942, all Pe-2s were equipped with nine fuel tanks, with a total fuel capacity of 1,484 litres. This only applied where all the tanks fitted were of metal construction. Some aircraft had Nos. 2 & 3 tanks of fibre construction, which reduced the total capacity to 1,411 litres.[3]

Kuva 15.- Polttoainejärjestelmä.

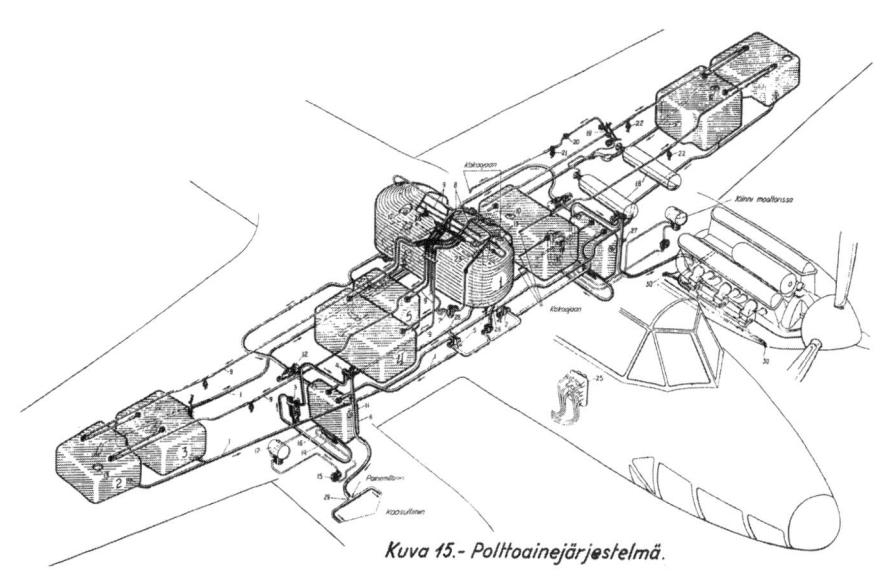

Diagram 4: Layout and location of fuel and hydraulic fuel distribution. (Russian Aviation Research Trust)

The ventrally mounted supplementary fuel tanks fitted to the Pe-2R gave her an extra 250 litres (74 Imperial gallons) capacity and extended the range to 1,700km (1,056 miles), more than ample for most Eastern front operations. (Russian Aviation Research Trust)

THE PETLYAKOV Pe-2

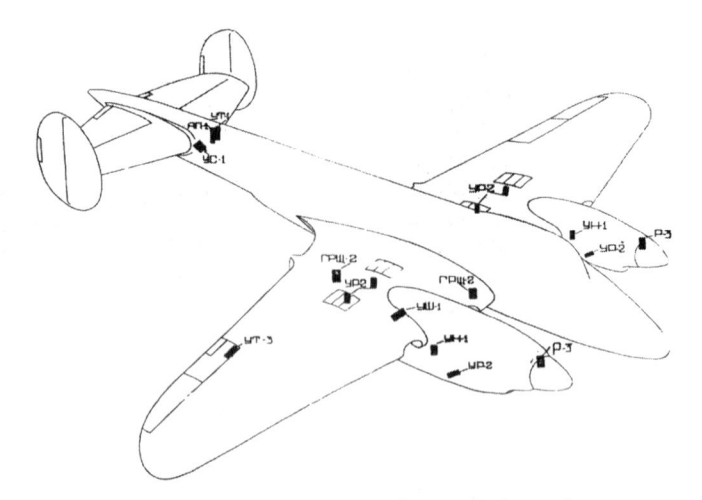

Kuva 9: Säätömoottorien sijoitus koneessa.

P-3 (R-3)	Potkurin säätäjä
УР-2 (UR-2)	Öljyn ja nesteen jäähdyttäjien säätö
УН-1 (UN-1)	Ahtimen vaihdemoottori
УШ-1 (USch-1)	Laskutelineen sähköinen säätö
ГРЩ-2 (GRScht-2)	Laskusiivekkeiden ja syöksyjarrujen säätö
УТ-3 (UT-3)	Siivekkeiden säätölevyn säätö
УС-1 (UC-1)	Vakaajan säätö
УТ-1 (UT-1)	Sivuperäsinten säätölevyjen säätö
АП-1 (AP-1)	Korkeusperäsimen säätölevyjen säätö (syöksyautomaatti)

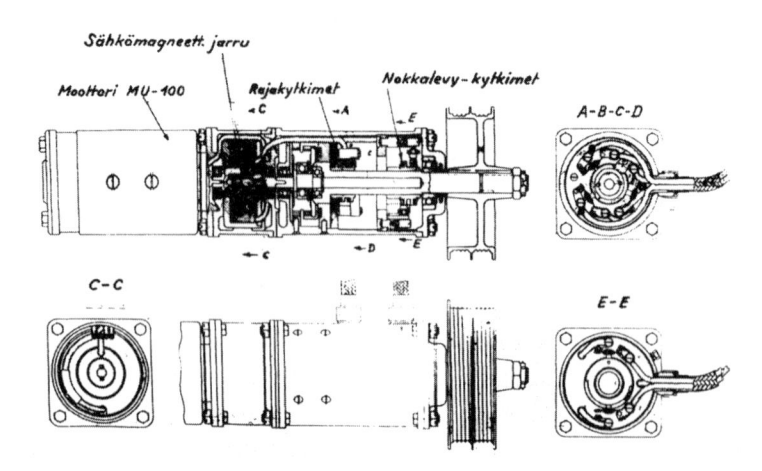

Diagram 7: The Pe-2 electric motor, distributor and detail. (Russian Aviation Research Trust)

THE Pe-2 DESCRIBED

Diagram 8: Pe-2 engine cooling system.
(Russian Aviation Research Trust)

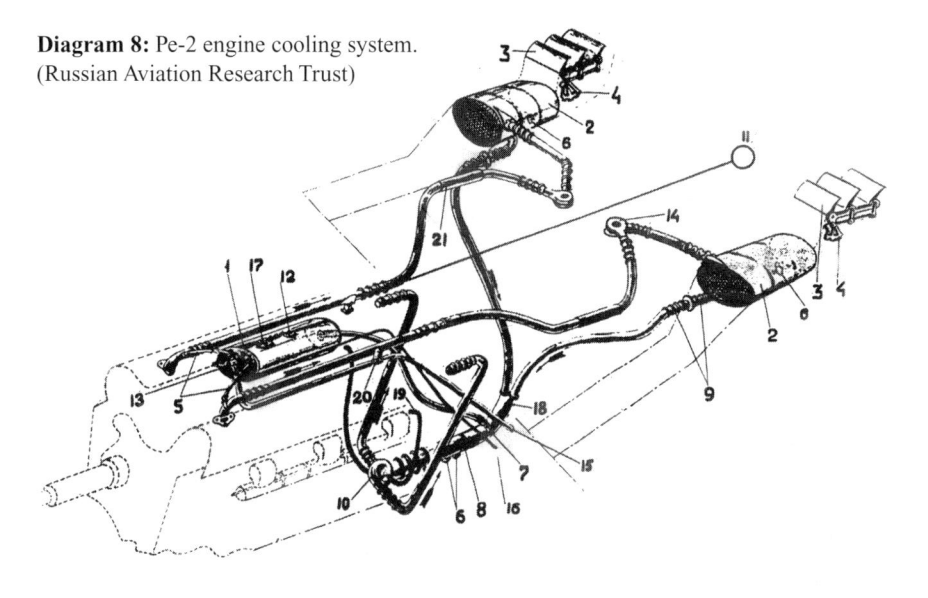

Kuva 17. - Jäähdytysjärjestelmä.

Electric Motors: Total of fifty, varying from two Kw-3 to 30 Kw electrically-driven motors, used for hydraulic pump system, actuation of hydraulically-operated undercarriage, ailerons, elevator, rudder trim tabs, wing flaps, dive brakes, radiator flaps, bomb-release mechanism, engine fuel pumps and engine superchargers. (Most extensive system fitted to Soviet warplanes up to that date, 1941).

Defence: *Initially* – Two fixed 7.62mm ShKAS machine guns in nose (with 500rpg carried). Single dorsal 7.62mm ShKAS rear machine gun on pivoted (Toropov) mounting (with 750rpg carried) instead of remote-controlled turret of original design. This gave 200° horizontal coverage, and 56° vertical sky arc coverage. Single ventral 7.62mm ShKAS rear machine gun with alternating port or starboard egress (with 750rpg carried), and fitted with 120° periscopic sight. Ammunition via chain running along fuselage wall, which easily jammed rendering aircraft 'blind' defensively in this area. Later rectified. Several armament alternatives became available depending on mission/function/availability. (See text)

Bomb Load: *Initially* – Six FAB-100 (100kg) bombs in three internal integral bomb bays, four in main fuselage and two aft of each engine nacelle; Two 100kg bombs externally on racks below centre wing section. Many variations carried later depending on target/mission/availability (See text).

THE PETLYAKOV Pe-2

Performance:	*Initially* – Maximum speed 336mph at 16,400ft (540km/h at 5,000m); 314mph at 6,560ft (506km/h at 2,000m).
Dive speeds:	With dive brakes extended – 373mph (600km/h); Maximum clean dive – 450mph (725km/h).
Range:	*Initially* – 621–931 miles (1,000–1,500km) according to loading.
Climb Rate:	3.5 min to 9,840ft (3,000m); *Initially* – 9.3 min 16,400 ft (5,000m); Later 7 min to 16,400ft (5,000m).
Ceiling:	*Initially* – 28,870ft (8,800m). Later – 29,530ft (9,000m).

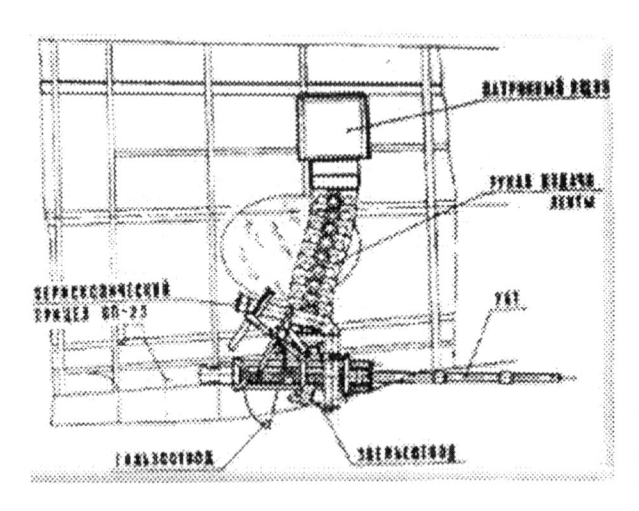

Diagram 12: The MN gun mounting. (Russian Aviation Research Trust)

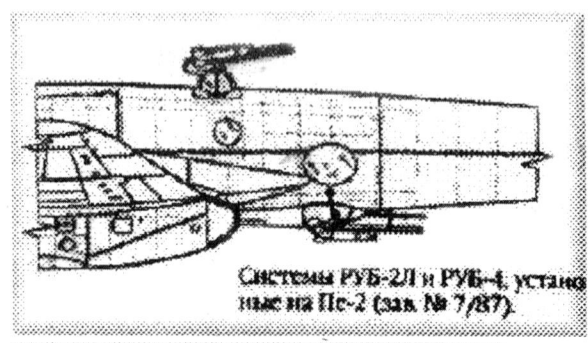

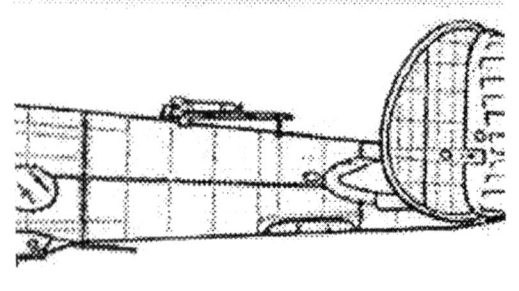

Diagram 13: The FZ gun mounting (Russian Aviation Research Trust)

Chapter Five

The Pe-3 fighter variant

Due to its speed, there was still a demand for the *Peshka* as a twin-engined fighter aircraft in the early 1940s. It should be remembered that, incredible as it may seem, the Soviet Union did not possess one single aircraft of this type in its armoury on the outbreak of war with Germany.[1] Influenced perhaps by the German Bf.110 long-range fighter, which had a good reputation at the time, the adaptation of the Pe-2 for a similar role was an obvious move. At the same time the demands of the production line dictated that only conversions of existing series production aircraft could be contemplated, rather than brand-new designs, and this also ensured that the Pe-2 was the logical choice, as did the *Peshka's* fighter design ancestry, the VI-100.

The One-Week Wonder!

On 2 August 1941 the GKO (State Defence Council) issued a directive instructing Petlyakov's OKB and GAZ 39 in Moscow, to produce a fighter variant of their

Close-up detail of the Pe-3 undergoing detailed examination at the Finnish Air Force Research Institute at VL. Assembly of the cockpit is revealed in this view. (Via Keski-Suomen Ilmailumuseo, Tikkakoski)

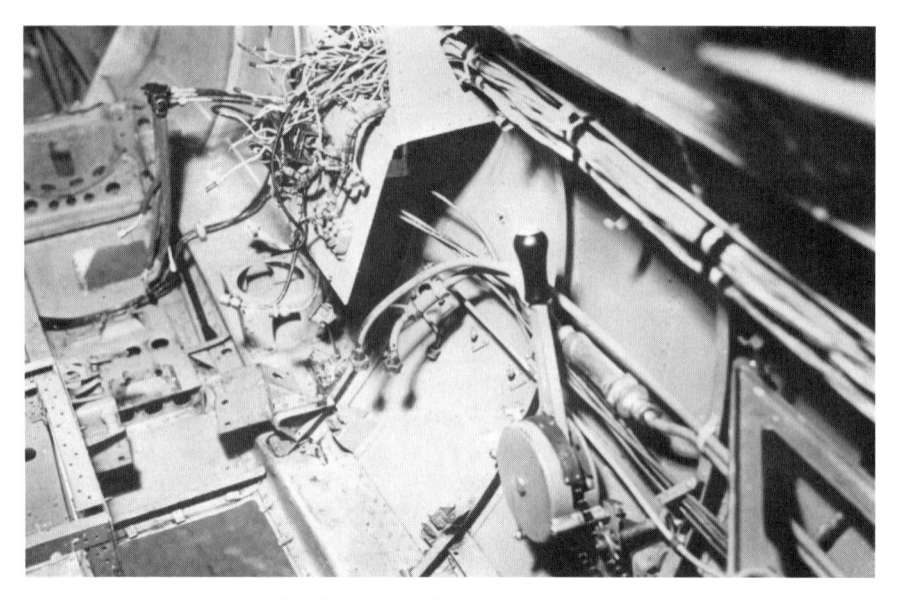

THE PETLYAKOV Pe-2

Looking aft along the inner fuselage of a Pe-3 showing wiring arrangement and construction detail. (Via Keski-Suomen Ilmailumuseo, Tikkakoski)

dive-bomber. They set a deadline for prototype delivery of 6 August! The due modifications were carried out on the sixth aircraft of the sixteenth production batch of Pe-2s being produced at GAZ 39, aircraft c/n 391606 becoming the prototype Pe-3.

Actual flying commenced on 7 August, with test pilot Fyodorov making the first flight development take offs.[2] One day later and the NII VVS RKKA test pilot, Colonel V.A. Stepanchonok, with *Ing*. Makarov as leading test engineer, undertook the pre-acceptance flight tests and then the Pe-2 went straight into her State Acceptance evaluation programme. The American designer 'Dutch' Kindleberger used to boast that the North American Mustang fighter was developed from scratch in one hundred days, and was not believed.[3] The Pe-3's conception, birth and first steps all took place within one week, and yet, like the Mustang, it was a winner.

The Modifications

Subsequently, several hundred machines were to be altered on the production line, simply and easily. Nothing in the basic construction changed; the rounded cross-section fuselage, 1.3m at its maximum diameter and 12.6m long, remained. So did the all-metal monocoque form built of 1.5 to 2mm thick D-16T, without stringers, in four sub-assemblies. The nose and centre-section alone altered along with the armament. The two-spar, all-metal wings, with the Schrenk flaps also remained, but the fitting of automatic slats to the leading edges of the outer wing panels was envisaged.[4]

THE Pe-3 FIGHTER VARIANT

Endurance and range were essential features of the new fighter, which was to be a two-seater, dropping the wireless-operator/navigator station. The existing eight wing fuel tanks of the Pe-2 could not be easily expanded to increase the extra volume of fuel required, and it was here that the most extensive redesign was necessary. There was obviously no time for detailed work and the massive changes to the production line that a proper re-think of layout would entail, and so a 'quick-fix' was adopted. Three additional fuel tanks were inserted into the fuselage, as close to the centre of gravity as possible. One 250-litre tank was located in the bomb bay, and the remaining pair, of 225-litre capacity,[5] in the now surplus rear gunner's cabin. This 700-litre extra fuel stowage gave the Pe-3 a theoretical 2,000-kilometre reach. The existing rear gunner's entry hatchway was retained in the new aircraft to facilitate the passage of engineers for ferry flights.

The other main changes were the elimination of the external bomb racks to give a smoother surface and more speed, the abandonment of the unnecessary dive brakes, which further cleaned up the undersides and the fitting instead of fully-automatic leading-edge slats mentioned earlier. The armament was changed from defensive to offensive with the addition of a nose-mounted armament of a 20mm ShVAK cannon, with 750rpg, and two 12.7mm UBK machine guns, with 150-rpg, which replaced the mixed ShKASs on the dive-bomber. Production Pe-3s had the ShKAS deleted, and the weight saved utilised by increasing the UBK's rounds carried to 250 per gun.[6] A single fixed ShKAS was mounted in the tail cone with 250rpg, and another was positioned in the navigator's cabin using the TSS-1 flexible mounting.[7]

The lack of offensive firepower was obvious to the designers, but they planned to rectify that deficit on later production runs when they expected to have more time for further modifications. This proved a false assumption, however. In the interim, the upper navigator's cabin ShKAS mounting was kept without alteration while, for rear ventral protection, the VI-100 arrangement of a single fixed ShKAS gun with 250rpg was to be fitted. On contemporary Pe-2s the same constricted cabin was also considered downright dangerous. The gun turret critically restricted the emergency escape route. The actual process of jettisoning the canopy to make an exit was difficult and, indeed, on many occasions, had proved fatally impossible.

A simplified bombing capability was also retained, with just two bomb racks located in the nacelle weapons bays and another pair under the main fuselage. This gave a limited capacity bomb-toting capability of 400kg in normal condition, with 700kg in overload condition. The Pe-3 could therefore carry into battle two 250kg and two 100kg bombs. However, in addition to the dive-brake shields and fittings, the ESBR-6 electrically-operated bomb-release mechanism was taken out, along with the ASShL-340 emergency mechanically-operated release unit, both to save weight. Ironically, in actual combat, the Pe-3 was used as much as a bomber as a fighter, if not more so in many naval units.

Another retrograde step was the replacement of the navigator's RSB-bis transceiver with the RSI-4 fighter type. The new equipment was decidedly inferior, having an effective range of just 100 kilometres (working to ground stations) and only 50-60 kilometres (working to other aircraft), which, on an aircraft with an 800-kilometre range, was useless. The RPK-2 HF/DF receiver unit also went by the board, as did the PR camera, again as weight-saving measures.

Performance, Problems and Production

These alterations were coupled with some slight aerodynamic styling changes. The glazed observation blisters set in both sides of the Pe-2 fuselage were eliminated, the wireless operator's cabin gun and glazed hatch were dropped and the area smoothed over, all of which resulted in better aerodynamics and a small loss of weight. These, in turn, resulted in a slight increase in speed. Colonel Kabanov conducted the four-day state evaluation programme from 10 August.

The figures that came out of the prototype's evaluation programme were a maximum speed of 530km/h at 5,000m, a service ceiling of 9,000m and a range of 2,150 kilometres. This was considered satisfactory for the intended job and, by 14 August 1941, GAZ 39 received authorisation to proceed to series production, with a pre-production batch of five machines to prototype standard by 25 August. Full-scale production was to follow immediately upon that.

Again, aircraft for the programme were taken from existing serial production and the first production Pe-3 was c/n 391902. She underwent the NII VVS acceptance evaluation trials in the period 29 August to 7 September, the flights being made from the Moscow Central field. Performance was almost identical to the prototype, with a slight increase in the maximum speed to 535km/h being attained.

This headlong rush was not achieved without complications of course. Corners could not be cut continually without some resulting difficulties. The pressing ahead to production was driven by dire need, and understandable, but, more haste, less speed, applied to aspects of the Pe-3 as with all else. The lack of properly prepared production drawings for many of the sub-assemblies, and the use of rough sketches instead, caused many headaches, with details being finalised actually on the shop floor! The major changes, the extra nose-mounted armament, the rear ShKAS gun mounting and the additional fuel tanks, all had to be improvised on the line, which led to hold ups.

The Flight Testing

Test pilot V. Stepanchonok conducted the State Acceptance evaluation flight testing in August 1941. Two forward-firing ShVAK were carried in the frontal section of the bomb bay on this aircraft[8] but, strangely these were not continued with. This seems odd when one of the biggest criticisms to be levelled was the sparseness of the final armament. Not only was it considered inadequate (compared to the equivalent German Bf.110C the Pe-3's firepower was puny, the Messerschmitt carrying four wing-mounted 7.9mm MG17 machine guns and two 20mm MG/FF nose-mounted cannon and still being 1,300kg lighter, the result of being designed for the job of course and not a bomber conversion), but firing tests showed up weaknesses. The extensive Perspex nose glazing of the Pe-2, considered necessary for dive-

THE Pe-3 FIGHTER VARIANT

bombing, was far from suitable in withstanding the blast effects of the heavier nose-mounted armament. Muzzle gas pressure caused considerable rippling and other damage under test conditions, which led to the replacement by a dural panel. When even this proved inadequate, a steel panel finally had to be substituted to overcome this problem.

Nor was this the end of the problem. The expelled spent cartridges and links from the UBK ejected into the slipstream and struck the leading edges of the wings and underside of the fuselage, in some cases fracturing the skin. Spent cartridges found their way into the gaping apertures of the coolant radiator intakes. Changing the ejector chutes failed to solve the problem completely and a collector box had to be provided.

Upgrading the armament was always going to be a requirement, offensively by the addition of the ShVAK cannon, defensively by beefing up the rear protection with the provision of the BT gun for the ShKAS. Aircrew protection was also below combat standard, and extra armour protection was worked in both forward and around the navigator's cabin area. The useless RSI-4 had to be quickly replaced with equipment of greater range. The Pe-3 lent herself to the photo-reconnaissance role, and several were fitted with aerial cameras for this purpose.

Meanwhile the dictates of the front meant that initial serial production Pe-3s followed the lines of the prototype as they were allocated to front-line units. For example, 95 SBAP was among the first to switch over from the Pe-2. This unit later became the sole Air Force unit to exclusively fly the Pe-3. However, their initial enthusiasm was dampened by actual combat use. The commanding officer of the regiment, Colonel S.A. Pestov, complained that lack of forward protective armour in the Pe-3 would mean that his regiment would be fortunate to survive intact after more than two missions! He called for enhanced protection on the lines of the NII VVS evaluation report.

The flow of Pe-3s had already undergone a compulsory cessation caused by the move of the GAZ 39 to Irkutsk. After the prototype, conversions had varied, from eighteen[9] in August 1941, to ninety-eight in September and a further eighty-two in October, giving a total Pe-3 tally of 197 machines.[10] Production was not resumed until April 1942, and this enforced breathing space enabled the recommended modifications to catch up with combat requirements. Meanwhile other considerations were under study.

Combat experience modifications

All the Pe-3's predicted shortcomings itemised by the NI VVS were soon confirmed as the result of actual combat experience. This led to widespread modifications, usually carried out in the field, and which were carried out piecemeal during October and November 1941, by service teams sent out from the plants with whatever was available at the time. Variation from unit to unit was therefore considerable.

The offensive armament was enhanced with the ShVAK located in the nose, with a second BK relocated to starboard, replacing the ShKAS there. The rear

THE PETLYAKOV Pe-2

The Pe-3 long-range fighter variant of the *Peshka*. This photo was taken by Major Frank Carney and logged with US Intelligence on 1 April 1947. In the post-war period, all Pe-2s and variants received the NATO codename 'Buck'. (US National Archives)

cabin glazing was removed in order that the navigator could operate a BT gun on a flexi-mounting and a DAG-10 dispenser was installed aft, with a stock of ten AG-2 parachute grenades.[11] These were launched into the path of attacking fighters where they exploded. While fresh and unexpected, they initially caused the Germans some losses. Extra armour was worked in and the CG moved forward, increasing the risk of nose-over on landings, so braking had to be restricted.

The pressing of the Pe-3 into service as a ground-attack aircraft during the German advance upon Moscow, however unsuitable, ensured enhanced ground-attack capability being introduced. From four to eight racks for the RS-82 rocket, and from four to six racks for the heavier RS-132 rocket, were fitted below the wings. Sometimes a mixed rocket loading of both types was employed.

Several DRAPs (Long-Range Reconnaissance Aviation Regiments) modified their Pe-3s specifically for this role at this period. The bomb racks were removed and replaced by extra fuel tanks. Cameras, both the AFA-B and AFA-1 types, were installed. Some units installed ventral racks for RS-82 rockets, which were fired to the rear as a defensive measure, either beneath the wings or after fuselage.

Night Fighter

The Pe-3 was hardly a month old when thought was being given to producing a night-fighter variant. The VVS's Aircraft Armament Scientific Test unit commenced evaluation trials in September 1941. Initially the flight-test team, test pilot Stepanchonok and his navigator, *Voyentechnik 1 ranga* (Military Technician 1st Class) Nos, initially investigated the effects of night firing on vision.[12] They quickly established that muzzle flash was blinding, making it impossible to use the K8-1 aiming sight. Flash suppressors were fitted to the gun muzzles and tested until the desired reduction was achieved to permit effective operation.

Because the Pe-3 night-fighter would be working in conjunction with friendly searchlight illumination, the effect of this was also analysed. It was found that, over Moscow in particular, the glare had a strong adverse effect on pilot orientation. The lights at times were powerful enough to cause eye watering and nausea, akin to physical impact. The lower cabin glazed area was therefore screened off, which much reduced this effect. Later, the very first use of interior UV lighting was adopted for the Pe-3, and instrument markings were made fluorescent. All these improvements were later extended into series production as standard.

Limited installation of the *Gneis-2* AI radar (fifteen sets only on the Pe-3, with others on the Pe-2 night-fighter variant) was later carried out on some of these aircraft, the *Peshka* being selected because the set was too heavy and of too large dimensions for single-engined fighters to embark.[13] This radar was first ready for air testing in June 1942 and, the following month, undertook State Acceptance evaluation over the Sverdlovsk region. They could pick up aerial targets at a range of 3.5 kilometres. Successful trials were followed by combat service evaluation, both over Moscow and, later, over Stalingrad. The set proved serviceable, but further trials were thought necessary. In the period February to May 1943, Gneis-*2* equipped Pe-3s of 2 Guards IAK PVO combat-evaluated the set over Leningrad and, as a result, it was approved for service in June of that year.[14]

The Pe-3*bis*

Strong criticism of the Pe-3 continued to be received from front-line units equipped with it. One squadron commander, Captain A. Zhat'kov, was so moved as to risk writing direct to the secretary of the Central Committee of VKP(b), G. Malenkov. Zhat'kov did not mince his words! He stated that, as a squadron commander, he felt he had a duty to inform on the 'poor quality of aircraft entering VVS service'. He affirmed that he and his fellow pilots were quite ready to fight the enemy with any aircraft they were given ('even this one'), but that men and machines were both costly and that to sacrifice so many of both for so little return was futile.

His criticism listed many faults with the Pe-3, but they generally followed the pattern already recognised from the NII VVS tests, viz., lack of armour protection, the need for the more powerful ShVAK cannon to replace the machine guns, the fitting of a turret-mounted ShKAS instead of the flexibly-mounted BT gun; all these were urgent requirements. He had duelled with enemy fighters and lost, only the fact that, when he prepared to bale out, his jettisoned canopy had struck the airscrew of his pursuer, forcing it and its companions to sheer off, had saved his life. Nor was his the only voice raised in protest at being sent to war in an inadequately equipped aircraft. The aircrew of 40 SBAP, busy converting to the Pe-3, were equally loud in their condemnation, and showered KB-39 with similar complaints.

THE PETLYAKOV Pe-2

The combined effect of this torrent of protest was the initiation by Malenkov of an order to the VVS command to instigate a searching and detailed examination of their complaints and come up with fast, and effective, solutions. The KB-39 team duly concentrated their efforts thus and the results of their labours were a completely new sub-type, the Pe-3bis.[15]

Specification

The principal change, as expected, was to the armament. Mounted in the unglazed nose was a pair of the new Berezin-designed universal machine guns (UBK), so-called because they were supplied complete with a modification kit that enabled them to be fitted to a whole series of aircraft, replaced the existing BK type machine gun.[16] Each of these had an ammunition outfit of 250rpg. In addition, a ShVAK cannon with 180 shells was fitted. The barrel of this gun protruded and was faired over with a conical probe.[17] In place of a ShKAS on a TSS-1 flexi-mounting, the *bis* shipped a UBT turreted gun with 180rpg.

To improve flight-handling performance slats were fitted to the outer wing panels. These had the most effect in the reduction of stalling tendency during the landing procedure. The recommended anti-glare screens were fitted to a much-reduced ventral glazing area. The pilot's cockpit was redesigned, reduced in profile and with the anti-crash frame moved forward by 0.5m. To decrease the flame risk a new system of inert, cooled exhaust gas to the fuel tanks replaced the nitrogen method.

Not everything that was requested, could be supplied, however, due to the extreme situation the Soviet Union found itself in the second half of 1941. The RPK-10 HF/DF receiver had to be omitted. The power plant, as we have seen in the Pe-2, remained unreliable in the extreme. In addition, some of the desired improvements had adverse affects elsewhere. For example, reduction in glazing gave better protection, but only at the cost of reduced vision, it was an unavoidable trade off. This made long-range navigation more difficult and tiring. The ShKAS cannon, a long-felt need, was found to produce up to 20 degrees of variation in the A-4 compass, which also added to the navigator's difficulties.

The prototype for the Pe-3*bis* was another series production aircraft from the line, c/n 392207, which was converted in September 1941. Again, test flying was conducted by A. Khripkov for the NI VVS during late September and October of that year. The modifications had increased the take-off weight by 180kilos, to 8,040 kilograms. Despite this, ground-level speed went up to 448km/h, but the price was paid at altitude, where the maximum speed again fell back to 520km/h.[18] A total of forty flights was made by this aircraft and the results were regarded as satisfactory.

As usual, various applications developed in the *bis* were extended to production aircraft, without any special indicators or breaks in the line flow. The pressures of the first years of the war with Germany meant that the Pe-3 was rarely used in its intended role and was, instead, pressed into service as a makeshift ground-attack machine. Hardly suitable for such a mission (complete lack of armour protection resulting in a high loss rate), the Pe-3 was nonetheless fitted with the four RO-82

THE Pe-3 FIGHTER VARIANT

rocket launchers, and others with an extra pair of RO-132 rocket-projectile launchers for the RS-82 and RS-132 rockets respectively, for use against German armour and soft-skinned vehicles. This, of course, negated any increase in speed, but that was of secondary consideration at this desperate period when stopping the Panzers was all that counted.

Defensively, the operational units themselves modified individual series production aircraft. Mobile companies temporarily assigned to the units' technical staff did this work. Thus ShVAK cannon were fitted, the UBT gun replaced the ShKAS machine gun, with the rear canopy simply deleted, as the new mounting screen was not on supply. The DAG-10 grenade launcher was fitted in the after-fuselage section for additional defence.

Production Changes

Before the Pe-3*bis* entered final production the Irkutsk team worked further changes into the design during the winter of 1941/42, which effectively, if not officially, resulted in a new variant. The power plant was the M-105R of 1,050hp, fitted with floatless (diaphragm) carburettors.[19] The alterations included improvements to armament, protection and undercarriage.

Armament

To overcome the problems as related with the nose-mounted cannon, both UBK weapons were relocated. They were paired in a specially designed sideways-hinged hatch, which was slung below the centre-section weapons bay. This hatch incorporated easy-access facilities to enable rapid and simple re-loading to be conducted in the field. Thus, it had a hinged, drop-down, front-frame section, which was released with the opening of the rear locks, bringing the ammunition containers down and out for ease of replenishment. The rounds-per-gun carried under this arrangement were 265 for the port gun and 230 for the starboard. The navigator's turret had been designed by GAZ 39 for the first prototype and held a wing-mounted UBK fitted with a pneumatic charging mechanism and 200rpg belt feeding. The gun was mounted on a standard Toporov mounting (designated variously as the VUB-1 or B-270).[20]

Various changes were introduced to enhance the aircrew's protection. The pilot's seat was given 10-13mm armour plating and extra plating was worked in front of him with two sloped 4mm thick steel plates, with a third of 6mm thickness behind the instrument panel. The floor of the cabin hatch was also armoured, not for external protection but internal in case the shock of landing accidentally triggered the pneumatically-charged UBK. The total weight increase from the extra protection thus built-in was 148 kilograms.

Reductions in weight to compensate for this rise were brought about by the removal of the anti-crash framework, the purpose of which was to enable the navigator more space to work the new mounting. The transfer of the armament into the centre-section meant that No. 7 fuel tank had to be made smaller, and its capacity was reduced to 100 litres. There was the provision of asbestos screening to this tank with a two-way effect. It shielded the fuel tank from overheating while the gun was being fired, and also helped prevent any leakage of fuel reaching the gun position, both of which could have deadly results. There was a change in the nose glazing with the dive-bombing requirement being phased out in favour of level aiming, and only a single nose panel was retained, along with two tapered side panels. The airscrews and two windshield panels were fitted with spirit-spray de-icing equipment.

In order to improve the directional stability, this prototype was given a 15 per cent increase in her tailfin/rudder assemblies, but this was never carried over into the serial production aircraft, presumably because it involved too much work and affected the line output too much. Test flights were made by Major S.I. Sofronov. Stability while landing, especially with almost empty fuel tanks, remained low, and the centre of gravity was found to have shifted forward with the introduction of the heavier nose armament and the armour protection. This nose-heaviness imposed restrictions on hard braking and reduced the anti-crash angle considerably. One of the test pilots, Colonel Kokinaki, recommended a longer main-wheel leg might help overcome this shift of weight. His idea was incorporated, and with the wheels in fully-extended position moved forward by 60mm, landing stability did indeed improve.[21]

These improvements were incorporated into the series production, which re-commenced in April 1942. Transfer of sub-assemblies from Moscow to the new factory enabled an additional eleven aircraft to be completed, bringing the total to that date to 207 machines plus the prototypes.

In May the second Pe-3*bis* prototype, c/n 40143900, began her flight-testing for NII VVS acceptance evaluation, flown by test pilot M. Nyukhtikov. The normal take-off weight of this aircraft was now 8,002 kilograms and the weight resulted in a drop in maximum speeds attained, which now became 438km/h at ground level and 527km/h at cruising height. Performance figures came out at a height gain of 540 metres in a combat turn, with turn time at 1,000 metres of 30 seconds, while climb-time to 5,000 metres was 9.65 minutes. These figures remained the norm for the serial production aircraft.

Actually, production numbers were tiny, GAZ 39 manufacturing just thirty-nine Pe-3*bis* in the rest of 1942. The factory was switched to the production of the Il-4 bombers in the autumn of that year, but enough parts had been produced to enable a further thirteen aircraft to be finished off in 1943 to clear the lines before production ceased for a while with a total run of just 134 Pe-3*bis* plus the two prototypes.[22]

Some of the early production models were allocated to 6 IAK PVO (Fighter Air Corps) for use as night fighters in defence of the capital during the period of the closest German advance. These aircraft were fitted with more powerful transceivers, airborne searchlights to both illuminate the target and for night-landings, and had RPK-8 ADF equipment added.[23]

There were other, one-off, hybrids that emerged from the serial production line in this period of experimentation and innovation. A very few such Pe-3s appeared in

THE Pe-3 FIGHTER VARIANT

the three-seater configuration for example.[24] Other details could vary; one aircraft mounted a single ShVAK, two UBs and one ShKAS, but omitted the ventral rear-gun position. It carried additional armour protection for the crew. This machine crash-landed in Karelia in 1943 and was restored to service by the Finnish Air Force.[25]

Although small in quantity the Pe-3*bis* was significant in that many of the changes introduced by this variant saw introduction into normal Pe-2 production; i.e. the streamlined pilot canopy, the trailing of the VUB-1 gun turret, the inert-gas fire-prevention kit, extension of the main wheels forward to reduce nose-down on landing. Changes, which were recommended but not carried over, were the increase in tail area and the leading-edge slats.

As mentioned, some Pe-3s were fitted with extra fuel tanks to extend their range, and given a pair of cameras, thus becoming photo-reconnaissance machines, and their relative success led to a special sub-type being introduced. However, for the Pe-3 herself, production ceased for the next twelve months.

Pe-3 – Production Re-started

Heavily used in combat, total front-line numbers soon fell to negligible proportions. The experiments with the Pe-2I and Pe-2VI had proven to be cul-de-sac and, anyway, the need for long-range fighters for the Navy in the Arctic and Black Sea, and as reconnaissance aircraft elsewhere, was not being met by modifications to serial production Pe-2s. On 23 May 1943, therefore, a GKO directive ordered GAZ 22 to resume production of the Pe-3, but with many of the advances and modification omitted, and using the M-105PF engine. Production was to start within a month to meet the front-line demand.

In specifying their requirements for the 'new' fighter, the VVS laid down more stringent parameters than the Pe-3 could possibly meet. They asked for a maximum speed of 650km/h, heavier offensive firepower, which included two 23mm (or even 37mm) cannon and three-to-five heavy machine guns and a range of 2,000 kilometres. Gone was the pressurised cabin, gone were the remotely-controlled guns, gone were the Dollezhal designed turbo-superchargers. In place was additional fuel, a 500-litre tank replacing the rear-gunner station of the Pe-2; a pair of ShVAK which replaced the bomb-bay 160rpg. While the nose-mounted UBKs were retained, a fixed tail-mounted ShKAS was to be installed.

Putilov realised that the Pe-3 could not possibly fill the bill, and told the NKAP so, adding that only a new design could do so. Already unhappy with his attitude and the deteriorating performance of the series production Pe-2, Putilov's opinions, although supported by Myasishchev, found no favour with the NKAP. More politically shrewd, the latter kicked the Putilov pet project, the Pe-2VI, into touch, moving its development to LII and then GAZ 26 before it was finally terminated. Meanwhile GAZ 22 proceeded to build the M-82-engined Pe-2 instead of the Pe-3. This merely delayed the day of reckoning, however, for, with the failure of that project also, the revised Pe-3 came to the fore once more, but it did so obliquely. In the autumn of 1943 the new-type Pe-3 development was resumed at GAZ 22

In order to meet demands for an improved navigator's cabin for the serial production Pe-2, as part of modernisations of the standard dive-bomber line, OKB-22 had designed a new version, designated the FZ station. This new station had been approved by the NII VVS for series production, but, with the idea of minimising technical delay to the remorseless demands of the Pe-2 production line, it was mooted that this innovation should be first introduced on the re-started Pe-3 variant. Any hitches here would not affect the monthly *Peshka* figures! A full-scale mock-up produced in November 1943 also featured a modified leading-edge wing profile, yet another attempt to improve the landing characteristics of the aircraft. However, once more, things turned out very differently.

False Dawn

When the first of the new Pe-3 batch, aircraft number 15/298, was rolled out in February 1944, there was little resemblance to the mock-up. The wing leading-edge modification had been dropped entirely; the NKAP had banned the installation of the FZ navigator station (the argument apparently put forward was that, as the Pe-2I did not require it, nor therefore did the Pe-3).[26] The frontal armour did not appear either. The armament was a varied mix. The new electrically-operated DEU remote turret was not available and a proposed twin-ShVAK central mounting from GAZ 22, did not materialise either. In their place the UBK nose gun was retained while two DAG-10 containers, which released ERG-2 parachute grenades, provided the sole lower rear defence. Only two MDZ-40 bomb racks were fitted, each capable of carrying a single 250kg weapon.

So far short of the new specification did the renewed Pe-3 fall that it was not submitted for State Evaluation testing. The production run reflected this and only nineteen aircraft (in two batches) were ever finally built by GAZ-22, all in the first quarter of 1944. What to do with even these few was the subject of an acrimonious dispute between the NKAP and VVS that was not finally resolved until the summer. Under the direction of Major (*Ing*) D. Smirnov, the NII VVS armament trials were finally conducted with c/n 15/298 during July and August 1944, but the results were almost uniformly dismal.

The armament was, as expected, criticised for its total lack of hitting power, while its bomb-carrying capacity was equally meagre; only two 250kg bombs could be carried on MDZ-40 racks. The promise by the GAZ-22 representative that production models would upgrade with a second ShVAK failed to impress the evaluation team. The aircraft's performance matched everything else; the VVS call for a maximum speed of 625km/h at altitude and a climb time of six minutes not being achieved by a wide margin. Indeed the new Pe-3 batch hardly differed from the current 300-plus production-batch Pe-2 dive-bombers coming off the line at that time, and these had a maximum speed of 515km/h at 3,500-4,000 metres and a climb time to 5,000 metres of 9.5 to 11 minutes.[27] The evaluation committee did not even bother to record the Pe-3's figures and their silence can be regarded as an eloquent representation of their feelings on the matter.

THE Pe-3 FIGHTER VARIANT

After an award ceremony this *Peshka* aircrew pose for the camera. Notice the extreme youth of these flyers. (M Mastov)

Front-line allocation

Once the decision had been taken, albeit reluctantly, to deploy the eighteen Pe-3s[28] the question was which units would receive them. The final choice was a pair of long-range reconnaissance aviation units, 40. and 98. APR GK KA (Aviation Reconnaissance Regiment of Red Army Supreme Council) which, by the time of receipt, had become 48. and 98. Guards Long-Range Reconnaissance Aviation Regiments respectively.

Pe-2 Tow-tugs

The Pe-2 was often used in subsidiary roles, one of which was a tow-tug for various experimental types. In 1943 one acted in this capacity to Professor M.KL. Tikhonravov's I-302 rocket-powered target-defence fighter at the Jet Engine Scientific Research Institute (RNII) before this project was aborted.

The first liquid-rocket-engined fighter aircraft to enter service was the Bolkhovitinov BI (after the two designers, Viktor Fedorovich Bereznyak, and Aleksei Mikhailovich Isaev, who worked under the direction of Aleksandr Yakovlevich Bolkhovitinov). This mainly wooden construction, low-wing cantilever monoplane was built around the Dushkin D-1A liquid-fuel rocket, powered by kerosene and nitric acid. Test flights commenced on 10 September 1941 and the test pilot, Boris Mikhailovich Kudrin, was towed into the air by a Pe-2 prior to gliding back to earth. The *Peshka's* passing connection with rocket power at this early date was to be replaced by a much more prominent role three years later.

THE PETLYAKOV Pe-2

Korolev's Rocket proposals

S.P. Korolyev, who was heavily involved in the development of the RD-1KhZ liquid-fuelled rocket engine, provided one last postscript to the Pe-3 design story. Flight development tests had already been conducted on a Pe-2, c/n 15/85,[29] to provide boosted acceleration.

In February 1944 Korolyev proposed that the Pe-3 could have her performance transformed by the fitting of two of these engines. Thus equipped, Korolyev claimed, the Pe-3 could reach speeds equal to the very latest fighter type. They would gain immensely from both rate of climb and operational ceiling.

Korolyev went further, postulating a single-seater version of the standard Pe-2 with the VK-105PF engines being fitted with these supplementary liquid-fuel rocket boosters.[30] This would have been the Pe-2RD. He also proposed a similar arrangement for the Pe-2VI, with turbo-superchargers; top speed was estimated to be a giddy 785km/h, but range had to be sacrificed and was reduced to just 1,000 kilometres. The tractor fuel kerosene and concentrated nitric acid oxidant was a volatile mix, the dangers of which Korolyev dismissed as without any 'adverse effects'. His bland views were not shared by the VVS who had practical demonstrations of the dangers involved, and those proposals followed the many others into the wastepaper basket, bringing the Pe-3 development story to a conclusion after 360 had been constructed.

Table 1: Development of the Pe-3

	Pe-3 (1941)	Pe3*bis* (1942)	Pe-3 (1944)
Power Plant	M-105R	M-105RA	VK-105PF
Nominal hp	1,050	1,050	1,210
hp at Altitude (m)	4,000	4,000	2,700
hp at Altitude (ft)	13,123	13,123	8,858
Overall length (m)	12,665	12,665	12,650
Overall length (ft)	41.55	41.55	41.55
Wingspan (m)	17,13	17,13	17,13
Wingspan (ft)	23.44	23.44	23.44
Height (m)	3,925	3,925	3,925
Height (ft)	12.87	12.87	12.87
Wing area (m^2)	40,8	40,8	40,8
Wing area (ft^2)	133.85	133.85	133.86
Weight (Empty) (kg)	5,730	5,815	n/a
Weight (Empty) (lbs)	12,532	13,060	n/a
Normal takeoff weight (kg)	7,860	7,870	7,920
Normal takeoff weight (lbs)	17,328	17,350	17,460
Overload takeoff weight (kg)	n/a	8,300	n/a
Overload takeoff weight (lbs)	n/a	18,298	n/a

THE Pe-3 FIGHTER VARIANT

Fuel capacity (litres)	2,200	2,078	1,900
Fuel capacity (gals)	484	457	418
Maximum speed ground level (km/h)	442	438	470[1]
Maximum speed ground level (mph)	274.65	273.31	292.05
Maximum speed (km/h)	535	530	540
Maximum speed (mph)	332.45	329.34	335.55
Landing speed (km/h)	n/a	140	n/a
Landing speed (mph)	n/a	87	n/a
Service ceiling (m)	n/a	8300	n/a
Service ceiling (ft)	n/a	27,230	n/a
Range (km)	2,150	200	1600
Range (miles)	1,336	1,242	994
Take off distance (m)	n/a	360	500
Take off distance (ft)	n/a	1,181	1,644
Landing run distance (m)	n/a	410	n/a
Landing run distance (ft)	n/a	1345	n/a
Main (Nose) armament	2 x BK[2]	1 x ShVAK	1 x UBK
Secondary ('Midships) armament	n/a	2 x UBK	2 x ShVAK[3]
Upper armament	1 x ShKAS[4]	1 x UBK	1 x UBT
Rear armament	1 x ShKAS	1 x ShKAS	1 x ShKAS[5]
External Bomb Capacity (kg)	2 x 250	2 x 250	2 x 250
External Bomb Capacity (lbs)	2 x 551	2 x 551	2 x 551
Nacelle bomb-rack capacity (kg)	2 x 100	2 x 100	n/a
Nacelle bomb-rack capacity (lbs)	2 x 220	2 x 220	n/a

Notes
1: Predicted speed.
2: Single ShVAK cannon added later
3: Only one on test aircraft
4: Replaced by BT later
5: Not carried on test aircraft.

Experimental Fighter Projects

The Pe-3 and the Pe-2 fighter adaptations were not the only fighter projects associated with the *Peshka*. We shall examine the later concepts elsewhere but early war-period ideas were the Pe-2I and the Pe-2VI.[31]

With serial Pe-2 dive-bomber production established at three factories, GAZ 22 and GAZ 39 in Moscow and GAZ 124 at Kazan, and with plans to extend production to yet a fourth factory, GAZ 400 at Kharkov, GKO expected to have adequate capacity to experiment with the design. The order issued in July 1940, therefore, not only authorised mass production of the Pe-2 but also included plans for both a small batch of ten to fifteen of a fighter-bomber variant, and an escort-fighter variant. This latter was to be built at both GAZ 22 and GAZ 39, and would be built without the pressurised cabins or turbo-superchargers.[32]

However, the German invasion soon eliminated the Kharkov plant and the two Moscow units had to move beyond the Urals. All of a sudden, there was no spare capacity whatsoever and both ideas were abandoned. Other fighter ideas continued to appear, however.

The Pe-2I (1941)

Almost concurrent with the early work carried out on the Pe-3 fighter variant herself, GAZ-22 came up with a more heavily-armed alternative as a competing private venture. In August 1941 the fifth aircraft of the thirty-third Pe-2 production batch, 5/33, was modified to this specification. While many of the changes carried out closely followed those adopted by the Pe-3 (elimination of the dive brakes; conversion to a two-seater aircraft with just pilot and navigator; installation of the fighter-type transceiver equipment, plating over side-cabin windows and ceiling hatch, and so on)[33] other modifications differed. The production model replaced the standard Schrenk-type split flaps by a special TsAGI-type.

The armament retained the existing Pe-2 nose guns intact but increased firepower by mounting two 20-mm ShVAK cannon, each with 160rpg, in the main weapons bay.[34] The rear defence deleted the tail-mounted ShKAS and substituted a fixed (5-degree depression), ventrally-mounted BK weapon, with 100rpg, which was emplaced in the standard Lu-Pe-2 rear-ventral mounting, instead of the BT. The ultimate intention was to replace this with, in turn, the same weapon mounted in a DEU remote-controlled barbette sighted via the OPKS aiming sight. The almost nominal bomb-load on the Pe-2I was restricted to just two 100kg bombs carried on DZ-40 racks inside the engine nacelles.

The intention was to push the maximum range up to 2,000 kilometres and to do this extra fuel bunkerage was provided. The centrally-mounted fuel tanks each had their capacity increased to 70 litres; two 180-litre drop tanks were carried on the modified under-fuselage bomb racks. With the elimination of the rear gunner, this space was occupied by a further fuel tank with 240-litre capacity. This resulted in an increase in internal fuel stowage to 1,810 litres compared to the standard Pe-2's 1,500 litres, which the external tanks further increased to 2,170 litres.

Despite all this, the Pe-2I failed to achieve the desired optimum range, even with the dropping of the forward armour protection for the aircrew, the deletion of the NKPB-4 night bomb-sight, dive-brakes and automatic dive-control unit. In fact, take-off weight actually *increased* to 8,239 kilograms compared to 7,860 for the Pe-3. On-board equipment included the RPKO-10 HF/DF (later also deleted),

THE Pe-3 FIGHTER VARIANT

the RSB-3*bis* transceiver, the SPU-2F intercom, oxygen equipment and AFA1M cameras on the first, and AFA-3 cameras on the second aircraft. Dive-bombing was conducted via the PBP-1 machine-gun aiming sight, while level bombing was conducted via the OPB-1r bomb-sight.

The NI VVS evaluation flights were conducted by test pilot Captain Vasyakin and took place in the period 27 August to 7 September 1941. The Pe-2I achieved an increase in speed over the Pe-2 bomber of just 32km/h, which was no surprise.

Comparison with the Pe-3 being produced by GAZ-39 at the same time showed the Pe-2I to be the superior machine. Certainly, the offensive armament was better. Performance figures, when released, also looked good, with an average 10km/h increase in speed at most altitudes over the Pe-3, plus a 30-second shorter climb time to 5,000 metres. Not without justification, KB-39 questioned these figures and an examination did indeed show that the trials were 'rigged' in favour of the KB-22 teams machine. Whereas the Pe-3 had conducted her evaluation tests in normal condition, the Pe-2I had been trialled minus the external fuel tanks, without the drag and weight factors those would have imposed.

Compared with the Pe-3 the Pe-2I had superior firepower, and there was little difference in crew protection, which was virtually nil for both.

Less biased was the simulated air-to-air combat the Pe-2I was put through, testing her abilities against both the MiG-3 fighter and the SB bomber. As an interceptor the Pe-2I had no difficulty in catching the bomber and carrying out attacks from all angles with ease. Unfortunately, her blind spot was poor manoeuvrability and she found it difficult to out-turn the bomber. Nor did the lack of forward protection evoke much feeling of safety in combat. Against the single-engined MiG, the Pe-2I was much outclassed. Her only hopes lay in a head-on attack (with again the lack of protection a stultifying factor working against this) or outright evasion by means of a shallow dive at full power. The Pe-2I, like most twin-engined, long-range interceptors, was *no* dog-fighting machine. Both the Pe-2I and the Pe-3 were inferior to the Bf.110 and even the SB, which had smaller minimum turn radius and faster rates of turn.

Those serial production Pe-2s taken from the line and made over as temporary fighters had an all-round capability to act as dive- and level-bombers, as reconnaissance aircraft, ground-attack and long-range escorts. In any case, the advantages of the Pe-2I were too small to cause upset to production. The Pe-2 serial production dive-bomber output had to be maintained at GAZ-22 above all else and the first Pe-2I fell by the wayside due to this and the subsequent evacuation eastward.

Pe-2VI (1941)

It was hardly surprising, considering the *Peshka's* origins as the *Sotka*, that projected high-altitude fighter variants were to feature time and time again in the Pe-2 story. The first known instance of this was an order issued in 1941 to the Petlyakov OKB to built a small batch of five such variants, equipped with pressurised cabins, and submit them to the State Evaluation Programme. By June 1941 a full-scale mock-up had been completed at GAZ 22, which was designated the Pe-2VI. With the move to the east in October all work stopped on this programme.

Yet the war, as it developed, quickly revealed that the VVS had a real need for a twin-engined fighter, but with endurance and range, rather than high-altitude capacity, as the prime requirements. Indeed standard Pe-2 dive-bombers were combat flown as long-range escorts from very early on the war, in lieu of anything better. Vital troop convoys bound for Sevastopol were given air cover against German dive-bombers well beyond the range of single-engined Soviet fighters, by the Pe-2s of 40. BAP. They were also used as long-range dive-bombers utilising the K-76 or K-100 bomb cassettes against German troop concentrations and bridgeheads along the Black Sea coast as the combat moved east.[35]

Pe-2VI (1942)

The death of Petlyakov and the appointment of A.I. Putilov as his successor had the side effect of re-instating the Pe-2VI on the *Peshka* Agenda. Dollezhal had designed a new and more efficient turbo-supercharger and these were to be fitted to the M-105PD engines for the new design. As envisaged, this aircraft was to be a single-seater with a pressurised cabin, and a stripped-down-to-essentials armament of one forward-firing ShVAK cannon, with 250rpg, and a remote-controlled machine gun in a tail barbette.

Design work continued on this aircraft but it was not until December 1942 that the new Pe-2VI received NKAP approval. They required that flight development trials should commence by the end of February 1943.[36] Work therefore proceeded very quickly. By the end of January 1943 all the project drawings were finalised and sent out to the workshops, and a full-scale mock-up was completed. On 1 February 1943 a special commission had inspected this mock-up and others. These included the pressurised pilot's cabin and the DEU-1 barbette with the UBK gun and the revised power unit for the inspection. The commission pressed for better armour protection for the pilot. The first three prototypes then quickly took shape, while a flying test-bed Pe-2 (c/n 12/138), equipped with M-105PD engines, were also ready. The commission, who recommended that the wing area be increased by 2.5 square metres, approved all these.

The prototype proved ready to commence her flight development trials by 10 February 1943.[37] She differed from the standard Pe-2 in that the outer wing panels were of wooden construction and combined a NACA 230 airflow section with the increased area asked for. This modification was to improve lower speed lift capability. These wooden sections were sub-contracted out, as the team had no proper facilities in the factory. Unfortunately, this led to delays by the sub-contractor, which held the programme up for a time. One of the three prototypes was therefore completed with the normal Pe-2 wing panels in order to get the trials moving. The Pe-2VI also had the extreme nose section (F-1) totally re-designed.

THE Pe-3 FIGHTER VARIANT

The first prototype was completed without the pressurised cabin, and was used principally for engine trials. The second prototype had to be engined with the M-105PF due to unavailability of the M-105PD, although the correct power plant was fitted retrospectively. In addition, yet another standard Pe-2 was used to evaluate the DEU-1 tail barbette.

The first test flight, therefore, did not take place until 30 April 1943. The new pressurised cabin was *not* a success, being subject to misting up and poor vision, while the test pilot complained of overheating and uncomfortable operating conditions. A second test flight, on 9 May, ended in a forced landing due to engine malfunction. Nor did the expected high-altitude results materialise from this power plant. Furthermore, as troubles never come in ones, the DEU-1 tests had revealed that the new barbette had poor sighting and its operating equipment was far from reliable.[38]

Putilov was now spending more and more time in nursing the Pe-2VI through these various trials and tribulations, and less and less time in attending to the more boring demands of speeding the serial production line and modernising the plant. In short, he took his eye off the ball as far as the NKAP was concerned. Apparently blind to the increasing frustration this attitude was causing in Moscow, Putilov pressed on with new proposals.

Putilov was well aware of the unreliability of the chosen power plant, and suggested building yet another prototype Pe-2VI, to be equipped with the M-82NV engine and TK-3 turbo-supercharger. These engines had the advantage of having already been flight-tested on another modified Pe-2 (c/n 19/31). Before this could be done, however, Putilov was replaced by Myasishchev. As we have seen the latter quickly had the design work transferred to the LII. They, in turn, passed it on to an aero-engine factory for specialised work, GAZ 26, but little work was done before the project was abandoned, and this time permanently.

In truth, the demand for such an high-altitude aircraft turned out to be far less than expected at this stage of the war, but a year later the fitting of the Pe-2VI with rocket motors was revived, but again to no avail.

Chapter Six

First Combat

The basic doctrine of the VVS lent itself to the Pe-2 dive-bomber's capabilities. The *Raboche-Krest'yanskaya Krasnaya Armiya* (RKKA – Workers and Peasants Red Army) draft *Field Manual* for 1939 stated quite categorically that 'Aviation is linked strategically and tactically to the ground forces.'[1]

The handful of existing operational Pe-2s were initially used badly, being merely sent to make up the numbers in the *Dal'nebombardirovochnaya aviatsiya Glavnovo Komandovaniya*, DBA-GK (Supreme Command Long-Range Bomber Force). This comprised five air corps, each containing two air divisions, along with two independent divisions. This mix of some 800 aircraft of all types was mainly inherited from the *Aviatsiya osobov naznacheniya* – AON (Special Purpose Air Arm), which had been done away with in 1940. This motley assembly was based mainly on back-area airfields, and thus survived the initial massacre by the Luftwaffe more than the front-line units. However, it was only a temporary reprieve

Close-up detail view of the *Peshka*, giving clear views of the forward fuselage-mounted guns, bomb racks etc. Reindeer are being employed to cart ammunition on sledges. (Via Keski-Suomen Imailumuseo, Tikkakoski)

FIRST COMBAT

for they were thrown in wholesale to try to stop the rout and the Bf. 109Fs took a very heavy toll of them from June 1941 onward. By August the DBA-GK had taken such heavy casualties that its air corps were dissolved and the survivors, 310 obsolete DB-3F bombers, ninety-two TB-3s and twenty-eight escort fighters, supplemented by nine of the new Pe-2s which had nothing in common with them, were assigned to various front-line commands.

The VVS bomber forces had undergone several organisational changes from 1938 onward as the various combat lessons were digested and analysed. In April 1939, in order to establish the new *Armeiskaya Aviatsiya* (Army Air Force) the existing air brigades were abolished and in their place a new formation, the *Aviatsionny Polk* (air regiment) was introduced. The *Pikiruyushchi Bombardirovochny Aviatsionny Polk* (dive-bomber air regiments) were made up of five squadrons of aircraft, each squadron having a strength of twelve aircraft. The standard sub-section for all the bomber units was the three-plane section (*Zven'ya*), calls for a more flexible four-plane formation, in two two-plane pairs (*Pary*) following Spanish Civil War experience, going unheeded.

This new arrangement as adopted, in theory, gave each air regiment a strength of sixty aircraft, plus reserve machines, but in practice few had actually attained that number by June 1941, the majority being well under strength. This was particularly so, of course, in the case of the Pe-2, even until the following year. The new groupings were an attempt to bring the air force more in line with the ground forces and thus four, five or six *Aviatsionny polk* comprised the strength of an *Aviatsionnoya Diviziya* (air division). In the case of the dive-bombers this was ultimately to lead to the formation of composite air divisions, with both fighters and *Peshka* squadrons then being assigned and attached to co-operate with their own ground army.

This set-up did not long last the tests of war. By July/August, 1941 the *Stavka* had already decided to re-organise the air regiments into thirty-two-plane units and air divisions into two regimental units (with two bomber and one fighter air squadron of ten aircraft apiece, each with its own dedicated ground army number), plus two bombers assigned to each of the respective regimental headquarters. On 20 August the *Narodnyy Komissariat Oborony* (NKO, or People's Commissariat of Defence) issued an order that all the air regiments receiving the new combat aircraft, including the Pe-2, were to be re-organised into homogeneous regiments of two nine-aircraft squadrons each, with two additional planes assigned to regimental HQ, giving a total of twenty.[2]

Although these units were how the bulk of the warplanes of the Soviet Union were to be organised, there was also the VVS-VMF (*Voenno-morskoi Flot* or Navy Air Force), which were always land-based; the Soviet Union built no aircraft carriers until the 1960s. They were designed to work with the Arctic, Baltic, Black Sea and Pacific fleets respectively. Their basic weapons were the torpedo-bomber for offence and fighters for defence, and they not only worked over the actual fleets, which rarely, if ever, put to sea, but also over the seaward flanks of the army; almost all their wartime operations were in this littoral. Allocations of the Pe-2 to Navy units were initially just a handful, some for reconnaissance purposes, but steadily their numbers increased and Navy dive-bomber units operated against German

THE PETLYAKOV Pe-2

A fighting Soviet dive-bomber aircrew, in full flying gear, pose atop their *Peshka,* which is adorned with combat citations following many front-line missions. (M Maslov)

forces principally in northern Norway and the Baltic during the war. In the same area the Fourteenth Army, charged with the defence of the vital Kola Inlet down to Kandalaksha, operated a composite light-bomber wing equipped with both SBs and Pe-2s, for example.[3]

As one might suspect, the actual flying was much regimented, with little or no allowance made for individual flair or self-expression.[4] Formations were strictly regulated by their *Zveno* (squadron leaders – this was a description and not a rank) and only reacted to direct visual signals from him during operations. This usually meant that if the leader was shot down the formation lost cohesion and purpose and became both vulnerable and ineffective. It was perhaps an invariable situation given the Soviet system based on fear and blind obedience so ingrained in every citizen from birth to death. Such tactics were also taught at the eighteen *Osoviakhim* training schools but, after the fiasco of the Finnish War in the winter of 1939-40, and the pending arrival of the new generation of warplanes, the Party Central Committee issued a resolution in February 1940 demanding an acceleration into service of these new aircraft. This required the training programme to turn out sufficient new pilots, of a higher standard, capable of crewing these aircraft. Three special reserve air regiments had been formed with this in mind, but were hampered by the initially limited production of the Pe-2 and the enforced shift eastward that followed the outbreak of the war with Germany.

Back in 1940 the two impending bitter enemies were still, nominally, allies, presiding over their rape and dismemberment of Poland. Thus reciprocal visits

FIRST COMBAT

were paid to each other's respective air factories where the latest aircraft of all types were examined by the visiting teams and many purchased for testing. That such visits were enlightening seems not to have been the case with those German and Soviet exchanges, for the wrong conclusions seem to have been drawn by both parties. On their part, although G.A. Ozerov claims that a Ju. 87 Stuka was among the Soviet purchases at this time[5] another Russian historian claims just the opposite, and that this dive-bomber was considered 'slow and obsolete' by the visiting party and rejected.[6] However, it was to be their bane. On the other hand while the Luftwaffe delegation viewed the Pe-2 production line at GAZ No.22 it does not seem to have made much impression on them, or, if it did, Göring, as usual, could not be bothered with it.

In any case, when Operation BARBAROSSA was launched on 22 June 1941, and the warplanes of the Soviet Union's Western Military District lost 738 out of their 1,086 operational machines in just one day, only forty-two Pe-2s were said to be on the front-line strength on the Western Front. This is not the whole story, however. In fact, a total of 391 Pe-2s were recorded as being 'in service' on this date, with 180 of them in the five border military districts. Many of these were not strictly operational but assigned in 'penny packets' to SB regiments which were commencing to re-equip. This was but part of the overall disaster, which saw some 1,811 VVS aircraft destroyed for the loss of thirty-five German.

The Soviet riposte was immediate, but fragmented and badly organised. Flying steadily in their massed and rigid ranks, sixty at a time, in wedge or line formations, the SBs proved easy meat for the Bf.109s and were massacred. Those who got through bombed straight and level at heights of between 2,000 and 3,000 metres with a resulting absence of accuracy which rendered their sacrifice useless.

Pe-2s stand ready on their dispersal area at a back-area airfield. (M Maslov)

THE PETLYAKOV Pe-2

In subsequent days the fast-dwindling numbers of SBs were ordered to press in much lower to achieve some hits on the massed columns of Panzers and motorised infantry, but this only resulted in a further culling at the hands of the Luftwaffe's flak gunners. These suicidal attacks rapidly used up most of the light bombers that had survived the initial destruction, and, more importantly, their trained, however poorly, aircrews.

Early *Peshka* operations

It was in August-September that the first units converted to the Pe-3. These were 40, 95 and 208 Bomber Aviation Regiments.

The first production aircraft were issued to 95.SBAP, which was commanded initially by Colonel S.A. Pestov and later by Major L.V. Kolomeitsev. The regiment had been raised in April 1940 and was originally supplied with the SB-2-M-103 bomber before becoming a dive-bomber outfit and changing to the Ar-2. In February/March 1941 the regiment re-converted to the Pe-2, being the first VVS RKKA unit to operate the *Peshka*. It was Pe-2s of this regiment which took part in the May Day flypast over Moscow.

On 21 June 1941, 95. SBAP was far from the front, being based at Kalinin airfield and so escaped heavy losses on the ground during the initial German air strikes.

Table 2: Pe-2s in service on 1 June 1941

Total	Active	Repair	Unit	Based	District	Division
18	17	1	58 BAR	Staraya Russia	Leningrad	2 Combined Aviation
4	4	-	72 BAR	Bessovets & Staraya Russia	Leningrad	55 Combined Aviation
5	5	-	50 BAR	Khapsau Estonia	Baltic	4 Combined Aviation
7	7	-	54 BAR	Vilnus	Baltic	54 Combined Aviation
8	8	-	13 BAR	Ross & Borisovschizna	Western	9 Combined Aviation
9	9	-	39 BAR	Pinsk & Zhabitsy	Western	10 Combined Aviation
37	37	-	16 BAR	Zheludok & Cherlena	Western	11 Combined Aviation
10	10	-	86 BAR	Trembovlya & Zubov	Kiev	16 Combined Aviation
36	36	-	48 BAR	Izyaslavl & Kaskov	Kiev	17 Bombardment Aviation

FIRST COMBAT

14	14	-	33 BAR	Belaya Tserkov & Gorodische	Kiev	19 Bombardment Aviation
15	15	-	52 BAR	Ovruch & Krasnaya Boloka	Kiev	62 Bombardment Aviation
5	5	-	45 BAR	Odessa	Odessa	20 Combined Aviation
27	25	2	5 BAR	Akkerman & Kulevcha	Odessa	21 Combined Aviation
5	5	-	132 BAR	Kirovograd & Ekaterinovka	Odessa	45 Combined Aviation
200	196	4	-	-	-	Totals

On the very first day of operations 5 BAP sent a force of seventeen *Peshkas* to bomb the vital Galitskii bridge over the Prut river while, on 16 July, 13 BAP was heavily involved near El'na.

In the case of the Pe-2, in spite of heavy losses, reinforcements raised the number available for combat on the Western Front to sixty aircraft by 10 July. Among the Pe-2-equipped regiments at the outbreak of the war were 95 BAD (46 SAD/BAD) in the Moscow Military District, which had been the first BAP to receive this aircraft on its establishment. There was also 48 BBAP (17 SAD), in Kiev Special Military District, which had been the second to receive the Pe-2, and 5BAP (21 SAD) in the Odessa Military District. Three Special Western Military District units were 13 BAP (21 SAD), 16 BAP (11 SAD) and 39 BAP (10 SAD). With regard to naval units, 40 BAP-ChF with the Black Sea Fleet actually took delivery of its first *Peshka* on 22 June.

A Pe-2 pilot poses with his aircraft's radio antenna. This photograph provides an excellent scale of the size and detailed composition of the antenna. (H Valtonen via Keski-Suomen Ilmailumuseo, Tikkakoski)

The standard training for tactical support aircrew, those who were destined to fly the Pe-2 or the Il-2, amounted to a shorter specialist course than those for fighter or long-range bomber aircrew. Replacements were available in large numbers but these were, in the main, even more badly prepared for the combat conditions they found themselves in.

THE PETLYAKOV Pe-2

> Less than 100 hours' classroom and airfield instruction, and about fifteen hours' flying instruction, meant that the course could be completed in two to three months. Dive-bombing, ground-strafing, the complications of Army co-operations and formation flying were the main items, as one would expect.[7]

Asher Lee went on to make the following statement:

> It is strange that an air force which believed in the theory and practice of maximum support for the ground forces paid relatively little attention in their training plans to the specialised art of tactical reconnaissance for ground troops. There were no specialist training schools for it in the pre-war period. Moreover, the Soviets had no pre-war equivalent to the British Lysander or the German Henschel, i.e. a specialist aircraft for Army reconnaissance work. Neither was there any specialist tactical reconnaissance units in the Soviet Air Force before 1943. The bomber, fighter and ground support units did their own reconnaissance or persuaded a long-range reconnaissance unit to photograph a dump or railway junction for them.[8]

This lack, if it really existed, was apparently soon to be rectified for the same author goes on to state that 'At Michurinsk in the Urals, hundreds of pilots were given a thorough, at times even a leisurely, flying training course on the Il-2 and the twin-engined Pe-2.'[9]

Even so, the Pe-2s were largely wasted at this time and they, too, were made to fly straight-and-level and bomb from altitudes that negated all their precision refinements, merely because tactics had not been developed to match the new aircraft. The intensity of their operations was such that the Pe-2s were recorded as flying three or four sorties per day against German tank columns in the Unecha, Starodub, Trubchevsk and Novgorod Seversk areas.[10] That the *Peshka* had great potential was soon confirmed by the pilots of the two RAF Hurricane squadrons, Nos. 81 and 134, who, from August, 1941, until October of the same year, worked with them out of Murmansk airfields protecting British convoys of war material and, from 24 September, escorting the Pe-2s on missions against German and Finnish ground forces. Even so, as late as November 1943, the British line was that the Pe-2's sole rôle was 'medium or high level attacks on the enemy supply aerodromes'.[11]

Also set up in the aftermath of the initial German attack was a special Test Pilot Regiment charged with the specific task of bringing the Pe-2 to perfection prior to generally re-equipping most light-bomber units with it.[12] One such Pe-2 unit was 411-PBAP-ON, which was commanded by Lieutenant Colonel V.I. Zhdanov.[13] This was just one of five regiments established with test pilots.[14]

Another unit equipped with the *Peshka* was 410-PBAP-ON, set up during the last days of June 1941 under the command of Lieutenant Commander A.I. Kabanov.[15] It was sent to the front on 5 July, working directly to Front assignment rather than

FIRST COMBAT

A Pe-2 taxiing along an improvised front-line airstrip. Like the German Junkers Ju. 87 *Stuka* and most contemporary Soviet aircraft of this period, the ability to sustain such rough treatment in the field was one of her major attributes. (Imperial War Museum, London)

through any air division in a desperate effort to stem the tide. It is a measure of the desperation that such cadres of highly-skilled pilots were thrown into the cauldron thus, there being no time to consider the long-term effects that the loss of such priceless men would cause. The price paid was a high one; the unit's losses were described as 'devastating'.

During the period 5 to 28 July thirty-three aircraft were lost. The remnants were assigned to 23 BAD in September but, by October, so few aircrews remained that the unit was disbanded and the few survivors went back to test flying.

Despite these examples, and others, one source says that the Pe-2s were highly valued despite 'all their teething problems'.[16] In fact, it would seem that the Pe-2 was more ready for dive-bombing combat than many of the pilots who flew her, or the commanders who so misused her during this period. Furthermore, with the seemingly relentless German advance upon Moscow itself, the first Luftwaffe air raids on the Soviet capital, although insignificant by the standards of the London Blitz, initiated what might be termed 'panic-measures'. A further special group was formed with Pe-2 and SB bombers with the aim of decoying further German bomber groups away from the city, although it is doubtful whether this ploy was ever effective. Still it was more drain on the *Peshka's* limited numbers. Equipped with searchlights these Pe-2s were also employed in locating, and then illuminating, German night-bomber formations, so that defending Soviet night-fighters could attack them more easily.[17]

Such use was probably justified, if just for their propaganda value alone, to steady the populace who daily expected to see the Panzers driving through Red Square, but they caused the inevitable shortages elsewhere.

THE PETLYAKOV Pe-2

Crashed Pe-2 being examined by German troops. (Denés Bernard)

If the Pe-2 losses were bad, those of the slow-flying SB regiments were worse and many such units quickly converted to the faster aircraft. Typical was 40 SBAP, which flew the SB on the North-West Front. In September 1941 it began to convert to the Pe-2 while at the same time losing half its strength to form the new 511 BBAP commanded by Major A.A. Babanov, equipped with the Pe-3.

The new aircraft were thrown into the conflict without reservation almost at once and suffered accordingly. In a series of attacks in a three-day period from 22 to 24 September, 40 BAP struck with precision at the vital rail junction at Staraya Russia, which was put out of action for a week. Three similar pinpoint attacks were made against Roslavl railway station and marshalling yards on 27 and 28 September by the Pe-2s of this unit, which caused enough disruption to force German trains carrying vital war supplies to make a two-to-three day diversion. Again, the dive-bombing attacks were resolutely pushed home despite intense flak opposition and Captain A.G. Rogov, the squadron commander, earned Hero of the Soviet Union status for his bravery. However, he was soon one of the victims, failing to return from another dangerous mission on 8 October. Captain V.B. Malofev replaced him, but he only survived four days before also being killed in action. By 15 December 40 BAP was so reduced that it was converted to a reconnaissance unit as 40 RAP, later becoming the long-range unit 40 DRAP.

Another SB unit was 9 BAP commanded by Major V. Lukin, based at Panevezhis on 22 June. After four days of continual action this regiment had been decimated and was withdrawn to re-equip with the Pe-2 and convert to the new, smaller, twenty-plane composition. The surplus aircrew were used to create the new 723 BAP, also allocated the Pe-2 as their mount.

FIRST COMBAT

A Pe-2 throws up a dust cloud while taxiing along a front-line airstrip, two M-105R engines power her. (Russian Aviation Research Trust)

The German battles of encirclement in the south, at Smolensk, Kiev and elsewhere, netted another million PoWs, and further wholesale expenditure of Russian aircraft in a failed counter-offensive failed to stem the tide. By 25 September the C-in-C of the Western Front, Colonel General I.S. Konev, had his bomber force reduced to an operational total of sixty-three aircraft, all but twenty of which were of obsolete types. Included in the modern aircraft inventory were just *five* Pe-2s. He sent an urgent signal to the *Shtab Glavnovo/Verkhovnovo Komandovaniya*, or *Stavka* (Supreme Command Staff), urging them to reinforce him with regiments of both Pe-2 and Il-2 aircraft if he was to have any chance of holding on.[18] The 81st Bomber Air Division had, by the end of September, been reduced to forty operational machines, of which twelve were the new fighter variant of the *Peshka*, the Pe-3.

The Pe-3 was introduced as a heavy fighter early in the production life of the aircraft, and although it was practically identical to the standard Pe-2, this version was cleaned-up aerodynamically and had her overall fully-laden weight reduced to 17,637lb (8,000kg) by eliminating the dive bomber's dive brakes, under-wing bomb racks; it was fitted with automatic leading-edge slats. However, speed remained much the same as the dive-bomber. This, however, gave her an excess in speed over likely opponents of 62mph (100km/h) over a Heinkel He.111 and 46mph (75km/h) over a Ju.88. To provide a punch capable of knocking down either of these Luftwaffe stalwarts quickly and easily, the Pe-3's armament was modified to include two fixed 20mm ShVAK cannon and two 12.7mm UBK machine guns.

Any advantages the Pe-3 might have were usually thrown away for, such was the desperation of the situation, they were more used as ground-attack aircraft with their cannon, and festooned with RS-132 rocket projectiles for use against tanks and armoured vehicles, than in their intended mission. Some were also siphoned off into the photo-reconnaissance units. These had two extra fuel tanks built in to increase range and carried two fixed cameras.

On 6 July 1941, 95 SBAP started to operate on the Western Front. Although the aircrew were by now fully familiar with their aircraft, they took heavy losses, so heavy in fact that by August the unit had to be withdrawn to refit. Between August and September 1941, 95 SBAP were re-equipped with the Pe-3. Their now superfluous air gunners were transferred to other units. Navigators had to master the intricacies of radio operating while pilots re-trained in fighter tactics. From their previous experience with the Pe-2 they knew that the Pe-3 only stood a chance as a fighter operating against slow types of German bombers and reconnaissance aircraft. Various tactical procedures were devised, from patrolling in pairs as situation surveillance posts, individually attacking lone enemy aircraft or guiding single-engined fighters by radio against larger forces. In this latter case, it resembled naval tactics where scouting forces led the main fleet into action and guided them to the enemy. Naval terminology had already been adopted in Germany where their Bf.110 was termed *Zerstorer* (destroyer) aircraft, while the Dutch air force termed their aircraft of this type as airborne light cruisers.

It was not hard to envisage a fast reconnaissance role for the Pe-3 with its longer range. For a while it was hoped that lack of strong defensive armament might be compensated for by typical autumnal cloudy weather conditions.

By 4 August 1941, 208 SBAP had been operating as a SB outfit since the beginning of the war, and had been in the thick of the fighting. They had lost

Peshka crews pose for the camera, including from the left, Lieutenant Stretsov, Second Lieutenant Samsonov and Captain Kirikov. (H Valtonen via Keski-Suoment Ilmailumseo, Tikkakoski)

fifty-five aircraft and thirty-eight crews by the beginning of August. By an order from C-in-C VVS, 208 SBAP, commanded by Captain Kolomyeytsev, was split into three new regiments, with twenty aircraft in each, and the original unit began conversion to the Pe-3.

In an order from C-in-C VVS dated 25 September 1941, 95 BAP was officially redesignated as 95 IAP and attached to 6 IAK (Fighter Corps) of PVO, a major fighter force defending Moscow. At this date it had a strength of forty aircraft compared to a normal complement for most air regiments of half that number. The following month, 208 BAP was also attached to this corps.

At the end of September 1941, 95 IAP carried out its first sorties. Six Pe-3 escorted C-47 transport aircraft with a British mission on board from Vologda to Moscow. Three attempts by German fighters to intercept these transports were repelled.

The 95 IAP was deployed at Naro-Fominsk on 30 September 1941 with a task of covering the approaches to Moscow and, by 2 October 1941, its total strength of about forty aircraft made a massed bombing attack on enemy troop concentrations fifteen kilometres from Byely. Farther south the Soviets' defeat was just as staggering and a million men were lost between July and October. Colonel General Konev, the C-in-C Western Front, was soon clamouring for some of the aircraft held back to defend Moscow, asking, on 25 September, for the *Stavka* to release a regiment of Pe-2s to help stem the flow. Yukhnov fell to the Germans on 6 October and the message was finally understood. One regiment of *Peshkas* was sent, joined soon after by a second, and they operated under General N.A. Sbytov in supporting the Mozhaisk Defence Line held by the Soviet Fifth Army.

On 3 October 1941 Senior Lieutenant Fortovov claimed the first kill by a Pe-3, destroying a Ju.88, while a second was destroyed by Lieutenant Kulikov. The following day the second squadron of 95 BAP, led by Major A.A. Sachkov, attacked an armoured column, claiming the destruction of twenty-three tanks and forty other vehicles. They dropped forty FAB-50 and FAB-100 bombs, then strafed. During their withdrawal, attacks by Bf.109s left one Pe-3 and one Bf.109 destroyed while another Pe-3 was damaged and crashed on landing with a wounded pilot.

More astoundingly, a Pe-2 commanded by Senior Lieutenant Gorslykhin fought with nine Bf.109s on 5 October and claimed to have destroyed three of them. Fortovov's Pe-3 became the first casualty for 95 IAP when it failed to return from a mission this day. His wingman had reported that his leader had sighted a lone enemy aircraft and, after ordering him to continuing patrolling over the set area, broke off to attack it, and was never seen again.

Operation TYPHOON

Operation TYPHOON, the final German drive on Moscow, was launched five days later and the Soviets found themselves overwhelmed as predicted, even though Colonel-General P.F. Zhigarev had nine bomber regiments with three more in reserve. Most of these aircraft were obsolete, and there had been, initially, only a mere *five* Pe-2s on the strength of General I.S. Konev's bomber force on

THE PETLYAKOV Pe-2

25 September 1941.[19] However, Fyodorov states that the Western Military District had 42 Pe-2s on its strength on day one of the war.[20] The Germans quickly took Oryol and then Briansk and by 6 October even Yukhnov had fallen. All available aircraft were rushed in, including two more Pe-2 regiments, drawn from the *Stavka* Reserve, to try to stem the tide. One such ad hoc ground-attack unit that proved most successful was set up under the command of General N.A. Sbytov. It consisted of one Pe-2 Regiment, the 46th Bomber Air Regiment, and two Il-2 units, the 65th and 243rd *Shturmovik* Regiments. They acted in direct support of the Soviet Fifth Army holding the Mozhaisk Defence line in front of Moscow.

Another Pe-2 unit, the 39th Bomber Air Regiment, commanded by Air Squadron Commissar First Lieutenant B.K. Morozovsk. On 5 October this outfit had completed their dive-bombing mission over the Western Front, and were returning to base, when they were 'jumped' by ten Bf. 109s. Unburdened by their bombs, the Pe-2s proved no walkover for their single-engined opponents and the Soviets claimed that three Messerschmitts were shot down in the resulting dogfight.[21]

One more Pe-2 outfit which distinguished itself at this time was 321 Close-range Bomber Regiment, commanded by Major S.P. Tyurkin, part of 77th Composite Aviation Division (SAD). One account states that the crews of this regiment 'developed the ability of dive-bombing angles of 30-40 degrees, while individual aircrews practised diving at an angle of 60 degrees.'[22] The good work conducted by this regiment was rewarded later when it was re-designated as 82nd Guards Bomber Air Regiment.

Seen in a snow flurry, groundcrews prepare to swing one of the props for a testing of the port engine while others work under the starboard engine. The spinners on this aircraft are painted white. (H Valtonen via Keski-Suoment Imailumuseo, Tikkakoski)

FIRST COMBAT

Based at Moscow Central airfield, 9 BAP flew both the Pe-2 and the Pe-3 from the middle of September through to February 1942 in defence of the capital. Another unit which used both aircraft was 54 BBAP commanded by Major Skibo. This regiment flew some 400 combat missions, during which they claimed the destruction of thirty-three German tanks, 780 motor vehicles and thirty-five wagons, in addition to exploding two enemy ammunition dumps and destroying six attacking fighters, all for the loss of just eleven of their own aircraft. Other regiments which fought with both the Pe-2 and Pe-3 on the Moscow front were 95 BAP, 208 BAP and 511 BBAP.

Also fighting during this period, 31 PBAP earned itself the distinction of being re-designated as 4 GvPBAP for its achievements. The 128 BAP, 603 BBAP and 745 BBAP were all Pe-2-equipped units used in Moscow's defence, while 132 BAP was assigned to the Kalinin Front from the end of October onward with a strength of thirteen Pe-2s and 150 BAP (which became the 46 BAD from August) was transferred from Transbaikal. Meanwhile, 46 BAD with their *Peshkas*, along with the Il-2-equipped 64 and 243 ground-attack regiments, formed a special air group under command of N.A Sbytov.[23] They operated in support of Fifth Army.

By 5 October 1941, 208 SBAP with the Pe-3 was attached to 6 IAK. Their principal mission was air cover of railway installations and distribution centres in the Moscow area. They also operated as fighter-bombers. During the next three months this unit conducted 638 combat sorties, claiming to have destroyed thirty-four tanks, 212 other vehicles, six trains and thirty-three German aircraft. In addition, it is claimed by Alexander Boyd that a group of 'special pathfinders' flying the Pe-2 was used to lure German bombers away from Moscow.[24] Their own losses included ten Pe-3s, with twelve pilots and nine navigators. For the part they played in the defence of Moscow the regiment received high praise from Army General Zhukov, GOC Western Front.

The Pe-2 was also fast enough to be employed as a photographic reconnaissance aircraft. This one, in an unusual paint scheme, has just returned from just such a mission over German lines in northern Norway and the crew is off for their de-briefing session. (SIB Photo Services)

THE PETLYAKOV Pe-2

As the German army approached Moscow during October, both 95 IAP and 208 BAP were used increasingly as fighter-bombers against enemy motorised columns. Between October and its withdrawal from the front line in December, 208 BAP claimed the destruction of twenty-eight tanks, 212 other vehicles, six trains and thirty-three enemy aircraft for the loss of ten Pe-3s. However, on 5 November 1941, Fortovov and his crew were lost, missing after taking off to intercept German aircraft.

Still the Russians slowed the enemy advance and, aided by the *Rasputitsa* (rainy season) which turned the roads into quagmires in which Panzers and horse-drawn supply wagons alike slithered and stuck, all-out attacks were launched by these units against German columns in the Tula area in November.

On 28 November 1941 a pair of Pe-3s, piloted by Senior Lieutenant L. Puzanov and Lieutenant V.S. Strel'tsov, were scrambled to protect Alexandrov railway junction. They intercepted three Ju.88s which were about to make dive attacks out of the cloud cover. The German trio split up and Puzanov destroyed one of them. Strel'tsov attacked another, receiving heavy return fire; he made a second pass and set one of its engines afire, then a third pass which brought the enemy down. However, Strel'tsov had been wounded by cockpit fragments in return and was blinded. Following his navigator's instructions he managed a safe landing before losing consciousness.

By the end of November 1941 Major A. Zhat'kov, already credited with the destruction of several enemy aircraft, became the new CO of 95 IAP. The Pe-3s had been field modified with the BT gun in place of the nose and rear flexi-mounted ShKAS machine gun. Some aircraft of this unit had been fitted with racks for two sets of four RO-82 rockets; others had an additional pair of RO-132s. The rockets could be fired in salvoes of two or four. Other aircraft had the AFA-B aerial camera fitted.

An unknown Pe-2 aircrew stand in a huddle on a forward airstrip in a snow flurry prior a mission. The typical *Peshka* crews' flying outfit for winter operations are clearly shown, with parachutes, helmets and boots. Note the navigator's map case. (H Valtonen via Keski-Suoment Ilmailumuseo, Tikkakoski)

100

FIRST COMBAT

Front-line refuelling underway at a forward air base in challenging weather conditions. Notice how the aircraft's normal markings and national insignia appear to have been almost obliterated. (Russian Aviation Research Trust)

Between December 1941 and January 1942 the main role was ground attack and they dropped over 1,500 bombs in that period. Despite this, they also continued to operate as a fighter unit when required.

Short-term need saw the establishment of 410 OBAP (Independent Dive-Bomber Regiment) in December, which was made up entirely of NII VVS test pilots. The 410 BAP had a mixed complement of Pe-2 and Pe-3 machines, but both were pressed into service as fighter-bombers attacking advancing German columns. They were also joined by 9 and, later, 54 and 511 BAPs, both Pe-3-equipped units.

Also that December 9 OBAP was among those who fitted DAG-10 grenade launchers firing AG-2 grenades; 39 Guards OBAP used their AG-2 grenades most successfully in shallow diving attacks on German truck convoys and concentrations.

Although the glittering towers of the Kremlin eventually came in sight of advanced German units, the enemy was finally held. Next month, on the night of 5/6 December, a massive counter-attack was launched and, for the first time in the war, the Wehrmacht had to go over onto the defensive, indeed was pushed back.

Formation Leaders

During the hasty re-organisation following the German invasion, many of the precious Pe-2s were used in the role of 'formation leaders'. Each bomber regiment was re-organised in two squadrons of nine aircraft each, with a pair of Pe-2s leading them to their targets. In the same manner many fighter regiments used the *Peshka* in that role.

THE PETLYAKOV Pe-2

Other winter battles

During the bitter winter of 1941/42, 125 BAP operated in the Leningrad sector, with dive brakes omitted, as photo-reconnaissance aircraft. In the period January-February 1942, as part of the Soviet counter-attacks in the Moscow area, which drove the Germans back, the Pe-2s made up approximately 25 per cent of the tactical bomber force employed. Pe-2 of 40 BAP worked as long-range escort fighters for transports carrying troops and supplies into Sevastopol. With the temporary halt of Pe-3 production and combat losses, 40 BAP was transformed into 40 DRAP and re-equipped firstly with the Pe-2 and later with the A-20B; 208 BAP followed their example.

The bitter cold and the terrible conditions affected the Luftwaffe far more than the VVS of course, but Soviet air strength declined both to the weather and shortages of spare parts and numbers of operational aircraft in each unit fell dramatically.

Pe-2 shot down in Russia in the operational area of KG 54 in 1942. (Major Franz Zauner of KG B54 via Franz Selinger)

FIRST COMBAT

A Pe-2 seized in Russia by a Hungarian fighter squadron on a Ukrainian airfield in 1943. (Frigyes Héfty ex Royal Hungarian Air Force via Franz Selinger)

Thus the end of January 1942 found the VVS on the Kalinin Front reduced to just ninety-six operational combat aircraft, of which five were *Peshkas*.[25] Consequently, although many German units were surrounded and cut off for a time, the Russians were unable to hold them and losses were less severe than might have been expected, the cold often causing more casualties than fighting in many units.

The end of this period found the respective *Peshka* strengths working over the main combat zones concentrated in 46, 54, 130, 511 and 603 BBAPs on the Western Front with 128 (7 SAD), 132 and 745 BAPs on the Kalinin Front. By March 1942 the battle lines had almost fought themselves to a temporary standstill.

By the spring of 1942, other than the reconnaissance aviation regiments, only 95 IAP and 9 BAP remained as total Pe-3 units, with the latter based at Moscow's central airfield, and used as escorts for VIP aircraft. During June and July 1942 this regiment converted to the Pe-3*bis*. Finally, 95 IAP, commanded by Major A.V. Zhat'kov, was transferred to the Maritime Aviation Command on 1 March 1942, by order of the People's Commissariat of Defence.

From May 1942 onward it was the intention to equip every one of the air armies on the front with at least one tactical-reconnaissance regiment of Pe-2s, but this took time to achieve.

Chapter Seven

Counter-Attack

The Soviet winter counter-offensive had created twin advances against Smolensk in the north and against Kharkov and Kursk in the south and although these were eventually, and at great cost, ultimately held by the Germans, the April thaw had seen deep inroads made into all their initial conquests. At the beginning of January 1942, for example, a major break-through of the German lines took place between Lake Volgo and Kalinin, and the German Ninth Army was outflanked. The resulting Battle of Rzhev lasted from 12 to 24 February before the situation was established. For the first time in the war German armies had been forced to retreat on a large scale; it was to prove an omen for the future and German military leaders later admitted that they had totally underestimated, or been misled, about both the strength and resilience of their Soviet enemy.

A three-man aircrew approach their *Peshka* on a snowy airstrip prior a mission as the ground team makes last-minute preparations for take-off. (Soviet Official)

Flaps fully lowered, this Pe-2 taxies back down a snowbound airstrip after another mission. The large oval intakes on the leading edge of the wings are clearly visible in this photograph. (H Valtonen, via Keski-Suoment Ilmailumuseo, Tikkakoski)

Pe-2s were still rare, although welcomed, birds. On the Kalinin Front at the end of January just five of them were in the line.

It was the turn of Stalin to become over-confident. Convinced that he had the enemy on the run he ordered a series of premature offensives, with Kharkov as the main objective. Initially successful, these were soon turned into disasters when the Germans out-generalled the Soviets once more and cut off no fewer than five Soviet armies when General von Kleist's Panzers trapped them west of the Donets and annihilated them. This was the biggest Soviet defeat in the war so far and the VVS's measure of air support proved very woeful.

Fresh German assaults

The Germans had new plans to renew the assault in the summer against the Crimea and, ultimately, on the oil-rich Caucasus, and even during the height of the Soviet counter-stroke were busily building fresh airfields in the south to support this drive.[1]

For their part the handful of Pe-2s had more than proved themselves although they were still only available in penny-packets and tactics were primitive. The strength of the German flak defences had forced a change in the bombing profile of ground-attack units, ground-level strikes being increasingly changed to gliding attacks from 1,000-foot altitudes, but still true dive-bombing was not practised.

By 5 March 1942, many members of 95 IAP received awards for their winter work. Major A. Zhat'kov and Captain N. Morozov, his navigator, received the Order of Lenin.

THE PETLYAKOV Pe-2

Transfer to the Arctic Theatre of War

On 7 March 95 IAP moved north to Vayenga airfield, one of the main bases of the Northern Fleet VVS. A month's training to familiarise themselves with maritime operations followed, including instrument-only navigation and identification and tactics used against enemy naval and maritime targets at sea.

Initially, the unit's role, under command of the Northern Fleet, was to provide fighter cover over British convoys bringing Allied Lend-Lease war material to Murmansk and the Kola Inlet ports. The Pe-3 had by far the best range for this type of work. With two engines, which decreased the risk of operating over the sea at distance from land, and the luxury of a navigator able to devote himself exclusively to this duty, as well as more extensive navigation instrumentation, it proved ideal. The only weakness was the lack of an efficient HF/DF receiver.

Experiments were conducted in 1942 to test the suitability of the Pe-3 in the maritime anti-submarine role. This proved far less successful and was only conducted because of the chronic lack of any more suitable aircraft on the Northern Fleet's strength at this time. The Pe-3s were adapted to carry four PLAB-100 depth charges, with hydrostatic detonators, on makeshift underwing racks. These depth charges were released and descended by parachute to the sea, where they then descended to a pre-set depth before exploding. However, the high-speed of the Pe-3 caused the failure of this system, the parachutes failed to open, while the restricted vision ventrally in these aircraft made sightings of U-boats very difficult. Attacks on surfaced U-boats were subsequently made on rare occasions, but never with a decisive result.

Changes of organisation

Further re-organisation also took place. By May 1942 production enabled the creation of front air armies harmoniously built up of just one aircraft type,[2] and the Pe-2 featured in these. Although obsolete light bombers were still employed, increasingly the *Peshka* was to become the standard front-line bomber, working as a dive-bomber in conjunction with the Il-2 units as a winning team. Similar specialisation on the most important new types was extended to the training and re-training flights and maintenance crews to ensure total dedication to keeping these important aircraft flying and building them up to regimental strengths in increasing numbers. This was taken to extremes with some of the above personnel concentrating exclusively on individual aircraft models, which produced highly skilled teams of experts, which later formed cadres for enormous expansion.

This began to bear fruit at the front. To support their winter offensive, the Soviets had also undertaken extensive airfield building and a total of thirty *Batak'on aerodromnogo obsluzhivaniya* (airfield service sattalions – BAO) were established to service the seven new *Raion Aviatsionnovo Bazirovaniya* (air-base regions – RAB), along with fuel and munitions dumps strategically placed at 200-mile intervals behind the front.

COUNTER-ATTACK

These were but part of the great re-organisation undertaken in the spring of 1942 which transformed the VVS into an effective fighting force, utilising the harsh lessons of war and near-defeat. Although many ad-hoc changes had taken place, it was recognised that the whole edifice had to be re-structured from top to bottom and, in the comparative lull that followed the winter campaigns, this was undertaken root and branch.

Known as the Novikov Reforms, after General A.A. Novikov who took over as commander of the VVS on 11 April, replacing General P.F. Zhigarev, the new man proved himself a dynamo and just the right choice for such a complex and urgent task. He had already visited and served on most of the fronts and added his own personal experience to the overall lessons to produce a lasting reform of great detail. This vital task, Novikov was to assert, was considered to be 'his sacred duty'[3] and was forced through at relative speed in the hope of being ready before the expected German summer offensive. The unique, for the Soviets, experiment of giving the military expert his head relatively unfettered by Communist political dogma and cant paid a handsome dividend in this case.

Although, like the RAF during the Battle of Britain, the Soviets did not spurn learning lessons from the superior Luftwaffe tactics, and adopting or adapting them to their own advantage, Novikov did not slavishly follow the Germans in everything. The VVS was to become even more tactically orientated than the Luftwaffe, and totally wedded to unstinting close support of the army. Lessons were learned here but, in fact, in this particular area of operations the Soviets, for once, had aircraft and tactics, and were soon to develop the tactics and the pilots, that were *superior* in many facets, to the Germans; the Pe-2 was a classic example of this.

One of the most important reforms was the creation in March 1942 of mobile *Vozdushnaya Armiya* (air armies) with a centralised VVS control and which were virtually an expansion of the *Udarnaya aviatsionnaya gruppa* (air assault groups – UAG), which they replaced. These new units, equipped with the best aircraft and crews, could be rapidly switched from one area of the front to another while still retaining their own kernel of expertise and unit, rather than having aircraft and units leeched off piecemeal. Such groupings were far more effective when used as integral entities and their skills were not diluted but concentrated against the enemy at the most useful points. First Air Army, commanded by General T.F. Kutsevlov, was the first of these new units, which was formed on 5 May, 1942 and was quickly followed by four others by the end of May 1942 (Second, Third, Fourth, and Eighth) and then two more in June (Fifth and Sixth), two in July (Fourteenth and Fifteenth), and the Sixteenth in August. All were built up with self-contained combinations of fighter, ground-attack and one or two regiments of Pe-2 dive-bombers, along with reconnaissance, training and liaison squadrons.

The NKO order initiating the first of these new formations read:

> For the purposes of improving the striking power of aviation and permitting successful employment of massed air strikes, combine the aviation resources of the Western Front into a single air army and designated it the 1st Air Army.[4]

THE PETLYAKOV Pe-2

With each air army's commander in effect working as a deputy of the associated frontal army commander, a virtually seamless co-ordination of air strikes with ground attacks was ensured and this proved highly efficient. This front-line re-organisation was coupled with the establishment of specialised reserve units, the Air Corps of *Stavka*, the *Rezerv Verkhovnogo Glavnokomandovaniya* (RVGK)) Reserves.[5] Initially these were exclusively fighter formations, but rapidly expanded until, by the end of the year, there were thirteen, three of which were Pe-2 units. Again, in the case of Pe-2 and other modern types, these corps comprised two or three air divisions with 120 to 270 aircraft, which took delivery of the aircraft from the factories and formed a highly-trained mobile reserve of warplanes able rapidly to reinforce any air army at critical times of high combat attrition.

At division and regimental level the key to success was, again, the formation and concentration on homogeneous units. The concentration of the Pe-2's squadrons into such organisations maximised the efficiency of not only the combat aircrews, but also of their maintenance, training and supply. As production got into its stride once more this also enabled regiments to individually expand, from twenty-two *Peshka*-strong in 1942 to thirty-two by the end of 1943, providing more hitting power, better trained and more concentrated. By this time, more than 50 per cent of front-line aircraft were of the new types.

The *Peshka*, by virtue of her outstanding speed for a bomber aircraft (at 335mph almost as fast as the latest German Messerschmitt Bf. 109E single-engined fighter) had found herself a new rôle by 1943, for, with the establishment of all air regiments equipped with new aircraft, and of two squadrons of nine planes apiece, two Pe-2s were usually allocated as formation leaders to guide the others to the target area.[6]

All this took place at a time when the Soviets were reeling from the second great German offensive which followed the failure of their own Demyansk, Kharkov and Crimea offensives in May and June 1942. Going back over to the defensive, a series of panic orders was issued from Moscow and the situation worsened. Field Marshal Fedor von Bock's Army Group B and Field Marshal Wilhelm von List's Army Group A punched their way eastward once more, with the initial objects of Voronezh and the Don, the reduction of the Crimea and Sevastopol and the occupation of the Caucasus. With these objectives, Hitler would have the grain of the Ukraine and the oil of Maikop to sustain his armies for further advances while making the Black Sea an Axis lake.

Navy Pe-2s

The Pe-2 series 110 of 73 BAP Red Banner Baltic Fleet (KBF) Aviation, which later became 12 Guards BAP was commanded by Colonel V. Rakov and, later, Major K. Usenko. The Black Sea Fleet's 40 BAP was led by Colonel I. Korzunov in 'Yellow 29'.

Despite continuous air operations, the Germans were largely successful. The Wehrmacht attacked the Kerch' Peninsula in May and, after fierce fighting, broke through to pound Sevastopol mercilessly until it capitulated on 4 July. Pre-emptive strikes against German airfields on the Kharkov were followed by a ground attack

COUNTER-ATTACK

which, for three brief days, made progress. Counter strikes by the Germans resulted in a massive defeat for the Russian armies at Barvenkovo. In June the Germans advanced east of Kursk and struck at Bryansk. Everything the VVS had in the area was thrown in with the exhortation to 'employ all of our ground-attack and bomber aviation to destroy the enemy's tank and motorised columns, annihilate his manpower, and thus support our troops'.[7]

Continuous strikes by ground-attack aircraft and bombers directed against this front, with some Pe-2 units mounting three or four sorties per day, failed to slow down the German advance on this sector either, although they claimed to have inflicted heavy losses. In particular attacks on the bridges across the river Don that carried the supplies for the German offensive, received bloody repulse. Between 17 and 22 August 8 VA made over 1,000 combat sorties against the Don river crossings, and lost 100 bombers in the process, with a further 210 losses of all types in the succeeding equally disastrous week.

Typical of the scale of loss taken by the Pe-2 units at this time is the experience of 86 BAP, commanded by Major F. Belyy. This regiment had been withdrawn from the front to Astrakhan eight months previously to rest and refit following earlier heavy losses. It returned to the front near Kirov on 17 August 1942 and, two days later, was committed to combat in an attempt to stem the German onslaught.

On 19 August, two formations of nine aircraft, led by the staff aircraft of Major Belyy, went into the attack with fresh zeal and confidence. That elation did not survive the day, only three of the twenty Pe-2s committed to battle surviving. Intercepted by German fighters and ravaged by strong flak defences the other seventeen aircraft were either destroyed outright or so damaged that they were forced to make crash-landings all over the area. One pilot, Lieutenant Andrey Terchuk, with his aircraft fatally hit, chose to crash it into a column of German tanks. Another aircraft had one of its bombs hit and the percussion wheel torn off, but somehow managed to crash-land without the bomb detonating on impact.[8]

The following day 86 BAP made another determined effort against the same targets, with predictable results. Their target was the river crossing at Duboiviy Ovrag, near Kalach. Again led by Major Belyy, just nine Pe-2s, all that could be scraped together, went in. Once more, they ran into German fighters over the target, losing two aircraft, one of which was Lieutenant Nikolay Mamatchenko's mount, which crashed into the river. A third Pe-2 was destroyed by flak, and only six machines returned.

A greater slaughter was inflicted upon 270 BAD that same day. Their fighter escort failed to turn up at the pre-arranged rendezvous point, but a large group of Bf.109s, from III./JG 3 and I./JG 53, were there instead. In the ensuing massacre, *every one* of the Pe-2s was destroyed.

Despite this the German Sixth Army, under General (later Field Marshal) Friedrich Paulus, penetrated through to the Stalingrad *Oblast* on the Volga river by 12 July, while farther south the Caucasus was entered. In the general rush to organise a last-ditch defence of the city that bore Stalin's name, General P.S. Stepanov and his staff were sent to the area to survey its air defence. He found it badly lacking and *Stavka* despatched ten new air regiments, including many Pe-2s, as reinforcement for Eighth Air Army. This meant that the defending Soviet air forces were more than 75 per cent equipped with modern aircraft for the first time. The *Peshkas* of Eighth Air Army, attacking in groups of ten to thirty aircraft, mounted over 1,000 sorties against the German spearheads in an attempt to slow their advance.

The German offensive planned for the summer of 1942 was tempered by the severe mauling they had received the previous winter. Thus the spoiling attacks mounted prematurely at Stalin's orders at Demyansk and Kharkov had first to be held and then reversed. These German victories were the prelude to the main menu planned by Hitler, the drive by Army Group B under Field Marshal Fedor von Bock from Bryansk towards Voronezh. In conjunction, Army Group A, under the command of Field Marshal Wilhelm von List, attacked via the Donets Basin across the Ukraine, spearheaded by Sixth Army under Paulus, across the Don and towards the Volga, with the oilfields of the Caucasus and the fabled city of Astrakhan on the Caspian Sea as an ultimate goal. The industry of the Donets, the wheat of the Kuban, and the oil of Maikop were the limited German strategic objectives that summer, and although the siege of Leningrad and Murmansk in the north continued, the main thrust was south-east.

In the blistering heat of the high summer of 1942, the German Blitzkrieg was successful for the last time in the war. The Germans and their allies rolled forward across the endless, featureless plain and by 8 August the Maikop oilfield had been taken, while on 23 August they had reached the banks of the Volga river just north of the city of Stalingrad. The city itself was a great industrial centre and bore the Soviet dictator's name.[9] As such it assumed almost mystical properties to attacker and defender alike. There was really no need for the Germans to storm the city; they had very wisely forbade doing any such thing in any other campaign. Surrounding it and cutting it off, before leaving it to wither on the vine, would have been normal policy and far more sensible. Instead, as if hypnotised, Hitler issued his 'Directive No. 45', which called for his by-now over-stretched armies to take both the Grozny oilfields and Stalingrad, simultaneously. But this time the Soviets had been given time to prepare and were ready to stem both blows.

Stalingrad's air defence re-organised

Being outnumbered by about four to one in the crucial battle zone around Stalingrad, the VVS had to revert to emergency measures to stem the flow. *Stavka* sent an operational group under Army Commissar P.S. Stepanov to re-organise the city's air defence. His group of officers included P.G. Grigor'yev, M.N. Karpuk, N. Kozhevnikov, A.N. Mal'tsev, I.I. Ospiov, I.P. Selivanov and S.A. Tyurev.[10]

Spanish Pe-2 pilot

An interesting sidelight on this colossal struggle, and the place of the Pe-2 in its outcome, is the death of one pilot before Stalingrad. He was Anselmo Sepulveda. During the Spanish Civil War he had flown a Soviet-supplied SB light bomber in

COUNTER-ATTACK

M-105R engines revving, a trio of Pe-2s turn onto a snow-cleared strip close to the front line during the winter fighting. Note the leader's radio aerial and the flaps of the two leading aircraft. (Crown Copyright)

combat missions with the Republican air force against General Franco's forces. In the spring of 1939 he just managed to escape over the border from Spain with the victory of the Nationalists, aided by Germany and Italy. He spent a short time in a French internment camp before emigrating to the USSR.

With the German invasion in June 1941, Sepulveda, like many expatriate Spaniards, volunteered to fight against Fascism once more. Many who joined were former fighter pilots and were sent to replace fighter pilot casualties. The cadets mostly went to the Kirovobad Flying School and then on to Polikarpov U-2 regiments. Only one Spaniard, it seems, was drafted to the dive-bombers and he was killed on a combat mission in late September or early October to the west of the city.[11]

Polbin's command

Among the reinforcements which joined the fighting was 150th Bomber Air Regiment commanded by Lieutenant Colonel Ivan S. Polbin, described as 'a master of sniper attacks'.[12] The *Peshkas* of this outfit soon made their presence felt; in four days' operations they were credited with the destruction of forty German tanks and fifty motor vehicles, all of which bought time for the defenders to prepare the incomplete outer defences.

One such dive-bombing is deserving of special attention. Behind the German lines, in an area known as the Morozovsk farm, a large fuel dump had been established to supply the advancing tank columns. It was so obviously a prime target that elaborate precautions were taken to protect it from air attack, and the Luftwaffe had drafted in several flak batteries, both heavy and light, while a nearby fighter airfield was set up specifically for aerial defence. Protective measures also

THE PETLYAKOV Pe-2

included comprehensive camouflage but, despite this, the site was targeted by the VVS. After several conventional attacks had failed totally, Polbin's *Peshkas* were assigned the task, and a ten-plane attack was made. Two of the Pe-2s survived both fighters and flak to arrive over the target and duly carried out precise dive-bombing which scored hits on the fuel tanks themselves, which duly ignited and burnt out. The loss of so much valuable tank fuel caused the Panzers leading the drive on Stalingrad to be halted at a crucial juncture of the battle and gave the Soviet defenders a few more vital days' breathing space.

Polbin led from the front, and continued to do so, but he was exceptional. The majority of corps commanders had tactical command or liaison tasks back at the ground control centres during major battles like this one. The improvements in radio control and contact ensured that the majority of divisional commanders remained in the safety of the ground bunkers directing operations and leaving the combat flying leadership to their junior subordinates. Polbin liked to see for himself just what was happening and then to design, and combat-test, his solutions in the field.

It was also during the Stalingrad fighting that the first women dive-bomber pilots enjoyed their combat debuts, with the 587th *Peshka*-equipped Bomber Regiment. This had originally been set up in the autumn of 1941 by Colonel Marina Raskova, a female air ace from pre-war days.[13]

With the Axis thrust now directed mainly from the south-west, another special operational group was established, and supported by Eighth Air Army, to strike at this further head of the German Hydra. Up to 600 sorties a day were mounted during the first days of August. Then the ground fighting became concentrated on a German thrust against the Soviet Sixty-fourth Army at Tinguta station. Again the

The modified tail-cone shape can be seen here, as well as the dorsal entrance-hatch and the engine vents on the upper surfaces of the *Peshka's* wings. (Russian Aviation Research Trust)

COUNTER-ATTACK

A typical Pe-2 mission over the Stalingrad front in the winter of 1942-43. Seen astern of the lead section are two aircraft of a three-plane section following, releasing their ordnance. (Robert Michulec)

Pe-2s joined in an all-out assault on both the tank columns and supporting German airfields from 5 August onward, flying 265 sorties in a single day. This day also saw the elongated Stalingrad battle zone split into two manageable areas, the Stalingrad Front and the Southeast Front with Eighth Air Army responsible for the former and Sixteenth Air Army under General S.I. Rudenko, for the latter.

Fierce fighting continued around Tinguta station, which changed hands several times, Eighth Army aircraft flying up to 600 sorties supporting both the retreat and counter-attacks. Halted there, the German advance changed shape and direction once again and struck at the city from Trekhostrovsky and Abganerovo. On the Don front a serious enveloping threat developed on 17 August when German attacks were made at Vertyachiy and Peskovatka. General Novikov switched vital bomber units of the Eighth Air Army to dispute these crossings. In the stifling heat of mid-summer groups of between ten and thirty Pe-2s, with ten to fifteen Yak-1 or La-5 fighters as escorts, were thrown against the German columns, the *Peshka* crews flying up to three sorties each day between 18 and 22 August. Despite their best efforts, and 1,000 sorties, they failed again, and the Germans established a bridgehead at Peskovatka, from where they broke out to reach positions on the Volga south of Stalingrad on 23 August. Pe-2 missions continued with renewed intensity but the Axis forces relentlessly closed in on the city.

From September onward bitter fighting developed with the defenders digging in amongst the rubble of the city and defending it tenaciously, block by block, building by building. The German onrush came to a halt as unit after unit was ground down and worn out. Both sides required the precision of their respective dive-bomber units to winkle out pinpoint targets in such conditions, with opposing

THE PETLYAKOV Pe-2

troops separated only by a street width and sometimes occupying different parts of the same factory.

The Pe-2s struck at the German support columns, artillery positions and rear-area ammunition and fuel dumps throughout this period. On 23 September they attacked German positions in the heart of Stalingrad and, next day, switched targets to the south of the elongated city which sprawled along the Volga riverbank. Strikes were guided in by Soviet ground forces using rockets, coloured smoke from mortars and tracer shells to indicate to the *Peshka* pilots the enemy positions to be hit. Liaison officers were sent in with radios to help co-ordinate such strikes more accurately and worked right up in the front line in this dangerous rôle. This was an innovation for the VVS but was to be used more frequently as the campaign progressed. It mirrored similar developments pioneered by the Luftwaffe and belatedly copied by the Western air forces in the Desert and Italy.

In order to keep the pressure intense on the Germans a new order was issued on 22 October 1942 that each regiment was to train five aircrews for bad weather and night operations. The Pe-2s so trained operated as single aircraft at intervals of up to fifteen minutes, so prolonging the agony and sleeplessness of the enemy.

Above left: Wartime Soviet painting of a squadron of Pe-2s under attack from German Me. 109 fighters in the vicinity of Stalingrad. (Soviet Official)

Above right: The Pe-2s strike! This picture is typical of the *Peshka's* inherent accuracy by which pinpoint targets would be taken out totally, causing the German armies enormous supply problems over their extended supply lines. As Russian roads turned to quagmires, rail links to bring up ammunition, fuel, men and supplies were doubly essential. Here, the remnants of one such German supply train lie in a wrecked marshalling yard after the Pe-2s had paid a visit. (Soviet Official).

COUNTER-ATTACK

Sometimes more aircraft were used, flying against the same target from differing directions and altitudes; attacks were often made in a silent glide with the engines shut off.

By early October the fighting had continued for months but still parts of the city held out. It was now that the decisive counter-blow was planned.

Penal Squadrons

A uniquely Soviet concept was the attempt to introduce the use of convicts and political internees in their own penal battalions in air operations. Bizarre as this might now appear in hindsight, in the desperate days of 1942 it was tried, and with no less a demanding aircraft as the *Peshka* at that!

The unit concerned was 204 BAP, which was first established at Kubinka, close to Moscow, on 29 May 1942. The divisional commander there was Colonel V.A. Ushakov, with V.M. Tolstoi as chief of staff. The divisional commissar was L.A. Dubrovin, who had served in a number of other air units prior to his allocation to the 204th. Initially the unit was made up from 2 BAP (which became 119 Gv BAP from 3 September 1943) commanded by Major (later Lieutenant Colonel) Grigorii Maksimovich Markov, 6 BAP (commander unknown) and 130 BAP (122 Gv BAP from 3 September 1943). The latter was commanded by Major (later Lieutenant Colonel) S.N. Gavrilov. To this nucleus was shortly added 38 BAP (commander unknown) and 261 BAP (which became 123 GvBAP on 3 September 1943), commanded by Major (later Lieutenant Colonel) Mikhail Ivanovich Martynov, thus becoming a five-regiment division.[14]

The unit first saw combat on 1 June 1942.[15] Interestingly, their escorting fighter protection was provided by the French *Normandie* Squadron, which was attached to 204 BAD. This arrangement had only lasted a short time before *Normandie* was transferred to 303 IAD. For a few months after that, 204 BAD was assigned 22 Gv NBAP, flying Po-2 night bombers, and 179 IAP, equipped with Hawker Hurricane fighters. This made for a unique seven-regiment division. However, from September 1943, the division reverted to a standard three-regiment outfit.

The division was heavily engaged in the fighting of that critical summer, being credited with some 2,000 sorties between June and August. During an intense two-day commitment near Zhizdna, north-west of Kaluga, they flew 300 sorties and were engaged in twelve major air battles, in which they claimed to have destroyed a dozen German fighter aircraft.

The Pe-2s of this unit flew the majority of their early missions with 600kg bomb loads according to Dubrovin, but this steadily increased to 800kg as the summer wore on. Outstanding *Peshka* pilots like Markov, Martynov, Major V.I. Dumchenko, Captain A.A. Lokhanov and Captain D.I. Bytkov, frequently exceeded these bomb weights, taking off with 900 to 1,000kg loading.

It was in August 1942 that this outstanding *Peshka* unit was ordered to establish a penal squadron within its organisation, on the same general lines as the army penal battalions. Assigned to it would be existing pilots and crews who had been found

THE PETLYAKOV Pe-2

guilt of slacking, insubordination and even cowardice! In order that these 'criminals' could redeem themselves with their blood and purge their guilt, the unit was to be given the most dangerous, even suicidal, missions to carry out.[16]

In vain did the commanding officer, his immediate subordinates and even the Kommissar, protest that this was madness. In the air things were vastly different than on the ground and only the willing, they felt, should be allowed the privilege of flying for their country. Indeed, cowards should lose that privilege. However, obedience to orders was exactly what a penal unit was supposed to reinforce, so all arguments were overruled and 261 BAP, commanded by Captain P.D. Osipenko, himself an outstanding and brave officer, was designated as the leader of the official penal squadron. Nobody was ever sent to 261 as a penal servitor and, after a discreet passage of time, they were able to report, without contradiction, that they had no slackers, cowards or any type of violators on their strength. Thus 'purged', if only by omission, 261 was permitted to return to its former normal designation and status.

Bombs on Target! The 587th Regiment subject a German-occupied factory area in the Stalingrad area to an attack. (Soviet Official)

During this period an American military delegation made a visit, on 6 September, but no convicts were on display to greet them. In January 1943 Ushakov was transferred from the unit to a HQ job with a bomber corps; his place was taken by Colonel Sergei Pavlovich Andrev. Markov himself was killed by enemy flak on 22 September and was succeeded at 119 Gv BAP (as it had by then become) by Major N.K. Zaitsev. Martynov was also transferred during the late summer and succeeded by V.I. Dymchenko.

Chapter Eight

New Tactics, New Defences, New Confidence

From Stalingrad onward the war in the air shifted decisively in favour of the Soviets. Their production was now going into top gear and the quality of the aircraft and the refinement of their tactics increasingly bore fruit and helped mitigate against the continued superiority of the quality of the German airmen.

Last-minute checks of the maps for this aircrew of the 128 Short-Range Bomber Air Regiment, working on the Kalinin front on 30 September 1942. (M Maslov)

THE PETLYAKOV Pe-2

Polbin's Experiments

Following his appointment, in November 1942, as commanding officer of his own aviation division, 150th Bomber Regiment, Polbin was free to develop his own strategy to improve the dive-bombing techniques, then still in their relatively rudimentary stages. The classic tactical attack he was later to perfect, the *Vertushka* (Dipping Wheel), was described by Soviet historians thus:[1]

> The Pe-2s approached their target in the three-plane 'Vee of Vees' formation and circled above it at a distance of about 500-600m from one another. One after another, in line astern, each *Peshka* took it in turns to dive down and carry out her attack;[2] in each case the angle of the dive was 70 degrees. This continuous series of assaults split the anti-aircraft defences and produced great accuracy. It was to become the main method chosen by all Pe-2 units as the war progressed, to take out small, or concentrated targets. It was also named the 'Polbin Revolver' by the aircrews at the front. During a single four-day period of operations in July 1942, Polbin's 150th Regiment was credited with the destruction of forty German tanks and fifty soft-skinned vehicles using this technique.

Despite their growing confidence and expertise, the *Peshka* was still not often operated in her designed dive-bombing rôle, the sniping of Polbin and others being the exceptions by an elite, rather than the rule, and so much of the Pe-2's potential was still being wasted as late as the autumn of 1942. However, that was to change dramatically in the months that followed.

The great structural reforms to the VVS initiated by Novikov from April 1942 until the middle of 1943 had an affect on the affiliation of BAPs to divisions. In effect, during this period Pe-2 regiments remained at the front until they were depleted. At that point the survivors were withdrawn to the rear to replenish both aircraft and aircrew. A short period, a few weeks only, of re-training and assimilation of this influx followed and then the regiment was returned to the mincer, but not always to the same division with which it had been serving previously. Allocation was dictated by the overriding needs of the front and the then current military situation.

This policy was changed from mid-1943 onward, the situation having changed. The Pe-2 regiments tended to stay in line with the replacement men and machines being fed into them at the front. This allowed for greater continuity between the regiments and their 'parent' divisions. However, as always, there were many exceptions to this general pattern with, for example, regiments being withdrawn to form the cadre of a completely new division as the air force expanded rapidly.

Unfortunately, the terms BAP, BBAP and SBAP seem to have been used with a large degree of interchangeability in the records of the period. On occasions, the same units have been given different prefixes in the same report or document. In theory the Pe-2 regiments should have been termed as PBAP but this seems rarely to have been the case.³

As an example of this flexibility, 587 PBAP left Saratov at the end of 1942, being assigned to 270 BAD. During the following year, this regiment was re-assigned to 223 BAD. In October 1943 this division and its component regiments were given Guards status as 4 GvBAD, including 125 'M.M. Raskova' *Borisov* GvBAP.

The principal Pe-2 training organisation was 8 ZAB (*Zapasnaya aviatsionnaya brigada* – or Aviation Depot Brigade), which comprised 3, 9 and 18 ZAPs.

Pe-2 and -3 Operations in Norway

The sole ice-free Soviet port of Murmansk on the Arctic Kola Peninsula was one of the foremost German aims as they launched BARBAROSSA. The German attacks along the coast from Norway through Finland failed repeatedly and resulted in a front frozen in trenches from 1941 until 1944. Hence much of the continued conflict was to be acted out between the German Luftflotte 5, led by GeneralOberst Stumpf, later Generalleutnant Kammhuber, and the air forces of the Soviet Northern Fleet (VVS-SF) and Red Army (VVS-RKKA).

The Red Army Air Forces of the Leningrad Military District were reorganised repeatedly following the German onslaught. On 23 August 1941 the Leningrad MD was divided into the Baltic and Karelian Fronts, the latter gaining responsibility for the Finnish and Murmansk Fronts. Up to November 1942 the Air Forces of the Karelian Front were attached to the armies of each sector of the front.

With their Pe-2 parked close to a wood in snowy conditions, this aircrew chat prior to a combat flight. (M Maslov)

THE PETLYAKOV Pe-2

In the Murmansk area this was Fourteenth Army, the air component of which first became 1st Composite Air Division (SAD) in late 1941. Then, in November 1942 it became 258 Air Division of the new Seventh Air Army under Lieutenant General I.M. Sokolov. Sokolov also controlled 257 SAD (from June 1944), 259 fighter Air Division (IAD, to December 1943), 260 AD, 261 AD and, finally, 324 IAD (replacing 259) – supporting the ground forces of Seventh and Fourteenth Armies.

In June 1943 the 258 AD was honoured by becoming the 1 Guards Composite Air Division.

The division remained in the Murmansk area, led by Colonel (*Polkovnik*) S.F. Pushkarev, but did not operate the Pe 2. The Seventh Air Army's main bombers, in 3 and 4 Regiments, were the SB and DB-3F, the former mostly being replaced in 1942-43 by Lend-Lease A-20s.

Pe-2 bombers entered service with Seventh AA in 1943, when 80 BAP joined 261 AD at Koleshma following conversion from the SB at Archangel. Commanding 80 BAP was Lieutenant Colonel G.P. Starikov. On 19 February 1944, under Polkovnik A.V. Minayev, 257 SAD was formed in the Onega area, including 716 PAP equipped with the Pe 2FT. Seventh AA, as well as the three air divisions of the neighbouring Thirteenth Air Army under Lieutenant General S.P. Rybalchenko, were strongly committed to the June 1944 offensive, which forced the Finns to leave the war and turn on their former German allies. By then the former naval 29 BAP had transferred to Seventh Air Army. In October 1944 these forces were moved to Murmansk to support the offensive against the Germans in the Petsamo and Kirkenes area.

Following this operation both 80 BAP and 716 PAP were awarded the battle honour 'Kirkenes'. In this context it can hardly be said that the Pe 2 played a significant role – but nevertheless the contribution to the fighting army cannot be overlooked.

A belly-landing in the snow for this white-painted *Peshka,* which only just made it back to her home base after engine damage over the front line. (M Maslov)

NEW TACTICS, NEW DEFENCES, NEW CONFIDENCE

In addition to Pe 2 bombers, Seventh AA had two directly subordinate reconnaissance squadrons equipped from 1942 with the Pe 2R. These were 118 ODAE, operating from Koleshma, and 108 ORAE at Afrikanda in the central Kola Peninsula.

The commander of 108 ORAE, Major V.I. Donchuk, went missing in his Pe 2R on a mission to Kirkenes on 21 October 1944, four days prior to the Soviet capture of the Norwegian mining town. Donchuk was posthumously made a Hero of the Soviet Union on 2 November 1944.

The Soviet Red Banner Northern Fleet Air Forces (VVS-SF), started the 'Great Patriotic War' with a single bomber squadron with SBs in 72 Composite Naval Air Regiment (72.MSAP. The main base was the three-airfield complex at Vaenga, called Warlamowo by the Germans, to the north-east of Murmansk. In July 1941 this MSAP was strengthened by the transfer of a squadron of early model Pe 2s from central Russia, shortly afterwards augmented by a squadron of DB-3Fs.

During 1941 the Pe-2 Squadron of 72 MSAP lost four aircraft and three crews in action. Their greatest success was the bombing of a bridge near Petsamo in September, setting off a tremendous landslide and seriously hindering a German offensive against Murmansk. On 18 January 1942 the unit was honoured for its role in the defence of Murmansk, by being redesignated 2 Guards Naval Composite Air Regiment (GvMSAP).

Following strong German attacks on the allied supply convoys to Murmansk and Archangel in the spring of 1942, the VVS-SF was ordered by Stalin to be increased in strength and a separate Naval Aviation Group – OMAG, was formed on 30 June 1942 specifically to support the convoy operation.

Daubed with mottled white snow camouflage, this Pe-2 of the 73 BAP, Baltic Fleet, is seen in February 1942. (Via Keski-Suomen Ilmailumuseo, Tikkakoski)

THE PETLYAKOV Pe-2

Major General A.G. Petrukhin assumed command over two fighter regiments; a mine-torpedo regiment and the Pe-2-equipped 28 BAP and 29 BAP. However, 28 BAP had a very short naval career, being transferred back to the VVS-RKKA inside a month, or so. It is not known whether any operations were conducted from Murmansk.

In March 1942 in Kazan 29 BAP was formed, consisting of two nine-aircraft squadrons. After brief operations in support of the besieged Leningrad, 1 Squadron transferred to Vaenga at the end of May, followed by the seven remaining Pe-2s of 2 Squadron, commanded by Captain Popov, on 22 June. The ground crew followed in TB-3 transports and trains and, after a brief stay in barracks, the crews moved into tents following heavy German attacks on the airfield. Their transfer to the Naval Air Force consisted of being handed new naval uniforms. One of the crews, that of Lieutenant George Yevelyev, participated in eight attacks prior to being shot down on 11 September. Three of these were horizontal attacks against the German-held Petsamo airfield, three against German coastal defences and two dive-bombing attacks against shipping off the coast of Norway. The attack when they were shot down was typical: seven Pe-2s escorted by four Yak-1s and four LaGG-7s took off to attack Petsamo airfield; they were intercepted by German fighters of III/JG 5 and two Pe-2s were shot down. Lieutenant Yevelyev had also thrice led fighter reinforcements from central Russian depots to the Murmansk area.

Unusual replenishments, as a caged bomb is unloaded from a reindeer-drawn sledge at a Fleet Air Base close to Murmansk. There is an excellent view of the extensive underside nose glazing of the Pe-2 and also the leading-edge inlet ports inside the engine fairing. (Sovphoto)

NEW TACTICS, NEW DEFENCES, NEW CONFIDENCE

In November 1942, 29 MBAP came under the control of 5 Naval Aviation Brigade which, in July 1943, became 5th Naval Aviation Division, commanded by Colonel N.M. Kidalinskiy. Squadron Commander Semyon Laptchenkov was made a Hero of the Soviet Union following his death in a convoy attack on 20 September 1943. Losses were heavy. During 1942 29 MBAP lost some fourteen Pe-2FTs and thirteen crews. Of these thirty-nine men only two became PoWs with the Germans. Losses in 1943 continued to be high: thirty aircraft and twenty-four crews – seventy men – were lost out of a complement of eighteen aircraft. Following this 29 MBAP was withdrawn to the Archangel area to reform, eventually to return to the control of the Red Army.

Replacing 28 MBAP, 121 BAP was transferred to the Northern Fleet in support of the incoming convoy PQ 18. The eighteen Pe-3s of 121 BAP arrived at Vajenga on 6/7 September 1942, led by the regimental commander, Major Miroshtishenko. The CO of 1 Squadron was Captain Saitschenko, while Captain Kalshnikov commanded 2 Squadron. Their first days at Vaenga indicated an unlucky unit. On 9 September they lost three of their aircraft to German bombing by I/KG 30. Their first operation was to take place on 11 September as PQ 18 had sailed from Iceland. The objective was the KG 30 bomber and KG 26 torpedo-bomber base at Banak in Norway. Nine Pe-3s took off at dawn, only to be intercepted by two Bf.109s of JG 5 in the vicinity of Lake Enare in Northern Finland. Four of the inexperienced Pe-3 crews fell to the two Germans' guns, in return for one Bf.109 missing.

A mobile bowser refuelling a Pe-2 of the 127 BAP on the Northern Front at Karelia airfield, close to besieged Leningrad (St. Petersburg) during the spring of 1942. (Robert Michulec)

THE PETLYAKOV Pe-2

Two Pe 3s managed to force land. Their crews tried to walk back, but that of Sergeant Solovov was captured after ten days. Junior Lieutenant Judin managed to parachute to the ground, and evaded capture for sixteen days. Junior Sergeant Samarin force landed close to Enare and succeeded in returning to Soviet-held territory. He was later to become an accomplished Pe-2R pilot with 118 MRAP. His aircraft was salvaged by the Finns and put into service as 'Pe-310'.

Aircraft losses were replaced by Pe-2FTs, and 121 MBAP accompanied 29 MBAP into 5 MAB in November 1942. Only a few more Pe-3 losses were recorded, two in December and two in February 1943. On 29 March 1943 five Pe-2FTs of 121 MBAP took off from Vaenga to attack a German supply convoy passing Persfjord on its way to Kirkenes. The nine armed ships of the convoy were escorted by fourteen naval units and a Ju. 88D of 1.(F)/124 from Kirkenes; as the Soviets attacked a pair of Bf.110s of 13.(Z)/JG 5 arrived and a fierce air battle began. One Pe-2 shot down the Ju. 88, but the Bf 110s were more of a match. The Pe-2FT of Junior Lieutenant Zabobin – serial 6/157 – was shot down and crashed just west of the town of Vardö. Junior Lieutenant Alexeij Chasovnikov, flying Pe-2 number 16 (serial 16/141), lost his gunner, Junior Sergeant Matveyev and managed a forced landing on the Kudal mountain north-west of Vardö. The German convoy sailed on, unmolested.

Chasovnikov and his bomb-aimer, Lieutenant Teterin, found themselves on a snow-covered mountain a long way from Murmansk. They nevertheless started to walk home across the mountain tundra. After five days they approached inhabited areas in the north-western end of the Varangerfjord, and sought assistance from a local farmer. The area was heavily garrisoned and the farmer dared not help them, but informed the Germans. The two had continued on their trek but, when the Germans tried to capture them, a firefight started and one of the Russians were killed.

Following this unhappy sortie, 121 MBAP was sent to the rear to reform, and was eventually returned to the Red Army, later to participate in the liberation of Kirkenes, and gaining that battle honour on 2 November 1944.

The reconnaissance resources of the VVS-SF were in the autumn of 1942 combined into 118th Naval Reconnaissance Aviation Regiment (MRAP) led by Lieutenant Colonel N.G. Pavlov. One Squadron got the Pe-2R in addition to A-20s for long-range recce duties. This unit also performed agent-dropping and re-supply tasks, also with their Pe-2s. While commanded by Lieutenant Colonel S.K. Litvinov, 118 MRAP was awarded the Order of the Red Banner on 31 October 1944.

In March 1942 the Northern Fleet was strengthened by the transfer of a dedicated long-range-fighter regiment, 95 IAP, equipped with the Pe-3 and commanded by Major A.V. Shatkov. Their first operation, a raid on Petsamo airfield on 26 April 1942, was a disaster for 2 Squadron. Five aircraft with their ten crewmen were lost to German fighters.

In all eleven *Peshkas,* with nine crews were lost in 1942, another eight with seven crews in 1943; a further three were lost during 1944, while one crew was lost in a flying accident. A squadron commander, Captain Viktor Streltsov, became a Hero of the Soviet Union on the Pe-3 on 22 July 1944.

NEW TACTICS, NEW DEFENCES, NEW CONFIDENCE

A ground officer checks the detail of a sortie with a Pe-2 flight crew prior to a combat mission over enemy lines. Note the tail markings of this aircraft. (M Maslov)

The unit remained with the VVS-SF for the duration of the war, and was awarded the Order of the Red Banner on 8 July 1945, while commanded by Major I.A. Olbek.

Another unit, briefly attached to the VVS-SF in 1942, was 13 BAP equipped with both Pe-2s and Pe-3s. During operations over the White Sea off Archangel during the arrival of convoy PQ 18 in September 1942, this unit lost three aircraft and crews. In November 1942 the unit was transferred from the OMAG to the Moscow area.

Strengths

The available statistics of the VVS-SF show that their Air Force received a total of eighty-two Pe-2 aircraft from 1941 through to 1945, fifty-five of these coming straight from factories, the remainder from other fronts. Thirty-six of these arrived in 1942 while a total of seventeen were lost, thirteen of them in action. Annual strength for the Pe-2 was reported to be three aircraft at the end of 1941, thirty-seven in 1942, six in 1943 and one at the end of 1944.

Simultaneously, the VVS-SF received a total of sixty-three Pe-3s between 1941 and 1945. Of these twenty came from Red Army air units in 1941, another eleven in 1943, while naval air units contributed twenty-eight Pe-3s in 1942 and three in 1943. A total of twenty-six were lost on operations, and nineteen on non-operational flights; four were written off for a total of thirty-nine Pe-3s.

Annual strength for the Pe-3 was thirteen at the end of 1941, twenty in 1942, twenty-one in 1943 and fourteen in 1944.

THE PETLYAKOV Pe-2

Pe-2 '101', the mount of Twice Hero of the Soviet Union, Lieutenant Colonel V I Rakov, commander of 12 Group PAP, Battle Fleet, summer 1944. (Via Keski-Suomen Ilmailmuseo. Tikkakoski)

Table 3: Northern Fleet *Peshka* Strength July-December 1942

Wing	Type	1-7-42	3-7-42	1-10-42	1-12-42
95 IAP	Pe-2	3	3	3	3
	Pe-3	12	10	7	20
28 AP	Pe-2	11	8	6	-
29 AP	Pe-2	12	8	9	14
121 AP	Pe-2	-	-	7	-
	Pe-3	-	-	5	9
28 AE	Pe-2	-	-	-	4
Totals		38	29	37	50

IAP – *Istrebitelnyi Aviacionnyi Polk*. AP – *Aviacionnyi Polk*. AE – *Avicionnaja Eskadrilija*. from Roman Larincew.

Table 4: Soviet Northern Fleet - Pe-2 & Pe-3 Combat Sorties 1942-1943*

Date	Type	No.	Target	Losses
10/01/42	Pe-2	1	General Attack sorties	
13/01/42	Pe-2	1	Vardoe Harbour	
14/01/42	Pe-2	1	Vardoe Harbour	
20/01/42	Pe-3	1	Kirkenes Harbour	
01/02/42	Pe-2	1	Vardoe	
02/02/42	Pe-2	1	Vardoe	
06/02/42	Pe-2	1	Vardoe	

NEW TACTICS, NEW DEFENCES, NEW CONFIDENCE

07/02/42	Pe-2	1	Artillery emplacements near Zapadnaja Litsa	
11/02/42	Pe-2	1	Bolschaja Litsa village	
13/02/42	Pe-2	1	Vardoe Harbour	
15/02/42	Pe-2	2	Motorised column near Vardoe	
15/02/42	Pe-2	1	Vardoe Harbour	
16/02/42	Pe-2	2	Vardoe Harbour	
19/03/42	Pe-2	1	Titovka	
19/03/42	Pe-3	2	Ibidem	
24/03/42	Pe-3	4	Titovka	
24/03/42	Pe-3	2	Ibidem	
24/03/42	Pe-2	1	Luostari airfield	
24/03/42	Pe-2	4	Ibidem	
03/04/42	Pe-2	1	Liinahamari Harbour	
03/04/42	Pe-3	2	Ibidem	
04/04/42	Pe-2	1	Vardoe	
04/04/42	Pe-3	14	Luostari airfield	
13/04/42	Pe-3	2	Ship at Liinahamari	
15/04/42	Pe-3	11	Ibidem	
15/04/42	Pe-3	3	Kirkenes Harbour	
23/04/42	Pe-3	1	Banak airfield	
23/04/42	Pe-3	4	Vardoe Harbour	
24/04/42	Pe-3	3	Ship at Kirkenes	
26/04/42	Pe-3	7	Hebuktmoen airfield	3
30/04/42	Pe-2	1	Vardoe	
12/05/42	Pe-3	2	Vardoe Harbour	
14/05/42	Pe-3	1	Destroyer near Sulterfjord	
14/05/42	Pe-3	1	Vardoe	
14/05/42	Pe-3	4	4 Destroyers near Suterfjord	
14/05/42	Pe-3	2	Vardoe	
16/05/42	Pe-3	4	Destroyer 35 miles north of Vardoe	
16/05/42	Pe-3	2	Ships in Vardoe harbour	
17/05/42	Pe-2	2	Vardoe Harbour	
17/05/42	Pe-2	2	Ships off Cape Skalnes	
18/05/42	Pe-3	1	Vardoe Harbour	
19/05/42	Pe-2	2	Patrol ship at 71-02 N/ 30-30E	
28/05/42	Pe-2	14	Luostari airfield	VVS

THE PETLYAKOV Pe-2

Date	Type	No.	Target	Losses
28/05/42	Pe-2	7	Luostari airfield	A
29/05/42	Pe-2	14	Kirkenes Harbour	VVS
29/05/42	Pe-2	1	Kirkenes Harbour	A
30/05/42	Pe-2	14	Hebuktmoen airfield	VVS
30/05/42	Pe-2	5	Hebuktmoen airfield	A
30/05/42	Pe-2	5	Ibidem	
01/06/42	Pe-2	14	Hebuktmoen airfield	VVS
01/06/42	Pe-2	5	Hebuktmoen airfield	A
02/06/42	Pe-3	2	Vardoe Harbour	
19/06/42	Pe-3	1	Vardoe	
19/06/42	Pe-3	1	Destroyer 71-05N/3030E	
25/06/42	Pe-3	1	Vardoe	
29/06/42	Pe-3	1	Vardoe	
29/06/42	Pe-2	2	Vardoe	
30/06/42	Pe-2	15	Luostari airfield	3
30/06/42	Pe-2	13	Ibidem	2
30/06/42	Pe-3	2	Ibidem	
01/07/42	Pe-2	2	Kirkenes harbour	
01/07/42	Pe-2	1	Vardoe	
02/07/42	Pe-2	4 + 2	Kirkenes	
03/07/42	Pe-2	1	Hebuktmoen airfield	
07/07/43	Pe-2	6	Escort Persfjord	
09/07/42	Pe-2	7	Vardoe	
10/07/43	Pe-2	8 + 3	Hebuktmoen airfield	
10/07/43	Pe-2	2	Vardoe	
11/07/42	Pe-2	4	Hebuktmoen airfield	
12/07/42	Pe-2	6	Hebuktmoen airfield	
13/07/42	Pe-2	5	Ships at Kirkenes	
13/07/42	Pe-2	2	Luostari	
15/07/42	Pe-2	3	Vardoe	
19/07/42	Pe-2	2	Ship at Kirkenes	
19/07/42	Pe-2	1	Kirkenes Harbour	
19/07/42	Pe-2	1	Petsamo	
20/07/42	Pe-2	3	Kirkenes Harbour	2
21/07/43	Pe-2	1	Ships near Vardoe	
21/07/42	Pe-2	2	Vardoe	

NEW TACTICS, NEW DEFENCES, NEW CONFIDENCE

23/07/42	Pe-2	5	Parkkina	1
24/07/42	Pe-2	2	Vardoe	
27/07/42	Pe-2	2	Escort Haviningsberg	
28/07/42	Pe-2	3	Ship in Bosfjord	
29/07/42	Pe-2	3	Ship near Makkaur	
30/07/43	Pe-2	2	Vardoe	
05/08/42	Pe-2	1	Makkaur	
07/08/42	Pe-2	1	Ship in Syltefjord	
07/08/43	Pe-2	2	Escort Peersfjord	
07/08/43	Pe-2	1	Havingsberg	
07/08/42	Pe-2	2	Escort sea	
08/08/42	Pe-2	2	Ship near Vardoe	
22/08/42	Pe-2	1	Havningsberg	
28/08/42	Pe-2	1	Havningsberg	
01/09/42	Pe-2	1	Ship in Syltefjord	
05/09/42	Pe-2	1	Ship near Vardoe	
05/09/42	Pe-2	2	Ship near Vardoe	
06/09/42	Pe-2	1	Ship near Kibergness	
06/09/42	Pe-2	2	Ship near Vardoe	
06/09/42	Pe-2	2	Ship near Kibergness	
07/09/42	Pe-2	1	Warship at Haviningsberg	
07/09/42	Pe-3	1	U-boat 90 miles north of Cape Kanin	
08/09/42	Pe-2	2	Ship near Vardoe	
09/09/42	Pe-2	2	Luostari airfield	
11/09/42	Pe-2	9	Luostari airfield	
11/09/42	Pe-3	9	Banak airfield	4
12/09/42	Pe-2	7	Luostari airfield	2
14/09/42	Pe-2	2	Havingsberg	
16/09/42	Pe-2	4	Ship near Skalnes	
16/09/42	Pe-2	2	Havningsberg	
27/09/42	Pe-2	4	Ship near Havningsberg	
27/09/42	Pe-2	1	Havningsberg	
28/09/42	Pe-2	2	Ship in 70-30N/30-45 E	
28/09/42	Pe-2	2	Ship near Havningsberg	
28/09/42	Pe-2	2	Havingsberg	
29/09/42	Pe-2	1	Havingsberg	
29/09/42	Pe-2	4	Escort Nordkyn	

THE PETLYAKOV Pe-2

Date	Type	No.	Target	Losses
01/10/42	Pe-2	1	Ship in 71-10N/29-00E	
04/10/42	Pe-2	2	Ship in 70-30N/30-45E	
04/10/42	Pe-2	2	Ship in 70-52N/29-50E	
05/10/42	Pe-2	6	Ship in Bussesund	
05/10/42	Pe-3	2	Ship in Bussesund	
06/10/42	Pe-2	1	Havningsberg	
10/10/42	Pe-2	1	Ships at sea	
30/10/42	Pe-2	1	Ship in 70-45N/29-40E	
31/10/42	Pe-2	2	Berlevaag	
31/10/42	Pe-2	3	Ship in 70-50N/29-40E	
06/11/42	Pe-3	1	Berlevaag	
07/11/42	Pe-2	3	Ship in 70-55N/29-20E	1
13/11/42	Pe-2	1	Berlevaag	
15/11/42	Pe-2	1	Makkaur	
27/12/42	Pe-2	6	Liinaharmari harbour	
28/12/42	Pe-3	1	Coastal Battery at Petsamo	
31/12/42	Pe-2	9	Ship in Liinaharmari	
08/01/43	Pe-3	6	Ship in Kirkenes	
10/01/43	Pe-2	6	Ship in Liinahamari	
15/01/43	Pe-3	8	Ship in Liinahamari	
23/01/43	Pe-3	3	Motorised column between Vardoe and Vadsoe	
24/01/43	Pe-2	5	Ship in Kirkenes	2
05/02/43	Pe-3	4	Escort Sultefjord	
14/02/43	Pe-3	1	Motorised column between Vardoe and Vadsoe	
17/02/43	Pe-3	3	Cutter near Sultefjord	
17/02/43	Pe-2	3	Cutter near Vardoe	
21/02/43	Pe-3	4	Minesweeper near Lille-Ekkeroy	
21/02/43	Pe-2	4	Escort Kirkenes	
28/02/43	Pe-2	3	Luostari airfield	
05/03/43	Pe-2	3	Luostari airfield	2
01/03/43	Pe-3	3	Escort Sultelfjord	
13/03/43	Pe-2	4	Luostari airfield	
28/03/43	Pe-3	2	Escort Kongsfjord	
29/03/43	Pe-2	8	Escort Persfjord	2
29/03/43	Pe-3	3	Escort near Cape Harbaken	

NEW TACTICS, NEW DEFENCES, NEW CONFIDENCE

29/03/43	Pe-3	3	2 minesweepers near Vardoe	
25/04/43	Pe-2	2	Escort at sea	
May-43			No operations	
Jun-43			No operations	
16/07/43	Pe-2	6	Ship in Syltefjord	
17/07/43	Pe-2	7	2 Troopships in Baatsfjord	2
20/07/43	Pe-2	13	Ship near Vardoe	1
23/07/43	Pe-3	2	U-Boat	
25/07/43	Pe-2	12	Ship near Vardoe	
06/08/43	Pe-2	6	Liinahamari Harbour	
14/08/43	Pe-2	6	Ship in Kirkenes	
23/08/43	Pe-2	6	Escort Petsamofjord	1
14/09/43	Pe-2	4	Luostari airfield	
15/09/43	Pe-2	1	Kirkenes	
19/09/43	Pe-2	4	Luostari airfield	
19/09/43	Pe-2	6	Ship near Vardoe	
27/09/43	Pe-2	6	Luostari and Svartness airfields	2
13/10/43	Pe-2	6	Escort Kibergness	1
03/11/43	Pe-2	6	Ship in Kirkenes	1
24/11/43	Pe-2	12	Hebuktmorn airfield	
02/12/43	Pe-2	3	Luostari airfield	1
02/12/43	Pe-2	3	Hebuktmorn airfield	
Total Sorties		590	**Total Losses**	33

* Information kindly supplied to the Author by Roman Larincew various dates 2001.

More Actions

On 15 April 1942, 95 IAP became increasingly employed in the bombing role against both enemy shipping and airfields in Northern Norway. Four Pe-3s led by Captain V.A. Kulikov attacked enemy shipping at the port of Linahamari with bombs and rockets. They claimed to have sunk a 4,000-BRT ship and damaged other ships and port installations without loss to themselves.

Five days later, on 20 April, a single Pe-3, piloted by Captain V.S. Strel'tsov, attacked a 5,000-tonne enemy tanker with bombs, which set her on fire, and then finished her off by rocket attack. Her sinking was subsequently confirmed by reconnaissance.

From April 1942 onward other duties performed were the dropping of supplies to an army reconnaissance unit working behind German lines. The supply

THE PETLYAKOV Pe-2

containers were carried on the wing bomb-racks and were carried out without loss. Due to increased German attacks on convoys from Britain heading for Murmansk, Arkhangel' and Molotovsk, the Soviet command set up a Special Maritime Aviation Group (OMAG) which included 95 IAP.

On 23 April the arrival of convoy PQ15 led to a number of pre-emptive strikes by the Northern Fleet VVS on the Germans' Luftflotte 5 airfields in northern Norway. One squadron of 95 IAP attacked Luostari airfield, claiming to have set on fire sixteen enemy aircraft there, and to have destroyed one of the intercepting Bf.109s, all without loss.

Seven Pe-3s sent to attack Hebugten airfield on the 26th were intercepted by a force of twenty-three Bf.109s. Captain B. Shishkin, the leader, made a head-on attack against this force firing his rockets into their formation, which enabled the rest of his unit to get through and make an accurate attack on the target. Reports from a PoW later revealed that four Ju.87s, one Ju.88, and one Bf.109 were destroyed in this attack, along with twenty other aircraft damaged. In addition, two hangars and two ancillary buildings were destroyed and fifteen ground personnel killed. The cost to the attacking force was also heavy, with five Pe-3s failing to return, one landing at a neighbouring base, and one pilot parachuting to safety. Only one aircraft returned to base.

From 29 April the surviving Pe-3s were employed on their long-range convoy protection duties over PQ 15 and escorted it into the White Sea. On either 14 or 16 May, with the Northern Fleet, four Pe-3s, led by Captain N. Kirikov, with Lieutenant V. Strel'tsov, were scrambled and led to the island of Vardoe where reconnaissance reported the presence of an enemy ship. They claimed to have sunk a German T-class destroyer, which was hit by several of the sixteen FAB-100 100kg bombs aimed at her. A second pass was made and two of the Pe-3s fired their rockets into her, finishing her off. Strel'tvov went on to become the only Hero of the Soviet Union earner of 95 IAP in a career that included 146 sorties, sinking three ships and damaging two others, destroying twelve enemy aircraft, nine tanks, two trains and forty-five vehicles.

A small number of Pe-3s joined 27 Reconnaissance Aviation Squadron (27 RAE) of the Black Sea Fleet VVS in the summer of 1942. This unit also operated the Pe-2 and A-20, these aircraft being used in both reconnaissance and long-range escort roles. Usually they fought at a disadvantage against German single-engined fighters.

Meanwhile, during July 1942, Pe-3s from the Northern Fleet were engaged in providing air cover to surviving ships from convoy PQ 17 which had been scattered by the Admiralty under threat of attack by the German battleship *Tirpitz*. Pe-3s were used to locate ships and then guide them towards the nearest naval escorts. In order to extend the area of their search and cover for the stragglers from this convoy a wooden-slatted airstrip was built on the coast of the Kola peninsula, strengthened with larch planks, and two or three sorties a day were mounted from it. Lack of the necessary night-flying equipment on the Pe-3 precluded their use after dark. On long flights most Pe-3s, which arrived back after dusk, had to force land due to this lack and several were lost in crashes.

Captain V. Volodin was leading a group of four Pe-3s on 13 July when they intercepted an enemy formation heading for the convoy and attacked in two pairs, one led by Volodin and the other by Lieutenant A. Suchkov. They used rockets, guns and cannon, claiming the destruction of seven Ju. 88s. In return Suchkov was hit and the controls taken over by his navigator. After an hour-and-a-half flight the damaged aircraft was safely landed at her base.

Tirpitz at her Altenfiord anchorage was the target for Pe-2Is on the night of 10/11 February 1944. Fifteen specially-adapted *Peshkas* took off from Vaenga airfield near Murmansk (now known as Severomorsk), each carrying a special 2,000lb (907.18kg) armour-piercing bomb which it was hoped would penetrate the battleship's tough hide. Unfortunately, weather conditions rapidly deteriorated after the aircraft had left and in the end only four of the bombers managed to reach the target through the subsequent murk and snow flurries. They caught the German defences off-guard and the covering smokescreen was not initially in place when this quartet made their attacks. To penetrate the ship's armoured decks, bomb release had to be from at least 4,000 feet (1,219.20m). The bombs fell in the right area and the Soviet authorities later claimed that at least one was a very near miss, but apparently no damage was inflicted.

Southern Operations

Even as late as July 1942, production was not keeping up with demand. Eight VA (Air Army), operating in the Stalingrad area, had just 8 per cent of its tactical bomber force made up of *Peshkas* (fourteen Pe-2s and a solitary Pe-3). Colonel I.G. Polbin's 150 BAP was moved into the area to lend their special expertise to the rout of German forces there. During the house-to-house fighting that went on street by street, the *Peshka* vied with the Stuka in delivering precision, pinpoint bombing, with the crews flying maps in hand to prevent hitting their own forces.

The Pe-3-equipped 121 IAP began operations in August 1942. The Pe-3 was also operated by reconnaissance units 28 ORAE and, later, 118 ORAE with the Northern Fleet VVS.

Northern Fleet combat

One Pe-3 from 121 IAP crash-landed in northern Finland on 11 September 1942. The navigator was killed but the pilot *Starshina* Samarin, survived and rejoined his regiment a few weeks later. The aircraft was salvaged, restored, and used by the Finnish air force with the LeLv 48. It was finally destroyed in an Pe-2 attack on Lapperanta airfield on 2 July 1944.

Convoy PQ 18 took place during September 1942.[4] In readiness, the Independent Maritime Air Group (OMAG) of the Northern Fleet VVS, was reinforced by two more Pe-3 aviation regiments, 13 and 121 IAPs. However, their value was limited as they had very little operational experience with the Pe-3 since their conversion, although 13 IAP had supported the earlier PQ 16 and QP 14 convoy operations with other aircraft. The OMAG reinforcements were augmented by 13 SBAP equipped with Pe-3*bis* led by Major V.P. Bogomolov. They were introduced to operations by experienced squadron commanders from 95 IAP and soon earned their spurs. The CO and Lieutenant A.I. Ustimenko each shot down one Ju 88.

The main *Peshka* involvement in this bitter air/sea battle covered the period 16-19 September 1942. First contact with QP 18 was by a Pe-3 from 13 IAP, led by

THE PETLYAKOV Pe-2

K. Usenko on 16 September and, during the following three days, a constant patrol was maintained. With only twenty-three Pe-3s available they operated in groups of four at a time. Two four-hour sorties were mounted each day, with a fifteen-minute gap between each.

On 18 September 1942 two German torpedo-bomber attacks were made against the convoy. One Ju.88 was claimed as destroyed by the Pe-3 escort, Usenko's crews. Having just repelled an attack by Ju.88s, 13 SBAP led by Major Bogomolov noticed a group of Fw.200Cs approaching the convoy from the opposite direction. 'It was too late to intervene in their torpedo runs' (Medved' and Khazanov) but Usenko managed to get close and set the outer starboard engine on fire. Because his crew was ordered to immediately return to the patrol area, the attack was discontinued without finishing off the *Kondor*. Out of a total of sixty-two sorties by German aircraft launched in this period, only one torpedo-bomber scored a hit; this was on the transport *Kentucky*, which was damaged and had to be sunk by the naval escort.

German attacks on a convoy at Molotovsk port on 19 September. Were repelled by four Pe-3s led by the unit's CO, claiming two Ju.88s shot down and others damaged from a force of twenty-four. Pe-3 losses were one damaged in air combat, with two more lost in dusk crash landings.

During the winter of 1942/43, 13 SBAP took heavier losses, though not from the enemy, but the elements. They were caught in a blizzard and, with inadequate navigation equipment, had to choose between baling out or belly landing. They lost a large number of aircraft to crash landings. So depleted was the unit by this disaster that it was disbanded on 5 November, and their few surviving Pe-3s were transferred to 95 IAP.

On 27 December 1942 a Pe-3 piloted by M.K. Verbitsky and navigator P.I. Seleznyev took the first Soviet photographs over Altenfiord. Three days later other units attacked the German supply airfields which reduced their effectiveness in supplying the besieged Sixth Army of General Paulus. On this date, a force of six Pe-2s attacked Tormosina airfield and claimed the destruction of no fewer than thirty Ju.52s.

By this period, also, Pe-2 tactics had been refined with concentrated formations of between thirty to seventy dive-bombers able to operate in strength, as opposed to small sections of three to nine as had hitherto been the norm. Polbin's *Vyertushka* (merry-go-round or carousel), a stacked-up circle or wheel, was put into practice here.

On 23 September 1942, a pair of Pe-3s of the Black Sea Fleet's 27 RAE fought a duel with four Bf.109s escorting German ships heading for the Crimea. Both Pe-3s were lost, one crash-landing on the Caucasian coast, the other ditching in the sea, but the crew were rescued. By the beginning of 1943 all the Pe-3s of the Black Sea Fleet had been lost in combat or accidents.

Baltic operations

In the 1942/43 winter campaign in the Baltic the Baltic Fleet VVS dive-bombers attacked and destroyed a vital bridge over the river Narva. The bridge took the Germans a month to repair and severely affected the supply route of their armies laying siege to Leningrad (St Petersburg).

Chapter Nine

Tilting the Scales – Stalingrad to the Donets

Pre-mission flight briefing by a *Peshka* aircrew, note the effective dappling effect of the camouflage netting over the aircraft. (Via Keski-Suoment Imailumuseo, Tikkakoski)

The result of the air battles on the Stalingrad front gave rise to fresh thinking on close-support air power in the higher echelons of the VVS. A detailed report on the conclusions reached and recommendations for future application was presented to Stalin on 3 February 1943 by General N.A. Zhuravlev after a briefing from Air Force commander A.A. Novikov on his return to Moscow from the front.

New thinking

Among the many ideas put forward to improve land/air co-operation in future combat were some that directly affected the combat mission of the dive-bombers.

1: During artillery barrages and softening-up bombardments prior to major land assaults and advances, it was suggested that forward aviation be released from the front and instead concentrated on disrupting the enemy command-and-control centres, such as headquarters and communication centres.

2: Once the actual infantry attacks went in then the dive-bombers should revert to their traditional role of targeting artillery and mortar positions, and other strongpoints.
3: An air reserve force should be held back and placed at the disposal of the army commander to use against enemy reserve forces.
4: To support important breakthroughs by tank and mechanised forces, close-support units should be attached to them directly, along with liaison officers and communications representatives to call them in and guide them to the target. This had long been the common practice for the German armed forces but was only now under consideration by the Russians (and was to be even more belatedly adopted by the Western Allies).
5: The limited combat radius (4,560km maximum) of the Pe-2 dive-bomber was its main weakness and it was proposed that a longer-range replacement be designed. This was because it had been found that, when the ground actions developed so that it was desirable to co-ordinate the air activity from two or three fronts, their lack of range meant that Pe-2s could not always be used from one front to support another.
6: A total re-organisation of the Pe-2 bomber divisions was called for, with the three regiments of twenty aircraft each being replaced by two regiments of thirty-two aircraft each.

Progress on other fronts

The cataclysmic defeat at Stalingrad led to other breakthroughs on other fronts as the overstretched German forces fell back all along the line. The situation in the north was eased with advances on the Leningrad and Volkhov fronts, supported by Thirteenth and Fourteenth Air Armies, which finally broke the blockade of the former city on 18 January 1943. Three days earlier, the North-western Front and Sixth Army under General F.P. Polynin had also gone over to the offensive against the Demyansk salient, which the Germans had held since winter 1941. The pressure he exercised forced the Germans to withdraw to the Lovat' river and this important German bridgehead was finally eliminated.

The First and Third Air Armies, under Generals S. Khudyakov and M.M. Gromov, supported the Kalinin and Western fronts which took the city of Rzhev on 3 March, Gzhatsk on 6 March, Vyaz'ma on 12 March and were approaching both Dukhovshchina and Spas-Demysansk by 1 April. In the North Caucasus Fourth and Fifth Air Armies commanded by Generals N.F. Naumenko and S.K. Goryunov, pushed the Germans back to a depth of up to 600 kilometres during February. The same progress was reported on the upper Don, where fifteen German divisions had been eliminated by the end of January. The Second and Fifteenth Air Armies, under Generals K.N. Smirnov and I.G. Pyatykhin supported the advance of the Voronezh Front towards Kursk and Kastornoye. Along the whole of the Voronezh-Kastornoye front the Soviet forces pushed the Germans back as far as Sumy by March, before the line was re-stabilised.

TILTING THE SCALES – STALINGRAD TO THE DONETS

Pe-2s of the 29th Bomber Air Regiment taxi out in 1943. (Juri Rybin via Hannu Valtonen)

Failure of the Kharkov offensive

Only in one sector, the vast Western Front, did the new confidence of the Soviet armed forces falter. On the South-western Front Seventeenth Air Army, commanded by General S.A. Krasovkiy, supported a massive offensive into the Donets Basin that commenced on 29 January. A similar advance on the Southern Front, to which Eighth Air Army, commanded by General T.T. Khryukin, lent its weight, supplemented this. By mid-February, these twin offensives had thrown the Germans back to the River Mius. However, they over-reached themselves. The Germans might have been chastened by events on the Volga, but they were still masters of mobile warfare and skillfully turned a Russian offensive into a retreat by executing a massive pincer movement from Krasnograd and Krsnoarmeyskoye against the South-western Front and from south-west of Kharkov against the Voronzh Front in March 1943. The Soviets fell back northwards on Kursk and eventually stabilised the line again at the end of the month. The result of these major exchanges was a large western-facing bulge in the Western Front, the Kursk salient.

Kuban air fighting

The Soviets, with 5,500 combat aircraft, now decisively outnumbered the Luftwaffe. Moreover, these planes were largely of modern type and were being reinforced at an accelerating rate. In contrast the Luftwaffe was a steadily decreasing asset, being switched not only from front to front to plug increasing gaps, but from theatre to theatre as the Allied invasions of, first, North-west Africa, then Sicily and then mainland Italy itself developed during 1943. With their confidence vastly increased, the VVS engaged in an air war of attrition over the Kuban in spring 1943, in which further advances in tactics were honed.

THE PETLYAKOV Pe-2

Throwing the Germans out of the North Caucasus and liberating the Taman' Peninsula had led to the establishment of a Soviet bridgehead at Novorossiysk from 4 February 1943. A naval assault landing party had been reinforced by Eighteenth 18 Army and resisted all German attempts to eliminate them by the reinforced German Seventeenth Army defending the lower Kuban River and the Taman', centred on Krymskaya. The Germans concentrated some of the best Luftwaffe units in this area to decide the issue and the Soviet Fourth and Fifth Air Armies, plus those of the Black Sea Fleet VVS under General V.V. Yermachenkov, totaling about 550 aircraft, opposed them. The Soviets opened their offensive to surround Krymskaya and Myskhako on 4 April. The result was fierce air battles, which commenced on the 17th of the month. From 20 April, heavy reinforcements from the Stavka Reserve were thrown into the contest, including the Pe-2s of II BAC under General V.A. Ushakov. The *Peshkas* main role was in supporting Fifty-Sixth Army.

After repelling the German offensive at Myskhako, the Soviets went over to the offensive on 29 April, and, on 3 May, eighteen groups of Pe-2s from 2 BAC attacked at ten-to-twenty minute intervals, targeting artillery positions at Verkhni Adagum and Neberedzhayevskaya. These precision attacks opened the way for an advance from the south and, by 4 May, Krymskaya was in Russian hands. On 26 May a new front opened with Thirty-seventh and Fifty-sixth Armies attacking the German Blue Line held by the German Seventeenth Army. Savage air battles resulted, which lasted through to June 7 when the fighting petered out. The Germans had held the Soviet offensive, but at heavy cost in aircraft, 1,100 in total.

Peshka pilot. This is Second Lieutenant A G Buzanov in the cockpit of his Pe-3. Note the oxygen equipment, the Soviet censor has blocked out his breathing apparatus in this photograph. (Via Keski-Suomen Ilmailumuseo, Tikkakoski)

TILTING THE SCALES – STALINGRAD TO THE DONETS

During the early summer repeated strikes were made at German airfields and, subsequently, at their lines of communications. The idea was to pre-empt the enemy's preparations for his summer offensive, which was known to be directed against the Kursk salient. Plans were laid to draw the German thrusts onto well-prepared and in-depth defences, grind them down and then to counter-attack. In preparation for this, enormous efforts were made to replace all obsolete aircraft with modern machines, and it was at this time that the Pe-2 dive-bomber almost totally replaced all other types in the active bomber fleet.

Early in May Sixteenth Air Army launched a crushing Pe-2 attack with fifty dive-bombers following detailed aerial reconnaissance over Lokot and the Brasovo railway marshalling yard. A large quantity of military supplies, several tanks and armoured vehicles and a supply train were all destroyed in this operation, hindering the German build up considerably.

In view of the fact that enemy armour was to be their principal target, the equipping of *Peshka* units with the new PTAB 2.5 – 1.5 (*Protivotankovaya aviabomba* – anti-tank aviation bomb), a hollow-charge weapon designed by I.A. Larionov in 1943, was a great advance. This weapon was light and small, inexpensive to manufacture and highly effective, even against the new German Panther and Tiger tanks.

During the three-month pause prior to the German assault, every effort was made to improve land-air communications, the aim being for every aircraft to be equipped with a radio. Increased aerial reconnaissance was another vital feature and the steady build up of German forces near Orel and Kromy was constantly monitored from 14 May onward. By the end of June the major clash of arms was imminent.

Peshka Men – Aleksei Fedorov[1]

Aleksei Fedorov became the commander of 9 SBAP in November 1941, remaining with that regiment until late 1942.[2] This SBAP had begun the war at Khodynka Field, Moscow, which was named for M.V. Frunze. It had re-equipped with the SB in the first month of the war. One of the best pilots at this time was Mikhail Antonovich Krivtsov, later to command 138 PBAP.

In August 1942 Aleksei was ordered to write a detailed article for the Air Force Newspaper based on his experiences of using the *Peshka* in its proper dive-bombing role. He explained how the best dive-bombing results could be obtained from the aircraft, and it is here that the chess analogy quoted at the front of this book was

Peshka ace Aleksei Fedorov. (Vladimir Patrov)

first used: 'With proper handling, the Pawn can advance to become a Queen.' This, of course, was a revelation to most *Peshka* pilots of the time.

Most of the veterans who survived had converted from the SB, a medium bomber in the main, and still considered themselves medium (low-level) bomber men and had little or no experience of a diving attack. The flood of replacement intakes was poorly trained in order to get them to the front. With such novices having only about twenty-to-thirty hours flying time of any kind under their belts, taking the tricky Pe-2 into a diving attack seemed totally beyond them. Many could not fly at night or in bad weather; the little time they had been allocated was confined to basic flying skills. Thus the introduction of the diving principle as a matter of course was bound to have got off to a slow start. Fedorov and Polbin were very much the exceptions rather than the rule and they taught by example and by results.

From late 1942 until September 1943 Fedorov flew with 39 PBAP, 202 BAD, based close to Stalingrad.[3] Organised in late October 1941, 202 BAD then comprised 39, 514 and 797 BAPs, all equipped with the Pe-2. Later 514 became 36 Guards Regiment and when 39 BAP became 39 RAP, it was replaced in the division by 18 BAP. Meanwhile 241 BAD comprised 24, 128 and 779 BAPs; in April 1943 this unit converted into a Pe-2 reconnaissance regiment.

Following this stint Aleksei was transferred once more, this time to 241 BAD as deputy commander, taking over full command of that regiment later.

Radar-equipped night fighters

In the period 1942/43 one independent squadron, equipped with Pe-2 and Pe-3s fitted with the *Gneis-2* AI radar, was engaged as night fighters against German transport aircraft attempting to supply the besieged Sixth Army at Stalingrad.

Experimental equipping of a Pe-2 with the German-originated Soviet *Gneis* radar set for night fighting. (Author's collection)

TILTING THE SCALES – STALINGRAD TO THE DONETS

In January and February 1943 the Soviet command recorded a number of instances of whole Pe-2 squadrons failing to return without a trace from sorties without a fighter escort. The most worrying incident of this kind involved fourteen Pe-2s from First VA; later investigations revealed that all these aircraft were shot down by enemy fighters. On 29 January 1943 a flight of Fw.190A-4s of III./JG51, led by Guenther Shack, returning from escorting Ju.87 dive-bombers, attacked eight Pe-2s over Novosiliya. Within ten minutes all eight bombers were shot down, five of them claimed by Shack alone.

By February 1943, 95 IAP was transferred to 5 MTAD, escorting torpedo-bomber missions, as both defensive escort and engaging enemy fighters. When no enemy aircraft were present the Pe-3s acted as flak-suppressors, leading the attacks with cannon and machine-gun fire and enabling the torpedo-bombers to carry out their attacks. A few Pe-3*bis*s were modified to lay down smokescreens to achieve the same effect. They had to learn the hard way just how dangerous this role was.

In a combined attack on 10 April 95 IAP Pe-3s became separated from their charges and four Bf.110. were able to get through to the torpedo-bombers, destroying one Il-4 and one Hampden of 24 MTAP.

On 25 April seven Pe-3s, under Squadron Commander Khaydarov, escorted five Hampdens of 24 MTAP in an attack on a German convoy of seventeen transports and escorts off Kongsfiord, which had a aerial escort of three Bf.110s and one He.115 floatplane. The He.115 was destroyed and the fighters chased off, two being claimed as damaged. The torpedo-bombers claimed the sinking of two transports (the Germans admitted loss of one *Leesee* vessel) and one escort. Two Pe-3s and one Hampden were lost.

In mid-1943, 121 IAP handed over its remaining Pe-3s to 95 IAP and was disbanded.

Pe-2 Tactics

The combat qualities of the front-line aviation regiments were rigorously honed for the battle. As well as the Carousel tactic, the Main Directorate of Frontal Aviation Combat Training, under General D.F. Kondratyik, which had been created in January 1943, devised other lessons. Methods of attacking small mobile ground targets were evaluated, and the increasing use of radio guidance of Pe-2s onto the target were practised constantly.

One hour before the expected Soviet counter-attack at Prokhorovka commenced at 0830 on 12 July, I BAC, commanded by Colonel I.S. Polbin, launched a pre-emptive strike against German armour. The resulting tank battle was the world's largest and Second Air Army's *Peshkas* were in the forefront.

When the time came for the main Soviet counter-blow, the dive-bombers were called up to give maximum support. This took place on 15 July in the Orel sector. Again, a quarter of an hour before the main assault seventy Pe-2s joined General M.M. Gromov's First Air Army Il-2s in attacks on artillery and strongpoints in front of Eleventh Guards Army. This set the pattern of the battle, with the dive-bombers making concentrated attacks in up to full division strength.[4]

THE PETLYAKOV Pe-2

Soviet pilot V A Khovoshilov, Hero of the Soviet Union from the Winter War with Finland in 1939-40. He flew SB-2s with the 48 SBAP, 7 Army, during that conflict and received his award on 27 March 1940. These photos show him and his Pe-2 preparing for and then flying a Pe-2 mission on the Zakavkaski Front in the winter of 1942-43. The crew are carrying out last-minute checks prior to tale-off. Note the lowered aircrew hatch. (Robert Michulec)

Khovoshilov and his aircrew boarding their aircraft. Note the detail of their flying gear, fur boots and parachutes typical of this period of the war. (Robert Michulec)

TILTING THE SCALES – STALINGRAD TO THE DONETS

Bloodletting on the Western Front

During the summer of 1943, in the Soviet counter-assault at the Kursk-Belgorod battle, there were sufficient Pe-2s to mount even larger-scale operations against German armour. General G.K. Zhukov requested the replacement of forty Pe-2s for Second and Fifth Air Armies prior to this offensive. On 16 July, 3 BAK (Bomber Air Corps) made 115 sorties over the central-front area of the battle, claiming the destruction of fifty-five German tanks, 229 soft-skinned vehicles, eleven anti-aircraft guns, three field guns, twelve machine-gun and mortar positions and seven fuel and ammunition dumps.

Also during the Belgorod-Kharkov operation a particular development of the Pe-2 evolution took place when, on 3 August, on the Stepnoi Front, Fifth Aviation Army units made two concentrated attacks on German front-line positions. The first attack was early that morning and was carried out by a force of fifty Pe-2s against the enemy's strongly-fortified positions and troops. It was timed for one hour thirty minutes before the Soviet ground attack went in.

The follow-up attack was just as devastating, if not more so, for, more than an hour later, and just before the Soviet assault jumped off from the start lines, a further force, of 100 Pe-2s, went in and caused devastation.

So successful were these massed dive-bomber assaults in breaching the German lines that exactly the same technique was employed by Second Aviation Army during other phases of the same battle.[5]

Close-in detail of the 250kg bombs in their racks with fuses in place. (Robert Michulec)

THE PETLYAKOV Pe-2

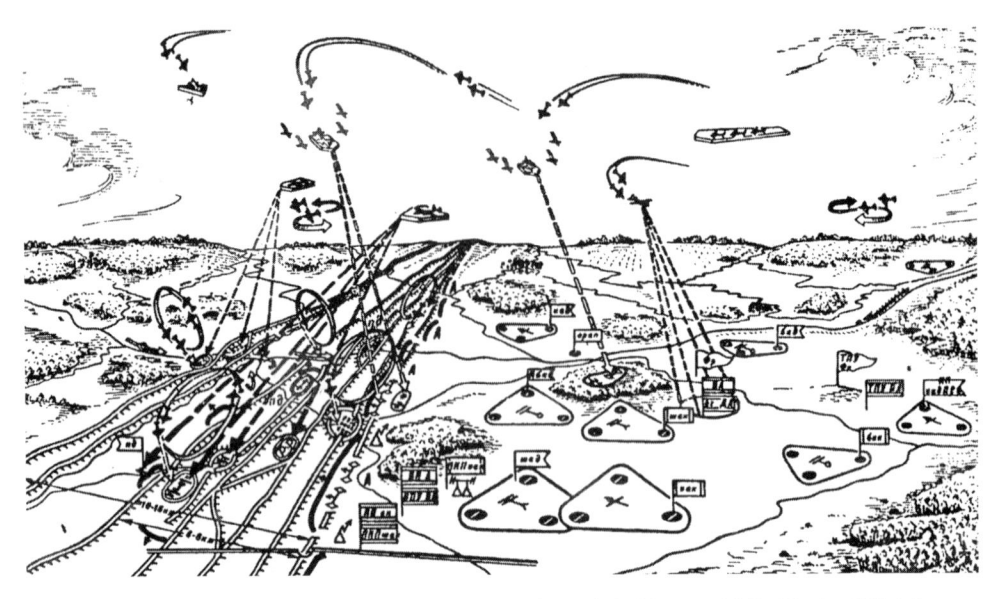

Diagram 16: Belgorod-Kharkov Battles – 1st Pe-2 attack 3rd August 1943. (Soviet Official)

The Pe-2's strike! The growing power of the *Peshka* to strike far and wide behind the German front line, disrupting communications and supplies is given evidence in this view of a dive-bombed German transport column in a snowbound village during the winter of 1943-44. (Soviet official)

TILTING THE SCALES – STALINGRAD TO THE DONETS

Photo-reconnaissance missions

Prior to the great summer offensive of June 1944, special camera-equipped Pe-2s flew numerous missions over the front line to garner vital information on enemy strength and dispositions. Operations by Fourth Air Army against encircled German forces near Minsk, on the Second White Russia Front, were typical, 163 IAP frequently providing their fighter escort on these missions. This unit was commanded by a famous fighter ace, Lieutenant Colonel Piotr Kozachenko, a Golden Star holder of the Hero of the Soviet Union. According to Dariusz Tyminski, the Pe-2s aircrew bestowed on Kozachenko the nickname of *Bat'ka* (Daddy), such was their great faith in his ability to protect them.[6]

Czeslaw Krzeminski gives an example of his work, which is revealing of the Pe-2's photo-reconnaissance mission methods.[7] On 9 November 1942 Kozachenko's group escorted a solitary Pe-2 over an area of important German troop concentrations. As usual, intense flak was encountered on the *Peshka's* first run over the target, but this suddenly stopped, heralding the arrival of German fighters on the scene. Despite this, the Soviet fighters managed to protect the Pe-2 during second and third runs. A fourth pass, however, pushed their luck a little too far. A Fw.190 managed to close unobserved by either the *Peshka* crew or her escorts until it was too late. Cannon fire from the German aircraft blew a large hole in the cockpit of the *Peshka* and the radio man was killed outright. In revenge, Kozachenko engaged the Fw.190, at close quarters and shot it down in short order.

A Pe-2 aircrew prepare for a sortie. These men are from 11 Independent Reconnaissance Air Regiment, 3 March 1944. (M Maslov)

THE PETLYAKOV Pe-2

A later model Pe-2 in flight; this is the reconnaissance variant. Note how the extensive nose glazing as been almost totally eliminated in this model. (S Kafafian)

The damaged Pe-2 managed to return safely to base with the vital photographs, and her surviving crew, unfortunately not named, received the personal thanks of Marshal Konstantin Rokossovsky, C-in-C on this part of the front, for their persistence and bravery in obtaining these vital photographs.

However, during the breakthrough to the Baltic coast, heavy attacks mounted by the Pe-2s against the ports of Gdansk and Gdynia, where the Germans were desperately evacuating trapped civilians and troops by sea, a similar escort mission on 18 March 1945 resulted in Kozachenko's death.

Chapter Ten

Heroines of the Skies

Despite the original communist idealism, which gave absolute equality to men and women to express themselves, and the fact that women in the Soviet Union certainly presented a different face to the world than those in western nations, there was no great movement to ensure that female pilots became a major factor in the VVS. Indeed, quite the contrary, for the Soviet Government in the 1930s and 1940s, while encouraging women to participate in flying as in everything, officially *discouraged* their participation in *combat* flying.[1] This was not, however, an outright ban, and many women did overcome the obstacles to reach combat squadron status.[2] The Germans had outstanding female test pilots, like Hanna Reitsch and Melitta Schiller both of whom worked on aspects of the Ju. 87 dive-bomber programme,[3] but no women pilots fought in combat; British and American women pilots performed valuable second-line duties as ferry pilots throughout the war but, again, were barred from combat. To the Japanese it would have been totally 'unthinkable' and thus it was that the Soviet air force was unique in having quite a large number of female combat pilots serving, many of whom achieved the highest honours during 'The Great Patriotic War'.

Pre-war three Russian women made aviation history, not only in the Soviet Union, but internationally. These outstanding pilots were Marina Raskova, Paulina Ossipenko and Valentina S. Grizodubova. The last-named was the daughter of Russian aviation pioneer Stepan Grizodubov, who, in 1910, had completed the design of his first aircraft, which he flew and tested himself. He had no son and

Marina Raskova, the famous Soviet airwoman who organized the formation of the all-female-piloted section of the 587 Dive-Bomber Regiment. She was tragically killed in an air crash in January 1943. (Soviet Official)

therefore Valentina, even as a child, was taken aloft with her father, so it is not surprising that, in 1928, she became one of the earliest Soviet women to receive a pilot's licence. She attended flying schools and applied herself so well that she was later appointed an instructor, subsequently becoming a pilot with the Gorky propaganda air squadron. By 1937 she had broken five international women's flying records. For these accomplishments she was awarded the Red Banner of Labour and the Order of the Red Star and, in December 1937, was elected a deputy in the Supreme Soviet.

Polina O. Ossipenko, born in 1907 in the Dniepropetrovsk region, was one of twelve children; her parents were semi-illiterate and very poor. On leaving school at seventeen she became a nurse, then a farmhand and finally a charwoman in a grain elevator. Nobody could have had a more adverse start in life. By sheer hard work, she was elected to the local Soviet in 1927 and this gave her the first chance of proper schooling at Kiev. A chance visit by an aviator to her remote village inspired her and she set her heart on aviation, enrolling in a training school near Sevastopol and graduating in 1932 with exceptional grades.

She served with the Kharkov garrison air unit, becoming a flight commander specialising in high-altitude flight, breaking all known women's records for altitude flying at that time when she reached 5.5 miles. In three successive days, 22 to 24 May 1937, she broke three international women's records. She was promoted to lieutenant. In 1936, she made a speech at the Kremlin concerning the participation of women in national defence, and the Commissar of Defence gave her permission to attempt a non-stop cross-continental flight from Sevastopol to Archangel. This brought her into contact with Valentina Grizodubova and the real heroine of this book, Marina M. Raskova. The three-woman mission, which took place in September 1938, was a great success and won great acclaim worldwide. Flying an ANT-37 Rodina (Motherland), they flew a distance of 3,672 miles (5,908km), which involved spending twenty-six hours and twenty-nine minutes continuously in the air, passing through eleven time zones in the process, before being forced to land. All became Heroes of the Soviet Union for this exploit, the first women ever to receive the honour. Their example opened the gates to other girls of like mind to try for the skies in both civilian and military aviation.

Captain Polina Ossipenko went on to become a leading test pilot but was tragically killed, along with the Spanish Civil War I-16 ace, A.K. Serov, when taking part in night-flying exercises in May 1941. Valentina Grizodubova continued her political as well as her aviation career, becoming Chief of the Aeronautical Authority, Foreign Division, while, as a colonel, commanding 31 GvBAP (Guards Bomber Air Regiment. Marina Raskova, a Red Air Force regimental commander, saw her work culminate in the setting up of one of the first all-women combat regiments, which saw combat service in the autumn of 1942.

HEROINES OF THE SKIES

Women pilots flew with both bomber and fighter units. Women pilots of the VVS flew in excess of 24,000 combat sorties during the war. Thirty women combat flyers became Heroes of the Soviet Union in the process. In the West only the open-cockpit Po-2 biplanes serving as night harassment bombers of 46 GvNBAP (Guards Night Bomber Air Regiment) under Major Ya.D. Bershanskaya (the 'Night Witches') and 586 Fighter Regiment, flying Yakovlev-3 single-engined fighters, under Major Tamara Kazarinova, received any publicity[4] but female pilots acquitted themselves with great bravery flying the Pe-2 dive-bomber also, and it is with their stories that this chapter is concerned. Sadly, Marina Raskova herself was killed in battle in 1943. So outstanding had been her work with the dive-bombers that her ashes were given full military honours when they were laid to rest at the most honoured

Natalia Fedorvna Meklin, Pe-2 pilot and heroine of the Soviet Union, proudly wears her many decoratioms. (San Diego Aerospace Museum)

place in the walls of the Kremlin, not far from those of Paulina Ossipenko. The interment of the Raskova remains was, in fact, the first state funeral rite held in the Soviet Union during the war. Like Ivan Polbin, she was later commemorated by the renaming of the Tambov Air School, where she underwent her original aviation training, as the Raskova Air School.

Here we can do a little to rectify that omission, but the subject requires a book in itself to do it justice.[5]

Although there was already a large number of female instructors with the *Obshchestvo sodeistviya oborone, aviatsionnomu I khimicheskomu stroitel'stvu*, or *Osoaviakhim*, (Society for the Support of Defence and Aviation and Chemical Construction), as well as the *Grazhdanski Vozdushny flot* (Civil Air Fleet) GVF pilots and navigators, and engineers already serving with the VVS at the time of the German invasion, it was Marina Raskova, who, in autumn 1941, drew many of them together and formed the three *Tamansky* (Women's) air regiments in which female pilots dominated; 586 Fighter Regiment, 587 (125 Guards) Bomber Regiment and 588 (46 Guards) Night Bomber Regiments.

These female pilots began conversion training on the Su-2 light bomber, but before they became an operational unit, learned to fly and tame the *Peskha*, as re-equipping with the dive-bomber got under way. In fact, 587 flew with mixed crews and male command staff, but was famed for its women pilots.

THE PETLYAKOV Pe-2

Table 5: Outstanding Women Pe-2 Pilots

Ania Artemova
Katia Batuchtria
Antonina Bonderova
Dasha Chalaya
Mariya Ivanovna Dolina-Mel'Nikova
Katerina Fedotova
Nadiezhda (Nadya) Nikifozovna Fedutenko
Klavdiya (Klavia) Yakovlevna Fomcheva-Levashova
Roofa Gasheva
Valentina Grizodubova
Liuba Gubina
Galina Junkovskaya (Markova)
Nina Karasova
Masha Kirillova
Valentina Kravchencko
Valya Kravchencko
Valya Matuchina
Natalia Fedorovna Meklin
Sonia Mosolova
Lena Ponomareva
Marina Raskova
Tonia Skoblikova.
Irina Soodova
Shenya ('Jennie') Timofeyeva
Alexandra Yegorva
Anna Zazoevskay
Antonia (Tonya) Leont'Yevna Zubkova

The Pe-2 unit not only featured women pilots, but bomb-aimers and navigators also. Much of the earliest fighting 587 was involved in was at Stalingrad, now known as Volgograd.

Bombs fall on target

Valentina Kravchenko, the regiment's navigator, recorded one mission, which took place in January 1943, thus:

Under the wing of my aircraft, torn to pieces, smoking from numerous fires, crippled by the January frosts, Stalingrad! The Pe-2s fly in from the direction of the Upper Achtuka lakes on our battle course for the city. Our target is the Tractor Factory complex. Now our bombs can be seen exploding in the heart of the factory and my heart is torn apart for the works itself, the pride and joy of our first 'Five Year Plan' which we must now destroy. However, we cannot allow the Fascists to rule there. Mission accomplished, we turn back to rejoin our colleagues.

Kravchenko gave snippets from all aspects of 587's operations in diary form.

Klavdya Fomchieva, one of the women Pe-2 pilots who became Twice a Heroine of the Soviet Union with her combat exploits. (Soviet Official)

July 1943, Western Front. The airfield of Ezovinia Yezovnia

Our crews get ready for their Battle Orders. The flight maps are placed in front of us. From where we navigators are standing, we can hear the roar of the engines as our air mechanics start up our aircraft and prepare them for the mission flight. As we receive the battle orders relayed to us from Headquarters, we navigators quickly mark our maps with the route and the target, and calculate the flying time. Our pilots have already received from our technicians the readiness reports on our aircraft, armament and radio-contacts.

The aircrews help the mechanics to hang heavy 250-500 kilo bombs on our aircraft. We work in close harmony, for they all know their jobs very well. Ania Artemova, Ira Zubova, Sonia Mosolova, Dasha Chalaya and others of our unit, all compete to be the first of the crews to complete loading, but the bombs are very heavy and we girls help each other to hang them on our respective aircraft and set the detonators.

Within a few minutes all the aircrews are in their aircraft. Heavily laden from wing tip to wing tip, our Pe-2s roll out, one after the other, to the actual take-off strip. The airfield is filled with the roar of

THE PETLYAKOV Pe-2

our engines, and the wet grass bends under the wind of our propellers as the first three planes commence the take-off run together. They seem to be tied to each other, as, in perfect harmony together, they pick up speed and simultaneously lift off the ground, retract their undercarriages and begin to climb.

Once the first trio has lifted off the second, third and fourth flights quickly follow. This type of group take-off requires from all the pilots a particular exactness and skill. Sitting serious and fully concentrated at their flight controls are Sasha Egozova, Valya Matuchina and Tonia Skoblikova. Slowly and surely, the various flights combine to form a solid column. The aircrews continue to strive for achieving the perfect formation, with strict intervals and distances between the flights.

Those who remain on the ground are certain, watching such precision, that their battle task will be fulfilled and that their bombs will fall right on target.

On this mission I am flying with Timofeyeva, a squadron leader in command of nine aircraft. I loved Jennie Timofeyeva very much. I liked her because she believed in me as a navigator, that during all the combat flights she made she was always deeply concerned about the wellbeing of everyone she led. She even took my attention away from my own observations and calculations by telling me to watch out for the rest of the crews following us. Sometimes such concern interfered with my work, but I always carried out her orders in this respect with pleasure, because she gave me these orders not out of any fear of having to account for any lost aircraft, but because of her great concern for her comrades-in-arms.

I loved her too, for her self-possession, thanks to which she skillfully executed the necessary air manoeuvres despite the strong enemy anti-aircraft fire and the uninterrupted attacks by their fighter interceptors. She always strove to save her aircrews and carry out her battle instructions whatever the difficulties. She also had very good co-ordination with the radio and machine-gun operator, Grishko, who was in charge of the squadron's communications.

Explosions behind us, on the right hand side! I inform Grishko, who confirms. 'Yes, Right' Timofeyeva briefly acknowledges and at once turns our aircraft in the necessary manoeuvre to get the correct height, direction and speed. More explosions, under us and to the left! I report and again, 'Yes' and a new turn. So, weaving through the flak bursts, we reach the target.

From this moment of contact Timofeyeva comes under the orders of her *Shturman* (navigator). Now you hear only the curt orders.

HEROINES OF THE SKIES

To keep that way! Two degrees to the left, one more to the left. 'Good! Good! Now!' I released. Our bombs fell directly on target. After I had unloaded Jennie keeps her course, but still weaving, using both height and speed, while I take photographs and give my last order of the mission. 'Change course.' We turn around and Timofeyeva is back in command.

I leave my instruments and look at Jennie. On her nose and upper lips are beads of sweat. Her face looks extremely strained because the leaving of the target zone after bomb release is almost always accompanied by enemy fighter attack. She is therefore worried for the following aircrews, especially those on the outside of our formation, as they can be left behind and isolated during the turn-around manoeuvre. Jennie slows our aircraft down as much as possible so that all our aircraft can close up with us.

Again we get reports from the radio-operator. 'Martiuchina went down, but there was no fire on the plane. Kizillova is lagging behind.' Only after crossing our front lines and we have evaded the enemy fighters, does Jennie finally ask, 'Well, how are things? Well bombed?' I give her the reply, 'Closely.'

Colonel Katerina Fedotova, seen here seated at the controls of her Pe-2 with the famous Swallow insignia. (Soviet Official)

Timofeyeva replies, 'The photos will show.' She does not like being praised.

During the return flight, once we are far from the front line, Jennie allows herself a little relaxation. She leans back against her bullet-proof seat back and flexes her tired wrist muscles, taunt from concentrating on the controls. Timofeyeva's reports, about the fulfillment of the Battle Orders, and the circumstances of each flight, are always extremely concise and exact. Mission accomplished.

October 1943. Leomdovo airfield (near Elna)

Our assembled aircrews stand still in mournful silence. Spasms are gripping many throats. Commissar Lina Eliseyeva speaks to us of our friends, who, only yesterday still living, have fallen in the battle for liberty and independence of our Motherland. The heart does not wish to reconcile with the harsh fact that Liuba Gubina, Anna Zazoevskaya and Lena Ponomareva will no longer be with us. It is painful to look up at Katia Batuchtria, Liuba Gubina's co-pilot. They were like sisters, always took care of each other, trusted one another and now Katia suffers heavily the loss of her good friend and beloved superior. Liuba Gubina died saving her crew. She gave both the navigator and ventral gunner the chance to bale out of her flak-damaged aircraft. As for herself, she did not have enough height remaining in order to safely parachute out of her damaged plane.

A rifle salute was fired into the air. Pilots, co-pilots and technicians of the Regiment take an oath on the grave of their dear friend to attack the enemy even harder and to avenge the deaths of their comrades-in-arms. That evening one did not hear the usual jokes and laughter. And only from the further corner of the accommodation, at first quietly and later more loudly, came the low controlled sobbing of Masha Kirillova reciting the dive-bomber pilot's lament.[6]

We join her, our girls sing well; the grief fades away with the song and the throat is not so dry. I sing with them all and leave them all, blue-eyed and dark-eyed, young and brave patriots. One song follows another and before long the aircrews are back preparing themselves for fresh combat, and our squadron leader, Klavdia Fomchieva, is making battle calculations for tomorrow's missions. Away in the other hut, Lina Yeliseyeva has bent over an oil lamp. She is our Commissar and she writes mournful letters to the relatives of Liuba, Anna and Lena.

HEROINES OF THE SKIES

Still October 1943, Leomidovo airfield

Today is a day of solemn significance for us; we are all joyful, full of life and bright faced. Soon all the personnel of our regiment will be lined up. At our Staff hut are gathering representatives of our Divisional Headquarters, of the Army Corps and of the Political Department of the Army. This is a meeting which will proudly assess and take stock of our dive-bombers' work so far. Our Regiment has carried out 414 combat missions, during which we had shot down thirty-eight enemy aircraft, while not a single enemy bomb has fallen on the area defended by the Regiment. All our personnel were awarded decorations and medals of the Soviet Union.

At the previous Party meeting of solemn farewell, the Party members also promised to work honestly and with self-denial at their wartime posts to carry high the Battle Honour of our Regiment. They also promised never to forget the friendships forged by the blood of our fallen friends.

Six of the leading female dive-bomber pilots pose for the camera. (Soviet Official)

THE PETLYAKOV Pe-2

A similar series of accounts was given by Galnia Olchovskaya, another woman navigator. She recorded the exploits of her unit, 2 Guards Bomber Air Corps, under the command of Nadiezhda Fedutenko, in the liberation of the town of Ozsha from the enemy, in which the Pe-2 squadron particularly distinguished themselves.

> On 26 June 1944, Nadiezhda Fedutenko led the squadron into battle, and made a very accurate dive-bombing attack on the vital rail junction at Ozsha. As a direct result of their attack was destroyed the ammunition and technical equipment of the German military echelons there, while the supply rail lines were very badly damaged and traffic to the front disrupted. It was a true 'Snipers' blow!'

The Right Stuff

Nowadays there is much debate about the role of women pilots in the military of both the UK and the United States. Grudgingly, female pilots have been accepted as capable of flying many of today's warplanes, but still their commitment to combat operations raises many doubts and objections, among the military and the western media alike. It is always presented as a new concept, but the truth is that Soviet women dive-bomber pilots were showing that they had 'the Right Stuff' more than *seventy* years ago!

Olchovskaya recalled the situation when the girl pilots first joined the *Peshka* squadrons to serve alongside their male counterparts.

> At last schooling and training finished and we found ourselves on a front-line airfield. The Division met us with a great deal of scepticism – the men pilots could not imagine that some girls as well as they could have mastered a complicated technical course and could carry out any battle tasks. But after our first flight they were convinced that we could fly not only as well as themselves, but sometimes even better!
>
> I particularly remember the first combat flight into battle. The honour to go first fell on our two female Pe-2 crews – I, with Nadya Fedutenko and Timofeyeva with Kravchencko. We joined the nine Pe-2s from another Regiment to give us a chance to get familiar with battle conditions in the company of experienced pilots. How worried I was before that flight! All my calculations had been made, the mission orders had been given and the aircraft began rolling out in readiness for take off.
>
> Nadya felt so sure and confident of herself in the air that I also got this feeling myself. Below us the burnt, but not surrendered, *Hero City* [she is talking about Stalingrad, of course]. When our bombs fell on the heads of the hated enemy we got the feeling of a fulfilled task.

Maintenance work being carried out on a mixed-crew squadron's Pe-2 at a front-line airstrip. (Soviet Official)

The target was destroyed and so the day of final victory comes a step nearer. Anti-aircraft shells followed us, but we all returned to our airfield without any losses.

On the same day our Regiment got another order. The three best aircrews, acting together, with the group of the neighbouring Dive Bomber Regiment, is to deliver a blow on the group of surrounded enemy troops in the northern part of the city. Nadya Fedutenko duly led her girls back into battle and dropped a further 1,200 kilos of bombs on the heads of the Nazis.

THE PETLYAKOV Pe-2

Further missions followed on all sections of the front.

Together with Nadya Fedutenko we bombed the enemy strongholds, artillery and infantry in both the Crimea and the Kiev districts. More than once we had to fight our way through the storms of anti-aircraft fire and rebuff attacks from enemy fighter planes. I remember one such incident on 26 May 1943. We had been given the task of destroying German artillery and heavy mortar batteries in the Kiev area. In spite of a strong curtain of anti-aircraft fire, we stubbornly pressed ahead to reach our targets. Suddenly one of our aircraft was sharply shaken, it turned its nose downward and started diving. Somehow, Nadya managed to regain control and straighten it up in the air. Relieved, I looked at her and noticed that from under her helmet a thin trickle of blood was flowing down her face. She had been wounded in the head, I realised. Only a few seconds flight time remained to the target. She noticed my worried look and said quietly, 'It is nothing. I will withstand it. You just aim more precisely.' When our bombs had been released, we saw big explosions and fires on the ground and the enemy battery was silenced. Fighting the pain Nadya kept our aircraft strictly on the designated course. She landed her aircraft, reported that the task had been carried out and, only after that had been carried out, did she allow herself to be taken to hospital.

For this exact and effective blow, which had assured the advance of our infantry, we received, while still in the air, the gratitude of the Army Commander of our ground forces. Nadiezhda Fedutenko was awarded her first award, the Order of War for the Fatherland, 1st Degree. Soon Nadya returned to the front again. In the summer of 1944, the fighting started in the Ozsha, Vitesbsk and Bozisov areas. These were days of intensive fighting when sometimes we had to conduct dive-bombing attacks two or three times daily.

At that time I was not flying with Fedutenko and her navigator was Tosia Zubkova. Before the war, she had nothing to do with aviation, being a third-year student at Moscow University. When she was twenty-one years old, in October 1941, she, together with her friends, went to the HQ of Komisonol and expressed her wish to go to the front. She was small, shy, and her soft character did not go well with a uniform. However, through stubbornness and hard work, she became a skilful navigator of a fighting plane. Fedutenko remembered her with these words: 'We have completed dozens of battle missions together and together we were awarded names of Hero of the Soviet Union.'

Peshka Women – Colonel Nadezhda *(Nadya)* Nikifozovna Fedutenko

Nadya was born on 30 September 1915 in the small hamlet of Rakitnoye in the Belgorod Region.

'Since I was a child I was always dreaming that I could become a pilot, from the very first time I saw an aeroplane which landed not far from our house,' Nadezhda Nikifozovna Fedutenko recalled. This incident, the plane which landed, made such a lasting impression on the small girl who was then, as in later years, small, but dark-eyed and full of vitality. That early wish to fly never left her in the years that followed.

'Our family lived in the village of Rakitnoe. My parents worked at a sugar refinery, where later I started working myself. I lived in a big and friendly family,' she continued. 'When at school I enjoyed all the schoolgirl things, like skipping and skating and easily took many first prizes in competitions for both.' She also liked horse riding; she enjoyed it for the speed and a competition of a brave team, horse and rider. And here again she managed to come first, leaving behind all her opponents of the same age, both male and female.

Peshka Women – Colonel Nadiezhda ('Nadya') Nikifozovna Fodutenko. (Soviet Official)

While still working at the refinery, Nadya was also studying in her spare time at the FZU (Technical College) to become a skilled turner, while her spare evenings were spent in the company of young model enthusiasts. Here she acquired her first detailed knowledge of aircraft and aeronautics. In addition, here, also, she received answers to the many questions she had; *why* it flies, *how* it is built, and *how* does a pilot direct it? Constructing her own light model aircraft Nadya was all the time thinking about real aircraft on which, one day, she was determined to fly herself.

As soon as she reached the age of eighteen she entered Tambov Flying College, and, after diligently applying herself, duly graduated with honours in 1935, and joined the Civil Air Fleet as a pilot. For more than six years, Nadya flew over the vast reaches of her immense country, transporting passengers and delivering materials for the building up of the Soviet aeronautical industry. She had to fly a lot, both by day and by night, and in all weather conditions, including fog and snowstorms when the only orientation remained the radio-beacon.

THE PETLYAKOV Pe-2

Her flying logbook recorded several thousand flight hours on various types of aircraft and, from the first days of the Great Patriotic War, Nadiezhda Fedutenko volunteered to go the front. In Kiev she joined the Special Group of the Civil Aviation Fleet and had to fulfill highly responsible tasks like the delivery of ammunition, military equipment, food and medications to Soviet troops cut off in the initial great German encirclements, flying deep behind enemy lines. She also evacuated many wounded soldiers on her return trips and delivered intelligence data on the enemy.

On these missions she usually was flying the P-5 aircraft, operating at low altitude, without any friendly fighter cover and not always having much in the way of local knowledge of the localities over which she flew. Her excellent piloting skills saw her through. On one occasion she was entrusted with the lives of the General Staff of the Briansk region, whom she flew to Kiev. 'At first I flew over the vast forest, almost touching the tree-tops,' she recalled, 'but soon the forest ended and suddenly from above out of the clouds I was jumped by an enemy fighter aircraft which threw itself into an attack on my lone transport plane.'

Immediately she became aware of the enemy Nadya abruptly changed course and the German pilot, misjudging, overflew his easy target. 'The fighter flew past, lifting clouds of dust on the ground from his exploding cannon shells. However, the enemy quickly made a sharp turn to renew his attack.

Scene from the mixed-group dive-bomber squadron. Male and female squadron members, pilots and crew mechanics, pose in front of a Pe-2. (Soviet Official)

Nadya flew even lower and manoeuvred just above ground level. A ravine loomed up ahead and she flew into it while, in the distance, she observed another forest. Another attack and her aircraft shook from the first hits, but it continued to fly. The engine was still intact and the steering was working, so everything was all right so far, Nadya thought, but the German fighter was all the time in sight.

Now the German pilot decided on different tactics and came in from dead ahead in a frontal attack. All the rage and anger bottled up inside her boiled over and Nadya had but one thought, 'To ram him, to ram him!' But she could not carry out her wish, due to her VIP cargo. 'I must get away.' In addition, the forest loomed up again, so she steered for a small gap through the trees and again the German aircraft flew past her, impotent to inflict further damage. She followed the track through the wood and into another ravine. Watching the trees with one eye and the enemy with another, she finally noticed, with relief that the German pilot had given up and had vanished to one side. 'He lost, he lost me at last,' Nadya happily concluded. Kiev city showed up on the far horizon. Now it was not far to the airfield and there were only a few minutes left to fly.

The plane landed safely and the senior officers climbed out, nervously trying to make jokes about their very lucky escape. 'We have, it seems, returned from the other world,' they told her, 'thanks to you, a second birth!' and each officer firmly shook her hand before leaving.

On another occasion it was necessary for Nadya to deliver a dangerous cargo of liquid fuel to the front. Her appointed landing strip was supposed to have been south-west of Kiev, near Rotmistrovka railway station. Fedutenko flew this mission with a lot of confidence, as now she knew the area well. She put the aircraft down, ran along the strip losing speed and stopped. However, what is this? Nobody was there to meet her. She climbed out and looked around. A group of armed men were running toward the plane. 'Nazis,' the thought came instantly. But, what to do? She jumped back into the plane, gave it full gas and took off, never mind that the wind was in the wrong direction for a take off. There was no time for the correct procedure; it would be too late.

The aircraft almost brushed the heads of the bewildered enemy as it lifted off. In a fury that they had failed to capture the Russian pilot they tried to spray the aircraft with machine-gun bullets but she had cheated death again. On landing she joked with her friends that it had been 'A landing right in the devil's teeth!' The technicians who examined her aircraft found forty-seven bullet holes in the machine.

Shortly after this exploit, Nadya was commandeered into the Raskovoy Regiment. As a military transport pilot, Fedutenko had sometimes spent seven to eight hours in the air. She brought more than 150 heavily wounded soldiers out of the encirclements. Her deeds could hardly escape the notice of those looking for outstanding pilots to fly the *Peshka* in combat. Nadya was ideal. Shortly after this, she was appointed a squadron leader of the Pe-2 dive-bombers.

She very soon found both affection and deep respect among the other girl pilots. Slim of build and with chestnut hair, with bright eyes, she was liked by everyone. 'A person with a great soul,' the other girls said about her.

'In those days I did not expect that I would last with her into battle more than once,' recalled one of her fellow pilots. 'Such pilots as Nadya Fedutenko, Jenia Timofeyeva and Lelia Sholochova, we green pilots looked at with great respect. They had a huge flying experience behind them and we eighteen-year-old girls had seen nothing much of life yet. We prepared long and hard for the front. Our friends had already fought with the enemy but we had only heard about it with some jealousy.'

Some of Nadya's exploits while flying the *Peshka* are recorded in these pages. She was wounded for the second time during attacks at Dvinsk. Her co-pilot on that occasion was Tosia Zubkova. However, Nadya continued flying the Pe-2 right to the very end of the war and proudly took part in the final Victory Parade in Moscow, a fitting culmination to a celebrated career. She was demobilised in 1946 and became an active party worker in both Khabarovsk and Irkutsk to 1954, before moving back to Kiev two years later. She died on 28 January 1978.

Her decorations included the Order of Lenin; the Order of the Red Banner (twice), and the Order of Patriotic War Class 1. Even a workers' team at the Volga Pipe Plant was named in her honour.[7]

Women Flyers – their place in history

While never coming to a definitive judgement about why the units were formed, Pennington seems to place the greatest importance on the role of Marina Raskova, the famous 1930s aviatrix, who had something of a cult following in the USSR and the ear of Stalin, whom she regarded as a personal friend. However, her own evidence challenges her conclusions here. As Pennington points out, there were some women already serving in male VVS regiments individually, even before the war, and some further women were integrated into those male units during the war.

So why the need to form three regiments of women, all them totally without military or combat experience, when they could have been integrated individually into established units, where they would have had the benefit of a leavening of combat veterans to mentor them? Obviously, the important thing was not that women should serve like men, alongside men, but that they should have their own segregated units. In addition, if it was important for the women to serve together, apart from men, then why did they form three regiments of different types, which would operate independently of each other, instead of forming an entire division of a single type of regiment, which could operate together? A further clue is that two of the regiments, 586 IAP with the Yak and 587 BAP with the Pe-2, had to accept the assignment of significant numbers of men. In fact, both regiments had to accept male commanders. In the latter case this was after their commander, Marina Raskova, was killed in a flying accident. The curious thing is that the women strongly resented the assignment of men.

It seems obvious that the prime motivations for formation of these regiments was ideology and propaganda, possibly given a push by the dynamic personality of Marina Raskova, who was personally friendly with Stalin. Pennington argues against this, pointing out that little propaganda use was actually made of the women's units. However, this may alternatively be explained by asserting that the units, in general, were not dramatically successful, even if this challenges one of Pennington's central claims. Although 587 BAP, ultimately, was honoured as 125 Guards Regiment, and seems to have performed creditably, it was no better than similar male regiments. A cynic might be tempted to speculate they might have received an 'affirmative action' Guards designation for average work.[8]

Peshka Women – Mariya Ivanovna Dolina-Mel'Nikova

Mariya was born on 18 December 1920 in the village of Sharovka in the Poltava district of the Omsk region of Siberia. She was typical of the post-revolutionary young women who were far more confident of themselves and what they wished to achieve under the new regime. On reaching maturity, she determined on a flying career and joined the state-sponsored Osoaviakhim. This enabled her to train with the flying club of that paramilitary organisation and she graduated

A much-decorated Pe-2 pilot, Mariya Dolina poses with her aircraft. (Soviet Official)

THE PETLYAKOV Pe-2

from the Kherson Flying School as a pilot in 1940. She became a flying club instructor herself, at both Dnepropetrovsk and Nikolayev, Ukraine.

With the German invasion, she volunteered for the Air Force and her first military flying was as a pilot with 296 Fighter Regiment (later 73 Guards Stalingrad-Vienna Regiment) under the command of Nikolay Baranov. She did not fly the fighters but instead piloted the lightweight, army co-operation plane, the U-2. Her duties were air liaison and ferrying officers and other VIPs between forward commands and bases. This was a dangerous duty close to the front line with marauding German fighters on the lookout for such easy targets. She also ferried wounded troops to back area hospitals and carried despatches. In the first six months of the war, she clocked up 150 combat flying hours and conducted 200 such sorties.

Such work was challenging enough, but Mariya determined on contributing more positively to the war and when the all-women 122 Air Group began to form under Marina Raskova, she was a natural volunteer. She joined 587 PBAP at Engels, close to Stalingrad, under the direct command of Raskova, and trained on the Su-2. Soon this aircraft was replaced by the more-exacting Pe-2 dive-bomber. The regiment itself first became operational in 1943, under the command of V.V. Markov, following Raskova's demise, and worked over the Stalingrad front.

The unit was subordinated to Fourth Air Army, North Caucasus before transferring to 5 Guards Air Corps, Sixteenth Air Army on the Third Byelorussia Front, and subsequently moved to 4 Guards Bomber Division of Third Air Army and the Baltic Front. Serving all through this period, Mariya fought at all the major battles as the advance towards Germany gained increasing momentum following Kursk. No fewer than seventy-two combat dive-bomber missions were carried out as the unit moved westward.

One of her many brushes with death took place on 2 June 1943 when her regiment was operating on the North Caucasus Front in Kuban. The nine Pe-2s were despatched to attack their targets but lost their eight fighter escorts, who broke away in thickening cloud to attack German fighters and did not regain contact. The dive-bombers continued to the battle zone without them and were met with heavy anti-aircraft fire. Nonetheless, they pressed home their attack with great tenacity. Mariya's aircraft took a direct flak hit on one engine, which totally incapacitated it. She bravely continued with one damaged engine and delivered her bombs.

On the way back the Pe-2s were jumped by more enemy fighters, both Fw. 190s and Bf. 109s and a swirling battle took place. Mariya's aircraft was hit by cannon fire in the other engine. The fire spread rapidly. Despite this, her gunners claimed to have destroyed at least two of their attackers. Mariya ordered her two crew members to bale out but they refused to abandon her and so she headed for Soviet lines, and made a belly landing in friendly territory close to a railway embankment. All three crew managed to escape before their aircraft blew up.

One notable attack, conducted against enemy troop concentrations at Zembin village on 28 June 1944, earned Mariya's regiment the title

125 M.M. Raskova Borisov Guards Dive Bomber Regiment for being directly instrumental in the forcing of the river Berezina and the taking of the town of Borisov. One exploit that brought her fame was the dropping of a message container on the liberated town urging that its inhabitants rebuild it promptly. This message was subsequently preserved and displayed for posterity in the town hall.

Mariya took part in the Moscow Victory Parade on 24 June 1945 and continued to serve as deputy commander of a post-war bomber regiment before her retirement from the service in 1950. Married as Mel'nikova, she continued to fly with the reserves and worked in the Riga City Party Committee. She had become an honorary member of the French *Normandie-Niemen* Regiment which had fought alongside her unit in many of their battles. She married a second time and, in 1983, moved to Kiev. She was also an executive member of the Ukrainian Branch of the War Veterans Committee. In May 1990 she was personally invited to Moscow by President Mikhail Gorbachev and pleaded for war veterans' allowances to be improved.

Much honoured, Mariya was in the course of her long career awarded the Order of Lenin, the Order of the Red Banner (twice), the Order of Patriotic War 1 Class and the Young Pioneers Groups of the Omsk Region were named in her honour.[9]

Table 6: *PESHKA* DATA

	VB-100	PB-100	Pe-2	Pe-3 bis	Pe-2R	Pe-2UT	Pe2 FT	Pe-2J
Year	Proj	Proj	1940	1941	1942	1942	1942	1944
Wingspan (m)	17	17.16	17.11	17.11	17.16	17.25	17.25	18.25
Wingspan (ft)	55ft 8 ins	56 ft 3 ins	56 ft 2in	56ft 2in	56ft 3-1/4 ins	56 ft 6 ins	56 ft 6 ins	56 ft 9 ins
Length (m)	12.5	12.78	12.78	12.5	12.5	12.78	12.78	12.93
Length (ft)	41 ft	41ft 11-1/2 ins	41ft 11-1/2 ins	41 ft	41 ft	41ft 11-1/2 ins	41ft 11-1/2 ins	42ft 4ins
Height (m)	3.95	4	4	3.95	3.95	4,00	4,25	4,25
Height (ft)	13 ft	13ft 1 in	13ft 1 in	13ft	13 ft	13ft 11 ins	13 ft 9 ins	13 ft 9 ins
Wing Area (sq/m)	40.5	40.5	40.5	40.5	40.5	40.5	40.5	41.9
Wing Area (sq/f)	495.95	495.95	495.95	495.95	495.95	495.95	495,95	451
Empty weight (kg)	-	5750	5852	5870	5852	5852	5870	6500
Empty weight (lbs)	-	12,678	12,903	12,941	12,903	12,903	12,941	14,330

THE PETLYAKOV Pe-2

	VB-100	PB-100	Pe-2	Pe-3 bis	Pe-2R	Pe-2UT	Pe2 FT	Pe-2J
Normal weight (kgs)	-	7680	8520	8049	8040	7680	8520	9000
Normal weight (lbs)	-	16,934	18,786	17,748	17,728	16,934	18,786	19,845
Speed (km/h)	-	560	540	675	657	540	581	657
Speed (mph)	-	347	336	419	408	336	361	408
At (m)	-	5000	5000	5700	5700	5500	5000	5200
At (ft)	-	16,405	16,405	18,700	18,700	18,045	16,405	17,060
Maximum speed (km/h)	-	450	428	450	450	460	460	485
Maximum speed (mph)	-	279.63	266	279.63	279.63	286	286	301
Stalling speed (km/h)	-	140	160	170	170	160	170	170
Stalling speed (mph)	-	87	99.5	106.6	106.6	99.5	106.6	105.6
Ceiling (m)	-	10,550	9500	10,500	11,000	10,500	10,500	10,500
Ceiling (ft)	-	34,614	31,170	34,450	35,810	34,450	34,450	34,450
Range (km)	-	1700	1500	1750	2000	1770	1770	2000
Engines (2)	M-105P (TK-3)	M-105P	M-105R	VK-107A	VK-107A	VK-105PAS	VK105PF	VL-17A
hp (each)	1050	1050	1100	1650	1650	1100	1260	1650
hp (each)	652	652	683.5	1,025	1,025	683.5	783	1,025
	-	-	AWE	AWE	AWE	AWE	AWE	
Armament Type	ShzKAS	ShzKAS	BS ShzKAS	BS SzKAS	BS	UBT	UBT ShzKAS	UBT
Calibre (mm)	7,62	7,62	12,7 7,62	12,7 7,62	12,7	12,7	12,7 7,62	12,7
	1	3	2 2	3 2	3	4	3 2	3
Type	LVAK	-	-	LVAK	SzWAK	-	-	Vk-23W
Calibre (mm)	20	-	-	20	20	-	-	23
	4	-	-	2	1	-	-	2
Bombs (kg)	-	600	1100	-	-	600	1200	3000
Bombs (lbs)	n/a	1,323	2,425.50	n/a	n/a	1,323	2,646	6,615.60
	-	-	-	RS-82	-	-	-	0
	-	-	-	6	-	-	-	-
Climb to 3,000 m (9,8540ft)			3.5 min					
Climb to 5,000 m (16,400ft)			7 min					

Table 7: *Peshka* Strengths at various dates during the Second World War

Date	Pe-2 & Pe-3 Operational	Pe-2 & Pe-3 Non-Operational	Recce Pe-2 & Pe-3 Operational	Recce Pe-2 & Pe-3 Non-Operational	Navy Air Arm Pe-2 & Pe-3 Operational	Navy Air Arm Pe-2 & Pe-3 Non-Operational	Navy Recce Operational	Navy Recce Non-Operational	Navy Spotter Aircraft Operational	Navy Spotter Aircraft Non-Operational
26/04/41	104	n/a	n/a	n/a	n/a	n/a	n/a	n/a	n/a	n/a
30/06/41	129	8	n/a	n/a	n/a	n/a	n/a	n/a	n/a	n/a
10/07/41	10	n/a	n/a	n/a	n/a	n/a	n/a	n/a	n/a	n/a
01/10/41	99*	25	45	18	n/a	n/a	n/a	n/a	n/a	n/a
05/12/41	172	58	41	21	21	8	0	0	0	0
01/05/42	303	82	78	31	28	8	1	0	0	0
01/07/42	379**	82**	28	9	56	23	0	0	1	0
19/11/42	519	86	109	34	73	19	5	1	1	0
01/07/43	853	73	224	43	70	14	14	2	2	1
01/01/45	1,314	67	345	43	125	13	20***	6***	49****	9****
10/05/45	1,129	190	308	32	139	14	17	4	27	0
09/08/45	374	32	89	10	181	8	4	1	10	0

NOTES
* Includes 4 Pe-2s converted to reconnaissance only

** Includes 3 Operational and 3 Non-Operational Pe-3s

*** Includes all types used, Pe-2, Pe-3, Ar-2 and DB3f

**** Includes Pe-3s, A-20s and Il-2s

n/a = not applicable or no information available

Source: *Soviet General Staff Historical Section, Moscow.*

THE PETLYAKOV Pe-2

Table 8: *Peshka* Supply at various dates in the Second World War

	Pe-2		Pe-3		Trainers UP3-2	
Date	Planned Deliveryies	Actual Deliveries	Planned Deliveries	Actual Deliveries	Planned Deliveries	Actual Deliveries
1941	2,194	1,671	179	196	0	0
1942	2,293	2,236	179	179	0	0
1943	2,291	2,311	0	3	80	107
1944	2,782	2,805	45	19	125	138
1945	1,160	1,208	0	0	400	426
Total	10,720	10,331	478	397	605	671

Source:
Soviet General Staff Historical Section, Moscow.

Table 9: *Peshka* losses during the Second World War

	Air Force			Navy*	
Date	Pe-2	Pe-3	Dates	Pe-2 lost per quarter	Pe-3 lost per quarter
1941	583	56	22-6-41 TO 21-6-42	49/8/4/0	0/0/6/0
1942	740	39	22-6-42 TO 21-6-43	33/29/13/0	0/0/12/0
1943	806	8	22-6-43 TO 21-6-44	24/40/21/0	0/0/8/0
1944	584	4	22-6-44 TO 31-9-45	5/56/3/3	0/0/4/0
1945	358	0	n/a	n/a	n/a
Total	3,071	107		288	30

Notes
* Black Sea, Baltic, Northern and Pacific Fleets

Source:
Soviet General Staff Historical Section, Moscow.

Chapter Eleven

The Fighting Finns

As was inevitable in such a huge conflict a number of Pe-2s fell into the hands of Russia's opponents. This was normal and, as part of the Luftwaffe's routine, any such new types that were captured were given a thorough evaluation by experienced German personnel and aviators.[1] So it was with the *Peshka*, and, because her performance was so exceptional for a dive-bomber, the Luftwaffe was naturally very eager to find out as much as they could about her, both strengths, which they could learn from, and weaknesses, which they could exploit. However, with some captured Pe-2s the Axis powers went even further, and brought them into combat service *against* the Soviets!

The first complete Pe-2 that the Germans got their hands on in flyable condition fell into those hands during the first weeks of battle in summer 1941. This aircraft was transported to the main Luftwaffe test centre (*E-Stelle*) at Rechlin, near Berlin where it was given a good overhaul and examination and one of the Luftwaffe test pilots, Friedrich Förschler, was allocated to conduct the initial tests and trials. Not much had been gleaned, however, when disaster struck. On 3 September 1941, while taking off from Müritz, there was a total engine stoppage, and the Pe-2 crashed and burned out completely, killing Förschler.

Altogether some eight further flyable *Peshkas* were taken over by the Luftwaffe, who first of all stored them in their vast war-booty dumps in autumn 1941, and took them to an overhaul unit near Prague, in the former Czechoslovakia, where Letov gave them a complete overhaul and broke them down with spare parts from many other wrecked, crashed and damaged Pe-2s, into kits. These eight were eventually offered by Germany to her Finnish allies, as 'flyable' aircraft.

Six Pe-2s were thus delivered to the Finnish Air Force between 6 July 1942 and 14 May 1943. The Finns found them far from combat-ready and gave them their own overhaul and, in some cases, almost re-build, at AL, the state aircraft factory at Tampere. They were given the Finnish Air Force designations Pe-211 to Pe-216.

To add to these, one of the long-range fighter version, a Pe-3, was captured by the Finns themselves when it was forced to make an emergency landing behind their lines at Inari in the north of the country on 11 September 1942. This particular machine was c/n 40106, of 121 IAP VVS SF, which came down in the sticky morass that was the northern tundra at that time, and so was relatively unharmed.

THE PETLYAKOV Pe-2

The under-wing dive-brakes are seen folded flat against the under-surface of the wing, as Finnish pilots and mechanics gather around this rebuilt *Peshka* prior to a trial flight. (Via Keski-Suom,en Imailumuiseo, Tikkakoski)

It lay where it came down for nine weeks until the first frosts of an early winter froze the ground hard enough for it to be evacuated, which was finally undertaken on 28 November. After a similar overhaul, it eventually joined the VL on 19 August 1943 as Pe-301.

The final Pe-2 of the eight also went to Rechlin, where it was painted in Luftwaffe colours and markings and given the German code NS+BA. Again overhauled by Letov at Prague this, too, was handed over to the Finnish Air Force, and flown by a Finnish crew from Olomouc to Finland on 29 January, 1944, to become, after another refit at VL, their Pe-217.

The Finnish Air Force (FAF) found these small numbers of Pe-2s very useful to their cause during what they termed 'The Continuation War',[2] especially in the strategic photographic-reconnaissance rôle in which they were primarily used. In particular, during the great Soviet summer offensive of 1944, captured Pe-2s were the only aircraft with the capability of overflying the vital Karelian isthmus, when solitary *Peshkas* in Finnish markings flew missions escorted by a pair of Messerschmitt Bf.109G fighters, which were just about capable of keeping up with them.

The Finns found that the engines were the weak point, with repeated problems and only a very limited number of spares and parts with which to maintain and repair them. This limited the number of *Peshkas* available to the Finns to just two most of the time. The Finnish pilots who flew them, however, were high in their praise for this aircraft, both its speed and ease of handling proving very popular with them.

Finnish Test Pilots' reports

Finnish testing of the captured Pe-2s took place at Malmi and the evaluations of those trials, coupled with captured Soviet aircrew interrogations and Finnish translations of the Petlyakov manuals, all combined to give another interesting series of eyewitness viewpoints of the Pe-2, which make an interesting comparison with the RAF's report from Squadron Leader Lapraik, detailed earlier.[3]

Cockpit arrangement

The pilot's seat, located on the port side of the cockpit, was armoured, and, although adjustable for height, and with an adjustable headrest, was considered by Finnish pilots to be cramped. The pilot's seating gave good visibility, both directly forward and to both sides, while, due to the main instrument panel being split and the floor of the nose largely transparent, an excellent and enhanced downward view also was available, so essential for accurate dive-bombing. However, the quality of the transparent panels was stated to be 'poor'.

The rudder pedals were adjustable, fore-and-aft, but the port pedal was situated so close to the instrument panel that, when full rudder was applied, the pilot's toes could be trapped. The wheel-type control column incorporated the bomb-release and forward machine-gun firing buttons as well as a brake lever. The machine-gun firing button was fitted with a flip-up safety cover latch to prevent accidentally shooting friendly aircraft and ground staff.

The pilot's domain in the Pe-2 (H Valtonen via Keski-Suomen Imailumuseo, Tikkakoski)

THE PETLYAKOV Pe-2

Looking forward from the pilot's seat gives a good indication of the perfect downward, but very vulnerable, forward view via the glazed lower-nose. The various instruments to port and starboard flank the control column seen on the left. (H Valtonen via Keski-Suomen Imailumuseo, Tikkakoski)

The main instruments were located on the port side of the split and contained:

1: Altimeter.
2: Artificial Horizon
3: Air-Speed Indicator
4: Rate-of-Climb Indicator
5: Direction Indicator
6: Turn-and-Bank Indicator.

The engine instruments were mounted on the starboard panel. Overall, the Finns considered the whole pilot's console very well designed and thought out.

Electrical Systems

As has been noted the Pe-2 employed widespread electrical systems for the first time on such a scale in a Soviet aircraft. The main systems were:

1: Trimmers: All electric, with their control buttons mounted on the port hand console, each with its respective light, which lit in its neutral position.

2: Flaps: All electric, with their control buttons also mounted on the port-hand console. PUSH lowered the flaps; PULL raised the flaps. A lever could be released which allowed for the selection of an intermediate setting. The maximum flap setting was 55-degrees and the time taken to lower maximum flap was between eight and ten seconds. Any changes in the *Peshka's* trim caused by the flaps was automatically corrected. With the flaps lowered less than 20 degrees, the trimmer stayed in 'neutral'. As a fail-safe device, the flaps could not be lowered while the undercarriage was in the UP position.

3: Dive Brakes: Electrically-operated. The slatted dive brakes opened to a full 90 degrees from the underside of each wing, and were large and very effective. Built of welded steel tube, each dive brake had a width of 1.8m and a height of 0.33m. It took between eight and ten seconds for the dive brakes to open fully. Once these brakes were opened more than 45 degrees, an automatic dive-recovery system kicked in with the elevator trim tabs opening to 4.5 degrees.

Once the bomb-release button was depressed (or, if it was not used due to an aborted attack or ground-strafing only attack, then a separate button connected to the same device), the trim tab automatically returned to a position of 1.5 degrees. Should the Indicated Air Speed (IAS) be under 600km/h, then 4G was not exceeded during the recovery and there was no 'Black-Out' by the pilot. The cockpit display included two indicator lights mounted on the instrument panel, one of which lit during a normal (3G) pull-out, while the other lit if 4G was being exceeded to warn the pilot.

4: Undercarriage: Electro-hydraulically operated. The operating lever for the undercarriage was mounted on the port half of the split consoles, with safety catches to prevent any accidental use while the aircraft was parked on the ground. Normal working saw the undercarriage fully lowered and locked in twenty seconds.

In the event of failure of the system, the Pe-2 was fitted with an emergency hand-pump to work the undercarriage in emergencies. The pilot's instruments contained three green lights, which lit when the undercarriage systems locked down. As a further precaution, a warning horn was activated in the cockpit if the Pe-2's engines were throttled down without the undercarriage being locked down.

THE PETLYAKOV Pe-2

Power Plant: The main power plant for the Pe-2 was a pair of Klimov M-105R V-12 supercharged engines, with the following power ratings:

(a) Nominal   1,020hp MS at sea level
(b) Maximum   1,100hp MS at 2,000m; 1,050hp MS at 4,000m

The port console contained the throttle levers, and had the mixture controls located aft of them. Manual mixture control was only permitted above the rated altitude. To lean the mix an (at that time) novel device, the Exhaust Gas Analyzer (EGA) was employed. This device measured the heat conductivity of the exhaust gas and the value thus obtained was compared with the boost pressure, the formula being tabulated, and the correct leaning mixture could be read off and applied. There were considerable problems with the EGA during the early years of use and these may have contributed to many of the engine failure accidents.

Each engine had a supercharger. These were not actuated by levers as on contemporary American aircraft but by means of electrically-operated shifting rams. The Finns found that, in their service, this device was not reliable, and VS replaced it with one of their own homegrown models, which worked perfectly.

Also electrically-operated were the radiator shutters, as well as the CSU control. By contrast, the pitch-change mechanism was of the conventional, pressure oil, type.

A vital requirement for any military (or civil) aircraft operating in Russia's winter weather conditions (as the Luftwaffe had found out to its cost, the hard way), was anti-icing. A single 1.5 (US) gallon tank of anti-icing fluid was mounted in the starboard engine nacelle. The pilot could direct this fluid from the tank to either airscrew by means of a cock mounted in his cockpit. The Klimov engine had six carburettors downstream of the supercharger and the fluid was pumped by pure bleed-air by the blower.

Detail of the tailwheel of a *Peshka*, showing the strong mountings and hydraulics. (H Valtonen via Keski-Suomen Imailumuseo, Tikkakoski)

Fuel: A total fuel capacity of 1,505 litres was contained in eleven separate fuel tanks (see Diagram18). Pneumatically-activated cocks were

THE FIGHTING FINNS

The engines are exposed to give a detailed view of a Pe-2 undergoing ground examination and testing at a Finnish air base. (K Koskensalo via Keski-Suomen Imailumuseo, Tidkkakoski)

mounted on the starboard wall of the cockpit. To reduce the risk of fuel fires, each tank could be pressurised with nitrogen. The observer, being in a better position to observe such dangers, and not the pilot, could also jettison some of the tanks from his after cockpit position.

Take-off Procedure

Assistance from the ground personnel was required for each aircraft sortie. The fuel cocks were opened and floor-mounted pumps primed both engines. In exceptional conditions of very cold weather, with the aircraft parked out overnight, the oil-cooler by-pass valve (mounted in the engine nacelle along with a valve, which provided extra lubrication) had to be opened. The battery and magnetos were switched on and the selector levers tuned to the required engine. The pneumatic starter valve was opened by mean of a mobile external pneumatics trolley. The booster coil button was depressed steadily until each engine was running smoothly. The Finns found the warm-up time for the Klimov 'prolonged'.

Once both engines were running nicely, the aircraft was taxied out. Here the Pe-2 performed best at 850-1,000rpm. 'There was no need for '*essing*'.' The Finns considered that the main undercarriage had good damping, but that the tail-wheel oleo had such a long stroke to it that, should the pilot pull back the stick in tight turns, the tail-wheel doors could be damaged! 'On a bouncy airfield the tail easily dug into the *terra firma*!' There was a marked tendency for the engines to overheat

THE PETLYAKOV Pe-2

Resplendent in her new markings, a captured Pe-2 is checked over by Finnish Air Force personnel at a wooded clearing close to the front line. (Defence Training Development Centre, Photographic Section, Helsinki)

if the taxiing was too prolonged, so usually the radiator shutters were kept open at this time.

The pilot had, as mentioned, excellent visibility, and could rely absolutely on his pneumatic wheel brakes, which were highly efficient. One unexpected problem was caused by the shortness of the main undercarriage legs. On primitive forward airstrips, this meant that any debris blown up by engines' slipstream could easily find its way into the carburettor air inlets and damage the delicate tail surfaces. The Finns found their own way of lessening this adverse effect by fitting VS dust filters to keep out its worst effects.

On take off, the pilot gave 15-20 degrees of flap, the necessity being to get the tail off the deck as quickly as possible in order that the aircraft was trimmed slightly nose-heavy, thus putting out the neutral position indicator lamp. There was always a marked tendency for the Pe-2 to swing to the starboard as it accelerated, and a firm rudder control was needed to counter this.

Acceleration was 'sluggish', the aircraft requiring a full length of runway to get airborne ('longer than any wartime Finnish Air Force aircraft'). During the Malmi tests the Finns recorded an average ground run of 380m at 7,550kg, using 20 degrees of flap. If flaps were not used, then the run was 630m to a height of 1,350 metres. At a weight of 8,520 kilos, with flaps used, the ground roll was 470m and to 20 metres height, 1,290 metres had to be traversed.

At about 160-180km/h the *Peshka* came unstuck and at an altitude of between 50-150 metres the flaps were raised. To reach 20-metres height required a lateral distance of more than 1,000 metres. If the IAS was 250km/h or less, the Pe-2 'mushed', another of its irritating habits which caught out many a novice pilot. With the undercarriage fully retracted, the three red lights glowed red in the pilot's cockpit.

Flying Characteristics

No detailed and scientific test flying was done in Finland specifically to study the Pe-2's flight characteristics, but reports from Test Pilot Aarne Siltavuori give some insights. The *minimum* Indicated Air Speed (IAS) speed required in order to maintain altitude was found to be 230km/h. At this speed or below, the aircraft was distinctly unstable and did not become fully stable until an IAS of 260km/h.

With regards the *Peshka's* cruising stability this was found to be good in pitch. However, Sitavuori reported that lateral and directional stability was not so good, although the aircraft was pleasant to fly in the straight and level. The instruments left something to be desired; indeed engine RPM synchronisation had to be done totally by ear as the instruments proved totally unreliable. The allowable RPM varied from 2,200 to 2,600.

Siltavuori thought that the turn radius was excessive, due to the high wing loading. He found the controls light, while the rudder was too light. 'In turns the rudder is hardly needed, even in a port turn, opposite rudder has to be applied. Too much rudder will cause increase of bank into the direction of the turn. If increasing bank is counteracted with ailerons, the aircraft will sideslip. If this is done at low speed, a spin is imminent. Incorrect turn is easy to induce, due to the very light rudder.'

From another source, the interrogation of a Soviet Pe-2 pilot lieutenant on 15 May 1942, it was confirmed that the *Peshka* would suddenly spin if too much rudder were applied. Normal recovery action was usually effective but the loss of height was about 500-600 metres.

Landing approach speed was at an IAS of 220km/h at the airfield boundary. The recommendation for Soviet pilots was to land power-on; otherwise the approach angle was so steep that height estimation proved very difficult. Landing speed itself was high although if at least 1,000 metres of runway were available the landing procedure itself was easy to accomplish. The Pe-2 was renowned for its hard 'bounce' and three-point touchdown was always advisable.

The Pe-2 was found to be unforgiving if the landing was not performed correctly and with precision. At an IAS of 200km/h, the rate of climb was barely 1.0-1.5km/s! Flaps could not be immediately raised to get you out of trouble as the aircraft 'mushed' considerably on retraction. The optimum landing distance from a height of 20 metres was found to be 1,000 metres and, without the application of the very hard braking system, ground roll was a further 600 metres. Use of the brakes reduced this to about 500 metres, while unprepared air strips as used close to the

THE PETLYAKOV Pe-2

Renowned for her heavy 'bounce' on touch-down, the *Peshka* was not an easy aircraft to handle and required a careful touch the whole time. The tailwheel on this uniquely marked aircraft has collapsed and one fin appears to have been left behind on the runway. (Russian Aviation Research Trust).

front line, reduced these distances considerably, at the expense of crew comfort and aircraft wear-and-tear. With the flaps raised, the touchdown speed was an IAS of 220 km/h and *at least* 1,500 metres of runway was required.

Finnish Test Pilots view of the Pe-2

Despite the above limitations, the Finnish test pilots freely acknowledged that the Pe-2 was one of the most advanced aircraft of its time. Most of the complex systems with which she was fitted worked extremely well during the trials, with the exception of the EGAs. In war service with the Finnish air force, some problems were to occur, primarily due to the use (unavoidable given the circumstances) of sub-standard materials in the construction.

T.P. Siltavuori's report was most enlightening, especially his criticisms: 'Flight characteristics have to be considered satisfactory in view of its poor power and wing-loading, which nullified its maneuverability.' As regards the *Peshka's* primary role, dive-bombing, he stated that: 'Visibility is good in all directions. The aircraft is a good dive-bomber in view of its handling and performance. Bomb shackling positioning was not the best possible.'

He concluded that: 'In evaluating its fighting abilities one must bear in mind that this aircraft demands very long, hard surface runways of at least 1200m in length. If flaps-up landing has to be made even that is too short for safety.'

THE FIGHTING FINNS

The aircrew of a Finnish Air Force Pe-2 chat to their groundcrew. Note the navigator's map board. (SA-KOVA)

Captured Pe-2s transferred by Germany to Finland

A total of seven Pe-2s from those that were captured relatively intact by the Germans were transferred to Finland after testing. Although deemed airworthy by the Luftwaffe, the Finns took no chances and stripped them all down and rebuilt them before committing them to combat duties. The seven aircraft were as follows:

Table 10: Finnish Pe-2s

Date Delivered	Finnish No.	Unit & Dates	Unit & Dates	Unit & Dates	Unit & Dates
19-12-41	Pe-211	1/LeLv48 6-7-42 – 28-2-44	2/PleLv48 1-3-44 – 3-12-44	PleLv 41 4-12-44 11-2-45	PleLv 45 12-2-45- 8-10-45
19-12-41	Pe-212	1/LeLv48 10-7-42-10-2-43	-	-	-
19-12-41	Pe-213	1/LeLv 48 1-8-42 -25-1-43	-	-	-

179

THE PETLYAKOV Pe-2

Date Delivered	Finnish No.	Unit & Dates	Unit & Dates	Unit & Dates	Unit & Dates
19-12-41	Pe-214	State Aircraft Factory 10-1-42 – 21-5-42	-	-	-
19-12-41	Pe-215	1/LeLv48 3-12-42 – 14-4-43	2/PleLv 48 15-4-44	-	-
19-12-41	Pe-216	1/LeLv48 14-5-43 – 28-2-44	2/PleLv 48 28-7-44	-	-
17-1-44	Pe-217*	2/PleLv 48 26-6-44 – 27-6-44	-	-	-

- This aircraft had served with the German Air Force and had the Luftwaffe codes NS + BA painted on delivery.

The initial batch of six Pe-2s was purchased from the German war-booty depots. The original idea was for all six, which were said to be in airworthy condition, to be flown directly to Finland from Pinsk airfield in eastern Poland. However, inspection revealed some damage to all the aircraft and this plan was dropped as being too risky; instead, all six were shipped by sea across the Baltic on 19 December 1941. All were sent to the State Aircraft Factory for thorough overhaul and inspection, arriving there on 10 January 1942, and given the Finnish designation Pe-200 series.[4] They were then put through air testing, during which one aircraft, Pe-214, was lost when it stalled during take off and crashed in the woods near the Tampere airbase. The remaining five were allocated to combat duties with a photo-reconnaissance flight of the FAF.

The main unit to employ the Pe-2/3s in Finnish service was the LeLv 48 (*Lentolaivue* = Flying Squadron). The squadron had been established at Luonetjärvi air base on 23 November 1941 and it was sub-ordinated to 4th Flying Regiment (*Lentorykmentti* 4). The initial commander of this unit was Lieutenant Colonel J. Harju-Jeanty, with Captain A. Pietarienen flight commander of 1 Flight, Lieutenant Y. Siirilä of 2 Flight and Captain T. Vasamies of 3 Flight.

LeLv 48 received its initial aircraft for training purposes for all of the newly allocated aircrew from LeLv 46, which was re-equipped with German Dornier bombers, and to supply the training needs of the whole of *Lentorykmentti* 4. The temporary photographic flight was set up on 2 May 1942, under the command of Captain E. Ahtianinen, and subordinated in turn to LeLv 48, and subsequently to LeLv 42. Initially this flight operated a mix of one Bristol Blenheim IV, two DB-3Ms and a Dornier 17. In mid-1942, it was split into two flights, 1 Flight becoming the Dive-Bomber Flight and 2 Flight reverting to a medium-bomber unit. The first of the refurbished *Peshkas* joined 1 Flight a month later.

THE FIGHTING FINNS

End of a dangerous foray. A Finnish *Peshka* aircrew exchange views at the end of a reconnaissance mission over Soviet lines, back at their base at Immola, 30 June 1944. (Defence Training Development Centre, Photographic Section, Helsinki)

Due to the experimental nature of their work and the need to familiarise themselves with the new aircraft, 1 Dive-Bomber Flight only managed to undertake one combat reconnaissance mission over Maaselka and Rukajarvi by the end of 1942. On 26 October, the Photographic Flight was re-united with the squadron but, by 21 November, winter had forced the curtailment of operations. This led to the dissolving of 3 Flight on the 29th, aircraft being transferred to a new training unit, *Täydennyslentolaivue* 17 (17 Complementary Flying Squadron). By 1 January, 1 Flight was under the command of Major A. Pietarinen and based at Onttola airfield with four active Pe-2s on its strength.

This flight was ordered to conduct a range of combat duties, including reconnaissance, photography and 'harassment bombing' in the Rukajärvi region as soon as weather conditions permitted combat operations to resume. On 30 April Captain O. Wickstrand was appointed the new Ccmmander of 1 Flight; he also commanded the photography flight which was formed for mapping purposes.

He was allocated another Pe-2 to strengthen his force for this purpose. During spring 1943 the Pe-2s were mainly employed in the Maaselkä area and daily reconnaissance and photography missions were flown at this period. The harassment bombing sorties conducted proved to be fruitless and a needless waste of resources and were stopped at the end of May, after only a few missions.

On 14 June Major K. Kepsu assumed command. Future targets for photographic mapping by the *Peshkas* were given as Carelia, Aland and the areas around both Helsinki and Kokkola, but combat pressure ensured that 1 Flight continued to concentrate its efforts in the Maaselkä region. The squadron's HQ was moved to Onttola on 15 July but by mid-November only two Pe-2s were still fit for service. One aircraft was retained by 1 Flight, the other was transferred to 2 Flight, but, by March 1944, any flyable Pe-2s were allocated exclusively to the latter unit. Meanwhile Captain J. Turpeinen had assumed command of 1 Flight in January 1944; in February the squadron commander was Major E. Ahriainen.

There was still vital work for the fast Pe-2s with the great Soviet summer offensive expected and, from 9 June 1944, the Finnish PEs were undertaking photo-reconnaissance missions of the Carelian Isthmus to keep track of the Russian onslaught. Each of these FAF *Peshka* sorties was given an armed escort of four Bf.109s, so strong had the Soviet fighter defences become. Even so, aircraft were lost and only one PE remained operational when the Finnish Government negotiated a ceasefire with the Soviet Union on 4 September 1944.

Under the terms of the treaty signed with Stalin, Finland was then obliged to turn on the Germans, and a single combat mission was flown by 2/PleVe 48 (*Pommituslentolaivue* = Bomber Squadron) by the sole operational PE aircraft in the Kemi-Tornio-Rovaniemi area on 2 October 1944.

In Finnish service from 6 July 1942 to 4 September 1944, Pe-2s had flown 125 combat missions, during which four aircraft of the seven were lost, with two more destroyed in accidents. Seven Finnish crew members had been killed and one became a PoW. The sole survivor, Pe-211, was moved to a depot at the end of 1944, but was still occasionally flown, the last time being on 4 April 1946, before it was finally pensioned off.

Finnish Pe-3

The only Pe-3 acquired by Finland was an aircraft captured intact at Inari on 28 November 1942. After refitting and trials this machine was delivered to 1/LeLv 48 on 15 February 1942 and was later transferred to 2/PL3Lv 48 on 5 June 1944. It met its end a few weeks later when, during the Soviet bombing attack on Lappenranta of 2 July, it was totally destroyed. This aircraft had logged some 222 hours 10 minutes in Finnish Air Force service at the time of its loss.

This Pe-3 variant that came into Finnish ownership arrived, not via Germany, but direct. This came about when the Soviet aircraft (s/n 40106) on a reconnaissance mission over Lapland, piloted by W/O V.I. Samarin with Senior Lieutenant Sustov as his gunner/observer, ran into difficulties and had to make a forced landing at Kauhalahti, in the area of marsh between Lake Inari and Nitsi.

THE FIGHTING FINNS

The aircraft came down in this soggy mass and was thus relatively undamaged. Both crew members survived the landing, Samarin eventually making it back to Soviet lines after stealing a boat and sailing it across the lake, followed by an eighteen-day trek across the Lapland wilderness.

The Pe-3 itself was eventually recovered from the bog and subsequently repaired and pressed into service by the Finnish Air Force as the Pe-301, and later in life was converted into a photo-reconnaissance aircraft with 1/PLeLV 48 during 1944.

Aircrew disembark their aircraft after a recce over Soviet airspace. (Defence Training Development Centre, Photographic Section, Helsinki)

PESHKA MEN – Captain Aimo Olavi Pietarinen, FAF

The foremost exponent of dive-bombing in Finland was Captain Aimo Olavi Pietarinen. He was the officer commanding 1 Flight, LeLv 48, during its formative years and a self-taught expert on the Pe-2 and tactics.

Born at Liperi on 15 June 1910, Aimo first got his pilot's 'wings' in 1932 and served as a lieutenant with the *Maalentoeskaaderi* (Land Flying Squadron) between 1932 and 1937. He was the acknowledged dive-bomber expert, flew many tests, and wrote many studies of the subject, which were presented as official papers. He used the Fokker C.X. aircraft for these trials, this being the first dedicated dive-bomber aircraft used by the FAF.

He was appointed as flying commanding officer of LeR 1 (Flying Regiment 1) which he led between 1938 and 1939, being promoted to captain in 1940, and again between 1941 and 1943, during which he developed dive-bombing techniques for the FAF. He was able to develop his ideas while also serving as CO of the *KoeLv* (Test Squadron) in 1941 and became a major in 1942.

Captain A O Pietarinen, Finnish Air Force, Commander of the I/*LeLv* 78 at Immola 1943. (H Valtonen via Keski-Suomen Ilmailumuseo, Tikkakoski)

Aimo later moved on to the command of LeR 4 during the war years, 1941-43 and became the squadron commander in LeR 4's Operational Training Unit (OTU), T-LeLv 17, in 1943. Further promotion followed and his appointment as Commanding Officer of the Flight Instruction Department at the FAF Flying School was confirmed in 1944.

Aimo continued to serve in the FAF post-war, rising to the rank of lieutenant colonel in 1952. In addition to dive-bombing, Aimo's interests in the academic and theoretical fields extended to nuclear physics and chemistry. In 1949 he had two books on these subjects published in Finland, *Chemistry in the Air Force* and *Nuclear Power and Nuclear Work*. Aimo died on 29 February 1956 while still on active service as a Departmental Chief at FAF HQ.

On the extreme southern front, 1,000 miles away, another of Germany's allies, Rumania, also captured several Pe-2s in fairly good condition, which they also tested at length. Similarly, Polish pilots were trained to fly the Pe-2, under Soviet commanders, but the war ended before any Polish-manned *Peshkas* took part in combat operations. However, post-war, the Soviet domination of Eastern Europe, which ultimately led to the Warsaw Pact and the long confrontation with NATO, saw the Pe-2 widely employed among Stalin's allies. These will be described in Chapter Fourteen.

Chapter Twelve

Production Line Progression

The Pe-2 was continually modified and developed as the war progressed. The *Peshka* quickly became easily the most numerous and important Soviet front-line bomber, although, for political reasons, this predominance was played down in the west. The fact that the two main land armies of both sides of the conflict placed such reliance on the dive-bomber was both embarrassing and uncomfortable to the RAF and USAAF, who had largely rejected the type. Instead, the Il-2 *Shturmovik* close-support aircraft was glamorised and the Pe-2 ignored. This bias, incredibly, still exists, even over seventy years later, among western historians still wedded to the myth of the Fairey Battle light bomber's role in the Battle of France and the Hawker Typhoon rocket strikes during the Falaise Gap action of 1944.

The production lines steadily increased their output as the war continued and new *Peshkas* soon far exceeded losses once the new factories got into their stride. This is the scene at the main plant in 1943. (Robert Michulec)

THE PETLYAKOV Pe-2

Just how much the *Peshka* came to dominate the VVS bomber force, and how unrepresentative western media coverage of the Il-2[1] was, and still is, can be seen by comparing construction figures.

Pe2/Pe-3	DB-3/IL-4	Tu-2
11,247	6,784	2,527*

* The bulk of these produced post-war.

Although the Tu-2 was operating as early as December 1942, when one solitary aircraft was used to take photographs of the Demyansk bridgehead, even by the summer of 1943, during the Kursk-Byelgorod battles, units like Colonel V.A. Sandalov's 285 BAD could only count eighteen Tupolevs on their combat strength. Another year on and, in May 1944, Colonel I.P. Skok's 334 BAD could muster a full complement of Tu-2s for operations, but the *Peshka* remained by far and away the main front-line bomber, as distinct from ground-attack aircraft, for the rest of the war.[2]

As the percentage of Pe-2s in combat service increased, and aircrew training in dive-bombing improved, it reflected on the average VVS bombing accuracy achieved, the 1944 figures being some 11 per cent better in this respect than the equivalent 1943 figures. This reflected the percentage of dive-bombing attacks carried out by the Soviet Air Force, as more pilots grew proficient at the technique. These percentages rose from 39 per cent in 1943, to 49 per cent in 1945. From 1943 the first Pe-2 bombing manuals had begun to be issued, and these were updated

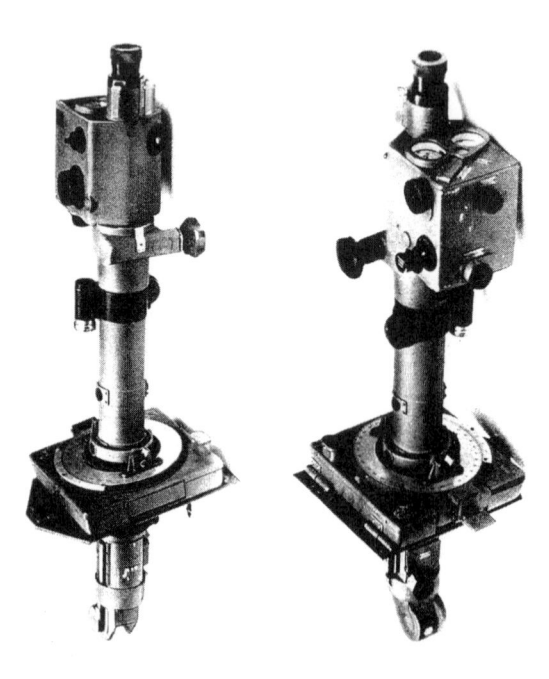

Although designed as a dive-bomber, the Pe-2 was frequently used as a low-level horizontal bomber at first, due to lack of fully trained and skilled dive-bombers pilots and the need to get the aircraft into action. The aircraft was fitted with an optical bombsight for this, the Goerz-Boykow OPB-2 system (left hand view) first introduced into the Soviet Air Force in 1937. A later improved version, with many modifications, is shown on the right. (*Flugzeuge, Flugzeugaustrüstung und Waffen der sowjetischen Luftwaffe, Heft II Flugzeugausrüng und Waffen, Der Oberbeichishaber der Luftwaffe, Fürungsatab Ic, Berlin, May 1942*)

PRODUCTION LINE PROGRESSION

A photo showing the early evaluation and flight testing of the Pe-2 2M-105, which took place in January and February 1941. The aircraft had been developed and built under the Order of 23 June 1940 of the Defence Committee of the Soviet People's Commissars, based on the VI-100 high-altitude fighter and was initially built at Aviation Factory No. 39 in Moscow. Overhead port three-quarter view. (M Maslov)

as the war progressed. The precision work of 2 Guards Bomber Air Corps was studied and attacks using dive angles of between 50 and 60 degrees were more and more implemented. Special instructions saw the Pe-2 operating more frequently in regimental and divisional strength against selected targets.

The recurring theme on the serial production line, as we have seen from numerous examples, was the need to maintain production to feed the expansion of the VVS, and replace losses. To this all-embracing end, everything else was largely sacrificed. Nonetheless, as the war progressed ever more successfully, opportunity was taken to update and incorporate improvements and modifications on a rolling basis. Although numerous official (and unofficial) designations were given to variations on the theme, for the larger part these upgrades were merely part and parcel of continuing production. They were not singled out for any special status. Often, also, designations bestowed, either contemporary or in retrospect, never had any official status on the line, and aircraft were referred to as coming from this series or that series.[3]

We examine here this progression as it was applied to the standard *Peshka* production line between December 1941 and 1945. By 1 December 1941, the Pe-2/Pe-3 delivery totals had reached 1,626 machines, with production being undertaken at GAZ 22, 39, 124 and 125.[4] By 1943 the majority of the older light bombers, the few Ar-2s, Yak-4s and the SBs, had either been combat or accident casualties, or withdrawn from front-line service due to their vulnerability, and used as transports or trainers.

THE PETLYAKOV Pe-2

Series Modifications History

Series 13: As related in more detail below, complaints from the front line brought about the modification of the armament very early on. Commencing with this production batch the 12.7mm UBK replaced the right-hand nose ShKAS gun. This switch was also extended to weapons mounted in the ventral position, which had been prone to jamming. These was replaced by a UBT. The UB gun had a higher muzzle velocity and fired a much larger bullet with more stopping power, although not equalling the German MG-FF.

Series 22: Aircraft produced from this production batch were fitted with the M-105RA engine and the VISh-61B airscrew, optimised for this power plant.

Series 83: The navigator's ShKAS gun was replaced by a UBT on a flexible mounting. This change had already been done in a few front-line regiments. The upgrade was also retrofitted to front-line units in the field as and when possible. A dedicated standardised armament kit was produced and special mobile teams worked from the plants to fit this to supplement this programme.

Series 105: The RPK-10, a more powerful HF/DF receiver with a conventional D/F loop, was fitted to replace the older RPK-2 which housed its antenna in a teardrop fairing and had only limited range. Those aircraft completed at the end of 1941 and in early 1942 had the RPK-2 fitted in those employed in the reconnaissance role only.

Series 110: From this batch onward the navigator's armament became the fleximounted UBT in a FZ turret. A portable ShKAS was also carried, which could be manhandled from one side of the aircraft to the other within 30 seconds to fire through small ports. In some cases, a strong gunner could handhold and fire this weapon from a dorsal port, which was fitted with a small hinged screen to provide limited protection from the slipstream. Extra armour protection was worked in and the electrical, hydraulic and fuel systems were all subject to improvement. These aircraft were often, incorrectly, retrospectively referred to by historians as the Pe-2FT.

Series 179: Another engine upgrade with the introduction of the 1,270hp M-105PF. The manifold pressure was readjusted to optimise operations at medium and lower altitudes, which, naturally, reduced efficiency at higher altitudes. This had the effect of increasing speeds up to the 4,000-metres level. At ground level, an increase of 25km/h was recorded. This enhancement was achieved despite the fact that the existing VISh-61B airscrew had been adapted specially for the older engine. The M-105R was withdrawn, so that all production could be concentrated on the M-105P for the Yak-1, Yak-7 and LaGG-3 single-engined fighters. The new M-105PF engine still had to make do with the same airscrew, which reduced its efficiency.

PRODUCTION LINE PROGRESSION

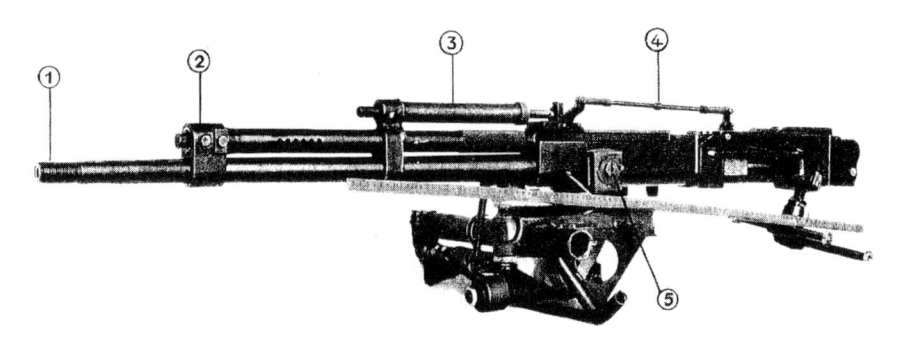

The standard defensive armament was built around various marks of fixed and flexible BS 12.7mm calibre machine-guns. Key – 1: Barrel; 2: Gas cylinder: 3: Compressed air cylinder for bypass passage; 4: Synchronized stanchion road; 5: Shield pivot. (*Flugzeuge, Flugzeugaustrüstung und Waffen der sowjetischen Luftwaffe, Heft II Flugzeugausrüng und Waffen, Der Oberbeichishaber der Luftwaffe, Fürungsatab Ic*, Berlin, May 1942)

A retrofit of the M-105PF was also carried out at unit level which led to physical problems because the reductor shaft of the PF engine was 60mm higher than that on the RA, making the cowlings incompatible. On the retrofits, the cowling had to be cut to accommodate them and the resultant gaps covered over by riveted inserts.[5]

Series 205: From this 1944 production batch onward, certain aircraft, 100 in total, but not in sequence, had their exhaust collector manifolds replaced with individual reactive exhaust ejectors. This was thought to have a marginal effect on improving overall speed.

In addition, the dive brakes were fitted with fairings for the first time. The antenna, combined with the pitot tube, was relocated to the front of the pilot's cockpit cabin. Sealing was applied to joints in an attempt to produce a smoother skin surface, thus reducing drag. The turret was redesigned.

Series 211: The teardrop-shaped fairings that covered the bomb racks were done away with and the racks concealed internally into recesses in the lower wing surface. Replacement of airscrew commenced with the adoption of the more efficient VISh-61P.

Series 249: A winter operations enhancement system was introduced, by which the fuel was diluted to make for easier starts at sub-zero temperatures.

Series 265: This series saw the introduction of the extended-range transceivers.

Series 275: Although, as previously related, used by certain *Peshka* units earlier in the war, from this batch onward production-line aircraft were equipped with two DAG-10 containers in the navigator's cabin. Each of these cassettes was loaded with five AG-2 grenades, for a total of ten.

These weapons were not a standard fit for the Pe-2 but fitted to select aircraft. Launched into the path of attacking fighter aircraft and descending by parachute, they were timed to explode within three-to-five seconds and the resulting detonations, if not deadly in themselves, had the effect of driving the attacking aircraft away from the vulnerable rear-ventral sector.

Series 301: An enlarged upper hatch for the wireless-operator/gunner, in order to improve the emergency escape capability, was fitted from this batch onward.

Series 354: The fitting of individual exhaust stacks, first introduced from the 205 production series, was made a standard fitting from this batch onward.

Series 359: Improvements incorporated included a revised oxygen supply and breathing outfit, new-style instruments and small aerodynamic modifications.

Series 382: A new winter ignition start kit was brought in to enhance the oil fuel modifications first fitted to the 249 batch.

Series 410: This 1945 batch introduced faired ports for the portable ShKAS machine guns.

Series 411: This production batch had all the gaps between the various fairings covered with tape in an effort to improve airflow and reduce drag.

Front-Line Demand

The complaint from many *Peshka* gunners that the under-fuselage machine gun was unreliable and subject to the frequent seizing-up of its belt-feed mechanism, often after just one shot, was the first major complaint to be rectified. A new, circular cartridge-box was introduced; this was mounted *above* the gun to remedy this fault. The armament was also revised with the installation of the MV-3 (MV = Mozharovsky and Venevidov designed) turret abaft the pilot's cabin.[6]

Despite prompt action here, the VVS appeared to be remarkably insensitive, in general, to complaints from front-line aircrew. Meetings were certainly held in which pilots and navigators were theoretically free to express their views. As befitted a totalitarian state, which brooked no dissent from the party line, only bland approval seemed to be expected and, initially, that was all that was forthcoming. However, there *were* notable exceptions. Brave men *did* begin to question the party line that everything was perfect and as it should be. Moreover, there were a few among those who heard such views who were themselves sufficiently motivated to take such criticisms to heart, and even to act on them in defiance of official policy.

PRODUCTION LINE PROGRESSION

One such was Leonid Leonidovich Selyakov, who was later to relate how this refreshing attitude came to affect the production parameters of the Pe-2.[7] Selyakov started his career pre-war, and later became deputy to Myasishchev, Chelomyey and Tupolev respectively. The culmination of his career was as chief designer of the Tu-134, but in the winter of 1941 he was working on the Pe-2 design team at GAZ 22.

His memory of those days was quite detailed and he recalled how it was the practice to hold meetings in the assembly workshop between the plant workers, VVS representatives and the young airmen from the front who were collecting new aircraft for their units. These were mainly rabble-rousing, morale-boosting events designed for mutual esteem between those fighting and those providing the weapons, in the traditional manner. Occasionally, however, young airmen, either politically naïve or fearless of the consequences, broke the mould and spoke out. Selyakov related one particular incident, on 18 February 1942, when this took place.

One young airman left the stage, visibly agitated and complaining loudly about all the talk of how they were fighting the enemy with good equipment and doing well, when in reality 'Enemy shoots us down like chickens'. Selyakov called this man aside and engaged him in quiet conversation, asking him outright specifically just what was wrong with the Pe-2. The young airman's reply was frank, explaining that the upper ShKAS machine gun was proving useless as a deterrent to enemy fighters. They were well armoured and could close to the attack with relative immunity from above. 'What is needed,' the airman stated, 'is a Berezin 12.7mm calibre weapon.'[8]

As Selyakov later recalled it, his reaction was to stay late at the plant and hold an impromptu meeting with fellow young designers P. Chugunov and Andrei Arkhipov, the latter being a weapons expert. He repeated the complaint and the request. The result was that for the next ten days this unofficial group worked on a mounting to replace the ShKAS, and, moreover, one which could be fitted in the field. By 28 February, the group, working in their own time, had agreed a design among themselves, which they called the FT (Front Demand) mounting, and were ready to test fire the weapon. Somehow, unchallenged, they collected the weapon and some ammunition and headed for the butts. They were exhausted from all the extra work, but still enthusiastic.

Selyakov hand-held the weapon for the test and pulled the trigger. Despite bracing himself, the shock of the heavy weapon firing knocked him backward, while retaining his grip on the trigger. 'The tracers formed an arc in the sky. I instantly realised that I would shoot away the whole assembly shop.'[9] He released the trigger and dropped the gun. This unofficial work and unauthorised testing, far from resulting in the group's censure, received the backing of an understanding factory management. Both the chief engineer, Mikhail Nikiforovich Korneyev, and the factory director, Vasili Andreyevich Okulov, lent their weight to the project. Within a short time proper company trials were held which proved the effectiveness and value of the FT mounting. Even the normally stringent State Acceptance evaluation tests were flouted and the mounting was rushed into series production.

Unit conversions to the new mounting were made with increasing rapidity and initial reports from front-line units confirmed the improvement in defensive capability. The first fittings of the factory-built FT mountings were carried out on 5 May 1942, to the *Peshkas* of 30 BAR commanded by Colonel Nikolayev, which at that time were operating in the Kerch area. This unit was intercepted by a force of Bf. 109s while returning from a mission and, as usual, the enemy confidently closed to within 300 metres to make certain of scoring a kill, knowing that they were safe to do so. Instead, the new FT mountings opened fire and at least three German fighters were claimed set on fire. The surviving Germans continued with their old tactics and were also hit and destroyed. It was a major vindication of the new weapon.

However, back in Moscow, officialdom was demanding that such unauthorised and unofficial procedures should cease immediately. The head of GU 10 (Main Directorate) of the NKAP (People's Commissariat of Aircraft Production) 'bombarded' GAZ 22 with telegrams demanding that production of the FT cease immediately. Those responsible for what was termed a 'private venture' were threatened with court martial if work did not cease at once. On the other hand, word had got around and front-line aircrew were threatening to refuse to accept new Pe-2s that were *not* fitted with this weapon. It was an impasse.

Selyakov recalled that he approached Okulov and asked him what he should do. The reply was, 'Carry on!' However, things could not remain as they were and, shortly afterwards, Selyakov was instructed to take his weapon and mounting to Moscow and 'convince' them of its merits. This was done, but he received the cold shoulder. For three days, he camped outside the office of Taraevich's office at the NKAP in Ulan Street. Eventually he got an appointment, but with Fedotikov of the Central Committee. He found that, behind the scenes, the matter had already been settled and the FT mounting had official blessing for full production at both Kazan and Savelovo. P.A. Chugunov, by then with the OKO (Experimental Design Department), was subsequently sent to Savelovo to initiate the work there and that plant eventually produced 1,010 FT mountings to fully re-equip the units in the field.

Finally, in June 1942, the department of operations and maintenance at the S.P. Gorbunov plant (NKAP SSR), issued bulletins Nos. 11 and 12 entitled *Replacement of upper mounting ShKAS gun by Berezin type (by repair works)*. It was finally acknowledged that the Berezin UBT machine gun in the FT mounting was designed by Selyakov and Chugunov and would 'improve the combat effectiveness of the Pe-2'.[10]

Proposals to fit yet a further dorsal mounting were put forward, but weight and CG considerations ruled out embarking yet a fourth member of the aircrew.

There were other ideas and schemes in which the Pe-2 was featured in the early years of her life.

PRODUCTION LINE PROGRESSION

Air Cushion undercarriage

One unique experiment was originated by TsAGI designer A.A. Nadiradze. He came up with an idea to replace the conventional undercarriage of the Pe-2, which was causing so much concern, with an air cushion substitute. As envisaged by his team, two large rectangular-shaped skis, each with an inflatable apron, were to be fitted. They could be retracted in flight into wells in the modified engine nacelles. A special system was attached to the M-105REN to inflate the air cushion prior to its use.[11] In 1941 a Pe-2 was so modified and tested by LII NKAP. It was deemed practicable and lent itself to operations from temporary or hastily-constructed airstrips near the front, which would have uneven or soft surfaces quite unsuitable for a normal undercarriage. Only the outbreak of war and the subsequent evacuation of LII ended what might have been a promising experiment, and it was never subsequently renewed.

Retractable skis

In 1942 a Pe-2, powered by the VK-105RA engine, was produced with fully-retractable skis, which withdrew flush with the engine nacelles. These worked well in practice, but the resulting loss of 40km/h and reduction in ceiling of some 500 metres offset any advantages gained and no production followed.

The ski fittings tried out on Pe-2 number 16-11 at Koltsovo air base in trials for arctic conditions. This aircraft subsequently crashed when the ski undercarriage collapsed in a heavy landing. (Russian Aviation Research Trust)

Pe-2M (1941)

Another experiment was the building of a prototype *Peshka* equipped with a turbo-supercharger, with the idea of future use with the M-105FNV or M-107 engines. This machine was also to feature a widened ventral fuselage centre-section to enable her to carry the FAB-500 bomb internally. Completed on 16 October 1941, it received the first designation of Pe-2M. Test pilot S.A. Shestakov and chief engineer A.A. Rosenfeld ferried her to another factory where the automatic slats were installed and air intakes were enlarged, but, despite this work, she was not further proceeded with.[12]

Pe-2*Sh*

There were various attempts made to produce a purely ground-attack version of the *Peshka*, and the *Sh* suffix (*Sh* = *Shturmovik*, Ground-Attack) was applied in each case. None of them came to anything. The first concept was for two ShVAK and one UB to be mounted in ventral positions. This aircraft was evaluated in 1941. Another version was a modified Pe-2, which had two ShVAK and two ShKAS, also ventrally mounted. These weapons could lay down forward fire at a 40-degree depression angle, but were fixed and could not traverse. No series production resulted. Yet a third variant was planned, which was to be armed with two ShVAK and two UB, all designed to deliver overwhelming firepower against massed enemy ground formations, but no production followed.

Other Modifications

The extent of the nose glazing on series production aircraft was steadily reduced. The tail right-angle section with its small glass windows was done away with and the whole tail cone was shortened.

By the end of 1941 an acute shortage of light alloys was manifest in the Soviet aircraft industry. This naturally impacted on the Pe-2 more than most contemporary warplanes. As a short-term fix, local companies designed a wooden fuselage tail section at Kazan for mass construction. These wooden structures began to be fitted on selected batches during the winter of 1941/42.

Pe-2 fighter

Quite apart from the Pe-3, a two-seater fighter version of the series Pe-2 was mooted. Engined by the VK-105R and fitted with additional fuel tanks the dive-brakes were deleted. Armament was two ShKAS, two UBS and two ShVAK with a single UBT in a lower-fuselage hatch mounting. There was no follow up to this concept.[13]

PRODUCTION LINE PROGRESSION

Table 11: Production Figures for the *Peshka* by Plant

Year	Plant 22 Moscow	Plant 39 Moscow	Plant 124 Kazan	Plant 125 Irkutsk
1940	-	1	-	-
1941	1120	303	104	144
1942	1937	587	-	-
1943	2423	5	-	-
1944	2944	-	-	-
1945	1634	-	-	-
Totals	10058	896	104	144
Grand Total: 11196*				

* Sources vary slightly - see *Aviation and Cosmonautics* Magazine, No. 5-6, 2004.

In-the-Field modifications

One long-range reconnaissance air regiment, 2 DRAP, sought to overcome rear-defence weakness against German interceptors in a novel manner. In October 1941 they installed four RS-82 air-to-ground rockets, reverse mounted, to fire ventrally aft. The rockets could be fired in salvo or individually to lay down a fragmentation barrage behind them into which the enemy flew.

Reconnaissance

The Pe-2 also quickly became the principal reconnaissance aircraft of the Soviet Air Force. This role embraced both specially-adapted serial production aircraft, taken as required from series batches, and a specialised variant, the Pe-2R. (R= *Razviedchik*). Both types omitted the dive brakes of course. To give these aircraft additional reach a pair of 290-litre belly-mounted drop tanks was fitted, to give an extra 500-kilometre range.

The standard aerial Soviet aerial camera was the AFA-B and both types carried this. More specialised equipment included the AFA-1 and the AFA-27T1 vertical-plane cameras, which enabled oblique photography to be carried out while, for night photography, the AFA-B was replaced by the NAFA-19. Some units were adapted to carry AFA-3C cameras; others employed United States' cameras supplied under Lend-Lease.

As well as extra radio equipment to send back reports to base, all these aircraft could employ the AK-1 autopilot. This locked the rudder and, when activated during the run, held the aircraft steady with only a 1-2-degree variation in course.

THE PETLYAKOV Pe-2

Unloading the large camera used by the photo-reconnaissance adaptation of the Pe-2. (Russian Aviation Research Trust)

Chapter Thirteen

The Great Offensive – June 1944

Once the Anglo-American landings on the French coast at Normandy had taken place in June 1944, adding another western front to the fighting in Italy, the Axis found itself at full stretch. To take advantage of this, the Soviet High Command had been planning their own summer offensive, designed to clear the remaining Axis forces from Russian soil, and knock Germany's allies out of the war for good.

The Campaign in White Russia

As early as spring 1944, detailed preparations for this great offensive began to be drawn up. The Germans were expecting the main Russian thrust to take place in the south but the Soviets had as their main aim the destruction of the German Army Group Centre, the liberation of Minsk and the whole of Byelorussia to the Polish border. Annihilation of the German Fourth Army was to be achieved by deploying overwhelming force. The front line to be attacked stretched for a distance of 1,100 kilometres, from Lake Nesherdo to Verba. Final discussions took place in the Stavka on 22/23 May.

To support the Russian First Baltic and First, Second and Third Belorussian Fronts, four air armies were to be deployed, these being First, commanded by General T.T. Khyrukin, Third, commanded by General N.F. Papivin, Fourth, commanded by General K.A. Vershinin and Sixteenth, commanded by General S.I. Rudenko. A fifth, General F.P. Polynin's Sixth Air Army, was to join in the second phase of the operation on the left wing of First 1 Belorussian Front. In total these five air armies would commit some 6,000 combat aircraft to the battle; this included over 1,000 dive-bombers and medium bombers, the bulk of them Pe-2s.[1] This mass was opposed by fewer than 1,500 German aircraft of Luftflotte 6, based at airfields centrally concentrated near Minsk, Baranovichi and Bobruysk.

To accommodate the huge numbers of aircraft deployed, some seventy new airfields had to be constructed and, as soon as these were ready, ten air corps and eight air divisions flew into them at the beginning of June in readiness. Lessons learnt from the previous winter's operations were promulgated down with strong emphasis on radio control of units down to local level to ensure flexibility in what was expected to be a very fluid and fast-moving operation of great complexity. The air group commanders were prevented from exercising too detailed a control of individual units; instead they would issue specific mission instructions down to air

THE PETLYAKOV Pe-2

A winter scene with the crew of a long-range reconnaissance aircraft posing in the winter sunshine on the port wing after a mission during the winter of 1943-44. The pilot (centre) is Anatoliy Popov. (Russian Aviation Research Trust)

corps and air division level, but leave the detailed combat-sortie allocations to their subordinates who could better react to local conditions.

The largest reinforcements were assigned to First Air Army supporting Third Belorussian Front and Sixteenth Air Army, acting in support of First Belorussian Front. The most notable was 132 BAD commanded by General I.L. Fedorov, which was directly subordinated to the Soviet Army Air Force commander. All the dive-bombers, totalling three air corps and two independent air divisions, were concentrated in First and Sixteenth Air Armies in order to concentrate their effect.[2] A total of 548 Pe-2s took part in the opening air assault on the southern sector, softening up the Germans' strongest defences. As usual, extensive photo-reconnaissance was conducted prior to the assault and a clear picture of German defences was obtained, which revealed their weaknesses at several key points.

To further assist in the enormously difficult task of assembling this great concentration of airpower over the battlefield, General Rudenko was assisted by a number of high-ranking VVS staff officers who included General I.L. Turkel', General P.P. Ionov, General G.K. Gvozdkov and General B.V. Sterligov. During a whole series of practice flights from rear-area airfields, the assembly and forming-up of entire bomber corps in the air was worked out for the first time. Analysis of the results of these exercises resulted in the decision to make a massed strike against enemy ground targets in divisional and regimental strengths.[3]

By 20 June 1944 most of the preparations had been completed. Both First and Sixteenth Air Armies were divided into two groups, designed to support the twin offensives of their respective ground troops on both First and Third Belorussian

THE GREAT OFFENSIVE – JUNE 1944

Fronts. The First Air Army had six air divisions allocated to the Bogushevsk area, and eleven assigned to the Orsha area, while Sixteenth Air Army had thirteen air divisions allocated to the northern sector Rogachev-Bobrusyk and seven in the southern area, Parichi.

The night of 23 June 1944 saw the launching of night attacks, followed up at dawn by continuous, round-the-clock close-support operations against German strongpoints, tanks and reserve units in the line of the various advances. In the first three days of operations in excess of 4,500 combat sorties were flown.

Under the direction of General F.Ya. Falaeyev, strikes were directed against a large enemy force cut off west of Vitebsk. On 24 June Sixteenth Air Army launched two mass attacks, with 162 and 163 Pe-2s, at 1200 and 1700 respectively, against German defences at Bol'shaya Krushinovka and Tikhinichi. These led to significant breakthroughs during the next two days, and mobile forces poured through the breaches in the German defences.[4]

One outstanding *Peshka* mission was conducted by 124 Guard Bomber Regiment who took out a vital bridge across the river Adrov, near Zabolotye, some six kilometres (four miles) west of Orsha. The flight leader, Second Lieutenant V.V. Zakharchenko, took a hit in the leg from a flak fragment during his dive on the heavily-defended target. Nonetheless, he carried on down and bombed the bridge. Assisted by his navigator, Second Lieutenant N.N. Tenuyev, the pilot managed to nurse his stricken aircraft back to his home field and landed successfully. Both men earned themselves the Order of the Red Banner for their courage.

Nor did the German airfields at Borisov and Dokudovo escape attention from the dive-bombers, with several attacks by the Pe-2s of First Air Army on both 25 and 26 June. Sixth Guards BAD hit Orsha airfield itself on 25 June, so effectively that the report of JG 51, based there, admitted that not a single German fighter took off and the squadron's command post was destroyed.

In-flight view of a Pe-2 with tailfin tips and unit code letter in white in yellow outline, with red star outlined in white. (Via Keski-Suomen Ilmailumuseo, Tikkakoski)

THE PETLYAKOV Pe-2

Fifth Guards Tank Army was supported by a bomber corps under General V.A. Ushakov which moved along the Minks-Moscow highway and rail link and routed the Germans near Borisov. That rout soon became a headlong flight and the Pe-2s culled the fleeing German forces ruthlessly.

To the north, Lithuania fell and the surrounded city of Vilnius was assaulted and taken between 7 and 13 July; 103 Pe-2s supported the final assault on the defences by fifty-one Il-2s. In southern Poland the picture was the same, with some 252 aircraft from 2 Guards Air Corps and 4 BAC opening the assault on 14 July. A mass armoured counter-attack by the Germans' 8th Panzer Division was met with withering dive-bomber assault with 4 BAC leading the attack on the German tank column at 1400, followed at five-to-eight minute intervals by wave after wave of Pe-2s; 4 BAC contributed 135 *Peshkas* to this massacre, diving in groups of five aircraft at a time, with the lead group flown by Polbin himself. Next came five aircraft of 8 Guards BAD led by Colonel G.V. Gribakin, the division's commander; then followed Lieutenant Colonel A.A. Novikov's 162 Guard Bomber Regiment. The dive-bombers formed up their carousel over the target, commencing their dives from 1,500 metres (4,920ft) and pulling out at 700 metres (2,300ft). In total 3,288 sorties were flown against the German force near Plugow that day and the carnage was great.

Tactics were refined as the great operation gathered momentum. The air support of tank and mechanised ground units moving at speed required increased flexibility. A schedule of continuous strikes was maintained with Pe-2s deploying against enemy targets in succession with only short, ten-twenty-minute gaps between each, allowing the reeling enemy no time to regroup.

On First Belorussian Front the Pe-2s were used as an aerial fire reserve and unleashed against targets of opportunity along the line of advance as and when

June 1944 and huge Soviet summer offensive is under way. Here ground teams prepare Pe-2s for another sortie at Kavelia airfield. (Robert Michulec)

necessary. The precision dive-bombing was used to break any isolated group of German defenders who managed to form a hedgehog island of defence against the tidal wave of the Soviet advance. The *Peshkas* operated in attack formations of nine-to-twelve aircraft at the behest of the forward air controllers stationed with the leading tank columns; this was the Germans' own method of 1940-42, used against them but with far greater numbers of aircraft and their weakened ranks were unable to withstand it.

The Bobruysk Cauldron

Another large German force, XXXV Army Corps, was encircled to the south-east of Bobruysk by 27 July, and reconnaissance indicated that this force was prepared for an attempted breakout, concentrating tanks, motorised artillery and transport along the Zhlobin-Titovka highway. A massed air strike was sent in by Sixteenth Air Army against this concentration, with devastating results. In all the Soviet Air Force committed 523 aircraft to this one mission, launched at 1815 that afternoon. The attacks continued until 2100 and, at the end of that period, some 150 German tanks, 6,000 motor vehicles and many artillery pieces were claimed destroyed or put out of action.[5] It was a devastating blow, and next day the remnants of the German pocket had been mopped up by the advancing ground forces. Bobrusysk

Aircrew sit in front of their Pe-2 which features the nose art of a bear with a large bomb, the motif of the 34 Guards Air Regiment, August 1944. (M Maslov)

THE PETLYAKOV Pe-2

itself fell on 29 July. First Air Army *Peshkas* were also involved in similar operations against another German force cut off in a forested area south-east of Minsk. Later in July elements of First Air Army were switched to reinforce the First Baltic Front, keeping the hard-pressed German forces continuously off-balance.

Sixteenth Air Army was equally heavily involved in the advance on Minsk itself. The German fortified areas at Orsha and Mogilev were eliminated and close air support of the Soviet First and Third Belorussian Front ground forces became the main concern of Sixteenth and Fourth Air Armies in this sector. The last bridge over the Berezina river was knocked out by 'sniper' attacks, with the Pe-2s diving from 900 metre (3,000ft) to score the vital hits, thus trapping large German forces of the Fourth Army on the eastern bank of that river. On 28 and 30 June these forces were subjected to a heavy scale of air attack, some 3,000 combat sorties being flown against them; by 3 July 4,000 sorties had been mounted. Unable to retreat and cut off, the way to Minsk itself was left open and advancing Soviet forces entered the city on 3 July. They then pushed on towards Vilnius, which fell on 13 July, Bialystok, which was taken on 27 July, and Brest, which was entered on 28 July. The whole Belorussian salient was cut off by mid-July and when the campaign official drew to a close on 29 August all of its original objectives had been achieved with a 600-kilometre advance, the crossing of the rivers Vistula, Neman, Narev and Berezina, and the virtual annihilation of Army Group Centre. It was the greatest defeat suffered by the German Army in the Second World War.

Bombing up a Pe-2 at a forward air base during the great Soviet offensive of 1944. The Russian dive-bombers played a major role in the classic manner in this grand '*Blitzkrieg* in Reverse' that carried the Soviet armies to the borders of the Third Reich. (Fotokhronika TASS, Moscow)

THE GREAT OFFENSIVE – JUNE 1944

Ukrainian Front

While the Belorussian campaign was still in progress more Soviet attacks were developing. On 13 July, the First Ukrainian Front erupted as Soviet forces launched their assault. Fierce fighting continued for several days and the Pe-2s of Second Air Army were heavily involved as part of the 3,000-strong fleet. The Soviet Thirty-eighth Army was subjected to a very strong German counter-attack on 15 July, and at one point threatened with being overwhelmed. An all-out effort was called for and some 2,000 combat sorties were mounted against the German forces, spearheaded by dive-bombing attacks by Pe-2s. The intensity of the air operations involved can be gauged when it is recorded that at one point almost 1,000 Soviet aircraft were over the battlefield. For five hours, this intense assault from the air went on, and no ground force could withstand such a battering. The German attack faltered and was halted, and the Soviet offensive resumed. By the winter, the Soviets had advanced to the very edge of the Third Reich. One last titanic effort would be required to finish the job.

Peshka Men: Abdiraim Izmailovich Reshidov

Abdiraim was born on 8 March 1912 at Mamashai, in the Crimea, to a minority Tartar peasant family. He completed the 5th Grade at school and then worked for a while on a collective farm. He joined the Red Army and, in 1933, at the age of twenty-one, entered the Osoaviakim Flight School, with the army and, in the following year, progressed to the Odessa Flight School. His service career followed the usual lines and he joined the Communist Party in 1939.

He served in both Finnish and Great Patriotic Wars and flew as a combat pilot for the entire period of the latter, completing almost 200 combat missions and being nominated for Hero of the Soviet Union. He served on the Finnish front throughout 1940, and was on the front line when the Germans invaded Russia on 22 June 1941. Although a dive-bomber pilot, he also became an air ace, with eight confirmed kills. He was the eventual recipient of the Order of Lenin, three Orders of the Red Banner and the Order of Aleksandr Nevsky for valour in aerial combat.

Peshka ace A I Reshidov. (Vladimir Petrov)

THE PETLYAKOV Pe-2

On 21 July, while bombing the corridor near Yamol-Soroki, he flew his aircraft at treetop level and conducted strafing attacks against a large concentration of enemy troops. He was subsequently credited with the destruction of thirteen enemy transport vehicles, and exterminated up to a battalion of German troops. For this devastating attack, the commander of the regiment personally commended his crew.

On 27 July, having just successfully bombed a large concentration of enemy troops and vehicles, he again flew his aircraft at an altitude barely above ground level and, with his machine guns, destroyed an additional ten motor vehicles and exterminated a further fifty to sixty enemy soldiers.

These successes were vouched for by other flight crews, intelligence photographs and ground forces, which confirmed their effectiveness. By this date he had already flown forty-seven combat sorties since the beginning of the war. Nor did the pace lessen and, from 20 August 1941, Reshidov flew an additional twelve combat sorties, taking his total combat flight hours to 103 hours 48 minutes.

On 22 August, as a part of an attack group, his crew bombed a German mechanised transport column at Tomakovka, and personally destroyed eight transports and their troops. The next day, also as a part of a larger formation, the crew bombed the German troops occupying the village of Khortitsa. An artillery spotting post was destroyed, and fifty to sixty enemy soldiers were killed as a result of their pinpoint attack.

On 3 September the precise dive-bombing of his crew into an enemy troop concentration near Nikopol exterminated fifty to sixty German soldiers and destroyed ten motor vehicles. Reconnaissance photographs confirm these results.

Three days later, on 6 September, again flying in formation, his crew bombed an enemy troop concentration in the populated location of Grushovka. Here, they destroyed one cannon, two vehicles and up to thirty German soldiers.

On 15 September 1941, while flying a reconnaissance mission near Nikopol-Stolovo-Krivoi Rog, Reshidov discovered a large enemy troop concentration near the village of Chaplino and Novo-Kamenka. His accurate placement of bombs exterminated twenty to thirty of the German infantry there. His reconnaissance mission was likewise carried out completely satisfactorily.

While on another reconnaissance mission in the area of Fedorovka-Militopol-Akimovka, near Volnovakh and Kuibishevo, on 15 October, Reshidov detected another large concentration of enemy troops. He bombed this column of transports moving towards Militopol, destroying two vehicles carrying soldiers and one transporting ammunition.

On 20 October he was flying a reconnaissance mission in the area Uspenskoe-Budennovka-Mariupol-Osipenko-Vonovakh. While conducting

THE GREAT OFFENSIVE – JUNE 1944

low-level bombing of an enemy troop concentration in Vonovakh, his plane suffered major damage from enemy anti-aircraft artillery, causing one engine to burst into flames. Reschidov managed to fly his burning aircraft 120 kilometres on one operable engine, no mean feat for a Pe-2, landing safely in Soviet territory. Even though the aircraft was subsequently engulfed in flames and burnt out, his crew was unhurt.

He continued to fly reconnaissance missions to locate a reported large enemy troop concentration. On 31 October he found this German force near Matveevka-Kurgan, radioed their position to headquarters and the regiment was despatched to bomb the enemy with little delay.

This mission brought Reschidov's squadron's mission total to over 170 since 20 August, and Reschidov was considered warranting the title of Hero of the Soviet Union for his work from the beginning of military action. Not only did the personnel of his unit urge this, but the whole 21st Division recognised his outstanding merit. According to the order of NKO N 0299, 1941, he was nominated for the third highest governmental award, HSU 'For his demonstrated courage, bravery, iron determination and heroism'.

This citation was approved all the way through to the Front Commander, Lieutenant General Malinovki (later Marshal of the Soviet Union and twice HSU himself). However, the citation was not approved at the top levels, and he was only awarded the Order of Lenin on 23 February 1942. That same day he was also awarded the Order of the Red Banner, which was the result of his nomination for the Order of Lenin. (In fact, so confident of his merit was his unit that he would be awarded the HSU, this citation was actually for his second Order of Lenin.)

This citation reads as follows:

> Since the military actions began on 22 June 1941, Comrade Reschidov has flown sixty-seven combat missions with a total combat flight time 89 hours, 20 minutes. From 20 August 1941 to the present, he has flown ten successful combat missions, their effectiveness confirmed by other aircrew and reconnaissance photographs. In all, he has flown forty-three highly successful combat missions since the beginning of the war, which have all been confirmed by other aircrew, photographs and observers. The Commanding Officer of the Regiment always tasks Comrade Reschidov with the most difficult and important missions, knowing that he will always successfully complete them.
>
> Since 20 August 1941, this squadron has over 150 confirmed combat missions. For his demonstrated courage and bravery in the battles for our Socialist Motherland, he is nominated for his second award of the Order of Lenin.

THE PETLYAKOV Pe-2

On 17 March 1942, while executing combat reconnaissance, Reschidov found a large concentration of enemy troops and automobiles in the locality of Sergeevka. Seizing the opportunity, he bombed the concentration. His attack resulted in the destruction of five automobiles and the complete demolition of a fuel depot. Again, on 19 May, while carrying out an offensive patrol with five aircraft, he bombed the runway at Konstantinovka, and destroyed eighteen enemy aircraft on the ground. While flying in a formation of four aircraft, on 20 May, Reschidov again bombed the runway at Konstantinovka, this time destroying twenty-two enemy aircraft on the ground.

In October 1943 Reschidov was sent to 8th Guards Cherkaskii Bomber Division, and promoted to the position of squadron commander. While there, he was recommended for yet another award – this time his Order of Aleksandr Nevsky, awarded in September 1944. His citation for the Nevsky reads as follows:

> While serving in the position of Squadron Commander during the Patriotic War on the Southern Front, Guards Major Reschidov, A.I., flew eight successful combat missions. While serving in the Patriotic War, Guards Major Reschidov has made a total of 151 successful combat missions, destroying the material and extermination the personnel of the enemy.
>
> Since receiving his last governmental award, he has flown an additional seventy-one combat missions. The precision bombing squadron led by Guards Major Reschidov has flown 186 successful combat missions on the 1st and 2nd Ukrainian Fronts. On four of these missions, his squadron tested a new method of bombing; while in a dive the aircraft circle one another.

This was a reference to the *Carousel* method, of which Reschidov was to become one of the masters.

On 28 October 1943 Reschidov led his new command against German troops, equipment and headquarters in the occupied city of Kirovograd. He led his bombing squadron to completely destroy ten large housing complexes, which had been turned into strong enemy fire-points.

Leading a flight of nine P-2 aircraft in the bombing of artillery and mortar emplacements in the locality of Bratolubovka, on 17 December, Reschidov destroyed three cannon and six large housing complexes, which had also been turned into strong enemy fire points.

By 29 April 1944 he was leading a formation of nine P-2 aircraft on a mission to bomb a concentration of enemy troops and equipment in the area of Bartuluk-Yassi. Bizarrely an estimated forty German Ju.87 dive-bombers, returning from a mission of their own, attacked them, in turn. Dive-bomber against dive-bomber! Despite the enemy's numerical superiority, and better maneuverability, Reshidov's unit successfully completed the bombing mission, and then turned on the German aircraft. Three Ju. 87s were claimed as shot down and the nine Soviet machines all returned unharmed, landing safely at their home airfield, with no losses and no damage.

Reschidov was again in action on 17 July, bombing a concentration of enemy tanks and automobiles in the locality of Plugov. He claimed the destruction of ten enemy tanks on his first bombing run.

On 16 January 1945 Reschidov was deputy flight leader of a group of fifteen aircraft, tasked with destroying the railway station and enemy logistics depot at Skarzisko-Kamenk. Leading six dives at the objective by the Carousel method the group destroyed seven complete railway trains loaded with troops and material, the train depot buildings, the inbound and outbound railway switches and set fire to an ammunition depot.

More action followed. Reschidov was leading a group of Pe-2 aircraft on a mission to exterminate the enemy forces and destroy fortified enemy positions in the city of Ratibor on 30 March. As a result of their precision bombing, sixty buildings were destroyed and seven major fires started. For their outstanding performance, the group received a personal commendation from the commander of 6 Guards Bomber Corps. For forty successful combat missions, all made after receiving his last governmental award, and for his demonstrated courage and bravery, he was nominated for the award Second Order of the Red Banner. The citation included the following:

> For seventy-one successful combat missions flown after receiving his last governmental award, for his demonstrated courage and bravery while carrying out his tasking, Guard Major Reschidov is recommended for the Governmental award, the second Order of the Red Banner.

His unit, 162 Guards BAP, fought on, all the way through to Berlin, seeing action the entire way. For these actions he was awarded his second Red Banner on 15 May 1945, this time as Deputy Commander of 162 Guards Vislenskii, Order of Bogdan Khmelnitski Bomber Regiment. His next citation reads at follows:

> For the exemplary fulfillment of combat tasking on the Front, for 161 successful combat missions, and for his demonstrated bravery and courage in the battles against the German invaders, he was awarded order of the Red banner in February 1942, Order of Lenin in February 1942, and Order of Aleksandr Nevsky in September 1944. Guards Major, Comrade Reschidov, has a very strong will and is an outstanding pilot of the Pe-2 bomber. Since the beginning of the Great Patriotic War, he has completed 191 successful combat missions. Many of these were dive-bombing missions, and thirteen of these missions consisted of precision bombing using the technique Carousel. Since he received his

THE PETLYAKOV Pe-2

last governmental awards, he has flown an additional forty successful combat missions, thirty-four of them in the Oppelskii Operation; and flying against enemy formations from Breslau to Berlin.

As squadron leader, he has perfected the coordination of the crews in his formations and support between the bombers and fighter escort. He has attained the most effective results in his missions and has received numerous commendations from superior commanders.

For his service in the war, he was finally awarded the title of Hero of the Soviet Union on 26 June 1945.

For the exemplary execution of combat duties on the front in the fight against German invaders, for 151 successful combat missions and for his demonstrated valour, bravery and courage he has been awarded with Order of Lenin, February 1941, order of Red Banner, February 1942, and Order of Alexander Nevsky, September 1944.

Guards Major Reshidov has a strong will and has mastered flying the dive-bombing aircraft Pe-2. From the beginning of the Great Patriotic War, he has made 166 successful bombing runs, 79 of them were executed as dive-bombing. Eleven times, he successfully completed missions using the new method Carousel. In this method, he would be above the object for 20-25 minutes, bombing small objectives during five to six bombing runs. He would then conduct one to two attacks at treetop level, finishing his mission destroying material and annihilating enemy troops with the fire of his machine guns. In numerous air-to-air combat engagements, he shot down eight enemy aircraft. For his courage, bravery and determination demonstrated in the fight against German invaders, he has numerous letters of gratitude from the commanders of fronts, commanders of armies and from the Supreme Commander, Comrade Stalin.

He has been awarded with the photo certificate 'To a Participant of The Great Patriotic War'. Guards Major Reshidov served with great valour, achieving numerous heroic deeds during his time in combat.

For successful combat missions, destroying the troops and materiel of the enemy, for courage, bravery and heroism demonstrated while executing combat tasks, he deserves to be awarded with the highest-governmental award, the title of HSU.

THE GREAT OFFENSIVE – JUNE 1944

> After the war ended, Reshidov, like so many brave wartime pilots, was transferred into the Reserves. He later went through the Admin and Tactical course 1949. He became a lieutenant colonel in 1954 and finally retired from the service in 1958 as a colonel. His working life was not over yet, however, and he subsequently served as Head of the Economic Section of Regional Statistical Administration of the Krimskaya Oblast until his final retirement from that in 1979. Colonel Reshidov died on 24 October 1984, in Simferpol, Ukraine, one of the great Pe-2 commanders.

Further actions

The remorseless drive westward by the Soviet juggernaut continued into the New Year, with the *Peshka* leading the way. In February 1944 a force of nine Pe-2s destroyed a bridge over the river Dnieper, near Rogachev, thus trapping the German forces in their bridgehead there. Pinned down and unable to withdraw, this enemy force was then destroyed by Soviet ground forces.

At the start of the Korsun'-Shevchenkov battle, 202 BAD attacked German forward air bases in Uman and Khristianovka. Meanwhile, in operations over the Black Sea the German AA cruiser *Niobe* was claimed sunk by the Navy VVS *Peshkas*.[6]

In March 1944 the *Peshkas* of 36 BAP were employed in precision dive-bombing attacks on crossings over the river Dniester. During operations in the Carpathian Mountains, dive-bombing proved particularly effective against the enemy holding the passes. Bridge-busting continued when the only exit from the Belorussian pocket, a bridge across the river Berezina, was destroyed by Pe-2 attack.

In May 1944 one Pe-2 crew of the Northern Fleet's 118th Reconnaissance Air Regiment (118 RAP), led by Captain R. Suvorov, was awarded HSU for over 300 recce sorties. They had located and reported the presence of over 800 vessels in port or on the open sea. During these operations they were credited with the destruction of three trains, thirteen tanks, seventy-five vehicles and shooting down four enemy aircraft.

On 30 June 1944 forty-four Pe-2s attacked an enemy airfield close to Borisovo and used their AG-2 grenades to destroy five Fw.190As there.

By the end of 1944, however, only about thirty-forty Pe-3s remained in service, flying almost exclusively with the reconnaissance aviation regiments. They were supplemented by other types in all active units. Since spring 1942 they had almost all been withdrawn from service with the PVO; 95 IAP of the Northern Fleet continued operating the type until the end of the war, notwithstanding this trend.

On 22 October 1944 a pair of Pe-3s, led by Captain Antonets, intercepted and destroyed two Ju.52/3m transport aircraft carrying German generals to Petsamo airfield.

THE PETLYAKOV Pe-2

Scene at the forward airfield of the 118 AP Sergeant Major (Mechanic) A N Ivanov (right) reports the serviceability of pilot Lieutenant Samarin's aircraft. (H Valtonen via Keski-Suomen Ilmailumuseo, Tikkakoski)

Chapter Fourteen

On to Berlin!

For the preliminary advance to the Vistula river, which commenced on 14 January 1945, Second and Sixteenth Air Armies could deploy a total of 4,770 aircraft of all types to support the First Front. The Pe-2 dive-bombers were in continuous on-call demand from the thrusting Soviet tank columns for the next few days and flew several combat sorties a day. On one occasion, a Soviet tank column had advanced beyond its support and became immobilised due to lack of fuel. A hasty 'Front-line Demand' call to 241 BAD led to an unusual mission for 779 BAR of that force, a re-supply run deep behind enemy lines. Mainly the *Peshka* targets were their favourites, 'sniper' objectives calling for 'thin-cutting' by the Pe-2s, strongpoints, fortresses, bridges, tanks, gun emplacements and mortar batteries.

Each German city was turned into a fortress in a futile attempt to hold back the Red Tide now sweeping over the Fatherland. In an attack on one such heavily-fortified area in front of the city of Breslau, Major General Ivan Semyonovich Polbin, that incomparable Pe-2 operator, met his premature death on his fortieth birthday, 11 February 1945 (see panel on page 215).

German attempts to use the frozen Vistula river as an avenue of escape were thwarted when the Pe-2s ice-bombed it for a distance of some twenty kilometres (12 miles) around Wyszogrod. By the end of February the Soviet armies were firmly entrenched along the eastern bank of the Oder river and were establishing bridgeheads in readiness for the final offensive to the west. In two days of intensive bombing on 5 and 6 March, Pe-2 dive-bombers of 24 Red Banner 'Orlov' BAR flew relays of bombing missions against the powerful German fortress at Küstrin (Kostrzyn). This they repeated when the final assault was made on this strongpoint during the crossing of the Oder and so successful were its dive-bombing attacks that the whole unit was awarded the Order of Suvrov (III).

A necessary precursor to the final offensive to capture the city of Berlin, heart of German resistance, was the exclusion of the powerful German forces occupying the fortified naval ports and harbours along the Baltic coast. The push to destroy the German armies in East Prussia, involving as it did the actual taking of German soil, was thought likely to prove costly and the maximum air support was to be offered the spearheading Soviet armies. The main German force was Army Group Centre, which was expected to offer fierce resistance. The Soviet forces allocated to this task were those of the Second and Third Belorussian Fronts and both Air Force and Red Banner Baltic Fleet aircraft were to be fully employed.

THE PETLYAKOV Pe-2

Sub-Lieutenant Alil Davel S Shein, of 118 BAP, with his Pe-2 marked '22' at Wajeaba-1 airfield. (Hannu Voltonen)

North Prussian Operations

The air groups involved were First Air Army, supporting Third Belorussian Front under General I.T. Chernyshev, and Fourth Air Army supporting Second Belorussian Front under General K.A. Vershinin. The two air armies had a combined total strength in excess of 3,000 aircraft, and had additional support from Third Air Army, First Baltic Front and Eighteenth Air Army, all co-ordinated by Marshal of Aviation F.Ya. Falaleyev. Against this great mass the defending Germans could only field some 775 aircraft.[1]

Part of the preparations for the attack consisted of an elaborate feint on the left wing of the Third Belorussian Front during the first ten days of January 1945. First Air Army co-operated in this ruse which saw the construction of dummy airfields and aircraft in the sector opposite Suwalki, and three bomber divisions conducted simulated air missions in the area to maintain the illusion of an attack being prepared in this sector. Meanwhile, the massive preparations for the real offensive were concealed from the enemy gaze by elaborate camouflage measures.

The actual attack commenced on 13 January on the Third Belorussian Front, and was extended the following day on Second Belorussian Front, and in each case was preceded by night sorties by First Air Army. A German counter-offensive against Fifth Army on 14 January was met by a further heavy air commitment, which held them. On 15 January the attacks were resumed along the line supported by 1,320 aircraft from First and Third Air Armies, which led to advances up to ten kilometres into the Germans' main defences. On 16 January two massive air strikes

ON TO BERLIN!

A trio of veteran Pe-2 pilots, with medals and ribbons testifying to their war service, pose in helmets and flying uniform in front of their mounts. (Russian Aviation Research Trust)

were made by 342 aircraft against the German second line of defence, which was followed up by a 248-plane strike a few hours later against the third line of defence. Some 2,800 combat sorties were flown by the two air armies on 16 January, which deployed five Pe-2-equipped BADs as part of their striking power. In a similar manner Fourth Air Army supported the advance on Second Belorussian Front between 15 and 17 January.

By the end of the month, a German garrison was surrounded and isolated at Torun and under heavy attack. A determined attempt at a breakout was made on 31 January and some 5,000 German troops tried to punch through encircling Soviet units. On 3 February Sixth Guards Bomber Air Division made a concentrated strike with a force of sixty-five Pe-2s on the enemy strongpoint of Preussisch Eylau, dropping over fifty-five tons of FAB-500 and FAB-250 bombs on the enemy defences. This same unit also conducted strikes at German airfields around the city.

Further prolonged and concentrated air strikes were made all day which caused heavy casualties to this force and halted them in their tracks, they were then finished off by further bombing sorties. Similar *Peshka* attacks were made against the fortifications of Heilsberg and, by 9 February Konigsberg, capital of East Prussia, had been invested on three sides and part of the Samland peninsula had been occupied, splitting the German defences into three isolated pockets. Fourth Air Army had flown 8,130 combat sorties and First Air Army had clocked up 9,740 combat sorties.[2]

THE PETLYAKOV Pe-2

Meanwhile, Warsaw had been liberated following the advance of the First Belorussian Front from 14 January. Two days later the weather cleared and repeated Pe-2 missions were flown. Colonel F.M. Fedorenko led 301 BAD in attacks by two Pe-2 groups that hit the marshalling yards at Lodz-Vostochnaya, which resulted in the destruction of fifty-four railway wagons, two mobile flak wagons and two locomotives. All vital rail movements through that supply bottleneck were halted. The Pe-2s also heavily hit the German 25th Panzer Division assembling for a counter-blow.

The second stage of the Soviet assault, the mopping-up of the German pockets of resistance, was launched on 10 February. Because of the intensity of the fighting, and the support of German naval forces in the Baltic, the air attacks were to be combined ones with the Baltic Fleet Pe-2s working in close harmony with the VVS units. In order to co-ordinate these attacks, which would see an intense concentration of air attacks in a relatively confined air space, the Soviet Air Force Commander, Chief Marshal of Aviation A.A. Novikov, with a special operations group, flew from Moscow to the HQ of Third Belorussian Front to oversee and direct the air side of the battle, two air armies, First and Third.

During the second half of March the Pe-2s of both air armies, operating in difficult conditions of fog and drizzle, gave support to the Soviet Samland Group which defeated the remaining enemy concentrations at Heilsberg and then prepared for the final assault on Konigsberg itself. For this First and Third Air Armies were joined by Eighteenth Air Army, two BACs (V Bomber, commanded by General M.Kh. Borisenko, and V Guards, commanded by General V.A. Ushakov) as well as the Pe-2s of the Baltic Fleet, commanded by General M.I. Samokhin. Together these forces totalled some 2,444 combat aircraft, of which 432 were Pe-2s.[3] The *Peshkas* of the Red Banner Fleet were especially tasked to take out any attempts at evacuation by German warships and transports, and prevent a 'German Dunkirk'.

The 130,000 German defenders of Konigsberg had strong defences, with four defence zones, 100 tanks and assault guns and 4,000 artillery pieces and mortars. There were about 170 combat aircraft based on the airfields of Gross Dirschkeim, Gross Hubnicken and Neutief and fifty-six anti-aircraft batteries. Against these defences, the VVS operated a detailed plan of air strikes according to a plan drawn up by First Air Army staff under Colonel N.P. Zhil'tsov. The attack was scheduled for 1 April and was preceded by two days of intense air strikes against the forts, pillboxes and strongpoints of the German defence lines as well as the elimination of the German air force. Some 5,316 combat sorties were flown and 2,620 tons of bombs dropped in that two-day period. The first day's mission saw the commitment of a first strike, which included 406 Pe-2s, and Tu-2s, mainly the former, as well as 133 Yak-9 fighter-bombers. This was followed by a similarly composed second strike a few hours later.

To cram such numbers into such limited air space, each air division was assigned its own air corridor and altitude to approach and leave the target zone. Intense photo-reconnaissance provided their HQs with detailed layouts of the city and fortifications in advance. Forward air controllers were employed on an unprecedented scale to facilitate close liaison with the attacking troops. In all, it was a large-scale rehearsal of the final air battle for Berlin itself. So much importance was attached to the air support for this battle that murky conditions led to the postponement of the attack until 6 April. Even this day proved far from satisfactory and only about a quarter of the planned 4,000 combat sorties were actually flown.

On 7 April the weather improved dramatically, and the full weight of the Soviet air fleet was deployed. Some 246 Pe-2s and Tu-2s made three massive and concentrated strikes against the main centres of German resistance to the west of the city and, by dusk, Soviet troops had broken through all the defence lines and were fighting on the outskirts of the city itself. A massed air assault by Eighteenth Air Army's heavy bombers was sent against the city itself, but was preceded by yet a further dive-bomber assault mounted by 118 Il-2 ground-attack and Pe-2 dive-bombers on the enemy airfields. Once the heavy bombers had struck, the Pe-2s and Tu-2s resumed their work with renewed intensity; the VVS flew more combat missions than they had ever done before that day, 5,000 sorties being recorded.[4]

The following two days saw similar Pe-2 missions repeated. Two mass strikes by a total of 2,000 aircraft were made on German positions west of the city on 8 April and the following day a final assault was made which resulted in the final fall of the fortress. Meanwhile Pe-2 strikes had been made on the main German naval base of Pillau and against the hordes of evacuation ships at sea, resulting in severe losses among troops and civilians embarked.

During the first four months of 1945 the Soviets had occupied large areas of East Prussia, Poland, Eastern Pomerania and Silesia and were massed along the rivers Oder and Neisse. The last act was imminent.

Peshka Men – Major General Ivan Semyonovich Polbin

Dive-bombing was one of the last aeronautical skills where the man was as important as any machine or electronic aid. Although much work had been done in the late 1930s, and on into the 1940s, in such diverse countries as Germany, the United States, Great Britain and Sweden, to design, build and perfect the perfect dive-bombing sighting device,[5] and although such instruments were completed, tested and found to be useful, in the end they did not find favour with those who flew the dive-bombers. To the end, the reliance was mainly on the pilot's own judgement and skill. Thus, it was that some men excelled at the art and stood out, even from the elite

Major General Ivan Polbin. (Soviet Official)

who surrounded them. The West termed them 'aces', the Russians 'snipers', so precise was their work.

One such outstanding dive-bomber was Twice a Hero of the Soviet Union Major General Ivan Polbin. He was to Soviet dive-bombers as Hans-Ulrich Rudel was to the German Stukas,[6] or Takashige Egusa was to the Japanese *Val*,[7] so outstanding as to be unique.

Ivan Semyonovich Polbin was born on 27 January (or 14 January under the old calendar) 1905 in Czarish prison in the Simbirsk region, his mother being incarcerated there as a revolutionist.[8] The small hamlet of Rtishchevo-Kamenka, Simbirsk Region, was his home town. He was Russian peasant by birth, growing up amidst the turmoil of the First World War and Russia's defeat, and the whirlwind of the Bolshevik revolutions, deposing and murder of the Czar and his family, and power struggles between Stalin and Trotsky after the death of Lenin in 1924.

He went to primary school and left to work on the land as a hired farm-worker. Later, he found more regular employment on the railways. All through this time he had dreamed of flying and aviation; it was his obsession. Therefore, it was no great surprise that, at the age of twenty-two, Ivan should take two steps to secure such a future. In 1927 he joined the Communist Party as a full-time member (essential if one was to gain admittance to the circle in which training was permitted) and joined the Red Army, but always with aviation, rather than a military, future in his mind. His ambition was thwarted because his lack of education, coupled with poor health, made him unfit for flying in the eyes of the Army.

Two years of determined effort (1927-28) were rewarded when, at his second attempt, Ivan entered the Vol'sk Amalgamated Aviation School for pilots and mechanics. This was one of the new colleges established at Orenburg, west of the Urals, for basic training and instruction for the GU-VVSRKKA (Military Air Forces of the Workers' and Peasants' Red Army).[9] To help spread the importance of aeronautics in the new Soviet republics, Pyotr Baranov formed the ODVF (Society of Friends of the Air Fleet). It had its own magazine, which was sent free to its 1.5 million members and Ivan Polbin, who was one of them, read each issue avidly from cover to cover.

In 1929 Polbin was sent to the Orenburg Military School for Pilots and graduated from there in 1931/32. He had done so well that he was one of the few graduates retained by the school as an instructor and, over the next five years, applied himself diligently to his chosen profession.

In 1933 Ivan was one of the instructors chosen to train and then command one of the new TB-3 four-engined long-range bombers. He continued to shine, rising to the command of his own *Eskadrilya* (squadron) at the age of thirty-two. By 1936 Polbin was serving as commander of a TBA *Otryad*, a force of ten aircraft. The *Otryad* became a BAE in 1938.

ON TO BERLIN!

Ivan had reached the rank of lieutenant colonel and commanded 150 SAP in the Far East when the first of several clashes with the Japanese occurred and gave Ivan his first taste of real combat.

The so-called Lake Khasan incident took place on 9 July 1938 and spasmodic fighting, including air operations, continued until 11 August when Japanese troops withdrew from the contested area. From 6 August Ivan Polbin's unit was in action almost constantly, supporting Soviet ground forces in this undeclared war.

The uneasy truce did not last long, and, commencing on 11 May 1939, a second, more serious, outbreak of fighting erupted between the two nations along the Halhin (Khalkhin) Gol river, on the border between Soviet Mongolia and Japanese-dominated Manchukuou (Manchuria). At this date Ivan was in command of 150th Air Regiment, which was equipped with the standard light bomber of the day, the Arkhangel'sky-designed Tupolev *Skorostnoi Bombardirovshchik*, SB (high-speed bomber), and which was one of three regiments under overall command of General Aleksandr I. Gunsev.

Under the overall command of General Ya.V. Smushkevic, who had recent live combat experience in Spain, the Soviets threw in some 600 aircraft against some 500 Japanese machines. The fighting intensified from 20 May and Polbin flew his first mission six days later, with his SBs attacking in formations sixty strong with an escort of I-15*bis*, I-153, and Polikarpov I-16 fighters. The air fighting was as fierce as the ground fighting and losses were severe on both sides. Here it was that the Soviets learnt (as the British were to learn soon after, with the massacre of their Fairey Battles and Bristol Blenheims of the same type – indeed all the other nations were to learn one by one) that the 'high-speed' concept, by which light bombers could penetrate enemy air space with comparative immunity, was but a fleeting ideal. Already the concept had been rendered null and void by the fact that the Japanese had, in the Type-97 (Ki-27) *Nate* fighter, an aircraft that could outpace, and therefore catch and destroy, the SBs.

To avoid unacceptable losses, therefore, Polbin adopted a high-altitude approach to the target, leading his bombers in at more than 6,000 metres, at which altitude the Ki-27 was less effective. Losses continued but less severely; of course, bombing accuracy rapidly fell away. On 20 August Polbin took part in a mass attack by more than 200 Soviet bombers in conjunction with General G.K. Zhukov's ground offensive. Such numbers swamped the Japanese defences and, from then on, the Soviet airmen enjoyed increasing ascendancy until the end of the fighting on 16 September. He was decorated with the Order of Lenin for his work at this time.

One thing these incidents did crystallise was the main future thrust of Soviet air power in that, after the failure of the high-speed, unescorted penetration mission, they concentrated wholeheartedly on the rôle of supporting the ground forces. Indeed the 1939 field edition of the *Raboche-Krest' yanskaya*

Krasnaya Armiya, RKKA (Workers' and Peasants' Red Army Field Manual), stated, unequivocally, that 'Aviation is linked, strategically and tactically, to the ground forces.'[10] From that attitude, the Soviet Air Forces were hardly to budge until the late 1940s. It also, as we have seen, gave impetus to the development of the dive-bomber.

Ivan Polbin had also learnt, at command level, at the sharp end, just what modern air fighting was like and he took those lessons to heart. When the German invasion took place in June 1941, Ivan, now a lieutenant colonel, (*Podpolkovnik*) and still in command of 150th Bomber Aviation Regiment in the Far East, survived the initial overwhelming massacres of the early days and, when his unit moved west in July to join the fray, it was as one of the few intact units equipped with modern aircraft, and *still* with combat expertise.

Early lessons had seen the quick abandonment of the standard sixty-plane formation used against the Japanese in 1939 and against the Germans in the summer of 1941, as being too costly. Instead, the *Stavka* re-organised the air regiments into more handy units of thirty-two aircraft each, with two such regiments to each air division. The lack of large numbers of *Peshkas* contributed to this decision, for there were still only a handful at the front.

Polbin first saw action against the Germans during the hard fighting at the Smolensk-Yartsevo pocket at the end of July where his regiment was part of a force of 370 bombers and 150 fighters assembled and thrown in regardless of loss to try to save the situation. In the event, they failed but Polbin's Pe-2s were among the few Soviet bombers capable of not only evading the defending Bf.109s, which they could outpace, but also of delivering bombing runs accurate enough to hit such small targets as Panzer columns and motorised infantry units moving up to envelop the trapped Russian armies. Polbin and his men flew an average of three to four sorties per day in this period. His unit was later in action at Velikie Luki and Rzhev.

One of the downsides to the otherwise superlative *Peshka* was its nasty tendency to spin to the right at the slightest relaxation on the part of the pilot. It was a real killer in this respect, particularly so among the many novices joining the bomber groups. So common was this occurrence that the Air Force issued special instructions to Pe-2 units, warning of this. Strict instructions were given to all pilots not to roll the aircraft as this led to the dreaded spin.

Polbin, however, determined to test the *Peshka* to the limit and conducted his own trials. It is a measure of the man that, when one of his junior pilots was due to be disciplined for disobeying this order, he had the man brought before him. Instead of tearing him to pieces, Ivan asked him a series of questions as to why, how and what had motivated this move and what had been the Pe-2's reactions as he had obviously survived. In essence, his junior had been following Polbin's example and putting his own life on the line to try and find cause and solution to the problem. He had deliberately sat down and worked out his own test programme and then carried it out. Far from censuring him, therefore, Polbin immediately took to the air and put his own *Peshka*

ON TO BERLIN!

through the same manoueuvres, ending up with a succession of continuous rolls, and landed safely. He put the results of both sets of tests into practice as, in successive months, he steadily perfected a new series of tactics to get the optimum performance out of the Pe-2. The results of this are recorded in these pages. Like most innovators, Polbin had a happy knack of knowing just when to break or bend rules to achieve results.

In the continuing action against the German spearheads of 3rd Panzer and 10th Motorised Divisions from 29 to 31 August, Polbin's Pe-2s of the 150th were instrumental in halting them for a crucial period. Again flying up to four missions a day, they destroyed more than 100 German tanks, 800 soft-skinned vehicles and twenty armoured vehicles for the loss of forty-two dive bombers. By September, Ivan had conducted 107 combat missions.

The 150th continued to feature in the defensive battles of October to December when the final German push on Moscow was halted, and Polbin was assigned to staff duties and theoretical studies of how to best use the Pe-2.

Given command of a BAD to put his ideas into practice in the field, Ivan was again in the forefront of activity during the winter counter-offensive that commenced on 5 December on the Kalinin Front. Following the Novikov study of tactics and other experimental work during spring 1942, Polbin's methods were crystalised in the *Vertushka* (Dipping Wheel or Carousel) plan of attack and the formation of Special Group No. 1.

Polbin was again involved in the bitter fighting at Verkhne-Businovki pocket in the late summer of 1942. In four days of continuous action, Polbin's Pe-2s claimed the destruction of forty tanks and fifty soft-skinned vehicles. A particular coup for his Pe-2s was an accurate attack on the main Panzer fuel supply dump at Morozovsk Farm, a very heavily defended target, which was nonetheless hit and destroyed in two deliberate *Peshka* dive-bombing attacks. This considerably slowed the German advance.

When the Kalach bridge over the river Don was captured by the Germans on 16 August, massed attacks by SBs and other light bombers failed conspicuously with heavy losses. In desperation Polbin's Pe-2s were sent in against 'the most formidable' German flak defences on the Eastern Front. They gallantly pressed home their attacks but failed to smash the bridge, and the German armies moved on towards Stalingrad and the Volga river. Polbin had meanwhile been appointed to the command of a new *Peshka* unit, 301st Bomber Aviation Division, part of Eighth Air Army and they flew 4,000 combat missions in the period 27 September-8 October on this front. During the Soviet counter-attack, which led to the encirclement and eventual total defeat of General Paulus's Sixth Army in the Stalingrad pocket from 19 November, Polbin again led from the front, as he always had.

His outstanding achievements were duly recognised. On 23 November 1942 he was made 'Hero of the Soviet Union' and added this accolade to a whole raft of awards and decorations, which included the Order of Lenin (twice); the Order of the Red Banner (twice), the Order of *Bogdan Khmel'niskii* and the

THE PETLYAKOV Pe-2

Order of the Patriotic War, First Class. None of these decorations seemed to impinge on his ego or his common sense and he continued to apply himself to perfecting dive-bomber tactics. Nor did he stop flying combat missions himself.

In March 1943 Ivan was appointed commander of 1 BAK (which from 5 February 1944, became 2 GBAK, and was re-designated as 6 GBAK on 26 December the same year). For the next great battle, which was to be the final German offensive against the Kursk salient in the summer of 1943, Polbin was promoted to Major General (of Guards) and placed in command of I Guards Bomber Air Corps, part of General S.A. Krasovski's Second Air Army on the Voronezh Front. When the Soviet counter-attack went in on 5 July, Polbin's Pe-2s spearheaded the land assault by sustained attacks on German tank concentrations and artillery positions in the way of Fifth Guards Tank Army. Polbin's divebombers blasted German defences on the steppe front at the end of August.

He was again promoted, on 20 October 1943, to Major General of Aviation and, at this time was involved in one of the strangest conflicts of his career in October, when, leading seventeen Pe-2s from a dive-bombing mission over the front line, he stumbled by chance on a force of eighteen German Ju. 87 Stukas about to commence their own dive attacks on Soviet troops below. He unhesitatingly led his Pe-2s to attack the Stukas to break up their attack, and they, knowing the *Peshka* had twice their speed, duly jettisoned their bombs and tried to escape back to their base at Berezovka. Polbin continued in pursuit, claiming to have shot down several of the Ju.87s en route. On reaching the German airfield, yet more Stukas were seen taking off and these tangled with the Pe-2s in a whirling dogfight of dive-bombers. In the ensuing meleé Polbin was personally credited with the destruction of two of the sixteen Stukas claimed shot down, for the loss of just one Pe-2.

Polbin's innovations continued to bear fruit. It was he who originated the 'Sniper' concept by which certain key targets, bridges, rail lines and ammunition columns, which needed exactness and precision, were hit, causing the enemy damage out of all proportion to the effort expended, whereas highaltitude level bombers rained down masses of bombs to no good effect. By 5 February 1944, special élite 'shock' units, like Polbin's I Bomber Air Corps, were given special status by the re-designation with 'Guards' title, and became II Guards Bomber Aviation Corps, one of only four Pe-2 outfits so honoured.

With more than 100 front-line combat dive-bomber missions under his belt, Ivan Polbin's thirst for action seemed unquenched. Not for him a liaison job back on the ground at HQ, he continued to fly the Pe-2 into the hottest action spots and, by the end of 1944, had clocked up 150 missions. He took part in the great June offensive, one notable attack on 14 July catching 8th Panzer on the move and causing what their commander, General von Mellenthin, described as 'devastating losses. Long columns of tanks and lorries went up in flames, and all hope of counter-attack disappeared.' The next day Polbin was heavily involved in the mass dive-bombing attacks at the vital Zalozhtse crossing, as related.

ON TO BERLIN!

Polbin's II Guards Bomber Air Corps continued to lead the way as the German army was rolled up, suffering the greatest defeat in its entire history. On 16 July he attacked troops at Sasov, Koltow and Bely Kamen, culminating in the surrender of the German forces in the Koltow Corridor.

On 20 August Polbin, received yet another honour, the Order of *Bogdan Khmelnitsky*, First Class, in recognition of his work in this offensive. By the end of that year, his regiment had carried out 4,661 combat sorties.

The westward advance continued in the early months of 1945 and in the assaults on the Oder river line Polbin, celebrating his fortieth birthday on 14 January, was again there leading his beloved *Peshkas* into attack after attack. On 17 January the towns of Przedborz and Radomsko were taken, the river Warta forced and the town of Czestochowa taken and Polbin distinguished himself in action. The Pe-2s again led the way as the Soviet army penetrated into Germany itself, on the 21st of the month. Polbin was mentioned in despatches during operations that resulted in the fall of Gleiwitz, Silesia, and was prominent in the taking of Beuthen. On 11 February he led dive-bombing attacks that opened the way for the investment of Breslau. There the German garrison made a firm stand and repeated air strikes were ordered to break their resistance. By the beginning of February Polbin had conducted 157 combat sorties but showed no wish to stop leading.

Thus it was that, on 11 February 1945, Ivan Polbin took off in his Pe-2 to carry out his 175th combat mission of the war, leading a force of nine dive-bombers. His targets were German artillery positions defending the city. As always Polbin's was the first dive-bomber off the stack, making a steep, 70-degree approach against a dug-in artillery position, which was holding up the Soviet advance. These guns had heavy flak defences and, as Polbin roared down, the very experienced Luftwaffe gunners caught his aircraft squarely in their sights. A veritable storm of exploding shells encompassed Polbin's aircraft and it never recovered from its final terminal dive, which ended atop a German AA gunsite, probably guided by Polbin. The *Peshka* itself hit the ground at full speed and burst into flames. Neither the Soviet aircrew nor the German gunners stood an earthly.

Therefore, the life of the Soviet Union's premier Pe-2 pilot came to an abrupt end in a blazing trail of destruction. Polbin had loved the *Peshka*, as he had loved flying. He had refused to shirk his duty, even when he could, quite honourably, have found a safer berth in a rear echelon. However, that was never his way, and his death may well have been as he would have wished it.

He was deeply missed at the Victory Celebrations a few weeks later following the fall of Berlin, a victory to which he had made a unique and very special personal contribution. His memory was honoured then by the award for a second time, posthumously, of Hero of the Soviet Union on 6 April 1945. He was described later as 'a talented leader, innovator and fearless pilot' and, for once, the communist superlatives were fully deserved. His name is still revered in the Russia of today, his old pilots' school at Orenburg being today known as 'The Polbin School' in memory of their greatest pupil.

THE PETLYAKOV Pe-2

The fall of Berlin

During April and May the final assault on Berlin took place and this culmination of the Great Patriotic War saw some 743 Pe-2 and Tu-2 bombers employed. Again the VVS co-ordinated the attack, leaving the Third Belorussian Front to plan the new offensive along the same lines on 9 April.

At the commencement of the battle, Sixteenth Air Army alone, the strongest in the VVS, contained 3,033 serviceable aircraft, including 533 Pe-2 and Tu-2 dive-bombers. Concentrated into this grouping were 113 and 138 BADs under the command of Colonel M.S. Finogenov and Colonel A.I. Pushkin HSU. There was also Second Air Army and Fourth Air Army. The attack was to be made along the whole line from Stettin to Penzig by the troops of First and Second Belorussian and First Ukrainian Fronts. As at Konigsberg, but on a larger scale, air formations from all three fronts had to be fed into the combat zone en masse, and each had to have its own zone of operations. This meant that 290 extra airfields had to be constructed hastily and associated dumps for fuel, ordnance and ammunition created to operate so many aircraft in such a concentrated area. A density of 170 aircraft per kilometre was envisaged for the crucial attack fronts of Fifth Shock and Eighth Guards Armies of First Belorussian front.[11]

By 7 April 1945 one Pe-2 of 72 ORAP had been modified to carry a fourth crewman to operate four additional cameras. Piloted by V.A.Temin, these photographs received worldwide coverage.

At dawn on 16 April the onslaught commenced and Sixteenth Air Army had to modify its operational plans due to low morning fog. The Pe-2 dive-bombers had to wait until after 0800 before they could commence their precision strikes, and the main bulk of the attacks did not take place until the afternoon.

On 18 April Pe-2 dive-bombers were sent in waves against German reserve forces attempting to move up from the area of Bidsdorf and Muencheberg. Attacking from

Good air-to-air view of *Peshkas* flying straight and level in typically loose formation on their return home from a combat mission in 1944. (Hannu Valtonen)

ON TO BERLIN!

the north-east Sixty-fifth Army crossed the Oder with strong dive-bomber support. Once the misty weather conditions improved, the Pe-2s were able to maximise their anti-tank tactics. The Fourth Air Army commander sent the following telegram to 5 BAK:

> Inform your flying crews that their bombing raid silenced the enemy artillery. Everything was afire in the target areas. Our ground units left cover and advanced rapidly.[12]

The fate of a large concentration of German forces discovered in the forested area of Birkholz, Buchholz, Halbe, Taupitz and Wendisch was salutary. This force was attempting to link up with the German Twelfth Army pushing in from the west in an attempt to break the ring around the capital. They achieved local superiority and broke through the Soviet cordon at Baruth. To retrieve the situation the aircraft of Second Air Army were called in on 26 April. The strikes were led by General P.P. Arkhangelsky's 4 BAK, spearheaded by a seventy-strong Pe-2 force. They claimed the outright destruction of eight tanks and fifty soft-skinned vehicles in the raid alone. Meanwhile *Peshkas* of 6 Guards BAK carried out dive-bombing assaults on the Dahm river crossings, which further disrupted the enemy's movements.

From 26 April the final assault on the remnants of the German Ninth Army's six divisions defending Berlin commenced. A 'control zone' was established over the city into which all attacking aircraft were routed via strict 'gates' and altitudes to the ever-changing, and pinpoint, targets. Each combat leader checked in via radio with the controller who assigned an entry route, re-directed them to a reserve target, or put them into a holding circuit pending a suitable target. The eastern gate was entered over the Grosser Müggelsee, while the northern gate was over the Shönwalde Wessensee with exits at various points around the city perimeter. This avoided many complications, but it did lead to predictability of the attack routes and Berlin's AA defences shot down some 527 aircraft of all types, including many Pe-2s, as a result.

General P.P. Arkhangelsky's 4 BAC led the assault that day, claiming the destruction of eight tanks and fifty motorised vehicles in the process. Some 200 sorties were flown while 6 Guards BAC dive-bombed crossings on the river Dahm, sealing off the area from attempts by the Germans to break the ring of steel around their capital.

On 27 April a hastily prepared military evacuation landing-strip near the Tiergarten was subject to one such precision attack by Pe-2s, and was rendered unusable. Many high-ranking officers were trapped in the shrinking defended area of the gutted city as Soviet troops pressed in street by street and house by house. On 30 April precision dive-bombing attacks continued, with *Peshkas* attacking the Gestapo HQ in Berlin.

The final Pe-2 combat mission in Europe took place on 7 May 1945, and was an attack on Sirau airfield from which German aircraft were seeking to escape to Sweden. With that strike, the *Peshka* completed its main task and had vindicated both the designer and dive-bombing itself.

THE PETLYAKOV Pe-2

A Pe-2 aircrew pose in full dress uniform by their aircraft after the award of medals at Insterburg, Germany, (re-named Chernyakkhovsk by the Soviets) April 1945. The marking on the aircraft's fuselage reads 'Taganrog Pioneer' showing that she was sponsored by the Communist Children's Communist Organisation of the USSR. (M Maslov)

Chapter Fifteen

Action in the Far East

Japan had made no moves whatsoever against the Soviet Union all through the bitter war period of June 1941 to May 1945. This had enabled the Russians to concentrate their entire effort against Germany, while railing at the Allies, who did all the fighting in the Mediterranean, Pacific and Asia, for not helping them more in Europe. But if the Japanese rulers had thought that this restraint would save them from Stalin's greed they were mistaken. Just as soon as the war in Europe had terminated to his satisfaction, he instructed the mass movement of troops and aircraft to the east, anxious to grab his share of the spoils as the Anglo-American task forces closed in on homeland Japan.

Operation AUGUST STORM

At midnight on 8 August, 1.5 million Soviet troops, with 5,000 armoured vehicles and supported by 4,000 aircraft launched a massive attack against the million-strong Japanese Kwantung Army based in Manchuria, which had only 1,215 armoured vehicles and 1,800 aircraft. There had been no activity on this front at all during the four years that Japan's ally Germany had been engaged with Stalin's hordes, and, thanks to that fact, the Russians had been able to ship the best divisions west without any risk to their eastern flank. Stalin was not the man to feel at all indebted by such facts and, with the war in the west won, was eager to grab as much as he could of the Japanese empire in the east before the Americans brought the war to a swift termination in the Pacific. The dropping of the Atomic bombs stirred the Soviets to frantic activity and war was declared as soon as an overwhelming force was in place. Some thirty divisions and nine brigades moved to the Far East from Europe, including the crack Fifth, Thirty-ninth and Fifty-third Armies and Sixth Guards Tank Army. Their air preparations were just as massive. From Europe were sent VI Bomber Air Corps under General I.P. Skok with 326 and 334 BADs and VII Bomber Air Corps under General V.A. Ushakov with 113 and 179 BADs as well as fighter and transport air divisions.

The smooth flow of these air reinforcements across such vast distances so quickly was eased by the careful planning which took place from 24 June onward. Specially selected officers from the VVS staff and directorates were lent

THE PETLYAKOV Pe-2

The dorsal 12.7mm machine-gun, with clip-fed ammunition belt, mounted atop the aft fuselage of the Pe-2B, which was the standard *Peshka* variant in 1944. (Russian Aviation Research Trust)

to these units and monitored the entire route to remove obstacles and hold-ups. Fresh and veteran crews were allocated, new aircraft were assigned to bring all units up to maximum strength, bombs and ammunition supplies were stockpiled and fuel reserves were built up to ensure unhindered close air support was both overwhelming and sustainable. Fresh ground personnel were also moved east to ensure the maximum level of operations was sustained.

At the end of June the Soviet Air Force commander, Chief Marshal of Aviation A.A. Nokikov, arrived in the Far East to oversee operations and, by 30 July, the various field headquarters were reinforced by high-ranking officers from the staff. Many new airfields were secretly constructed behind the front and elaborate camouflaging was undertaken to keep the Japanese from finding out the exact details of the huge aircraft build up. Combat units only deployed to the front-line airstrips at the last moment prior to hostilities, flying in at low heights and maintaining strict radio silence. They were then quickly dispersed and camouflaged again before they could be spotted.

Split between the three fronts, the Transbaikal, First and Second Far Eastern, the Soviet Air Force's Twelfth Air Army had some 1,334 aircraft under Marshal of Aviation S.A. Khudyakov on the first front alone. Ninth Air Army under General I.M. Sokolov was deployed on the First Far Eastern front and Tenth Air Army under General P.F. Zhigarev, with Colonel S.K. Fedorov in attendance, was deployed on the Second Far Eastern Front. The general composition of Soviet Air Force units was as Table 12:

ACTION IN THE FAR EAST

The rear turret of the Pe-2FT, with the 12.7mm UBT machine-gun in extreme left position to fire out to port. (Russian Aviation Research Trust)

Table 12: Composition of Soviet Air Force Units on the Far Eastern Front, July 1945[1]

Air Army	Air Corps	Air Divisions						Independent Regiments	Total Combat aircraft
		Bomber	Attack	Fighter	Composite	Transport	Total		
9	1 BAC	3	2	3	-	-	8	4	1,137
10	1 CAC	1	2	3	2	-	8	2	1,260
12	2 BAC	6	2	3	-	2	13	2	1,324
Total	-	10	6	9	2	2	29	8	3,721

The Transbaikal force attacked first. Operating from Outer Mongolia across the Gobi desert, the role of this massive force was to strike south across Inner Mongolia taking Peking and Ch'eng and advancing to the sea at the border of Manchukuo and China. Air support was paramount with 95 per cent of all Twelfth Air Army committed totally to support and cover the advancing troops. The Pe-2s were initially given the task of eliminating Japanese air strength on their forward airfields on the first day of combat and then attacking the enemy rear area and lines of communications to isolate the front from the main reserves.

From 8 August this plan proceeded with ruthless speed and efficiency. A northern wing, with Thirty-sixth Army, pinched out Hailar in the north-west and placed it under siege, while the central thrust across the Greater Hsingan mountains, outflanked the Japanese Forty-fourth Army by sweeping past S-lun on the Ch'ang-

THE PETLYAKOV Pe-2

Peshkas lined-up on a Far Eastern airbase during the crushing Soviet Far-Eastern Campaign of 1945 against the Japanese. (Russian Aviation Research Trust)

ch'un and Shen-yang before delivering a final thrust down the Dairen promontory to take Port Arthur and avenge the old Czarist humiliation of forty years earlier. Some 2,361 combat sorties were flown in support of this advance and some 710.7 tons of bombs had been expended.

In the Dunin fortified region a similar concentrated strike was mounted by 19 BAK with 108 aircraft. They scored direct hits on four pillboxes, two command bunkers and an ammunition dump, killed 130 Japanese troops and opened the way for a successful ground assault.

In the east the Ninth Air Army Pe-2 mission role was laid down as the destruction of Japanese fixed fortifications at Dongning, Donxingzheng, Mishan and Pograncicheskiy, which were known to be numerous and strong, and attacking Japanese battlefield troop deployments. Massed Pe-2 strikes were planned in advance for these initial objectives to be destroyed and then continuous air support and cover for the thrusting Soviet columns was to follow in the grand manner developed since 1942 in Europe.

Ship Targets

All through July and August 1945 the 34 BAP dive-bombers attacked the ports of Rasin and Seysin in Korea, claiming to have sunk three Japanese transports and two oil tankers, and five more transports.

ACTION IN THE FAR EAST

On 9/10 August 10th Dive-Bomber Division attacked Unegi and Najin harbours, and also Chongjin. The frigate *Yashiro,* corvette *Kaibokan 87* and sixteen merchant ships of 57,325 tons were sunk or damaged.

Again, on 10 August the Japanese corvette *Kaibokan 82* was sunk by dive-bombers SSW of Kumsudan, NE Korea. More victims followed; on 15 August, the Japanese frigate *Kanju* was sunk off Wonsan.

Finally, on 18 August 1945, the Pe-2's hit the Japanese corvette *Kaibokan* 213, which sank off Pusan.

Soviet Navy Pe-2 missions

From contemporary accounts the *Peshkas* encountered little in the way of meaningful air opposition from their Japanese Army counterparts during the brief campaign in the Far East in August 1945. Most recorded losses are attributed to anti-aircraft fire or normal operational damage causes With regard to the naval *Peshkas* of the Pacific Ocean Air Flotilla, who bore the brunt of the air action during the seizure of Sakhalin and the Kurile Islands, and the subsequent drive down the coast to take northern Korea, the situation was similar. The naval airmen flew a total of 474 sorties and lost fifty-seven aircraft, but only thirty-seven of these to enemy action. Of the fifty-five casualties suffered, twenty-three pilots and thirty-two aircrew, none was attributed to Japanese interceptor action.

On 9 August the *Peshka,* operating in strengths of sixty to seventy aircraft at a time, was heavily engaged against Japanese troop concentrations along the front line. They also flew operations against concentrations in rear areas, along with air bases, rail junctions, marshalling yards and railway depots at Hailar, Haishuitang, Hotou, Solon and Wuchaguo, and waterborne transport on the river Sungari. Some 30 per cent of the massive air photo and visual reconnaissance that was such a feature of the attack was conducted by the Pe-2s.

A typical intense *Peshka* mission took place on 10 August when General M.N. Kalinushkin personally led 120 sorties by 34 BAD against Japanese fortifications and strongpoints at Hutou, enabling the Soviet thirty-fifth Army to take the city the same day. Next day, 11 August, some sixty Pe-2s were sent against heavy concentrations of Japanese troops which air reconnaissance had identified in the Muling area. The weather was poor all the way to the target but, nonetheless, this heavy strike went in with great precision and the dive-bombers caused heavy losses to the enemy, as well as massive disruption, preventing an organised counter-attack.[2]

On 15 August, for example, twenty-nine Pe-2 dive-bombers of 55 BAP made an attack at 1330 on the railway station and junction at Ranan (Nanam). A pair of Japanese J2M fighters attempted to offer resistance, but were intercepted by escorting Yak-9 fighters of 19 IAP, who destroyed one, while the survivor fled the scene. Later that same day, at 1719, another dive-bombing attack was mounted by 3 BAP, with thirty-four Pe-2s, also escorted by Yak-9s of 19 IAP. They attacked another vital rail junction at Funei (Nuren), meeting only token opposition. Another J2M was destroyed, piloted by Lieutenant Grib.[3]

On the First Far Eastern front the Japanese concentrated strong forces around Mudanjiang to form a fortress area to cover the withdrawal of their troops from Baoqing and Jiamusi. There the Japanese stood and fought well, and even counter-attacked, bringing the Russian advance to a halt for the first time. Ninth Air Army was tasked with crushing this spirited resistance and a large number of strikes were made against these stubborn forces.

On day two of the operation Thirty-fifth Army reached the heavily-fortified area of Khutou and were halted by fierce Japanese resistance. A concentrated attack was made by eighty-one Pe-2s of Colonel K.A. Mikhaylov's 34 BAD on enemy pillboxes, artillery and mortar positions and strongpoints, which largely silenced them. As a result, after two days fighting, the Soviet ground troops broke through and took the whole region. The same *Peshka* outfit hit the vital Mudantzyan (Mutanchiang) railway station, hub of Japanese transport for their counter-attack against Fifth Army, and heavily disrupted the flow of traffic to the front. They joined in the five days' heavy fighting that saw the fall of this vital region.

Notable among the attacks on Mudanjiang was a Pe-2 strike against Japanese troops concentrated at the main railway station on 14 August. Bad weather again threatened to spoil their efforts but Lieutenant Colonel Plotnikov, in command of 59 BAR, was undeterred. On meeting appalling conditions en route to the target, with a cloud base of under 100 metres, Plotinikov, rather than abort his important mission, detoured to the north to go around it. The 59th descended to a height of fifty metres following the ground for 100 kilometres until they finally broke out into good visibility. They then turned back to the target and delivered a highly accurate and telling attack which wrecked the railway station and caused much chaos and heavy losses to the defending Japanese, before returning safely to base.

On the eastern front the Second Soviet army attacked across the Amur past Aihun and linked up at Tsitsihar on 19 August with the Thirty-sixth from the west. Meanwhile Fifteenth army pushed south-west in conjunction with attacks from Thirty-fifth Army across the Usari river and First, Fifth and Twenty-fifth Armies, which punched through south of Lake Khanga towards Mu-tan-chiang and Kirin. Another thrust was made along the coast south via Rashin, Seishin towards Pyongyang in Korea and a final halt was not made until the 38th Parallel, which would thereafter divide a communist North from a democratic South in that unhappy land, until then a Japanese vassal state.

Peshka Men – Major General Pavel Artem'evich Plotnikov

One of the most outstanding Pe-2 pilots was Pavel Plotnikov, who rose to great heights in the post-war air force. Born on 4 March 1920, in the small village of Gon'ba, near to the city of Barnaul in the Altai region, he was a typical peasant's son. With no advantages other than a quick brain, clever hands and a

ACTION IN THE FAR EAST

dedication to improve himself, Pavel attended the primary and secondary state schools before graduating.

The first work that Pavel found for himself was as a metal craftsman but he grew tired of this and, in 1938, volunteered for the Soviet Army. He set his eye on aviation and, two years later, successfully graduated from the Novosibirsk Flying School as a pilot. With the outbreak of war with Germany such young flyers were in great demand, but with a low life expectancy. However, Plotnikov's quick brain set him aside and, in October 1942, he was appointed assistant to the squadron commander of 82 GBAP (*Gvardeiskyi Bombardirovochnyi Aviatsionnyi Polk* – Guards Bombardment Aviation Regiment). This unit was part of 1 GBAD (Guards Bombardment Aviation Division), of II GBAK (Guards Bombardment Aviation Corps) in Fifth Air Army, serving on the Second Ukrainian Front. There it was that Plotnikov made his reputation as a dive-bomber pilot par excellence during the hard-fought campaigns of 1942 and 1943.

By May 1944 Plotnikov had flown 225 combat missions in the *Peshka* and had destroyed three enemy aircraft in aerial combat. Rewards came thick and fast. He was made Hero of the Soviet Union on 27 June 1944. Promoted to *Kapitan* (captain) and appointed as Squadron Commander of 81 GBAP, part of 1 GBAD, VI GBAK, Second Air Army on the First Ukrainian Front. With this unit, Plotnikov carried out a further eight combat missions in the Pe-2 and, on 19 August 1944, was again awarded the title Hero of the Soviet Union, an outstanding achievement.

With the end of the war in Europe and the fall of Berlin, Plotnikov, now a lieutenant colonel in command of 59 Bomber Air Regiment, was transferred to the Far East where his unit performed outstandingly in the brief and decisive campaign against Japan in the late summer of 1945, notably at the battle for Mudanjiang.

He was withdrawn from front-line duties and passed through the Higher Officer Flying-Tactical School, graduating in 1945, before further staff and flying duties. He graduated from the Military Air College in 1951 and the Military College of the General Staff in 1975 as a major general, before being transferred to the active reserve as befitted his age.

During his long and distinguished career Pavel Plotnikov was awarded the Order of Lenin, three Orders of the Red Banner, the Order of *Aleksandr Nevskyi*, two Orders of the Patriotic War First Class and the Order of the Red Star, as well as twice becoming an HSU. His bust in bronze stands today in Barnaul city to mark the achievements of this peasant boy turned flying ace and respected air force commander.

Chapter Sixteen

Variations on a Theme

Successful and widespread as the Pe-2 design was, it readily lent itself to a wide number of variants and experimental aircraft, some of which were produced in large numbers, others being merely 'one-offs'.

Pe-2F

This design originated early on in the history of the *Peshka* but the outbreak of war with Germany, the enforced move east with its associated problems, the lack of skilled workers, and the need to concentrate production on the basic types to ensure adequate numbers were supplied to the fighting units, all led to postponement of development.

The origins of the requirement were inherent from the speed (under six months) and manner in which the original VI-100 high-altitude fighter had been converted into the Pe-2. This had been done, as we have seen, very successfully, but it was clear that there remained serious problems which would require rectification. This was recognised very early on and the two main areas scheduled for revision were the comparatively small bomb load which could be carried into combat and the notoriously bad landing characteristics of the *Peshka*.

The inherent accuracy of dive-bombing over low-level or other forms of ordnance delivery were marked and fully recognised by the VVS which was to develop mainly into a tactical air force during the war, with the Pe-2 as its main warhorse. Even so, with a bomb capacity of just 600kg in normal combat configuration, and even in maximum overload configuration of a maximum of 1,000kg, the Pe-2 was considered underladen in comparison to other twin-engined bombers, for example the German Junkers Ju.88 (also a twin-engined dive-bomber) and the American Douglas A-20 (a standard medium bomber). The internal bomb bays restricted the size of the bombs capable of being toted to a mere 100kg, which reduced the hitting power of each strike. Moreover, the maximum bomb load could only be carried by using external bomb racks, which negated much of its speed margin, considered one the Pe-2's greatest assets.

The other defect, the weakness of the landing gear and undercarriage, coupled with the much commented upon 'bounce' of the aircraft on touch-down, was also a product of the hasty conversion from the original fighter concept. This factor had two adverse effects on operational use of the Pe-2; in the first place, even

VARIATIONS ON A THEME

Naval ratings and artificer working on a Polish Navy Pe-2FT in the late 1940s. This photo gives a good detailed view of the engine assembly. (Robert Michulec)

experienced pilots found it difficult to control, and with the rapid influx of brand-new pilots in increasing numbers, it became increasingly a matter that affected serviceability and even casualties. That it was not to be taken lightly can be illustrated by one typical example, that of the experience of 8. ZAB (Reserve Aviation Brigade) as late as 1943 which estimated that one-third of the Pe-2s out of service at any one time were because of landing accidents, a clearly unacceptable rate of attrition.[1]

Speed as defence

There was a third consideration, which was to influence the Pe-2F concept. From experiences in the Far East, the air war in China and the Spanish Civil War, most of the world's leading military aviation powers had concluded that the high-speed bomber, in the words of Prime Minister Baldwin to Parliament in 1932, 'would always get through'. Radical developments were taking place in the late 1930s which seemed to reinforce this article of faith, and the German Junkers Ju.88, the British de Havilland Mosquito and other wartime designs were to be developed in line with this thinking. Soviet thinking was influenced by the latter experience, whereby the SB bomber had, on occasion, managed to escape from enemy fighters by simply putting the nose down and outrunning them. This seemed a viable alternative strategy to that of equipping bombers with heavier and heavier defensive armaments to enable them to fight their way through. The bankruptcy of that line of thought was not shown up until the experiences of the RAF in 1939/40 and of the Luftwaffe over southern England in 1940. However, high speed in itself, although desirable, was limited by the design of the aircraft and, above all, the efficiency of the engines.

While the standard production Pe-2 might, under certain conditions, evade the Bf.109E in 1941, development never stood still. A speed of 560-580km/h at 4,000-5,000 metres might suffice for a time, but not forever, nor for long. If the engine power and thrust of the airscrew are assumed constant, speed increases in inverse proportion to the square root of the air density, and air density in inverse proportion to the altitude. The result is that an aircraft flying at 12,000 metres can fly at twice the speed as that at just above ground level. For every plus there is a minus of course; at the high altitude the aircrew thrust decreases and the speed falls off.[2]

In order to bolster the high-altitude performance of the piston engine in the late 1930s/early 1940s, either a mechanically-driven centrifugal supercharger or a turbo-supercharger was required. The Soviets were well advanced on the use of the latter method; indeed Petlyakov had already installed two TK-2 turbo-superchargers on each of the VI-100's M-105 engines, and was well acquainted with the merits of the system. No problem was therefore envisaged in fitting two of the improved TK-2F turbo-superchargers to the M-105F engines envisaged for the Pe-2F.

A preliminary study was initiated by Petlyakov in spring 1941. The figures produced gave revised figures, estimating that each engine would be capable of developing up to 1,300hp, and that this would be maintained up to an altitude of 7,000 metres. This would result in a maximum speed of 600km/h, better than either the Bf.109E-7 or 109F-2 fighters, which were at that time the fastest interceptors known to be available to the Germans.

Re-design and Mock-up

The other problems were addressed by Petlyakov at the same time. To help with the landing problems and the re-design of the undercarriage, the low-wing Pe-2 was to become a mid-wing aircraft. The fuselage was lowered by 0.3metres in relation to the wing, but this alteration to the mid-section of the fuselage did not affect either extremity, both the nose (F-1) and tail sections receiving only the minimum of modifications to allow a smooth match.

This shift freed up space by eliminating the centre-plane spars from the weapons bay. As a result, the bomb capacity increased, with alternative combinations of either a single FAB-500, a pair of FAB-250 or six FAB-100 bombs being capable of being internally carried. Against this, the extra weight, in turn, necessitated an increase in the size of the main wheels, infringed upon space there, and led to the total elimination of the engine nacelle weapons bays. While this meant that the total internal payload remained the same at 600kg, the fully-laden condition, with a single FAB-500 carried on each of the two MDZ-40 external bomb racks, increased to 1,500kg.

The fitting of the TK-2F turbo-supercharger did not affect the wing panels, other than adding two small fuel tanks.

In May 1941 this mock-up was inspected by a VVS commission and approved. Four factories were producing the Pe-2 and one of these, No. 22 GAZ, received the go-ahead to build two prototype Pe-2Fs forthwith. By June the full set of drawings for this pair of aircraft had been readied and work had commenced on various sub-assemblies. Even at this stage, further consideration was being given to yet another variant of the Pe-2F, with the M-107 engines developing 1,600hp as the two main power units.

With the go-ahead, work was quickly initiated, only to be sidelined with the German invasion. For a while everything at GAZ 22 was concentrated on producing standard aircraft quickly and most progress on the prototypes languished. Despite this, the first prototype was completed by September 1941, while the sub-assemblies for the second machine were also completed. However, with Moscow itself threatened, the programme was again temporarily disrupted as the factory moved east. The solitary completed aircraft had never taken to the air; nonetheless test pilot S. Shestakov with leading engineer A. Rozenfel'd, got it airborne and flew to Kazan and safety. There followed a further period of relative stagnation, which the death of Petlyakov only enhanced.

Resumption of development

The brief period of A.M. Izakson's reign at GAZ 22 led to further modifications of the Pe-2F concept. The design featured larger coolant radiators, these having a wider air intake to increase the airflow. On the Pe-2F these air intakes were fitted with a feature completely new to the Pe-2 series, an adjustable flap. Another new feature was the introduction of intermediate radiators, which were located between the turbo-superchargers and the carburettors.

The fuel system was overhauled, improved protection was introduced and the number of fuel tanks increased to twelve.[3] The air gunner's hatches were altered, in line with production Pe-2s. Following operational experience, the upper hatch was enlarged, while the lower hatch was given armour protection, and changed so that it could be opened outward

Principally a helicopter and autogyro designer, Izakson's aptitude did not lend itself to designing an experimental dive-bomber. Nonetheless, he made several notable changes, not least to the Pe-2F's armament. The contemporary production line Pe-2s were equipped with the UBT machine gun on a FT flexible mounting, and were converting to the VUB-1 turret and deleting the anti-crash pylon as a result. The Pe-2F switched from the TSS-1 turret with the ShKAS gun to the VUB-2 turret mounting the UBT machine gun (but retained the pylon).

The turret for the UBT machine gun had been developed and introduced into serial production by a young leading designer on the OKB 22 team, Leonid Leonidovich Selyakov.

THE PETLYAKOV Pe-2

Disappointing Results

These changes having been absorbed, a series of thirty-four flights were conducted at NII VVS by test pilot Major A.M. Khripkov. These airborne trials commenced in April 1942 with the company flight development and continued into May with the State Acceptance evaluation combined programmes. The Pe-2F proved a heavier machine, at 8,350kg showing an increase over the standard Pe-2 of between 500-600kg. This extra weight, coupled with the reduced flap area, increased both the take-off and landing speeds. Performance figures were disappointing. Rate of climb to an altitude of 5,000 metres was 7.8 minutes. Service ceiling was 6,500 metres. The maximum speed attained at ground level was 485km/h, while at 6,500 metres it reached 560km/h, some 40km/h less than had been predicted. At most levels, handling characteristics showed no marked difference with the standard model, although an improvement in stability was noted, but was coupled with a reduction of maneuverability.

One worrying feature was the unreliability of the propulsion unit which, on three occasions, necessitated forced landings. The old bugbears re-appeared in the turbo-superchargers – oil leaks, blade and impeller-casing-ring fracturing – all manifestations of bad manufacturing and inspection still in evidence. The limitations of the engine-control systems showed themselves even under normal conditions. The air pressure flow from the turbo-superchargers was adjusted by the manifold pressure control system which failed to function more often than not. This meant that it was left to the test pilot to manually control the fuel/air mix ratio. That was an onerous task requiring great concentration and delicacy, as during take off, for example, the mutual interdependence of both engines' parameters required careful balancing to avoid over-boosting, and the pilot had other tasks to occupy him. This was compounded by the fact that the dynamic characteristics of the port and starboard engines differed requiring shrewd, and swift, guesswork on the throttle.

Other old Pe-2 problems were encountered on the prototype, the M-105 engine crankcase oozing oil, frequent burning out of the spark plugs, and the indifferent performance of the cooling flow of the exhaust stacks. To these old chestnuts were added new design faults relating to the re-designed bomb bay. The loading of ordnance in the enlarged bays should have been simpler; in fact, it was worse, even dangerous. (According to Markovsky and Medvyed, one of the armourers had to stand beneath the loaded bomb to control this loading procedure!)[4]

All these negatives might have been acceptable, although requiring rectification, had the main thrust of the new design been attained, i.e. better performance. However, an analysis of comparative altitude/speed figures between the standard M-105F-engined Pe-2 and the Pe-2F, made by leading engineer Shashkov, came to a depressing conclusion. Shashkov was able to demonstrate that, within the height range between ground level up to 5,000 metres almost no improvement whatsoever had been achieved. These results ended the first phase of the experiment. Series production was out of the question. Instead a new modification of the design, this time employing the M-107 engine as the power plant, was authorised.

Izakson did not survive this fiasco, being replaced as head of the design team by the more experienced A.I. Putilov in May 1942.

Thus, the M-107-engined Pe-2 (referred to as the Pe-2D) was supposed to become Putilov's contribution to the problem.

Pe-2D

The final recommendation by the NII VSS examination body on the Pe-2F was that the test machine and the second prototype both be fitted with M-107 engines. This done, they were then to proceed with the evaluation programme once more, but now under the more appropriate design leadership of Putilov working under V.A. Okulov's directorship and with Lieutenant Colonel (*Ing*) Romanov as the senior military representative at GAZ 22.

The first task of this team was to persuade the NKAP to make available two sets of the M-107 engine, from which higher speeds were confidently expected. These drove the R-7 constant-speed unit (3,200-rpm) driving a variable-pitch airscrew of 3.6-metre diameter. GKO resolution 2346, issued on 25 September, and signed by Major (*Ing*) M.A. Savkin, chief engineer of No. 1 Department (Aircraft and Engine Procurement) of the Main Procurement and Technical Supplies Directorate of the VVS RKKA (UZSiM GUZiTS VVS RKKA), increased the programme to three M-107 modified aircraft. Full company flight development was to be completed by 15 December that year.

The first of the M-107-powered Pe-2s (c/n 5-134) was ready on 30 September and made her debut flight with the new power plant the following day. With a 1,500kg bomb load, and a defensive armament of three BT and one DAG-10 guns, take-off weight was 8,750kg with a range of 1,700 kilometres. This initial test was concluded with no problems other than difficulties with the R-7A airscrew constant-speed module.

However, any premature celebrations were soon dampened as the flight programme continued. Over the next month almost every flight had to be terminated prematurely with a forced landing due to the unreliability of the M-107. Nor was the simple replacement of each engine by another M-107, fully inspected and reliable, deemed to be the answer. Putilov discovered in the course of these trials that the heat-exchange rate of the M-107 was far greater than that of the M-105. To compensate for this fact a more efficient, and physically larger, coolant radiator would have to be fitted. This, in turn, would mean re-designing the wing panels to accommodate the bigger units as the standard Pe-2 wing profile could not accommodate them. The long-term answer to the problem was seen to be the arrival of the new M-107A engine. All work on the three Pe-2/M-107 prototypes was therefore put on hold indefinitely.

THE PETLYAKOV Pe-2

The saga of the M-107A

This engine first reached GAZ 22 at the end of 1942 but no work was done on the three prototypes for the many months. The reason for this lack of activity appears to have been a lack of sufficient skilled workers at the plant to carry out the many specialised tasks with which it was entrusted, the overriding one remaining the output of the series production to feed the front. Another factor, which has been said to have diverted effort away from Pe-2/M-107A trio, was Putlilov's obsession with his M-105PD-engined VI high-altitude fighter.[5] This led to NKAP disillusionment with Putlilov in his turn. They decided he was also the wrong man for the job and, on 15 May 1943, they issued order number 298, removing him from his post and naming P.O. Sukhoi as his successor.

This order was not complied with and Putilov continued in the role for a few weeks more. The impasse was only ended with the replacement of Putilov in his turn by Vladimir Mikhaylovich Myasishchev as the chief designer at 22 OKO, which took place in June 1943. A fresh Order, No. 367 dated 22 June, read that 'in order to improve the work of the no. 22 GAZ KB and to ensure a faster production of the modified Pe-2 with improved flight-technical parameters', V.M. Myasishchev was to be appointed as chief designer; that A.I. Putilov was to be relieved from duty and that the director of GAZ 288, Kutyepov, was to be transferred along with Myasishchev from GAZ 288 to concentrate the main design staff and 22 Experimental Workshop into GAZ 22 OKB.[6] They gave as priority proceeding with the high-altitude combat aircraft development, its equipment and armament, for which a subsidiary department was to be set up at GAZ 482 in Moscow.[7]

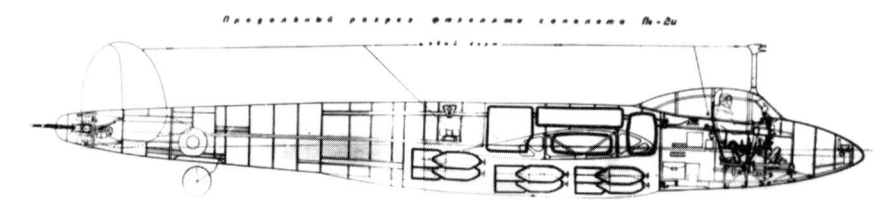

Diagram 14: Standard bomb and fuel dispositions – profile view. (Russian Aviation Research Trust)

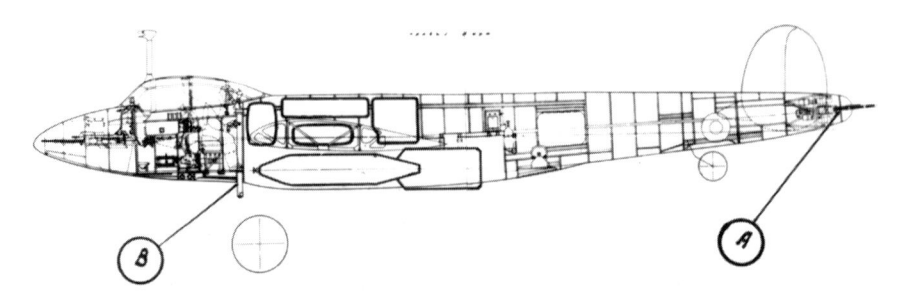

Diagram 15: Layout for 2,000lb bomb loading – profile view. (Russian Aviation Research Trust)

VARIATIONS ON A THEME

With this further change of leadership, the M-107A engines at last began to be installed in the Pe-2. Even this did not entirely introduce momentum into the programme, however, and problems with the new engine continued to stall any progress.

Finally, the decision was taken to remove the Pe-2/M-107A[8] from GAZ 22 to the aero-engine plant GAZ 26 for development and here she remained for the next four months. At the end of that time, during which Myasishchev had been as committed as his predecessors with endeavouring to increase the performance of the standard Pe-2, the new chief designer came up with a whole raft of new proposals, which he termed his 'August Programme'. These were presented to the NKAP; among the variants included was an M-107-engined Pe-2, which he now referred to as the Pe-6. This designation did not originate with Myasishchev, however, for a Pe-2 with M-107 engines was first mentioned in a document signed by Petlyakov himself in 1941.[9]

NKAP alternatives

The Pe-2 was being produced faster than ever in the re-located factories, which, on paper was just what was required. In truth, however, production standards had fallen and continued to fall. The new labour force consisted largely of youths, women and unskilled pensioners, drafted in to work long, tiring twelve-hour, round-the-clock shifts on poor diet. Many lacked the basic strength for the job as well. Unreliability was not confined to engine problems: matters affecting performance, like surface finish, deteriorated. Moreover, the call from the front had remorselessly laden the *Peshka* with more and more armour protection, greater defensive armament, additional instrumentation, all of which detracted from her biggest asset, her speed.

For example, a test on a random sample aircraft, c/n 15-95 built on 19 June 1942, and equipped with the bulkier turret housing the UBT machine gun, found a maximum speed of 488km/h. This was 42km/h *less* that c/n 10-35 produced in August 1941. Lieutenant Colonel Romanov broke this speed loss down as follows:

10-12km/h lost due to the drag of the Toporov gun turret.

2-3km/h lost due to the drag caused by the side-gun mounting.

3km/h lost due to the replacement of the AV-5L type airscrew by the VISh-61B.

16-20km/h lost due to poorer production finish with resultant aerodynamic drag.

This falling of speed in the Pe-2 was becoming more and more obvious in 1943. The NKAP called in both the LII NKAP and the TsAGI to offer remedies. The result was a number of experimental aircraft, modified with varying degrees of success.

THE PETLYAKOV Pe-2

19-78

The first aircraft selected by these organisations was c/n 19-78. In September 1942 this aircraft had been modified by changes, which included the profile of the oil-radiator tunnels, tightening the fit of flaps and other moving surfaces and the fitting of individual exhaust ejectors. Another experiment saw the sealing of the gaps in the fixed-skin panels of the wings, fuselage and nacelles to improve airflow and reduce drag.[10]

The test programme was a two-phase operation. The first test flights took place in September 1942, and the maximum speed rose to 531km/h. By the time of the second flight test, which took place in March 1943, refinements had managed to increase this again, to 547km/h. Both climb rate and landing response were also claimed as 'improved'.

16-163

Following the first phase testing with 19-78, TsAGI made GAZ 22 introduce the sealed external joints and gaps adaptation to the SK programme's production line. Such sealing was extended to internal applications as well. A more aerodynamic fairing of the VUV-1 gun turret was in introduced, along with flush-wing bomb racks. The first aircraft to emerge from the factory in this configuration was c/n 16-163, and her recorded maximum speed improved from 476 to 508km/h.

2-187

Following the second round of modifications with 19-78, these further improvements were added to a production line aircraft, c/n 2-187. When she emerged from the April 1943 line, she was tested and her maximum speed had been raised from 475 to 522km/h. This was conclusive enough to have the further changes incorporated to the SK programme line forthwith. An NKAP directive, No. 206, was issued, and from the 205th production batch onward, which appeared in June 1943, most of these features were included.

The one part of the TsAGI/LII programme that was not implemented involved the sealing of the thin-skin panel joints. It was found that, due to the vibration these were subject to, this application was just a waste of time, as the sealant peeled off within four or five hours. This was therefore abandoned.

19-205

Also from the 205th production batch, one M-105PF equipped aircraft, c/n 19-205, was selected for further research by the TsGAI. It was test flown from the line and, at the second altitude level for that engine, 3,700 metres recorded a maximum speed of 521km/h. Improvements to this aircraft were put in hand with the overall aim of increasing the maximum speed, *at all levels*, by at least 30km/h.

VARIATIONS ON A THEME

The measures taken were as follows:

1: Coolant-radiator capacity increased.
2: Coolant-radiator tunnel form changed.
3: Supercharger air intakes were transferred inside the oil-radiator tunnels.
4: Individual exhaust ejectors, with fairings, were introduced.
5: The frontal profile of the airscrew was narrowed to further reduce drag.
6: The navigator's canopy glazing was smoothed and elongated to reduce drag.
7: Surface areas were thinly layered over with nitric putty.
8: The front 1/3rd of the wing surface was polished and painted.

Evaluation flight testing of 19-205 with these various embellishments commenced in October 1943 with test pilot M.L. Gallay at the helm. The programme produced figures that encouraged TsGAI to think they were on the right track, 548km/h at a height of 3,600 metres being recorded. This was still 3km/h below their self-imposed target and further fine-tuning was done by altering the shape of the supercharger air intake. This done, Gallay took her back up and, by the end of the month, a maximum speed of 551km/h was achieved.

Despite this encouraging figure, Leading-engineer Heifetz thought that he could still improve upon it. The aircraft was subjected to yet a tenth modification, with the installation of an experimental, 2.8-metre-diameter VISh-61T airscrew. This done, the maximum speed was pushed up to 555km/h. The downside to this was that these airscrews proved less efficient at ground level, increasing the distance required for the *Peshka* to get airborne. Even so TsAGI and LII recommended the application of the majority of the ten improvements to the series line as soon as possible.

Despite the recommendations, 22 OKO failed to implement them all. They duly incorporated fairings for the dive brakes and the relocation of the antenna mast to the forward windscreen frame, which their own experiments had indicated were of greater value, as well as those already added to the 205th batch. Later they added individual exhaust ejectors, but not many of the other recommendations. But the factory soon fell back into their old ways with sub-standard work being recorded on both airframe and at the engine manufacturers negating all these superficial changes. When two production line Pe-2s, c/n 1-338 and c/n 6-343, were taken for test flights a year later, in mid-1944, the top speed had fallen back to 496km/h again.

The 'August Programme' of 1943

In addition to the Pe-6, Myasishchev's programme included the following modified variants for consideration: the Pe-2A, Pe-2B, Pe-2V, Pe-4, and Pe-4A. Let us examine each of these in turn, along with their associated ramifications.

THE PETLYAKOV Pe-2

The Pe-2A

A production aircraft, c/n 7-187, had been used as a test-bed for the new FZ gun turret, which had the enlarged pilot/navigator cockpit canopy. This was to be the basis of the Pe-2A, but was also to include a number of features designed to enhance the aerodynamic performance of the aircraft. The exhaust ejector fairings were to be modernised and coolant-radiator ducting was to be re-designed. To improve the airflow the tail plane was extended beyond the fins. Flush filters were provided for the carburettor air intakes, while pipes for the inert gases fire-extinguisher system were inserted in the wing. Finally, an emergency winch-retraction system was provided for the dive-brake system. Another Pe-2 from the line, c/n 17-176, equipped with M-105PF engines, was to be the lead aircraft incorporating these changes. The intention was for a 7,800kg take-off weight and a targeted maximum speed of 540km/h.

Conversion work was completed by September 1943, and the company flight development trials commenced, with test pilot A.G. Vasil'chencko at the helm. Flight testing was disappointing; none of these 'improvements' was sufficient to attain 540km/h, which meant that the standard production Pe-2 remained the faster aircraft. Two further modifications of 17-176 failed to improve matters. Therefore, although the flight-test report claimed that both the aircraft's speed and combat characteristics had been improved, the Pe-2A was not considered worthy of further work, other than to convert her into a second Pe-2B.

The Pe-2B

Also equipped with the M-105PF engine, this variant incorporated the various recommended aerodynamic improvements, which originated from TsAGI. The recommendations they had made, and which had been independently tested on c/n 19-205, including the new pilot/navigator cockpit with the FZ mounting, were

Head-on view of the Pe-2B. This makes an interesting comparison with the same view of the original Pe-2 (M Maslov)

VARIATIONS ON A THEME

Peshka No.19-223, a standard Pe-2B, is seen here at the State Testing Ground on 17 July 1944.(M Maslov)

almost all to be incorporated. There were to be new airscrew spinner cones, which would blend more efficiently with the nacelles to reduce drag. The cowling panels were modified to achieve similar results. The oil radiators and the engine air-intake ducts were moved to the leading edges of the wings. The whole wing forward section up to the front spar was re-profiled to combine the VVS leading-edge airflow section edge, extending to the forward spar with NACA-230/12 airflow section. Detachable outer wing panels were fitted. These had a 0.92-metre greater span and a 0.846m^2 greater area. These modifications, it was estimated, would reduce premature airflow separation at lower speeds

The armament was not altered at all. Take-off weight would go up to 7,900kg, but a maximum speed of 560km/h was hoped for. Some of this weight was accounted for by the addition of extra fuel tanks, which would extend the Pe-2B's range to 1,200 kilometres.

Delays, delays and yet more delays

The trial aircraft selected for these modifications was c/n 19-223. The intention was that, if these ideas worked out as planned, the Pe-2B would become the production standard for the 1944 Programme. This intention was, largely, thwarted by the fact that several changes to the planned design were made. Some of this was again due to shortage of skilled workers. The demands of the front line were unremitting and the staff of the experimental workshop was transferred to series production,

THE PETLYAKOV Pe-2

with the obvious result that some of the work was badly delayed, or, worse, totally abandoned. Both the wing forward section and the transfer of the oil radiators to their new positions in the wings went by the board as a result. In addition, the supercharger air intake was relocated inside the oil radiator tunnel, with the 'chin' beneath the engine reductor gearbox.

Other delays were not manmade but due to the weather. A particularly harsh winter was a feature of 1943/44. There were frequent blizzards and the air temperature plummeted below –35 C. and the runways at Kazan were made unserviceable for long periods of time. The factories continued to churn out production line Pe-2s,[11] which, in turn, were forced to sit unflown on the runways, further adding to congestion and restricting test operations. Even when the succession of blizzards finally abated, the resultant thaw turned the area into a morass, equally unfit for flying operations. Not until the end of February 1944 did conditions ease and the programme get underway again, but now hopelessly late.

When the flight-test programme did finally commence the results once more fell far short of what had been expected. A maximum speed of 524km/h was the best result from the initial run, some 36km/h under the target. The aircraft was put through a detailed examination to ascertain the drag effect to improve matters. All protrusions were looked at to see if they could be streamlined, the location of the coolant and oil-radiator flaps were subjected to change and experiment, even the shape and size of their apertures being adjusted to try to squeeze a few more knots from the design. All this tweaking gradually pushed the speed up a further 10km/h, but no more. Even so, the Pe-2B was presented for State Acceptance evaluation in this unsatisfactory condition. In truth Myasishcev's motivation was elsewhere by now, and more concerned with the development of the Pe-6.

Peshka No. 14-225 was the result of State testing at Factory No. 22. She featured two VK-105PF engines, driving VISh-105SVP airscrews of 3.1inch diameter, along with a modified wing. (M Maslov)

VARIATIONS ON A THEME

Unfortunately, yet again, a longstanding, and apparently irredeemable, manufacturing defect now re-appeared which set back the programme yet further. Cracks were discovered in the engine-mounting frames, which necessitated the return of 19-223 to the plant for repair. Not until June 1944 was the Pe-2B finally delivered to NII VVS. Here it eventually passed the tests and was recommended as fit for serial production, but time had passed her by. The NKAP was much more impressed with yet another new variant, the Pe-2I, and the Pe-2B was rejected outright. This aircraft was fitted with the VK-109MF engine as a flying test-bed.

The Pe-2V

This design took the Pe-2B concept several stages further. As well as incorporating all the intended modifications to the power plant described for the former, it was intended to increase both the aircraft's bomb-carrying capacity (with a bomb bay capable of carrying either a single FAB-500 or two FAB-250 bombs) and its range. The latter was to be brought about by increasing fuel bunkerage with extra tanks, the former by lowering the centre section by 300mm. As usual, in order to carry the extra weight these changes would involve, with take-off weight increased to 8,800kg, a strengthening of the landing gear was required. Large wheels and strong shock absorbers were to be introduced.

To compensate for the planned improvements of hitting power and reach, the defensive armament was sacrificed, with just three flexi-mounted 12.7mm machine guns constituting the total firepower. This would not have been welcomed in the front-line units, but they were destined never to see the Pe-2V. Paper studies concluded that, even with all the considerable amount of re-working it would involve over and above those planned for the Pe-2B, the difference in speed which would result would be minimal. The Pe-2V was therefore quietly shelved.

The Pe-4

GKO resolution no. 3622, issued on 21 June 1943, called for the production of 100 Pe-2/M82F radial-engined aircraft. This used the designation Pe-4, but it never became official. The plan called for an output of fifteen machines in August, thirty-five in September and a further fifty in October.

Radial-engined *Peshka*

Among the many problems generated by the enormous increase in military aircraft for the VVS once the war with Germany had got underway was the acute shortage of power plants. The engine factories had, as we have seen, been moved eastward and quickly had got back into their stride, despite the hazards of a largely unskilled labour force. It was the quantities of suitable engines that threatened to undermine the whole expansion programme. The M-105 engine, as well as being required in

THE PETLYAKOV Pe-2

The radial-engine equipped Pe-2 M-82 (this one is 22-1-232) seen at the *Nauchno-ispytatel'nyi Institut* (Scientific Test Institute or NII) at Kratovo. The aircraft was undergoing evaluation from January to March 1943. This aircraft attained a maximum sea-level speed of 472km/h (293.3 mph), slightly faster than the standard M-105 powered *Peshka*. (Viktor Kulikov)

increasing amounts for the Pe-2, also powered aircraft of equal importance, like the Yak-1, Yak-7 and LaGG-3 fighter planes.

One possible solution did present itself in 1942, and that was the availability of the twin-row, air-cooled M-82 radial 14-cylinder engine, designed by A.D. Shvetsov OKB. Series production of this engine had begun at GAZ 19 at Perm in 1941, and by the end of that year 1,000 had been produced.[12] As with all new designs, there were teething problems which required flight-testing to iron out, but finding a design team to conduct these proved difficult. Its overall dimensions were reduced to enable it to be used on fighter aircraft. Eventually Tupolev was to use it to replace the AM-37 on the Tu-2, while N.N. Polikarpov adopted it for the I-185, but that would be in the future. The NKAP was eventually forced to issue command-directives for all OKB-supported aircraft types to produce M-82 variants.[13]

One aircraft which had used this engine was the Su-2 light tactical bomber, but it had not proved very successful and all production was due to terminate from the middle of that year, leaving a surplus of capacity at the factory producing them. No alternative aircraft was in series production with this engine and the manufacturers therefore approached the design team at GAZ No. 22. They suggested that the extra power of the M-82 would enhance the performance of the Pe-2. There was even hope that, in the event that this proved to be the case, then part, or maybe even the whole, of the *Peshka* programme would switch over.[14] Early projections were not so optimistic. It was calculated that the Pe-2 with the M-82 engine, rated 1,700hp for take off, 1,400hp nominal power at 2,000 metres and 1,330hp at 5,400 metres would turn in a lower performance than those fitted with the M-105RA and M-015PF engines.

VARIATIONS ON A THEME

The Experimental 19-31

Despite this, the idea was not rejected outright. The need for an alternative power plant seemed obvious at the time, and a team was formed under L.L. Selyakov to evaluate it further. Further theoretical projections, taking into account many proposed modifications, suggested that, maybe, a better performance Pe-2 might well result. A Pe-2 (19-31) from the 31st production batch built at 125 GAZ at Irkutsk in 1941, had already been set aside for tests with a simplified armament, the VUB-2 mounting carrying the UBT gun. This machine was therefore selected for modification as the test-bed for the M-82 trial.

The resulting modified aircraft was ready by the autumn of 1942. The M-82 was of slightly greater weight than the M-105, and, naturally, presented a larger cross-section area. The designers had to totally re-work the forward section of the engine nacelle and the nacelle bomb racks were deleted. The team still had to strengthen the engine-mounting framework to take the extra weight. Oil radiators were incorporated into the outer wing panel root sections. The VISh-61B airscrew was replaced by the AV-5L-118A, which had larger spinner cones, with Hucks starter dogs.

In compensation, the original wing-mounted coolant radiators were no longer needed, and their removal allowed the fitting of an additional pair of 100-litre fuel tanks. Defensive armament was subject to considerable change also. A VUB-2 turret prototype, which mounted the BK cannon, was built into the navigator's cabin, replacing the hand-held flexibly-mounted machine gun of the wireless operator/gunner and the ShKAS machine gun mounted in the aircraft nose. The more advanced RPK-10 DF receiver was also fitted. The main undercarriage was shifted forward by some 60mm with the lengthening of the legs in order to maintain the original 26-27-degree taxiing attitude and prevent nose-overs.

The completely new design shifted the Pe-2's centre of gravity (CG) forward and some 68kg of lead ballast had to be incorporated into the tail fuselage section to compensate. The overall weight of the aircraft was estimated to have been increased by 600kg from all this. Notwithstanding this weight increase, once company flight development commenced at Arskoye Polye airfield near Kazan, it was found that the overall performance had indeed improved. On 30 June 1942 19-31 arrived at the LIS (flight test department) and some defects were put right. This led to the first test flight which took place on 21 July. By September a further seventeen flights had followed, totalling fifteen hours' flying time.

The new radial-engined *Peshka* had a shorter take-off distance; take-off and landing characteristics were improved, service ceiling was better and the maximum attainable speeds at all altitudes showed increases. At 3,250 metres a maximum speed of 545km/h was attained.

However, in the six-month development programme that followed, these plus items were found to be tempered by several adverse factors, which much reduced the euphoria. In particular, the radial was dogged by oil starvation problems. Analysis of repeated failures revealed that this was due to oil leakages, which led to an accumulation in the lower cylinders. This caused hydraulic shock to the pistons and cylinder heads, with resultant structural damage to the cylinder heads. This was prevalent at altitudes of 3,000 metres and over. Associated additional problems were found to be that the oil radiators were unreliable and caused rough engine running at low-power settings.[15]

Problems were also encountered with the AK-82 carburettor. With the supercharger setting at second speed the engines malfunctioned and at flights above 4,500 metres severe vibration set in. The increase in power led, not totally surprisingly, to increased engine torque and a biased tail-wheel had to be installed to counter this.

Measures taken to alleviate some of these faults were the reduction of the cross-section area of the cowling ring, the strengthening of the cowling panels and inlet ducting, and the adoption of the oil-supply system used on the Tu-2. All these measures were done to improve the thermal exchange interaction of the M-82. They had the effect of reducing engine temperature to what were considered safe limits, but the price was a reduction in speed at 3,000 metres to only 530km/h.

Not all the problems were material, according to at least one source. Lieutenant Colonel Romanov, the head VVS representative at GAZ 22, sent in a report to his chiefs at the GUZiTS VVS in December 1942 which was quite damning of the attitude prevalent at the time. He accused the chief designer and the director of lacking interest in the Pe-2/M-82 programme. Far from a careful step-by-step evaluation of its merits and defects, the experimental workshop was said to be rushing through the work just 'to get rid of it'. There was no system to the LIS flight-testing, and so defects already located were repeated and repeated. He accused leading engineer Rozenfeld of being 'sluggish, more concerned about the calculations and accounts than of real work'.[16]

Air trials

After six months of this, in April 1943, the experimental radial Pe-2 was flown over to Kol'tsovo airfield from GAZ-22 for comprehensive flight- and ground-testing by an official NII-VVS team. The test pilot for these trials was Major A.M. Khripkov, and he put the machine through her paces. In the period from January to March 1943 some fifty test flights were made.

It was found that the higher the altitude the greater the speed increase obtained by the radial over a standard M-105PF Pe-2 taken from the February 1943 production batch and one of the latest American Lend-Lease medium bombers, the Douglas Boston III. At ground level the difference between the two types of *Peshka* was a mere 7km/h (458km/h compared with 451km/h), but at medium altitudes this improved and was also superior to the Douglas import. (At 6,200 metres this was 547km/h for the M-82-powered Pe-2; 486km/h for the M-105PG Pe-2 and 530km/h at 4,500 metres for the Boston.)

Nor was this all. In both rate of length of take-off run, climb and maximum service ceiling, the M-82 proved the superior aircraft. The radial *Peshka* with the M-82 at boost, took off in 490 metres against 620 metres for an M-105RA-powered equivalent. The radial could climb at a steeper angle to 5,000 metres, and could do so 1.5 to 2.5 minutes faster than the Boston, while the ceiling improved by 300/800 metres. Against a gain of 450-500 metres in a combat turn by the standard Pe-2, the radial gained 800 metres. The asymmetric power flight characteristics were much improved, making for a smoother flight. With one engine cut the radial flew better than the standard production line *Peshka*. Only the longitudinal and directional stability suffered by comparison.

Again, initial enthusiasm from these statistics had to be measured against a whole raft of reported defects. Khripkov reported that the larger size of the radial-engine nacelles reduced pilot vision on either flank considerably. Even with a skilled and experienced pilot at the helm the always tricky landing of the Pe-2 became even more of a hazard with the radial. Being heavier, the M-82-powered *Peshka* landed at higher speed. Trials were conducted with power and without power, and both proved equally testing tasks. As already noted, at low setting the engines ran rough and great skill and delicacy was required in handling them for touchdowns. It was a dangerous time, made worse by the fact that the M-82 often seized up completely at this crucial juncture. Khripkov survived this occurrence on several occasions; it was doubtful whether many of the fresh-faced pilots pouring out of the wartime pilot schools would be as fortunate.

Equally unpredictable as the landing could be the power-boost control. It frequently engaged for only a short period, and then ceased. Sometimes it failed to engage at all! The resultant total engine failure that could result was hardly encouraging. Overall, it was the total unreliability of the engines themselves that presented the most constant of problems. The oil leaks and defects have been commented upon, and these did not improve over the life cycle of the trial. The fuel-mixture-control malfunctioned regularly, oil radiators ruptured. So unreliable were these engines that they were a positive danger. Poor construction and testing of both engine and radiator alike was endemic. The front cooling louvres jammed either open or shut. Excessive vibration was reported at certain speed settings. Fuel consumption was high, leading to a shortening of range and endurance.

Even as humble a component as the VG-12 spark plugs were equally prone to failure; indeed, this was a scandal. On one occasion a total of 210 spark plugs failed on this single aircraft. While, officially, the life of the M-82 radial engine produced by the GAZ-19 was given as 100 flying hours, in practice every five or six hours produced a spark-plug failure.

This was in the air, but the radial-engined Pe-2 had first to get airborne. The ground crew were soon complaining about the time it took for these engines to warm up prior to take off. In winter conditions this could take three to four hours, making meaningful combat operations at the front out of the question. The oil-radiator drain valves, found to be in constant use due to the above problems, were poorly designed and hard for the mechanics to access.

The result was that, even allowing for some decided advantages, the conclusion of the first NII-VVS report on 19-31 filed by Lieutenant Colonel (*Ing*) Shashkov was that it was not yet fit for operational employment. The recommendation, however, was that Kazan should rectify all the many faults they listed and that, once this had been done, small batches of what they termed the Pe-4,[17] should be built and combat evaluated. A single bomber regiment was to be equipped with the Pe-2/M-82 while the leading aircraft of the batch should be put through another State Evaluation Programme.

Limited Production

These aircraft were built with the M-82-112 engine, fitted with VISh-105V airscrews. The usual practice was followed by the factory in that, as with both reconnaissance and trainer variants, these Pe-2/M-82F aircraft were not subject to a special production batch, but modified with existing batches as the time and opportunity arose. Thus, the first such 'Pe-4' was c/n 1-226, and four more followed from batches 227 to 243 in August 1943. The first complete batch powered by the M-82F was 244. The final ten aircraft were not delivered until 1944. Total run was thirty-two aircraft, but only two dozen of these were ultimately presented by the factory for VVS acceptance. These aircraft also featured the production line improvements then being built into the normal production machines, and had the antenna mast mounted atop the windscreen and the revised navigator cabin-mounted gun turret.

These aircraft featured several changes over the trial aircraft. They continued to drop the nose-mounted ShKAS and the navigator's flexi-mounted ShKAS, although this raised protests from operational units, where they were considered desirable, especially the former which was much used for ground strafing. They carried the modified VUB-1 gun turret. The nacelle-mounted bomb bays were, in contrast, put back. A wider upper hatch was built into these aircraft, a feature later adopted by production line Pe-2/M-105PFs. Some redistribution of weights involved shifting the battery and oxygen bottles aft to the tail section while the lead ballast was dropped. Finally, a steel slab was built into No.13 bulkhead at the third fuselage section.

Other improvements were planned and approved by V.M. Myasishchev under the August 1943 development plan, with the provisional designation of Pe-4A. This projected design would have featured an enlarged bomb bay for greater payload capacity, and would have involved a re-design of the centre section of the fuselage. The FZ gun turret would have been incorporated with a re-designed canopy. Nothing came of these ideas at this stage and the 'Pe-4A' was never more than a paper concept.

The first production Pe-2/M-82F, 1-226, did not survive its company flight-testing. It crashed following an engine con-rod failure in flight and was a total write off. Therefore, the NI-VVS conducted their first tests on 1-232 in February 1944, with the aircraft flown by veteran test pilot Major General P. Stefanovsky. The results were disappointing. Compared to the trial aircraft, 1-232 turned in a lacklustre performance, with a lower speed of 526km/h at the mid-altitude range of 3,000-4,000 metres. This was established as being due to continued carburettor and fuel-mix-control unit problems at altitudes above 3,000-4,000 metres. As a result the engines could not be run at their full potential. (This despite the fact that the new version of the M-82 with the 2ASh-82FN direct fuel injection system, was deemed to have just about eliminated this problem on single-engined fighters.)[18]

Stefanovsky himself commented that the radial-engined Pe-2 showed commendable ability to fly on asymmetric power at 8,300kg weight, with the undercarriage retracted and extended. The glide-angle he found to be steeper, due to the greater revs on the throttled-back engines. However, in his view, the Pe-2/M-82 remained just as complex and difficult to handle and fly as the production Pe-2/M-105PF.

This persistent unreliability led to a lack of interest in the new radial-engined Pe-2 idea. Ironically, even greater factors in abandonment of the project were now a *shortage* of the M-82F, rather than the earlier excess. The engine was in demand again for the Lavochkin La-5 fighter aircraft, which the GKO (State Defence Council) deemed to be a greater priority. Later the Tu-2 bomber was also to be equipped with this power plant. In addition, shortages were being experienced in oil radiator production and so official authorisation was denied. Moreover, by the time the trials had been completed, the original bottleneck in M-105 engine production had been overcome. With an adequate supply of the normal Pe-2 engine, and the operational complications of introducing two very different types of engine for servicing of the same aircraft, the idea was taken no further.

Combat Evaluation

Despite this, the twenty-four accepted Pe-2/M-82s did see some limited combat service. Introduced for service trials in small batches of three to five aircraft to various front-line units from spring 1944 onward, they were given a thorough workout. The increased ceiling and extra speed provided by the radials saw the most practical employment of these unique aircraft with reconnaissance air regiments, with the dive-brakes removed; indeed, even with orthodox dive-bomber regiments, they were almost *exclusively* so employed. One factor in this assignment was that, as these recce units only operated their aircraft singly, or, at most, in pairs, the problems of engine harmonisation to achieve formation flying, was largely eliminated. The bulk of the two-dozen machines went to 8 RAB (8 Air Reserve Brigade) and they, in turn, trickled them out to front-line units.

One unit, which used them, was 99 Guards Independent Reconnaissance Air Regiment (99 Gv. ORAP). Another operator of this type was 39 ORAP, which had three on its strength for a time. The commander of 4th Guards Bomber Air Division (4. Gv. BAD), Major General F. Kotlyar, HSU, himself an air reconnaissance specialist, adopted one of the Pe-2/M-82Fs as his own personal aircraft.

THE PETLYAKOV Pe-2

End of the Experiment

This apart, no great enthusiasm for the radial-engined Pe-2 manifested itself from the front-line units which operated it. The unreliability of the engines, the oil fuel problems, the slow-starting in winter conditions, the added complications on maintenance in the field and lack of spare parts were all causes of frustration, while the elusive extra performance, only rarely achieved, failed to compensate.

No more than thirty-three machines (one trial and thirty-two production) were produced and GAZ-22 was instructed to concentrate on churning out more of the Pe-3 fighter variants, equipped with the VK-105PF engine, which is described elsewhere.

The Pe-4A

This proposal was a refinement of the Pe-4 variant. The central fuselage section was to be built as that of the Pe-2F to increase weapons capacity, and a new canopy was to be fitted incorporating the FZ turret. The protracted problems and ultimate failure of that project foredoomed the Pe-4A which never became more than a paper project.

Pe-2VI. (1943)

Having her origins as a high-altitude fighter aircraft, the Pe-2 was a natural choice when thought was given to intercepting the Luftwaffe's high-flying Ju.86 reconnaissance machines and the like which overflew Moscow in 1943. The Germans were known to be developing the Ju.288 as their own high-altitude bomber, and the immunity of such aircraft while over Soviet territory caused much burning of midnight oil to find a solution.

The brief was for an interceptor capable of attacking Luftwaffe reconnaissance machines at heights of between 13,000-14,000 metres. The final outcome was the Pe-2VI (*Vysotnyi istrebitel'* – high-altitude fighter), which was the brainchild of the team led by Vladimir M. Myasishchev. Pared down to basics the Pe-2VI was equipped with a single pressurised cockpit, which featured the blister-type canopy.

The hoped-for ceiling was 12,000 metres from the VK-105PF engine fitted with the V.A. Dollezhal superchargers. The Putilov-designed pressure cabin was a welded AMtsp alloy unit (semi-cold worked), built separately and then attached to the fuselage. External glue-fillers were applied for aerodynamic smoothness. This cabin occupied the whole nose section and was air-fed from the PTSN centrifugal blower. An alternative cabin was designed by Aleksei Yakovlevich Shcherbakov[19] and also flights tested on Pe-2.[20] However, as the blower unit was not fully developed by the time of the trials, which took place in spring 1943, only a 10,500-metre altitude was achieved.

Another variant, with improved armour fitted abaft the navigator and beneath the pilot, had been reported over the northern sector of the Karelian front in the spring of 1943 by Colonel K.V. Yanarmo of the Finnish Air Force in a letter to the Central House of Aviation, dated 16 March 1968.[21]

With the turn in fortunes later in the war, the specialised need for this aircraft was deemed to have passed. Finding a suitable power plant led to considerable experimentation, however.

Pe-2 No. 19/223

This was a standard Pe-2B taken over for in-flight testing in 1944. She was fitted with two VK-105PF engines, driving VISh-105 SB-01.1 airscrews of 3.1-metre diameter and underwent a series of trials in the summer of 1944 at the State Testing Centre.

Pe-2 No. 14/226

As a result of trials with 19/223, another aircraft was taken from the production line at Factory No. 22 as a test-bed in 1944; this aircraft was also fitted with two VK-105PF engines, driving the VISh-105SVP airscrew of 3.1-metre diameter. Originally this machine had been used to evaluate a booster system of water injection into the intake manifolds. That experiment was a flop, and so this aircraft was adapted for a totally different experiment. This new trial series resulted in the experimental re-winged Pe-2. The full report of these trials makes revealing reading.[22]

The trials were conducted by Leading pilot – Assistant Head of Department No. 3 for flying work – Lieutenant Colonel V. Zhdanov, with leading engineer of Department No. 3 of Nll of Red Army VVS, Engineering Major E.Ja. Matitsin. The aims of the tests were:

1: To reveal the specific features of piloting technique of the aeroplane with modified wing.
2: To determine the aeroplane's flight characteristics.

The trial aircraft was built at Factory No. 22 in September, 1943 and differed from the normal serial production Pe-2s by modified wing only. The main points of modification of the serial wing were:

1: The nose part of BSS profile of the wing outer part was changed to NACA-230 profile on the part up to 25% of the wing chord.
2: The wing area was increased on 0.846m^2, and span – on 0.92m by increasing the tip fairings of the outer wing parts.
3: There were also minor changes made in the front spar (in jigs only) in the inlet channel of the water-cooler tunnel and in the middle parts of the ribs.
4: Wing centre plane as well as the other parts of the outer wing panels were *not* changed.

THE PETLYAKOV Pe-2

On 29 May 1944 the aeroplane arrived at Red Army NII VVS for the performance testing, and test flights commenced on 7 June, continuing through until the 13th. In that period twenty-six test flights were conducted, with a total flying time of 13 hours, 45 minutes. The flight evaluation threw up the following points.

1: The serial Pe-2 with modified wing had sharply increased longitudinal stability during take off. The aeroplane did not roll on wing when pulling up at low speed, thus making the take-off itself 'significantly easier and less dangerous' than the serial Pe-2s.
2: The minimum flying speed decreased for the climbing regime and the lateral stability considerably improved. Minimum acceptable airspeed at climb was 200km/h. At the further decrease of airspeed up to 195-190km/h, the aeroplane lost controllability and dropped her nose. The most efficient airspeed for climbing practically did not change (with landing gear and air brakes retracted).
3: Horizontal flight was possible up to airspeed of 220km/h. At the further decrease of airspeed, the aeroplane drops the nose (landing gear and air brakes retracted).
4: It was easier to perform flying with one dead engine due to the increase of airspeed range. Maximum acceptable airspeed with one dead engine was 235-240km/h. At the further decrease of airspeed the pedal loads increased and trim-tab effectiveness was not sufficient to remove those loads, and the controllability reduced. The maximum airspeed for flying with one dead engine was found to be 300km/h (with landing gear retracted, airscrew of the dead engine at highest pitch and a flight weight of 8,447kg). An available airspeed reserve of 60-56km/h was sufficient to allow climbing in such condition.
5: The minimum acceptable gliding airspeed (with landing gear and air brakes retracted) was 235km/h. Any decrease of airspeed made the aircraft less stable in flight, and the nose dropped at 220km/h. Gliding with the landing gear and with air brakes set at 50-degree angle, could be performed at 200km/h airspeed, but, again, a further decrease to 180km/h saw the aircraft drop her nose. Gliding approach was therefore only recommended at airspeeds of 220-225km/h.
6: When landing with fully extended flaps, the efficiency of the elevator was not found to be sufficient to make a three-point landing. Landing was best performed with the brakes extended to 40-45 degrees. In the case of high-level flaring out or bouncing, the aircraft did not roll on wing, which was most significant.

The conclusions reached by test pilot Lieutenant Colonel V.I. Zhdnaov on 16 June was that:

a) The Pe-2 aeroplane with modified wing had a significantly wider range of airspeeds and better lateral stability compared to the serial production Pe-2.

b) That the aeroplane became safer in piloting at low airspeeds in all flying regimes. The modified wing eliminated the significant shortage of Pe-2 aeroplane rolling on wing at low airspeeds.
c) It was recommended that, as soon as possible, the modified wing be implemented into serial production, as this would reduce the number of accidents in service units and ease the training of aircrew on the Pe-2.

Major General Kabanov's own conclusions, delivered on 14 June, were similar in essence.

a: The aircraft had become significantly easier in piloting than those with the standard wing profile.
b: The aircraft became easier on take off and landings (which was especially important) due to the fact that it no longer had the tendency to roll on wing. The landing run was steady, but, even so, when landing with fully-extended flaps, the efficiency of the elevator was still not sufficient for a three-point landing.
c: The aircraft's minimum airspeed decreased significantly and her behaviour at minimum airspeed improved considerably. These facts increased the flying safety of the Pe-2, which previously was one of the strictest.
d: With one engine cut out, the modified aircraft flew much better and this would improve reliability and flying safety in combat conditions.

Kabanov added that 'I think that installation of such a wing on the serial production aircraft would considerably decrease the number of accidents and accelerate the training of flight crew for the Pe-2.'

The conclusions reached on the best piloting techniques to take advantage of the new profile were also laid out in detail.

1: Installation of the modified wing on the Pe-2 changed the character of the aircraft behaviour at minimum airspeeds just above the stall. When a normal Pe-2 production model reached minimum airspeed, there occurred strong buffeting of the empennage, twitching of all tail control surfaces, then the aircraft nose dropped sharply and rolls on wing. In the same conditions, the aircraft with the modified form, small jerks of the tail control surfaces appear, the aircraft drops the nose only. After stalling, the aircraft quickly regained stability and controllability.
2: At the regimes of climbing and gliding the minimum flying airspeed decreased by 15-20km/h.
3: Aeroplane stability improved in all flying regimes.
4: The modified aircraft became much easier to pilot, especially on take off and landing, because of the elimination of the roll on wing tendency of the standard Pe-2.

5: When flying with just one engine, the range of airspeeds increased by 20-25km/h.
6: When landing with fully-extended flaps, the efficiency of the elevator still remained insufficient for a three-point landing.

On the flying characteristics:

1: Maximum airspeeds, rate of climb, take-off and landing characteristics on the Modified-wing Pe-2 did not appreciably change compared to the serial production Pe-2.

A final conclusion was delivered by Lieutenant General of Engineering Aviation Losyukov on 22 June.

1: The modified wing provided the following features:
   a) improved aircraft behaviour on the minimum airspeeds – the aeroplane does not roll on wing (as happens on serial aircraft), which significantly simplifies the piloting technique and improved flying safety.
   b) Simplified take offs and landings.
   c) Decreased critical airspeeds of the aircraft by 15-20km/h.
   d) Increased the range of airspeeds by 20-25km/h when flying with one engine only.
   e) Did not practically worsen any of the aircraft's existing flying characteristics.

The recommendation was therefore for the installation of the modified wing in production *Peshkas* forthwith.[23]

Despite the enthusiasm of the report, the NII VVS did nothing other than 'duly note' it. Shakhurin at the NKAP would not do anything to complicate series production, and such radical changes in wing form would have that result. He was not alone; nobody had the enthusiasm to explain to GKO any slowing of the planned delivery quantities of the Pe-2, and even more reluctant to face Stalin with such facts. The Pe-2 might be progressively falling behind in technology, but the machines were coming off the lines as demanded. They, and their young crews, were deemed expendable. This idea was, therefore, abandoned like so many others.

Pe-4 (1944)

Following the experiments with Pe-2 No. 14/226, eighteen similar Pe-4s (as they were officially, but confusingly designated) were built in 1944. They were adapted from the standard Pe-2FT but fitted with the VK-105PF engine. Again, the variant was not further developed.

VARIATIONS ON A THEME

Pe-2R

Resulting from good results with adapted Pe-3s, a special Day/Night Photo-Reconnaissance variant, the Pe-2R (*Razvedshchik* – reconnaissance), was introduced. Stripped of most of the armament and cleaned up, these machines were equipped in their place with two supplementary fuel tanks, which provided the Pe-2R with an extra 64 Imperial gallons (290l) of fuel, sufficient to extend the range to 1,056 miles (1,700km).

Later models were equipped with a new automatic course-keeping device, the AK-1 (*Avtomat kurs* – automatic course), which was designed to keep the aircraft on a constant pre-set course, especially useful for night work. Soviet designers claimed that it achieved a high accuracy, keeping the aircraft within 1 or 2 degrees of the true course and thus easing the strain of long-range missions. The photographic equipment comprised three cameras, mounted both vertically and obliquely, to map a swathe of enemy territory with good coverage.

Pe-2P

In 1944 another photo-reconnaissance variant appeared, This was an experimental three-seater daytime reconnaissance aircraft. Designated as the Pe-2P (P= Photographic), it was equipped with multiple cameras and had a flying range of 1,700 kilometres due to extra fuel tanks. The power plant was the VK-105PF, and the defensive armament was three Berezin machine guns, but it carried no bombs. Loading was 1,200kg, with speeds of up to 580km/h at 4,000 metres. Climb rate was 8.8 minutes to 5,000 metres. Weight was 7,603kg. The single prototype was never used operationally. Another aircraft with the same designation was under construction at the same time, which featured the VK-107A engine and was armed with three ShVAK cannon for defence. Range was estimated to be 2,000 kilometres with a weight of 9,848kg and a top speed of 630km /h at 5,600 metres. This latter never materialised.[24]

Pe-2K

An intermediate variant, which Sharov asserts was designated as the Pe-2K,[25] combined features from the series Pe-2 and the experimental P-2I. the F-1 engine/propeller combination, F-3 and empennage of a series Pe-2, the centre-wing section, outer-wing panels, engine nacelles and undercarriage of the Pe-2I. This one off passed flight tests and was to be introduced as a step in the process of gradually transferring a series plant to a Pe-2I plant production line.

Pe-2 *Paravan*

This was a barrage balloon wire-cutter design from the Myasishchev period. A five-metre long, one-metre sharp trihedral pyramid made of duralumin tubing

THE PETLYAKOV Pe-2

The barrage-balloon cable-cutter attachment fitted to some Pe-2s, which became the Pe-2 *Paravan*. (Russian Aviation Research Trust)

was fitted to the fuselage nose, from the tip of which steel cables with sharp serrated cutting edges led to the wing-tips. Although fully equipped and photographed, this device was *never* tested in practice.

Rocket-powered *Peshka*

There had been a long tradition in the history of Soviet aviation of using rocket-power to assist with take off and experiments had been continual since the early 1920s. The wartime value of reducing the take-off distance of combat aircraft was obvious, both from the increasing demands of the actual bomb payload to the need for front-line units to take off from primitive airstrips close to the front.

By 1942 an OKB team, nominally led by V.P. Glushko, had produced the liquid-fuelled RD-1. In fact, the inventor was really Sergei P. Korolev, former head of the RNII (*Reaktivno-issledovatel'ski institut* – Reaction-Motor Research Institute), and later to be deified as a Soviet Space pioneer. At this time he was yet another incarcerated aeronautical political prisoner.

This engine was a liquid-fuel rocket which could be used as a booster for take off or during actual combat. The fuel was a mix of kerosene and nitric acid and the *Peshka's* internal bomb bay was altered to accommodate a 1,984lb (900kg) fuel tank. This gave a maximum of ten minutes burn time and was electrically ignited. The RD-1 could develop 661lb (300kg) of thrust in short bursts. The idea was to use the system to facilitate take off, climb, and evasion.

Fitted to the tail of 15/185 in 1942 under Korolev's direct supervision, he also flew the trial missions as onboard technician to observe results at firsthand. Despite his work and dedication, because he was in Communist eyes a criminal and a taint on the system, his invention was credited to the more acceptable scientist, Valentin P. Glushko, with Korolev as his deputy.[26]

The Pe-2, increasingly becoming the prime bomber equipping the VVS, was a natural choice for such a study. Early in 1943, as part of Glushko's team as deputy chief designer, Korolev was charged with applying the current technology to the *Peshka* as a booster.[27]

VARIATIONS ON A THEME

Close-up detail of the tail end of the RD-1 rocket-powered experimental aircraft. (Russian Aviation Research Trust)

Korolev produced a theoretical study with aerodynamical calculations comparing the potential performance of the Pe-2 engined by the RD-1 of 300kg static thrust against the same aircraft equipped with the VK-105RA piston engine. His figures indicated an improvement of 88km/h of maximum speed at ground level at 542km/h. He also predicted that an 80-100-second burst by the RD-1 at an altitude of 7,000 metres would accelerate the *Peshka* by 108km/h. For RATO (Rocket-Assisted Take Offs) operations, the rate of climb was very much improved, while the overall distance required to leave the ground would be reduced by some 70 metres.

Prototype 15-185 Built

In spring 1943 and under the combined direction of V.M. Myasishchev and S.P. Korolev, work commenced on converting a Pe-2, number 15-185, to accommodate the RD-1. Modification of a standard Pe-2 was extensive. The rocket engine itself was mounted on an attachment to the tail end of the aircraft. In order to distribute the weight and maintain of the original CG (centre of gravity) the associated oxidant tank was located in the *Peshka's* bomb bay, and the kerosene and nitric acid tanks were fitted in the wing roots and central fuselage. Part of the aircraft's piston-engine power was used to operate the pumping system. The main engine had a 700-litre fuel supply under this arrangement. Auxiliary systems and pipework had also to be incorporated into the fuselage.

The extra weight of all these additions, rockets and fuel, totalled some 1,050kg. Empty weight was 6,044kg. This gave a take-off weight of 8,200kg on modified aircraft. Armed with two 500kg bombs carried on the external racks, this increased

THE PETLYAKOV Pe-2

to 9,215kg. The machine, dubbed the Pe-2RD, and also known as the VM-15, was then ready for evaluation.

For the trials, the standard crew provision was unaltered, but the places of the navigator and gunner were taken by Korolev himself and another technician.

Propulsion method

The RD-1 liquid-fuel rocket operated on nitric acid and tractor-grade kerosene. Once lit, the RD-1 consumed 50 litres of oxidant and 25 litres of kerosene per minute. Burning 90kg of fuel per minute for a maximum ten-minute period, it developed 300kg of thrust. The rocket unit itself, designated the RU-1 (*Raketnyj Uskoritel'*), was self-contained.

The RD-1 could only be ignited by the test pilot himself, G. Vasilchenko, but in an emergency the power could be immediately terminated by *any* of the crew members should it prove necessary. By 24 May 1943 the design had been finalised.

The trials

Initially, a number of ground tests were carried out to ascertain whether the system worked reliably. This done, the trials moved on to the more dangerous

The newly-liberated Polish *Instytucie Lotnictwa* (Aviation Institute) at Warsaw was quickly put back into operation to develop a military jet engine of its own (based on captured German materials and designs which had fallen into Polish hands at the end of the war). The engine was flight-tested in 1946 on a Series 359 Pe-2, supported by a tubular framework that raised it 2m (6.6ft) clear of the fuselage to avoid blast damage. Work had not proceeded very far before the Soviet Union stepped in and informed Poland that all jet engines would be supplied by them! The project was immediately halted. (Andrzej Morgala)

flight-testing stage. The first test flight was made on 1 October 1943. A two-minute run of the RD-1 increased the Pe-2RD's acceleration by 92km/h (52mph). Two days later, the engine was switched on at 365km/h and run for three minutes successfully. The only problem encountered was increased stick pressure, as one would expect. On 4 October, the first of six successive experimental take offs using the rocket engine with a one-minute burn time was undertaken and was followed by five more. The test pilot for the programme was M.L. Gallai. These confirmed the decreased take-off run, reduced to just 446 metres, and the increased rate of climb with the rocket lit. In total, 110 test flights took place over the two-year period of the trials. Their breakdown was as follows:

>Test with rocket motor switched on: 29
>Equipment Check Tests: 14
>Rocket-Motor Ignition Tests: 67

Analysis of these tests followed each series of flights and further modifications were made as a result of their findings, and tested in their turn. It was found that, at high altitudes, the electrical ignition of the fuel mixture was unreliable and inconsistent. The RD-1 was modified by V.P. Glushko's scientists to a chemical ignition (*Khimicheskoe zazhiganie*) method, designated as X3, whereby the fuel components self-ignited. This improved reliability considerably, the modified rocket engine being designated as the RD-1X3 (alternately known as RD-1KhZ).

Double-rocket proposal for the Pe-3 fighter

By February 1944 Korolev was proposing that the Pe-3 be used with a two-rocket installation, with a pair of RD-1KhZ rocket engines which would give a total thrust of 600kg. They would be located at the rear of the VK-105 engine nacelles. The Pe-3 would be modified into a high-altitude interceptor by the fitting of a single pressurised cabin and turbo-superchargers. These alterations would have resulted in a take-off weight of 9,325kg (20,558lb), but Korolev put forward estimated performance figures of 785km/h at 15,000m (488mph at 49,215ft) for such a conversion.

This would turn the Pe-3 into a 1,000-kilometre long-range fighter. The primary object of this exercise was the interception of high-altitude enemy reconnaissance aircraft. Initially the idea was to be pioneered using a Pe-3 fitted the M-105 engines, which it would use to attain an altitude of between 9,000 and 11,000 metres, where it would assume level flight. On sighting the high-flying enemy aircraft above him the pilot would first boost his piston-engines, which would be fitted with turbo-compressors, to full, then turn on the rocket motor to fire him up to the required altitude (15,000m) above the target plane and attack from above. It was expected that a level speed of 785km/h would be possible at such altitudes.

THE PETLYAKOV Pe-2

For the final version of this aircraft, two single-chamber-type rocket motors would be installed at the rear of the engine mountings. This would aid maintenance and examination. The six pressure-sealed tanks, carrying 1,750kg of nitric acid, were to be mounted in the centre-section. These tanks were to be fitted with an emergency drainage system in the event of battle damage or accident. Forward of the pilot's pressurised cockpit would be the 300kg capacity kerosene tank and there were to be installed the usual specialised pumping systems to the motors.

The main offensive armament for this proposed interceptor would be a pair of 20mm cannon located in the former bomb bay. A pressurised cabin would replace the pilot and navigator's canopy, and the *Peshka* would have come full circle. Korolev considered that some lightening of the fuel, equipment and armament weight requirements would be necessary to compensate for the extra weight involved, which included 2,100kg of rocket fuel. Even so, the new interceptor's flying weight was expected to increase from 8,500kg to 9,325kg. Breakdown of the weights was:

Pressurised cabin installation:	100kg
Rocket Units:	250kg
Rocket Fuel etc.	2,100kg
Turbo-compressors:	200kg

Korolev also initiated a project to fit auxiliary rocket motors to the Pe-2I to boost her two M-107A engines as a high-speed fighter or bomber. With the approaching fall of Germany these, and other interceptor projects, no longer had the same relevance or imperative and remained just paper dreams. The Pe-2 testing had continued, however.

Results

The rocket-powered Pe-2 test programme continued until May 1945 and the end of the war in Europe. Even by early 1944, Korolev was satisfied the system had merit. Myasishchev and the plant's director were sufficiently upbeat to present 15-185 for trials in front of VVS-KA representatives. The trials were gauged a real success in that they showed that such an auxiliary rocket engine could be employed safely to reduce take-off distance, improve rate of climb and assist in pushing aircraft to new horizons of speed and height. The cause was not helped by an explosion in the system during a flight in 1944, which almost cost Korolev his life. His idea was not proceeded with, nor was a similar one for conversion of a Pe-2I and the final RD-1KhZ trial took place in May 1945.

However, this whole rocket-assisted Pe-2 programme paved the way for the subsequent development of such high-performance military aircraft as the La-7R, the Su-7 and the Yak-3R, all of which were equipped with the RD-1 and RD-1KhZ rocket engine.

VARIATIONS ON A THEME

Experimental aircraft used as a flying test-bed for the VRG-430 pulse-jet engine mounted on struts. This engine was a facsimile of the German Argus-Schmidt 109-014, used on the V-1 flying bombs against England, several of which were captured at the Huta-Bankowa plant at Dombrowa Gurna and at the Ferrum plant near Katowice, Poland. They were built under the 10X programme by a team under designer Tshelomey, using imprisoned German scientists and technicians, and were tested from the Kratovo base from 1946 onward. (Zdenek Titz)

RATOG

In 1943 a Pe-2 with the solid-fuel RATOG was built and evaluation flights were conducted by test pilot M.L. Gallay. This concept never proceeded beyond the experimental stage, however.

Ejector-seat trials

Several Pe-2s were used in early Soviet experiments to produce a satisfactory ejector seat during 1946. Modification was minimal.

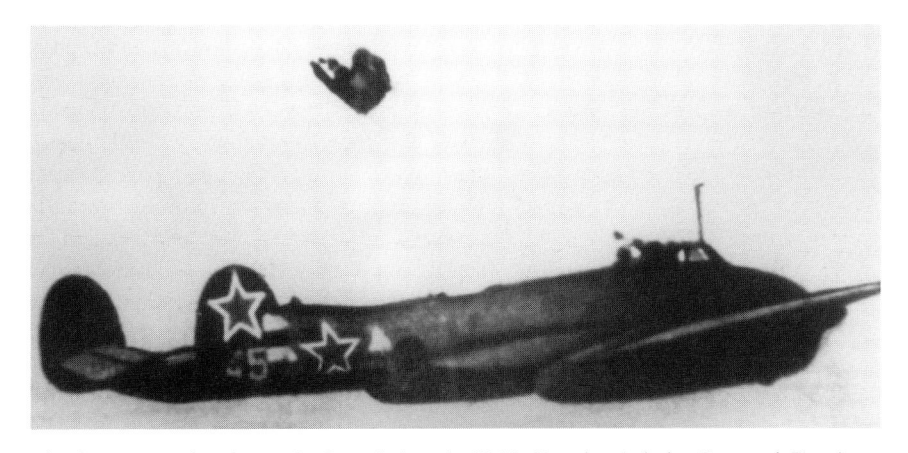

Ejection-seat testing from a Pe-2 carried out in 1946. (Russian Aviation Research Trust)

THE PETLYAKOV Pe-2

Pe-2 UT (UPe-2)

The specially adapted two-seater *Uchebnyi trenirovanii* (Advanced trainer) version was the Pe-2UT. The second pilot's cockpit was positioned in tandem, immediately abaft the fairing, in place of the turret and fuel tank number one. It was raised up above the original rear-gunner's position, giving the instructor an excellent view. The aircraft was fitted with dual controls.

Although a trainer, a limited armament of two UBS and two (fixed) ShKAS guns was carried. There was also some bombing capability, in either a 600kg internal or a 500kg external configuration. The engine was the M-105PF fitted with VISh-61B propellers. Production commenced in 1943. The prototype passed its state acceptance trials in April 1943. Some 671 UTs were finally built, which exceeded the original number planned. It was later designated as the Upe-2 in Polish service post-war.

Chapter Seventeen

Pe-2 Colour Schemes

This is a vexed subject and one that raises the hackles of serious historians and model-makers, as well as the usual anonymous, rivet-counting troglodytes that proliferate on the net and review pages. While we can ignore the latter group and leave them to their incestuous back-stabbing, we *can* briefly outline this complicated subject for the sake of the former. The comments made by Marcus Wendel on the quantification and cataloguing of production runs can just as easily be applied to the question of paint schemes. Wendel states, quite correctly, that:

> The Soviets were in a rush during the war and were not only loose in assignment of revision numbers to aircraft, but also continually tweaked production without much concern about block codes. Such practices tend to cause confusion in maintenance and production, but they were in a desperate hurry and felt they could put off worrying about such niceties.[1]

The Background

One secondary source for Soviet colour schemes is Mikhail Maslov, whose book contains a chapter entitled *Painting Schemes*.[2] Although he is mainly concerned with the principal subject of his book, a fighter aircraft, some of his statements relate to all military aircraft. Maslov maintains that until 1937 only a single standard finish for military aircraft existed, which was green upper surfaces and 'greyish-light blue' for under surfaces. It was the involvement of Soviet aircraft in actual combat conditions during the Spanish Civil War and other incidents, which led to the first questionings of this standard.

The principal switch, and especially for fighter aircraft, was away from concealment on the ground toward an attempt at concealment in the air. At a meeting held in summer 1937 between the GUAP (*Glavnoe upravlenie aviatsionnoi promyshlennosti* – Chief Administration of Aircraft Industry) and VIAM (*Vsesoyuzniy institut aviatsionnykh materialov* – All-Union Scientific Research Institute for Aviation Materials) this change of emphasis was embodied thus:

> All surfaces of monocoque fuselages and also the lower wing surfaces are to be painted a matt silver-aluminum colour. The upper surfaces of the wings and fuselages having a faceted form are to be painted in defensive (green) colour.

THE PETLYAKOV Pe-2

The use of this scheme was tempered in some cases by the ideas of Nikolai Polikarpov who had earlier advocated a light blue or dull silvery tint, and this latter was duly applied by Aircraft Factory No. 1. The lesson learned from the Khalkin Gol incidents in the Far East led to a hasty re-appraisal, dispersed aircraft featuring this colour scheme being prominent on their airfields from a great distance. On 23 May 1940 the State Defence Committee of the USSR issued Resolution No. 220, which reintroduced the '*Chaiki*', green upper and light blue under surfaces as the norm from June/July of that year. Two days later the NKAP (People's Commissariat of the Aircraft Industry) issued Order No. 228. From 10 June all machines from factories 83, 99, 125, 126 and 153 were to conform to the following patterns:

a: Upper surfaces of wings and tail unit, top and sides of fuselage – Green (Grass).
b: Lower surfaces of wings, tail and fuselage – Pale Light Blue (Cloud)

Existing aircraft were *not* to be repainted. The producers of the lacquer paints were ordered to co-ordinate their production accordingly through the offices of the GUAS-KA (Main Administration of Aviation Supply).

In June 1941, on the eve of the German invasion, this standard scheme was modified and green-painted upper surfaces of military aircraft were camouflaged with patches of black, with national markings obscured.

In 1947 an NKVD report was issued on the whole question of camouflage paint schemes and the various paints, emulsions etc., both used and recommended, along with the pattern requirements, during the whole period 1920-45. When this report finally became available to the public its details were incorporated, almost totally, in a series of articles by Vasili Vakhlamov and Mikhail Orlov, published in *M-Khobbi* magazine.[3] These articles were translated by George M. Mellinger in 2001 for the benefit of English-speaking enthusiasts and provided a wealth of detail. However, much of this information was subsequently dismissed by Erik Pilawski, who is an acknowledged expert in the field of Soviet aviation camouflage and paints. Mr Pilawski has spent many years examining the aircraft of this period first-hand, taking paint samples from more than 140 aircraft and studying more than 13,800 photographs, including more than 9,100 negatives from various Russian archives and records. He concluded that the NKVD reports, on which these articles were based, were written in retrospect by officials who lacked first-hand knowledge. Mr Pilawski states that, in the case of the Pe-2 largely for the entire course of the war, and for the 1944-45 period most especially, the last NKAP recommendation (the so-called 'Last Minute' Regulation issued at the end of 1944, incorporated in part in Order No. 5590/0207), 'was truly not worth the paper it was printed on'.[4]

Whether this is the case or not, certainly Mr Pilawski's second point has much validity and that was that, even though the various directives were issued at regular intervals, their actual promulgation, both in the aircraft factories and at the front line, was at best, patchy and at worst non-existent. Again, this non-compliance was

Pe-2 COLOUR SCHEMES

not so much wilful disobedience of bureaucratic instructions as the unavoidable exigencies of the period. In the factories, the pressure was totally concentrated on keeping the production lines rolling, the non-availability of specialist paints and materials specified and the like and related factors. Even Vakhlamov concedes that some of the schemes discussed did not go into use.

This author considers that the data in Vakhlamov and Orlov is of considerable interest, providing that it is treated with reservation. I consider that much of this theoretical information very likely did not translate into fact, but it provides a fair insight into the official thinking and theory on this subject at that time.

Even as early as summer 1940 there was ample evidence that the new painting instructions were not being carried out, especially with regard to bomber aircraft at both 125 and 126 Aircraft Factories. Nor was everyone in the VVS-KA convinced of the actual effectiveness of the newly-developed paints to aid concealment. Colonel Romanov, of the Rear Section of the Staff, reported to his Chief of Staff, Corps Commander Arzhenukhin, on 28 May, that, far from blending the aircraft so painted into the background, in some conditions of sunlight, the new paints produced a sheen that enhanced their visibility. Consternation was obvious and new standards providing for single- and multi-colour camouflage, with emphasis on a matt finish, indistinct and 'fairly dark', were called for. Thus, under Order No. 081 dated 9 June 1940, a 'Commission for the determination of standards of coverings for protective and deformative (sic) finishes for aircraft', was established with representatives from all the diffuse institutes, with Romanov as chairman, a post assumed by Colonel V. Suyazin after the former's abrupt demise shortly afterwards.

On 29 July it was determined that tests involving not just two- or three- colour variations would be tested, but that four- or even five-colour schemes would be examined, based on (a) Dark Brown, (b) Green, (c) Sand, (d) Grey Earth, (e) Yellow-Green and (f) Dark Green. The combinations and patterns would vary according to the military district the aircraft were currently operational in. Despite protests on the complexity of adopting such a variety of combinations, in view of the burden this would place on both manufacturer and aircraft factory, this decision was pressed ahead with. Chief of the VVS of the Red Army, Major General P.V. Rychagov signed Order 154 to this effect on 3 August 1940. The standard light bombers of the time, the SBs, with the dark-green upper and light-grey under surfaces were duly over-painted in these combinations and observed in a range of conditions and habitats. The results seemed conclusive. Both in the air and on the ground the four- or five-colour combination was found to give the best concealment.

As a result of these trials the SB units were issued with three four-colour schemes and one five-colour scheme, thus:

1: Sand /Green (4BO)/ Dark Green/Dark Brown
2: Sand/4BO/Yellow-Green/Dark Brown
3: Sand/4BO/Dark green/Grey-Brown
4: Sand/Grey-Brown/Yellow-Green/4BO/Dark Brown

However, between the decision on the paint schemes and their implementation across the board were bestrewn myriad problems. Manufacture of the required aero-laks (laquers) and aero-enamels, new formulae and technical standard requirements, availability of the required colours of powdered pigments to the two main producers (Factory No. 36 and the Krasnopresenenskii Lacquer and Paint Factory) proved insurmountable. As Vakhlamov and Orlov conceded, 'not one of these multi-coloured schemes was ever introduced into serial production'.

The Reality

Despite all the orders, instructions and resolutions, for this entire period and up to the eve of the war, the Soviet aviation industry continued to produce aircraft with the green upper and side surfaces and light-blue under surfaces. Plans to force the introduction of the new schemes, even by using unsuitable paints in the interim, were embodied in NKAP Order No. 417ss on 6 May 1941, which determined that camouflaged uppers and light-grey lower surfaces would be introduced from 1 October. These, however, went by the board. Marshal Stalin forced the issue in typical fashion. Determined to ensure that aircraft on front-line airfields facing the Germans were properly protected, he banged heads together figuratively, with the unspoken threat of doing it actually if something were not done. Prompted by a report from the central committee on the lack of such concealment, he had the heads of the NKAP and VVS summoned to the Kremlin for a meeting on aircraft camouflage. Stalin gave them three days to sort out what they had been discussing and fulminating on for three years.

Both factories and front-line units were told to implement the schemes forthwith, but it was already too late. Among the thousand upon thousand of Soviet combat aircraft torched on the ground in the opening days of Operation BARBAROSSA, none wore the new camouflage scheme. The first examples appeared around 13 July[5] but this was a classic case of belatedly closing the stable door.

According to the memoirs of Technical Lieutenant Vadim Vasil'evich Pshenichnov, who served at Chief of PARM-1 No. 1087, the maintenance units were under-staffed, under-supplied, and under pressure.

> During that period there was no time to think about finishes. Paint was smeared over only the damaged surfaces. That continued until the spring, even the summer of 1942, which the situation ... became notably quieter.[6]

Here he is talking about a fighter regiment, 562 IAP PVO, but the same situation applied to all units, including the Pe-2 regiments. Pshenichnov adds that, with the arrival of winter, 'All the aircraft were painted white. They used chalk, so very roughly ground you could hardly say it was pulverised, and painted with brushes.' Some spirit had to be added to this mixture of chalk, casein and water to stop it congealing in the sub-zero temperatures. Come spring it was wiped off again.

Pe-2 COLOUR SCHEMES

Thereafter, the standard two-colour schemes, with many local variations, continued to be the norm. Attempts were made from time to time, when the intensity of operations permitted, for experiment in the field. Thus, it is recorded that, in June 1942, twenty Pe-2s were painted in a new three-colour scheme originated by GYZiTS VVS KA (Main Administration of Requisition and Technical Supply of the Air Force). The camouflage appears to have won the approval of local commanders both at the front and in the rear echelons, but was not generally adopted. The factories doggedly continued to pour out increasing numbers of Pe-2s and Pe-3s but all in the standard two-colour green-black-upper, light-blue-lower schemes right through the first two years of the Great Patriotic War.

The Scheme of Aircraft Camouflage Finishes – July 1943

The first practical changes in camouflage schemes to be generally initiated in wartime conditions came about with Order NKAP SSRR & VVS Red Army No. 389/0133, issued on 3 July 1943 and signed fifteen days later. This was designed to mark a watershed in the whole area of military aircraft paint schemes.[7] This scheme was specific and laid down not just the colours and the actual marks of paint to be employed, but the very patterns themselves to be adopted.

Under this specification the Pe-2s were to have their upper surfaces painted with a three-colour scheme, with green, light brown and dark grey, with two variants of finish, while the under surfaces were to retain the usual light blue. Implementation was authorised from 1 August, but there was no requirement to repaint existing stocks of aircraft; that could be done on their next refits back at the PARM-1 (Aircraft Maintenance Shops) of the individual regiments. Once again, the actual putting into practice of the new camouflage scheme was tardy and even non-existent. The overriding need, as always, was for production targets to be met, and improved. Applying a three-colour-paint job to the upper surfaces of the Pe-2 took much longer than the ordinary painting, even supposing that supplies of the required colour paints were stocked. In many instances, it can be assumed that a Nelsonic blind eye was turned to the demands from Moscow, which were considered both impracticable and impossible on the shop floor.

The next edict came on 1 October 1944. By then the VVS was very much in the ascendant. Need for concealment on forward airfields remained, but the threat was much reduced: a pattern for attacking aircraft heading deep into central Europe was the main requirement. This change seemed to embody the absolute mastery of the air that the Soviets had obviously achieved by this stage of the war.

Thus it was that GKO (The Supreme Command) issued Resolution No. 6639 which contained a proposal from the Military Council of the VVS KA to move to a single camouflage finish for all types of military aircraft, based on that already outlined for fighter planes. This resulted in the issuing of a joint order, No. 5590/0207, from the NKAP SSR and VVS KA on 6 October, entitled 'A New Aircraft Camouflage Finish'. The album of schemes was issued, with the usual proviso that only new factory-production and combat aircraft under repair would

THE PETLYAKOV Pe-2

Three Pe-2FTs on a grass strip with bomb-bay doors agape. The red star of the national insignia is outlined in white on all these aircraft. (Russian Aviation Research Trust)

be affected, thus resulting in a continuation of the same units flying into battle with a wide variety of finishes.

With specific regard to the Pe-2, the old three-colour paint scheme of 1943 adapted by the painting over of the green areas with grey-blue, and the light brown with dark grey, save for the area of the left tail. Once again, in practice, this 'Last-Minute' scheme was adapted to an even lesser extent than the earlier ones. Erik Pilawski observed that these recommendations had a 'miniscule' effect. He doubted whether these recommendations were circulated to any of the aviation factories, stating that there appear to be no records of any factory receiving them. He also stated that photographic evidence also failed to record any sign of its implementation either, noting that a series of photographs taken at Zavod 22 on 1 May 1945, just a week before the end of the war in Europe, show enormous numbers of Pe-2s and Pe-3s. [8] The series revealed a large number of three-colour NKAP types, intermixed with some older Pe-8s on the production line being finished in the three-colour pattern of 1943 and that no two-tone samples can be seen green/dark green aircraft and the odd one or two of indeterminate coloration. It would appear that the war had terminated before any Pe-2 units had adopted the grey/grey 'fighter' pattern.

The main thing to be borne in mind in all this is that the NKAP schemes were recommendations and *not* directives; they were optional not compulsory and, due to lack of materials, time or interest, were as often as not ignored. Ulf Audun Larsstuvold told me that 'I have inspected seven different Pe-2/3 wrecks

Pe-2 COLOUR SCHEMES

from the VVS-SF: they all invariably had the blue underside with green/blackgreen oversides! *None* had any grey or brown at all!'[9]

The brief war against Japan in the Far East took place another two months down the line of course. Erik Pilawski told the author that there is 'persistent written evidence in many VVS records (especially factory and unit records) of an "Eastern" camouflage.' The colour AMT-1 is mentioned, along with AMT-1 and another darker colour, which, if confirmed would indeed be 'a curious and striking mix'.[10]

Interiors and Components

These were subjected to less change than the external camouflage patterns of course. The Pe-2s followed the general layout as the various internal photographs in this volume show.

Chapter Eighteen

The Final Developments

Pe-2I

Perhaps the most notable contribution made to the Pe-2 story by Vladimir M. Myasischev during his tenure as Chief Designer at Petlyakov was the Pe-2I. This was a day-bomber variant which was planned to operate in the medium bomber role of less accurate, but more easily trained for, level bombing in the Western mould, and capable of carrying a wider range of ordnance. In theory, it turned out well but, in practice, the *Peshka* soon reverted to the classic dive-bombing role to attain the desired battlefield results. Thus the Soviet experience was exactly the opposite of the Western one, which had refused to contemplate building specialist aircraft for close air support and had relied instead on carpet bombing. Such types were typified by the RAF Battle, Blenheim, Boston and the like and the USAAF B-25 Mitchell, A-20 Havoc and Martin B-26 Marauder, none of which could claim accuracy of bombing very high on their list of attributes.

By 1943 two things were clear to the VVS: that the air war was being won numerically, but that German technical innovations were counteracting this numerical superiority in many ways.[1] In the case of the Pe-2, it was clearly the most important dive-bomber aircraft in service, and would continue to be so. The older type light bombers had suffered heavy losses and were being progressively phased out. The new bombers, and especially the Tu-2, were still only being produced in penny-packets and would not yet replace the *Peshka* in service. (Not until the immediate post-war period did the Tupolev bomber take over the lead position in this role; by then the Pe-2 was being retired very quickly, while the production of the Tu-2 finally got underway in serious numbers.)

So, although the position of the Pe-2 remained paramount, the repeated tinkering with the series production, and the many failed attempts at specialised variants we have examined, had not solved the dilemma that the 1944 Pe-2 was still slower than the 1941 Pe-2, but that opposing fighter aircraft were now much swifter. The standard evasive tactic of the *Peshka* in the early years of the war, the shallow dive away, had worked against the Bf.109E, but it was failing totally against the Bf. 109G-6 and Fw. 190A-4.

There appeared two ways to combat this trend: make the *Peshka* even heavier by continually adding to her defensive firepower and relying on that to fight off the German attacks, or follow the British initiative with their de Havilland

THE FINAL DEVELOPMENTS

The low, lean profile of Vladimir M Myasishchev's major contribution to the Pe-2 story, the Pe-2I 'Mosquito' day-bomber. These variants were built at Aviation Factory No. 22. (M Maslov)

Mosquito, and abandon defensive armament totally, relying completely on speed to avoid losses.

The VVS, in general, continued to favour the first option. Already the basic defensive armament had grown, from four ShKAS 7.62mm machine guns in 1941 to five such weapons, including three of the heavier 12.7mm calibre, along with grenade ejectors, and other defensive weapons. That the air force would be extremely reluctant to follow the British example totally was obvious, and Myasishchev himself acknowledged this fact, as delicately as he could, in a OKO 22 report which stated that 'theoretical notions of limiting the defensive armament of a day bomber, *in view of the established traditions*,[2] cannot immediately be favourably introduced'.[3]

To be fair, there was also serious, and legitimate, doubt about the true value of the Mosquito. Although given enormous publicity in the UK press as morale-boosting propaganda with some notable exploits, losses were never featured. There was also the hard fact that the existing Pe-2 engine, the M-105, even with the new boosters fitted, was at the end of its potential. The fact that the Pe-2s frequently had to operate without fighter escort reinforced the view that they would have to stand up for themselves as they could not outrun the enemy interceptors. Weight increase was inevitable, with such increase in firepower (a 1943 VVS study for a new dive-bomber predicted an overall 2,500kg war loading) and of range, and therefore fuel-carrying capacity could not be reduced to compensate; this slowing-down process could only continue in a vicious circle.

The catalyst for change was the issuing, on 12 January 1944, of GKO resolution No. 4943. This defined the VVS's Tactical and Technical Requirements for the new high-speed dive-bomber requirement for 1944, after OKO had commenced project study in October 1943. This had led to two serious responses. Myasishchev's

THE PETLYAKOV Pe-2

The Pe-2I 'Mosquito' day-bomber version of the *Peshka*, with two VK-107A engines (rated at 1,000hp for take-off), driving VISh-107LS airscrews of 3.1m diameter. (M Maslov)

response was the Pe-2I and Tupolev's was the SB. On 14 January 1944 came NKAP order No. 22. Four days later the design received the go ahead for two prototypes to be completed by 22 February; one week later the mock-up was approved by the State commission.

Myasishchev's compromise – the Pe-2I

Although popularised by post-war western historians as the 'Soviet Mosquito',[4] it can be seen that Myasishchev's team of 22 OKO had to compromise. They did so reluctantly because they had no choice, but they did so. They were also quite successful in using various ploys of construction and assembly that employed many of the series Pe-2 parts (*temporarily so,* as they envisaged things) to disguise the fact that the new bomber was, in many ways, a new concept and not so much a variant of the *Peshka*.

The basic parameters for the new dive-bomber were therefore set in stone before design commenced. These were:

(1) An improved power unit was required;
(2) A new airframe configuration was essential to maximise the effects of (1);
(3) Defensive armament *had* to carried and could not be excluded, and, as always,
(4) Series production remained inviolate and any effects a new type of *Peshka* might have it had to be eliminated, or at least, minimised.

Let us examine each of these factors in turn and Myasishchev's thinking and solutions to each.

THE FINAL DEVELOPMENTS

The engine problem

With the M-105, even when boosted, at the end of its development potential, with the experiment with the M-82 radial no longer a viable option and with the rocket and RATOG experiments long-term, unproven, and complex, alternatives, the design team at 22 OKO was forced to seek a solution elsewhere.

The abandoned Pe-2F project seemed to provide the quick answer to the powerplant dilemma, with its experience with the liquid-cooled M-107A engine. This was powerful enough to do the job but, like so many Soviet engines of this period, reliability had left very much to be desired. The difficulties with oil leakages and overheating had resulted in no more than four-to-five hours of flight time being averaged between each failure. This was obviously unacceptable but, if these problems could be overcome, then the revised M-107A, the new VK-107A seemed to provide the only fast solution.

The VK-107A developed 1,675hp[5] at an altitude of 1,500 metres and, at 4,500 metres 1,500hp. These engines were fitted with two-speed compressors and constant-speed units. Each of the pair drove a VISh-107TL5 three-bladed airscrew, of 3.1-metre diameter. In comparison with the serial Pe-2, these engines were mounted 0.2 metres further forward. Four rows of individual exhaust ejectors were mounted, two atop the engine and one on each side of the lengthened and streamlined nacelles. The coolant radiators were positioned in the leading edges of the aircraft's centre-section, with the oil radiator and engine air intakes located in the leading edges of the outer-wing panels. Electrically-operated control flaps were provided, replacing the louvres on the serial Pe-2,

Port three-quarter view of the Myasishchev-designed Pe-2I day-bomber variant of the *Peshka*. (M Maslov)

THE PETLYAKOV Pe-2

and giving a more reliable control of the engine-coolant temperature. Underwing vents expelled the air from the radiators.

However, merely upgrading the engines alone would be insufficient, and so new airframe design changes were implemented in conjunction with the armament revision.

Armament

It was necessary for the weight-saving reduced two-man crew (pilot and navigator) of the Pe-2I to be capable of operating the continued, if modified, defensive armament with much the same efficiency as before if VVS requirements were to be met in this regard. For the future, Myasishchev was relying on the successful development of the electrically-operated DEU gun mounting, mounted aft in a remotely-controlled barbette for rear protection.[6] This weapon was designed by *Ing.* A. Zhuravlenko and was nearing the end of a long development programme. Until this weapon was ready, the UBK machine gun, as used on the standard Pe-2, was substituted. With a 100-round magazine, this gun ranged through a 16-degree traverse, an 18-degree elevation and a 12-degree depression, these parameters covering the principal areas of attack most commonly assumed by German fighters from existing combat experience.

The navigator in two separate modes controlled the rear barbette gun. To cover the lower-rear quadrant the gun was aimed with the OPSK periscopic

Head-on view of the 'Mosquito'. The Myasishchev-designed variant of the Pe-2 only carried a two-man aircrew, pilot and navigator. The rear-seat man also operated the remote 12.7 calibre rear machine-gun in the tail. The water and oil coolers were transferred to the wings on this model. (M Maslov)

THE FINAL DEVELOPMENTS

sight; for fire against targets in the upper-rear quarter, the navigator used the K8-T collimator sight.

For forward fire a more powerful weapon was required; the pilot would operate the fixed UB-20 cannon. It was to be positioned under the pilot's seat, which was designed to prevent muzzle glare in night action. Again, as this weapon was not immediately available, the prototypes had to substitute the serial production UBK machine gun initially.

There was also provision for a pair of DAG-10 parachute-grenade dispensers. These fired off a pattern of 1.8kg grenades in the path of the pursuing enemy, which exploded and laid down an area of steel fragments in its path. Hardly sophisticated, it had already been used in combat conditions, where, perhaps due to a measure of surprise, it had achieved recorded results on occasions.

Re-design

Just as the engines for the Pe-2I were influenced by the abandoned Pe-2F, another aborted project, the two-man Pe-2D, influenced the re-jigged design considerations. We have seen how GAZ 22 proceeded from November 1943 onward, with improvements to the aerodynamics of the *Peshka*, based on c/n 7-187, with the enlarged cabin incorporating the FZ (Front-line Task)[7] gun turret housing a UBT, revised engine cowlings and coolant radiator ducting. The early abandonment of preliminary work on sub-assemblies for this project was due to the arrival of the new Pe-2I concept, which took over many of its features.

In order to present an acceptable picture of production continuity, the Pe-2I, as has been mentioned, used many parts and sub-assemblies of the series line. This ensured that existing jigs and tooling would not need to be replaced at the outset. Thus, existing outer-wing panels were little modified from standard, being of combined airflow section. Fuselage tail section and tail surfaces likewise followed the series procedure with an adjustable tail plane incidence angle, being of 45 degrees in horizontal flight, opening automatically to -3 degrees once the flaps were extended beyond 22-25 degrees. These unchanged areas formed part of the design as presented. Secretly Myasishchev had a future agenda, which would see even these replaced as the programme continued, and he specifically assigned the designing of their replacements to one of his team, L.L. Selyakov.[8] Even so, *some* changes were to be made here also. Some features were simply dropped, like the dive brakes and associated dive-recovery equipment.

Main features of the Pe-2I were that it was a cantilever, mid-wing monoplane of all-metal construction. The centre section was NACA 23012 airflow section, with small radiator-coolant air intakes inset on the leading edge, and this blended into the standard B-BS airflow section at the trailing edge. This section was enlarged, increasing overall wing area by 1.2-m^2. The outer-wing panels remained of combined airflow section. The resulting aircraft was 30mm wider in fuselage diameter and longer in overall length.

THE PETLYAKOV Pe-2

Inside the streamlined enlarged cockpit, the pilot had 10mm thick back-seat armour plate, with a 8mm thick armoured headrest, while the navigator was also provided with armoured back and headrest as well as two vertical panels to give some protection, lacking in the series version. The total weight of the protective armour totalled 85kg.

The undercarriage remained as for the series production Pe-2 except that larger wheels were adopted in order to take the strain of the extra take-off weight. The oleo shock-absorber travel was increased which slightly reduced that famous 'bounce'. Otherwise, internally, it was much the same, except that the fuel tanks on the prototype incorporated the 'First Zone' fire-extinguisher system. By this method, cooled inert exhaust gases were restricted to the fuel tanks. Under the 'Second Zone' system, which came in on the second prototype ('doubler') a fuel gas neutralising chamber was added next to the fuel tanks. The need for greater range led to the installation of further fuel tanks, increasing the overall capacity to 2,590 litres.

The weapons bay was enlarged and lengthened, making it capable of carrying a single FAB-1000 M43 bomb internally. This weapon did not quite fit even then and the bomb's tail fins had to be shortened before it could be accommodated thus. Externally, the Pe-2I was capable of carrying various combinations on a pair of MDZ-40 underwing racks, either a single FAB-500 or pairs of FAB-250 or mixes of smaller bomblets. While the normal war load went down to 500kg, the maximum

Close view of the day-bomber variant, the Pe-2I. The main difference from the standard Pe-2 was that the fuselage diameter was increased by 30mm and lengthened overall by 1m. The bomb-bay was enlarged for the possibility of accommodating a FAB-1000 bomb installation (and later a FAB-2000). The number of fuel tanks was increased to a total capacity of 2,000 litres. (M Maslov)

THE FINAL DEVELOPMENTS

loading increased considerably. Although dive brakes were omitted, horizontal, glide- (40-degrees) or dive- (70-degrees) bombing was envisaged.

In achieving this enlarged capacity, which increased the aircraft's overall length by a metre and maximum diameter by 0.3-metres and raising the centre-section by the same amount, L.L. Selyakov recalled that this was done without actually moving the centre-section at all. What they did was cut part of the lower-spar beams and replace them with bowed inserts; this halved the height of the spar above the aircraft axis. The changing of the fuselage cross-section from circular to oval form accounted for the increase in diameter.

Selyakov's memories

Selyakov was later to record his own version of what took place. As he recorded it, the evaluation of the Mosquito aroused considerable interest in the Soviet Union and Myasishchev was asked to proceed with development of a Pe-2 variant on the same general principles. Leonid Selyakov joined the team. He recalled that enabling the Pe-2I to carry the FAB-1000 bomb caused considerable design problems. Because it was a low-wing monoplane, it was difficult to insert such a large weapon into the bomb bay without major reconstruction.

Selyakov's solution was to replace the straight lower steel spar strips by others of bowed form. 'The height of the spar at centreline was reduced to half. The fuselage volume was increased by changing its circular cross-section to that of oval form in its lower portion.'[9]

With a normal take-off weight hoisted to 8,430kg, and to 9,600kg in overload condition, take-off distance came out at 430 metres and 410 metres respectively. A climb rate of 6.8 minutes to 5,000 metres was recorded but speeds were disappointing, showing virtually no increase on the series Pe-2. Estimated speeds were 649km/h at 5,850 metres against 525km/h at ground level.

Official vetting

By the end of February 1944, the official commission inspected the mock-up. At this date the first prototype was about 70 per cent complete and also subject to a critical examination. Predictably, the main dissatisfaction generated was at the armament, the commission failing to be impressed by the substitute UBK and demanding the installation of the UB-20 in the second prototype without fail! The first prototype was rolled out on 10 March.

First air trials

On 6 April 1944 test pilot A.G. Vasil'chenko commenced the Company Flight Development testing programme in the still unpainted first prototype.[10] Two flights were made on that day, followed by single flights on the next two days.

THE PETLYAKOV Pe-2

The conditions tested were take-off capability, in-flight stability over all three axes, general airborne handling and the landing ability of the heavier aircraft. Results were mixed, the landing and take-off distances both increasing by far more than predicted. Directional stability was, in contrast, found to be much improved over the Pe-2, while other in-flight parameters remained much the same. The engines ran without faults, with temperature control within the expected tolerance band.

There followed a one-week lull while the aircraft was taken back to the workshop for minor faults to be rectified and for painting. This done, the programme resumed with the emphasis this time being on climb rate, speed at various altitudes and similar aspects. However, during preliminary engine running, there was a problem, with metal fragments found in the engine oil, indicating damaged bearings. This necessitated changing the engine concerned.

Second prototype

Attention then shifted to the second prototype, now almost completed, and this was subjected to static structural testing. Again the results were negative and showed up weaknesses in the wing which led to the fitting of stronger wing spars. All the modifications demanded for this second machine by the official inspectors were carried out, except for the fitting of the UB-20 cannon, which was still not ready. Once again, despite specific orders to the contrary, the inferior UBK had to be substituted. This weapon was re-positioned under the pilot's seat on the port side.

The remote control UBK 12.7 calibre tail machine-gun mounted in the Pe-2I. This stripped-down photo gives a view of its operating with two directional servos indicated. (M Maslov)

THE FINAL DEVELOPMENTS

Two external bomb racks, capable of carrying 250kg or 500kg bombs, increased the maximum bomb load to 2,000kg. The armour protection was all emplaced, however, and this aircraft showed a small increase over the first in take off weight.

Mass-balancing and spring loading was introduced to the elevator-control systems, without appreciable effect. There were some changes to the cockpit glazing to enhance ventral sighting, and the airscrews were given de-icers. As a gesture to enhance rear defence, a DAG-10 parachute-grenade dispenser was added. The transceiver was moved from the tail section up to the navigator's position, a battery was deleted and more powerful electric generators were added. Total fuel stowage was reduced by 50 litres.

In view of what had come to light to date, the design team produced two further proposed modifications to the second prototype. These were the fitting of a different engine and the introduction of a new tricycle nose-wheel undercarriage. In the event, nothing actually came of either proposal. After completion on 30 April, the second prototype completed the company flight-testing and was ferried from Kazan to NII VVS but during the journey suffered damage, which set back its State trials until 12 August 1944.

Trials resumed

The damaged engine replaced, the first prototype resumed flight-testing, again with Vasil'chenko at the controls. She underwent stringent State testing during the period 10 May to 10 July 1944. The empty weight of the new type was 7,014kg, with a flight weight of 8,983kg, with overload maximum of 9,928kg. The results were outstanding, *exceeding* the expected maximum speed at the second altitude height by some 14km/h. Only the de Havilland Mosquito B.IX and B.XVI had gone faster at this time, and then at a much higher altitude. No wonder 22 OKO rejoiced. The Pe-2I was the fastest light bomber in the world with a service ceiling of 11,000 metres and a range of 2,275 kilometres.[11]

The Soviet flight test report read that the Pe-2I was 'acceptable for the average pilot. In general has considerable advantages comparing to the Pe-2 aircraft already in service. Aircraft's maximum airspeed is higher than any native bomber aircraft.' This airspeed met 'the Government Defence Committee's Order of 12 January, 1944'. The final section stated that the Pe-2I 'can be recommended for the acceptance in Red Army Air Force service after obligatory improvements of take-off/landing characteristics'.

The word passed up the chain to the highest level.[12] Stalin took note and the word was passed back down through the aviation department of the Party Central Committee, to the NKAP and on to the VVS command itself that nothing should hinder Myasishchev's continued work on this project. All of a sudden, the elusive VK-107A engine suddenly became readily available to the team, and the work pressed forward. A State Acceptance evaluation programme was arranged almost immediately.

The very experienced team of test pilot A.M. Khripkov, Navigator Romashko, and leading engineer Major G.V. Gribakin, who had both been associated with the

THE PETLYAKOV Pe-2

Pe-2 from the very outset, were selected by the NII VSS to conduct these trials. The first evaluation flight of the first series took place on 10 May. The whole series, which followed, continued through June 1944. The newness of the VK-107A was very apparent in this period, and there were instances of cylinder-head seals splitting, over-revving and the almost inevitable oil leakages. These problems led to no fewer than six engine changes in the space of two months, an average life span of less than 100 hours. Such a high attrition rate would normally lead to a marked falling-off of performance.

Such proved not to be the case in this instance and the performance figures achieved continued to impress. Maximum speeds recorded were 556km/h at ground level, 617km/h at the first altitude limit and 656km/h at the second altitude limit. Rate of climb was marginally poorer than predicted, coming in at seven minutes to attain a height of 5,000 metres. Landing characteristics showed a marked improvement, thanks to the revised airflow section that had been adopted, which meant speed was lost more gradually in the descent, making for easier control. On the down side, with a 500kg bomb load, the range was still 125 kilometres under the desired minimum.

Planned improvements included new wing-tip sections, which would increase the wingspan to 17.8 metres and the total wing area to 43.5m^2. This gave greater lift and, together with a planned decrease in the extra weight of some 100-150kg, would improve on even the already greater control. Whereas the serial Pe-2 continued to present tyro pilots with enormous difficulties and unexpected problems during touchdown, Khripkov predicted that even pilots of 'intermediate flight proficiency'

An excellent broadside view of the Pe-3 long-range reconnaissance version of the *Peshka*, which was known to NATO in the immediate post-war period as 'Buck'. The Red Star insignia is now outlined in white and the upper-surface camouflage scheme can be seen quite clearly. This photo is from the files of the US Recognition Branch, Navy Department, Washington D.C. (US National Archives, Washington DC)

would be able to handle the Pe-2I. He concluded that the type showed 'a considerable advance' over the current serial Pe-2.[13]

Further trials were carried out with four more aircrews, test pilots A.I. Kabanov with navigator N.P. Tsvetkov; P.M. Stefanovsky with navigator P.I. Perevalov; V.I. Zhdanov with navigator Litvinchuk and M.A. Nyukhtikov with navigator Starykh. Zhdanov went into considerable detail, complaining about the pilot's cabin being cramped, with poor vision to port. General vision was good but for dive-bombing there was a blind ventral sector forward. He described the braking system as weak and liable to overheating. Take off and lift off was smooth and he found the controls responsive throughout the range. He felt the aileron and elevator forces were too great, but directional stability was good, roll stability and longitudinal stability neutral. Turning was steady and landing was simpler than the standard Pe-2.

The concluding NII VVS report summed up by stating that 'provided that its take-off characteristics are improved and the defects recorded are eradicated', the Pe-2I with the VK-107A engines was an aircraft that could be recommended for acceptance into service.

Air-to-air combat simulation

The deeply-held reservations of the VVS on the comparative lack of defensive armament still held sway, despite all the enthusiasm. The Air Force determined to evaluate the new defence system in a series of simulated air-to-air combats using captured German fighter aircraft. For this a Bf.109G4 with a Daimler-Benz DB 601 engine was used in attack profiles at various levels. The results made predictable reading. In the horizontal flight envelope at heights below 7,000 metres, the interceptor failed on several occasions to get into any attack position whatsoever, as, flat out, the Pe-2I was the faster machine. Better interception results were obtained over the target area with the Pe-2I committed to the bombing run. Here the Bf. 109G frequently got into an attack position, but *only* from astern in the rearward zones of fire, which would be fully covered by the new barbette gun. If the Pe-2I attempted to either put her nose down or run, or nose up into an evasive turn, the German fighter scored because it could accelerate faster than the Soviet bomber.

Test pilot Pominal'ny reported that he could only successfully attack during a climb or descent, while in level flight the Pe-2I at all altitudes up to 7,000 metres, had a speed advantage over the enemy.

Nonetheless, the C-in-C of the VVS RKKA, Marshal of Aviation A.A. Novikov, concluded in June 1944 that the Pe-2I's defensive armament was too weak, and needed to be improved. This judgement was almost pre-ordained of course. The only other defect he commented on was the increased take-off distance required by the new bomber. In view of plans to produce a night-fighter variant, this also required attention.

Apart from these points, the VVS showed only enthusiasm and recommended series production. The State Acceptance trials were deemed a success and, in May, GKO resolution 5947 ordered GAZ 22 to commence building five pre-production aircraft. Myasishchev was given a couple of pats on the back in appreciation, being promoted to major general (*Ing*) and awarded the Order of Suvorov, Second Class.

By mid-August, the second prototype had been repaired sufficiently for her to join in the State Evaluation programme, which commenced on 27 July. Test pilot A.M. Khriplkov flew a total of forty-nine test sorties, with leading engineer G.V. Gribakin and navigators Filippov and Romashko.

By 21 November the conclusions reached were that the Pe-2I had many attributes. She could dive steadily 'at angles up to 70⁰', was steady in turns, but required skilful speed control in turns with a vertical bank. This latter, in fact, was one of the two basic weaknesses of the whole *Peshka* concept. There was always major slip effect on the bank and the ailerons were not always capable of countering this. In cases of asymmetric power surges or sudden alterations in one of the engines, the Pe-2 would bank sharply, on extreme occasions ending up inverted![14] Such sudden upsets often proved as fatal during take offs as the notorious 'bounce' was on landings. Once the State trials were finalized, the first prototype was issued to the LII NKAP, which had earlier evaluated a Mosquito B.IV with Rolls Royce 21 engines. They found that the Pe-2I was 90km/h faster than the Mosquito in a similar laden condition. The second prototype was issued to GAZ 482.

Conflicting Priorities

Amid all the euphoria the seeds of disappointment were already being sewn. Its own success and the conflicting needs and priorities that flowed from it swamped OKO 22. Summarised they were as follows:

1: The GKO demand to produce the pre-production batch to a 15 October 1944 deadline.
2: The VVS insistence on a review of the defensive armament.
3: The problems with the development of the DEU gun barbette.
4: The complication of introducing a heavy fighter variant into the programme.
5: The problems associated with the VK-107A engine and the priority of its use for the Yak-9U fighter aircraft over the Pe-2I programme.
6: Finally, and still the most decisive, the *continued* all-embracing priority of continuing serial production, no matter what.

Let us examine how these affected the outcome of the Pe-2I programme.

The Plans … and the Reality!

The VVS plan for the Pe-2I envisaged the following:

(a) The completion and passing by State Acceptance by the second of the prototypes. This was satisfactorily concluded in November 1944.
(b) The completion and passing by State Acceptance of the five pre-production aircraft by the deadline set. This was *not* achieved. The first of this batch of

THE FINAL DEVELOPMENTS

five machines was not rolled out at GAZ 22 until the end of February 1945, fourteen *weeks* behind schedule. The remaining four aircraft followed at ten-day intervals. This compared with current serial production at the plant of seven-to-nine machines *per day*. This sluggish performance resulted from the reluctance of factory director V.A. Okulov to prioritise this batch, or transfer the necessary resources in both skilled personnel and material, to their completion. The need of the line remained paramount in his mind. A second factor was the unreliability of the DEU barbette, still largely experimental. The second pre-production aircraft, c/n 2-1001, had to have her barbette replaced on no less than *seven* occasions before one was fitted which worked properly. Not one of the pre-production aircraft was accepted by the VVS inspection, due to the high number of faults found in all of them. Work to rectify the faults was never pressed forward to get them into a combat-ready condition. They were abandoned by June 1945, by which time the war in Europe had terminated.

(c) The construction, completion and State Acceptance of a third prototype, in the new configuration of a heavy, long-range fighter. This added to the complications, of course. This aircraft was to be armed with a pair of forward-firing NS-45 cannon, with 45rpg, mounted in a ventrally-located weapons tray. This system was completed and delivered to GAZ 22 in November 1944. Despite this, the third prototype was never built, Myasishchev, quite properly, decided that this system could just as well be trialled in the first prototype. The VVS agreed to this but the system was subjected to strict and continuous scrutiny; as a result numerous defects were found and rectification insisted upon. By June 1945 the need for such an aircraft was deemed to have passed and it was cancelled. Furthermore, series production of the Pe-2I would require one-third of the Pe-2 drawings to be changed along with a similar amount of changes to existing production jigs and tooling. As a result, the heavy fighter version of the Pe-2I was stillborn.

(d) The introduction of first serial production batch of the Pe-2I was scheduled for completion early in the New Year. The first such aircraft was due on 15 January 1945 and the last on 10 February. In-service evaluation trials would then iron out the remaining defects and GAZ 22 was then to proceed to full serial production of the model. This plan was also destined to fail when, on 5 July, the third aircraft of the series was badly damaged in an accident caused by an engine con-rod fracture. At that late date, this proved to be the straw that was to break the proverbial camel's back.

(e) NKAP order no. 358, issued on 27 May 1944, called for OKO 22 to project and build two further prototypes to an even more ambitious specification. This new type was to be capable of a maximum speed of 700km/h at an altitude of 6,000 metres; to have a 1,000kg internally carried bomb-carrying capacity, and a range of 2,000 kilometres. This pair was to be ready for their acceptance trials by December 1944. The designation of these two machines was later given variously as the DB-2VK-108, the DSBVK-108, but more usually as the DB-108.

THE PETLYAKOV Pe-2

Recognition views of the Pe-2 in various poses taken from the Russian Aircraft Recognition Manual held in a US Intelligence File dated 1941. (US National Archives, Washington DC)

Solutions ... and yet more Problems

On 10 July 1944 Myasishchev was able to inform Shakhurin that all the defects listed by NII VVS had been readied for elimination. The reduction gearing between the engine and airscrew had been altered, together with further streamlining of the nacelles, and with the introduction of an extra 100hp boost. The total airframe weight had been brought down by 300kg, while the wing area had been increased by 1.2m2. In this new configuration the first prototype was re-evaluated at LII in February 1945, and showed increases in performance.

Special Armament Recommendations

As a result of Novikov's concerns about the defensive capability of the Pe-2I, a special examination team from the Zhukovsky Military Aviation Academy (VVA) was brought in. It comprised Major Generals B. Goroshenko and S. Kozlov of the engineering aviation service (IAS), and the scientist Colonel (*Ing*) V. Pugachv.[15] The conclusions they reached were hardly helpful; in their view the aircraft would be equally viable as a totally-unarmed aircraft on the lines of the British Mosquito, or with a moderate armament, by which they defined four 20mm cannon, one in the nose, one the tail and a twin in an upper gun turret.

THE FINAL DEVELOPMENTS

It was not really a choice. Myasishchev knew what the VVS really wanted; he also knew what he wanted. He had decided to go for the middle option and depend on an aerodynamically clean aircraft, with the single tail cannon. Having chosen this route he found himself immediately thwarted by the faults which began to plague production of the DEU barbette on which he had staked everything. Firstly, there were the problems associated with the remote-controlled aiming of the weapon, compounded by the distance between the two – the parallax angle problem. This meant that the lining-up of the target had to be offset at a degree decided by the gunner's best estimation. Secondly, the weapon system, as devised, carried a total ammunition supply of just 100 rounds, which was quickly fired off, especially as it was not locked on to the target at the outset. This meant that, in a long-running engagement, all reserves of shells were quickly expended leaving the aircraft defenceless.

More resources and more time *might* have resolved both these problems had not the DEU itself developed seemingly insurmountable problems of its own. The feedback system of the control impulses between the sighting device and the barbette itself were found to have a time lag between operation and response. This translated into a 2-degree angular differential, which had to be added to the offset already required. Under inflight conditions, this differential increased progressively, making accurate shooting impossible. This fault seemed incapable of any quick resolution and, as it made the Pe-2I an unarmed bomber, to which concept the VVS was totally and implacably opposed, the whole project foundered totally and finally stuttered to a halt.

Again, Selyakov has his own memories of these events. He later stated that, during the project development, the aerodynamics group was headed by Emmanuil Anatol'yevich Osherov, whom Selyakov described as a 'clever and sympathetic man, but also very cautious'. He recalled a continuing dispute between the pair of them. Following detailed calculations, Osherov concluded that the maximum speed to be expected would only be 620km/h as against the official requirement of 640km/h. Selyakov countered this gloomy prognosis, declaring that the design speed would easily be attained, but Osherov remained unconvinced. The outcome, as remembered by Selyakov, was that on the full trials the Pe-2I achieved a maximum speed of 656km/h. 'The Pe-2 "I" became the fastest Soviet bomber of the Great Patriotic War. Regrettably, it emerged too late.'[16]

In January 1945 a draft for a GKO resolution instructed GAZ 22 to use the time prior to converting to Tu-4 (B-4) production to build a number of Pe-2Is with the VK-107A engine. The planned schedule was an initial run of twenty-five such aircraft, followed by further batches of fifty per month. On 5 February NKAP 42 ordered that the prototype of these, converted from the second Pe-2I prototype, was to be ready for State Acceptance evaluation by 31 March. They were to be armed with one fixed, forward-firing UB-20 cannon, with two more cannon of the same type covering the upper and ventral rear arcs for defensive fire. They were later re-designated as the Pe-2M (see below).

In spring 1945 OKB 482 submitted a proposal for the Pe-2I to be re-engined with the AM-39F engine, with a *reduced* armament. Nothing more was heard of that particular proposal.

Myasishchev was forced to bow to the inevitable and comply with his masters' wishes. This led to the Pe-2M concept, (*not* to be confused with the earlier, unofficial, use of this designation to describe the experiments with the radial engine).

Jet-propelled *Peshka*?

As another obscure echo of the Pe-2I story the development of the first Soviet jet aircraft brought about one final mention. In the last months of 1945 work was proceeding at five separate plants on this important programme. The evaluation and restoration of captured German jet aircraft, the Me.262 fighter-bomber and the Arado Ar.234 bomber among them, being part of the overall plan, along with the development of the MiG-9 and Yak-15. The homegrown RB-1 (RB-17) four-engined jet bomber was one of the strands that the Myasishchev OKB was involved in during its final days of existence.

Due to Myasishcev's knowledge of the German turbojets, the OKB thought about marrying them up with the Pe-2I's airframe as one way to achieve a quick solution. The combining of the technical aspects of the Pe-2I and the Me. 262 were what fascinated people like Selyakov, but only for a short time. Further analysis of just what this match would involve soon dampened the initial enthusiasm. The technical needs of any jet aircraft imposed demands upon its airframe that far exceeded the now elderly *Peshka* design. It was soon obvious that it would be faster, and cheaper, to start afresh.

The Pe-2I remained one of the great might-have-beens of the war and there never was a Soviet 'Mosquito', nor was the jet-propelled *Peshka* more than a passing idea.

The Pe-2M (1945)

The second Pe-2I prototype was converted into the first prototype for the new Pe-2M which was to revert to a three-man-crew configuration, carry extra protective armour plating, and have better vision, with a newly-designed rear cabin. Wing taper was altered, with increased wing-tip area. A new oleo shock-absorber traveller was fitted to the undercarriage. A range of 2,300 kilometres with an internally carried 1,000kg bomb load was expected, plus a top speed of 625km/h at an altitude of 5,000 metres.

With the DEU fiasco the rear barbette idea had to be jettisoned and the new bomber's defensive armament was re-jigged once more; the VU-5-20 turret housing a heavy electro-mechanical power-assisted UB-20 cannon, with a 200-shell ammunition supply, re-emerged for rearward cover. A second similarly electrical power-assisted UB-20 was carried in a ventrally positioned LUS-20 mounting. This necessitated the reintroduction of the three-man *Peshka*, with the navigator

THE FINAL DEVELOPMENTS

controlling the former weapon and the wireless-operator firing the second. It was found that the upper mounting severely restricted the ability to jettison the canopy for an emergency escape. Forward-firing armament consisted of a fixed UB-20 cannon, with 120 rounds, placed under the cabin. All these weapons carried a big punch, but, even when servo-assisted, they proved cumbersome and hard to keep on the target.

With three men, the armour-protection requirements increased. Offensively the Pe-2M featured an enlarged main bomb bay, capable of carrying the FAB-1000 M43 bomb with uncut fins. This pushed the maximum weight up to 12,000kg. In turn, this imposed a penalty on the rest of the aircraft, with the undercarriage and wheels hard pressed to hold it up fully laden. Nor were the VK-107A engines still up to the job, proving increasingly unreliable and prone to faults. Con-rods tended to crack after only forty-seven to fifty-four hours' service, while the coolant and oil leakages were unremitting.

The Prototype

The converted prototype was readied by 1 March 1945, and company flight-development testing, with a team comprising test pilots F.F. Opadchi and A. Pal'chikov, leading engineers N. Lashkevich and K. Popov, flight development engineer A. Nikonov, technician V. Byelousov and flight engineer A. Artamoshin, commenced on 7 March. The trials continued into April, being marred by a forced landing due to a fire in the starboard engine at 4,500 metres. Pal'chikov and Lashkevich were able to get the aircraft down safely and the fire was extinguished. In spite of this episode, the company trials were declared successful. Re-engined with the VK-108 the Pe-2M underwent further flight testing in May, and in the same month was evaluated by the NII VVS. Due largely to the unreliability of the new cannon built by GAZ 43, the aircraft was rejected.

Having given the VVS what they wanted, however, Myasishchev felt justified in omitting the necessity of the State Acceptance programme for the new aircraft. In February 1945, therefore, and with NKAP backing, he went straight into an initial production batch, which was based upon the Pe-2M as it stood, in an attempt to make up some of the wasted time. It was another race that GAZ 22 lost. Despite the best efforts the first quartet of Pe-2M-based aircraft were not rolled out until June when a very different situation naturally prevailed. There was now no need to cut corners. All at once, 'Quality' rather than 'Quantity' became the watchword, a total reversal of priority. Therefore the NI-VVS re-imposed the State Acceptance programme and the first aircraft of the batch, c/n 1-1002, was delivered into the expert hands of the Khripkov/Gribakin test team.

The evaluation programme

The results of Khripkov's flight testing revealed that, not too surprisingly, the Pe-2M had better all-round qualities than the serial Pe-2, but was inferior in most respects to the Pe-2I. At the second altitude level the c/n 1-1002 turned in a respectable top speed of 630km/h. It took a full 1.8 minutes longer to climb to 5,000 metres and reach was reduced by 225 kilometres. The price of the required VVS firepower was thus made obvious.

Termination

Even as Khripkov was throwing the Pe-2M around the skies over GAZ 22, decisions were being made in Moscow, which were to render all their best efforts null and void. The Pe-2 programme was to be stopped immediately. Damage to the Pe-2I, the explosion aboard the RD-1KhZ experimental aircraft, c/n 15-185, the crash of the second prototype DB-108, and the decision to replace the series Pe-2 with the Tu-2,[17] plus termination of hostilities, all played a part in this decision.

Even so, the Pe-2M's final report was ambiguous to say the least. This report concluded that the aircraft, as fitted with the 2VK-107A engines, failed to meet the requirements. Having failed the evaluation due to a long list of faults, c/n 1-1002 was, nevertheless, to be returned to the plant for eradication of defects and further modification.

If this hinted at some distant reprieve, it was not to be, and all four Pe-2Ms spent their brief lives at GAZ 26 and GAZ 482 as test beds for various experiments.

DB-108

It will be recalled that, during the heady days of May 1944, with the first Pe-2I results resounding all the way from the Kazan to the Kremlin, a further ambitious bomber project based on the improved *Peshka* had been promulgated. This was confirmed by NKAP order 358 issued in August 1944 for OKB 22 to develop a new bomber fitted with the VK-108 engine, developing 1,850hp take-off power and 1,500hp at an altitude of 4,500 metres. The chief project designer was G.V. Smirnov. Drawings for the project were completed by 10 September and a mock up was approved. The roll-out of the (unarmed) prototype took place on 30 December 1944.

Myasishchev's team met the design parameters by increasing the size of the Pe-2I's bomb bay so that it would be able to carry internally the specially-shortened FAB-2000 M44 weapon. This led to the adoption of the mid-wing configuration.[18] (In fact, the prototype used the centre-section taken intact from the incomplete airframe of the third Pe-2I prototype and proved incapable of accommodating the mock-up bomb provided!)

The extra weight generated by this bomb would be catered for by the introduction of VK-108 engines driving VISh-108L-20 four-bladed airscrews. These engines had already been flight-tested on the Pe-2F at GAZ 26, and they were of roughly the same dimensions as the VK-107A. A new two-speed supercharger, which had Polikovsky-designed adjustable blades was fitted to these engines, and helped raise the power output by between 150-200hp.[19] They also featured modified engine nacelles. Bomb loading would increase to 2,000kg. Estimated performance figures were a maximum speed at 9,000 metres of 700km/h with a service ceiling of 12,000 metres. The take-off distance was expected to be 450 metres while operational range would be 2,500 kilometres, with an extended ferry range with drop tanks of 3,500 kilometres.[20]

In view of the expressed views of the C-in-C, defensive armament, which had, tactfully, remained unspecified in the original NKAP order, was substantial. Two alternative weapons systems were proposed by the designer, either of which would meet Novikov's requirements. The initially preferred option was for one fixed forward-firing UB-20 cannon and one remote-controlled UB-20 aft in the DEU barbette, with a 120-round ammunition supply. With the consideration that the heavy fighter option might also be applied later to this aircraft, an alternative package had a twin NS-37 or NS-45 cannon located in the weapons bay, with a 50rpg ammunition supply.

The cockpit canopy was further refined, with a lower but wider profile, with a large underneath glazed area introduced to facilitate navigation and bomb aiming. All crew were given 10mm armour protection on the backs of their seats, with 8mm thick armour headrests and 5mm armour seat plating.

Delays and Interruptions

Design work got underway in July/August 1944, with assembling of the prototype following by September. (The aircraft was also referred to as the DVB-1008 and the DBV-2VK-108). By cannibalising the Pe-2I programme, progress was relatively speedy at this stage and the prototype was rolled out just before New Year's Eve. Despite this, the first flight did not take place until 5 March 1945. Part of the reason for this delay was another intervention by 42 NKAP concerning the defensive armament.

On 5 February an order was received at Kazan that the second DB-108 prototype was to be equipped with a stronger armament. An additional UB-20 cannon was to be installed firing down from a ventral position, while a UBT machine gun on a flexible mounting was to be added to the wireless-operator's responsibilities.[21] This was complied with and the second machine was completed on 25 May 1945. Problems continued with the OKB-43 turret, which carried a pair of ShVAK guns and its development ceased.[22]

Disaster!

The first prototype was destined to have a tragically short lifespan. A con-rod failure knocked out the starboard VK-107A engine, which had been fitted pending VK-108s becoming available on 24 March, but far worse was to follow. Under the control of test pilot Vasil'chencko, and with leading engineer L.A. D'yakonov as his crew, he took off on a flight development flight on 5 June. Before long the port engine cowling fell off and fire broke out in the VK-107A engine, which was proving just as unpredictable and dangerous as all such Soviet engines we have recorded in the Pe-2 story. At an altitude of 1,500 metres the situation was serious, but not yet fatal. Vasil'chencko broadcast that he was making an emergency landing on the remaining engine.

The experienced pilot accelerated and made his approach to the field, dropping down to low level. He might well have brought his mount down safely despite the odds, had not a Pe-2, a series production aircraft on routine test, not suddenly appeared, cutting across his line of flight. An instinctive reaction avoided a mid-air collision but the delay, and lack of sufficient altitude, resulted in loss of control with no room for further recovery. The DB-108's starboard engine struck the roof of a building in the nearby village, bringing the aircraft down on top of it. The crash killed three civilians, two of them children, and also D'yakonov.

Somehow, Vasil'chencko was dragged from the wreckage with heavy injuries but recovered in hospital and survived. A subsequent enquiry laid the blame fully on the flight development department at Kazan for allowing routine flying to take place while a test flight was underway. In truth, although this certainly made the disaster certain, the unreliability of the VK-107A was equally to blame.

DB-108 abandoned

As a result of this crash the NKAP ordered the construction of another prototype to take its place, designated as the DB-I-108, to be completed by 25 April; flight development was to continue with it. This was not to be. Insistence by the VVS that the armament must include the electrically-operated barbettes, which were still in the experimental stage, was part of the reason. Also, shortly after this tragedy, came the switch by GAZ 22 to concentrate on further UPe-2 trainer and, later, to Tu-2 production. Myasishchev and the corel of this design team were moved back to Moscow, being re-located at GAZ 482, which had been established the year before.

Myasischev still did not give up initially. A further refinement designated as the DB-II-108 was submitted to the VVS in May 1945. The VVS had long put forward demands for a separate navigator's cabin to be positioned in front of the pilot, to give the former an improved field of vision for both navigation and bomb aiming. Myasishchev saw such a switch as enabling the abandoning of the existing periscopic bomb-sight and its replacement with the more advanced collimator night and all-weather bomb-sight.

To accommodate the increased four-man aircrew, a whole new three-man cabin was to be devised, with the rear gunner in separate accommodation aft. Myasishchev was enthusiastic about the advantages such a system would provide, stating to Shakhurin that a long-range variant, with enlarged outer-wing panels of greater area, would reduce take-off distance by 50 metres, increase ceiling by 500 metres and extend range by 700 kilometres. A small decrease in estimated top speed of 10-12km/h would be acceptable.[23] He requested permission to prepare a mock up of the new cabin, to have GAZ 482 build and fit the same to the second prototype, to construct another prototype, and to obtain two VEU-2 barbettes and two NEU-1 flexible gun mountings from OKB 140.

THE FINAL DEVELOPMENTS

Looking even further ahead, Myasishchev envisaged engine improvements by installing boosted VK-108F engines developing 2,100hp take-off power and, further, fitting VK-109 engines, as well as pressurised cabins, from the VB-VK-109 prototype then under construction at GAZ 482. This was all so much dreaming and never to be realised. Although the second prototype was dismantled and moved with the team to the new site, the project was, in effect, at an end. It was to form the basis of yet two further, and this time final, variations on the extended *Peshka* theme.

New long-ranger fighter and high-altitude bomber concepts

A successor the Pe-3 had long been under discussion. In general, the VVS had fought a tactical war as expected, but the examples presented by the long-range penetrations into German air space by night and by day by the bombers of the RAF and USAAF had raised questions in Moscow. Whereas the night area bombing of the British had done little other than lay waste to German towns and cities, the precision daylight attacks by the USAAF were a different matter. Heavy losses had been taken, but the introduction of the North American P-51 long-range escort fighter had made such missions a viable proposition. The Soviets were acutely aware that they had no such long-range escort in their armoury should they decide to mimic western policy. Although the efforts of the Soviets' own long-range bomber force (the ADD) had been comparatively small in comparison, this had forced them to adopt the British method of relying on darkness to shield them, a policy that became less and less effective with the introduction of German AI radar.[24]

Range ceased to be a problem as the war moved closer to the borders of the Third Reich, but the ability to operate radar-equipped and all-weather patrols over enemy air space remained a desirable quality. In 1944 the NII VVS had outlined the requirements needed for such an aircraft, which was designated as the DIS. This machine would be a twin-engined design with the VK-107A engine as its power plant. At the same time the more powerful VK-109 engine was to equip another new project, the high-altitude bomber known variously as the VB-2VK-109, VDB-2VK-109 or, more usually the VB-109.

The DIS (12) escort fighter

The initial specification for this aircraft had described it as a two-seat fighter-cruiser and PVO interceptor.[25] The prototype was built by GAZ 22 and the armament installed by GAZ 482. Powered by two air-cooled engines, it would have a maximum speed of 625km/h at ground level and 700km/h at altitude, coupled with a range of 3,000 kilometres. Offensive armament would comprise a pair of 45mm VYa cannon and two UBK. This new fighter would also carry two sets of the Soviet AI radar, the *Gneis-3*, a rather bulky item of equipment.

Despite the end of the war in Europe, the project was still deemed desirable. The original specification was tightened up in NKAP order No. 270, which was issued on 29 June 1945. The three-seater, low-wing configuration of the Pe-2 was to be followed.[26] Maximum speed for the first prototype at high altitude was to be 660-670km/h with the 1,700hp VK-107A, but the engine-mounting framework of a second prototype was deliberately built so that it could later adopt the VK-108 engine, then under development. With this power plant, the maximum speed estimate increased to 690-700km/h.

De-icing equipment was to be included on the leading edges of the wings, tail empennage, cockpit windscreen and airscrew blading, for all-weather capability while twin 45mm cannon, which had been provided for the third production Pe-2I, were to provide the armament of the first prototype. Production requirements were for a nose battery of two 20mm cannon, a belly pack with two 37- or 45mm cannon and a rear upper turret carrying another 20mm cannon. The earlier experiments undertaken with the Pe-2I to reduce the take-off distance required were also used. This resulted in Myasishchev recommending the wing centre section incorporate a 2-degree-incidence angle.

Another innovation brought about because of criticisms by the mock-up commission, were the replacement of metal fuel tanks with tanks of soft-cell type, with a total capacity of 3,000kg, which would have given a range of 4,100 kilometres.[27] This led to further design changes to the fuselage. Finally, in order to recover the centre of gravity (CG), the outer wing panels featured a small sweepback. Normal take-off weight was now 9,850kg, with a maximum loading of 11,700kg. However, the additional fuel tanks subsequently failed to be installed, which again reduced actual range to 3,600 kilometres.

By 18 December 1945 the first prototype had commenced company flight-development testing, while the second prototype was taking shape. This latter had been ordered under NKAP directive No. 270, dated 29 June 1945. A heavy nose-mounted armament of two 37- and two 20mm cannon was to be mounted, with a third 20mm cannon for rear defence. A maximum speed of 625km/h at 5,700 metres was sought. The range was specified as 3,200 kilometres on internal tanks, extended to 4,000 kilometres with drop tanks.[28] In this second machine the modification of the navigator's cabin by extending it 0.1-metres rearward was necessitated by the need for it to accommodate the VEI-1 upper gun barbette. This shift, in turn, required modification to the nose section to re-align the CG.

The second prototype was due to be completed by 1 July 1945, but the subsequent transfer of most of the OKB 22 team back to Moscow resulted in a hugely scaled-down effort and the programme was put on hold. On 10 November test pilot F.F. Opadchi was assigned to conduct the company flight programme on this aircraft by NKAP order No. 436 and the deadline for completion was extended to 10 February 1946.

The VB-109 high-altitude bomber

The origins for this aircraft had been the May 1944 NKAP order which had included the DB-108 project as already noted. The designated power plant was M.K. Yangel's new VK-109 engine, with two-stage centrifugal impellers of the variable-speed system adjusting the flow into the engine manifolds. They were expected to develop 2,075hp at ground level and 1,530hp at an altitude of 8,000 metres.

THE FINAL DEVELOPMENTS

Here again it called for two prototypes to be developed and built, but the design team gave a lower priority to the VB-109 for the usual reason; a reliable high-altitude-rated engine and associated turbo-supercharger were not available. Thus, the mock up was not completed for inspection at GAZ 482 until February 1945, and approval followed on 5 March. Work commenced on the prototype itself in April.

In the event, the planned high-altitude VK-109 engines, promised for January 1945, failed to materialise until thirteen months later. In the interim, the prototype was engined by two VK-108s. Top speed at an altitude of 5,800 metres was expected to be 660km/h with these engines. Once the VK-109 engine was installed, the maximum speed was expected to increase to 720km/h at an altitude of 9,000 metres, with a service ceiling of 12,500 metres.

The main feature was, naturally, the two-seat pressurised cabin, which, for the first time in a Soviet aircraft design, incorporated an internal heating unit. UV lighting would illuminate the cockpit interior. A de-icing unit with a hydraulically-operated wipe was provided for the pilot's windshield, in a similar manner to the VI. The compressed air was fed by way of an inter-cooling device into the carburettors. Yet another long delay was caused by the failure of GAZ 26 to supply these compressors for many months. This bomber was built to carry the concrete-penetrating FAB-2000 bomb to attack heavily-fortified targets.

Further delay was caused by several changes to the proposed defensive armament. In the light of experiences with the Pe-2I, Pe-2M and DB-108, this was continually under review. The planned start date for the VB-109's State Acceptance evaluation of April 1945 therefore slipped by and it was not until August that the first prototype was rolled out of the plant. Take-off weight for this machine was 13,580kg. The company flight-development testing was even more delayed and even ground testing did not get underway until December 1945.

These were proceeding at a leisurely peacetime rate when the carpet was suddenly pulled from beneath the whole Myasishchev OKB. Myasishchev's confidant, Shakhurin, was suddenly placed under arrest, disappeared and M.V. Khrunichev took over his post. Rumours began to abound that, tainted by association, OKB 482 might be closed. At this time Myasishchev was taken ill and unable to keep in touch with events as much as he would have wished. Initially the signs seemed good. The deputy chief of the NKAP, N.S. Shishkin, issued order no. 43 on 6 February 1946, which authorised flight development of the VK-108-engined VB and test pilot L. Yungmeyster was assigned for this programme.

It was a false dawn. Abruptly, on 20 February 1946, Khrunichev himself issued NKAP order 61, which announced that 'due to the lack of any aircraft in serial production at the plant',[29] the whole operation was to be disbanded forthwith. Most of the existing OKB 492 staff were to be transferred to S.V. Il'yushin's OKB 240, which was to be expanded.[30] Myasishchev himself only learned of his fate by accident while on sick leave. He at once protested to both A.A. Zhdanov of the Party Central Committee and to Khrunichev himself. He sent a long memorandum to both men on 26 February and another to the *SovMin* deputy chairman L.P. Beriya on 15 March. All this was in vain; they ignored him, and, worse, denigrated his achievements and work. He was eased into a sinecure post as dean of the aircraft

THE PETLYAKOV Pe-2

design faculty of the MAI and all contact with the VVS ceased. Thus the long and complex story of the *Peshka* in the Soviet Air Force came to an end.[31]

Table 13: Comparison of Final proposed types- Pe-2I, Pe-2M, DB-108 & VB-109

	Pe-2I	Pe-2M	DB-108	VB-109
Year	1944	1945	1945	1945
Crew	2	3	2	2
Intended Power Plant	VK-107A	VK-107A	VK-108	VK-109
Take-off power (hp)	1650	1650	1800	2075
Rated power (hp)	1500	1500	1700	1800
at altitude (m)	4500	4500	4500	6000
at altitude (ft)	14763.60	14763.60	14763.60	19684.80
Overall length (m)	13.78	13.65	13.80	14.00
Overall length (ft)	45.209	44.7829	45.275	45.931
Wingspan (m)	17.175	17.175	17.175	17.8
Wingspan (ft)	56.34	56.34	56.34	58.39
Height (m)	3.95	3.95	3.95	3.95
Height (ft)	12.959	12.959	12.959	12.959
Wing area (m^2)	41.7	43.16	43.16	43.16
Wing area (ft^2)	448.85	464.57	464.57	464.57
Weight – empty (kg)	7014	7458	6821	7508
Weight – empty (lbs)	15463.08	16441.90	15037.57	16552.13
Weight – take-off kg)	8983	10170	8736	9900
Weight – take-off (lb)	19803.95	22420.78	19259.38	21825.54
Weight – overload (kg)	9928	12044	9801	11900
Weight – overload (lb)	21887.26	26552.20	21607.28	26234.74
Fuel (kg)	1925[1]	1820	1640	1740
Fuel (lb)	4243.85	4012.37	3615.54	3836.00
Max. speed ground level (km/h)	565	545	580[2]	593[2]
Max. speed ground level (mph)	351.09	338.66	360.41	368.49
Max. speed (km/h) at (m)	656	630	700[2]	720[2]
Max speed (mph) at (ft)	407.48	391.48	434.98	447.40
Service Ceiling (m)	9350	8500	10000	12500
Service Ceiling (ft)	30,675	27,886.	32,808	41,010
Max. range (km)	2275	2050	2400	2200
Max. range (miles)	1413.68	1273.87	1491.36	1367.08

THE FINAL DEVELOPMENTS

Takeoff length (m)	650	685	n/a	n/a
Takeoff length (ft)	2132.52	2247.34	n/a	n/a
Landing distance (m)	790	n/a	n/a	n/a
Landing distance (ft)	2591.83	n/a	n/a	n/a
Forward armament	2 x ShVAK	1 x UBK[3]	1 x UB-20	1 x UB-20
Upper armament	n/a	1 x UB-20	1 x UB-20	1 x UB-20
Ventral armament	n/a	n/a	1 x UB-20	n/a
Tail armament	n/a	n/a	1 x UB-20	n/a
Bomb load –external (kg)	2 x 500	2 x 500	2 x 500	2 x 500
Bomb load – external (lb)	2 x 1102	2 x 1101	2 x 1102	2 x 1102
Bomb load – internal (kg)	1 x 1000	1 x 1000	1 x 2000	1 x 2000
Bomb load – internal (lb)	1 x 2204	1 x 2204	1 x 4409	1 x 4409
Bomb load – total (kg)	2000	2000	3000	3000
Bomb load – total (lb)	4409	4409	6411	6411

Notes:

1: Prototype 1,844kg.
2: Estimate only.
3: Third prototype would have carried two NS-45.

Statistics:

The official figure for the number of Pe-2s and completed was 11,426 (11,427 in some sources) with about 500 Pe-3 fighters and Pe-2R reconnaissance machines and, at their peak, they comprised 75 per cent of all Soviet twin-engined bombers in service.

The AG-2 aerial grenade was claimed by the Soviets to be responsible for about 20 per cent of all aerial kills obtained by the Pe-2 in combat. This weapon ejected a grenade, which exploded about 80 metres (260 ft) astern of the aircraft and scattered shrapnel in the path of the pursuer.

The Pe-2 series 205 configuration had aerodynamic improvements made in 1943 to enhance performance, including redesigned oil-cooler cowlings, new carburettor intakes, better attachment of the VUB-1 turret to the main canopy and the aerial mast moved forward onto the windscreen. The engines were M-105PF with VISh-61 props.

The series 211 had new bomb racks and faired dive brakes but was otherwise similar to the 205.

Length: 205 series – 12,525mm long, 17,16 mm wide.
Long tail coned Pe-2s were 12,660mm long

Pe-2 series 110 12,525mm
Wingspan 17,116mm

PESHKA MEN – Vladimir Mikhailovich Myasishchev

A close associate of Petlyakov, Vladimir Mikhailovich Myasishchev was later to take over the Pe-2 project, initiate the many improvements to the design, and undertake the many variations called for after reports were received from the front-line regiments. As such, his part in the *Peshka* story is a major one. But he went on to become one of the Soviet Union's most respected aeronautical innovators, being honoured with the titles of Hero of Socialist Labour in 1957, Doctor of Engineering Sciences in 1959 and Honoured Scientist and Engineer of the RSFSR in 1972.[32]

Born in 1902, Vladimir Myasishchev, like his mentor on the Pe-2 project, was an outstanding pupil and student and graduated from the *Moskovskoe Vysshee Tekhnicheskoe Uchilishche*, MVTU (Moscow Higher Engineering School) in 1926. He also joined the Tupolev Design Bureau, working within the TsAGI, and among the many projects on which he worked and developed his talents were the TB-1, the TB-3, and the massive ANT-20 *Maksim Gorkii*. In 1934 he was appointed Chief of the Experimental Aircraft Brigade in the Design Department of the TsAGI section, charged with all aspects of experimental aircraft research. One of the first results of his team's work there was the ANT-41, later the T-1, torpedo-bomber.

He was charged with the adaptation and construction of the licence-built Douglas DC-3 transport, known as the Li-2, between 1937-1938, at the Khimki Plant No. 84, near Moscow. This was successfully achieved but any taint by Western Imperialism, even when one had been ordered to liaise in order to achieve production of a superior aircraft, was fatal in the Kafka-type paranoia prevalent in the late 1930s in the Soviet Union and, in 1938, he was arrested by the NKVD and imprisoned. He was taken to the TsKB-29 NKVD Design Bureau where he joined many of his equally innocent colleagues (those lucky enough to survive with their lives that is), among them Petlyakov. Myasishchev joined the wing department of Petlyakov's department.

Like Petlyakov he was 'pardoned' in 1940 and was appointed as Head of the Design Bureau which was developing the DVB-102 long-range and high-altitude bomber in parallel with Tupolev's Samolet-103, later the Tu-2. This work continued when the plant was evacuated eastward to GAZ No. 166 at Omsk, and later, at GAZ No. 22 at Kazan, but lack of a suitable power-plant capable of carrying the desired combat load of 3,000kg at the necessary height and range made for slow progress. When the dire war situation pushed

Vladimir M Myasishchev, Soviet Aircraft designer. (San Diego Aerospace Museum)

THE FINAL DEVELOPMENTS

such projects into the background, due to the need to concentrate on more vital and easily attainable objectives, Myasishchev was given a new assignment. The death of Petlyakov had been followed by the brief appointments and removals of two successors. The first was A.M. Izakson, who lasted only a few months, and was replaced in April 1942 by A.I. Putilov, who was in turn moved on in the summer of 1943, and went to work as the head of the Delta Wing Research Group at the TsAGI until 1948.

On 23 June 1943 Myasishchev took over as Chief Designer at the Kazan Plant, No. 22, and began to implement additional modifications in design and armament on the Pe-2 and further enhanced its mass production. Myasishchev's work at this time was by no means confined to the *Peshka*, however, for he was also continuing his experimental work on the DVB-102 at Plant No. 486. At the same time he was initiating a whole string of new Petlyakov aircraft, over a wide range of types that included not just dive-bombers, but also fighters, reconnaissance, trainer, ground-attack and 'Paravan' wire-cable-cutters to deal with barrage balloon defences. Thus, the period 1943-46 saw the introduction of such aircraft as the Pe-2B, the Pe-21, the Pe-2M, the DIS, and the DB-108. The fact remained that most of these types were destined to remain experimental one-offs, because the demands of war would not allow any interruption in the flow of tried-and-tested warplanes to the front.[33]

With the coming of peace and the beginning of the 'Cold War' period Myasishchev spread his expertise to a new generation. He was appointed Chairman of Aircraft Design as a Faculty Dean of the Moscow Aviation Institute (MAI) and was a Professor of Aeronautical Science from 1947. Between 1951 and 1960, in a period of rapid development of jet aircraft, Myasichev headed up the GAZ (Experimental Design Bureau) No. 23 and oversaw the introduction of turbojet and turboprop into service, along with the M-4, 3M and M-50 aircraft developments.

The striking and aerodynamically beautiful M-4 strategic bomber developed at GAZ No. 23 at Fili, first appeared in public during the May Day Flypast in 1954. Powered by AM-3 axial-flow engines and with a range of 9,000 kilometres, some 160 were built, but this was not one of Myasishchev's better designs, falling well short of the 16,000-kilometre range the requirement had called for. An attempt to remedy some of the problems by fitting the Solovy'ev turbofan engines, and by retrofitting in-flight refuelling ability, also failed to save it. Some of these bombers were assigned to the *Aviatsiya Voenno-Morskovo Flota*, A-VMF (Soviet Navy's Air Arm), and modified as long-range photographic- and electronic-reconnaissance aircraft, and were first seen eavesdropping on Western naval forces during Operation TEAMWORK in September 1952. Others were built as aerial refuelling tankers in 1967, but overall the *Mya-4* (known to NATO as the Bison) was really a failure.

Nor was Myasishchev's next project anything but a disaster. This was the beautiful M-50 bomber, powered by four Solvy'ev turbofans. Featuring a delta-wing configuration, the M-50, given the NATO designation Bounder, made a gave rise to all kinds of alarmist stories in the Western media, it being reported as nuclear-powered and capable of circumnavigating the world several times non-stop without refuelling.

It featured revolutionary new features, which combined a low-drag airframe with powerful unreheated engines, capable of flying at speeds 50 per cent faster than any existing bomber aircraft. In truth, Myasishchev was trying to achieve the impossible. The configuration chosen, although outwardly awe-inspiring, was notoriously poor in efficiency in both subsonic and high supersonic speeds, due to the transonic drag rise.

As the 201-M, Myasishchev's new creation made her first flight on 16 September 1959. The Bounder attained an altitude of 15,320 metres (50,253 feet), with a load of 10,000kg (22,050lb). More was to follow. On 29 September she carried a load of 55,220kg (121,760lb) and in the course of further trials broke several payload-to-height records. However, the improvement over the *Bison* in no way justified the severe penalty in optimum lift/drag ratio and affected her range adversely. She was beautiful, but again Mysasishchev had failed.[34]

An attempt to salvage something from the wreckage was made by fitting the Bounder with reheat on the inboard power-plant, with the outer engines mounted on pylons extending from the wing-tips. In short bursts this improved speed to Mach 1.4, but it was unsustainable for prolonged operations. Although shown off at the Tushino Air Display in 1961, where it again made a deep impression on Western journalists, the M-50 was another turkey. The development of the Soviet rocket command and the development of ICBM technology had already ruled such bombers obsolete anyway. Myasishchev's reputation had suffered two severe blows and Nikita Khrushchev decided no more time and money should be wasted, and he 'put Myasishchev out to grass as Head of TsAGI'.[35]

Appointed Chief of the TsAGI in 1960, this was an honorary position Myasishchev held for seven years. Between 1967 and 1978 he worked again as General Designer of the Experimental Machine-building Plant (EMZ) where he headed up work on increasing the range of aircraft by the use of the laminar-flow principal, as well as implementing the introduction of new composite materials in aircraft construction. Under his directorship, such diverse projects as the high-altitude, subsonic M-17 Stratosphere aircraft and the VM-T *Atlant* carrier aircraft came to fruition.

He was awarded the Lenin Prize in 1957, and down the years was highly decorated, receiving no less than three Lenin Orders, the October Revolution Order, the Suvorov Order, Second Degree, the Labour Red Banner Order and many other commemorative medals for his work and achievement. In 1958 he was elected as a Deputy of the Supreme Soviet of the USSR, and served in that capacity until 1966.

Vladimir Myasishchev died in 1978, at the age of seventy-six, much revered, and in memory of his lifetime's work for the Russian Aeronautical Industry, of which the Pe-2 was a major part in his early years, the Experimental Aircraft Design Bureau and Construction complex near Moscow is named the *Myasishchev* Plant.

Chapter Nineteen

The *Peshka* in Foreign Service

As mentioned earlier, post-war, many of the Eastern European nations which came under Soviet sway as reluctant 'Allies' with their Communist governments installed and kept in place by Stalin's army and the KGB, had the bomber arms of their air forces equipped with the Pe-2.

Polish *Peshkas*

Although no actual Free Polish Air units were equipped with the Pe-2 during the Second World War, their involvement and organisation commenced in August/September 1944, with the Germans being driven from Polish soil by the Red Army.[1] The first induction began at Kharkov and Polish Pe-2 air regiments were established conforming strictly to the Soviet mould, 1 Polish BAD being based at the headquarters of the Soviet 184 BAD, commanded by Lieutenant Colonel M.I. Martynov.[2] This Soviet unit had not seen any action,[3] nor had it any assigned units at this time. each with a parent unit. Final Pe-2 operators were thus:

> 458th Soviet Bomber Regiment (formerly equipped with the SB, but inactive since 1942) = 4th Polish Bomber Regiment
>
> 719th Soviet Night Bomber Regiment (formerly equipped with the R-5) = 3rd Polish Night Bomber Regiment
>
> 11th Soviet ZAP (Replenishment) Regiment (a new unit) = 5th Polish (Replenishment) Regiment.

Of these, 3 BAP worked up at Kazan, 4 BAP at Vypolzovo, near Moscow, and 5 BAP at Kirovograd under 11 ZAP. By February 1945 none was ready for action, due to lack of fuel and of acceptable flying weather, and at this time they formally transferred to the Polish Air Force.

Up until then, these units had only used Russian personnel, the first Polish trainee aircraft not joining them until 1945. The Polish formations thus formed were, as above, 3rd, 4th and 5th PLB (*Pulk Lotnictwa Bombowego* = Regiment of Bomber Aviation), all under 1st DLB (*Dywizja Lotnictwa*) of I Polish Aviation Corps (MKL).

THE PETLYAKOV Pe-2

Post-war, the Polish armed services were widely equipped with various later marks of the *Peshka*. These are UTis (note cockpit) undergoing maintenance at their home Polish base. (Robert Michulec)

The numbers of Pe-2s allocated to these Polish formations was small and only slowly increased; by April 1945, the division had ninety-eight crews with seventy Pe-2 and UPe-2 aircraft, but further numbers of both were added to the end of the war, when they totalled only ninety-nine machines. The Polish trainees found the whole process long and difficult and, in truth, were not fully qualified even at the end of the courses. By the end of the war in Europe in May 1945, some 107 Pe-2s were accredited to the Soviet controlled *Lotnictwo Wojska Polskiego* (People's Polish Air Force) but only sixty-seven were operational due to lack of fully trained aircrew.

Only 4 BAP was ready for daylight operations, with just six of its crews certified for night-flying missions. Even then, the command staffs appear to have been all, or mainly, Russian aviators, seconded to the Polish Air Force. In fact, their formation had been a sop while the Soviet army consolidated its grip on their homeland, having evicted their fellow occupiers from 1939, the Nazis, and replaced them with their own forces. Thus, no Polish Pe-2 unit was considered fit for combat action by 10 May 1945 and the end of the war in Europe. The Polish Pe-2 strength as at 1 May 1945 was:

THE *PESHKA* IN FOREIGN SERVICE

A Polish aircrew pose in front of their aircraft, which is either a UP3-2 or a Pe-2Uti at their home base, around 1947-48. (Robert Michulec)

Table 14: Polish Pe-2 allocations on 1 May 1945

Polish Unit	Pe-2s on strength (*)	Other types	Personnel Strength
2 Independent Flight (SEL)	1	N/A	N/A
Staff 1 MKL	1	N/A	N/A
Staff 1 DLB	1	N/A	N/A
3 PLB	30 (32)	1 UPe-2	280
5 PLB	30 (32)	2 La-5	288
Pilots Military School (OSL)	12 (18)	-	-
15 ZAP	2 (12)	-	-

* Correct Establishment strength.

The following commanders and commissars commanded these units respectively:

3 PLB Pplk – Michal Bazanow (Commander) and Pplk Ivan Lebiediev (Commissar)

4 PLB – Major P. Bieloglazow (Commander) and Major Toropczyn (Commissar)

5 PLB – Major Mikolaj Dolgobajew (Commander) and Major Mikolaj Lucenko (Commissar)

THE PETLYAKOV Pe-2

The known aircraft allocated to 3 and 4 PLBs was:

Table 15: Soviet Serials of Pe-2s allocated to Polish Pe-2 units

3 PLB		4 PLB		7 SPBN		OSL
1-397	20-392	10-392	13-355	14-368	18-400	18-387
4-395	7-442	18-330	17-355	8-370	7-370	1-396
20-395	4-441	16-331	3-356	15-363	4-428	11-393
6-399	16-402	17-334	4-356	7-368	18-396	5-395
13-398	4-400	7-348	5-356	5-389	15-354	17-393
8-401	1-395	1-350	13-356	18-370	15-066	11-394
6-417	9-397	8-350	15-365	11-361	1-371	
6-401	13-359	3-351	18-356	13-359	17-399	
17-396	2-389	13-351	19-356	18-433	1-354	
5-389	19-399	1-353	1-357	2-365	6-399	
6-396	17-399	14-353	8-357	4-441	3-351	
11-395	18-433	1-354	13-357	13-398	19-356	
3-403	4-428	9-354	7-358	8-368	17-355	
13-396	3-400	12-354	14-358	16-393	16-399	
5-389	10-395	14-354	15-354	5-368	8-371	
3-403	17-397	16-354		1-395	4-368	
4-441	9-400	4-355		3-400	5-356	
19-391	16-399	10-355		17-396	13-351	
				3-369	7-348	
				16-383	17-334	

Table 16: Soviet Serials of UPe-2s allocated to Polish Pe-2 units

3 PLB		4 PLB		7 SPBN	OSL	SEL-MW
20-418	20-392	-	-	10-470	20-404	10-418	20-416
10-470				20-392	20-354		

After the war Polish Military Aviation was completely re-organised and 4 and 5 PLBs were decommissioned between January and March 1946. At about the same time (February 1946), 3 PLB was re-designated as an Independent Regiment of Diving Bombers (SPBN). This unit, at least, saw some limited combat action in the period 1946-47 against the insurgent forces of the Ukrainian Liberation Army (OUN) in south-eastern Poland. It survived as such for the next eleven years, until as late as 1957.

A totally new Polish Pe-2 unit, the Independent Aviation Flight, (SEL-MW) was formed by the Navy on 28 October 1948. Its initial establishment was a core of three *Peshkas*. These also remained in service for Warsaw Pact operations

THE *PESHKA* IN FOREIGN SERVICE

The Pe-2 was getting rather long in the tooth by the early 1950s but was still retained in front-line service with some Communist air forces. Here one fully laden Polish aircraft is subject to scrutiny at an 'Open Day' at an Air Force base, although one assumes the bombs are not armed but just for show! (Robert Michulec)

for a lengthy period, not being finally replaced by Ilyushin Il-28 bombers until the mid-1950s.

Table 17: Pe-2 Strength in Polish service

Type	1-4-45	1-6-45	1-10-45	1-1-46	1-7-47	1-12-47	1-9-49
Pe-2FT	79	107	113	111	49	45	49
UPe-2	4	4	11	9	9	11	6
Total	83	111	124	120	58	56	55

Total numbers in service at any one time, were never large and at typical periods were as:

Table 18: Total numbers of Pe-2/Upe-2 in Polish units

Unit	1-8-47			1-12-47			1-9-49		
	Pe-2	Upe-2	Total	Pe-2	UPe-2	Total	Pe-2	Upe-2	Total
7 SPBN	37	5	42	35	6	41	40	4	44
OSL	12	4	16	10	5	15	6	1	7
SEL-MW	-	-	-	-	-	-	3	1	4
Total	49	9	58	45	11	56	49	6	55

THE PETLYAKOV Pe-2

Nice photo of a *Polskie Wojska Lotnicze* (Polish Air Force) UP3-2 at the snow-covered Officers School, Deblin. Notice the solid nose and the instructor's cockpit, with a sliding canopy, mounted high behind the main cockpit. There are no dive brakes or waist-gun positions. (Andrzej Morgala)

Bulgaria

Some ninety-eight Pe-2s served in the Bulgarian Air Force (*Vâzdushni Voyski= VV-Air Army*) from April 1945 until 1956 when the Ilyushin Il-28 (NATO Codename Beagle) twin-jet bomber replaced all surviving Pe-2s and Tu-2s.

In the immediate aftermath of the war, the Bulgarians changed their national markings on their aircraft, from the wartime black St Andrew's Cross in a white square, associated with their alliance with the Axis, to a new scheme of a red disc

An extremely rare photograph of Pe-2FTs of the Bulgarian Air Force in 1945. The figure '10' is either yellow or light blue. The three-tone upper camouflage is not typical of the period and the foreground aircraft sports the post-May 1945 markings, consisting of a red disk surround by a white circle with a green horizontal bar across, adopted by the *Vâzdushni Voyski* in May 1945, in place of the former black St Andrew's Cross on a white square. In addition, the Bulgarian tricolour – white (top), green (centre) and red (bottom) – was applied in the form of three horizontal stripes across the top part of the fin and rudder. (Dénes Bernád)

THE *PESHKA* IN FOREIGN SERVICE

Bulgarian officers discussing tactics prior to take-off of the two Pe-2UTs seen in the background, operated by the Bulgarian Air Force. (Krassimir Marinou Stefanov)

in a white circle with a green horizontal bar across it. They also had the Bulgarian tricolour, which was, from top to bottom, white/green/red, painted on the top part of the Pe-2s' fins and rudders in the form of horizontal stripes. These markings were later replaced by the standard Communist insignia as that country toed Stalin's line as part of the Warsaw Pact.

In 1947, as part of their wartime reparations, the Bulgarians were forced to cede fifty-nine of their *Peshka* fleet to Yugoslavia. The survivors soldiered on for a while, the last being retired from service as late as 1956.

Czechoslovakia

The P-2 was coded as the B-32 by the Czechs (B = *Bitevni* - Bomber). The 1st Czechoslovak Mixed Air Division was officially formed in the Soviet Union on 25 January 1945 and was subordinated to the Soviet Eighth Air Army commanded by General N.V. Zhdanov. The division itself was a mixed one, consisting of one fighter and one dive-bomber regiment. This latter was not finally formed until the war in Europe was over. Following the agreement reached between the Soviet Union and Czechoslovakia, deliveries of the aircraft commenced the year after. The *Letecký pluk 25 'Atlantický'* (25th Bomber Regiment 'Atlantic' or 'Biscay' Flying Regiment) being formed on 1 May 1946,[4] but did not actually receive this name until 8 March 1948, carrying the unit code VÚ 5224 until that date. The *Letecký pluk 25* belonged to *6. Bojová divize* (6th Combat Division) commanded in 1947 by *pplk* (*podplukovník* = Wing Commander) Josef Snajdr. The regiment comprised three flights (*Letka*) and some aircraft assigned to regimental HQ.

Aircraft assigned to the HQ flight were coded 'LO-xx', aircraft from *1.letka* as 'LV-xx', aircraft from *2. letka* as 'MU-xx', and aircraft from *3. letka* as 'NT-xx'.

THE PETLYAKOV Pe-2

The CB-32s and B-32s served in *1. letka* and *2.letka* while other units employed the Aero C-3Bs (Czech-built Siebel Si-204Ds).

The Czech air force took delivery of thirty-two Pe-2 FTs and two Pe-2UPe-2 aircraft in May 1946, which they re-designated as the B-32 and CB-32 respectively. *Letecký pluk 25* was initially based at Prague-Kbely air base for its set-up and trial period, before moving to Havlièkùv Brod air base in summer 1946. By September of that year they had moved again, this time to the Èeské Budejovice air base and, in November 1946, to Plzeò-Bory air base. At the beginning of 1947 the unit returned to Havlièkùv Brod.

To recap, they were initially assigned to the 25th at that time under the command of plk. Jan Klán, but he was relieved by Lieutenant Colonel Jan Kostohryz in September 1946 with their base located at Havlièkùv Brod. They formed half of the 6th Air Division under Colonel Josef Snajdr.[5] These were brand-new aircraft and were flown to the Kbely air base, close to Prague. There, between 20 June and 1 August 1946, the Czechoslovak pilots were trained by two Soviet instructors, Captain Pantyeleyev and Lieutenant Katayev. The ground personnel to service and maintain the Pe-2s were also trained in situ by Soviet teams at the same time.

In September 1946 the 25th Bomber Regiment was transferred Èeské Budejovice and, subsequently, in November, to Plzeò-Bory. The number of Pe-2s operational proved insufficient for normal operations and they were supplemented with Siebel Si 204D (Aero C-3B) aircraft. In 1951 the unit was commanded by Jan Vopalecky who later recalled that 'As with every Soviet aircraft, built for war attrition and harsh conditions, the Petlyakovs were tough birds, which could put up with almost everything.'[6]

The Pe-2 served with the air force of Czechoslovakia at the end of World War II and for several years after that. This photo gives a clear view of the dive-brakes, wing form and landing gear on one such Czech dive-bomber. (Jiri Rajlich via Milan Krajor)

THE *PESHKA* IN FOREIGN SERVICE

Table 19: 25th Bomber Regiment – Pe-2 Serials – Summer 1947. 1st Flight – Serial LV, 2nd Flight – Serial MU)

Type	Serial Numbers of operational aircraft. (12 more in reserve)
UPe-2	LV-1, LV-2
Pe-2 FT	LV-5, LV-6, LV-7, LV-8, LV-9, LV-10, LV-11, LV-12, LV-13, LV-14, MU-3, MU-4, MU-6, MU-10, MU-11, MU-12, MU-13

These serial numbers were carried on the lower wing surfaces in black. Later the Pe-2s were painted olive-green on upper surfaces with light-blue under-surfaces with the national insignia on the top outboard section of the wings and on the rudders, codes in white on the rear fuselage and in black on the under-wing surfaces outboard of the dive brakes. The squadron badge (modelled on the RAF design but without the crown, of course) was on the nose.

The 25th returned to Havliekův Brod on 1 October 1947 when their aircraft had again been re-designated, the Pe-2 becoming the B-32 and the UPe-2 the CB-32. This code was merged with the original Soviet production number painted on the tail-plane (e.g. B-32-5-409). By 15 March 1948 the operational strength of the Pe-2s was twenty-eight machines.

Probably Havlickav Brod air base in the late 1940s. In the back is a MU-11 aircraft. The Pe-2 belonged to 2.*Letka* of *Letecky pluk* 25 also. Note the unit badge on the nose. This badge was based on the badges of 68 and 311 Squadrons RAF and were quickly done away with after the Communist *putsch* of 1948. (Archiv Stepánek Stanislav)

THE PETLYAKOV Pe-2

The commanding officer of *Letyecky pluk* 25 in 1947 was *pplk* Jan Kostohryz. He had been awarded the DSO while serving as commander of No. 311 Squadron RAF in September 1945 and became *Mjr* (*Major* = Squadron Leader) but was replaced by a new commanding officer after February 1948, the date of the communist takeover. All loyal Czechs who had served their country flying with the RAF during the Second World War were treated as traitors by the Communists, purged from the ranks and persecuted during the late 1940s and 50s, many being arrested. The unit was formally disbanded at the end of March 1950.[7] All surviving Pe-2s were then transferred to *Letecky pluk* 41.

On 16 March 1949, the new 41st Reconnaissance Regiment was formed at Milovice-Bozi with the merger of Nos. 41, 43 and 44 Reconnaissance Regiments and some Pe-2s were transferred out of 25th Bomber Regiment to this new outfit. The 41st moved to Havlièkùv Brod in June 1949 but, on 1 May 1950, was once again renumbered as 47th Reconnaissance Air Regiment and transferred to Prague-Kbely and then again to Brod in September. At this latter date, there were mixed B-32 and B-36 (Mosquito FB. VI) aircraft on its strength.

The main difficulties encountered by the Czech Air Force in keeping their *Peshkas* operational was the unreliability of their power-plant, the two VK-105PF (coded M-105 by the Czechoslovak Air Force) engines. The twelve reserve aircraft had to be cannibalised for spare parts, and often complete engines, because the repair facility at Malesice was not adequate to cope with the number of failures. There was a plan to replace the poor quality Russian engines with former German Jumo 211 F engines driving VS-11 propellers, but nothing ever came of this.

From February 1949 onward, changes and improvements were introduced including the fitting of new hydraulic controls to the landing gear. The two CB-32 trainers were rebuilt and because of extra training requirements some of the reserve B-32s were modified as trainers with dual controls at the Letov factory. By 1950, when Stanislav Štepánek visited Havlièkùv Brod, he saw the B-32s partly stripped down, parked just beyond the entrance gate. They were no longer in a flyable condition at that time.[8]

There were also moves for the replacement of the existing armament. This was initiated by the large stock of bombs, bomb racks, machine guns and ammunition abandoned by the Luftwaffe during the war, which was still in excellent condition and which could be used.

One of the Pe-2s was experimentally armed with two former German 13mm MG 131 (vz. 131/13N) machine guns in the nose, replacing the two front UBS machine guns. She also had rear-firing 7.92mm machine guns instead of Russian guns, and was equipped with ETC bomb racks for 70kg and 250kg bombs.

All of the Czechoslovakian Pe-2s were equipped with former German FuG 16ZY (LR-16ZY) radios and FuG 25a (LR-25a) IFF equipment. One other Pe-2 was modified as a photo-reconnaissance aircraft and fitted with vertically-mounted Fairchild cameras.

The last serviceable Pe-2s in the Czechoslovak Air Force ended their days with 47th Reconnaissance Regiment in early 1951 and none of the planned

THE *PESHKA* IN FOREIGN SERVICE

Seen here at the Museum of AA Artillery at Janecka, which no longer exists, is a CB-32 carrying the unit code of LV-3, but which actually belonged to 1.*Letka of Letecky pluk* 25. It would appear that the code of LV-3 is not correct and that this particular aircraft carried the code LV-1 in service. The ultimate fate of this aircraft is unknown at the time of writing; the author contacted many people, but nobody knew where she is now, if indeed she still survives. Jiri Rajlich, director of the Aviation Museum in Prague (at Kbely airfield) says this aircraft is not in store at his museum, although other planes from that collection, an Me. 262 and an La-7, still survived in 2003. (Archiv Stepánek Stanislav)

new deliveries from the Soviet Union ever took place. The last known flight of the type was recorded in February 1951, when factory test pilot Frantisek Kládek flew a CB-32 at the Kbely repair base (*Letecke Opravny Kbely*). The last two CB-32s served at the Military Educational Establishment for Mechanics and with the Military Educational Establishment of Anti-Aircraft Artillery respectively in the early 1950s. Both were later scrapped. One of the UPe-2 conversion trainers was for many years on exhibition at Olomouc in splendid condition. Sadly, since 1957, this aircraft has been totally dismantled, a great loss to aviation history.

Hungary

A few examples of the Pe-2 (NATO codename *Buck* served briefly with the *Magyar Legiero* (ML) Hungarian Red Air Arm in 1956. They carried the Red Star with a 1cm white border and individual aircraft number in black, which had been introduced in 1951, but never used operationally.

THE PETLYAKOV Pe-2

A Hungarian Pe-2 crew with their aircraft in the early 1950s. (Mirek Wawrzynski)

Yugoslavia

Under President Tito a communist government was established in post-war Yugoslavia and all opposition ruthlessly eliminated. For a time the Yugoslavs toed the Soviet line as dictated by Moscow and were duly supplied with weapons of war, including small batches of Pe-2s. The first aircraft were allocated in 1944 and formed 'The Yugoslav Bomber Regiment', as it was initially titled. The base at Sombor was established to set up 4 *Bombarderska Divizija*, which comprised 41 and 42 *Bombarderski Puk*.[9] The first aircrews were sent to Engels in the USSR, and their subsequent training and familiarisation base was at Pokrovsk. During the summer of 1945, their routine was interrupted by the brief war with Japan.[10]

There were two batches of aircraft allocated to Yugoslavia in total, of sixty-four and eighty-nine aircraft respectively, for a grand total of 153 machines, and these included fifty-nine handed over by Bulgaria post-war. Two versions were supplied, both the Pe-2 FT and the UPe-2. The Pe-2s supplied to the Yugoslavs were armed with the standard three 12.7mm UBS machine guns and one 7.62mm Ska.

THE *PESHKA* IN FOREIGN SERVICE

One of the first Pe-2s, from an allocation of seventy-three, to arrive in Yugoslavia from the Soviet Union, is shown here at the Sombor air base in 1946. Deliveries to the Air Force of the Yugoslav Liberation Army commenced in the second half of 1945 and continued to June 1946. After the 'Resolution of Informbiro' in 1948, relations between the two communist countries were broken and the Soviets terminated deliveries of all spare parts for these aircraft. (Kolekcija Zdenko Kinjerovac via Dr Zvonimir Freivogel)

The Yugoslav aircrew training was a continuing affair, and their time at Pokrovsk lasted from November 1944 to January 1947. The first operational aircraft entered service with the Yugoslav Air Force in 1946, and continued in service until the last was retired in 1954. The USSR-based training ceased at the latter date with Tito's split with Moscow in 1948, and no further aircraft, nor any replacement spares or parts, were received after that date.

As a result 41 *Bombarderski Puk* moved its base to Pleso, near Zagreb in 1948 and was re-named 97 *Avijacijski Puk*. In May 1949 this unit shifted base once more, this time to Zemunik. Some Pe-2s were also operated by 715 *Samostalna Izvidzacka Eskadrila* (Indeendent Reconnaissance Squadron between 1949 and 1952. The Yugoslav Pe-2s were painted dove-grey on the upper surfaces but light blue below, which was typical of that nation's colour schemes in the early 1950s and later.[11]

After Tito adopted a more independent line, the Soviet Union cut off replacement parts and spares for these machines, but some soldiered on for a considerable time in front-line units. However, severe problems began to be experienced in the late 1940s and early 1950s as parts became worn or damaged and could not be replaced. Replacements were sought from war surplus in the West and the first de Havilland Mosquito FB VI and NF 28s were received in April 1952. This programme continued steadily and the last Pe-2 was finally phased out of front-line service in 1954.

THE PETLYAKOV Pe-2

France

The *Normandie-Niemen* fighter squadron of expatriate French pilots and aircrews fighting on the Russian front under command of the Soviets had been long established, albeit only in small numbers. By the end of 1944 the expansion of this fighter force was under serious consideration, with the aim to increase in size to that of a full composite air division for the final push into Germany. The aim was to add a *Bretagne* BAP equipped with the Pe-2 dive-bomber, with French aircrew and Russian ground personnel. Some thirty-one Pe-2 and three Pe-2UT aircraft were initially allocated to this new unit and training was begun in March 1945, at Klokovo airfield, near Moscow. However, the unit had been disbanded before the end of the Second World War in July, without ever becoming operational.[12]

Red China

Reports in many post-war reference books that the People Liberation Army Air Force (PLAAF) was supplied by its Soviet mentor with the Pe-2 seem, in fact, to be without any firm foundation. (As recently as 2001 the type was said to have been supplied to Communist China, according to Marcus Wendel, and the date of 1949 is given by Hans-Heiri Stapfer the same year, with their use continued until the mid-1950s.) This might well be true but there appears to be little or no documentary evidence and no proof has been supplied to back the claims.

By the time the Communists had seized power from the Nationalist Chinese, Pe-2s had been largely phased out in the Soviet Union and had been replaced by the Tu-2. Numbers of the later *were* certainly handed over to the Chinese and feature in books on the Red Chinese Air Force with one Tu-2 being preserved in their air museum, but there seems to be little such mention of the Pe-2. Of course numbers of *Peshkas*, surplus to requirements, *might* well have been handed over and used from 1949, but, from my own research and that of friends of mine, it would appear that very few, *if any,* Pe-2s could have ever seen much active service in the air force of China.[13]

Chapter Twenty

The Survivors

From January 1946 Pe-3s continued to operate with the Northern Fleet VVS, with No. 3 squadron, of 574 Independent Maritime Reconnaissance Aviation Regiment (574. OMRAP). They did not start converting to the A-20G until July 1946 and the last Pe-3s were only withdrawn from service in the early 1950s. Turbojet Il-28 bombers finally replaced them. From all the thousands produced just one Pe-2 survives intact in Russia today, in addition to one in Poland, one in Norway, one in Bulgaria and one in Yugoslavia.

Russia

The most well known is a Pe-2FT (M-105R), which is an indoor static display in quite good condition at the Gagarin Military Air Academy at Momino. The exhibit is located at the Zhukovsky area of the Air Force Academy. This particular

Good overhead view of the preserved Pe-2 at the Monino Museum near Moscow shows off wing construction detail. (Victor Kulikov)

THE PETLYAKOV Pe-2

Excellent front view of the preserved Pe-2 at the Monino Museum. The display includes examples of the engines, bombs and starter trucks. (Victor Kulikov)

aircraft was built in 1940. As far as can be ascertained, it saw no combat or military service but went to the Museum from the construction plant in the late 1940s or early 1950s.

A second was frequently reported, condition unknown, kept in store at Severomorsk, to the north-east of Murmansk. Access to the latter, in a still very sensitive military area, is very difficult. However, it transpires that this aircraft was, in fact, a Pe-3 fighter of 95 MIAP, recovered for the Fiftieth Anniversary of Operation DERVISH, the first British convoy of war materials sent to Murmansk in 1941.

Mikhail Souproun led a team of enthusiastic volunteers from the Pomor State University at Archangel on a search for known Pe-2 aircraft from 95th Fighter Regiment in order to restore them. By 1992 they had located the wrecks of no less than nine Pe-2s and Pe-3s, as well as forty-three other types, including three Hawker Hurricanes, one Supermarine Spitfire, three Junkers Ju. 88s, two Junkers Ju. 87 Stukas, four Messerschmitt Bf.109s, and two Focke-Wulf Fw.190s, among others. All were duly handed over to the county administration for transportation to the aviation museum at Archangel when Dr Souproun left Archangel for duties in Moscow in 1993. When he later returned, he told me 'all our aircraft had disappeared.' (Later on, from foreign publications, I found some traces of them in a private collection in the UK!).[1]

Mikhail decided to send what material he had left to the Historical Aviation Society in Bodø, northern Norway. Among them were some unique coloured photographs of instruments and equipment inside the cockpit of the Pe-2 in Monino Museum.

THE SURVIVORS

The vogue in recovering Second World War aircraft continues. In 2009, for example, a known crash-site for one Pe-2 (Serial 19/104) which was shot down by Fw.190 fighters of 2./JG 51 near Senkovo, a village south of Lake Ozero Bolshoy Ivan, was excavated. It had been part of a force of nine *Peshkas* from 2/202 BAP under Captain E.A. Konyaeva en route to attack the rail centre at Chernozem. They were intercepted by twelve German fighters and six Pe-2s were claimed destroyed by the Germans. This was an exaggeration, however, as only three *Peshkas* were actually lost, 3/104, 6/115 and 19/104. At a depth of some eight metres the tail section of this machine was found and later a gun turret was brought to light.

Bulgaria

A Bulgarian Pe-2 is held by the National Aviation Museum at Krumovo close by Plovdiv International Airport. On outside display, it is not in good condition.

Poland

One Polish Pe-2FT survives as a static display, but not in too good a condition, outside at the Polish Army museum *Wojska Polskiego* near Warsaw to this day. Unfortunately, internal access is not possible.

The preserved Polish Pe-2 on her stand outside the Military Academy near Warsaw. Note the 'clipped off' nose on this machine. (Russian Aviation Research Trust)

THE PETLYAKOV Pe-2

Yugoslavia

One Yugoslavian survivor now resides at the *Vazduhoplovni muzej* (Air Force Museum) at *Aerodrom Beograd*, but is not accessible to the general public, viewing for serious researchers being by appointment only. Mr Cedomir Janic is the leading expert based there. Apparently, the exhibit is not on display but stored away in sections and not assembled.

Norway

The remains of Sr Lt Chasovnikov's Pe-2FT lingered on Kudal Mountain. The Germans fetched the instruments and radios; the rest was eventually forgotten. A group of Norwegian Defence Museum supporters salvaged the aircraft with the help of a 330 Squadron Sea King from Banak in summer 1988. The wreck was displayed at the fiftieth anniversary of Banak airfield that August, prior to being transported to Bodø where it was stored while restoration of the engines and minor parts were started. Parts were collected from other wreck sites, in particular the remains of Sergeant Solovov's Pe-3 east of Kirkenes.

In 1991 a breakthrough was reached when contacts in Archangel provided the restoration team with the original Russian manuals for the aircraft and engines.

The most complete of the four Pe-2 wrecks found in north Norway and being worked on at Bodo by Birger Larsen and the Bodo Aviation Historical Society, which was formed in 1989. When I visited in the early 2000s work was fully underway but since then has lapsed to a large extent. This particular Pe-2 FT, 16-141, was from 121 BBAP and was lost on 29 March 1943 after attacking a German coastal convoy off Hardbaken. This photo shows the snow-filled wreckage at Kudalsfjellet, Langryggen. (Ulf Larsstuvold)

THE SURVIVORS

The building of the National Aviation Museum, which opened in 1994, slowed the restoration work, which only recommenced in 2001. Now the forward fuselage and cockpit area is soon to be finished.

In 1997 another salvaged Pe-2 was bought by Widerøe Captain Klas Gjolmesli and brought to Bodø. This was salvaged from a lake near Murmansk, but its restoration is now on hold. The fate of two Pe-3 wrecks of 95 IAP, salvaged near Archangel in 1991, is still unclear, but they may have been sold by the Russians.

A Soviet Pe-2FT, which force-landed in Norway in March 1943, is currently under restoration at the Norwegian National Aviation Museum, Bodø.[2] In addition, parts from three other *Peshkas*, which also crashed in Norway, have been recovered, while a fifth Pe-2 was recovered from the Murmansk area by a Norwegian team.

The details of each of these machines are as follows:-

1: A Pe-3 of 95 MIAP was part of the escort for three Il-4s that attacked Honningsvag harbour at 1735 hours on 19 July 1943. Two small ships were sunk in this attack but all four Soviet aircraft were intercepted and shot down by Bf. 109s of 4/JG5 from Banek. The Pe-3 wreckage was found near Jal'gavarri (533E, 798N) in summer 1987 and further visits were made in 1989 and 1990 to recover mainly engine parts and landing gear.

2: On 29 March 1943 a German convoy was attacked outside Hardbaken. At least two of the attackers were lost, one being a Pe-2 FT, from 121 BAP, piloted by S. Sgt Jurij V. Sveshnikov, with navigator J. Lt Nikolai V. Zabobin and wireless operator Sgt Leonid V. Grjazev, was shot down and all three aircrew were killed in the crash, which was close to the railway line where it crosses the Shiunslakkeloa stream, north of Domen (255E, 053). The site of the crash was visited in 1987 but very little was found of the aircraft. The vanes for the turret were salvaged for use in the Pe-2 project. Nothing now remains.

3: The main project aircraft was the second Pe2-FT shot down on 29 March, 16/141, also from 121 BBAP, and piloted by 28-year-old Jr Lt Aleksie Ivanovitsj Tsjasovnikov, with 27-year-old navigator Lt Nikolaj Petrovits Teterin and wireless operator Jr Sgt. Igor Ivanovitsj Matvejev (21). Sent to strike German shipping off Hamningberg, Finnmark it was intercepted by German fighters and fatally damaged going down in deep snow on a spur to the east of the Sandfjorddalen range (050E, 216N). Two of the crew survived but were captured by German troops who reached the crash site shortly afterward.

The wreck proved to be the most comprehensive Pe-2 found in Norway. Expeditions were mounted in 1987 and 1988. The front and tail sections and the two engines were recovered by a Sea King helicopter of No. 330 Squadron of the Royal Norwegian Air Force in the latter year and taken to Bodø. The centre section and left wingtip remain at the site today.

4: A wreckage of another Pe-3, from 95 MIAP, which crashed on 11 September, was found scattered over a wide area in the Bugoyfjor area of Gallutjakka (698E, 425). The two main sections were visited in 1988 and the tail section

THE PETLYAKOV Pe-2

and two 12.7mm machine guns were recovered at that time, along with many other parts. The right wingtip of this aircraft was lifted by an UH-1B helicopter but had to be put down again some miles to the east, in position 761E, 423N. Some useful parts for the engine restoration and smaller parts for the gun mounting and fuselage remain to be recovered.

Since 1991 the Bodø Aviation Historical Society has been collecting parts from all these machines for the restoration of a Pe-2. The process started in 1991 but had to be put on hold for several years due to other priorities at the museum. The bulk of the restoration has been 16/141 and the pilot's seat, along with the steering stick, rudder pedals and top gun turret were displayed in the Museum. Sheet-metal repair work on the forward cockpit section had taken place. Skinning was replaced and interior details underwent restoration. The cockpit section was completed and the whole forward section placed on exhibition along with a restored engine (and a copy of my original book). Unfortunately, when the main proponent and enthusiastic backer of the project, Tor E. Olsen, retired from the Museum, the entire project lapsed.

Another Pe-2, 2/225, coded 33, from 29 BAP VVS and piloted by Junior Lieutenant Zajtsev, with Junior Lieutenant Spiridonov and Technician Borovoj as his crew, was hit by AA fire at Luostari and came down on the ice at Lake Koshkajavr, Kola 02 Municipality on 2 December 1943. On 4 October 1996 this machine was salvaged and later sent to Bjørg Gjølmesli, an airline captain with Widerøes Airlines, based at Jakobsli. It was transferred at Bodø and in January 2004 was sold to Vintage Wings Corporation at Arlington, Virginia, via Jeffrey Thomas, an American Airlines pilot, and an assistant to Paul Gardner Allen.

Preserved *Peshka* at Morino Air Museum

Seen on display at an unknown museum is one of the early Pe-2FT (*Frontovye trebovanye* = front-line demand) models, which featured the reduced nose glazing and rear 12.7 UBT gun turret. (Russian Aviation Research Trust)

THE SURVIVORS

Hungarian Site Reclamation Project

A total of four known *Peshka* crash-sites are on record in Hungary, but of these three were the victims of AA fire and went into the ground and nothing meaningful was recoverable. The fourth had a rather different story, which continues to this day. At the beginning of 1944 the Soviet army made overwhelming attacks against the Axis defences from Balatonakaratya to Budapest, and broke through in several places. The Germans desperately despatched armoured divisions south form Poland to try to hold the line. The transporting of these units naturally led the Soviets to mount numerous reconnaissance missions to locate and then attack them while still in transit,

At 1453 on 11 December 1944 a solitary Pe-2 on such a reconnaissance mission approached the eastern part of Balaton from the direction of Siofek at an estimated height of 5,000 metres (15,000ft). Before this aircraft could reach the designed target zone it was surprised and intercepted by a section of Bf.109s, led by *Hauptmann* Helmut Lipfer. On the second pass, the Bf.109s scored fatal hits on the *Peshka,* which started to burn steadily, then exploded. The burning debris smashed into the lake and the lakeside, next to Balatonakenese. Some elderly people from Balatonakenese clearly remembered the attack and the impact, even after fifty years, and could point out the impact point.

The years move on and, in 1990, the local scuba diving club, Amphora, started to make a detailed search for the wreck. They soon located the impact point from the eyewitness reports and, with the co-operation of the local water management authority (VIZIG *Közép-dunantúli Vízügyi Igazgatoság*), organised a recovery plan. They quickly discovered, to their surprise, that the main wreckage lay only 1.5 metres (4.5ft) deep. So shallow was it that it was considered a hazard for local shipping and even for swimmers. (It later came to light that two swimmers who jumped overboard from a boat at this spot in the 1960s had smashed their skulls on the wreckage and had died of their wounds.) Additional potential hazards of pollution were considered to be due to leakage from the aircraft's fuel tanks, although none were ever discovered. In any event, VIZIG decided to make a clean sweep of everything to be on the safe side.

Following several probing dives, the main part of the wreckage was lifted on 14 September 1994 after VIZIG had closed that area of the lake to shipping. Following representations from both the Hungarian War Veterans' Association and the Embassy of the Russian Federation, every attempt was made to secure any possible human remains. Despite the passage of so much time, remains were discovered of what was thought to be the cockpit floor. In fact, it was the centre section of the wings but this was unclear below water to the recovery team.

In all, the search and lifting operation lasted for two weeks, but failed to locate the fuselage or the stabilisers in the 100-metre (300ft) zone of wreckage. It was supposed that these had been lifted at some time in the preceding fifty years but no firm records of such recovery were discovered. A report, dated 1945, stated that an aircraft wreck (type or make not identified) had been found between the Military Recuperation

THE PETLYAKOV Pe-2

Home at Balatonkenese and the shore of Balaton and that all the parts had been taken for scrap in 1946. It was assumed that the wreckage on the lakebed was the residue of this. All they finally lifted were the port wing and associated debris. It was assumed that the heavier engines had sunk into the mud and silt of the lakebed.

With research work in conjunction with the Embassy of the Russian Federation it was determined that the remains belonged to the three-man Pe-2 of Seventeenth Air Army's 39th Reconnaissance Regiment, shot down that fatal day. The pilot and co-pilot were later identified as two 23-year-old lieutenants, Vaszilij Rogyinocics Jelishoy, who hailed from Usztyi-Kamenka village in the district of Perm, and Ivan Jefimovics Uhatov, from Amur. The gunner was Viktor Szergejevics Tyislenko, a 34-year-old from Krahovec Szumen. All had died instantly when the aircraft exploded in the air.

The wing recovered is now in storage at the Military Museum, Kecel. It was struck by a truck in transit but only suffered minor damage. The hope was to display the wing in a Budapest Museum but lack of sponsorship has thwarted this, although there are plans in the initial stages to mount an exhibition of all military aircraft wrecks found in Hungary. No Second World War aircraft remain in the country; everything that survived was collected and processed for scrap in the post-war period.

A photograph showing the original salvage work on the wreck of the Pe-2 shot down by Hauptmann Helmet Lipfer into the lake at Balatonakenese, Hungary and recovered in 1994 (VIZIG). Preserved Polish Pe-2 on external view near the Wojska Polskiego, Warsaw.

Remnants of Pe-2 recovered from Lake Balatonakenese (Lujos Legrady)

Appendix 1

Pe-2 Units

Abbreviations:

VA	Air Army
MD	Military District
RVGK	Supreme High Command Reserve
BAK	Bomber Air Corps
SAK	Composite Aviation Corps
BAD	Bomber Air Division
SAD	Composite Air Division
RAG	Reserve Air Group
UAG	Shock Aviation Group
BAP	Bomber Air Regiment
BBAP	Close Range Air Regiment
SBAP	Fast Bomber Air Regiment
PBAP	Dive Bomber Air Regiment
LBAP	Light Bomber Air Regiment
RAP	Recon. Air Regiment
DRAP	Long Range Recce Regiment
AP Pogody	Weather Recce Regiment
IAP	Fighter Air Regiment
AP-DD	Long-Range Air Regiment
G (prefix)	Guards
-SF	Northern Fleet
-KBF	Baltic Fleet
-ChF	Black Sea Fleet
-TOF	Pacific Ocean Fleet
">"	Indicates transferred to
"<"	Indicates transferred from

Dates in parentheses ( ) are approximate, based only on a particular identification in a text. 'German source' indicates data taken from 'SU *Fliegertruppe im Einsatz*' German intelligence document, but not yet corroborated in a Soviet source.

Air Armies

1. Western Front 6/42
   Third Belorussian Front 5/44
2. Bryansk Front 6/42
   Voronezh Front 8/42
   Southwest Front 12/42
   Voronezh Front 2/43
   First Ukrainian Front 11/43
3. Kalinin Front 6/42
   First Baltic Front 11/43
   Third Belorussian Front 5/45
4. Southern Front 7/42
   North Caucasus Front 8/42
   Transcaucasus Front 9/42
   North Caucasus Front 2/43
   Independent Coastal Army 12/43
   Second Belorussian Front 5/44
5. North Caucasus Front 7/42
   Transcaucasus Front 10/42
   North Caucasus Front 3/43
   Steppe Front 8/43
   Second Ukrainian Front 11/43
6. Northwest Front 7/42
   Stavka Reserve 12/43
   Second Belorussian Front 4/44
   First Belorussian Front
   Stavka 10/44
7. Karelian Front 12/42
   Stavka 12/44
8. Southwest Front 7/42
   Stalingrad Front 8/42
   Southern Front 1/43
   Fourth Ukrainian Front 11/43
   Stavka 6/44
   First Ukrainian Front 8/44
   Fourth Ukrainian Front 9/44
9. Far East Front 9/42
   FE Coastal Group 1/44
10. Far East Front 9/42
11. Far East Front 9/42
    disbanded 1/45
12. Transbaikal Front 9/42
    Far East Front 8/45
13. Leningrad Front 12/42

Pe-2 UNITS

14 Volkhov Front 9/42
    Stavka 3/44
    Third Baltic Front 5/44
    Second Baltic Front 11/44
    Stavka 12/44
15 Bryansk Front 8/42
    Second Baltic Front 11/43
    Leningrad Front 4/45
16 Stavka Reserve 9/42
    Don Front 10/42
    Central Front 3/43
    Belorussian Front 11/43
    First Belorussian Front 3/44
17 Southwest Front 12/42
    Third Ukrainian Front
18 ADD 1/45

Bomber Aviation Army

| 1 | BAA-VGK | Kalinin Front 8/42-9/42 | 221, 222, 293 BAD |

Bomber Air Corps

1	GBAK	(<2)	1 VA 10/43	4 G, 5 G BAD
			3 VA 8/44	
			>5 GBAK 26/12/44	
2	GBAK	(<1)	5 VA 3/44	1 G, 8, G BAD
			8 VA 8/44	
			2 VA 9/44	
			>6 GBAK 26/12/44	
5	GBAK	(<1G)	3 VA 1/45	4 G, 5 G BAD
			15 VA 3/45	
6	GBAK	(<2 G)	2 VA 1/45	1 G, 8, G BAD
1	BAK		Kalinin F 10/42	263, 293 BAD
			14 VA 2/43	
			2 VA 4/43	
			5 VA 8/43	
			>2 GBAK 5/2/44	
2	BAK		Stavka 11/42	223, 285 BAD
			16 VA 12/42	
			2 VA 4/43	
			4 VA 5/43	
			1 VA 8/43	
			>1 GBAK 2/9/43	

THE PETLYAKOV Pe-2

3	BAK		Stavka 11/42	241, 301 BAD
			3 VA 2/43	
			16 VA 5/43	
			6 VA 8/44	
			16 VA 9/44	
4	BAK		2 VA 3/44	202, 219 BAD
			6 VA 10/44	
			2 VA 12/44	
5	BAK		16 VA 10/44	132, 327 BAD
			4 VA 1/45	
6	BAK		1 VA 4/45	326, 334 BAD
			12 VA 8/45	
7	BAK		12 VA 8/45	113 DBAD, 179 BAD

Bomber Air Division (BAD)

1	GBAD	(<263)	1 BAK 3/43	80, 81, 82 GBAP
			2 GBAK 3/44	
3	GBAD	(<204)	1 VA 10/43	119, 122, 123 GBAP
			Stavka 10/44	
			3 VA 11/44	
			12 VA 9/45	
4	GBAD	(<223)	1 GBAK 10/43	124, 125, 126 GBAP
5	GBAD	(<285)	1 GBAK 10/43	35, 127, 128 GBAP
6	GBAD	(<270)	8 VA 11/43	10, 134, 135 GBAP
			Stavka 6/44	
			1 VA 7/44	
8	GBAD	(<293)	2 GBAK 3/44	160, 161, 162 GBAP
34	BAD		9 VA 9/42	
53	BAD		Far East F 10/41	
			9 VA 9/42	
66	BAD		Southern F 1/42-5/42	
82	BAD		2 A-Far East F 9/41	
			11 VA 9/42	
83	BAD		25 A-Far East F 1/42	
			10 VA 9/42	
132	BAD		Crimean F 9/41	63, 277, BAP
			5 VA 7/42	
			4 VA 5/43	
			8 VA 5/44	
			6 SAK 6/44	
			Belorussian MD 10/44	
			5 BAK 1/45	
179	BAD		Stavka 5/45	
			7 BAK 8/45	

Pe-2 UNITS

183	BAD	Kharkov MD 9/44-12/44	319, 540 BAP
		16 VA 1/45	
188	BAD	Moscow MD 3/44–9/44	367, 373, 650 BAP
		15 VA 9/44	
202	BAD	3 BAK 11/42	36 G, 18, 797 BAP
		3 SAK 1/43	
		7 SAK 4/43	
		2 VA 8/43	
		4 BAK 3/44	
204	BAD	1 VA 6/42	2, 130, 261 BAP
		>3 GBAD 2/9/43	
211	BBAD	3 VA 7/42	930, 991 NBAP, 128 BAP
		> ShAD	
219	BAD	4 VA 6/42	6, 35, 38 BAP
		Stavka 9/43	
		Moscow MD 10/43-2/44	
		4 BAK 3/44	
221	BAD	8 VA 7/42	57, 745, 794 BAP
		1 BAA-VGK 8/42-9/42	
		1 BAK 10/42	
		Stavka 11/42	
		17 VA 12/42	
		Stavka 4/43	8 G, 57, 745 BAP
		6 SAK 5/43	
		5 BAK 10/44	
		16 VA 11/44	
223	BAD	2 VA 6/42	20, 334, 587 BAP
		2 BAK 11/42	
		>4 GBAD 10/43	
237	BAD	Moscow MD 6/44	
241	BAD	6 VA 7/42	24, 121, 128, 779 BAP
		3 BAK 12/42	
244	BAD	Bryansk F 7/42	45, 449, 860, 861 BAP
		2 VA 9/42	
		Stavka 12/42	
		17 VA 3/43	260, 449, 455, 541 BAP
		1 GBAK 8/44	
		17 VA 10/44	
254	BAD	10 VA 9/42	
		>SAD 10/42	
260	BAD	7 VA 12/42	80, 137 BAP, 668 NBAP
		>SAD 3/43	
263	BAD	1 BAK 10/42	46, 202, 321 BAP
		>1 GBAD 17/3/43	
270	BAD	8 VA 7/42	52, 135 BBAP, 275, 779 BAP

327

THE PETLYAKOV Pe-2

			10 G, 86, 284 BAP
		>6 GBAD 23/10/43	
276	BAD	13 VA 12/42	34 G, 58, 140 BAP
		1 VA 11/44	
		>2 GBAD 17/3/43	
280	BAD	14 VA 9/42	
285	BAD	3 VA 8/42	35 G, 134, 205 BAP
		1 VA 9/42	
		1 BAK 10/42	
		2 BAK 12/42	
		>5 GBAD	
293	BAD	Stavka 8/42	780, 804, 854 BAP
		1 BAA-VGK 9/42	
		1 BAK 10/42	
		>8 GBAD 2/5/44	
301	BAD	3 BAK 1/42	96 G, 34, 54 BAP
304	BAD	5 SAK 3/43	

Bomber Air Regiments

(Aircraft types confirmed used by a regiment are listed alongside. Pe-2s are listed only where their use has been confirmed. For the other regiments, Pe-2 use is unconfirmed but possible; in some cases probable.)

4	GBBAP	(<31)	7 Army 3/42	Pe-2
			280 SAD (9/44)	
			188 BAD (2/45)	
8	GBAP	(<5)	5 RAG 5/42	Pe-2, A-20
			219 BAD 5/42	
			4 VA 8/42	
			Trans Caucasus MD 9/42-4/43	
			221 BAD (5/43)	
10	GBAP	(<33)	Southwestern F 4/42	SB, Pe-2, A-20B, Tu-2
			Manoeuvre Gp -Southwestern F 5/42-6/42	
			270 BAD 9/42	
			6 GBAD 11/43	
			Moscow MD 5/45	
12	GBAP		219 BAD (8/44)	Pe-2
13	GBAP	(<43)	Southwestern F 4/42	Su-2, Pe-2, A-20C
			8 VA 7/42	
			Siberian MD 9/42-5/43	
			Moscow MD 6/43	
			321 BAD (8/43)	

Pe-2 UNITS

34	GBAP	(<44)	13 VA 12/42 276 BAD 1/43	Pe-2
35	GBAP	(<150)	285 BAD 11/42 5 GBAD (10/43)	Pe-2
36	GBAP	(<514)	202 BAD 11/42)	Pe-2
80	GBAP	(<46)	1 GBAD 3/43	Pe-2
81	GBAP	(<202)	1 GBAD 3/43	Pe-2
82	GBAP	(<321)	1 GBAD 3/43	Pe-2
96	GBAP	(<99)	301 BAD 6/43	Pe-2
114	GBAP	(<137)	1 GSAD 9/43 7 VA 1/45	Pe-2, A-20
119	GBAP	(<2)	3 GBAD 9/43	Pe-2
122	GBAP	(<130)	3 GBAD 9/43	Pe-2
123	GBAP	(<261)	3 GBAD 9/43	Pe-2
124	GBAP	(<10)	4 GBAD 10/43	Pe-2
125	GBAP	(<587)	4 GBAD 10/43	Pe-2
126	GBAP	(<224)	4 GBAD 10/43	Pe-2
127	GBAP	(<134)	5 GBAD 10/43	Pe-2
128	GBAP	(<205)	5 GBAD 10/43	Pe-2
134	GBAP	(<86)	6 GBAD 11/43	Pe-2
135	GBAP	(<284)	6 GBAD 11/43	Pe-2
160	GBAP	(<780)	8 GBAD 3/44	Pe-2
161	GBAP	(<804)	8 GBAD 3/44	Pe-2
162	GBAP	(<854)	8 GBAD 3/44	Pe-2
1	BAP		Western F 7/41-8/41 23 BAD 9/41-1/42	SB, Pe-2
2	SBAP		Northern F 6/41 Volga MD 1/42 13 VA (5/43) 204 BAD >119 GBAP (9/43)	SB, Pe-2
3	BAP		Western F 7/41-8/41 23 BAD 9/41-1/42	SB
4	BBAP		Stalingrad MD 1/42	U-2, Pe-2
5	SBAP		21 SAD 6/41 Stalingrad MD 2/42 >8 GBAP 3/7/42	DB-3. SB, Pe-2
6	BAP		12 BAD 6/41 North Caucasus MD 2/42 Stavka 5/42 132 BAD 6/42 204 BAD 219 BAD (8/44)	SB, Pe-2
8	BAP		Volga MD 1/42	SB, Pe-2

THE PETLYAKOV Pe-2

9	SBAP	Stalingrad MD 2/42 2 VA (11/42), German source NW Front 6/41 (Volga MD?) 7/41-9/41 Moscow MD 10/41-12/41 Stavka 1/42-2/42 2 AD-ON (11/42-1/44) Moscow MD 1/44	SB Pe-2 Pe-3
10	SBAP	41 BAD 6/41 Stavka 1/42 2 RAG 3/42 Stavka 4/42 2 RAG 5/42-7/42 Moscow MD 8/42 223 BAD 5/43 >124 GBAP (10/43)	SB, Yak-4, Pe-2
12	BBAP	Western Front 6/41 Siberia MD 7/42 3 VA 12/42 Stavka 2/43-3/43 Moscow MD 4/43-8/43 3 VA 9/43 Stavka 11/43 Moscow MD 12/43 334 BAD 5/44	Pe-2 Tu-2
13	BAP	9 SAD 6/41 11 SAD 8/41-9/41 Moscow MD 10/41 Volga MD 1/42-2/42 Siberian MD 3/42-4/42 >RAP 5/42	SB, Ar-2, Pe-2
14	BAP	Moscow MD 6/41 Northern F 7/41	SB
16	BAP	11 SAD 6/41 Volga MD 1/42 Stavka 6/42 222 BAD 7/42 >AP-DD 10/42	SB, Pe-2 B-25C
18	SBAP	Northern Front 6/41 54 A-LG Front 1/42 Moscow MD 10/42 202 BAD 11/42 Stavka 3/43	SB, Pe-2
20	BAP	Southwestern F 6/41 3 VA (7/43), German source	SB

Pe-2 UNITS

21	BAP	51 Army 9/41	SB
23	BAP	Northern F 6/41 2 VA (7/42), German source	SB
24	BBAP	13 BAD 6/41 Bryansk Front 10/41 61 SAD (11/41) 223 BAD Moscow MD 10/42 241 BAD 3/43-EOW	SB, Pe-2
25	BAP	Northern F 6/41	SB
30	BBAP	Western F 9/41 Volga MD 1/42 Siberian MD 4/42 Stavka 8/42 293 BAD 8/42 8 VA 9/42	Pe-2
31	SBAP	NW F 6/41 7 A 10/41 > 4 GBAP 12/6/41	SB, Pe-2
32	BAP	Volga MD 1/42 Stavka 5/42-6/42 2 RAB 7/42 Stavka 10/42	SB, Pe-2
33	SBAP	19 BAD 6/41 Southwestern F 3/42 >10 GBAP 3/7/42	SB, AR-2, Pe-2
34	BAP	4 SA Bde. 6/41-9/41 Western Front 10/41 Stavka 3/42 S. Ural MD 7/42 Moscow MD 10/42 301 BAD (8/44)	SB, Pe-2
35	SBAP	NW F 6/41 North Caucasus MD 1/42 Moscow MD 2/42 2 RAB 3/42 1 UAG 4/42-7/42 Volkhov F 8/42 Moscow MD 5/43-10/43 219 BAD (8/44)	SB, Pe-2
37	SBAP	31 SAD 6/41 Volga MD 1/42-5/42 Stavka 6/42 222 BAD 7/42 >AP-DD 10/42	SB, Pe-2 B-25C

THE PETLYAKOV Pe-2

38	SBAP	28 SAD 6/41 Volga MD 1/42 Stavka 4/42 2 RAB 5/42-6/42 204 BAD 219 BAD (8/44)	SB, Pe-2
39	BAP	10 SAD 6/41 43 SAD 9/41 Volga MD 1/42 North Caucasus MD 2/42 Volga MD 5/42 Moscow MD 8/42 Volga MD 10/42 202 BAD (2/43) 17 VA 4/43 > 39 RAP 5/43	SB, Pe-2
41	BAP	56 A-Southern F 12/41 Trans Caucasus F 1/42 North Caucasus MD 3/42	SB
43	LBAP	12 BAD 6/41 6 A-Southwestern F 3/42 >13 GBAP	SB, AR-2
44	SBAP	2 SAD 6/41 LG F 3-6/42 Zhdanov Group 7/42-8/42 >34 GBAP 11/21/42	SB, AR-2, Yak-4, Pe-2
46	BAP	NW F 6/41 49 A-Western F 2/42 Stavka 6/42 263 BAD 10/42 >80 GBAP	SB, Pe-2
48	BBAP	17 SAD 6/41 Volga MD 1/42 Trans Caucasus MD 7/42 Stavka 2/43-3/43 218 BAD (8/43)	Pe-2, A-20C, A-20G
50	LBAP	24 A-Reserve Front 9/41 Trans Caucasus MD 2/42 Stavka 4/42 Moscow MD 5/42	Pe-2
52	BBAP	76 SAD 10/41-2/42 Volga MD 3/42-4/42 Manoeuvre Gp -Southwestern F 5/42-6/42 270 BAD 7/42-8/42	Su-2

Pe-2 UNITS

53	BAP	Karelian Front (9/42)	SB, Yak-4
54	BAP	NW F 6/41-7/41	SB
		(Volga MD?) 8-19/41	Pe-3
		Western Front 11/41	
		Stavka 12/41	
		54 A-Western F 2/42	
		Volga MD 3/42	Pe-2
		Moscow MD 6/42	
		241 BAD 3/43-EOW	
55	BAP	Far East MD 6/41	SB, Pe-2, Tu-2
		NW F 3/42	
		13 VA (5/43)	
		Stavka 12/43	
		15 VA 1/44	
		113 BAD (12/44)	
58	BAP	2 SAD 6/41	SB, Pe-2
		Volga MD 1/42	
		Stavka 4/42	
		NW F 5/42	
		6 VA 12/42	
		276 BAD 5/43	
		6 VA 12/43	
		276 BAD (6/44)	
59	BAP	FE Front 6/41	SB, Pe-2
60	BAP	Moscow MD 6/41	SB
61	BAP	NW Front 6/41	SB
63	BAP	NW F 6/41	SB, A-20B, A20G, Pe-2
		Volga MD 1/42	
		Stavka 6/42	
		Trans Caucasus MD 7/42	
		132 BAD (5/44)	
68	BAP	4 VA (6/43), German source	
77	BAP	15 VA (9/42), German source	
80	BBAP	Arkhangel MD 6/41	SB, Pe-2
		32 A-Karelian F 4/42	
		260 BAD 12/42	
		261 SAD (6/44)	
		7 VA 12/44-1/45	
82	BAP	Arkhangel MD 6/41	SB, Pe-2
86	SBAP	Southwestern F 6/41	SB, Pe-2
		Stalingrad MD 2/42	
		8 VA 7/42	
		>134 GBAP 10/23/43	
92	BAP	Southwestern F. 6/42	Pe-2
		8 VA 6/42	

333

94	BBAP	>reforming in rear 7/42 Southwestern F 6/41 Stavka 2/42 Moscow MD 3/42 228 ShAD 5/42 270 BAD 6/42 Moscow MD 8/42	SB, Pe-2
95	BAP	46 SAD 6/41 Western F 7/41 Moscow MD 9/41 >IAP 10/41	Pe-2 Pe-3
96	BAP	Moscow MD 1/42 13 VA, (1/43), German source	Pe-2
99	BBAP	4 RAG 10/41-6/42 270 BAD (9/42) 16 VA 9/42 Moscow MD 10/42 223 BAD 11/42 >96 GBAP 6/16/43	SB, Su-2, Pe-2
108	BAP	3 VA (1/43), German source	
121	BAP	13 BAD 6/41 2 UA Volkhov F 1/42 3 RAG 3/42 2 RAG 4/42 241 BAD 3/43	SB, Pe-2, Pe-3
125	BAP	13 BAD 6/41 LG F 10/41 2 SAD 12/41 Stavka 3/42 Volga MD 5/42 222 BAD 7/42 >AP-DD 10/42	SB, Pe-2 B-25C
128	BBAP	12 BAD 6/41 3 UA-Kalinin F 3/42-5/42 211 BAD 6/42- Moscow MD 12/42 241 BAD 3/43-EOW	SB, Pe-2
130	BBAP	13 BAD 6/41 Moscow MD 11/41 Western F 2/42 204 BAD >122 GBAP	SB, Pe-2
132	SBAP	45 SAD 6/41-8/41 Kalinin F 11/41-3/42	SB, AR-2, Pe-2, Tu-2

Pe-2 UNITS

		Moscow MD 4/42	
		Siberian MD 4-8/42	
		Kalinin F 11/42-1/43	
		Stavka (Southwestern Front)	
		2/43-5/43	
		Moscow MD 6/43-11/43	
		Volga MD 12/43	
		334 BAD 6/44	
133	BAP	Northern F 6/41	SB, Pe-2
134	BAP	46 SAD 6/41	SB, AR-2, Pe-2
		Western F 9/41	
		Volga MD 2/42	
		Siberia MD 6/42	
		Stavka 7/42	
		285 BAD 8/42	
		>127 GBAP	
135	BAP	Southwestern Front 6/41	SB, Su-2
		21 A-Southwestern F 3/42	
		270 BAD 6/42-8/42	
136	BBAP	19 SAD 6/41	Yak-2, Pe-2
		46 SAD 10/41	
		Southwestern F 3/42	
		Stavka 4/42	
		Volga MD 5/42	
		Stavka 7/42	
		4 VA 8/42	
137	BBAP	1 SAD 6/41	SB, Pe-2, A-20C
		14 A-Karelian F 3/42	
		260 BAD 12/42	
		258 SAD 3/43	
		>114 GBAP 8/24/43	
138	BAP	2 RAG 1/42	SB, Pe-2
		Moscow MD 2/42	
		2 RAB 5/42	
		Moscow MD 11/42	
140	BAP	Volga MD 1/42	Pe-2
		Moscow MD 7/42	
		8 VA 8/42	
		Stavka 2/43-3/43	
		276 BAD 12/42	
150	SBAP	Transbaikal F. 6/41	SB, Pe-2
		46 BAD 8/41	
		Moscow MD 3/42	
		8 VA 8/42	

THE PETLYAKOV Pe-2

		Moscow MD 9/42	
		285 BAD 11/42	
		>35 GBAP 11/21/42	
175	BAP	Volga MD1/42	
		Western F 3/42	
		Stavka 11/42	
188	BAP	219 BAD 5/42	Pe-2
202	BAP	Northern F 6/41	SB, Pe-2
		Stavka 1/42	
		North Caucasus MD 2/42	
		Moscow MD 9/42	
		263 BAD 10/42	
		>81 GBAP	
203	BAP	15 VA (10/42), German source	
204	BAP	Western Front (5/42),	
		German source	
205	BAP	Volga MD 1/42	Pe-2
		Karelian F 5/42	
		2 RAB 6/42-7/42	
		13 VA (5/43)	
		>128 GBAP	
208	BBAP	Moscow MD	SB, Pe-2
		>IAP 10/41	
209	BAP	12 BAD 6/41	SB
		40 A-Southwestern F 3/42	
		Voronezh Front (8/42),	
		German source	
213	LBAP	North Caucasus MD 1/42	
214	BAP	Moscow MD (6/41)	SB, Pe-2
224	BAP	Stavka 1/42	Pe-2
		Stalingrad MD 2/42	
		Moscow MD 9/42	
		223 BAD (9/43)	
		>126 GBAP 10/43	
225	BBAP	3 RAG 12/41-1/42	Yak-4
		4 A-Volkhov Front 1/42	
230	BAP	38 A-Southwestern F 3/42	SB
		Stavka 5/42	
		S. Ural MD 7/42	
243	BBAP	Moscow MD (2/44), German source	
244	PBAP	Bryansk F 11/41	Pe-2
		Volga MD 1/42	
		Trans Caucasus MD 5/42-4/43	
		8 VA (4/44), German source	

Pe-2 UNITS

260	BAP	Volga MD 1/42 Siberian MD 10/42-5/43 244 BAD (9/44)	Pe-2, A-20C, A-20G
261	BAP	Moscow MD 1/42 Stavka 7/42 204 BAD (8/43) >123 GBAP 9/3/43	Pe-2
267	BAP	7 VA (3/43), German source	
275	BAP	Moscow MD 1/42 270 BAD 6/42 Stavka 7/42	Pe-2
277	BAP	North Caucasus MD 9/41 56 A-Southern F 1/42 North Caucasus MD 4/42 Trans Caucasus MD 7/42 132 BAD	SB, Pe-2, A-20B
279	BAP	Moscow MD 1/42 Stavka 7/42 16 VA 4/43 Stavka 5/43-6/43 3 VA 7/43	
284	BAP	S. Ural MD 1/42-8/42 270 BAD 9/42 >135 GBAP 10/23/43	Pe-2
288	BBAP	21 SAD 6/41 57 A-Southern F 5/42 4 VA 11/42	Su-2, Pe-2, A-20
289	BBAP	63 SAD 6/41 Southwestern F 3/42	
301	BAP	15 VA (3/43), German source	
309	BAP	3 VA (5/43), German source	
317	BAP	17 VA (1/43), German source	SB
319	SBAP	2 A-Far East F 4/42 183 BAD 9/44	Pe-2
321	BBAP	77 SAD 10/41 Volga MD 1/42 202 BAD (10/42) >82 GBAP	SB, Pe-2
326	LBAP	Volga MD 1/42	
350	BAP	5 VA (8/43), German source	
356	BAP	2 VA (3/43), German source	
362	BAP	15 VA (9/44), German source	
366	BAP	56 A-Southern F 12/41 219 BAD 5/42	Pe-2, A-20B

THE PETLYAKOV Pe-2

367	BAP	132 BAD (6/42-5/43) Trans Caucasus MD 8/43 132 BAD (2/44) 188 BAD (3/44)	SB, Pe-2, A-20B
368	BAP	5 VA (4/43), German source	
373	LBAP	Stavka 1/43 3 VA 6/43 188 BAD (3/44)	Pe-2
385	LBAP	Moscow MD 4/43 Stavka 5/43 2 VA 6/43 14 VA (1/44), German source	
387	LBAP	Moscow MD 4/43-7/43 2 VA (10/43), German source	
406	LBAP	Moscow MD 12/42 8 VA 4/43 3 VA 12/44, German source	Pe-2
410	BAP	Western F 7/41-8/41 23 BAD 9/41-1/42	Pe-2
411	BAP	Stavka	Pe-2
423	BAP	8 VA (2/44), German source	
426	BAP	8 VA (12/43), German source	
440	BAP	5 VA (9/44), German source	
444	BAP	4 (or 5) VA (3/43), German source	
449	BAP	North Caucasus MD 3/42 Trans Caucasus MD 7/42 244 BAD 8/42	Pe-2, A-20B, A-20G, Tu-2
454	BAP	17 A-Transbaikal MD 3/42 Trans Caucasus MD 7/42-3/43 2 VA 4/43 Stavka 10/43-11/43 Moscow MD 12/43 334 BAD 6/44	Pe-2 Tu-2
455	BAP	36 A-Transbaikal F 3/42	
456	BBAP	36 A-Transbaikal F 3/42	
457	BAP	Transbaikal F 4/42 T Caucasus F 1/43	
458	BAP	5 VA (9/42), German source Moscow MD 7/44	
459	BAP	Western F 9/41 5 RAG 5/42 4 VA 9/42	SB
507	SBAP	51 Army 10/41 Volga MD 3/42	Yak-4

Pe-2 UNITS

		3 RAB 5/42	
		2 RAB 6/42-7/42	
		4 VA (5/43), German source	
511	BBAP	10 SAD 10/41	Pe-3
		Stavka 12/41	
		Western F 2/42	
		Stavka 6/42	
		Moscow MD 8/42-2/43	
		Volga MD 3/43	
		> 511 RAP 4/43	
512	BAP	3 VA 3/43	Pe-2
514	PBAP	NW F 3/42	Pe-2
		Moscow MD 8/42	
		>36 GBAP 11/21/42	
527	BAP	Volga MD 1/42	
		Stavka 5/42	
		Moscow MD 12/42	
		16 VA (7/43), German source	
530	BAP	5 VA (10/43), German source	
540	BAP	Central Front 3/43	Pe-2
		183 BAD 9/44	
541	BAP	36 A-Transbaikal F 3/42	
		12 VA 8/45	
581	SBAP	15 A-Far East 4/42	
585	BAP	56 A-Southern F 12/41	
		4 VA 10/42	
587	BBAP	122 SAD 1/42	Su-2, Pe-2
		Volga MD 2/42-6/42	
		223 BAD 7/42	
		>125 GBAP (10/43)	
603	BBAP	19 A-Western F 2/42	Pe-2, Pe-3
608	BBAP	Karelian F 1/42	Pe-2
		>disb. 12/42	
632	LBAP	Volga MD 3/42	
633	LBAP	Stavka 1/42	
		6 A-Southwestern F 3/42	
		8 VA (9/42), German source	
635	LBAP	Stavka 2/42	
636	LBAP	Stavka 1/42	
		Bryansk F 3/42	
640	NBAP	Ural MD 1/42	U-2, Pe-2
		3 RAB 4/42-7/42	
		15 VA 8/42	
643	BBAP	Stavka 2/42	
		4 UAG 5/42	

THE PETLYAKOV Pe-2

645	LBAP	Volga MD 1/42	
		Stavka 3/42	
		2 RAB 4/42	
		11 A-NW F 5/42	
		Moscow MD (2/44), German source	
647	LBAP	Volga MD 1/42	
		12 A-Southern F 4/42	
650	LBAP	North Caucasus MD 1/42	U-2, Pe-2
		37 A-Southern F 5/42	
		8 VA (3/44), German source	
		188 BAD 3/44-	
664	LBAP	Stavka 1/42	
		Kalinin F 2/42	
682	LBAP	Stavka 1/42	
		40 A-Southwestern F 3/42	
		4 VA (11/42), German source	
684	BAP	Stavka 2/42	SB
		4 UA-Kalinin F 3/42	
		3 VA 6/42	
696	BBAP	Stavka 1/42	
		2 UA-Volkhov F 2/42	
		13 VA (8/43), German source	
699	LBAP	Stavka 2/42	
		NW F 3/42	
711	LBAP	1 UA-Western F 12/41	
		5 A Bryansk F 3/42	
		Voronezh Front (8/42), German source	
712	LBAP	Stavka 2/42	
		Western F 3/42	
713	LBAP	Volga MD 2/42	
		Western F 4/42	
717	LBAP	2 UAG 5/42-6/42	Pe-2
		6 VA 10/43?	
		242 NBAD (12/44)	
		4 VA 9/42	
723	BBAP	Volga MD 8/41	Pe-2
		NW Front 10/41	
		Volga MD 1/42	
		Stavka 3/42	
		7 Stavka UAG 4/42-5/42	
		Moscow MD 10/42-4/43	
		Moscow MD 8/43	
730	LBAP	Stavka 6/42	
732	LBAP	Stavka 2/42	

Pe-2 UNITS

		Western F 3/42	
		15 VA (3/43), German source	
733	LBAP	Stavka 1/42	
		61 A-Western F 2/42	
742	BAP	Crimean F 5/42	Pe-2
		5 VA (9/42)	
745	BAP	Stavka 2/42	Pe-2, A-20B
		30 A-Kalinin F 3/42	
		Stavka 4/42	
		Trans Caucasus MD 5/42-7/42	
		221 BAD 8/42	
750	LBAP	Volga MD 1/42	
		56 A-Southern F 4/42	
755	BAP	16 VA (10/43), German source	
757	BAP	15 VA (11/42), German source	
759	BAP	16 VA (8/43), German source	
762	LBAP	4 VA 9/42	
766	LBAP	Volga MD 4/42	
771	BBAP	Stavka 2/42	Pe-2
		1 RAB 3/42	
		1 UAG 4/42-7/42	
775	LBAP	Moscow MD 3/42	
778	BAP	Volga MD 4/42	Pe-2
		1 VA 12/42	
		15 VA (8/43), German source	
779	BAP	North Caucasus MD 3/42	Pe-2
		270 BAD 6/42	
		Stavka 7/42	
		16 VA 9/42	
		Moscow MD 10/42	
		204 BAD (2/44)	
		241 BAD 3/43-EOW	
780	BAP	North Caucasus MD 3/42	Pe-2
		3 VA 4/43	
		Stavka 7/42	
		293 BAD (8/43)	
		>160 GBAP 2/5/44	
782	BBAP	35 A-Far East F 4/42	
783	LBAP	51 A-Crimean F 5/42	
793	BBAP	Trans Caucasus MD 4/42	
		Kalinin Front (7/42), German source	
797	BAP	Moscow MD 10/42	Pe-2
		202 BAD (5/45)	

THE PETLYAKOV Pe-2

799	BAP	?	Pe-2
803	BAP	Stalingrad MD 3/42	
		Stavka 7/42	
		2 VA (5/43), German source	
804	BAP	Volga MD 5/42	Pe-2
		293 BAD 11/42	
		>161 GBAP 2/5/44	
841	LBAP	Stavka 6/42	
853	BAP	Stalingrad MD 3/42	
854	BAP	Stalingrad MD 4/42	Pe-2
		293 BAD (8/43)	
		>162 GBAP 2/5/44	
859	BBAP	Trans Caucasus MD 5/42	
892	BBAP	North Caucasus MD 6/42	
		Volga MD 8/42	
		Moscow MD 9/42	
902	BAP	Far East F 6/42	
		Southern F 3/43	
935	LBAP	14 VA 9/42	
968	LBAP	Karelian F 9/42	
		7 VA 12/42	
970	LBAP	Transbaikal MD 9/42	U-2, Pe-2, A-20G
		16 VA 10/42	
974	BAP	Trans Caucasus F 9/42	
988	LBAP	Stavka 10/42	
		15 VA 11/42	
		Stavka 12/42	

Long-Range Reconnaissance Regiments (DRAP)

47	GDRAP	(<2)	ADD 3/43-3/44	Il-4, Pe-2, Tu-2
			Moscow MD 4/44-6/44	
			1 VA 7/44	
			ADD 8/44	
			4 VA 9/44	
			Belorussian MD 10/44-12/44	
48	GDRAP	(<40)	ADD 3/43-3/44	Pe-2, Pe-2/M-82, A-20B,
			Moscow MD 4/44-6/44	B-25, Pe-3*bis*, Yak-9R
			Odessa MD 7/44-5/45	
98	GDRAP	(<4)	ADD 5/43-3/44	Pe-2, Pe-3*bis*, A-20, Li-2,
			Moscow MD 4/44-5/44	P-39, U-2
			2 VA 6/44	
99	GDRAP	(<32)	15 VA 7/43	Pe-2, Pe-2/M-82

Pe-2 UNITS

164	GDRAP	(<366)	4 VA 5/44	Pe-2, A-20B
1	DRAP		ADD 9/41	SB, Pe-3, Tu-2
2	DRAP		ADD 9/41	Pe-2, Pe-3*bis*, Tu-2
			>47 GDRAP 3/43	
3	DRAP		Western F 2/42	Yak-2, LaGG-3, Pe-2, Pe-3
4	DRAP		17 VA 1/43	Pe-2, Pe-3*bis*, A-20B, B-25
			>98 GDRAP 6/16/43	
			ADD 2/43	
8	DRAP		8 VA 6/42	Su-2, Pe-2
10	DRAP		1 VA 1/43	Pe-2
11	DRAP		3 VA 8/42	Pe-2, Pe-2/M-82, Tu-2
15	DRAP		Moscow MD (till 7/43), German source	
16	DRAP	(<RAP)	16 VA 2/44	Pe-2, A-20C, Yak-9R
32	DRAP		15 VA 12/42	Pe-2
			>99 GDRAP 6/16/43	
40	DRAP	(<SBAP)	ADD 1/42	Pe-2, Pe-3*bis*, A-20B, B-25
			16 VA 11/42	
			>48 GDRAP 2/8/43	
72	DRAP	(<RAP)	6 VA 4/44	
			Stavka 11/44	
260	DRAP		Moscow MD (till 7/43), German source	
366	DRAP		4 VA 3/43	SB, Pe-2, A-20B
			>164 GDRAP	
742	DRAP	(<RAP)	18 VA 3/45	
859	DRAP	(<RAP)	Moscow MD 7/44-9/44	Pe-2, Tu-2
			Stavka 10/44	
			2 VA 11/44	
			4 VA 12/44	
859	AP- DR Pogody		4 VA 1/45	
			Stavka 3/45	

Reconnaissance Regiments (RAP)

40	GRAP		5 VA (till 2/44), German source	
193	GRAP	(<50)	2 VA 9/44	Pe-2, Il-2m
5	RAP		2 VA (till 10/43), German source	
6	RAP		9 VA 9/42	
7	RAP		10 VA 9/42	
10	RAP		1 VA 7/42	R-5, Pe-2, Il-2m
			> 10 DRAP	
12	RAP		12 VA 9/42	
13	RAP	(<BAP)	Volga MD 5/42	Pe-2, Pe-3, Yak-9D

THE PETLYAKOV Pe-2

16	RAP	(<325 AE)	13 VA 12/42 16 VA 12/42 >16 DRAP 2/44	Pe-2
20	RAP		1 VA (till 1/44), German sources	
39	RAP	(<BAP)	17 VA 5/43	Pe-2, A-20
50	RAP		2 VA 12/42 >193 GRAP	Pe-2, Il-2m
62	RAP		5 VA (till 5/44), German source	
72	RAP	(<BAP)	6 VA 12/42-12/43 Moscow MD 1/44-3/44 >72 DRAP	Pe-2
88	RAP		NW Front (till 5/42), German source	
90	RAP		Orel MD 3/44-7/44 1 VA 11/44	Pe-2
93	RAP		6 VA 3/44	
149	RAP		Trans Caucasus MD 4/42	
168	RAP		Far East F 6/41	
215	RAP		Stavka 11/41	
395	RAP		16 VA (till 7/43), German source	
511	RAP	(<BAP)	Volga MD 4/43-6/43 Stavka 7/43 5 VA 8/43	U-2, Li-2, Pe-2
526	RAP		1 VA. (till 6/43), German Source	
536	RAP		4 VA 4/44	
742	RAP		5 VA 7/42 4 VA 5/43 Stavka 7/43 13 VA 3/44 14 VA 5/44 >742 DRAP	Pe-2
799	RAP		Far East F 9/42	
859	RAP		Moscow MD 1/44-6/44 >859 DRAP 7/44	Pe-2

Naval Aviation units

1	MTAD	ChF 7/43 >2 GMTAD 5/5/44	5 G, 36 MTAP, 119 RAP, 11GIAP
2	MTAD	TOF	4, 49, 52 MTAP
5	MTAD	SF 8/43 >1 GMTAD	24, 35 MTAP, 29 BAP, 255 IAP

Pe-2 UNITS

8	MTAD	KBF 7/43	
		1 G, 51 MTAP,	
		12 GBAP, 21 IAP	
10	PBAD	TOF	
		34, 55	PBAP, 19 IAP
13	BAD	ChF 4/44	
		29, 40	BAP, ô3 IAP
12	GPBAP (<73)	8 MTAD-KBF 6/43	Pe-2
13	GBAP (<119MRAP)	2 MTAD-ChF 2/44	Il-4, A-20C, A-20G
12	BAP	KBF	SB
17	BAP	15 SAD-TOF	
28	BAP	SF 7/42	Pe-2
29	BAP	SF 7/42	Pe-2
		5 MTAD-SF 8/43	
		13 PBAD-ChF (1944)	
33	PBAP	TOF	
34	BBAP	10 PBAD-TOF	SB
		>34 GBAP 8/26/45	
40	BAP	63 BABde-ChF 6/41	SB, Pe-2
		1 MTAD 7/43	
		13 BAD (10/44)	
55	BAP	10 PBAD-TOF	
73	BAP	10 SABde-KBF 6/41	SB, AR-2, R-10, Pe-2
		8 BABde-KBF 10/41	
		>12 GPBAP 5/31/43	
94	BAP	SF	SB, Pe-2
221	BAP	SF 7/42	
15	RAP (14, 43, 44 esk.)	KBF 6/41	
		MBR-2, Yak-7U,	
		Yak–1M/-7/-9,	P-47D, Pe-2, A-20B, B-25, B-25G
30	RAP	ChF 10/42	LaGG-3, P-40K, Yak-1,-9
			Il-4, Pe-2, A-20B, A-20G

Polish Air Force

1	SAK	Kharkov MD 11/44
		1 BAD, 2 ShAD, 3 IAD
3	SAK	Volga MD 2/45
1	BAD	1 SAK 12/44
		3, 4, 5 BAP
2	ShAD	1 SAK 11/44
		6, 7, 8 ShAP

THE PETLYAKOV Pe-2

3	IAD	1 SAK 11/44	
		9, 10, 11 IAP	
1(4)	SAD	1 Pole Army 1/45	
		1 IAP, 2 NBAP, 3 ShAP	
3	BAP	1 BAD 12/44	Pe-2
4	BAP	1 BAD 12/44	Pe-2
5	BAP	1 BAD 12/44	Pe-2

(Received 110 Pe-2 & 5 UPe-2)

Appendix 2

Pe-2 Unit Commanders

1	BAK	Lt Gen.	Vladimir Aleksandrovich Sudets 10/42-3/43
		Maj. Gen.	Ivan Semenovich Pol'bin 3/43-
	2 GBAK	Maj. Gen.	Ivan Semenovich Pol'bin 2/44-2/45
	6 GBAK	Maj. Gen.	Ivan Semenovich Pol'bin 12/44-2/45
		Maj. Gen.	F.I. Kachev 2/45-3/45
		Col	D.T. Nikishin 3/45-EOW
2	BAK	Maj. Gen.	Ivan Lukich Turkel' 10/42-6/43
		Maj. Gen.	V.A. Ushakov 7/43-4/45
	1 GBAK	Lt Gen.	V.A. Ushakov 9/43-4/45
	5 GBAK	Lt Gen.	V.A. Ushakov 12/44-4/45
3	BAK	Maj. Gen.	A.Z. Karavatski 9/42-EOW
4	BAK	Maj. Gen.	P.P. Arkhangel'ski 1/44-EOW
5	BAK	Maj. Gen.	M.Kh. Borisenko 9/44-EOW
6	BAK	Maj. Gen.	I.P. Skok 4/45-EOW
7	BAK	Lt Gen.	V.A. Ushakov 4/45-EOW
34	BAD	Col	K.A. Mikhailov (8/45)
132	BAD	Col	A.Z. Karavatski (5/42)-
		Maj. Gen.	I.F. Fedorov 1/43-EOW
179	BAD	Maj. Gen.	A.M. Duboshin (8/43)
183	BAD	Col	M.A. Sitkin 6/44-EOW
188	BAD	Col	Anatolii Ivanovich Pushkin 2/44-EOW
202	BAD	Col	S.I. Nechiporenko (12/42-4/44)
		Col	V.I. Aleksandrovich -EOW
204	BAD	Lt Col	S.P. Andrev (3/43)-
3	GBAD	Lt Col	S.P. Andrev 9/43-
208	NBAD	Col	L.N. Yuzev (11/42)-EOW
211	BBAD	Col	P.P. Arkhangel'ski 7/42-
219	BAD	Col	I.T. Batygin 5/42-
		Col	P.N. Anisimov -EOW
221	BAD	Col	Ivan Diomidovich Antoshkin 6/42-3/43
		Col	S.F. Buzylev 3/43-EOW
223	BAD	Col	I.K. Kosenko (6/42)
4	GBAD	Maj. Gen.	Feodosii Porfir'evich Kotlyar 5/43-EOW
241	BAD	Col	I.G. Kurilenko (2/43)-
		Col	Aleksei Grigor'evich Fyodorov 10/43-EOW

THE PETLYAKOV Pe-2

244	BAD	Maj. Gen.	V.I. Klevtsov (6/43)-
			M.Z. Melamed (1943)
		Col	Kripinkov (-8/44)
		Col	P.V. Nedosekin (8/44)
260	BAD	Col	I.D. Yudonin 11/42-3/43
263	BAD	Col	Fyodor Ivanovich Dobysh (1/43)
1	GBAD	Col	Fyodor Ivanovich Dobysh (3/43-6/44)
270	BAD	Col	S.A. Egorov 6/42-2/43
		Col	Grigorii Aleksevich Chuchev 2/43-
6	GBAD	Col	Grigorii Aleksevich Chuchev 10/43-EOW
276	BAD	Maj. Gen.	A.P. Andrev 12/42-(9/44)
280	BAD	Col	N.N. Buyanskii (1/43)
285	BAD	Col	Vladimir Aleksandrovich Sandalov (9/42-9/43)
	5 GBAD	Maj. Gen.	Vladimir Aleksandrovich Sandalov
293	BAD	Col	Gurii Vasil'evich Gribakin (7/43)-
8	GBAD	Col	Gurii Vasil'evich Gribakin 2/44-EOW
301	BAD	Lt Col	F.M. Fedorenko (2/43)-EOW
2	BAP	Maj.	G.M. Markov (5/43)
	119 GBAP	Col	G.M. Markov
		Maj.	Zaitsev (9/44)
		Lt Col.	Borisov (9/44-)
3	BAP	Maj.	Chavilo (5/42)
4	BAP	Lt Col	Zhmatachenko (9/44)
5	SBAP	Maj.	Nikolai Gavrilovich Serebryakov 1939-40
		Col	Feodosii Porfir'evich Kotlyar SOW-
8	GBAP	Col	Feodosii Porfir'evich Kotlyar 3/42-
		Lt Col	G.I. Popov (6/44)-
6	BAP	Maj.	V. I. Lukin (6/42)-
		Maj.	Kacheleii (9/44)
9	SBAP	Maj.	V. Lukin SOW-11/41
		Maj.	A. G. Fyodorov 11/41-9/44
10	BAP	Lt Col	Grigorii A. Nikolaev (5/43)
124	GBAP	Lt Col	Grigorii A. Nikolaev -9/44
12	BAP	Maj.	P.Kh. Kozyrev (11/42)-9/43
		Lt Col	M.P. Vasyanin 9/43-9/44
13	BAP	Capt.	Vasili Pavlovich Bogomolov 7/41-4/42
18	BAP	Col	Kotnov (9/44)
24	BAP	Col	G.I. Belitskii SOW-
			P.I. Mel'nikov
		Maj.	Ivan Nikolaevich Gorbko -5/42
		Lt Col	Arsenii Ivanovich Sokolov 5/42-EOW
30	BAP	Lt Col	M.A. Sitkin (9/42)
31	PBAP	Lt Col	F.I. Dobysh (10/41)-
	4 GBAP	Lt Col	F.I. Dobysh 12/41-
		Maj.	Morozov (9/44)

Pe-2 UNIT COMMANDERS

32	BAP	Maj.	Bugaii (9/44)
33	BAP	Col	F.S. Pushkaryov SOW-
10	GBAP	Col	F.S. Pushkaryov 3/42-
		Lt Col	Burbilo (9/44)
		Col	Dergunov (1944)
34	BAP	Lt Col	P.A. Parfenyuk (2/44)-
		Lt Col	V.A. Novikov (2/45)-
35	BAP	Maj.	Vetokhin (9/44)
37	BAP	Lt Col	K.F. Katarzhin (4/42)-7/42
	>AP-DD		
38	SBAP	Capt.	Artamonov 1939
		Maj.	Osipenko (9/44)
39	BAP	Col	Aleksei Fyodorovich Fyodorov (2/43)-10/43
43	BAP		
13	GBAP	Maj.	I.G. Chuk 3/42-
44	BAP	Lt Col	V.I. Kochevanov (11/41)-
34	GBAP	Lt Col	M.N. Kolokol'stev 11/42-(6/44)
46	BAP		
80	GBAP	Lt Col	N.A. Rybalchenko (9/43)
		Lt Col	Starikov (9/44)
		Lt Col	Nikolai Sergevich Zaitsev -EOW
48	BAP	Lt Col	V.P. Kolii (8/44)-EOW
50	SBAP	Maj.	Vladimir Vasil'evich Smirnov 1940
52	BBAP	Col	T.P. Kosenko SOW-
		Maj.	Anatolii Ivanovich Pushkin 10/41-8/42
		Maj.	Fyodorov (8/43)
54	BAP	Maj.	Skibo 2/42-
		Lt Col	Mikhail Antonovich Krivtsov -1/44
55	BAP	Lt Col	A.F. Artemov (3/43)
		Col	Morozov (10/43)
58	BAP	Maj.	N.G. Serebryakov
		Maj.	I.S. Aniskin (3/43-9/44)
63	BAP	Maj.	Trotskii (9/44)
68	BAP	Maj.	Koniaev (6/43)
80	BAP	Maj.	S. I. Starichevskii (11/42)-
		Lt Col	G.P. Starikov (7/44)-
86	BAP	Col	F. Belyii (8/42)-
134	GBAP	Maj.	Viktor Mikhailovich Katkov (3/44)
94	BAP	Col	Nikolaev (1941)
95	BAP	Col	S. A. Pestov 6/41-10/41
99	BAP		
96	GBAP	Col	A.Yu. Yakobson 6/43-
108	BAP	Maj.	Zakhanenko (1/43)
121	BAP		Ivan Ivanovich Konets SOW-

THE PETLYAKOV Pe-2

125	SBAP		Doyar SOW-
		Maj.	Vladimir Aleksandrovich Sandalov (11/41)
128	BAP	Capt.	N.I. Laukhin (3/42)
		Lt Col	Mikhail Mikhailovich Voronkov (10/43)-EOW
130	SBAP	Maj.	I.I. Krivoshapka -6/22/41
		Capt.	Ivan Petrovich Kolomichesko 6/23/41-
122	GBAP	Col	S.N. Gavrilov
		Capt.	Andrev (9/44)
132	BAP	Lt Col	A. Khlebnikov (9/42)-
		Lt Col	Bugaii (6/44)
134	BAP		
127	GBAP	Col	Kolachenkov (9/44)
		Lt Col	Dubinkin (9/44)-
135	BBAP	Col	G.M. Korzinnikov SOW-
			Boris Vladimirovich Yansen
137	SBAP	Col	I.D. Udonin SOW-10/41
		Maj.	V.V. Kotov (11/42)-
		Maj.	Ivanov (8/44)
114	GBAP	Maj.	A.N. Volodin (10/44)
138	BAP	Maj.	Mikhail Antonovich Krivtsov 7/42-
140	BAP	Lt Col	I.N. Aniskin
		Lt Col	G.T. Grechukhin (1/44-9/44)
150	SBAP	Maj.	Ivan Semenovich Polbin SOW-10/42
35	GBAP	Maj.	V.A, Novikov 11/42-
		Lt Col	P.S. Svenskii
202	BAP		
81	GBAP	Lt Col	V.Ya. Gavrilov (8/43)
203	BAP	Maj.	Starost'enko (10/42)
205	BAP	Lt Col	N.Ya. Gorelov (3/43)
128	GBAP	Col	Dubinkin (9/44)
224	BAP		
126	GBAP	Lt Col	Mikhail Andrevich Zhivolup (9/43)
225	BAP	Lt Col	V.A. Belov (10/41)-
244	BAP	Maj.	Kisdov (4/44)
260	BAP	*Lt Col*	*Sabelin (9/44)*
261	BAP		
123	GBAP	Maj.	V.I. Dymchenko 9/43-
275	BAP	Maj.	Voronkov (2/42)
277	BAP	Capt.	Filatov 9/41-
		Maj.	Kornev
		Maj.	Shcherbatykh (9/44)
284	BAP	Maj.	Dmitri Danilovich Valentik 1/42-
135	GBAP	Lt Col	Dmitri Danilovich Valentik 10/43-(4/44+)
		Lt Col	Terent'ev (9/44)
		Maj.	Fyodor Prokof'evich Palin -EOW

Pe-2 UNIT COMMANDERS

288	BAP		I. Gorokhov (1942)
		Maj.	Bautin (8/43)
309	BAP	Lt Col	Minov (5/43)
319	BAP	Lt Col	N.G. Sutyagin -EOW
321	BAP	Maj.	S.P. Tyurikov (10/41)-3/43
82	GBAP	Maj.	S.P. Tyurikov 3/43- (1/44)
		Maj.	Yaniskin (4/44)
		Maj.	Anatolii Vasil'evich Golitsin -EOW
367	BAP	Maj.	B.N. Slivko -EOW
373	BAP	Maj.	Zilverstov (9/43)
		Maj.	M.D. Postnov -EOW
385	BAP	Maj.	Ivanov (1/44)
406	NBAP	Lt Col	Boris Zakharovich Zumbulidze (4/44)-EOW
410	BAP	Col	A.I. Kabanov 7/41-10/41
444	BAP	Maj.	Shirov (3/43)
449	BAP	Maj.	Malog (9/44)
452	BAP	Maj.	G.S. Kucherkov (5/44)
		Lt Col	A.A. Panichkin (11/44)
453	BAP	Lt Col	Ya.P. Prokof'ev
454	BAP	Lt Col	Khlebnikov (9/44)
		Maj.	N. E. Ostreiko -EOW
459	BAP	Capt.	Dvoriankin (5/43)
507	BAP	Maj.	Pinaev (5/43)
511	BBAP	Maj.	A.A. Babanov 9/41-5/42
514	BAP		
36	GBAP	Maj.	P.S. Lozenko 11/42-
		Maj.	Mozgovoii (9/44)
527	BAP	Maj.	Dedov (57/43)
540	BAP	Lt Col	S.I. Prikhod'ko -EOW
587	BAP	Maj.	Marina Mikhailovna Raskova -1/43
		Lt Col	Valentin Vasil'evich Markov 2/43-
125	GBAP	Lt Col	Valentin Vasil'evich Markov -EOW
588	NBAP	Maj.	Evdokia Davydovna Bershanskaya 12/41-
46	GNBAP	Maj.	Evdokia Davydovna Bershanskaya 2/43-EOW
593	NBAP	Lt Col	M.A. Lisov (10/41)
596	NBAP		
60	GNBAP	Maj.	A.A. Ovodov 2/43-
597	NBAP	Maj.	Pinegin (9/44)
603	BAP	Capt.	Emel'yanov (5/42)
608	BAP	Maj.	V. V. Kotov (9/42)-11/42
640	NBAP	Maj.	Poleshchuk (9/44)
645	BAP	Maj.	Krasnoshchakov (2/44)
650	BAP	Col	Kuzenko (3/44)
		Lt Col	A.A. Vdovin -EOW
713	BAP	Capt.	Daikov (9/44)

THE PETLYAKOV Pe-2

717	NBAP	Lt Col	V.E. Kalinin (3/45)
745	BAP	Maj.	Frolov (9/44)
		Lt Col	G.I. Popov (1/45)-
778	BAP	Col	Bortsov (8/43)
779	BAP	Lt Col	A.V. Khramchenkov (12/43-1/45)
780	BAP	Lt Col	F.D. Lushaev -2/44
160	GBAP	Lt Col	F.D. Lushaev 2/44-
793	BAP	Maj.	Kalashnikov (7/42)
797	BAP	Lt Col	Bondranaskii (9/44)
803	BAP	Maj.	Kalmin (5/43)
804	BAP	Maj.	A.. Semenov (8/43)-2/44
161	GBAP	Maj.	A.M. Semenov 2/44-
854	BAP	Lt Col	Aleksandr Aleksevich Novikov (8/43)-2/44
162	GBAP	Lt Col	Aleksandr Aleksevich Novikov 2/44-(8/44)
970	NBAP	Lt Col	N.F. Pushkarev (2/43)
2	DRAP		
47	GDRAP	Lt Col	T.R. Tyurin 2/43-
4	DRAP		
98	GDRAP	Lt Col	B.P. Artem'ev 6/43-
8	DRAP	Maj.	M. M. Podgornov 6/42-
		Col	Kishkin (9/44)
10	DRAP	Col	Rodin (9/44)
11	DRAP	Maj.	G. A. Mart'yanov (6/44)
12	RAP	Lt Col	Tol'machev (8/43)
13	RAP	Lt Col	Vasili Pavlovich Bogomolov 5/42-11/42
		Maj.	V.I. Duzhii (1/44)
		Lt Col	I.A. Mekhanikov (4/44)
16	RAP	Col	D.S. Shestyuk 12/42-
20	RAP	Maj.	Novikov (8/43)
32	RAP		
99	GRAP	Maj.	N.P. Shchenikov 6/43-
39	RAP	Lt Col	Stepanov (9/44)
40	DRAP		
48	GDRAP	Lt Col	P.M. Sadov 2/43-
		Lt Col	Lozenko (5/44)
50	RAP		
193	GRAP	Col	G.G. Bystrov
		Col	Mironov (9/44)
62	RAP	Lt Col	Strukovets (5/44)
72	RAP	Lt Col	Ivan Dmitrievich Zavrazhnov -8/43
		Lt Col	A.Ya. Gavril'chenko 12/43-(1/45)
366	RAP	Maj.	A.P. Bardev (9/42)
164	GRAP	Maj.	A.P. Bardev
511	RAP	Maj.	A.A. Babenov 5/42-

Pe-2 UNIT COMMANDERS

526	RAP	Maj.	Domoshetsii(6/43)
742	RAP	Maj.	N.E. Sergienko 6/42-
859	DRAP	Maj.	Orlov (9/44)
1	Polish BAD	Col	Martynov -EOW
29	PBAP-ChF	Lt Col	Zhiromyatnikov (9/44)
34	PBAP-TOF	Capt.	Nikolai Ignat'evich Druzdev -EOW
40	BAP-ChF	Col	A.G. Mokhirev 6/41-7/41
		Maj.	V. F. Zlugarev 7/41-
		Lt Col	I.E. Korzunov
55	BAP-TOF	Maj.	Fyodor Nikiforovich Radus -EOW
73	BAP-KBF	Col	Anatolii Il'ich Krokhalev SOW-11/42
		Lt Col	M.A. Kurochkin 11/42-12/42
		Col	Vasili Ivanovich Rakov 12/42-1/44
12	GBAP	Lt Col	M.A. Kurochkin 1/44-7/44
		Lt Col	Vasili Ivanovich Rakov 7/44-1/45
		Maj.	Konstantin Stepanovich Usenko 1/45-EOW
15	RAP-KBF	Lt Col	Filipp Aleksandrovich Usachev (9/44)-EOW
30	MRAP-ChF	Lt Col	Kh.A. Rozhdestvenskii (4/44)
50	DRAP-TOF	Maj.	Ivan Vasil'evich Sidin -EOW
95	RAP	Maj.	A.V. Zhatkov 3/42-5/44
		Maj.	A.I. Ol'bek 5/44-EOW
115	MRAP-TOF	Maj.	I.G. Nekhaev -EOW
116	MRAP-ChF	Col	Vasili Ivanovich Rakov 1/41-4/42
		Maj.	I. G. Nekhaev 4/42-
118	MRAP-SF		V.N. Vasil'ev SOW-
119	MRAP-ChF	Lt Col	N.G. Pavlov (5/43)
13	GMRAP	Lt Col	Nikolai Aleksevich Musatov 1/44-EOW

Appendix 3

Pe-2 Pilot Biographies

Abramov, Pyotr Petrovich, born 26 December 1915 in Poltavchenskoe, Krasnodar Region, in a peasant family. In 1933 completed communications FZU at Rostov-on-Don. In 1937 completed Bataisk Civil Aviation School and flew for GVF. Entered Army in 1941. CPSU 1942. Went to the front in July 1941. Gds Captain in 81 GBAP; during war flew 300 missions. HSU 23 February 1948. Retired as Major in August 1946.

Aksyonov, Konstantin Filippovich, born 18 August 1918, at Proletarskaya Stanitsa, Rostov Region, in worker family. CPSU 1945. Middle school. Aeroclub. Lathe operator in factory. Army in 1940. Omsk flight school 1941. To front in October 1942. Sr Lt Dep. Sqdn Cdr 82 GBAP. To March 1945, 130 sorties, Wounded by flak 26 March 1945 over Upper Silesia. HSU 27 June 1945. Reserves in 1946.

Aleksev, Grigorii Fedotovich, born 22 January 1918, in Istoshino, Tyumen Region, in a peasant family. Joined the army in 1939; in 1940 completed Radio/Air-gunner School. CPSU after war. At front from June 1941. During war Starshina radio-air gunner with 128 BAP. 217 missions, Shot down 7 aircraft & destroyed 15 on ground. HSU on 15 May 46. After war left military.

Andryushin, Yakov Ivanovich, born 17 April 1906 in Stavpropol' in a working class family. Completed his education in a workers' faculty in Krasnodar. Army in 1931. Lugansk flight school 1933. CPSU in 1942. Winter War. At front from start of war. By March 1943, Capt. & Sqdn Cdr. of 128 BAP. 149 sorties. HSU 24 August 43. Major, retired in 1946.

Anpilov, Vasilii Dmitirevich, born 29 March 1915 in Kineshma, Ivanovo Region, in a peasant family. Completed 9th grade and 2 courses at a hydrology *technikum*. Worked as an economic planner. Army 1935. Voroshilovgrad flight school 1937. Occupation of eastern Poland and Finnish War. CPSU 1941. At front from June 1941. By December 1941 was Lt & Sqdn Cdr. In 225 BBAP (3 RAG). 124 sorties. HSU 17 December 1941. Ended war as Lt Col. KIA 26 November 1945.

Anpilov, Anatolii Andrevich, born November 7, 1914 in Staryii Oskol, Belgorod Region, in a working-class family. He completed a year of a *technikum*, and in

Pe-2 PILOT BIOGRAPHIES

1933 was called to the army. In 1936 he completed flight school at Stalingrad. Occupation of eastern Poland and Winter War. At front from start of war. CPSU in 1943. By February 1944 was Captain & Sqdn Cdr of 779 BAP. 185 sorties. HSU 1 July 44. Air Force Academy in 1948. Maj. Gen. retired in 1971.

Antipov, Mikhail Nikolaevich, born in 1923 in Lipetsk in a working-class family. Middle school education. Army in 1940. Khar'kov flight school in 1941. At front from October 1942. CPSU 1943. By end of war Sr Lt & dep. Sqdn Cdr of 707 ShAP. 329 sorties. HSU 818 August 1945. Remained in service after the war but died on 1 June 1947.

Argunov, Nikolaii Filipovich, born 14 April 1919 in Kochenovo, in a peasant family. Middle school education. Army in 1939. Chelyabinsk Military Aviation Academy for Pilots and Observers in 1940. CPSU in 1941. At front from start of war. October 1944 Sr Lt & squadron navigator. 35 GBAP. 172 missions. Shot down over Klaipeda by flak on 11 October 1944. HSU posthumously on 23 February 1945.

Arkhangel'ski, Nikolai Vasil'evich, born 10 April 1921 in Osevo, Kurgan Region, in a working-class family. Middle school education. Lathe operator & studied at Shadrin Aeroclub. Army in 1940. Completed Chkalov military flight school. June 1942 to front. CPSU in 1943. June 1944 Lt & Sqdn Cdr in 57 BAP (221 BAD). 210 sorties. 1 kill. HSU 26 October 1944. 14 January 1945 KIA. Aircraft damaged and he crashed it into supply dump.

Armashev, Grigorii Ivanovich, born 28 January 1914 in Saint Petersburg, in a working-class family. Completed middle school and worked in factory. Army in 1932. After completing 2 courses at the Leningrad Artillery School, transferred to aviation. Orenburg Navigators' School in 1936. Winter War. CPSU 1940. In action from June 1941. By June 1943 was Major & Regtl navigator of 261 BAP. 85 missions. Regt destroyed more than 200 tanks, 44 artillery pieces and 300 motor vehicles. HSU 24 August 43. Lt Col retired in 1946.

Azarov, Pyotr Luk'yanovich, born 14 August 1922 in Zinovino, Smolensk Region. Peasant. Lived in Moscow from 1930. Middle school and FZU. Worked as factory mechanic. Completed Aeroclub. Army 1940. Engels 1942. Front in November 1942. Lt 134 GBAP (6 GBAD). To March 1945 158 missions (133 recce). HSU 19 April 1945. CPSU 1945. Reserves 1949.

Babushkin, Aleksandr Vasil'evich, born 20 December 1920 in Krasino-Uberezhnoe, Tula Region, in a peasant family. Completed middle school and joined the army in 1939. In 1939 he completed the Melitopol Military Aviation School. He was in combat from June 1941. CPSU 1943. By March 1, 1945, he was a captain and a squadron navigator of 10 RAP. He flew 163 reconnaissance missions, about a third of them aerial photography. He was awarded the HSU on April 19, 1945. Shortly after, he joined the CPSU. Air Force Academy in 1950. Colonel retired 1977.

Bakhvalov, Georgii Pavlovich, born 10 January 1914 in St Petersburg in a working-class family. Completed a geology *technikum* and worked as a geologist. Army in 1937. Orenburg Aviation Academy as an aerial observer in 1938. At front from June1941. By June 1943 Capt. & senior observer with 11 ORAP on Kalinin Front. 169 sorties. HSU 4 February 1944. CPSU 1944. Lt Col retired 1960.

Balabanov, Anatolii Ivanovich, born 1 January 1912 in St Petersburg in a working-class family. Completed middle school and an FZU. Army in 1935. Kacha flight school in 1936, Flight Commanders' course in 1941. CPSU in 1943. At front from June 1941. April 1945 Major & Sqdn Cdr of 135 GBAP. 322 sorties, 147 of them long distance and high-altitude reconnaissance. HSU 29 June 45. Lt Col retired 1954.

Balashov, Vasilii Dmitrievich, born 10 February 1921 in Dor, Kalinin Region, in a working-class family. Completed middle school and worked as a metal worker. Army in 1938. Voroshilovgrad Flight School in 1940. Went to the front in 1941. By May 1943 was Capt. & Sqdn Cdr in 8 ORAP. 210 sorties, 45 during battle for Stalingrad. HSU 24 August 1943. After war worked in DOSAAF. CPSU 1955. Col retired 1967.

Bardev, Aleksandr Petrovich, born 4 April 1910 in Ekaterinoslav in a working-class family. After completing middle school studied at Dnepropetrovsk Communist University. ÜPSU 1930, Army in 1932. Flight school in 1934. Russo-Finnish war. At front from October 1941. By Oct. 1942 Major & Sqdn Cdr in 366 BBAP. (219 BAD) 105 sorties. HSU 13 December 1942. Lt Col retired 1958.

Barskii, Andrei Ivanovich, born 12 October 1912 in Varvarino, Tula Region, in a peasant family. Completed middle school and studied at the Moscow Institute of Collective Farming. Navy in 1935. Eisk Naval Aviation Academy in 1937. Russo-Finnish war. Went to the front in October 1943. By May 1945 Gds Capt. & Sqdn Cdr in 12 G PBAP-KBF. 101 sorties. Destroyed 2 transports individually and shared in 15. HSU 15 May 1946. Lt Col retired in 1956.

Belikov, Pyotr Vasil'evich, born 22 February 1916 in Orekhovo, Voroshilovgrad Region, in a Ukrainian peasant family. He finished primary school and a Rabfak. Army in 1938. Yelitopol' Aviation Academy in 1940. Bombardier-gunner. At front from June 1941. By January 1942 was Sr Lt in 240 ORAE (Northwest Front) 119 sorties. HSU on 21 July 1942. Major retired in 1946.

Bobrov, Leonid Nikolaevich, born 20 January 1920 in Raiskoe, Donetsk Region, in a Ukrainian peasant family. Finished middle school and an FZU. Army in 1939.

Pe-2 PILOT BIOGRAPHIES

Voroshilovgrad flight school in 1940. At front from June 1941. CPSU 1944. By March 1945 was Gds Major & Sqdn Cdr of 134 GBAP. 172 sorties. HSU 19 April 1945. Lt Col to reserves in 1973.

Bobrov, Nikolaii Aleksandrovich, born in 1921 in Penza in a white-collar family. He completed middle school in Moscow and entered university. Army 1939 and completed flight school for aviation specialists. Candidate member for CPSU. At front from June 1941. Sr Sgt Radio-air gunner with 44 SBAP on Leningrad Front. By June 1942 67 sorties and 12 air battles. Killed on 12 July 1942 when pilot crashed burning aircraft into enemy artillery battery. HSU posthumously on 10 February 1943.

Bochin, Pyotr Antonovich, born 12 May 1920 in Kresty, Kalinin Region, in a Karelian peasant family. Completed the 7th grade and a construction *technikum*. Worked as a planer while studying at an Aeroclub. Army in 1939. Completed flight school at Voroshilovgrad. Was with an active unit in June 1941. CPSU in 1942. By Sept 1943 Lt in 10 GBAP. 365 sorties. HSU 1 November 1943. Flew against Japan in August 1945. Lt Col retired 1963.

Bogutskii, Viktor Stepanovich, born 18 February 1923 in Vysokogorodetsk, Krasnoyarsk Region, in a peasant family. Secondary education. Army in 1941. Omsk flight school 1942. To front in 1943. CPSU 1944. Sr Lt 99 GORAP, completed 120 sorties. KIA 28 February 1945. HSU 18 August 1945.

Boiko, Grigorii Evdokimovich, born in 1918 in Ozeryanovka, Donets Region, in a Ukrainian peasant family. Beginning secondary education. Army in 1938. Voroshilovgrad flight school 1940. In action from June 1941. Candidate member CPSU. Senior Lieutenant in 514 PBAP (NW Front) 158 sorties. KIA 7 June 1942. HSU 21 July 1942.

Borisov, Vasilii Dmitrievich, born 1 September 1918 in Ivanovka, Penza Region, in a peasant family. Completed the 7th grade and 2 courses at a Rabfak. Worked as a factory despatcher. Army in 1939. Taganrog flight school 1940. At front from 1941. By Sept. 1944 Captain in 8 ORAP. 198 sorties. Twice shot down in flames. HSU 23 February 1945. CPSU 1945. Colonel retired 1960.

Boronin, Ivan Konstantinovich, 25 September 1909 in Titovskii Farmstead Tsaritsyn Region, in a peasant family. Completed the 5th grade and worked as a tractor driver on a state farm. Army in 1931. Khar'kov flight school 1935. CPSU 1938. Finnish War. To front in October 1941. By Sept 1942 Major & Sqdn Cdr in 366 BAP. 156 sorties. HSU 13 December 1942. Killed 12 March 1944.

Brazhnikov, Ivan Moisevich, born 14 November 1915 in Orenburg in a working-class family. Completed the 8th grade and became an actor in the local theatre.

Army in 1937. School for junior aviation specialists in 1941. At start of war sergeant & senior radio operator/air gunner in 132 SBAP (45 SAD). During bombing mission in June his bomber was shot up by enemy fighters, Brazhnikov shot down 1 enemy. After completing bombing mission, crew baled out of burning bomber and returned to base on foot. HSU 27 March 1942. CPSU 1942. Major retired 1946.

Buchavyii, Valentin Romanovich, born 20 July 1919 in Levaya Rossol', Voronezh Region, in a peasant family. Completed school at an FZU, and then worked as a metalworker in a factory. Army 1939. Voroshilovgrad Flight School 1940. At the front from start of war. By end of war was Sr Lt & deputy Sqdn Cdr in 34 BAP. 222 sorties. HSU 15 May 1946. Was Komosmol member but never joined Party. Retired as Captain in 1955.

Bukhanov, Aleksei Dmitrievich, born 8 March 1923 in Astashikha, Gor'kii Region, in a peasant family. Completed the 7th grade and worked in a factory. Army 1941. Engels Flight school 1942. To active unit in February 1943. By 25 April 1945 he was a lieutenant and flight commander of 36 GBAP. 168 sorties. HSU 27 June 1945. CPSU post war. Released from service 1946.

Bulanov, Aleksandr Parfyonovich, born 7 February 1914 in Teikovo, Ivanov Region, in a peasant family. Secondary education. Army in 1937. Krasnodar Military Aerial Navigators' Academy in 1939. To front in June 1942. By May 1945 Capt. & squadron navigator in 334 BAP. 241 sorties, including 86 to the partisans, with 32 landings in the enemy rear. CPSU 1945. HSU 15 May 1946. Colonel retired 1973.

Bystrykh, Boris Stepanovich, born 28 March 1916 in Mysovaya, in the Buryat Region, in a working-class family. He completed the 8th grade and the Balashov Commercial Flight School. From 1939, he flew as a civil pilot in the Tyumen region of the Far East. Army 1940. To active unit in June 1941. By 1 September 1942 was Sr Lt in 99 BAP. Candidate CPSU member. 168 sorties. HSU 5 November 1942. Was killed on 3 June 1943 while making a forced landing in enemy-controlled territory.

Chagovets, Grigorii Ivanovich, born in 1922 in Novoaleksandrovka, Northern Caucasus Region. Completed an aviation *technikum* and an Aeroclub. Navy 1941. Eisk Naval Aviation Institute 1943. To the front in June 1943. By September 1944 was Komsomolist, Lt in 15 ORAP-KBF. 165 sorties, of which 66 were aerial photography. 13 air combats, 1 air victory. KIA during his 166th sortie 16 September 1944. HSU 5 November 1944.

Chelpanov, Vasilii Nikolaevich, born 12 March 1918 in Kholm, Novgorod Region, in a working-class family. Middle school. Army 1936. Perm flight school 1938. Finnish War. CPSU 1939. To front in June 1941. Lt & dep. Sqdn cdr

Pe-2 PILOT BIOGRAPHIES

in 24 BBAP (61 SAD). 60 sorties. 27 November 1941 Crashed his burning aircraft into enemy troop concentration. HSU 14 February 1943.

Chernykh, Ivan Sergevich, born 2 August 1918 in Petukhii, Kirov Region, in a peasant family. Completed 6th grade and an FZU in Tomsk. Worked as a metalworker in a machine-building factory. Completed an Aeroclub. Army 1938. Novosibirsk flight school 1940. To the front in June 1941. Jr Lt in 125 BAP. Komsomolist. 62 sorties. Crashed his burning aircraft into enemy troop concentration 16 December 1941. HSU 16 January 1942.

Chernysh, Pyotr Prokof'evich, born 20 April 1919 in the Krasnogorovka workers' settlement, Donets Region, in a Ukrainian working-class family. 7th grade & FZU. Worked as a milling-machine operator. Studied at an Aeroclub. Army 1938. Voroshilovgrad 1941. At the front from June 1941. CPSU 1945. By April 1945 was Sr Lt and Flight Cdr in 81 GBAP. 172 sorties. HSU 27 June 1945. Advanced Officers' course 1947. Col retired 1975.

Chesnokov, Fyodor Sergevich, born 28 April 1922 in Telyatinkii, Moscow Region, in a peasant family. Completed the 7th grade and an FZU. Worked as a lathe operator in a machine-building factory. Completed an Aeroclub. Army 1940. Kirovabad flight school 1941. To the front in April 1942. By May 1943 was Jr Lt & flight cdr in 367 BAP. 171 sorties, of which 145 were at night. 1 air victory. Destroyed 21 aircraft on the ground. HSU 24 May 1943. CPSU 1944. Completed Officers' advanced course 1947. Col retired 1967.

Chervyakov, Vladimir Ivanovich, born in 1923 on Chervyakov Farmstead, Penza Region, in a peasant family. 7th grade, Army 1940. Engels Flight School 1942. To front in May 1942. By November 1943 was Jr Lt in 48 GORAP. 102 sorties. HSU 4 February 1944. CPSU 1944. Col retired 1967.

Danilov, Aleksei Vasil'evich, born 1 June 1923 in Vyazovy Vrag, Saratov Region, in a peasant family. Completed 7th grade and 3 courses in a River *technikum* by 1940. Studied at an Aeroclub. Army July 1940. Kirovabad flight school 1941. To front in August 1942. CPSU 1943. By 9 May 1945 was Lt in 161 GBAP, 179 sorties, 82 of which were dive-bombing missions. HSU 27 June 1945. Air Force Academy 1952. Major retired 1956.

Danyushin, Nikolaii Aleksevich, born 30 October 1919 in Yartsevo, Smolensk Region, in a working-class family. He completed secondary school and an Aeroclub, and then worked as physical education instructor at his school. Army 1939. School for Junior Aviation specialist in 1940. To front in June 1941 as radio operator/air gunner. CPSU 1943. By February 1945 was Starshina in 4 GBAP. 170 sorties and 33 air combats. 3 individual and 10 shared kills. HSU 18 August 1945. Discharged to reserves in November 1945.

THE PETLYAKOV Pe-2

Davidenko, Grigorii Ivanovich, 17 April 1921 in Staryii Korvaii, in a Ukrainian peasant family. Completed secondary school and worked in his native village until entering the navy in 1939. Levandovskii Naval Aviation Academy in 1941. To the front in July 1942. ÜPSU 1943. By January 1944 was Lt and navigator in 44 AE of 15 OMRAP-KBF. 215 sorties. 13 air battles. HSU 22 January 1944. Failed to return from mission 8 May 1945.

Davidenko, Stepan Pavlovich, born 20 November 1911 in Aleksandro-Grigor'evka, Donetsk Region, in a Ukrainian working-class family. Completed 7th grade. CPSU 1928. Completed a two-year Party school in 1930. Worked in a mine. Army 1930. Course for bombardier-gunners at Orenburg 1932. Krasnodar school for aviators and air observers 1933. Fought at Lake Khasan in 1938. Was in an active unit in June 1941. By October 1943 was Captain & Sqdn navigator in 24 BAP. 180 sorties. HSU 4 February 1944. Officers Higher Navigators' school in1952. Lt Col retired 1957.

Davydov, Sergei Stepanovich, born 25 October 1907 in Kamyshin, Tsaritsyn Region, in a working-class family. Completed beginning secondary school and worked in a shoe factory. Navy 1929. CPSU 1932. Eisk naval aviation school and a navigators' course through the Levandovskii Naval Aviation Academy. Was sent to a combat unit in June 1942. By June 1944 Capt. & Sqdn navigator in 12 GPBAP. 101 sorties. Destroyed 2 transports, 2 escort ships, 2 fast landing barges, a trawler and a gunboat. Personally shot down 3 enemy aircraft. HSU 22 July 1944. Killed in the course of duties on 5 August 1945.

Davydov, Viktor Iosifovich, born 17 December 1920 in Shcheglovka, in the Donets Region, in a working-class family. Completed the Donetsk Metallurgical *Technikum* and worked as an electrician. Army 1938. Voroshilovgrad flight school 1940. Sent to front in June 1941. CPSU 1944. By the beginning of 1945 was Capt. & dep. Sqdn Cdr in 72 ORAP (16 VA). 163 sorties, of which 108 were photo-reconnaissance missions deep in the enemy rear. HSU 15 May 1946. In 1949 completed course in night and blind flying. Became Sqdn Cdr and promoted to Lt Col. Killed in flying accident 23 May 1952.

Deineko, Stepan Petrovich, born 22 December 1918 in Khoroshe, Ekaterinoslav Region, in a Ukrainian peasant family. Completed the 6th grade and an FZU. Metalworker. Army 1937. Voroshilovgrad flight school 1938. CPSU 1940. To front in December 1941. By 1 May 1943 was Captain and Deputy Sqdn Cdr in 367 BAP. 200 sorties. HSU 24 May 1943. 15 February 1914 over Kerch his bomber was hit and he crashed it into a transport.

Del'tsov, Pavel Andrevich, born 26 January 1917 in Ivanovo-voznesensk, in a working-class family. Completed a technical academy, and became an apprentice machinist. Army 1935. Voroshilovgrad flight school 1937. Finnish war 1939-40.

Pe-2 PILOT BIOGRAPHIES

In action from start of war. CPSU 1943. By October 1943 was Capt. and Sqdn Cdr in 24 BAP. 202 sorties, HSU 13 April 1944. Postwar became commander of an aviation regiment. Lt Col retired 1957.

Demchenkov, Filipp Trofimovich, born 27 October 1915 in Steikii, Smolensk Region, in a peasant family. Completed the 7th grade and worked at a Moscow electrical power station. Bataisk Civil Airfleet Flight School 1939. Flew as Civil Airfleet pilot in Southern Kazakhstan. Army 1940. At front from start of war as Jr Lt with 150 SBAP (46 SAD). By December 1941 146 sorties. HSU 4 November 1942. CPSU 1942. Air Force Academy 1949. Lt Col retired 1958.

Demidov, Vasilii Aleksandrovich, born 12 April 1921 in Vitebsk, in a Belorussian white-collar family. He completed the 10th grade and study at the Vitebsk Aeroclub. Army 1940. Omsk Flight School 1942. To front in March 1943. By 1 March 1945 was Sr Lt and flight commander in 10 ORAP (1 VA). 226 sorties. His crew fought 16 air combats. HSU 19 April 1945. CPSU 1946. Air Force Academy 1955. Col retired 1961.

Doling, Mariya Ivanovna, born December 18, 1920 in Sharovka, Omsk Region, in a Ukrainian peasant family. She finished the eighth grade. She got her wings from the Kherson Aviation School in 1939 and became a flying instructor. In 1941 she volunteered for the army. In 1942 she completed military flight school at Engels. In 1943 she joined the Communist party. By January 1945, she was a Guards Captain and a deputy squadron commander of 125 GBAP. She completed 63 sorties, dropping 45,000kg of bombs. In 6 air combats, she (and her crew) shared in the destruction of 3 enemy fighters. She was awarded the HSU on August 18, 1945. After the war, she became the deputy commander of a BAP, but was retired in 1950.

Domnikov, Vasilii Mikhailovich, born 4 November 1918 in Efimovka, Orel Region, in a peasant family. Completed 7th grade. Studied at a *technikum* and an Aeroclub. Army 1939. Krasnodar flight school 1940. At front from first days of the war. CPSU 1943. By April 1945 Capt. & squadron navigator in 34 GBAP. 215 sorties. KIA 8 April 1945. HSU 29 June 1945.

Donchuk, Vasilii Ivanovich,[1] born 10 December 1910 in Kiev in a Ukrainian working-class family, but was raised in children's home. Secondary education. Lived in Khabarovsk from 1931. CPSU 1932. Studied at an Aeroclub and then completed the Eisk Civil Airfleet Academy. Flew as an Aeroflot pilot until called to the service in 1937. He flew at Lake Khasan in 1938. Went to the front in November 1941. By October 1944 was Major and commander of 108 ORAE flying on the Karelian Front. 270 sorties. Killed on 21 October 1944. Posthumous HSU on 2 November 1944.

Druzdev, Nikolaii Ignat'evich, born 8 May 1918 in Kalinino, Georgia, in a peasant family. Completed a village school education. Studied at the Tbilisi Aeroclub.

THE PETLYAKOV Pe-2

Navy 1937. Eisk Naval Aviation Academy, and then assigned to Pacific Ocean Fleet. By August 1945 was Capt. and Regtl Cdr of 34 PBAP-TOF. Regiment flew 211 sorties and sank 2 tankers, 3 transports, and 4 wharves, 3 petrol-storage facilities, and 4 railway trains. He personally sank a tanker, destroyed a supply dump and a railway bridge. HSU 14 September 1945. After war Naval Academy. Col retired 1957.

Dunaevskii, Konstantin Dmitirevich, born 27 May 1922 in Rzhev, in a white-collar family. Completed secondary school. Studied at the Bataisk Aviation Academy and then worked in the Far East. Army 1940. Chkalov military aviation school 1941. To front in December 1943. CPSU 1945. By April 1945 was Sr Lt and flight commander in 47 GORAP. 106 sorties. 23 April 1945 MIA. HSU 18 August 1945.

Dzhunskovskaya (Markova), Galina Ivanovna,[2] born October 6, 1922 in Yurkovka, Kiev Region, in a Ukrainian peasant family. In 1938 she completed a medical academy and two courses at the Moscow Aviation Institute. In 1941 she volunteered for the army and, in 1942, completed training as a navigator. She went to the front in January 1943 with 587 BAP (later 125 GBAP), where she flew as navigator for Mariya Dolina and Klavdiya Fomichyova. During 1943 she joined the Communist party. On 23 June 1944, she was shot down by flak, but managed to bale out and returned to her regiment with minor injuries. By December 1944 she was a Guards Senior Lieutenant and a squadron senior navigator. She had flown 62 sorties. She and her crew were credited with 2 fighters shot down in 5 air combats. She was awarded the HSU on August 18, 1945. She remained in service until 1949, when she retired with the rank of Major.

Efremov, Vasilii Sergeich, born 14 January 1915 in Tsaritsyn, in a working-class family. Completed the 7th grade in 1929, and an FZU in 1932. Army 1934. Flight school 1937. Finnish war 1939-40. In action from June 1941. By February 1943 Capt. & Sqdn Cdr In 10 GBAP. 293 sorties. HSU 1 May 1943. CPSU 1943. Second HSU on 24 August 1943 for 340 sorties, Crew destroyed 32 aircraft on their airfields, and shot down 4 aircraft in air combat. Air Force Academy 19949. Served as a deputy Regtl Cdr instructor at an Aviation Academy, and a test pilot. Col retired 1960.

Eletskikh, Gavril, Nikiforovich, born 8 April 1919 in Petrovskie, Lipetsk Region, in a peasant family. Completed a pedagogical academy and worked as a teacher. Army 1939. Khar'kov Military Aviation Academy 1940. To front in June 1941. CPSU 1942. By February 1944 was Capt. and Sqdn navigator in 8 ORAP (8VA). 167 sorties. HSU 1 July 1944. Air Force Academy in1949 and then worked there as instructor. Candidate Degree in Military Science and Assistant professor. Col retired 1979.

Eroshenko, Viktor Ivanovich, born 9 March 1921 in Evpatoriya, Crimea, in a Belorussian working-class family. Commenced secondary school. Army 1937.

Pe-2 PILOT BIOGRAPHIES

Kacha flight school 1938. Flew 47 sorties during Finnish war. At front at start of war. By May 1945 Major and deputy Cdr for flight skills (*Insp-letchik po tekhnike pilotirovaniya i teorii poletov*) 35 BAP. 205 sorties, including 87 reconnaissance missions. 12 air combats. Crew shot down 3 aircraft. HSU 27 June 1945. CPSU 1946. Air Force Academy 1952. Col retired 1961, and worked in civil aviation.

Ershov, Vladimir Aleksevich, born 28 May 1923 in Moscow in a working-class family. Secondary education. Army 1940. Krasondar Unified Pilots' and Observers' Academy 1942. To front in February 1944. By February 1945 was Sr Lt in 16 ODRAP (16 VA) 104 sorties. HSU 15 May 1946. CPSU 1946. Left service 1946.

Evdokimov, Grigorii Petrovich, born 2 September 1919 in Ozhgii, in what would become the Udmenrt ASSR, in a peasant family. Completed a pedagogical academy. Army 1938. *Ühelyabinsk* Air observer Academy 1940. To front in August 1941. CPSU 1943. By April 1945 was Capt. and Sqdn navigator in 449 BAP. 270 sorties. HSU 18 August 1945. Air Force Academy 1954. Col retired 1966.

Evtushenko, Nikifor Timofevich, born 7 February 1917 in Staraya Osota, Kirovograd Region, in a Ukrainian peasant family. In 1937 completed an agricultural *technikum*. Army 1937. Melitopol Military Aviation Academy 1940. Joined CPSU. At front from July 1941. By August 1944 was Capt. and Sqdn navigator in 99 GORAP (15 VA), had completed dozens of reconnaissance flights. HSU 19 August 1944. Lt Col retired 1946. Worked for MVD in Riga until 1957.

Fadev, Aleksandr Il'ich, born 23 April 1911 in Pokrovskoe, Moscow Region, in a peasant family. Completed a construction *technikum* and an Aeroclub. Army 1934. Odessa flight school 1936. Occupation of eastern Poland 1939. Finnish War 1939-40. CPsU 1940. At front from June 1941. By March 1945 Major & Sqdn Cdr in 96 GBAP. 168 sorties. 69 group air combats. HSU 15 May 1946. Advanced course through Air Force Academy 1951. Col retired 1957.

Fak, Fyodor Kuz'mich, born 13 September 1913 in Dubovskii, Rostov Region, in a Ukrainian working-class family. Completed 7th grade and an FZU. Worked in a locomotive-building factory. Army 1935. Kharkov military aviation school 1937. To the front in 1941. Jr lt & Sqdn chief of signals in 150 BBAP (46 SAD). By January 1942, 204 sorties, 101 of them at night. HSU 5 May 1942. CPSU 1942. Officers' Higher air navigation school 1950. Lt Col retired 1959.

Fat'yanov, Andrei Efremovich, born 14 September 1906 in Novodmitrievka, Simbirsk Region, in a peasant family. Agricultural worker. Army 1928. Flight school 1931. Finnish War 1939-40. Sr lt & Deputy Sqdn Cdr 5 OSBAP (14 Army) 6 sorties. On 4 February 1940 landed his bomber behind enemy lines to rescue the crew of another bomber, which had force-landed. HSU 6 May 1940. At the front from 1941. KIA September 1942.

THE PETLYAKOV Pe-2

Fedorenko, Nikolai Vladimirovich, born 6 December 1907 in Zavodovka, Odessa Region, in a Ukrainian peasant family. Completed a village school and then worked as a gardener on a collective farm. Army 1929. Orenburg flight school 1931. CPSU 1931. Course for paratroop instructors at Voronezh in 1938. Fought at Khalkin Gol. Advanced officers' course through the air force academy in 1941 At the front from 1941. By October 1944 was Lt Col & chief navigator of 3 BAK (16 VA). 173 sorties, of which 39 as formation leader. 35 air combats. HSU 15 May 1946. Advanced course for Chief Navigators in 1952. Col retired 1955.

Fedutenko, Nadezhda Nikiforovna, born 30 September 1915 in Rakitnoe, Belgorod Region, in a peasant family. She completed the seventh grade and an FZO, while studying at an Aeroclub. In 1935, she completed the Civil Airfleet Flight School at Tambov, and then went to work as a civilian pilot. In 1940 she joined the Communist Party. In 1941 she volunteered for the army. Went to the front in June 1941, and flew an R-5 of one of the Civil Airfleet units, which had been marshalled to support the army flying cargo and liaison missions. In 1942 she completed the military flight training at Engels, together with the other women who were assembled by Marina Raskova. She was assigned to the 587 BAP (later 125 GBAP) flying the Pe-2. She flew her first bombing mission on 28 January 1943, near Stalingrad. By December 1944 she had risen to the rank of Guards Major, and had been given command of the 1st squadron. She had flown 56 sorties. She was awarded the HSU on 18 August, 1945. In 1946 she left the service.

Fil'chenkov, Sergei Yakovlevich, born 18 March 1915 in Bol'shie Vorob'i Kalinin Region, in a peasant family. Completed a village school, and worked in a bread factory. Studied at an Aeroclub. Army 1938. Gunner-bombardier school 1940. At front from 1941. CPSU 1942. By July 1944 was Jr Lt & a navigator in 128 BAP. 212 sorties. 1 individual and 4 shared air victories. HSU 16 October 1944. Released from service after the war.

Fishchuk, Vasilii Maksimovich, born 15 July 1921 in Chernorudka, Zhitomir Region, in a Ukrainian peasant family. Completed a pedagogical *technikum*. Army 1939. Kharkov Military Aviation Institute for Aviators and air Observers 1940. At front from August 1941. By May 1945 was Sr Lt and flight navigator in 160 GBAP. 165 sorties. 2 air victories. HSU 27 June 1945. CPSU 1945. Officers' Advanced Course 1956. Col retired 1960.

Fomichyova, Klavdiya Yakovlevna, born 25 December 1917 in Moscow in a white-collar family. She graduated from middle school and an Aeroclub. Then she worked as a bookkeeper at the State Bank in Moscow. Joined the army in October 1941 and completed her military flight training at Engels in 1942. She went to the front in January 1943 with 587 BAP (later 125 GBAP). Shot down by flak on 23 June 1944. When her navigator had difficulty in baling out, Fomichyova delayed

Pe-2 PILOT BIOGRAPHIES

her own escape until the last minute. She landed alive but badly injured. However, she recovered and returned to duty. By December 1944 she was a Guards Captain and commander of the 2nd squadron. She had flown 55 sorties. She and her crew were credited with 11 fighters shot down in group air combat. She was awarded the HSU on 18 August 1945. After the war, she served as a flying instructor at the Air Force Academy and the Borisoglebsk Flight Academy. She retired in 1955 with the rank of Colonel.

Franchuk, Karp Yakovlevich, born 13 October 1915 in Vishnopol', Charkas Region, in a Ukrainian family. Completed an agricultural mechanization technikum. Army 1938. Melitopol Military Aviation Institute for Air Observers 1940. At front from June 1941. CPSU 1941. By November 1944 was Captain & Sqdn navigator in 650 BAP. 301 sorties. 3 air victories. HSU 18 August 1945. Lt Col retired 1954.

Gapenok, Nikolai Ivanovich, born 17 April 1919 in Glinishche, Vitebsk Region, in a Belorussian family. 9th grade. Balashov Civil air Fleet Flight School 1939. Army 1939. Military flight school 1940. Active unit from June 1941. CPSU 1943. By March 1945 was Guards Captain & deputy Sqdn cdr in 81 GBAP. 165 sorties. HSU 27 June 1945. Air Force Academy 1951, and then worked there as instructor. Doctor of Military science. Col retired 1979.

Gataullin, Anvar, born 23 February 1923 in Perm' in a Tatar working-class family. Completed one year at Perm Aviation technikum. Army 1940. Omsk flight school 1942. To front in June 1943. By October 1944 was Sr lt in 99 GORAP. 110 sorties. On 10 October 1944 while photographing enemy positions near Dobele, Latvia, his aircraft was hit by flak and set afire. He sought to crash his aircraft into an enemy artillery position, but he survived. Before his aircraft hit ground, the fuel tank exploded, blowing him out of the cockpit. His parachute harness caught on a tree. HSU 18 August 1945. Lt Col retired 1955.

Gavrilov Pyotr Ivanovich, born 29 June 1907 in Kutluk-Zyudostov, Azerbaijan in a working-class family. After completing the 5th grade worked in the fish trade. Army 1929. CPSU 1931. Kacha flight school 1934. Flew at Khalkin Gol. At front from June 1941. By August 1943 was Major & Sqdn cdr Of 99 GORAP. 130 sorties. HSU 2 September 1943. Lt Col retired 1956.

Gavrilov, Vladimir Nikolaevich, born 18 April 1921 in Petrograd in a working-class family. Completed the 10th grade and studied at the Leningrad Institute of Water Transport. Navy 1939. School for junior flight specialists in 1940. Levanevskii Naval Academy in 1941. To front in March 1942 as Sergeant & bombardier-gunner in 24 MTAP-SF. Komosmol. On 14 January 1943 during a raid on Vardo, Norway he sank an 8,000-ton ship, but the aircraft was shot down in the process and crew lost. HSU 22 February 1943.

THE PETLYAKOV Pe-2

Gavrilov, Vladimir Yakovlevich, born 16 April 1908 in Severnii Rudnik, Donetsk Region, in a working-class family. Finished school in an FZU and worked as a lathe operator. Army 1928. CPSU 1929. Completed Military Weapons technical School in 1931. Borisoglebsk Flight School 1935. At the beginning of the war, he had just completed 2 years at the Air Force Academy, with distinguished result. At front from June 1941. Maj. & regular Cdr of 804 BAP (293 BAD) (161 GBAP from 5 February 1944). From the middle of November 1942 to February 1943 flew 17 sorties. HSU 1 May 1943. After war General Staff Academy. Commanded an aviation division and then was instructor at the Lenin Military Political Academy. Retired as Colonel.

Geleta Vasilii Arkhipovich, born 8 May 1918 in Chertoriya, Vinnitsa Region, in a Ukrainian peasant family. Studied at the Ukrainian Library Institute. Army in 1938. Melitopol Military Aviation Academy in 1940. Active unit from 22 June 1941. CPSU 1943. By May 1945 was Sr Lt & Sqdn navigator of 797 BAP. 169 sorties. HSU 27 June 1945. Air Force Academy 1950, and then worked there as instructor. Colonel retired 1973.

Globe, Mikhail Maksimovich, born 24 July 1921 in Topolyovka, Vladimir Region, in a peasant family. Worked on a collective farm until entering the army in 1940. Engels flight school 1942. To front in March 1943. CPSU 1944. By December 1944 was a Capt & dep. Sqdn car in 11 ORAP. 133 sorties and 14 air combats. HSU 18 August 1945. Air Force Academy 1954. Colonel retired 1975.

Glinski, Sergei Nikolaevich, born 25 September 1913 in Yagodno, Pskov Region, in a peasant family. Completed secondary school. Army 1932. Leningrad Military-Theoretical School for Aviators 1933. Orenburg flight school 1935. Retained as instructor. CPSU 1939. Advanced Course for Command Staffs 1942. To front in March 1943. By April 1945 Major & Sqdn Cdr in 34 GBAP. 146 sorties. HSU 29 June 1945. Left service in 1948.

Glushkov, Ivan Vasil'evich, born 29 December 1918 in Verkh-Bobrovka, Altai Region, in a peasant family. He completed two years' study at a pedagogical *technikum*. In 1936 he joined the army. Perm aviation school 1938. At front from June 1941. CPSU 1943. By May 1945 Major & Sqdn Cdr in 10 ORAP. 317 sorties, of which 31 were night-bombing missions in the R-5, and 241 were bombing missions in the Pe-2. HSU 19 April 1945. Air Force Academy 1955. Lt Col retired 1960.

Glyga, Grigorii Semyonovich, born 17 November 1913 in Aleksevo-Orlovka, Donetsk Region, in a Ukrainian peasant family. 7th grade. Worked as a bookkeeper. Army 1935. In 1938 completed an officers' course and commissioned a junior lieutenant. Kharkov Military navigation school 1939. At front from August 1941. By April 1945 Major & Regtl navigator of 81 GBAP. 136 sorties. HSU 27 June 1945. Left service 1946.

Pe-2 PILOT BIOGRAPHIES

Gnedoii, Aleksandr Aleksevich, born 22 November 1914 in Tsarytskin Kut, Zaporozh'e Region, in a Ukrainian working-class family. He completed a year at the Kiev Rural Mechanization and Electrification Technikum. Navy 1934. Flight school 1936. Finnish war 1939. CPSU 1940. At front from first days of war. By mid-October 1944 Capt. & Sqdn car of 40 BAP-ChF. 140 sorties. Sank minesweeper, submarine, 6 barges, a transport and a trawler, and destroyed a railway bridge. Also destroyed 15 aircraft on the ground. HSU 6 March 1945. Naval Academy 1951. Colonel retired 1960.

Golitsin, Anatolii Vasil'evich, born 29 June 1908 in Petrakovo, Yaroslavl' Region, in a working-class family. Completed the 7th grade and a course for production forming. CPSU 1929. Army 1930. Stalingrad flight school 1937. Finnish war 1939-40. Advanced course for squadron commanders in 1941. At front from June 1941. By Sept. 1944 was Major & Regtl Cdr of 82 GBAP. 96 sorties. His regiment flew 1,025 sorties. HSU 27 June 1945 demobilised 1946.

Golubnichii, Ivan Polikarpovich, born 9 March 1923 in Armavir, Krasnodr Region, in a working-class family. Completed beginning secondary school. Army 1940. Taganrog flight school 1942. Davlekanovsk Military Academy for Aerial Reconnaissance in 1943. To front in March 1943. CPSU 1944. By end of war Capt. & Deputy Sqdn Cdr in 47 GORAP. 108 sorties. HSU 15 May 1946. Air Force Academy 1958. Colonel retired 1966.

Goncharov, Yakov Ignat'evich, born 23 March 1914 in Kozlovka, Mogilyov Region, in a Belorussian peasant family. Completed the 7th grade and worked on a collective farm. Army 1931. Nerchinsk School for Junior Aviation Specialists in 1937. Flew at Khalkin Gol. At front from start of war. CPSU 1942. By March 1945 Sr Lt & Sqdn chief of communications 96 GBAP. 221 sorties. Shot down 1 individual and 3 shared victories. HSU 15 May 1946. Major retired 1954.

Gorbko, Yuri Nikolaevich, born 23 March 1908 in Novograd-Volynskii, Zhitomir Region, in a Ukrainian working-class family. Completed secondary school and worked as a metalworker. Army 1929. CPSU 1930. Borisoglebsk flight school 1932. During Finnish war Capt. & Sqdn Cdr in 50 SBAP (18 SBA Bde.). By January 1940 32 sorties. HSU 21 March 1940. At front again from August 1941. KIA 27 May 1942.

Gorbunov, Aleksandr Matvevich, born 21 September 1921 in Arapovka, Simbirsk Region, in a working-class family. Completed his secondary education, and worked in a factory. Army 1939. Krasnodar Air observer school 1940. To front in December 1941. CPSU 1942. By January 1943 was Lt gunner-bombardier in 367 BAP. 133 sorties. HSU 1 May 1943. Air Force Academy 1946. General Staff Academy 1959. Major General in 1966. Still in service in 1989 in MoD.

THE PETLYAKOV Pe-2

Gorkunov, Mikhail Stepanovich, born 5 September 1915 in Nadezhdino, Khar'kov Region, in a Ukrainian peasant family. He completed an FZU and worked in a factory while studying at an Aeroclub. Army 1937. Voroshilovgrad flight school 1938. CPSU 1941. At front from December 1941. By January 1943 Capt. & Sqdn car in 367 BAP 144 sorties. HSU 1 May 1943. 6 May 1943 Failed to return from mission.

Goryachkin, Timofei Stepanovich, born 4 March 1922 in Chamzinka, Mordvin ASSR, in a Mordvin peasant family. 9th grade. Army 1941. Engels flight school 1943. To front June 1943. By end of was Sr Lt & flight cdr in 99 GORAP. 101 sorties, 10 air combats, 2 individual victories. HSU 15 May 1946. CPSU 1947. Air Force Academy 1954. Colonel retired 1969.

Grechishkin, Vasilii Nikolaevich, born 13 January 1911 in Ol'ginka, Tula Region, in a peasant family. Completed primary school, and then worked as a metalworker. Army 1931. Completed Kharkov Military Aviation School. Finnish war 1939-40. CPSU 1939. Was at front from the first days of the war. Maj. & Sqdn Cdr in 34 GBAP. 152 sorties. On September 30 1943, his bomber was shot down by flak. He crashed his bomber into an enemy artillery position. HSU 4 February 1944.

Gubanov, Maksim Gerasimovich, born 18 January 1920 in Titovka, Altai Region, in a peasant family. After completing a mining and metallurgical *technikum*, he worked as a bookkeeper. Navy 1939. Naval Aviation Academy 1941. Went to front in October 1942. CPSU 1944. By March 1945 was Capt. & navigator in 12 GBAP-KBF. 86 sorties. HSU 6 March 1945. Krasnodar Higher Officers' Navigation School 1951. Lt Col retired 1959.

Gubin, Nazar Petrovich, born in 1918 in Zorgol, Chita Region, in a peasant family. Completed his education in a FZO, and worked as a demolitions worker in a local coal mine. Army 1939. Completed school of Aircrews in 1940. Went to front in October 1941. Sergeant radio-operator/air gunner and Komosmol member in 125 BAP. Completed 5 sorties. On 16 December 1941 his crew crashed their burning aircraft into a German target. HSU 16 January 1942.

Gulyaev, Nikolai Semyonovich, born 1 August 1921 in Novoselkovo-Vtoraya, Donets Region, in a peasant family. Completed the 7th grade and worked as a metal parts fitter. Army 1938. Borisoglebsk Flight School, 1940. At front from June 1941. CPSU 1944. By April 1945 was Sr Lt and deputy Sqdn Cdr in 80 GBAP. 163 sorties. HSU 27 June 1945. Air Force Academy 1955. Promoted to Colonel and commanded AP. Then to responsible staff duties. Died still in service 31 March 1967.

Gusenko, Pavel Yakovlevich, born 16 July 1914 in Ekaterinoslav in a Ukrainian working-class family. Completed study at a railway *polytechnikum* and an Aeroclub. Army 1936. Voroshilovgrad flight school 1938. Flew at lake Khasan 1938. Khalkin Gol 1939, Finland 1939-40. CPSU 1939. At front from June 1941. By June 1944

Pe-2 PILOT BIOGRAPHIES

was Capt. Sqdn Cdr in 81 GBAP. 196 sorties. 29 September 1944 crashed burning bomber into enemy railway station near Preshov, Czechoslovakia. HSU 26 October 1944.

Il'in Il'ya Ivanovich, born in1910 in St Petersburg. CPSU 1931. Navy 1933. Leningrad military-theoretical school for aviators and Eisk Naval Aviation School. Baltic Fleet. Finnish War 1939-40. In war from 1941. By August 1943 was Capt. & Sqdn Cdr in 119 MRAP-ChF. 270 sorties. Destroyed 8 supply dumps, and 3 minefields. HSU 16 May 1944. KIA 3 May 1944 in battle for Sevastopol.

Ivanov, Aleksei Alekksandrovich, born in 1922 in Mar'ino, Kalinin Region, in a peasant family. Completed secondary school. Army 1940. Completed Khar'kov Aviator's School. In action from June 1941. Sr Sgt bombardier-gunner and Komosmol member. 52 BAP. 17 sorties. On 27 November 1941 in spite of being mortally wounded during a bombing mission fulfilled his duties and dropped his bombs on the target. HSU 27 December 1941.

Ivanov, Leonid Petrovich, born 31 August 1921 in Staraya Tayaba, Kuibyshev Region. Completed the 9th grade. Army 1940. Engels Flight School 1941. CPSU 1942. To the front June 1942. By April 1945 Captain & Sqdn Cdr in 193 G ORAP (2 VA). 305 sorties, photographing 11,000km sq., 11 ground attacks, 14 air combats. 1 air victory. HSU 27 Jun3 1945. Higher officers' air tactics course 1945. Air Force Academy 1951. Lt Col retired 1961.

Ivanov, Nikolai Maksimovich, born 28 November 1918 in Pashkovskaya, Krasnodar Region, in a peasant family. Completed the 9th grade in 1938 and an Aeroclub. Army 1938. Krasnodar Military navigators' Academy 1940. At front from June 1941. CPSU 1943. By October 1944 was Sr Lt & air observer 50 ORAP (2 VA). 199 sorties. HSU 16 October 1944. Tambov Military Aviation Academy for Aviators 1947. Central Air tactics course for command staffs 1955. Died in service 6 October 1959.

Ivanov, Vasilii Konstantinovich, born 7 June 1921 in Mukhanovo, Gor'kii Region, in a working-class family. Completed secondary school and an Aeroclub. Worked as a draftsman. Army 1940. Engels flight school 1942. To front in January 1943. CPSU 1943. By May 1945 Sr Lt & deputy Sqdn Cdr 160 GBAP. 164 sorties. HSU 27 June 1945. Promoted to Captain. Remained in service. Died 9 July 1949.

Ivanov Vitalii Andrevich, born 14 April 1923 in Vladimir in a white-collar family. Completed secondary school in Novosibirsk in 1940. Army1940. Perm. Flight school 1941. Was instructor at Maikop flight school. To front in May 1942. CPSU 1943. By April 1945 was Sr Lt and Flight Cdr in 4 GBAP. 232 sorties. 10 air combats. HSU 18 August 1945. Zhukovskii Air Force Engineering Academy 1953. Was instructor and then did scientific research work. Lt Col retired 1957.

THE PETLYAKOV Pe-2

Ivashkin, Vasili Il'ich, born in1908 in Yushta, Ryazan' Region, in a working-class family. Completed a year in a *technikum* and worked as a boilermaker. CSU 1931. Army 1932. Leningrad military-theoretical Aviators' School 1932. Engels flight school 1934. Finnish war 1939-40. At front from June 1941. Major & deputy Sqdn Cdr in 608 BAP. 31 sorties. KIA 18 May 1942. HSU 22 February 1943.

Kabanov, Evgenii Ivanovich, born 20 November 1918 in Begichevo, Voronezh Region, in a peasant family. Completed a *technikum* and then worked as a supervisor in the local roads department. Navy 1939. S.A. Levandovskii Naval Aviation Academy 1941. To front in November 1942. CPSU 1944. By June 1944 was Sr Lt & flight navigator in 12 GPBAP-KBF. 103 sorties. Sank 1 transport individually, and 2 transports and an escort ship shared. 1 aircraft shot down. HSU 22 July 1944. Air Force Academy 1951. Honoured Military Navigator of the USSR. Maj. Gen. retired 1974.

Kalinichenko, Semyon Zinov'evich, born 30 September 1915 in Prizovoe, Dnepropetrovsk Region, in a Ukrainian peasant family. Completed 3 years at a RABFA and 1 course at a Transportation institute. Army 1936. Krasnodar Unified Pilots and Observers Academy 1940. CPSU 1941. To front in December 1941. By mid-January, 1945 was Captain and Sqdn navigator 367 BAP. 240 sorties. 26 aircraft, 47 Tanks and Self-propelled guns, 17 batteries of Field artillery and flak. HSU 18 August 1945. Krasnodar higher navigators school 19949. Lt. Col. retired 1958.

Kaminski, Ivan Ilarionovich, born 8 November 1919 in Mosory, Vitebsk Region, in a Belorussian peasant family. 9th grade. Army 1939. Engels Flight School 1941. To front in August 1942. By March 1945 was Sr Lt and Flight Cdr in 10 ORAP. 239 sorties. HSU 29 June 1945. CPSU 1946. Capt. retired 1947.

Kapitonov, Vasilii Efimovich, born 25 April 1917 in Sutokii, Pskov Region, in a peasant family. Completed the Leningrad highway *technikum* in 1936, and did road construction. Army 1938. School for junior Aviation specialists 1939. Finnish war 1939-40. At front from June 1941. Sr Sgt air gunner-radio operator in 33 SBAP (19 BAD). 111 sorties by February 1942. Shot down 4 fighters. HSU 27 March 1942. Completed flight school 1942, Rustavi Aviators' school 1945. Flew in Japanese war August 1945. CPSU 1945. Higher air tactics course for sqdn cars in 1947. Lt Col retired 1960.

Karpenko, Ivan Trofimovich, born 14 December 1916 in Lisichansk, North Caucasus, in a Ukrainian working-class family. Completed the 7th grade and an FZU, and worked as a metalworker. Army 1934. Voroshilovgrad flight school. CPSU 1939. Served in Far East. In August 1945 was Major and deputy Cdr of 52 PBAP-TOF (2 MTAD). Personally sank 2 transports and 4 landing barges. HSU 14 September 1945. Air Force Academy 1952. Lt Gen. in 1962. Died 1970.

Pe-2 PILOT BIOGRAPHIES

Karpov, Aleksandr Dmitrievich, born 10 January 1921 in Pyatigorsk, North Caucasus, in a peasant family. Completed secondary school. Navy 1940. Eisk Naval Aviation Academy 1942. To the front in 1943. CPSU 1944. By end of August 1944 was Lt & flight Cdr in 30 RAP-ChF. 251 sorties. HSU 6 March 1945. Air Force Academy 1955. Col retired 1972.

Khal'zev, Aleksandr Ivanovich, born 7 September 1921 in Novosibirsk, in a working-class family. Completed 9th grade and an Aeroclub. Army 1940. Engels Flight School 1941. To the front in October 1942. CPSU 1943. By May 1944 was Sr Lt & Deputy Sqdn Cdr 63 GNBAP (132 BAD). 300 sorties. Destroyed 28 aircraft on the ground. 1 air victory. HSU 19 August 1944. Air Force Academy 1950. Lt Col retired 1958.

Kharitonov, Vladimir Mikhailovich, born 7 January 1919 in Pskov, in a working-class family. Completed the 7th grade and worked as a master in a watch-making factory. Studied at an Aeroclub. Army 1939. Balashov flight school 1941. To the front in February 1942. CPSU 1944. By September 1944 was Sr Lt in 10 ORAP. 175 sorties. 12 air combats, 3 air victories. HSU 23 February 1945. Advanced Officers' Course 1953. Lt Col retired 1960.

Khoroshilov, Vladimir Aleksandrovich, born 20 July 1915 in Odessa in a working-class family. Completed 2 courses at a workers' faculty. Was a Komosmol worker. Army 1932. Completed flight school 1933. Military school for flight Cdrs 1936. During Finnish War was Sr Lt & flight Cdr in 48 SBAP. 45 sorties. HSU 21 March 1940. At the front from June 1941. Advanced course for Command Staffs 1950. Maj. Gen retired 1970.

Khrustalyov, Pavel Ivanovich, born in 1922 in Barabinsk, Novosibirsk Region, in a working-class family. Secondary school. Army 1940. Kacha flight school 1942. To the front in November 1942. By October 1944 was Sr Lt and senior air observer in 99 GORAP. Candidate CPSU. 109 sorties. On 10 October 1944 crashed his burning aircraft into an enemy artillery position. HSU 18 August 1945.

Khvostunov. Andrei Grigor'evich, born 27 October 1919 in Galkino, Vladimir Region, in a peasant family. Completed 7th grade and worked as a metalworker in a factory. Completed an Aeroclub. Army 1937. Perm flight school 1938. To the front in July 1941. By mid-January 1942 was Jr Lt and Flight Cdr in 150 SBAP (46 SAD). 210 sorties. HSU 5 May 1942. Col retired 1959, and worked in civil aviation.

Kibalko, Vasilii Vasil'evich, born 14 January 1918 in Odessa in a Ukrainian working-class family. Completed the 7th grade and an FZU and worked as a smelter in a shipbuilding yard. By 1936 completed 3 courses at a pedagogical institute and in 1937 an Aeroclub. Army 1937. Odessa flight school 1938. Took part in occupation of eastern Poland 1939. At front from June 1941. CPSU 1942. By the beginning of 1943 was Capt. & Deputy Sqdn Cdr in 10 ODRAP (1 VA). 100 sorties bombing and long-range reconnaissance. HSU 24 May 1943. Air Force Academy 1949. Commanded a regiment, and then deputy Cdr of air division. Senior instructor in tactics at the Frunze Academy. Col retired 1978.

Kirilenko, Vasilii Ivanovich, born 14 October 1919 in Druzhkovka, Donets Region, in a Ukrainian working-class family. Completed a machine-building *technikum*. Army 1938. Voroshilovgrad flight school 1939. At front from June 1941. CPSU 1944. By August 1944 was Sr Lt and flight Cdr in 98 GORAP. 235 sorties. HSU 26 October 1944. Major retired 1950.

Klochko, Nikolai Antonovich, born 19 September 1907 in Voronezh Settlement, Sumy Region, in a Ukrainian working-class family. Completed primary school and worked as a telephone/telegraph operator at a mine. Army 1929. CPSU 1930. Khar'kov Military Aviation School for Pilots and Observers 1933. Finnish war 1939-40. To the front in September 1939. By end of war was Major & Flight Inspector for Pilot Training of 276 BAD. 192 sorties. HSU 29 June 1945. Lt Col retired 1954.

Kolesnikov, Aleksei Vasil'evich, born 17 March 1921 in Makedonovka, Voroshilovgrad Region, in a Ukrainian peasant family. Completed the 7th grade and studied at the Voroshilovgrad Aeroclub. Army 1938. Voroshilovgrad military flight school 1940. To front in September 1941. CPSU 1942. By mid-November 1943 Sr Lt in 118 ODRAE. 168 sorties. HSU 4 February 1944. Higher Air Tactics course 1948. Lt Col retired 1950.

Kolesnikov, Nikolai Danilovich, born 22 April 1921 in Temryuk, Krasnodar Region, in a working-class family. Completed the 8th grade and worked as a lathe operator. Navy 1939. Eisk Naval Aviation Academy 1941. To front in July 1943. By mid-1944 was Sr Lt and flight Cdr in 12 GPBAP-KBF. 100 sorties, sank 2 transports, 2 trawlers, 2 warships, and destroyed 2 artillery batteries, 12 trucks, and 2 ammunition dumps. HSU 5 November 1944. CPSU 1944. Promoted to Captain. Released from service 1947.

Komarov, Sergei Petrovich, born 12 June 1922 in Tokarevo, Ryazan' Region, in a peasant family. He completed 2 courses at an industrial *technikum* before joining the army in 1940. Completed Konotop Military Aviation Academy in 1943. To front in June 1943. By February 1945 was Lt in 16 ODRAP. 237 sorties. CPSU 1945. HSU 15 May 1946. Air Force Academy 1955. Colonel retired 1975.

Kondrashin, Andrei Kuz'mich, born in 1916 in Dubovich'e, Ryazan Region, in a peasant family. Completed secondary school. Navy 1936. Eisk Naval Aviation Academy. At front from June 1941. CPSU 1942. By the end of 1943 Capt. & Sqdn

Pe-2 PILOT BIOGRAPHIES

Cdr of 40 PBAP-ChF. 311 sorties. Sank 6 transports, totalling 12,300 tons, 7 fast landing barges, 3 dry goods barges, 3 cutters, 1 FLAK gun, 21 trucks, and 17 aircraft on the ground. HSU 31 May 1944. KIA 11 January 1944 over the port of Odessa.

Konkin, Mikhail Parfent'evich, born, 25 July 1915 in Berdyansk, Zaporozh'e Region, in a Ukrainian working-class family. Completed secondary school and then worked as a metalworker. Army 1935. Voroshilovgrad flight school 1936. To front in June 1941. CPSU 1942. By mid July 1942 he was a Sr Lt and Sqdn Cdr in 4 DRAP. 70 sorties. Shot down 3 aircraft. HSU 23 November 1942. Major retired 1948.

Kononenko, Vasilii Ivanovich, born 9 April 1921 in Taganrog, in a working-class family. Completed secondary school. Army 1938. Krasnodr Military Navigation Institute 1940. At front from June 1941. CPSu 1942. By July 1943 was Captain and flight navigator in 10 ORAP. 196 sorties. HSU 4 February 1944. Air Force Academy 1946. Became instructor in Air Force Academy 1951, and a Candidate Degree of Military Science, and department head. Col retired 1973.

Kopeikin, Igor' Valentinovich, born 8 July 1920 in Aksyonovo, Bashkiriya, in a peasant family. Completed secondary school. Army 1939. To front in June 1941. CPSU 1943. By October 1944 was Starshina gunner-radio operator, and Sqdn chief of signals in 35 GBAP. 180 sorties, more than 50 air battles, 2 individual and 8 group aerial kills. HSU 23 February 1945. Released from service. Studied at the Moscow Institute of Railroad Transportation, and from 1952 became an officer in the KGB.

Kornev, Ivan Aleksandrovich, born 26 November 1907 in Selaevo, Kaluga Region, in a peasant family. Completed primary school. Army 1929. CPSU 1931. Lugansk flight school 1932. In 1935 a course through the Eisk Military Aviation Institute. Fought at Lake Khasan in 1938. To the front in August 1938. By end of war Major and deputy Cdr of 63 NBAP (132 BAD), a unit which flew twin-motor bombers despite its NBAP designation. 57 sorties. On 25 April 1945 his bomber was hit by flak and he was badly wounded. Ordered his crew to bale out while he remained with the aircraft. HSU posthumously 18 August 1945.

Korolyov, Matvei Grigor'evich, born 22 November 1909 in Pokrovskoe, Moscow Region, in a working-class family. Completed 7th grade and worked at a variety of jobs, including driver. Army 1931, CPSU 1932. Odessa flight school 1934. At front from June 1941. By May 1945 was Major & Sqdn Cdr in 160 GBAP. 161 sorties. HSU 27 June 1945. Higher Officers' air tactics course 1945. Assigned to flight inspectorate. From 1948 test pilot. Lt Col retired 1956.

Korzunov, Ivan Egorovich, born 3 May 1915 in Ekaterinoslav, in a working-class family. Completed his education in a Rabfak, and then worked in a Moscow sawmill.

THE PETLYAKOV Pe-2

Navy 1934. Eisk Naval Aviation School, 1936. CPSU 1939. In action from June 1941. By April 1943 Major & Sqdn Cdr in 40 PBAP-ChF. 191 sorties. HSU 24 July 1943. General Staff Academy 1955. Colonel General. Died in service 29 October 1966.

Kosenko, Yuri Khrisanfovich, born in 1922 in Chistyakovo, Donets Region, in a Ukrainian peasant family. Navy 1940. Eisk Naval Aviation Institute 1942. To front in November 1942. By mid-May 1944 was Lt and flight Cdr in 12 GBAP-KBF. 76 sorties. Killed while bombing enemy ship 17 May 1944. HSU 31 May 1944.

Kosinov, Semyon Kirilovich, born 2 February 1917 in Uspenka, Kursk Region, in a peasant family. Completed 7th grade and worked on a collective farm. Army 1935. Tambov Infantry Institute 1938. Khar'kov Military Aviation Institute 1940. At front from start of war. Komosmol. Lt gunner-bombardier in 125 BAP (2 SAD). 61 sorties. On 16 December 1941, his aircraft was hit by flak. Crew dropped bombs on enemy, and then crashed burning bomber into enemy column. HSU 16 January 1942.

Kostrikin. Afanasi Georgievich, born 14 May 1914 in Kozlovka, Voronezh Region, in a peasant family. Completed a maritime biological *technikum* and worked on a state fish farm. Army 1936. Completed air observer school. Finnish war 1939-40. CPSU 1941. At front from start of war. By September 1943 was Captain and navigator of 224 BBAP. 100 sorties, 8 of them deep in the enemy rear. 35 air combats. Scored 3 individual and 8 shared aerial kills. HSU 28 September 1943. Air Force Academy 1948. Col killed in car accident 2 November 1961.

Kostylev, Aleksandr Nikolaevich, born 2 November 1908 in Peskovka, Kirov Region, in a working-class family. Completed 7th grade and FZU, and in 1929 a CPSU school. Was secretary of regional Komosmol. CPSU 1929. Army 1930. Orenburg flight school 1936. Course for Kommissar-aviators in 1938. Finnish War 1939-40. B. Kommissar. Was Kommissar of 50 SBAP. 41 sorties and political work. HSU 21 March 1940. At front from June 1941. Became Regtl Zampolit. Was wounded in action. Flew 11 different types of aircraft. Col retired 1953.

Kotlyar, Feodosii Porfir'evich, born 27 August 1904 in Vyazamskaya, Khabarovsk Region, in a working-class family. Completed 4th grade. Army in 1926. CPSU 1928. Completed Orenburg flight school. Frunze Academy in 1938. Occupation of Eastern Poland 1939. Finnish War 1939-40. At front from June 1941. Major General. In May 1943 was appointed commander of 4 GBAD. Remained in position to end of war. Under his command, the division flew 2,210 sorties. Kotlyar personally flew 118 sorties during this period. HSU 29 June 1945. After war completed Air Force Academy and General Staff Academy. Held a number of important command positions. Lt Gen retired 1960.

Pe-2 PILOT BIOGRAPHIES

Koval'chuk, Ivan Ivanovich, born 18 January 1918 in Pavlovka, Vinnitsa Region, in a Ukrainian peasant family. Completed Vinnitsa medical *technikum*. Navy 1936. Eisk Naval Aviation Academy 1938. At front from June 1941. CPSU 1942. By September 1944 was Capt. and Sqdn navigator in 30 RAP-ChF. 285 sorties. Personally destroyed 5 tanks and 7 artillery batteries. HSU 6 March 1945. Naval Academy 1955. Col retired 1957.

Kovalenko, Anatolii Yakovlevich, born 23 January 1919 in Yakimovka, Gomel Region, in a Belorussian peasant family. Completed an automobile *technikum* and then worked as a motor mechanic. Army 1939. Khar'kov Military Aviation Academy 1940. At front from June 1941. By November 1944 was Sr Lt and air observer in 742 ORAP. 160 sorties. ASU 23 February 1945. CPSU 1945. Captain released from service 1946.

Kovanev, Ivan Fyodorovich, born 1 August 1910 in Posevkina, Voronezh Region, in a peasant family. Completed 6th grade and worked as the head postal clerk for a collective farm. Army 1931. CPSU 1932. Leningrad Military Theoretical Aviators' School 1933. Stalingrad flight school 1935. Took part in occupation of eastern Poland and Finnish War 1939-40. In action from start of war. By March 1944 Major & Sqdn Cdr in 34 GBAP. 198 sorties, 34 of them at night. HSU 19 August 1944. Advanced Course for Kommand Staffs 1949. Col retired 1957.

Kovsharov, Ivan Akimovich, born 28 October 1911 in Glybotskoe, Gomel Region, in a Belorussian peasant family. Completed a zoological *technikum* and then worked as a livestock breeder on a state farm. Army 1936. Orenburg Pilots' and Observers' School 1938. Khalkin Gol 1939. Winter War 1939-40. CPSU 1940. At front from June 1941. By December 1941 was Lt and Sqdn navigator in 225 BBAP. 99 sorties. HSU 17 December 1941. Air Force Academy 1944. Lt Col retired 1961.

Kozhemyakin, Mikhail Stepanovich, born 24 January 1913 in Verkhnesolyonyi, Rostov Region, in a peasant family, but early in life the family moved to the Akhtyubinsk Region. Completed a construction *technikum* and then worked as a construction worker. Army 1935. Orenburg Military Aviation Academy 1937. Finnish war 1939-40. CPSU 1939. At front from June 1941. By end of War Major & navigator of 38 BAP. 122 sorties. HSU 27 June 1945. General Staff Academy 1956. Col retired 1960.

Kozlenko, Pyotr Aleksevich, born 7 June 1916 in Bogoyavlensk, Nikolaev Region, in a Ukrainian peasant family. Completed the Leningrad fish industry *technikum*, and worked in the Nikolaev fishing industry. Army 1938. Krasnodar Military Navigation Academy 1940. To front in June 1941. By end of war was Captain and Sqdn navigator in 24 BAP. 165 sorties. HSU 15 May 1946. CPSU 1946. Krasnodar higher officers' navigation school 1949. Col to the reserves 1960. Retired 1975.

THE PETLYAKOV Pe-2

Kozlov, Aleksei Vasil'evich, born 25 February 1913 in Ekateinoslav, in a Ukrainian working-class family. Completed a railway *technikum*. Army 1932. Completed Sevastopol air observers' school 1934. Discharged 1935. Employed as construction worker. Recalled to army 1941. At front from June 1941. By December 1943 was Sr Lt and flight navigator in 118 ODRAE (7 VA). 127 sorties. HSU 4 February 1944. Seriously injured in aviation accident 3 March 1944. Retired for disability April 1944.

Kozlov, Valentin Georgievich, born 20 August 1917 in Aleksandropol' in a working-class family, but in childhood moved to Siberia with family. Completed 6th grade and went to work in a mine. Finished his education in an FZU, then operated a crane in a foundry. Army 1939. Novosibirsk flight school 1940. At front from June 1941. CPSU 1942. By April 1945 was Major and Sqdn Cdr in 6 BAP. 170 sorties. HSU 27 June 1945. Major retired 1956.

Krivolutski, Nikolai Efimovich, born 18 December 1922 in Verkhnyaya Esaulovka, Krasnodar Region, in a peasant family. Completed 2 courses at a financial-economic *technikum*, and an Aeroclub. Army 1940. Omsk flying school 1943. To the front in August 1943. By the end of the was Lt in 98 G ORAP. 120 sorties. HSU 15 May 1946. CPSU 1946. Secondary school 1947. Air Force Academy 1954. Worked in MOD central apparatus. Col retired 1975.

Krivoruchenko, Aleksei Nikitovich, born 15 March 1918 in Ivanovka, Voroshilovgrad Region, in a Ukrainian peasant family. Completed a railway *technikum*. Army 1938. Voroshilovgrad flight school. At front from 1941. CPSU 1943. By February 1945 was Major & Sqdn Cdr in 72 ORAP. 154 sorties. HSU 15 May 1946. Lt Col retired 1959.

Kruchenykh, Sevast'yan Petrovich, born in 1909 in Anatol'evka, Nikolaev Region, in a Ukrainian family. Completed secondary school. Navy 1931. CPSU 1932. Completed Voroshilovgrad flight school. Served in Black Sea Fleet. In action from June 1941. By July 1943 was Major & Sqdn Cdr in 119 MRAP. 135 sorties. HSU 24 July 1943. Officers' Higher air tactics course 1950. Lt Col retired 1966.

Krupin, Andrei Petrovich, born 25 May 1915 in Petrograd, in a white-collar family. Completed a course at a highway *technikum*, and then worked as a metalworker. Army 1937. Chelyabinsk Military Aviation Institute for aviators in 1940. At front from June 1941. CPSU 1942. By February 1943 was Captain and squadron navigator in 99 BAP. 199 sorties. HSU 1 May 1943. Promoted to Major. In 1947 entered Air Force Academy. 30 July 1949 killed in flying accident.

Kudryavtsev, Sergei Sergevich, born 5 October 1920 in Sorozh, Kostroma Region, in a peasant family. Completed a *technikum*. Army 1938. Chelyabinsk Military Aviation Institute for Air Observers 1940. To front in June 1941. By March

Pe-2 PILOT BIOGRAPHIES

1945 was Sr Lt & flight navigator in 373 BAP. 306 sorties. HSU 18 August 1945. Promoted to Captain. CPSU 1945. After war released from service.

Kurzenkov, Aleksandr Georgievich, born in 1920 in Tashirovo, Moscow Region, in a working-class family. Completed 8th grade and an FZU in Moscow and an Aeroclub. Worked as a lathe operator in a car factory. Navy 1939. Eisk Naval Aviation Institute. CPSU 1943. By September 1943 was Lt and Flight Cdr in 44 AE-15 MRAP-KBF. 203 sorties. 13 air combats. Damaged an escort ship and a gunboat. HSU 22 January 1944. MIA near Liepaya, Latvia 8 May 1945. He was shot down in a Pe-2 by Gerhard Thyben of *JG-54* who was flying to refuge in Sweden. This was probably the last German aerial victory of the war.

Kuz'menko, Nikolai Ivanovich, born 9 August 1914 in Beryozovka, Chernigov Region, in a Ukrainian peasant family. Completed 7th grade and 3 courses at an agricultural mechanisation *technikum*. Army 1935. Voroshilovgrad flight school 1937. CPSU 1940. Course for flight commanders in 1941. At front from June 1941. By end of war Major & deputy Cdr for flight preparation of 140 BAP. 162 sorties. HSU 29 June 1945. Higher officers' air tactics course 1947. Air Force Academy 1956. Maj. Gen retired 1963.

Kuznetsov, Nikolai Vasil'evich, born 6 December 1912 in Saratov in a working-class family. Completed 7th grade in 1929 and a food industry FZO in 1931. Studied at an agricultural mechanisation institute. Army 1934. Engels flying school 1934. Finnish war 1939-40. ÜPSU 1940. At front from June 1941. By February 1945 was Major & Deputy Cdr for flight crews of 58 BAP. 329 sorties, 143 bombing missions and 128 special missions. HSU 29 June 1945. Air Force Academy 1955. Col retired 1960.

Lapshenkov, Semyon Vasil'evich, born in 1913 in Ekaterinovka, Kaluga region, in a peasant family. Completed an FZU and studied at the Moscow Machine-building Institute. CPSU 1932. Navy 1934. Eisk Naval Aviation Institute 1936. Finnish War 1939-40. At front from June 1941. Major & Sqdn Cdr in 29 BAP-SF. 55 sorties. Individually sank minelayer and 3 transports, and shared 2 transports. Destroyed 8 aircraft on the ground. KIA 21 September 1943. HSU 31 May 1944.

Lashin, Georgii Ivanovich, born 1 May 1920 in Sekretarka, Penza Region, in a peasant family. Secondary school. Army 1940. Kirovobad flight school 1943. To front in November 1943. CPSU 1944. By May 1945 was Lt in 861 BAP. 236 sorties, of which 121 were reconnaissance missions. His crew was credited with 3 aircraft shot down. HSU 18 August 1945. Promoted to Sr Lt Killed in flying accident 18 April 1946.

Lashin, Mikhail Afanas'evich, born 7 November 1918 in Dzhurovka, Bryansk Region, in a peasant family. Completed 7th grade. Army 1937. Melitopol Military

Aviation Institute for Navigators 1940. At front from June 1941. CPSU 1943. By April 1945 was Captain and Sqdn navigator in135 GBAP. 266 sorties. 1 individual and 2 shared aerial victories. HSU 29 June 1945. Air Force Academy 1950. Became Chief of Voroshilovgrad Higher Military Aviation Institute for Navigators. Honoured Military Navigator of the USSR. Maj. Gen. retired 1973.

Leont'ev, Vasilii Aleksandrovich, born 11 January 1917 in Staropyshminsk, Ekaterinburg Region, in a peasant family. Completed school in an FZU and worked as a metalworker. After completing an Aeroclub, he worked as a flight instructor. Army 1937. Perm flight school 1938. CPSU 1939. During Finnish War 1939-40 flew 38 sorties. In action from June 1941. By end of war Sr Lt and Deputy Sqdn Cdr in 24 BAP. 165 sorties. HSU 15 May 1946. Captain retired 1948.

Lezzhov, Ivan Ivanovich, born 20 September 1923 in Kashira, Moscow Region, in a peasant family. Completed a mechanical *technikum*. Army 1940. Tambov flight school 1942. To active unit in April 1943. By January 1945 was Lt & Sqdn navigator in 98 GORAP. 147 sorties. HSU 29 June 1945. CPSU 1947. Air Force Academy 1950. General Staff Academy 1965. Promoted to Major General; became head of a department at the Zhukovskii Air Force Engineering Academy and a Candidate of Military Science. Still teaching late 1980s.

Lisitsyn, Dmitri Fyodorovich, born in 1913 in Odintsovo, Moscow Region, in a working class family. He finished 7th grade and an Aeroclub, and worked as an Aeroclub flight instructor. Army 1939, and that same year finished military flight school at Groznyi. Retained as instructor. To the front in April 1943. CPSU 1944. By September 1943 was Sr Lt in 98 GORAP. 88 sorties. On 30 July 1943 during a mission, his aircraft was hit and set afire, and Lisitsyn was seriously wounded. Nonetheless, he flew his burning aircraft back to friendly lines and landed in a field, saving the valuable reconnaissance information. HSU 28 September 1943. Captain retired 1947.

Litvinov, Fyodor Pavlovich, born 12 April 1912 in Velikomikhailovka, Belgorod Region, in a peasant family. Completed secondary school. Worked as a brigadier-joiner in a factory in Kharkov. Army 1932. Completed flight school in Kharkov. CPSU 1939. Participated in occupation of Eastern Poland in 1939, and the Finnish War 1939-40. At front from June 1941. In 1943 completed an accelerated course at the Air Force Academy & returned to front. By May 1945 was Major & Sqdn Cdr in 162 GBAP. 83 sorties. On his last mission on 22 April 1945, he was wounded and the controls of his aircraft were damaged. However, he continued to lead his squadron and successfully completed the mission, and then returned home to his own base. HSU 27 June 1945. Col retired 1961.

Lobozov, Vasilii Andrevich, born in 1913 in Vasilyovo, Smolensk Region, in a peasant family. Completed 7th grade and an FZU. Worked in Smolensk and then Moscow. Army 1935. Initially trained as an aircrew man at Voronezh, and served as gunner-radio operator. Served as a volunteer in Spain during 1936-37, where he completed 153 sorties. After his return, he completed flight training at Stalingrad and was assigned to the 40 BAP-ChF. Was in action from June 1941. By March 1944 was a Major and deputy commander for flight training of the 30 RAP-ChF. 185 sorties. He had participated in the defence of both Odessa and Sevastopol and in the bombing attacks on the Constanza oil refineries, the Danube bridges, and other targets in Romania at the beginning of the war. HSU 16 May 1944. In July 1944 completed a Higher Officers' Course of the VVS-VMF. He was killed 30 November 1944.

Loskutov, Viktor Georgievich, born 27 September 1923 in Yanaul, Bashkir ASSR. Completed secondary school. Navy 1941. Naval Aviation Institute 1944. To the front in May 1944. Served in Black Sea & Baltic Fleets. Took part in war against Japan as Lieutenant of 34 BAP-TOF. Sank a transport and destroyed an armoured train, a bridge and a supply dump. HSU 14 September 1945. CPSU 1951. Higher Officers' air tactics course 1952. Major retired 1962.

Luk'yanets, Andrei Nikitovich,[3] born 15 September 1922 in Zhukovka, Kiev Region, in a Ukrainian peasant family. Completed secondary education in1940 and in July went into army. Krasnodar Navigators' School in1941. By the end of 1942 was lead navigator for a flight. By end of war was Guards Senior Lieutenant in 160 GBAP. 164 sorties. HSU 27 June 1945. Krasnodar Higher Navigator School in 1949. Lt Col to reserves 1974.

Luk'yantsev, Vasilii Petrovich, born 21 August 1913 in Mar'inskaya Stanitsa, Stavpropol Region, in a peasant family. He completed 9th grade and the Bataisk Civil Air Fleet School in 1937. Worked as a flight instructor at the Taganrog Aeroclub. Army 1941. To the front in September 1941. CPSU 1942. By June 1943 was Captain & Sqdn Cdr in 10 ORAP. 167 sorties, 86 of them long range. 12 air combats. Personally shot down 1 aircraft, and his crew claimed 2 more, and 5 more kills in group air battle. HSU 4 February 1944. Air Force Academy 1946. Lt Col retired 1957.

Luzgin, Aleksei Andrevich, born 1 February 1920 in Zagorod'e, Vitebsk Region, in a Belorussian peasant family. Completed secondary school and an Aeroclub, and worked on a railway passenger line. Army 1939. Tambov flight school 1941. To an active unit in March 1943. CPSU 1943. By the end of the war was a Lieutenant and flight Cdr in 98 GORAP. 106 sorties. HSU 15 May 1946. Lt Col retired 1960.

Lyadov, Grigorii Grigor'evich, born 5 December 1921 in Krasnaya Sludge, Perm Region, in a peasant family. Completed secondary school and joined Army 1939. Chelyabinsk Military Aviation Academy 1940. To the front in October 1941. CPSU 1943. By April 1944 was Captain and air observer in 511 ORAP. 115 sorties. Particularly distinguished himself in operations on the right bank of the Dnepr. KIA 31 April 1944. HSU 26 October 1944.

THE PETLYAKOV Pe-2

Lyalin, Vasilii Konstantinovich, born 9 January 1920 in Dvurechnaya, Kharkov Region, in a Ukrainian white-collar family. Completed a machine-building *technikum* in 1938 and worked in a tractor factory. Army 1938. Melitopol air observer school 19940. At front from June 1941. CPSU 1943. By 25 October 1943 was Capt & Sqdn navigator in 8 ORAP. 171 sorties. HSU 13 April 1944. Air Force Academy 1952. Col retired 1961.

Lykhin, Sergei Egorovich, born 25 October 1914 in Lykhino, Kirov Region, in a peasant family. Completed secondary school. Worked as a clerk in the fire department. Army 1936. Orenburg air observer school 1937. At front from June 1941. By the end of February 1944 was a Captain and squadron navigator in 742 ORAP. 165 sorties. Personally destroyed 4 enemy aircraft. HSU 1 July 1944. CPSU 1944. Krasnodar higher officers navigation school 1947. Lt Col retired 1958.

Lyulin, Sergei Mikhailovich, born 17 September 1915 in Kulachikha, Ivanovo Region, in a peasant family. Completed primary school and an FZU. Worked as a lathe operator in a machinery-building factory. Army 1937. School for junior aviation specialists 1937. Took part in occupation of eastern Poland and Finnish War 1939-40. Khar'kov air observer school 1941. At front from June 1941. CPSU 1943. By September 1944 was Captain and Sqdn navigator in 124 GBAP. 110 sorties. Scored 3 individual and 7 group aerial victories. On 14 September 1944, en route to target, his bomber was hit by flak and set afire. Plane continued to target and dropped its bombs successfully on a railway station, and then was crashed into a column of tanks. HSU 18 August 1945.

Maikov, Nikolai Ivanovich, born 30 April 1918 in Yaroslavl in a working-class family. Completed 7th grade and an FZU, and worked in a locomotive factory. Studied at an Aeroclub. Army 1940. Tambov flight school 1941. To the front in August 1942. CPSU 1943. By November 1943 was Lt & flight cdr in 134 GBAP. 68 sorties. HSU 1 November 1943. Captain retired 1947.

Maiski, Dmitri Vasil'evich, born 1 January 1917 in Aleksevka, Tambov Region, in a peasant class family. Completed two courses at a Rabfak. Army 1936. Stalingrad Military Aviation Institute 1939. To the front in June 1941. CPSU 1941. By March 1942 Sr Lt & flight Cdr in 514 BAP. 78 sorties. HSU 31 July 1942. KIA 10 January 1943.

Makarenko, Aleksei Iosifovich, born 16 May 1920 in Petrovskoe, Stavropol Region, in a working class family. Completed 7th grade. Worked as a glider mechanic at the Maikop Aeroclub. Army 1939. Taganrog flight school, 1941. Kirovabad flight school 1943. To front in May 1943. CPSU 1944. By May 1945 was Sr Lt in160 GBAP. 161 sorties. HSU 27 June 1945. Major retired 1954.

Makhrinov, Grigorii Fyodorovich, born 15 February 1921 in Lisogorka, Rostov Region, in a peasant family. Completed 7th grade and an FZU. Worked as a

Pe-2 PILOT BIOGRAPHIES

milling-machine operator. Army 1938. Voroshilovgrad flight school 1940. At front from start of war. CPSU 1943. By February 1945 was Captain & flight Cdr in 72 ORAP. 75 bombing and 115 reconnaissance sorties. HSU 15 May 1946. Air Force Academy 1954. Maj. Gen. retired 1973.

Malashenkov, Grigorii Stepanovich, born 15 October 1919 in Pogibelka, Smolensk Region, in a peasant family. Completed secondary school. Army 1939. Kharkov military aviation institute 1940. To the front June 1941. CPSU 1944. By February 1945 was Captain and Sqdn navigator in 745 BAP. 320 sorties. HSU 15 May 1946. Air Force Academy 1952. Was senior navigator of a Regt and a division. Head navigator of an Aviation District. Honoured Military Navigator of the USSR. Col retired 1974.

Malikov, Il'ya Antonovich, born 4 August 1921 in Istobnoe, Lipetsk Region, in a peasant family. Lived in Noginsk, where he finished secondary school and worked as a lathe operator. Army 1940. Flight school at Kirovabad in 1940. To front in July 1942. CPSU 1944. By February 1945 was Sr Lt & flight Cdr in 128 BAP. 86 sorties. HSU 15 May 1946. Captain retired 1946.

Malin, Anatolii Petrovich, born 14 August 1916 in Tambov in a peasant family. Completed 5th grade and an FZU. Worked as metalworker. Army 1934. Completed Saratov Armoured Institute 1938. Chakalov Military Aviation Institute 1940 as navigator. Finnish War 1939-40. At front from June 1941. CPSU 1943. By March 1945 was Captain & Sqdn navigator in 140 BAP. 182 sorties. HSU 29 June 1945. Officer's higher navigation school 1947. Major retired 1957.

Malushchenko, Mitrofan Egorovich, born 23 July 1912 in Chutovka, Poltava Region, in a Ukrainian peasant family. CPSU 1939. Graduated from Kharkov State University in 1940. While at university received territorial military training, with a specialty as a gunner-bombardier. Received a position as an instructor of Marxism-Leninism in a teacher-training institute. Called to army in June 1941 and sent to the front. By May 1945 was Captain and Sqdn navigator in 134 GBAP. 207 sorties. HSU 29 June 1945. Major retired 1947.

Mamai, Nikolai Vasil'evich, born in 1914 in Gorodishche, in the Cherkass Region, in a Ukrainian peasant family. Completed 7th grade. Army 1933. Kharkov air observer school 1936. CPSU 1941. To the front in October 1942. By March 1945 Captain and navigator of 82 GBAP. 139 sorties. Credited with 11 group aerial kills. HSU 27 June 1945. KIA 16 April 1945.

Martynov, Evgenii Vasil'evich, born 12 February 1924 in Chernevo, Moscow Region, in a peasant family. Completed 9th grade and an Aeroclub. Army September 1941. Chuguev Flight School 1943. To the front in October 1943. By April 1945 was lt & flight Cdr in 98 G ORAP. 170 sorties. HSU 18 August 1945. CPSU 1945.

THE PETLYAKOV Pe-2

Higher air tactics course 1949. Central Air Tactics course 1955. Commanded an IAP, but from 1962 commanded a VTP. Lt Col retired 1964.

Martynov, Mikhail Ivanovich, born 18 November 1909 in Elshanka, Orenburg Region, in a peasant family. Completed 7th grade and a Communist Party School. Army 1930. CPSU 1931. Vol'sk aircrew and mechanics school 1931. Borisoglebsk Flight School 1933. During Finnish war was Captain & Sqdn Cdr in 48 SBAP. 46 sorties, including bombing from low altitude during limited visibility. HSU 21 March 1940. During SWW flew 126 sorties. Advanced Course for Command Staffs through Air Force Academy in 1944. Was assigned to Polish Air Force. General Staff Academy 1951. Served in various command positions. Lt General retired 1970.

Matrunchik, Iosif Vasil'evich, born 21 January 1903 in Kaikovo, Minsk Region, in a Belorussian peasant family. Completed 6th grade and worked as a labourer. Army 1925. CPSU 1928. Orenburg flight school 1932. Borisoglebsk flight school 1934. Finnish war 1939, Captain & Sqdn Cdr in 18 SBAP. More than 60 sorties. HSU 20 May 1940. During SWW commanded a BAP. From October 1942 Inspectorate of Flight Proficiency of a BAD. Killed 9 May 1945.

Medvedev, Aleksandr Nikolaevich, born 23 November 1918 in Protasikha, Gorkii Region, in a peasant family. Completed a *technikum* and then worked as director of the club at the Gorkii Automobile factory. Army 1938. CPSU 1939. Melitopol Military Aviation Institute 1940. In active unit from start of war. By October 1944 was Major & Regtl navigator of 122 GBAP 234 sorties. Shot down 5 aircraft individually and 3 with the group. HSU 18 August 1945. After war completed Air Force Academy and General Staff Academy. Became Col Gen. and 1st deputy Chief of the Main Staff of the VVS. Died in 1984.

Melakh, Efim L'vovich, born 26 July 1918 in Odessa, in a Jewish working-class family. He completed 8th and worked as a metalworker in a machine-building factory in Odessa. In 1937 he joined the army and in 1938 competed flight training at the Odessa Military Aviation School for Pilots. He was sent to the front in August 1942. During 1943, he joined the Communist Party. By October 1943 he was a Captain and commander of a Zveno of the 47G ORAP. He had completed 80 sorties of long-range reconnaissance and bombing missions. Melakh was awarded the HSU on February 4. 1944. He remained in service after the war, completing the Advanced Course for Command Staffs at the Air Force Academy, and then became a regiment commander. He had reached the rank of Colonel when he retired in 1960.

Melanin, Grigorii Andrevich, born 22 January 1918 in Aleksandrovski, Novosibirsk Region, in a working-class family. Completed a topography *technikum* and then worked as a photographer. Army 1939. Orenburg military aviators school 1941. To the front in November 1941. CPSU 1943. By September 1944 was

Pe-2 PILOT BIOGRAPHIES

Captain & air observer in 10 ORAP. 180 sorties. HSU 23 February 1945. Higher officers' navigation school 1952. Col retired 1960.

Mel'nikov, Ivan Semyonovich, born 4 September 1914 in Balyklei, Tambov Region, in a peasant family. Completed a pedagogical course and then worked as secretary for the village soviet. Army 1935. Ryazan Infantry school 1938. Kharkov Military Aviators Institute 1939. At front from June 1941. By January 1945 was Captain and senior air observer in 98 GORAP. 106 sorties. CPSU member. HSU 29 June 1945. Major retired 1960.

Mikhailov, Vasilii Nikolaevich, born 3 February 1910 in Kazan in a working-class family. Completed 7th and worked as an unskilled worker until entering the army in 1928. Infantry school in 1929. CPSU in 1930. In 1934 Orenburg Air Observer School. Later completed Eisk Naval Aviation School. Took part in occupation of Eastern Poland in 1939. In action from June 1941. By December 1941 was a Major and navigator of 125 BAP. 75 sorties. HSU 10 February 1943. Killed 6 July 1943.

Mikhev, Grigorii Yakovlevich, born 7 January 1919 in Petropavlovsk, Northern Kazakhstan, in a working class family. Completed 10th grade. Army 1937. Krasnodar Military Aviation Institute 1939. To the front in June 1941. By March 1943 was Capt. & flight navigator in 10 ODRAP. 114 sorties. HSU 24 May 1943. CPSU 1943. KIA 5 February 1945.

Miletski, Veniamin Mikhailovich, born 23 October 1918 in Kaskelen, in what was later to be the Alma-Ata Region, in a peasant family. Completed 2 courses at a mining institute. Army 1939. Finnish War 1939-40. Tashkent Military Aerial navigation School 1941. At front from October 1941. CPSU 1942. By March 1945 was Captain & Sqdn navigator in 373 BAP. 305 sorties. HSU 18 August 1945. Released from service 1945.

Miroshnichenko, Nikolai Prokof'evich, born 20 October 1920 in Petrovsk, Stavropol Region, in a Ukrainian working-class family. Grew up in Kirgizia, where he completed a construction *technikum* in Frunze and an Aeroclub. Army 1940. Chkalov Flight School 1942. To the front in June 1942. CPSU 1944. By March 1945 Sr Lt & Sqdn Cdr in 34 GBAP. 160 sorties. HSU 29 June 1945. KIA 8 April 1945.

Mirovich, Anatolii Ivanovich, born 19 June 1914 in Kazanka, Nikolaev Region, in a Ukrainian peasant family. Completed an aviation *technikum*. Army 1935. Completed flight school Kharkov Military Aviation Institute and the Advanced Course for Command Staffs at the Engels Military Aviation Institute. At front from June 1941. CPSU 1941. By May 1945 was Captain and Deputy Sqdn Cdr in 98 GORAP. 113 sorties. HSU 29 June 1945. Air Force Academy 1951. Instructor at Air Force Academy 1956-1969, when he retired as a Colonel.

THE PETLYAKOV Pe-2

Mishanov, Nikolai Dmitrievich, born 1 December 1918 in Kurovo, Kalinin Region, in a working class family. 7th grade. Worked as telephone repairman. Army 1939. Voroshilovgrad flight school 1940. At front from June 1941. CPSU 1943. By March 1945 Captain and Deputy Sqdn Cdr in 96 GBAP. 169 sorties, of which 42 were reconnaissance and bombing missions deep in the enemy rear. 38 group and 14 individual air combats. Shot down 2 aircraft. HSU 15 May 1946. After war attended Air Force Academy. Col retired 1965.

Mizinov, Mikhail Petrovich, born 18 November 1918 in Pyatino, Ul'yanovsk Region, in a peasant family. Completed 9th grade. Army 1937. Ckhalov Military Aviation Institute 1940. At front from June 1941. CPSU 1942. By April 1943 was Sr Lt and flight Cdr in 128 BAP. 210 sorties. HSU 24 August 1943. Higher Air Tactics' Course 1949. Air Force Academy 1955. Col retired 1959.

Mordin, Vasilii Aleksandrovich, born in 1918 in Khotevo, Bryansk Region, in a peasant family. Navy 1936. Eisk Naval Aviation Institute. At the front from 1941. CPSU 1942. By November 1942 was Captain in 40 BAP-ChF. 202 sorties. Destroyed 30 trucks, 13 aircraft on the ground, 5 artillery pieces and 4 mortar batteries, a barge and a landing craft. HSU 24 July 1943. After war continued in service. Major, perished 8 July 1949.

Morgunov, Yuri Vasil'evich, born 19 August 1921 in Yasenevo, Moscow Region, in a peasant family. Completed 7th grade and worked as a lathe operator. Studied at an Aeroclub. Army 1940. Chkalov flight school 1942. To front in January 1943. By December 1943 Jr Lt and flight Cdr in 48 GORAP. 98 sorties. HSU 4 February 1944. CPSU 1944. Air Force Academy 1954. Col retired 1976.

Mosienko, Sergei Ivanovich, born 27 July 1921 in Andrevka, Donets Region, in a Ukrainian peasant family. Completed 8th grade and worked as a Young Pioneers leader. Army 1940. Tambov flight school 1942. To the front in March 1943. CPSU 1944. By December 1944 was Sr Lt in 11 ORAP. 131 sorties. HSU 11 August 1945. Air Force Academy 1955. Academic courses in 1970. Became chief of Air Rescue Service Administration. Maj. Gen. retired 1985.

Musatov, Nikolai Aleksevich, born 19 November 1911 in Kamenka, Tula Region, in a peasant family. Completed 2 courses at an industrial construction *technikum*, and worked as an electrical repairman. CPSU 1932. Navy 1933. Eisk Naval Aviation School 1935. Finnish War. At front from June 1941. By May 1945 was Lt Col and Cdr of 13 GBAP-ChF. 247 sorties. HSU 15 May 1946. Air Force Academy 1951. Maj. Gen. retired 1961.

Musinski, Nikolai Stepanovich, born 18 April 1921 in Bol'shoe Vederinkovo, Volga Region, in a woodcutter's family. Completed 2 courses in a Rabfak in Arkhangelsk. Army 1939. Began flight study at Perm flight school, but finished

Pe-2 PILOT BIOGRAPHIES

at Stalingrad flight school in 1940. To the front in June 1941. By April 1942 Lt in 128 BBAP. 103 sorties. 2 air victories. HSU 30 January 1943. Major retired 1956.

Muzhailo, Nikolai Timofevich, born 20 April 1918 in Ozyora, Poltava Region, in a Ukrainian peasant family. Completed a pedagogical institute in1939 and worked briefly as a teacher. Army in 1939. Aerial gunner-radio operator school in 1940. To front in 1941. CPSU 1942. By May 1945 was Lt & chief of signals in a squadron of the 8 GBAP. 332 sorties. He and his crew shot down 10 enemy fighters. HSU 15 May 1946. Major released from service 1946.

Myasnikov, Evgenii Aleksandrovich, born 25 May 1920 in Vyazovka, Saratov Region, in a peasant family. 10th grade. Army 1939. Balashov flight school 1941. To the front February 1943. CPSU 1943. By May 1945 was Sr Lt & Sqdn Cdr in 449 BAP. 300 sorties. ASU 18 August 1945. Air Force Academy 1954. Col retired 1960.

Naneishvili, Vladimir Vardenovich, born 28 February 1903 at Rioni, Georgia, in a Georgian white-collar family. Completed a humanities *technikum*. Army 1925. Leningrad Military-Theoretical School for Aviators 1926. Kacha flight school1928. Finnish war 1939-40 as Col commander of 18 SBA Bde. Under his leadership unit flew 1,247 sorties. HSU 21 March 1940. At front from June 1941. Commanded an Air Division and later an air corps. Colonel General from 1944. General Staff Academy 1949. Retired from 1957. Worked as Chief of Administration of GVF of Georgia.

Naumov, Vasilii Nikolaevich, born 4 July 1917 in Slin'kovo, Yaroslavl, in a peasant family. Completed an auto-mechanisation *technikum*. Army 1938. Melitopol' Military Aviation Institute 1940. To the front in December 1941. CPSU 1942. By February 1944 was Sr Lt and Sqdn navigator in 367 BAP. 204 sorties. HSU 13 April 1944. Major retired 1957.

Navrotski, Mikhail Aleksevich, born 3 July 1911 in Chapaevka, Zaporozh'e Region, in Ukrainian peasant family. Primary education and an FZU, and worked as a metalworker. Army 1933. Course for signals officers 1938. Kharkov flight school 1939. At front from June1941 as Lieutenant and aircraft navigator in 132 SBAP. In July 1941 destroyed a bridge across the Dnestr delaying the enemy attack. He accomplished this feat even though the aircraft had been damaged by flak. HSU 27 March 1942. CPSU 1943. Captain retired 1954.

Nemkov, Ivan Andrevich, born 15 March 1914 in Bol'ahaya Boyovka, Orel Region, in a peasant family. Navy 1935. Eisk Naval flight school. Finnish War 1939-40. To the front in May 1942. By May 1943 was Sr Lt & flight Cdr in 15 ORAP-KBF, and Candidate CPSU. 101 sorties. KIA 3 May 1943. HSU 24 July 1943.

THE PETLYAKOV Pe-2

Nikolaenko, Nikolai Mefodievich,[4] born 28 June 1917 in Pologi-Verguny, Kiev Region, in a Ukrainian peasant family. Completed secondary school and two years at an industrial *technikum*. He worked as a welder. Army in 1938. Completed school for aviation specialists in 1939 and flew 35 bombing sorties in Finnish war. At front from June 1941. Soon after start of war, his crew was re-assigned from a bomber to a reconnaissance regiment. CPSU 19942. By June 1944 was a Senior Lieutenant and head of signals in the 50 ORAP (2 VA). 243 sorties, including 12 bombing missions. Shot down 1 aircraft. HSU 26 October 1944. By end of the war had flown more than 300 sorties. Retired as major 1960.

Nikolaenko, Vladimir Mironovich, born 2 May 1920 in Tereshki, Poltava Region, in a Ukrainian railroad worker's family. Completed a transportation *technikum* and an Aeroclub in Poltava. CPSU 1939. Army 1939. Taganrog flight school 1941. To the front in May 1942. By the end of 1943 was Jr. Lt. in 98 GORAP. 90 sorties. On 17 January 1944 was killed in an air battle against 6 enemy fighters. HSU 13 April 1944.

Nikolaev, Georgii Georgievich, born 3 March 1919 in Sotino, Tula Region, in a peasant family. Completed a pedagogical *technikum* and worked as a teacher. Army 1937. Engels Military Aviation Institute 1941. To the front in September 1941. CPSU 1941. By February 1942 was Jr lt & flight Cdr in 288 BBAP. 46 sorties. Destroyed 4 tanks, 75 trucks, and silenced a flak battery. HSU 6 June 1942. KIA over the Kuban 2 June 1943.

Nikulin, Dmitri Egorovich, born 19 September 1914 in Shchyokino, Kirov Region, in a peasant family. Completed a village school and worked on a collective farm, and then at the local MTS. Army 1936. Completed a course for Junior Lieutenants. CPSU 1941. At front from June 1941. By June 1944 was Sr Lt and Chief of Signals of 99 GORAP. 137 sorties, of which 30 bombing and 107 reconnaissance. HSU 19 August 1944. KIA 10 October 1944.

Novikov, Aleksandr Alekseevich, born 23 April 1907 in Belovodsk, Lugansk Region, in a peasant family. 6th grade. Army 1929. Kacha flight school 1931. CPSU 1932. To the front in May 1943. Was Col & Cdr 854 BAP (162 GBAP from 5 February 1944). By May 1945 120 sorties. HSU 27 June 1945. Retired 1957.

Novikov, Gennadii Ivanovich, born 20 January 1915 in Taiga Poselyok, Kemerovo Region, in a railway worker's family. Completed 7th, an FZU, and an Aeroclub. Worked as a locomotive machinist. Army 1938. CPSU 1939. Novosibirsk flight school 1940. To the front in October 1942. By April 1945 was Captain and Sqdn Cdr in 82 GBAP. 97 sorties, of which 80 were dive-bombing missions. 17 air combats. 3 shared aerial victories. HSU 27 June 1945. Higher Air tactics course 1945. Major, released from service 1946.

Pe-2 PILOT BIOGRAPHIES

Nurpeisov, Plis Kol'rel'dievich, born in 1919 in Takhtakupyr Aulkarakalpak ASSR, Uzbekistan, in a Kazakh peasant family. Completed a course at a *technikum* and worked as a teacher. Army 1939. Melitopol' Military Aviation Institute. To the front in December 1943. Was Sr Lt and Komsomolist. Air observer in 47 GORAP. 100 sorties of long-range reconnaissance, including 10 missions over Berlin. MIA after a sortie over Berlin on 23 April 1945. HSU 18 August 1945.

Onishchenko, Viktor Pavlovich, born 30 December 1921 in Kozeletsk, Chernigov Region, in a Ukrainian white-collar family. 10th grade. Army 1940. Chkalov Aviators school 1941. To the front in November 1942. CPSU 1943. By June 1944 was Sr Lt and flight navigator in 134 GBAP. 185 sorties. HSU 29 June 1945. Krasnodar officers' higher navigation school 1947. Air Force Academy 1954. Col retired 1972.

Oprokidnev, Boris Konstantinovich, born 5 October 1921 in Tyumen, in a white-collar family. Lived in Sverdlovsk from 1932. 10th grade. Studied at a mining institute. Army 1939. Completed a Military Aviation Institute. To the front November 1941. CPSU 1944. By August 1944 was Sr Lt in 511 ORAP. 140 sorties. KIA 2 April 1945. HSU 15 May 1946.

Orlov, Mikhail Yakovlevich, born 21 May 1916 in Golubinka Farmstead, Rostov Region, in a peasant family. Completed a mining *technikum*. Army 1937. Kharkov Military Aviation Institute for Navigators 1940. At front from June 1941. CPSU 1942. By April 1945 was Captain & Sqdn navigator in 336 BAP. (4 GBAD-18 VA). 408 sorties. HSU 15 May 1946. Major retired 1955.

Orlov, Vitalii Ivanovich, born 15 April 1923 in Belye Berega, Bryansk Region, in a white-collar family. Completed middle school. Army 1941. Kacha flight school 1942. To the front September 1943. By April 1945 was Sr Lt & flight Cdr in 98 GORAP. 210 sorties, many of them escorting artillery spotter aircraft. 19 air combats. 4 air victories. HSU 31 May 1945. CPSU 1946. Air Force Academy 1956. Col retired 1965.

Orlov, Yakov Nikiforovich, born 25 November 1917 in Nesterovka, Novosibirsk Region, in a Ukrainian peasant family. Completed 7th grade and worked as an electrical metals worker in the mine at Karaganda. Army 1940. Tambov flight school 1942. To the front in 1943. CPSU 1944. By November 1944 was Sr Lt & flight Cdr in 11 ORAP. 154 sorties. HSU 23 February 1945. Higher air Tactics course 1952. Major retired 1957.

Ostaev, Aleksei Egorovich, born 15 December 1905 in Sokhta, south Ossetia, in an Ossetian peasant family. Completed middle school. Worked as metalworker on railway. Army 1930. CPSU 1931. Flight school 1933. During Finnish War was a Senior Lt in 58 SBAP. By March 1940, 30 sorties. Was shot down on

THE PETLYAKOV Pe-2

19 February 1940, but was able to avoid capture and returned to his own airfield. HSU 21 March 1940. To the front in June 1941. Rose to rank of major & Deputy Sqdn Cdr. KIA 1 July 1942.

Palin, Fyodor Prokof'evich, born 5 June 1916 in Kobrinovo, Cherkass Region, in a Ukrainian peasant family. Completed an agronomics *technikum*. Army 1935. Kacha flight school 1937. At front from June 1941. CPSU 1943. By April 1945 was Major & Cdr 135 GBAP. 168 sorties. HSU 19 April 1945. Officers' Higher Air Tactics Course 1947. Advanced academic courses through the General Staff Academy 1958. Maj. Gen. retired 1961.

Panin, Boris Vladimirovich, born 30 December 1920 in Nizhni Novgorod in a working-class family. Completed 9th grade and worked as a metalworker. Army 1940. Engels Flight School 1941. To an active unit October 1942. Candidate CPSU. By August 1943 Jr Lt & flight Cdr in 82 GBAP. 57 sorties. Crew scored 3 victories. KIA in air battle 4 August 1943. HSU 2 September 1943.

Parshin, Fyodor Ignat'evich, born 27 September 1915 in Nizhnechirskaya Stanitsa, Tsaritsyn Region, in a peasant family. Balashov GVF flight school 1937. Worked as a civil pilot at Krasnodar. Army 1940. At front from June 1941. CPSU 1942. By July 1944 was Captain & Sqdn Cdr in 128 BAP. 210 sorties. 2 individual air victories. HSU 26 October 1944. Lt Col retired 1950.

Pasynkov, Grigorii Vasil'evich, born 19 September 1922 in Ardon, Northern Ossetia, in a working-class family. Completed grade and the Ordzhonikidze Aeroclub. Navy 1940. Eisk Naval Aviation Academy 19941. To front in 1941. CPSU 1943. By February 1944 was Lt and Deputy Sqdn Cdr in 12 GPBAP-KBF. 96 sorties. HSU 31 May 1944. Naval Academy 1956. Col retired 1959.

Pavlov, Mikhail Nikitovich, born in 1919 in Lipovets, Orel Region, in a peasant family. Completed 7th grade and worked on a collective farm. Army 1939. Krasnodar Military Aviation Institute for Navigators 1940. At front from June 1941. CPSU 1943. Jr Lt & Sqdn navigator in 128 BAP. 213 sorties. KIA 6 October 1943. HSU 13 April 1944.

Pavlov, Nikolai Dmitrievich, born 11 October 1916 in Beryozovka, Saratov Region, in a peasant family. Completed 7th grade and a railway institute. Worked on the railway. Army 1939. School for junior aviation specialists 1940. Participated in Finnish War. To front in 1941. CPSU 1943. By July 1944 was Jr Lt & Flag-Air gunner-radio operator in 4 GBAD. 4 individual and 6 shared air victories. HSU 26 October 1944. Military Air Transport Academy 1952. Col retired 1964.

Peregudov, Aleksei Ivanovich, born 12 March 1913 in Prigorodnyi, Ryazan Region, in a peasant family. Completed 7th grade and a professional technical

Pe-2 PILOT BIOGRAPHIES

school. Worked as a lathe operator in a Moscow factory, and later worked on a state farm. Army 1935. Completed a school for aircraft mechanics, and then a school for aircrew. CPSU 1939. Finnish War 1939. At the front from October 1941.Captain & sqdn navigator in 34 GBAP. 220 sorties. KIA 30 September 1943 when aircraft shot down & pilot crashed it into enemy artillery battery. HSU 4 February 1944.

Pivnyuk, Nikolai Vladimirovich, born 5 September 1917 in Nikolaev, in a Ukrainian working-class family. Completed 10th grade. Army 1936. Kacha flight school 1938. At the front from August 1941. CPSU 1942. By April 1942 Sr Lt & flight Cdr in 128 BBAP. 97 sorties. HSU 30 January 1943. Officers' Higher Aviation School 1944. Grodnensk Military Aviation Institute 1946. Lt Col retired 1958.

Plashkin, Boris Iosifovich, born 20 October 1917 in Petrograd in a working-class family. Completed middle school. Army 1935. Leningrad Military Electro-technical Institute 1938. Kharkov Military Aviation Institute 1939. Finnish War 1939-40.At the front from 1941. Sr Lt bombardier/gunner in 514 BAP. Candidate CPSU. 157 sorties. KIA in air battle 15 March 1942. HSU 21 July 1942.

Plotnikov, Pavel Artem'evich, born 4 March 1920 in Gon'ba in a peasant family. Completed middle school and worked as a metalworker. Army 1938. Novosibirsk flight school 1940. To the front in October 1941. By May 1944 was Sr Lt & Deputy Sqdn Cdr in 82 GBAP. 225 sorties. 3 air victories. HSU 19 August 1944. Promoted to Captain. Became Sqdn Cdr. CPSU 1944. By March 1945 additional 80 sorties. Second HSU 27 June 1945. Officers' Higher Air Tactics Course 1945. Air Force Academy 1951. General Staff Academy 1960. Honoured Military Aviator of the USSR. Maj. Gen. retired 1975.

Podkolodov, Viktor Gavrilovich, born 18 January 1918 on Malaya Ershovka Farmstead, Tsaritsyn Region, in a Ukrainian peasant family. Completed secondary school. Army 1936. Stalingrad Military Aviation Institute for Pilots 1939. To the front in June 1941. ÜPSU 1942. By June 1943 was Captain & Deputy Sqdn Cdr in72 RAP. 119 sorties. 1 victory. HSU 8 September 1943. KIA in air battle 9 July 1944.

Pogorelov, Vasilii Parfir'evich, born 18 August 1919 in Novospasovka, Rostov Region, in a Ukrainian peasant family. Completed middle school and worked as a miner. Army 1938. Voroshilovgrad flight school 1940. To the front in August 1941. CPSU 1941. By January 1942 was Sr Lt & dep. Cdr of 240 ORAE (NW Front). 119 sorties. HSU 21 July 1942. Killed 10 March 1943.

Pokolodnyi, Vasilii Dmitrievich, born 21 July 1916 in Filippovka, Kharkov Region, in a Ukrainian working-class family. Completed 7th grade & FZU. Worked as a metal assembly worker. Army 1934. Flight school1937. CPSU 1939.

THE PETLYAKOV Pe-2

Finnish war 1939-40. At front from June 1941. By beginning of 1942 Sr Lt & flight Cdr in 24 BBAP (61 SAD). 102 sorties. 1 air victory. 22 March 1942 shot down over Bryansk and made forced landing. Was killed while trying to cross the lines back to friendly territory. HSU 14 February 1943.

Polbin, Ivan Semyonovich, born 27 January 1905 in Rtishchevo-Kamenka, Simbirsk Region, in a peasant family. Completed primary school and became a railway worker. CPSU 1927. Army 1927. Orenburg flight school 1931. 1939 was Lt Col & commander of 150 SAP at Khalkin Gol. To front in July 1941. By August 1942 107 sorties. HSU 23 November 1942. Maj. Gen. & Cdr of 6 GBAK. By February 1945 157 sorties. KIA in an air battle over Breslau 11 February 1945.

Polevoi, Ivan Stepanovich, born 7 January 1907 in Nikolaevka, Nikolaev Region, in a Ukrainian peasant family. 6th grade. Army 1929. CPSU 1932. Flight school 1936. At front from June 1941. By August 1944 was Major & deputy Cdr of 132 BAP. 125 sorties. Killed 20 August 1944. HSU 23 February 1945.

Pomazunov, Aleksandr Ivanovich, born 25 August 1915 in Verkhnii Saltov, Kharkov Region, in a Ukrainian peasant family. Completed 3 courses at the Kharkov pedagogical institute. Army 1936. Eisk Naval Aviation school for aviators and air observers 1937. Khalkin Gol 1939. Advanced Course for Command Staffs 1940. At front from June 1941. CPSU 1944. By May 1945 was Major & senior navigator 1 GBAD. 136 sorties. HSU 27 June 1945; retired 1946.

Popov, Anatoli Fyodorovich, born 26 December 1917 in Perm, in a working-class family. Secondary school. Army 1936. Chkalov Military Aviation Academy in 1940, and the Ryazan' advanced navigators' school in 1941. At front from October 1941. CPSU 1942. By Oct. 1943 Capt. and deputy Sqdn Cdr of 47 GRAP. 80 sorties. HSU 4 February 1944. Air Force Academy in 1952. General Staff Academy in 1959. Colonel retired 1970.

Pozdnyakov, Aleksei Petrovich, born 24 March 1918 in Ekaterinodar in a working-class family. Completed secondary school. Army 1937. Melitopol Military Aviation Institute 1940. To front in 1941. By December 1941 was Lt & sqdn navigator in 125 BAP (1 SAD). 74 sorties. CPSU 1942. HSU 10 February 1943. Borisoglebsk Military Aviation Institute 1945. Col retired 1961.

Pstygo, Ivan Ivanovich,[5] born 10 April 10 1918 in Sukhopoly, Bashkir ASSR, in a Belorussian peasant family. He completed middle school, and in 1936 joined the military. In 1940 he completed the Engels Military Aviation Academy. On the first day of the war, he was a Lt commanding a Zveno of the 211 BBAP, equipped with the Su-2. He flew his first mission on the first day of the war. He joined the Communist Party that same year. Later he commanded a squadron, and still later a regiment of Shturmovik. He flew 96 missions. He graduated from the General Staff

Pe-2 PILOT BIOGRAPHIES

Academy in 1957, and later commanded an aviation division, a corps, and then an air army. In 1967 he became deputy commander of the air force for preparedness. In 1978 he was assigned to the minister of defence. He was awarded the HSU on 7 April 1978. In 1983 he retired to the General Inspectorate. He received the title Honoured Military Pilot of the USSR.

Pushchin, Mikhail Nikolaevich, born 20 October 1911 in Ekaterinodar, in a working-class family. Completed secondary school. CPSU 1932. Army 1934. Stalingrad flight school 1937. At the front from June 1941. By October 1944 was Captain & flight inspector for flight proficiency in 5 GBAD. 224 sorties. HSU 23 February 1945. Col retired 1954.

Pushkin, Anatoli Ivanovich,[6] born 30 May 1915 in Sukonnikovo, Moscow Region, in a working-class family. Worked as a lathe operator in a Moscow motor pool. He joined the army in 1933 and completed Voroshilovgrad flight school in December 1934. Initially he was assigned to Smushkevich's 40 Aviabrigada at Vitebsk, where he flew with an R-5 Eskadrilya. However, very quickly, in 1935 he was transferred to Smolensk to transition to the new SB bomber. At the start of 1938 Pushkin was reassigned to 12 OSBAE commanded by T.T. Khryukin, which was preparing to send SB crews to aid the Chinese against Japan. In March 1938 Pushkin and the other volunteers flew to Alma Ata. From there they were flown across the mountains in a TB-3 to China. After several days of travel, they found themselves in Lanchow, where they received SB bombers. This SB unit, which also included Chinese crews as well as Russians, flew bombing missions against Japanese shipping, and missions against the Japanese army on the Yangtze. Pushkin flew 20 sorties in China, mostly as Khryukin's right wingman, though he also led at least one mission, which turned into a disaster. He was to lead a flight of 5 SBs, the other 4 of which had Chinese crews. On take off one aircraft nosed-over on the ground, a second aborted the mission because of engine trouble, and a third because the landing gear would not retract. Pushkin and one wingman continued until they were intercepted by Japanese A5Ms. Pushkin's aircraft was shot down and he made a forced landing, while the Chinese pilot turned and fled back to base to report Pushkin's death, prematurely as it happened. The 'dead' Pushkin and his crew returned to the regiment several days later.

Upon his return to Russia in August 1938 Pushkin was assigned as inspector for flight skills of the 31 SBAP. With this regiment he flew against no opposition during the brief Polish campaign of September 1939. Then, in December 1939, his regiment was sent to strengthen the forces committed against Finland. During the war against Finland, Pushkin flew 18 sorties. During 1939 Pushkin joined the Communist Party.

At the end of the campaign Pushkin was sent to the Kharkov military district as the deputy commander of 135 BBAP, newly forming with the Su-2, a large regiment with a full 6 squadrons. During 1940 Pushkin trained the pilots of

THE PETLYAKOV Pe-2

his regiment, and also helped convert the pilots of other regiments, 135 BBAP serving as a de facto operational training unit. In December 1940 he was sent to the Air Force Academy at Monino, to attend a year-long course for training future regiment commanders. Due to the international situation, the course was shortened and accelerated, and Pushkin graduated on 19 June 1941. At the start of the war, he returned to his regiment and flew his first sortie on 5 July. In spite of the intense activity, because of their excellent training, 135 BBAP suffered relatively light losses during the summer 1941 retreat. However, a 6-squadron regiment proved too bulky, and in September, the decision was made to split the regiment into two. This second regiment was designated 52 BBAP, and Pushkin was appointed commander from 1 October 1941. They flew on the Southwestern and Southern Fronts as part of 76 SAD until March 1942, when the regiment was ordered to hand over its surviving aircraft to other units, and to return to Molotov (Perm) in the Volga MD to receive new aircraft. On 15 May 1942, 52 BBAP returned to the Southwestern Front with an up-engined version of the Su-2. On 12 August 1942 Pushkin was awarded the HSU, and a few days later was re-assigned as deputy commander of the newly organising 270 BAD a component of 8 Air Army of the Stalingrad Front. In January, after the conclusion of the battle of Stalingrad, Pushkin was sent to Orenburg for a six-month course for future division commanders, returning to 270 BAD in July. In February 1944 he was promoted to colonel and assigned as commander of 188 BAD, which was forming in the Moscow MD as a new formation. After months of training and waiting in reserve, 188 BAD was assigned to 15 VA in August 1944 for the Riga offensive. Pushkin and his division remained in action for the rest of the war. Pushkin flew a total of 120 sorties from July 1941, 22 of them in the Pe-2 and the rest in the Su-2. Pushkin's Su-2, from March 1942 was an M-82 powered version, No. 19116, camouflaged in light green and dark earth-gray. On the tail fin was a small white lightning flash and, on the rudder, the white number 100. Beneath the cockpit, in red letters outlined in white was the inscription *Podarok frontu ot trudyashchikhsya Stalinskogo r-na g. Molotova* (A gift to the front from the workers of the Stalin District of the City of Molotov).

After the war Pushkin led his division back to Georgia where it was to be based near Tbilisi. During the post-war years, the division converted first to the Tu-2 and then to the Il-28. In 1954 Pushkin graduated from the General Staff Academy and held a series of command positions before retiring as Lieutenant General in 1975.

Pyrkov, Yurii Ivanovich, born 5 October 1923 in Balakovo, Saratov Region, in a working-class family. Completed 9th grade and an Aeroclub. Army 1941. Engels Flight School 1942. To front in March 943. By May 1945 was Sr Lt & flight Cdr in 134 GBAP. 135 sorties. HSU 29 June 1945. Released from service as invalid 1946. CPSU 1948.

Rakov, Vasilii Ivanovich,[7] born 8 February 1909 in Kuznechkovo, Kalinin Region, in a white-collar family. Completed secondary school and an FZU. Navy 1928.

Pe-2 PILOT BIOGRAPHIES

Leningrad Military-Theoretical Aviators' School 1929. Flight School 1931. CPSU 1932. Finnish War 1939-40, was Major & sqdn Cdr of 57 SBAP-KBF. HSU 7 February 1940. Graduated from Naval Academy 1942. Lt Col, he commanded an aviation brigade of the Black Sea Fleet. Was wounded during the last days of the defence of Sevastopol. Later flew with 13 BAP and then 73 BAP-KBF (12 GBAP from 31 May 1943). In January 1944, he was assigned as Deputy Commander of 9 ShAD-KBF. By July 1944 68 sorties. In early July 1944 was returned to 12 GPBAP as regiment commander. Second HSU 22 July 1944, after raid on the German cruiser *Niobe*. In January 1945 was withdrawn from combat and ordered to the General Staff Academy, which he completed in 1946. Doctor of Naval Science 1967. Taught at Naval Academy until 1971. Maj. Gen. retired 1971.

Reshidov, Abdraim Izmailovich, born 8 March 1912 in Mamashai. Crimea, in a Crimean Tatar working-class family. Completed 5th grade and worked on a collective farm. Completed Osoaviakhim flight school. Army 1933. Odessa flight school 1934. CPSU 1939. At front from June 1941. By February 1945 was Major & deputy Cdr 162 GBAP. 166 sorties. Crew scored 8 air victories. HSU 27 June 1945. Officers' advanced air tactics course 1949. As Col retired 1958.

Rolin, Nikolai Mikhailovich, born 27 October 1914 in Pol-Uspen'e, Orel Region, in a white-collar family. Completed a teaching institute in Kursk in 1938, and worked as a teacher and a director of a middle school. Army 1939. Kharkov Military Aviation Institute 1941. To the front in October 1941. CPSU 1944. By March 1945 was Sr Lt & sqdn navigator in 34 GBAP. 175 sorties. HSU 29 June 1945. Major retired 1955.

Romanov, Evgenii Pavlovich, born 5 April 1920 in Vyksa, Gorkii Region, in a white-collar family. Completed secondary school. Army 1939. Kharkov Military Aviation Institute 1940. Krasnodar unified Military Aviation Institute 1941. Advanced course for command staffs 1942, and another Military Aviation Institute in 1943. To the front in March 1943. CPSU 1945. By the end of March 1945 was Sr Lt & senior air observer in 47 GORAP. 88 sorties. HSU 18 August 1945. Col retired 1957.

Rozhkov, Aleksandr Evgen'evich, born 8 June 1914 in Moscow in a white-collar family. Completed secondary school. Navy 1935. Eisk Naval Aviation Institute 1938. At front from 1941. CPSU 1942. By September 1944 was Captain & deputy Sqdn Cdr in 30 RAP-ChF. 224 sorties. Sank a transport and 2 escort ships. Destroyed 4 aircraft. HSU 6 March 1945. Naval Academy 1952. Col retired 1969.

Rud', Nikolai Maksimovich, born 19 December 1922 in Dal'nerechensk, Primorskaya Region, in a white-collar family. Secondary school. Army 1940. Chkalov flight school 1941. To the front in June 1942. CPSU 1943. By August 1944 Lt in 745 BAP. 190 sorties. HSU 16 October 1944. Captain retired 1953.

THE PETLYAKOV Pe-2

Rudenko, Andrei Avksent'evich, born, 16 December 1918 in Ekaterinburg, in a Ukrainian working class family. Completed 9th grade. Army 1936. Chkalov flight school 1938. To front in June 1941. By October 1944 was Capt. & flight Cdr. in 164 GORAP. 262 sorties. HSU 23 February 1945. CPSU 1949. Central Air Tactics Course 1956. Col. retired 1960.

Ruzhin, Vladimir Mikhailovich, born 28 July 1919 in Khlystunovka, Cherkass Region, in a Ukrainian peasant family. Completed 8th grade and worked as a rural film projectionist. Army 1938. Voroshilovgrad flight school 1041. To front in September 1941. CPSU 1944. By January 1945 was Sr Lt & deputy Sqdn Cdr in 367 BAP. 202 sorties. HSU 18 August 1945. KIA 26 July 1945.

Saevich, Timofei Aleksandrovich, born 23 February 1919 in Sukhopol', in the future Bashkir ASSR, in a Belorussian peasant family. Completed 9th grade. Army 1936-1948. Rejoined army 1940 and completed Engels flight school in 1942. To front in March 1943. CPSU 1943. By September 1944 was Capt. & flight Cdr in 11 ORAP. 157 sorties. HSU 23 February 1945. Officers' advanced course 1949. Col retired 1964.

Samochkhin, Anatolii Vasil'evich, born 1 May 1914 in Buinsk, in the later Tatar ASSR, in a working class family. Completed 9th grade and FZU. Ul'yanovsk School for flight instructors 1939 then worked as instructor for Aeroclub. Army 1941. To front in September 1941. CPSU 1941. By January 1942 was Lt. in 289 BBAP (63 SAD). 115 sorties. HSU 27 March 1942. Air Force Academy 1946. Lt. Col. retired 1961.

Samochkhin, Nikolai Ermolaevich, born 1 October 1913 in Granitnoe, Donets Region, in a peasant family. Completed middle school. Army 1934. Military flight school 1936. Finnish War. At front from June 1941. CPSU 1942. By May 1943 was Captain & flight Cdr in 11 ORAP. 171 sorties. HSU 2 September 1943. Captain retired 1947.

Sandalov, Vladimir Aleksandrovich, born 26 January 1906 in Saint Petersburg in a white-collar family. Completed 9th grade and a Communist Party school. Worked for a distinct Komosmol committee. Army 1926. Leningrad Military-Theoretical School for Pilots 1927. CPSU 1928. Orenburg flight school 1929. Higher advanced course for command staffs 1939. Finnish War 1939-40. At front from June 1941. Lt Col & Cdr of 125 SBAP. By November 1941 47 sorties. HSU 6 June 1942. General staff academy 1952. Maj. Gen. retired 1959.

Sapozhnikov, Mikhail Aleksandrovich, born 23 November 1920 in VerkhnyayaTura, Sverdlovsk Region, in a working-class family. Completed 7th grade and an Aeroclub. Worked as metalworker at the Cheboksarai automotive factory. Army 1940. Engels flight school 1941. To front in October 1941.

Pe-2 PILOT BIOGRAPHIES

CPSU 1942. On 16 September 1942 was shot down and captured, but managed to escape and return to his regiment. By November 1943 was Jr Lt in 48 GORAP. 113 sorties. HSU 4 February 1944. Higher air tactic course 1951. Col retired 1960.

Saranchyov, Nikolai Georgievich, born 11 November 1906 in Yalta, in a working-class family. Completed middle school. Worked as a viti-culturalist on a state farm. Army 1926. Kacha Flight School. During Finnish War was Captain & sqdn Cdr in 35 SBAP. 10 sorties. HSU 19 January 1940. During SWW was test pilot. Lt Col killed during a combat assignment 4 January 1944.

Savoshchev, Ivan Ivanovich, born 1 December 1913 in Afanas'evo, Tula Region, in a working-class family. Completed 8th grade and an FZU, and worked as a metalworker. Army 1935. Melitopol Military Aviation Institute 1940. To the front in September 1941. CPSU 1943. By February 1944 was Major & Regtl navigator in 8 ORAP. 140 sorties. HSU 1 July 1944. Krasnodar higher navigators' school 1947. Higher air tactics course 1953. Lt Col retired 1961.

Seleznyov, Pyotr Ivanovich, born 15 May 1920 in Myshkovo, Smolensk Region, in a peasant family. Completed 3 courses at a *Technikum*. Army 1938. Melitopol Military Aviation Institute 1940. At front from June 1941. CSPU 1944. By June 1944 was Captain & sqdn navigator in 118 RAP-SF. 173 sorties. 1 air victory. His observations led to the sinking g of 20 transports and 35 warships. HSU 22 July 1944. Air Force Academy 1953. Col retired 1956.

Seliverstov, Fyodor Petrovich, born 18 June 1917 in Kulikovka, Saratov Region, in a peasant family. Completed a pedagogical institute and worked as a teacher. Army 1939. Balashov flight school 1940. At the front from June 1941. CPSU 1943. By August 1944 was Captain & Deputy Sqdn Cdr in 10 ORAP. 157 sorties. HSU 23 February 1945. Col retired 1958.

Semak, Pavel Ivanovich, born 16 August 1913 in Petrovka, Chernigov Region, in a Ukrainian peasant family. Completed 7th grade. Worked as a shift foreman for a printing shop. Army 1935. Flight school 1937. Finnish War 1939-40. To the front in June 1941. CPSU 1943. By September 1944 was a Captain & Sqdn Cdr in 4 GBAP. 186 sorties. Destroyed 11 aircraft on the ground and in the air. HSU 23 February 1945. Col retired 1954.

Sen'kov, Tit Grigor'evich, born 2 April 1917 in Starokozhevka, Mogilev Region, in a Belorussian peasant family. Completed a livestock *technikum*. Army 1937. Krasnodar Military Aviation Institute 1940. To front in June 1941. CPSU 1943. By June 1944, was Captain & Sqdn navigator in 81 GBAP. 123 sorties. HSU 26 June 1944. Higher Officers' Aviation School 1948. Advanced Course for Staff Officers 1954. Air Force Academy 1958. Col retired 1960.

THE PETLYAKOV Pe-2

Serbin, Fyodor Petrovich, born 13 July 1919 in Vechorki, Poltava Region, in a Ukrainian peasant family. He completed a veterinary *technikum* and worked as a veterinarian until entering the army in 1939. In 1940 he completed the Khar'kov Military Aviation Academy. He was at the front from June 1941. By the end of the war he was a Guards Senior Lieutenant and a Squadron Navigator of the 80 GBAP. He flew 186 missions, and in 28 air battles he shot down 3 enemy aircraft individually, and shared 2 more with his unit. He was awarded the HSU on 27 June 1945. In 1953 he graduated from the Military-Political Academy. He remained in service until 1961 when he retired with the rank of Colonel.

Sergenkov, Nikolai Semyonovich, born 8 May 1916 in Upino, Smolensk Region, in a peasant family. Completed an Agronomics *Technikum* and worked as an agronomist. Army 1938. Melitopol Military Aviation Institute 1940. To front in June 1941. CPSU 1942. By 1943 was Captain & sqdn navigator in 99 GORAP. During the period of the battle of Kursk, and the period of preparation, photographed 626 km^2 of enemy-occupied territory. HSU 2 September 1943. KIA in air battle 28 February 1944.

Sergev, Vsevolod Pavlovich, born 5 May 1917 in Rodnichol, Saratov Region, in a peasant family. Completed 8th grade and an FZU, and worked as metalworker while studying at an Aeroclub. Army 1938. Engels Military Aviation Institute 1940. To front in November 1942. By the end of November 1943 was Lt and Flight Cdr in 48 GORAP. 98 sorties. HSU 4 February 1944. CPSU 1944. Advanced air tactics course of officers in 1951. Col retired 1960.

Shapovalov, Aleksandr Timofevich, born 9 November 1916 in Uspenka, Lipetsk Region, in a peasant family. Completed 8th grade and an FZU. Army 1938. Completed school for junior aviation specialists. To front from June 1941. CPSU 1942. By February 1942 was Starshina and Sqdn. signals chief in 36 GBAP. 182 sorties. 3 air victories. HSU 1 July 1944. Engels Military Aviation Institute for Pilots 1947. Advanced course for officers 1952. Major retired 1961.

Shcheglov, Stepan Stepanovich, born 22 July 1914 in Kurilovka, Saratov Region, in a peasant family. Completed 5th grade and an FZU. Army 1932. Junior aviation specialist school 1933. Navigators' course 1938. Finnish War 1939-40. At front from June 1941. CPSU 1942. By May 1945 was Captain & sqdn navigator in 128 BAP. 173 sorties. HSU 15 May 1946. Retired 1953.

Shcherbina, Nikolai Semyonovich, born 23 January 1920 in Debal'tsevo, Donets Region, in a Ukrainian working-class family. Completed 7th grade and an FZU. Then worked as a pattern maker for a mine. Army 1939. Boroshilovgrad flight school 1940. At front from June 1941. CPSU 1943. Completed an advanced course for commanders in 1944. By September 1944 was Sr Lt and Deputy Sqdn Cdr in 36 GBAP. 169 sorties. HSU 23 February 1945. Higher officers' air tactics course 1953. Lt Col retired 1969.

Pe-2 PILOT BIOGRAPHIES

Shein, Pavel Stepanovich, born 18 June 1921 in Druzhino, Saratov Region, in a peasant family. Secondary education. Navy 1939. Completed Naval Aviation Institute. At the front from August 1941. CPSU 1942. By mid-September 1943 Jr Lt navigator-radio operator in 28 RAE (118 RAP-SF), 105 sorties. HSU 22 January 1944. KIA 16 May 1944.

Shevkunov, Anatolii Konstantinovich, born 19 June 1921 in Maikop, Krasnodar Region, in a working-class family. Completed two courses at the Krasnodar medical institute, and an Aeroclub. Army 1939. Taganrog flight school 1941. To the front in February 1943. By September 1943 was Lt & Flight Cdr in 449 BAP. 142 sorties, of which 134 were at night. Scored 2 air victories. CPSU late 1943. HSU 1 July 1944. Capt. released from service 1946.

Shumeiko, Avksenti Andrevich, born 1 January 1908 in Stertenka, Primor'e Region of the Far East, in a Ukrainian peasant family. Educated in a village school. From 1919-1922 was a member of a partisan detachment, and fought in the civil war. After the civil war, he worked for the Cheka and furthered his education in a Workers' Faculty. Also worked as a miner and as a lathe operator. Army 1929-1935. Took part in the fighting over the Far Eastern railway line in north-western China in 1929. CPSU 1931. Eisk flight school 1933. After discharge worked as civil aviation pilot. Recalled to military in 1941. At front from June 1941. By June 1944 was Major & deputy Cdr of 12 BAP. On 9 June 1944 he distinguished himself while bombing enemy troop concentrations on the Karelian Isthmus. KIA 10 June 1944. HSU 2 August 1944.

Sirenko, Ivan Lavrent'evich, born 25 March 1910 in Parafevka, in the future Bashkir ASSR, in a Ukrainian peasant family. Completed 7th grade. Worked as a blacksmith in a locomotive factory. Army 1931. CPSU 1932. Vol'sk air mechanics school 1932. Kacha flight school 1937. Finnish War 1939-40. To the front in June 1941. By may 1945 Major & deputy Cdr. of 34 GBAP. 153 sorties. HSU 29 June 1945.Lt. Col. retired 1953.

Sklyarov, Ivan Andrevich, born 10 September 1920 in Grabovo, Kazakhstan, in a Ukrainian working-class family. Completed 7th grade. Worked in the Red Star mine in the Donets region. Army 1938. Voroshilovgrad flight school 1940. To the front in June 1941. By February 1942 was a Lt in the 33 SBAP (19 BAD). 87 sorties. HSU 27 March 1942. CPSU 1942. After war continued in service in the Navy. Col retired 1965.

Skugar', Vladimir Antonovich, born 15 July 1914 in Zhabyki, Mogilev Region, in a Belorussian peasant family. Completed a *Rabfak* and worked in a Moscow factory. Navy 1935. Eisk Naval Aviation Institute 1938. CPSU 1940. At the front from June 1941. By January 1944 was Captain & Deputy Sqdn Cdr in 30 RAP-ChF. 295 sorties. HSU 16 May 1944. Naval Academy 1955. Col retired 1961.

THE PETLYAKOV Pe-2

Slivka, Anton Romanovich, born 9 August 1918 in Podvysokoe, Kirovograd Region, in a Ukrainian peasant family. Completed 7th grade and FZU, and worked in a meat-packing plant. Army 1938. Voroshilovgrad flight school 1940. At front from June 1941. CPSU 1942. By November 1943 was Sr L. & flight Cdr in 118 ODRAE. 173 sorties. HSU 4 February 1944. Air Force Academy 1949. General Staff Academy 1959. Maj. Gen. retired 1975.

Smirnov, Aleksei Pantelevich, born 17 March 1917 in Bykovo, Kalinin Region, in a peasant family. Completed 7th grade and studied at an agricultural mechanisation *technikum* in Leningrad. Army 1936. Orenburg Military Aviation Institute 1940. To the front in June 1941. CPSU 1942. By September 1942 Captain & Sqdn Cdr in 99 BBAP. 207 sorties. HSU 5 November 1942. Air Force Academy 1949. Col retired 1971.

Smirnov, Vladimir Antonovich, born 10 August 1920 in Loshchemlya, Kalinin Region, in a peasant family. Completed 9th grade and worked as a metalworker in a Leningrad factory. Army 1938. Kharkov air navigators' school 1940. To front in April 1942. CPSU 1943. By November 1943 was Captain & sqdn navigator in 72 RAP. 135 sorties. HSU 13 April 1944. KIA 9 July 1944.

Smirnov, Nikolai Fyodorovich, born 22 December 1915 in Kineshma, Ivanovo Region, in a working-class family. Completed an industrial *technikum* and worked as a mechanic's assistant in a linen combine. Army 1936. Voroshilovgrad flight school 1937. Occupation of Eastern Poland and Finnish War. To the front in June 1941. By November 1942 was Sr Lt & flight Cdr in 366 BAP. 300 sorties. HSU 1 May 1943. CPSU 1943. Air Force Academy 1949. General Staff Academy 1956. Later taught at Air Force Academy. Col retired 1970.

Sobkovski, Grigori Platonovich,[8] born 21 June 1921 in Malaya Snetinka, Kiev Region, in a Ukrainian peasant family. Secondary education. Army in 1940. Krasnodar air observers' school in 1942. CPSU in 1944. Went to front in February 1944 as air observer with 16 ODRAP. By February 1945 Senior Lieutenant. 102 sorties. HSU 15 May 1946. Completed party school in 1952. Colonel retired in 1975.

Sokolov, Valentin Petrovich, born 27 December 1915 in Kharkov, in a white-collar family. Completed 7th grade, a *Rabfak*, and an FZU. Worked as a metalworker and later a brigadier in the Kharkov locomotive factory. Army 1936. Eisk naval aviation school 1937. Occupation of eastern Poland 1939. CPSU 1940. Higher navigators' school 1941. At front from June 1941. By May 1945 was Captain & sqdn navigator in 47 GORAP. 194 sorties. HSU 15 May 1946. Col retired 1974.

Solovyov, Mikhail Georgievich, born in November 1923 in Klyuchi, Saratov Region, in a peasant family. Middle school Army June 1941. Engels flight school. To the front in July 1943. CPSU 1944. By June 1944 was Lt in 50 ORAP. 122 sorties. HSU 26 October 1944. KIA 13 November 1944.

Pe-2 PILOT BIOGRAPHIES

Sorokin, Vitalii Andrevich, born 25 November 1921 in Orsk, Orenburg Region, in a white-collar family. Completed 10th grade and an Aeroclub. Army 1940. Chkalov flight school 1941. To the front in May 1943. By March 1945 was Lt & flight Cdr in 24 BAP. 74 sorties. 11 January 1945 – completed a bombing mission even after his bomber was hit by flak and he was seriously wounded, then managed to land his aircraft back at base. HSU 15 May 1946. Sr Lt retired 1946. CPSU 1947.

Starostin, Nikolai Fyodorovich, born 13 September 1920 in Konstantinovski Poselyok, Yaroslavl Region, in a working-class family. Lived in Rybinsk where he completed 10th grade and an Aeroclub. Army 1939. Krasnodar Military Aviation Institute 1940. At the front from June 1941. CPSU 1942. By October 1943 was Sr Lt & Sqdn navigator in 128 BAP. 236 sorties. 1 air victory. HSU 4 February 1944. Killed 7 May 1945.

Stepin, Kuz'ma Ivanovich, born 24 October 1913 in Pogorelovka, Bryansk Region, in a peasant family. Completed a machine-building *technikum* and then worked in a factory. Army 1935. Completed Military Aviation Institute for Airmen and Air Observers 1938. To front in August 1941. CPSU 1943. By September 1943 was Captain & sqdn navigator in 98 GORAP. 85 sorties. HSU 28 September 1943. Krasnodar higher navigators' school. Officers' advanced course through the Air Force Academy 1955. Col retired 1960.

Stol'nikov, Nikolai Maksimovich, born 4 May 1916 in Lozovaya-Pavlovka, Voroshilovgrad Region, in a Ukrainian working-class family. Completed 7th grade and 3 courses at a *Rabfak*. Worked as a lathe operator. Army 1935. Voroshilovgrad flight school 1937. In Finnish war was Lt in 31 SBAP (16 SBAB). Completed 6 sorties and shot down 3 enemy aircraft. HSU 7 April 1940. Flew again during SWW. After war was a regtl cdr and then transferred to test flying. Col retired 1957.

Stratievski, Nathan Borisov, was born 22 December 1920 in Odessa in a Jewish working-class family. He completed a course at the Moscow Electromechanical Institute of Transport Engineers. He entered the army in 1939 and completed a school for junior aviation specialists in1940. He was in action from June 1941 as a bomber crewman. In 1942, he joined the Communist Party. By August 1944 he was a lieutenant and chief of communications for one of the squadrons of 96 GBAP (301 BAD - 3 BAK-16 Air Army). He had completed 232 sorties. He received the HSU on 23 February 1945. After the war Statievski entered the Military Institute of Foreign Languages which he completed in1949. Then he taught English in the Kharkov Military Aviation Institute for Navigators. In 1956 he was released to the retired reserves with the rank of captain.

Strelkov, Vladimir Dmitrievich, born in 1922 in Kineshma, Ivanovo Region, in a working-class family. Completed 10th grade. Army 1940. Kirovabad flight school 1941. To the front in July 1942. CPSU 1943. By May 1945 was Lt and flight Cdr in 82 GBAP. 146 sorties. HSU 29 June 1945. Sr Lt released from service 1946.

THE PETLYAKOV Pe-2

Struzhkin, Ivan Vasil'evich, born 11 April 1914 in Ulkino, Vologda Region, in a peasant family. Studied at a land improvement *technikum* and then worked as an irrigation specialist. Army 1935. Voroshilovgrad flight school 1937. Khalkin Gol. 1939. Finnish War, 1939-40. At the front from 1941. CPSU 1941. By February 1942 was Sr Lt and Deputy Sqdn Cdr in 514 PBAP. 123 sorties. Promoted to captain. Killed 6 April 1942. HSU 21 July 1942.

Sudakov, Vladimir Konstantinovich, born 23 July 1921 in Pochinki, Gor'ki Region, in a peasant family. Completed 10th grade. Army 1940. Completed gunner-radio operator school. At the front from June 1941. CPSU 19942. Completed officers' advanced school. By March 1945 was Captain & deputy Cdr for air gunnery service in 122 GBAP. 182 sorties. 4 individual and 3 shared air victories. HSU 29 June 1945. Air Force Engineering Academy 1952. Became assistant professor. Col retired 1983.

Sugrin, Valentin Vasil'evich, born 4 April 1922 in Vatalino, Vologda Region, in a peasant family. Completed 9th grade. Army 1941. Novosibirsk flight school 1942, and a Military Aviation Institute in Davlekanovo, Bashkir ASSR in 1943. CPSU 1943. To the front in March 1943. By March 1945 was Sr Lt and flight Cdr in 47 GORAP. 108 sorties. HSU 18 August 1945. Air Force Academy 1955. Col retired 1976.

Sukhanov, Mikhail Andrevich, born 5 November 1921 in Novodevich'e Kuibyshev Region, in a peasant family. 10th grade. Navy 1940. Naval Aviation Institute 1943. To front in July 1943. CPSU 1944. By September 1944 was lt & flight navigator in 12 GPBAP-KBF. 100 sorties. HSU 5 November 1944. Air Force Academy 1951. Col retired 1974.

Sulev, Viktor Aleksandrovich, born 3 March 1921 in Rostov-na-Donu in a white-collar family. Completed secondary school and studied at the Bataisk GVF Aviation Institute. Army 1939. Stalingrad Military Aviation Institute 1941. To front in June 1941. CPSU 1944. By end of the war was Sr Lt and flight Cdr in 13 GBAP, 179 sorties. HSU 29 June 1945. Air Force Academy 19954. Col retired 1962.

Suvorov, Rodion Mikhailovich,[9] was born 1 April 1914 in the settlement of Visim, Sverdlovsk Region, in a working-class family. He completed 7th and an FZU and worked as a construction worker at Nizhnyi Tagil. He joined the army in 1939, and completed his basic flight training at the Perm Military Aviation School. In 1940 he graduated from the Engels Military Aviation Academy. He was in action from June 1941 and by May 1944 had risen to the rank of captain, commanding a squadron of 118 RAP-SF. Although in this unit he may have flown a number of different types of aircraft, he was mainly known as a pilot of the Pe-3, the long-range fighter version of the Pe-2 bomber. On 31 May 1944, he was awarded the HSU for the completion of 264 missions over the Arctic wastes and seas. By the end of the war he had flown over 300 sorties. He was credited with having located 800 German

Pe-2 PILOT BIOGRAPHIES

vessels, and destroying 3 trains, 13 tanks and 75 motor vehicles. He shot down 4 German aircraft, though it is uncertain whether all four were personally shot down by Suvorov himself using the Pe-3s forward-firing armament, or whether this total might also include aircraft claimed by his defensive aerial gunners. In 1948 Suvorov retired with the rank of major.

Svirchevski, Vladimir Stepanovich, born 28 January 1920 in Kramatorsk, Donets Region, in a Ukrainian working-class family. Completed secondary school. Worked as a factory technician. Army 1939. Voroshilovgrad flight school 1940. At front from June 1941. ÜPSU 1943. By the summer of 1943 was Sr Lt & flight Cdr in 11 ORAP. 135 sorties. HSU 24 August 1943. Higher air tactics course 1951. Col retired 1959.

Sviridov, Aleksei Andrevich, born 17 April 1919 in Stupishino, Tula Region, in a peasant family. Completed 7th grade and an FZU, and worked as a metalworker at a machine-building plant. Completed an Aeroclub. Army 1938. Engels Military Aviation Institute 1939. To the front in June 1941. CPSU 1942. By October 1943 was Sr Lt & sqdn Cdr in 128 BAP. 205 sorties. 6 October 1943 was wounded by flak while bombing Gomel station and died. HSU 13 April 1944.

Tagil'tsev, Vladimir Mikhailovich, born 2 April 1922 in Biisk, Altai Region, in a working-class family. Completed 8th grade and an Aeroclub. Army 1940. Omsk flight school 1942. To the front in June 1943. By the end of the war Sr Lt & flight Cdr in 161 GBAP. 163 sorties. HSU 27 June 1945. Captain retired 1948.

Tarasevich, Konstantin Mikhailovich, born 17 January 1922 in the village Taras Shevchenko, Chernigov Region, in a Ukrainian peasant family. Completed secondary school. Army 1940. Kharkov air school for airmen and air observers 1941. To front December 1941. CPSU 1942. By March 1945 was Captain & sqdn navigator in 58 BAP. 576 sorties. KIA 22 April 1945. HSU 29 June 1945.

Taryanik, Grigori Aver'yanovich, born 3 January 1913 in Ekaterinoslav, in a Ukrainian working-class family. CPSU 1932. Completed a metallurgical *Rabfak* in 1933. Operated a rolling mill in a Dnepropetrovsk steel factory. Army 1933. Stalingrad flight school 1936. Course for Komissar-aviators 1939. Occupation of Eastern Poland & Finnish War 1939. At the front from June 1941. Squadron Komissar in 260 BBAP. By December 1941 more than 50 sorties. HSU 16 January 1942. Officers' Advanced Course at Air Force Academy 1944. Col retired 1960.

Temnov, Viktor Pakhomovich, born 24 January 1916 in Bogorodskoe, Saratov Region, in a peasant family. Completed 7th grade and an FZU, and worked as a metalworker in Leningrad. Army 1934. Kharkov Military Aviation Institute 1938. Occupation of Eastern Poland and Finnish War. At the front from June 1941. CPSU 1943. By October 1944 was Captain & Sqdn navigator in 164 GORAP. 177 sorties. HSU 23 February 1945. Lt Col retired 1960.

THE PETLYAKOV Pe-2

Terenkov, Nikolai Anastas'evich, born 15 December 1915 in Aleksandrovka, Lipetsk Region, in a peasant family. Completed 2 courses at a railway *technikum*. Army 1934. Tambov Infantry Institute 1938. Fought at Lake Khasan 1938. Chkalov Military Aviation Institute 1940. At the front from June 1941. CPSU 1942. By mid-February, 1944 was Captain & sqdn navigator in 34 GBAP. 207 sorties, of which 47 were at night. HSU 19 August 1944. Completed Officers' air tactics courses 1945 and 1953. Lt Col retired 1960.

Tikhomirov, Il'ya Kuz'mich, born 23 March 1910 in Nikonovo, Kalinin Region, in a peasant family. Completed 7th grade. Army 1932. Air observer school 1937. CPSU 1938. Finnish War 1939-40. Training course for aviation navigators 1941. At the front from June 1941. By February 1942 was Sr Lt and chief of communications in 24 BBAP (61 SAD). 95 sorties. KIA 10 March 1942. HSU 14 February 1943.

Tkachevski, Yuri Matvevich, born 19 June 1920, in Pavlovo, Gorki Region, in a white-collar family. Completed 10th grade. Army 1939. Kharkov Military Aviation Institute 1940. To the front in June 1941. By November 1943 Sr Lt and air observer in 48 GDRAP. 98 sorties. HSU 4 February 1944. CPSU 1944. Released from service 1946.

Tobolenko, Mikhail Nikolaevich, born 5 July 1922 in Azarovka, Smolensk Region, in a peasant family. Completed middle school and an Aeroclub. Army 1940. Tambov flight school 1941. To the front in September 1941. By May 1944 was lt & flight cdr in 15 ORAP-KBF. Candidate CPSU. 188 sorties. HSU 22 July 1944. KIA 7 April 1945.

Tokmakov, Evgenii Petrovich, born 29 September 1916 in Chita in a working-class family. Completed civil aviation flight school 1939. Worked as civil pilot based at Karaganda. Army 1941. To front in June 1942. CPSU 1943. By November 1943 was Captain & Sqdn Cdr in 72 RAP. 129 sorties. HSU 13 April 1944. Major released from service 1946.

Trifonov, Boris Pavlovich, born 28 April 1915 in Nizhni Novgorod, in a working-class family. Completed the Gorki Industrial-economic *technikum*, and worked as a planner at an automotive factory. Army 1934. Kharkov flight school 1937. Occupation of eastern Poland 1939. During Finnish War was a Sr Lt & flight Cdr in 58 SBAP. By February 1940 had flown 45 sorties. HSU 21 March 1940. CPSU 1941. At front from June 1941 as Sqdn Cdr. Lt Col retired 1959.

Trusov, Mikhail Trofimovich,[10] born 15 November 1940 in Beryozovka, Tambov Region, in a peasant family. Completed 5th and was a worker before entering the army in 1929. In 1931 he joined the Communist Party. He completed flight school at Stalingrad in 1933. In 1939, he was a captain

Pe-2 PILOT BIOGRAPHIES

serving as a deputy squadron commander in the 44 SBAP when the war with Finland erupted. By February 1940 he flew 16 combat sorties. On one mission in February one of his squadron's aircraft was hit by flak and force landed on a frozen lake near the front lines. After completing his bombing mission, Trusov landed his own bomber on the ice and rescued the crew. He took off again under fire from Finnish troops and brought his friends to safety. He was awarded the HSU on 21 March 1940. He was again sent to the front in June 1942 after completing the advanced course for command staffs. He was promoted to major and served during the war as a regiment commander. He was released from the service in 1945.

Tsaregorodski, Aleksei Andrianovich, born 3 March 1918 in Il'inka Voronezh Region, in a peasant family. Completed a pedagogical institute taught in a primary school. CPSU 1939. Army 1939. Kharkov Military Air Navigation Institute 1940. At front from June 1941. By March 1945 was Captain & sqdn navigator in 96 GBAP. 176 sorties. HSU 15 May 1946. Released from service 1947.

Tsisel'ski, Mikhail Petrovich, born 20 May 1909 in Stoikovo, Cherkass Region, in a Ukrainian peasant family. Completed middle school and an FZU, and worked as a metalworker in a locomotive repair factory. Army 1932-1938. CPSU 1932. Irkutsk aircraft-mechanic school 1934. Eisk Naval Aviation Institute 1936. Rejoined the military 1939. At front from 1941. By December 1944 was Captain and backup sqdn navigator in 12 GPBAP-KBF. 296 sorties. HSU 6 March 1945. Major retired 1948.

Tsurtsumiya, Aleksandr Pekhuvich, born in 11908 in Golaskuri, Georgia, in a Georgian peasant family. Completed middle school. Army 1929. Borisoglebsk flight school 1934. CPSu 1937. At the front from 1941. By December 1941 was Major & sqdn Cdr in 40 BAP-ChF. 87 sorties. KIA 29 December 1941. HSU 22 February 1944.

Turikov, Aleksei Mitrofanovich, born 3 February 1920 in Zal'kovo, Smolensk Region, in a peasant family. Completed a pedagogical institute and worked as a teacher. Army 1938. Melitopol Military Aviation Institute of Air Observers 1940. At the front from June 1941. By February 1943 was Captain & sqdn navigator in 99 BBAP. 145 sorties. 6 air victories. HSU 1 May 1943. CPSU 1943. Borisoglebsk Military Aviation Institute of pilots 1945. Air Force Academy 1954. Col retired 1960.

Turkov, Nikolai Yakovlevich, born 22 May 1913 in Orenburg in a Mordvin white-collar family. Completed 3 courses at a grain-milling *technikum*. Navy 1938. Nikolaev Naval Aviation Institute 1939. CPSU 1939. At front from June 1941. By June 1944 was Captain & Sqdn Cdr in 118 RAP-SF. 195 sorties. HSU 22 July 1944. Naval Academy 1949. Col retired 1956.

THE PETLYAKOV Pe-2

Tuzov, Mikhail Filippovich, born 1 November 1907 in Bol'shoe Syr'kovo, Moscow Region, in a peasant family. Lived in Moscow. Completed a *Rabfak* and worked as a solderer in a lamp factory. CPSU 1931. Army 1933. Voroshilovgrad flight school 1934. Finnish war 1939-40. At front from June 1941. By August 1944 was Major & Sqdn Cdr. in 4 GBBAP. 181 sorties. 2 air victories. HSU 23 February 1945. Lt Col retired 1954.

Tyulenev, Ivan Nikolaevich, born 25 November 1915 in Borykovo, Kalinin Region, in a working-class family. Completed 6th grade and an FZU. Worked as a metal worker. Army 1934. Kacha flight school 1936. Finnish War 1939-40. CPSU 1941. At the front from June 1941. By July 1943 was Captain & Sqdn Cdr in 367 BAP. 156 sorties. HSU 24 August 1943. Higher Air Tactics Course 1947. To Navy in 1950 where he commanded an air division. General Staff Academy 1956. Col retired 1958.

Tyurikov, Sergei Petrovich, born 12 September 1910 in Rzhev, Kalinin Region, in a working-class family. Completed 6th grade and worked in a flax mill. Army 1931. Kharkov military aviation school 1938, CPSU 1938. Occupation of eastern Poland and Finnish War. To the front in June 1941. By February 1945 was Major & Regtl navigator of 4 GBBAP. 179 sorties, 20 air combats, 3 air victories. HSU 18 August 1945. Higher officers' school for navigators 1947. Lt Col retired 1958.

Usachyov, Filipp Aleksandrovich, born 1 October 1908 in Tasevo, Krasnoyarsk Region, in a peasant family. Completed 7th grade and worked on a collective farm. CPSU 1931. Army 1932. Flight school 1932. At front from June 1941. By April 1945 was Lt Col and Cdr of 15 ORAP-KBF. 142 sorties. HSU 20 April 1945. Col retired 1956.

Usenko, Konstantin Stepanovich,[11] born 20 April 1920 in Kirovsk, Donets Region in a Ukrainian working-class family. He completed the seventh grade and a chemical *technikum* and then worked as a technician in a chemical plant until entering the military in 1938. He completed flight school at Voroshilovgrad in 1940. In autumn 1940 he was sent to the 13 SBAP (9 SAD) as a junior lieutenant. He was in combat with the front from the start of the war. At first the regiment flew the Tupolev SB and the Ar-2. However, the regiment's aircraft were destroyed during the first days. By July it received the Petlyakov Pe-2, which it used in the dive-bombing role. Just between the periods July 16 to August 19, 1941, he completed 41 sorties, and fought 37 air combats. He destroyed 4 tanks, 22 trucks, 3 trains, and 6 artillery batteries, 3 DOT bunkers, 7 supply dumps, a hangar, and other targets. His crew claimed 4 fighters shot down during air combat. In early September 1941 his aircraft was badly hit during a mission and set afire. Instead of baling out over occupied territory, Usenko and his crew flew their burning bomber back over friendly lines before baling out. Usenko was the last to bale out and was badly burned, requiring time in the hospital. At the end of 1941, 13 BAP was withdrawn from the front lines for rebuilding in the deep rear.

Pe-2 PILOT BIOGRAPHIES

In May 1942 the regiment received the Pe-3 and was re-designated as a RAP. From July to November 1942 the regiment flew patrols over the Arctic convoys. In 1942 he joined the Communist Party. In August 1943 he was re-assigned to 12 GPBAP-KBF (73 BAP before 31 May 1943). In late January 1944 he was promoted to Captain and command of 1st squadron. By September 1944 he had flown 95 missions. He was awarded the HSU on November 5, 1944. In January 1945 he was promoted to Major and given command of 12 GBAP-KBF, when the regimental commander was sent to the General Staff Academy. By the end of the war Usenko had flown 156 sorties over the Baltic, in addition to those flown earlier. After the war he remained in service and graduated from the Naval Academy in 1953. He retired as a Colonel in 1960.

Ushakov, Viktor Georgievich, born 1 March 1914 in Ekaterinoslav, in a working-class family. Completed 6th grade and an FZU. Worked as an electrical metals worker. Army 1934. Voroshikovgrad flight school 1936. Khalkin Gol 1939. CPSU 1940. To front in July 1941. By August 1942 was Captain & sqdn Cdr in 150 BAP. 180 sorties, of which 97 were at night. HSU 23 November 1942. Advanced officers' course at Air Force Academy 1950. Colonel killed in the line of duty 5 November 1956.

Vazhinski, Aleksandr Grigor'evich, born 27 February 1910 in Maikop in a working-class family. Completed primary school and worked as an electrician. Army 1933. Khar'kov flight school 1936. CPSU 1942. Front in July 1943. By April 1945 was Major & sqdn Cdr in 6 BAP (219 BAD) 116 sorties. HSU 27 June 1945. Released from service in 1947.

Valentik, Dmitrii Danilovich, born 23 February 1907 in Raikovo, Vitesk Region, in a Belorussian peasant family. He completed three courses at a Rabfak and worked in his native village. Army 1929. Orenburg flight school 1931. Course for commanders of flights at Borisoglebsk in 1936. In Finnish War 1939-40 was capt. & cdr of 3rd Sqn of 5 SBAP (14 Army). His squadron flew 26 missions and in 3 air combats shot down 5 enemy fighters (Note: this was the squadron, not Valentik himself). HSU 7 May 1940. During SWW was Lt Col and BAP commander. 115 sorties. Colonel retired 1955.

Vishenkov, Vladimir Mikhailovich, born 15 May 1922 in Khar'kovo, Smolensk Region, in a peasant family. 10th grade. Army 1940. Engels flight school 1941. Went to front in August 1942. CPSU 1943. By November 1943 was Sr Lt 8 DRAP. 133 sorties. HSU 13 April 1944. Air Force Academy 1952. General Staff Academy 19958. Colonel Retired 1975.

Vlasov, Ivan Pavlovich, born 15 July 1912 in Teryaevka, Penza Region, in a peasant family. Secondary education. CPSU 1932. Army 1934. Vol'sk & Borisoglebsk flight schools. During Finnish War Capt. & Sqdn Cdr 50 BAP (18 SBA Bde.). 52 sorties. HSU 21 March 1940. Flew during SWW. Col. Killed in flying accident 6 February 1957.

THE PETLYAKOV Pe-2

Voronkov, Mikhail Mikhailovich, born 17 January 1910 in Dmitrievski, Donetsk Region, in a Ukrainian miner's family. Completed a *Rabfak* and 2 courses at a pedagogical institute. CPSU 1929. Army 1931. Flight school 1934. During Finnish war was Capt. & sqdn Cdr in 50 SBAP. 56 sorties. HSU 21 March 1940. During SWW commanded a PBAP. Lt Col retired 1968.

Vysotski Pyotr Iosifovich, born 12 January 1916 in Shiryaevo, Sumi region, in a peasant family. Completed 7th grade and worked as metalworker. Army 1935. Kacha flight school 1937. Finnish war 1939-40. CPSU 1941. At front from start of war. By middle of 1944 Major & Sqdn Cdr of 80 BBAP (261 SAD). 143 sorties. HSU 2 November 1944. Killed in flying accident 12 January 1946.

Yalovoi, Ivan Pavlovich, born 8 January 1919 in Avdot'evka, Dnepropetrovsk Region, in a Ukrainian working-class family. Completed 9th grade and an FZU and worked as an electrical repairman in a pipe factory. Completed an Aeroclub. Army 1937. Kacha flight school 1938. At front from June 1941. CPU 1943. By February 1945 was Major & sqdn Cdr in 745 BAP. ó26 sorties. HSU 15 May 1946. Higher officers' air tactics course 1947. Studied at Air Force Academy. Col retired 1960.

Yanitski, Vasilii Ivanovich,[12] born 28 February 1916 in Staryi Kuak, in the future Tatar ASSR, in a peasant family. Completed 7th grade and worked on collective farm. Completed two courses at a *technikum*. Completed the Tambov Civil Aviation Flight Academy in 1939. Worked as Aeroflot pilot in eastern Siberia. Army 1940, and completed course for advanced plight training. To front in June 1941. Lt and Deputy Sqdn Cdr in 52 BBAP (270 BAD). On 20 June 1942, while attacking enemy troop concentrations, his Su-2 was hit by flak and he was wounded in the side. He pressed on with his mission and, after dropping his bombs, managed to return and land at his home base. HSU 12 August 1942. CPSU 1943. Air Force Academy 1946. Then teacher at Borisoglebsk Aviation Academy. Col retired 1970.

Yashchuk, Rostislav Davydovich, born 4 January 1915 in Chernigov, in a Ukrainian working-class family. Completed the Leningrad Chemical-Technological Institute. Army 1937. Chelyabinsk Military navigation Institute 1940. CPSU 1941. To the front in August 1942 as air observer. By October 1943 was Sr Lt in 47 GORAP. 75 sorties. HSU 4 February 1944. Lt Col retired 1957.

Yatskovski, Serafim Vladimirovich, born 2 January 1917 in Tbilisi, in a working-class family. Completed 7th grade and an FZU in Leningrad. Completed an Aeroclub in1934 and then worked as a flight instructor in Dushanbe. Army 1939. Poltava military aviation school 1941. At the front from June 1941. CPSU 1943. By March 1945 was Captain and Deputy Sqdn Cdr in 164 GORAP. 230 sorties. 2 individual aerial victories. HSU 18 August1945. Was wounded and released to the reserves, but returned to active service in 1951. Completed Air force Academy. Lt Col retired 1963.

Pe-2 PILOT BIOGRAPHIES

Yurchenko, Fyodor Sergevich, born 21 February 1913 in Topil'no, Cherkass Region, in a Ukrainian peasant family. Completed 7th grade and worked on a collective farm. Army 1935. Kharkov Air observer school 1937. Khalkin-Gol 1939. CPSU 1939. At front from June 1941. By May 1942 was Captain & sqdn navigator in 44 SBAP. 143 sorties, 116 of them at night. HSU 10 February 1943. Died of wounds 16 October 1943.

Yur'ev, Leonid Vasil'evich, born 29 June 1915 in Platovo, Kursk Region, in a working class family. Completed an FZU and a Rabfak, and then worked as a lathe operator. Army 1937. CPSU 1939. Krasnodar Military Navigators Institute 1940. At front from June 19941. By January 1944 was Sr Lt and senior air observer of 98 GORAP. 90 sorties. 17 January 1944 KIA. HSU 13 April 1944.

Yurkin, Nikolai Ivanovich, born 18 November 1918 in Yamnoe, Bryansk Region, in a peasant family. Completed a medical assistants' school. Army 1939. Novosibirsk flight school 1940. To the front in August 1941. CPSU 1943. By September 1943 was Sr Lt & flight Cdr in 98 GORAP. 113 sorties. HSU 28 September 1943. Col retired 1960.

Zaitsev, Nikolai Sergevich, born 6 December 1911 in Samara in a working-class family. Completed middle school. Army 1929. Borisoglebsk flight school 1932. At Khalkin Gol 30 sorties. At front from June 1941. By April 1945 was Lt Col & Regtl Cdr 80 GBAP. 111 sorties. HSU 27 June 1945. Higher Officers' Air Tactics course 1948. CPSU 1953. Col retired 1958.

Zapadinski, Aleksandr Semyonovich, born 6 June 1914 in Kal'nik, Vinnitsa Region, in a Ukrainian peasant family. Completed an agricultural mechanisation *technikum* in1935 and then worked as a mechanic on a local MTS. Army 1936. Melitopol Military Aviation Academy 1940. To front in September 1941. CPSU 1942. By November 1943 was Sr Lt air observer in 118 ODRAE (7 VA, Karelian Front). 148 sorties. HSU 4 February 1944. Higher Officers' Navigation School 1947. Major retired 1957.

Zavadski, Vladimir Georgievich, born 13 January 1919 in Cherkasovo, Vitebsk Region, in a Belorussian working-class family. Completed middle school. Army 1939. Engels Military Aviation Academy 1940. CPSU 1940. At front from June 1941. By April 1944 was Sr Lt & dep. sqdn Cdr in 511 ORAP. 115 sorties. HSU 26 October 1944. Major retired 1955.

Zavrazhnov, Ivan Dmitrievich, born 11 November 1906 in Ryazan, in a working-class family. Completed primary school. Army 1924. Ryazan flight school 1927. CPSU 1931. Higher air tactics school 1938. Occupation of Eastern Poland 1939. Finnish War 1939-40. At front from start of war. By August 1943 was Lt col & Cdr of 72 ORAP. 54 sorties, 1 air victory. KIA 28 August 1943. HSU 28 September 1943.

THE PETLYAKOV Pe-2

Zevakhin, Mikhail Stepanovich, born 12 September 1922 in Gorevskaya, Kirov Region, in a peasant family. Completed 7th grade and studied at an Aeroclub. Army 1939. Perm flight school 1940. To front in May 1942. CPSU 1943. By September 1943 was Sr Lt & flight Cdr in 11 ORAP. 198 sorties, 122 bombing missions, and 76 reconnaissances. KIA 13 January 1944. HSU 4 February 1944.

Zhivolup, Mikhail Andrevich, born 22 July 1909 in Kovsharovka, Khar'kov Region, in a Ukrainian working-class family. Beginning secondary school. Worked as truck driver. Army 1929. CPSU 1931. Minsk flight school 1933. Borisoglebsk flight school 1935. 65 sorties during Finnish War. At front from start of war. By September 1943 was Lt Col and Cdr of 126 GBAP. 107 sorties. HSU 28 September 1943. After the war commanded a regiment and then a division. Higher Officers' Air tactics course 1948. General Staff Academy 19954. Maj. Gen. retired 1960.

Zhmaev, Nikolai Romanovich, born 8 May 1916 in Miass, Chelyabinsk Region, in a peasant family. Completed an FZU and worked as a metalworker. Army 1937. Junior aviation specialist school 1938. Fought at Khalkin Gol. At front from start of war. CPSU 1942. By April 1945 Starshina. Chief of squadron communications in 36 GBAP. 300 sorties. Shot down 3 individual and 5 shared victories. 12 aircraft destroyed on ground. HSU 27 June 1945. Demobilised at end of war.

Zhmurko, Ivan Matvevich, born 29 August 1914 in Stepashki, Vinnitsa Region, in a Ukrainian peasant family. Completed a village school and then worked as a bookkeeper. Army 1935. Khar'kov Infantry academy 1938. Khar'kov Aviation Navigators' Academy 1939. Finnish War 1939-40. At front from start of war. CPSU 1943. By April 1945 was Captain and sqdn navigator in 35 GBAP. 206 sorties. HSU 15 May 1946. Krasnodar Higher Officers' navigation school 1949. Killed in line of duty 4 August 1955.

Zholudev, Leonid Vasil'evich, born 27 May 1917 in Luzhki, Pskov Region, in a peasant family. Completed 9th grade in a factory school, then worked in a construction trust in Leningrad. Army 1936. Orenburg Military Aviation Academy 1939. CPSU 1939. To front in July 1941. By February 1945 was Capt. and sqdn Cdr in 35 GBAP. 193 sorties. HSU 18 August 1945. Air Force Academy 1950. Series of responsible command and staff positions, including staff assignment to Warsaw Pact forces command. Honoured Pilot of USSR. Lt General retired 1976.

Zinchenko, Nikolai Aksyonovich, born 29 November 1918 in Vishnyovyi Dol, North Caucasus in a Ukrainian family. Secondary school. Army 1937. Voroshilovgrad flight school. Finnish war Junior Lt 50 SBAP (18 SBAB- 7 Army). 21 sorties. HSU 21 March 1940. At front from June 1941. CPSU 1941. Air Force Academy 1943. Shot down in air battle and KIA 26 February 1944.

Pe-2 PILOT BIOGRAPHIES

Zlydennyi, Ivan Dmitrievich, born 14 April 1919 in Kopanskoe, Orenburg Region, in a Ukrainian peasant family. Completed a medical assistants' school. Army 1939. Orenburg military aviation academy 1940. To front July 1941. CPSU 1941. By July 1944 was Sr Lt and senior air observer in 99 G ORAP. 148 sorties. HSU 19 August 1944. Military-Political Academy 1954. Col retired 1975.

Zolin, Ivan Leon'tevich, born 20 July 1907 in Klyuchi, Perm Region, in a peasant family. Completed 3rd grade. In 1929 was one of the first to go to a collective farm. and became local Komosmol secretary. Later District Komosmol secretary. CPSU 1932. Army 1933. Orenburg military aviation academy 1933. At front from start of war. Sr Lt and Deputy Sqdn Cdr 242 BAP. 28 sorties. 23 September 1941 was shot down and crashed his burning aircraft into enemy target. HSU 6 June 1942.

Zubovka, Antonina Leont'evna, born 12 October 1920 in Semion, Ryazan' Region in a peasant family. She completed 3 courses at the Mechanical-Mathematical Institute of Moscow State University. In October 1941 she volunteered for the army, and in 1942 completed training as a navigator at Engels. She went to the front in January 1943 with 587 BAP (later 125 GBAP). During 1944 she joined the Communist party. By March 1945 she was a Guards Senior Lieutenant and a squadron senior navigator. She had flown 56 sorties. She and her crew were credited with 2 fighters shot down in 5 air combats. She was awarded the HSU on 18 August 1945. Left the service in September 1945.

Zumbulidze, Boris Zakharovich, born 7 June 1945 in Gori, Georgia, in a Georgian orking- class family. Completed *Rabfak* in 1924 and called to army. Completed infantry school 1927. CPSU 1929. Air Observer school 1932. Flight school 1935. In action from June 1941. By April 1945 was Lt Col & Regtl Cdr of 406 NBAP. More than 100 sorties. HSU 29 June 1945. Retired 1954.

Appendix 4

Glossary

Abbreviation	Russian Title	English equivalent
AA	*Armeiskaya Aviatsiya*	Army Air Force
AD	*Aviatsionnoya Diviziya*	Air Division
ADD	*Aviatsiya Dal'nevo Deistviya*	Long-Range Aviation (from March 1942 - formerly DBA)
ADF	n/a	Airborne Direction Finding
AE	*Avicionnaja Eskadrilija*	Reconnaissance Aviation Squadron (Yugoslavia)
AFA	*Aviatsionnyi FotoApparat*	Aviation Camera
AGOS	*Aviatsiya, Gidroviatsiya I Opytnoe Stroitel'stvo*	Aviation, Hydro-Aviation and Experimental
AK	*Avtomat Kurs*	Automatic course
AON	*Aviatsiya osobov naznacheniya*	Special Purpose Air Arm
AP	*Aviatsionny Polk*	Air Regiment
AP Pogody	*Aviatsionny Polk Pogody*	Weather Reconnaisance Regiment
AP-DD	*Aviatsionny Polk-Dal'nyaya Dvukhmestny*	Long Range Air Regiment
APR GK KA	*Aviatsiya Razviedchik Polk Glavnovo Komandovaniya Krasnaya Armeiskaya*	Aviation Reconnaissance Aviation Regiment of Red Army Supreme Council
A-VMF	*Aviatsiya Voenno-Morskovo Flota*	Soviet Navy Air Arm
Ap	*Avijacijski Puk*	Yugoslavia
A-PVO	*Aviamatka- Protivo Vozdushnaja Oorona*	Aviation - protective air defence
ASShL	*Avarijni sbrasivatel' shturmana s lyebyodkoi*	Emergency release mechanism (operated by) navigator with winch (to open bomb bay hatches)
BAD	*Bombardirovochnaya aviatsionnaya diviziya*	Bomber Air Division
BAK	*Bombardirovochnaya aviatsionnaya korps*	Bomber Air Corps
BAO	*Batak'on aerodromnogo obsluzhivaniya*	Airfield Service Battalions

410

GLOSSARY

BAP	*Bombardirovochnyi Aviapolk*	Bomber Air Regiment
BBAP	*Blizhni bombardirovshchik Aviatsionnaya polk*	Close Range Air Regiment
BBS	*Blizhni bombardirovshchik Skorostnoi*	High-speed close-range bomber
Bd	*Bojova Divize*	Combat Air Division (Czechoslovakia)
Bd	*Bombarderska Divizija*	Bomber Division (Yugoslavia)
Bp	*Bombarderski Puk*	Bomber Squadron (Yugoslavia)
CG	n/a	Centre of Gravity
ChF	*Chyornaye Morye Flotta*	Black Sea Fleet
CPSU	*Vsesoiuznaia Kommunisticheskaia Partiia*	Communist Party of the Soviet Union (Party Member)
DAG	*Degtyarev aviatsionny Gosudarstvenny*	Degtyarev (aircraft gun designer – state produced)
DBA	*Dal'nebombardirovochnaya aviatsiya*	Long-Range Bomber Aviation (*re-named ADD in March 1942*).
DBA-GK	*Dal'nebombardirovochnaya aviatsiya Glavnovo Komandovaniya*	Supreme Command Long-Range Bomber Force
DEU	*Dal'nebombardirovochnaya E U*	
DLB	*Dywizja Lotnictwa*	Polish Aviation Force
DRAP	*Dal'nebombardirovochnaya Razvedchik Aviacionny Polk*	Long Range Reconnaissance Aviation Regiment
EMZ	*Eksperimental'nii Mashinostroitel'nii Zavod*	Experimental Machine-building Plant
ESBR	*Elektrosbrasivatel'*	Emergency electrically-operated release mechanism
FAB	*Fugsasnaya AviaBomba*	Demolition Bomb
FT	*Frontovoye Trebovaniye*	Front Line Demand
FZ	*Frontovoye Zadani*	Front Line Task
FZU	*F Zavod Univirsityet*	Technical University
GAZ	*Gousudarstvenny Aviatsionny Zavod*	State Aircraft Factory
GBAD	*Gvardeiskyi Bombardirovochnyi Aviatsjonnyi*	Guards Bombardment Aviation Division
GBAK	*Gvardeiskyi Bombardirovochnyi Aviatsjonnyi Korpus*	Guards Bombardment Aviation Corps
GBAP	*Gvardeiskyi Bombardirovochnyi Aviatsjonnyi Polk*	Guards Bombardment Aviation Regiment
GKO	*Gosudarstvennyy Komitet Oborony*	State Defence Committee

THE PETLYAKOV Pe-2

Abbreviation	Russian Title	English equivalent
Gneis	PNB-1 (based on German FuG 220 set)	Radar Detection and Interception
GUAP	Glavnoe Upravlenie Aviatsionnoi Promyshlennoti	Main Administration of Aircraft Industry
GUAS	Glavnoe Upravlenie Aviatsionnoi Sluzhba	Chief Directorate of Aviation Service
GU-VVS	Glavnoe upravlenie-Voenno-vozdushnye sili	Chief Directorate – Air Force
Gv	Gvardeiskyi	Guards
GVF	Grazhdanki Vozdushny flot	Civil Air Fleet
GYZiTS VVS KA		Main Administration of Requisition and Technical Supply of the Air Force
HSU (GSS)	Geroi Sovetskogo Soiuza	Hero of the Soviet Union
IAK	Istrebitelnyyi Aviacionnyi Korps	Fighter Aviation Corps
IAP	Istrebitelnyi Aviacionnyi Polk	Fighter Aviation Regiment
	Ishak	Donkey
KB	Konstruktorskoe byuro	Design Bureau
KBF	Krasnaya Baltiskaye Morye Flotta	Red Banner Baltic Fleet
KOSOS	Konstruktorski Otdel Opytnovo Samolyotostroeniya	Experimental Aircraft Design Section
KZ	Khimicheskoe zazhiganie	Chemical ignition
LBAP	Lyokhki Bombardirovohnaya Aviacionnyi Polk	Light Bomber Air Regiment
LeLv	Lentolaivue	Flying Squadron (Finnish)
LeP	Letecky pluk	Bomber Regiment (Czechoslovakia)
LII	Leno-issledovatel'skii Institut	Flight Research Institute
LIS	Leno-issledovatel'skii Samolyotostroeniya	Flight Test Station
MD	n/a	Military District
MDZ	Mnogotochechni derzhatel' zamkovij	Multi-point bomb holder on locks
MKL	Mieszanego Korpusu Lotnictwa	Polish Aviation Corps
MN	Mazharousky & Venevidov	Mazharousky & Venevidov designed aviation gun mounting
MVTU	Mkoskovskoe Vysshee Teknicheskoe Uchilishche	Moscow Higher Technical School

GLOSSARY

NII-VVS	*Nauchno-spytael'ny Insitute - Voenno-vozdushnye sili*	Scientific Test Institute of Soviet Air Force
NII	*Nauchno-ispytatel'ny*	Scientific Test Institute
NKAP	*Narodnij Kommissariat Tiazholoj Promyshlennosti*	Peoples Commissariat for Heavy Industry
NKO	*Narodnyy Komissariat Oborony*	Peoples Commissariat of Defence
NKPB	*Nochi dastaoprimichatyel'nasti*	Night Aviation bomb sight
NKVD	*Narodnij Komissariat Vnutrennik Del*	Peoples Commissariat for Internal Affairs
Obt	*Oblast*	Soviet political-administrative unit/area
OKB	*Opytno Konstructorskoe Buro*	Experimental Design Bureau
OKO	*Osdbyj Konstructorkjij Otdel*	Special Design Section
OMAG	*Osdbyj*	Special Naval Aviation Group
ORAE	*Osoboe Razvedchik Aviacionnyi Eskadrille*	Long-range Reconnaissance Aviation Squadron (Navy)
ORAP	*Osoboe Razvedchik Aviacionnyi Polk*	Special Reconnaissance Air Regiment
Osoaviakhim	*Obshchestvo sodeistviya oborone, aviatsionnomu I khimicheskomu stroitel'stvu*	Society for the Support of Defence and Aviation and Chemical Construction
OTB	*Osoboe Tekhnicheskoe Byro*	Special Technical Bureau
P	*Pikiruyushchi*	Dive
	Pary	Two-plane section
PB	*Pikiruyushchi Bombardirovochny*	Dive Bomber
	Peshka	Chess Pawn
PBAP	*Pikiruyushchi Bombardirovochny Aviatsionny Polk*	Dive Bomber Aviation Regiment
PLB	*Pulk Lotnictwa Bombowkego*	Regiment of Bomber Aviation (Polish)
pplk	*podplukovnik*	Wing Commander (Czechoslovakia)
Ppk	*Podpolkovnik*	Lieutenant-Colonel
PTAB	*Protivotankovaya aviabomba*	anti-tank aviation bomb
PTsN	*Protivotankovaya Tsentral'noe Nauchny*	Experimental Anti-tank weapon.
PVO	*Protivovozdushnaya oborone*	Air Defence
R	*Razvedshchik*	Reconnaissance

413

THE PETLYAKOV Pe-2

Abbreviation	Russian Title	English equivalent
RAB	*Raion Aviatsionnovo Bazirovaniya*	Air-Base Regions
RAG	*Rezerv Aviatsionnovo Gruppa*	Reserve Air Group
RAP	*Razvedchik Aviatsionnovo polk*	Reconnaissance Air Regiment
	Rasputitsa	Rainy Season
RATO	*Raketny-A T*	Rocket-Assisted Take-off
RKKA	*Raboche-Krest'yanskaya Krasnaya Armiya*	Workers and Peasants Red Army
RKKVF	*Raboche-Krest'yanski Krasny Vozdushny Flot*	Workers and Peasants Red Air Fleet
RNII	*Reaktivno-issledovatel'ski institut*	Reaction Motor Scientific Research Institute
RO	*Roketnyi Orudie*	Rocket Projectile
RSB	*Radio stanciya bombardirovochnaya*	Bomber radio set
RSI	*Radio stanciya istrebitel'naya*	Fighter radio set
RS	*Raketny Snaryad*	Rocket Missile
RU	*Raketnyj Uskoritel'*	Rocket
RVGK	*Rezerv Verkhovnogo Glavnokomandovaniya*	*Stavka* (Supreme High Command) Reserve
SAD	*Smeshannii Aviatsionnaya Divisiia*	Composite Aviation Regiment
SAK	*Smeshannii Aviatsionnaya Korps*	Composite Aviation Corps
	Samolyet	Aircraft
SBAP	*Skorostnoi bombardirovshchik Aviatsionnaya polk*	Fast Bomber Air Regiment
SEL-MW	*Samodzielna Eskadra Lotnicza- Marynarki Wojennej*	Independent Aviation Flight (Polish Navy)
	Seriinyi	Series
SF	*Syevyer Flotta*	Northern Fleet
ShKAS	*Shpital'nyy-Komarnitskiy aviat sionnyy skorostrel'nyy (pulemet)*	7.62-mm rapid-fire aircraft machine gun designed by Shpital'nyy and Komarnitskiy
	Shturman	Navigator
	Shturmovik	Ground-Attack
ShVAK	*Shpital'nyy-Vladimirov aviatsionnaya krupnokalibernaya (pushka)*	20-mm heavy aircraft cannon designed by Shpital'nyy and Vladimirov
	Sotka (Sotnya)	one hundred

GLOSSARY

SPB	*Skorostnyi Pikiruyushchii Bombardirovshcik*	Fast Dive Bomber
SPBN	*Skorostnyi Pikiruyushchii Bombardirovshcik Naznacheniya*	Independent Regiment of Dive Bombers
Stavka	*Shtab Glavnovo/ Verkhovnovo Komandovaniya*	Supreme Command Staff
STO	*SpetsTekhOdyel*	Special Technical Department
	sto	hundred
TAR	*Tamansky*	Womens Air Regiments
TASSR	*Tatarskaia Avtonomnaia Sovetskaia Sotsialisticheskaia Respublika*	Autonomous Tatar Republic
TOF	*Tikhi Akian Flotta*	Pacific Ocean Fleet
TsAGI	*Tsentral'nyi Aero-Gidrodinamicheskii Institut*	Central Institute for Aerodynamics and Hydrodynamics
TsIAM	*Tsentral'nyi Institut Aviatsionnovo Motorostroeniya*	Central Aero-engine Institute
TSS	*Turel' skorostnogo samolyota*	Fast aircraft gun mounting
UAG	*Udarnaia Aviatsiia Gruppa*	Shock Aviation Group
UBK	*Universal'ny Berezina Kryl'evoj*	Berezin-designed Universal Aviation 20-mm cannon (wing-mounted)
UBT	*Universal'ny Berezina Turel'nij*	Berezin-designed multipurpose machine-gun turret modification
UZSiM GUZiTS VVS		
UT	*Uchebno Trenirovochnyi*	Advanced trainer
VA	*Vozdushnaya Armiya*	Air Army
VI	*Vysotnyi Istrebitel'*	High-Altitude Fighter
VIAM	*Vsesoyuzny Institut Aviatsionnyich Materiialov*	All-union Scientific Research Institute for Aviation Materials
VISh	*Vint c 'zmenyaemovo shaga*	Variable-pitch propeller
VNOS	*Vozdushnoye nablyudeniye, opoveshcheniye I svyaz*	Air Observation, Warning and Communications.
VK	*Vladmir Klimov*	(Aircraft designer)
VKP(b)	*Vsesoyuznay a kommunisticheskaya partiya (bol'shevikov)*	All-Union Communist Part of the Soviet Union (Bolsheviks)
	Voyentechnik 1 ranga	Military Technician 1st Class
VUB	*Vozdushnaia Ustanovka Berezina*	Toporov-designed gun mounting
VV	*Vazdushni Voyki*	Bulgarian Air Force
Vm	*Vazduhoplovni muzej*	Air Force Museum (Yugoslavia)

THE PETLYAKOV Pe-2

Abbreviation	Russian Title	English equivalent
VVS-VMF	*Aviatsiya Voyenno-morskogo flota*	Navy Air Force
	Vertushka	Dipping Wheel
VVS	*Voenno-vozdushnye sili*	Military Air Force
VVS-RKKA	*Voenno-Vozdoshnye sili- Raboche-krest 'yanski krusny aeroflot*	Workers and Peasants Red Air Fleet
ZAB	*Zapasnaya aviatsionnaya brigada*	Aviation Depot Brigade
ZOS	*Zemmoye obespecheniye samoletovozhdeniya*	Ground-based navigational aide.
ZOK	*Zavod Opytnii Konstruktsii*	Experimental Design Plant
	Zveno	Squadron Leaders
	Zven'ya	Three-plane section

Appendix 5

Some Pe-2 Aces

Name	Unit	Sorties	Details
Kuznetsov, N.V.		360	7 ships, 5 tanks, 5 aircraft, 11 carriages, 21 cars, 1 locomotive, 2 warehouses, 3 bridges, many strongpoints, etc.
Zholudev	150 BAP (37 Gv BAP)	200+	
Kopeykin, I.V. (Gunner)	150 BAP (37 Gv BAP)	200+	Several aircraft in 60+ air combats
Gapeyonok, N.I.	202 SBAP (*1 GvBAP)	198	
Sayevich, T.A	110 RAP	186	
Danilov, A.V.	161 GvBAP	178	24 in Finland
Scheglov, S.S. (Navigator)	128 BAP	173	10 in Finland
Rakov, V.I.	30 AG, 12 GshAP, 9 ShAD	170	12 ships
Sirenko, I.V.	34 GvBAP	155	Some aircraft
Pavlov, N.D. (Gunner)	4 GvBAD	150	62 air combats 4 certains, 6 probables
Polbin, I.S.	150 BAP, 301BAD, 1 (2G, 6G) BAK	147	See Panel
Logvinenko, A.P.	95IAP (Pe-3)	146	4 tanks, 3 ships, 9 tanks, 45 cars, 2 trains
Dzunkovskaya, (Markova) G.I.	125 GvBAP	125	2 aircraft
Kochetkov, K. (Gunner)	9 BAP	125	43 air combats – 15 aircraft
Gusev, V. (Gunner)	150 (37 G) BAP	?	10 aircraft
Sergetev, V.P.	48 Gv APDR	98+	1 aircraft
Pozdnyakov, A.P.	125 BAP	75	
Dolina, M.I.	587 BAP, 125 Gv BAP	63+	3 aircraft
Fomichyova, K.J.	125 GvBAP	55	11 aircraft
Lapshenkov, S.V.	29 BAP	55	8 aircraft, 4 ships sunk, 2 damaged.

Appendix 6

Further reading

Efremov, V S, *Eskadril'I letiat na gorizont* (Eskadrils fly toward the horizon), Voenizdat, Moscow, 1984.

Fedorov, A G, – *Do poslednego starta* (Until the last start) – Voennoe Izdagtel'stvo (Voenizdat Military Publishing), Moscow, 1965.

Fedorov, A G, *Sud'boiu stalo nebo* (Destiny became the sky), Moskovskii Rabochii, Moscow, 1972.

Silant'ev, Vladimir, *Vozdushnye razvedchiki; Zapiski Aviamekhanika* (Air Reconnaissance; Notes of an Aviation Mechanic), Molodaia Gvardiia, Moscow, 1983.

Sinitskii, A, G/Glebov, M, M/Zharko, V T, *Vozdushnye razvedchiki* (Air Reconnaissance), Izdatel'stvo, Belarus, 1987

Tsupko, P, *Nad prostormami severnykh morei* (Above the open spaces of the Northern Seas) - Molodaia Gvardiia, Moscow, 1981.

Notes

1. Inspiration Imprisoned

1. Stalin heads the league table by a very wide margin, in the number of his own people slaughtered, with an incredible 21 million Russian citizens being put to death at his orders, or dying as a direct result of his policies; this puts in the shade even Hitler's destruction of 6 million Jews and other ethnic 'undesirables' in Nazi Germany; Chairman Mao's culling of his fellow countrymen in China and Pol Pot's *Khymer Rouge* annihilation of his own nationals during the 'Killing Fields' period of Cambodian history. Such events are still very much with us, viz. the summary executions, rape and mass expulsions attributed to Serbia's Slobodan Milosevic, the one-million-plus tribal killings in Rwanda-Burundi; and more recently the mass slaughters in Democratic Republic of the Congo and in Somali.
2. *Peshka* is diminutive of Pe, which coincides with the word 'pawn', consonant with Pe. In Russian, the suffix *shka* is used to emphasise small size.
3. See Flight Lieutenant H. Griffiths, *The RAF in Russia*, London, 1942. He reported that 'in an operation that lasted as long as an hour they had to go all-out to keep station' with the Pe-2, and also stated that the *Peshka* 'climbed and flew at a rate that astounded our boys considerably'. The Air Ministry, busy rubbishing the dive-bomber at every opportunity, did not *want* to hear these facts, of course.
4. See Memo from Assistant Chief of the Air Staff, dated 3 March 1943. (AIR 20/4249) National Archives, London. 'We have no knowledge of the dive-bombing technique they employ in operating the Pe-2, nor has the Pe-2 been popularised as had the IL-2.' This was all totally untrue, for the Air Ministry had on their desks for the previous eighteen months a very detailed report from Squadron Leader Lapraik, 'P.E.2. Twin-Engined Dive Bomber, Report', dated 11 September 1941. (Air Intelligence 2 (g)- IIG/132/2/27. Contained in AIR 40/29. National Archives, London.
5. For details of all these experiences, see Peter C. Smith, *Dive Bomber!*, Ashbourne and Annapolis, 1982. Also Peter C. Smith, *Impact! The Dive Bomber Pilots Speak*, London and Annapolis, 1981.
6. See Colonel N. Denisov, *Boyevaia Slava Sovetskoi Aviatsii*, (*Fighting Glory of Soviet Aviation*) Moscow, 1968.
7. The Russians called this aircraft the SB followed by the engine fitted, i.e. SB-M100, SB-M105 etc. etc.

419

8. See Peter C. Smith, *Douglas SBD Dauntless*, Crowood Aviation Series, 1997.
9. See Peter C. Smith, *Straight Down!; the A-36A at War*, Manchester, 1999.
10. See Peter C. Smith, *Vengeance!; the Vultee Vengeance Dive Bomber*, Shrewsbury and Washington DC, 1986.
11. There has been speculation that ANT-58 might have been Tupolev's ironic choice for he had been imprisoned in Cell 58 at the Butyrkii prison for a time, but this seems unlikely and the designation merely followed on from the ANT-57 four-engined dive bomber.
12. For details of these successes, see Peter C. Smith, *Junkers Ju. 87 Stuka*, Crécy, 2011.
13. For the most complete description and history of the ANT-58-62, and the subsequent production model, the Tu-2, see Herbert Léonard, *Le Toupolev Tu-2*, Editions Heimdal, Bayeux, France, 1998.
14. See Colonel Vladimir Lesnitchenko, *Combat Composites, Russia's Operational Mother-Ships*, article in *Air Enthusiast* magazine, No. 94, London, November/December 1999.
15. *Ibid.*
16. Some American sources claim that Pe-2s led by Captain A. Tsurtsulin (sic) attacked the Ploesti oilfields 'destroying millions of tons of oil products. The sea boiled with oil for days afterwards (sic).' I don't think so.
17. See J.L. Roba & C. Craciunoiu, *Seaplanes over the Black Sea*, 1995.
18. See Field Marshal Erich von Manstein, *Lost Victories*, London, 1958.
19. See Peter C. Smith, *Stukas over the Steppe*, London, 1999.
20. The Sukhoi Su-2 and Su-6 aircraft are sometimes, totally incorrectly, referred to in Western history books as 'dive-bombers'. They were not, being designed as *Blizhnii bombardirovshchik* (Short-Range Bomber) and later adapted to perform as the *Shturmovik*, performing poorly in both guises, but they *never* acted as dive-bombers. A small dive-bomber batch of five of the N.N. Polikarpov-designed SBP was produced, but a series of accidents halted any further work in this direction.
21. See Shavrov, V.B., *Istoriya konstruktsiy samolyotov v SSSR (History of aircraft design in USSR) 1938-1950, Vol. 2* Mashinostroyenie, Moscow, 1978.
22. See Alexander Boyd, *The Soviet Air Force since 1918*, New York, 1977.
23. See Goncharov, V.N.; article in *Technika Vozdushnogo Flota (TVF)*, April 1991.
24. See Goncharov, op. cit.
25. See Kosminkov, Konstantin, 'From "Sotka" to "Peshka"', article in *Kryl'ya Rodiny*, March 1994.
26. In 1932 the former *Aviatsiya, Gidroviatsiya I Opytnoe Stroitel'stvo* AGOS (Aviation, Hydro-Aviation and Experimental Design) changed to *Konstruktorski Otdel Opytnovo Samolyotostroeniya* KOSOS (Experimental Aircraft Design Section). See Alexander Boyd, *The Soviet Air Force since 1918*, London, 1977.
27. Op. cit.
28. See V.B. Shavrov, *History of Aircraft Construction in the USSR, Vol. 2*. pp. 166-8; also A.S. Yakovlev, *Fifty Years of Soviet Aviation Industry*, in *Science*, Moscow, 1968, pp. 107-11.

NOTES

2. Many Starts, Many Endings

1. See, Air Ministry, *The Rise and Fall of the German Air Force (1933 to 1945)*, A.C.A.S.[I], London, 1948.
2. See Ionov, Kombrige P.P., *Fighter Aviation*, Moscow, 1940.
3. See Kotyel'nikov, Vladimir, *Heavy fighters by Petlyakov,* article in *Aviatsiya I Kosmonavtika,* Vol. 37, Moscow, May-June 1998
4. See Kosminkov, op. cit.
5. Kotyel'nikov, *Heavy fighters by Petlyakov,* op. cit.
6. Shavrov, Vol. 2, op. cit.
7. Kotyel'nikov, Vladimir, *Heavy fighters by Petlyakov*, op. cit.
8. See *Ing.* V. Kondratyev, *Petlyakov VI-100*, article in *Krilya Rodiny*, 1982.
9. Kotyel'nikov, *Heavy fighters by Petlyakov,* op. cit.
10. See Kotel'nikov V.R. and Leyko, O. Yu., *Pe-2 evolution*, article in AS 90/MAI publications, 1993.Translated and made available to the author by the Russian Aircraft Research Trust.
11. Goncharov, op. cit., gives the date as 20 December.
12. Kotyel'nikov, *Heavy fighters by Petlyakov,* op. cit.
13. See Kosminkov, op. cit.
14. Kotyel'nikov, *Heavy fighters by Petlyakov,* op. cit.
15. Kotyel'nikov, *Heavy fighters by Petlyakov,* op. cit.
16. Kotyel'nikov, *Heavy fighters by Petlyakov,* op. cit.
17. Goncharov, op. cit.

3. *Sotka* becomes *Peshka*

1. See Air Ministry, *Dive Bombing Techniques with High Speed Aircraft of Clean Aerodynamic Design,* OR, 2 April 1936 (AIR 2 655/831592 08862), Public Record Office, Kew, London.
2. The inaccuracy of RAF bombing was notorious, so much so that a special committee was set up to sort fact from fiction. The Butt Report came out in the summer of 1941 and was scathing. 'Mr Butt concluded that of all the aircraft recorded as having attacked their targets, only one-third had got within *five miles* of them.' Even over the French ports (mainly Brest and Lorient), just a short hop over the English Channel, 'about two-thirds of the aircraft reported to have attacked the target had actually been within five miles of it'. Over the Ruhr, the proportion was reduced to one-tenth. A French port, he estimated, was more than twice as easy to find as a target in the interior of Germany, but a target in the Ruhr was four times as difficult to locate as one elsewhere in Germany. In full moon, two-fifths of the aircraft reported to have attacked their targets had 'got within five miles of them. Without a moon the proportion fell to one-fifteenth.' See Professor Sir Charles Webster and Dr Noble Frankland, *The Strategic Air Offensive over Germany 1939-45*, 4 volumes, London, 1961. Sir Henry Tizard, Rector of Imperial College, London, and Chairman

THE PETLYAKOV Pe-2

of the Aeronautical Research Committee and Chairman of the Committee for the Scientific Study of Air Defence summed it all up in a speech he gave to the Royal United Services Institution in August 1946, in which he declared: 'The actual effort in manpower and resources that was expended in bombing Germany was greater than the value in manpower of the damage caused.' Professor Patrick M. S. Blackett recorded that 'Immediately after the war the US Bombing Survey was sent to Germany to find out what had been achieved. A very strong team (which included two men who were subsequently advisers to President Kennedy – J. K. Galbraith and Paul Nitze) produced a brilliant report, which was published in September 1945. Without any doubt the area, bombing offensive was an expensive failure. About 500,000 German men, women and children were killed but in the whole bombing offensive 160,000, US and British airmen, the best young men of both countries, were lost. German war production went on rising steadily until it reached its peak in August 1944. At this time, the Allies were already in Paris and the Russian armies were well into Poland. German civilian morale did not crack.' Article in *Scientific American*, April 1961 edition. See also Oliver & Boyd *Studies of War*, Edinburgh, 1962. Lord C.P. Snow concluded, after quoting a minute dated 15 February, 1942, by the Chief of the Air Staff, Air Chief Marshal Sir Richard E.C. Peirse, emphasising that aiming points should be defined as areas and not (for example) specific factories or war plants, wrote that 'As a piece of information, what percentage of American and English realised that this was their countries' intention? It is a very interesting example of collective moral responsibility. In the long future, perhaps the history of our times, and our methods of making war, will be written by some Asian Gibbon: if so, "The Strategic Air Offensive" will provide him with a good many of his most sardonic laughs.' Pamphlet, *A Postscript to Science and Government*, Oxford, 1962, p.49.

3. Kotel'nikov and Leyko, op. cit.
4. Kondratyev, op. cit.
5. The ShKAS machine gun had become the standard Soviet aircraft defensive machine gun since its introduction into service in 1935. Of 7.62mm calibre, it had a firing rate of 1,800rpm, a muzzle velocity of 825m/sec and a weight of 10kg.
6. Kotel'nikov and Leyko, op. cit.
7. See Official History, *The Soviet Air Force in World War II*, translated by Leland Fetzer, Edited by Ray Wagner, New York, 1973.
8. The Universal'nyi Berezina, was a 12.7mm calibre, gas-operated, multi-purpose machine gun designed by a team under M. Ye. Berezin from 1935 onward. Six prototype BS (Berezina Sinkhronnyj = synchronised) took place in 1939. The UB was a fixed installation fitted to the I-153 and the I-16 fighters firing through the propeller disc. They replaced the SShK (Degtyaryov-Shpaign Krasnoj) machine gun and had increased muzzle velocity and higher rate of fire coupled with reduced weight. By 1940 these had been modified into three variants, the UBS, with a 800rpm rate of fire, a fixed installation; UBK

NOTES

(K = Kryl'yevoj) a wing-mounted installation and the UBT (T = Turel'nyj = Flexible) mounting.

9. See Richard C. Lukas, *Eagles East: The Army Air Forces and the Soviet Union, 1941-1945*, Tallahassee, Florida, 1970.
10. See Morgala, A., *Polskie samoloty wijskowe*, Wydawnictwo MON, Warsaw, 1977.
11. This section is based on Il'dar Valeev and Rave' Kashalapov, *The Death of Petlyakov* in *Aviatsia* Magazine No.2, 1994, translated and kindly made available by the Russian Aviation Research Trust.
12. In the event the Tu-2 was later taken out of production at Omsk and replaced by the Yak.
13. Passenger trains had very low priority on the rail networks at this time, having frequently to be shunted into sidings to allow the passage of vital troops, arms and war materials to the front. A two-day trip might possibly in such circumstances take almost a week. Petlyakov was in no mood to consider such a delay.
14. Shestakov had made his name pre-war with his ground-breaking flight to the USA piloting the *Strana Sovetov*.
15. Alexander Bolnykh tells of the cruel joke that had wide circulation among Soviet pilots at this time: 'Petlyakov has built an excellent aircraft. And the landing gear he has tested himself!'

4. The Pe-2 Described

1. Squadron Leader Lapraik, *P.E.2. (sic) Twin-Engined Dive Bomber, Report*, op. cit.
2. Interestingly, test reports in Soviet documents give different figures to those quoted here. In these, the maximum diving speed of the Pe-2 was limited to 720km/h at a 60-degree diving angle. However, during the actual testing, Pe-2s in dives reached a maximum recorded speed of 760km/h. Information to the author via Nigel Eastaway, 14 November 2000.
3. Information from Andrey Mikhailov, 14 August 2000.

5. The Pe-3 fighter variant

1. Kotyel'nikov, Vladimir, *Heavy fighters by Petlyakov*, article in *Aviatsiya I Kosmonavtika*, Issue 37, May-June, 1998.
2. See Medved', Alexander N. and Khazanov, Dmitri B., article, *Unknown Pe-3*, in *Aviatsiya I Vremya*, Moscow, 1996.
3. See Smith, Peter C., *Straight Down! The North American A-36 dive-bomber at war*, Crécy Publishing, Manchester, 2000.
4. See Kotyel'nikov, V.R. and Leyko, O.Yu., *Pe-2 evolution*, article in *AS 90/ MAI publications*, 1993.
5. Kotyel'nikov, Vladimir, *Heavy fighters by Petlyakov*, op. cit.
6. Medved' and Khazanov, op. cit.

THE PETLYAKOV Pe-2

7. Kotyel'nikov, Vladimir, *Heavy fighters by Petlyakov*, op. cit.
8. Kotyel'nikov, V.R. and Leyko, O.Yu., *Pe-2 evolution,* op. cit.
9. Medved' and Khazanov, op. cit.; but Kotyel'nikov, Vladimir, *Heavy fighters by Petlyakov*, op. cit., states 16.
10. Medved' and Khazanov, op. cit.
11. Kotyel'nikov, Vladimir, *Heavy fighters by Petlyakov*, op. cit.
12. Medved' and Khazanov, op. cit.
13. The Soviet Union was woefully behind both the UK and Germany in the development of airborne radar. The USSR was helped by the capture of both ground equipment of Junkers Ju.88 night-fighters equipped with radar air-interception equipment, especially the *FuG* 220 set, which they copied as the PNB-1, but the Junkers was a much larger aircraft than the *Peshka*. The Soviet Air Force named all their radar sets after stones or crystals; *Gneis* is a grey, striped, crystalline slate with a granite-type composition.
14. Kotyel'nikov, V.R. and Leyko, O.Yu., *Pe-2 evolution,* op. cit.
15. Although an official designation, the suffix -*bis*, was often omitted from the records as they were taken from serial production Pe-2 batches and modified as expedient. Therefore, although some 300 Pe-2*bis* aircraft had been produced by 1944, they were not always recorded as such by block numbers. Some, indeed, were engined by the M-105PF and other power plants, or differently armed.
16. It also replaced the existing BS and BT types used by other Soviet combat aircraft at this period.
17. Kotyel'nikov, Vladimir, *Heavy fighters by Petlyakov*, op. cit.
18. However, Kotyel'nikov, Vladimir, *Heavy fighters by Petlyakov*, op. cit., states 530km/h.
19. Kotyel'nikov, Vladimir, *Heavy fighters by Petlyakov*, op. cit.
20. Also, incorrectly, as the FT, see V.B. Shavrov, op. cit.
21. Medved' and Khazanov, op. cit.
22. Kotyel'nikov, Vladimir, *Heavy fighters by Petlyakov*, op. cit. These Pe-3*bis* aircraft received serial numbers in the 40 six-figure series. This sequence broke down thus: - 40= Pe-3*bis* aircraft; 01 = 1st production batch; 01 = first aircraft of the batch.
23. Kotyel'nikov, Vladimir, *Heavy fighters by Petlyakov*, op. cit.
24. Kotyel'nikov, V.R. and Leyko, O.Yu., *Pe-2 evolution,* op. cit.
25. See Chapter 11.
26. Medved' and Khazanov, op. cit.
27. Medved' and Khazanov, op. cit.
28. The nineteenth machine built apparently never received VVS acceptance.
29. See Chapter 16.
30. See Chapter 5.
31. Note that the 1941 Pe-2I was a totally different aircraft to the Pe-2I developed later in the war and discussed elsewhere. As with the Pe-2M, and other variants, the use (both official and unofficial) of the *same* suffix for *different* variants being a constant headache for *Peshka* historians.

32. See Kotyel'nikov V., *Heavy fighters by Petlyakov,* op. cit.
33. See Kotyel'nikov V., *Heavy fighters by Petlyakov,* op. cit.
34. These mountings were removed from Il-2 wing stations.
35. See Kotyel'nikov V., *Heavy fighters by Petlyakov,* op. cit.
36. Medved' & Khazanov, op. cit.
37. But Kotyel'nikov, V.R. and Leyko, O.Yu., *Pe-2 evolution,* op. cit. states 1 April 1943.
38. See Kotyel'nikov V., *Heavy fighters by Petlyakov,* op. cit.

6. First Combat

1. M.N. Kozhevnikov, *The Command and Staff of the Soviet Army Air Force,* op. cit., p.26.
2. Ibid.
3. See Jackson, Robert, *The Red Falcons; the Soviet Air Force in Action, 1919-1969*, Brighton, 1970, p.87.
4. To be fair this was typical of most air forces during peacetime: it always took hard combat lessons before flexibility was tolerated, witness the RAF Fighter Command's early commitment to the rigid three-plane formation so inferior to the Luftwaffe's two-plane (*Rotte* or cell) structure.
5. See G.A. Ozerov, *Tupolevskaaya Sharaga* (The Internee Tupolev Design Bureau), Frankfurt, 1971.
6. See A.S. Yakovlev, *Tsel' Zhizni* (The Aim of Life), Moscow, 1967. It is of interest to note that even though the Soviets did not purchase the Ju.87, their Japanese allies did, two examples being shipped to Japan pre-war and tested, see Peter C. Smith, *The Junkers Ju.87 Stuka*, Crowood Aviation Series, Ramsbury, 1998. However, stories that the famous Aichi D3A1 dive-bomber were based on the Ju.87 are totally false; see Peter C. Smith, *The Aichi D3A1/2 Val*, Crowood Aviation Series, Ramsbury, 1999.
7. See Asher Lee, *The Soviet Air Force*, London, 1950, p.62.
8. Ibid.
9. Ibid.
10. See Ray Wagner (Ed) and Leland Fetzer (Trns) *The Soviet Air Force in World War II,* op. cit., p.56.
11. See John Stroud, *The Red Air Force*, London, 1943, p.22. Also Robert Jackson, *The Red Falcons*, op. cit., p.217, where the Pe-2 is described as a 'Light bomber and night fighter'. Asher Lee states that the Pe-2 was 'a splendid all-purpose machine for night fighting, reconnaissance and ground-attack. The modified all-purpose version was called the Pe-3 (*sic*)'. Not a hint from any of these British sources that the *Peshka* was first and foremost a dive-bomber. Later Lee changes her designation yet again, describing the Pe-2 and the Pe-3 as 'almost the equal of their counterpart the German Me.110', p. 144.
12. See P.M. Stefanovski, *Trista Neizvestnykh*, (Three Hundred Strangers), Moscow, 1968.

13. See Christer Bergstrom & Andrei Mikhailov, *Black Cross, Red Star*, Vol. 1, 2000.
14. Non-Pe-2 test-pilot-manned regiments set up at the same time were 401 and 402 IAPs equipped with the MiG-3 and the 430 ShAP flying the Il-2.
15. The test pilots *sals* formed 401 and 402 IAPs equipped with the MiG-3, and an unidentified ShAP, which was flying the Il-2.
16. See Von Hardesty, *Red Phoenix; The rise of Soviet Air Power 1941-1945*, Washington DC, 1982, p.22. Asher Lee, in contrast, states that there were 'virtually no major snags to report in the 1942-5 period. Petlyakov's Pe-2 and Pe-3 continued in service, and at the time of writing (1948) they are still being supplied to the Soviet Satellites, notably the Polish, Czechoslovak and Romanian Air Forces'. *The Soviet Air Force,* op. cit. p.91.
17. Alexander Boyd, *The Soviet Air Force since 1918,* op. cit.
18. See I.S. Federov, *Nachalo Moskovsky bitvy*, article in *Voyennoistoricheskiy zkhurnal*, Issue 10, 1966, p.66.
19. At this date even the DBA-GK (*Dal'nebombardirovochnaya aviatsiya Glavnovo Komandovaniy*a or Supreme Command Long-Range Bomber Force, had nine Pe-2s on its strength and, needless to say, these were quickly switched to their designed tactical role as the Panzers stormed eastward.
20. Fyodorov, A.G., *Aviatsiya v bitve pod Moskvoi* (in the Battle for Moscow, Nauka, Moscow, 1985.
21. *The Soviet Air Force in World War II,* op. cit. p.71.
22. See A.G. Fedorov, *Letchiki na zashcite Moskvy*, Moscow, 1979.
23. See von Hardestry, *Red Phoenix; The Rise of Soviet Air Power 1941-1945*, Smithsonian Institution, Washington, DC, 1982.
24. Boyd, Alexander, *The Soviet Air Force since 1918*, London, 1977.
25. See A.G. Fedorov, *Aviatsiya v bitve pod Moskvoy* (*Aviation in the Battle for Moscow*), Moscow, 1971.

7. Counter-Attack

1. Air Ministry Pamphlet, *The Rise and fall of the German Air Force (1939 to 1945)*, ACAS [I]), 1948.
2. *The Soviet Air Force in World War II,* op. cit. p.92.
3. See S.I. Rudenko, *Kril'ya pobedy*, (*Wings of Victory*) Moscow, 1973, pp.86-7.
4. *The Command and Staff of the Soviet Army Air Force,* op. cit., p.74.
5. *The Soviet Air Force in World War II,* op. cit., p.71.
6. See A.G. Fyodorov, *Aviatsiya v bitve pod Moskvoi (Aviation in the Battle for Moscow)*, Moscow, 1975.
7. *The Command and Staff of the Soviet Army Air Force,* op. cit., p.74.
8. See Lieutenant Aron Shapiro's account, quoted in Chazanow, *Nad Stalingradem*, Russian Central Military Archive TsAMO, Podolsk. Translated by Christer Bergstrom and Andrey Mikhailov, *Black Cross/Red Star: Air War over the Eastern Front*, 2001.

NOTES

9. The city had originally been name Tsartisyn, and had been the scene of Stalin's defeat of the White Russian army under General Denikin in the autumn of 1918, and much the same circumstances; no wonder the Soviet dictator felt confident of repeating the outcome. He had 1.25 million fresh troops in place behind the Volga and was producing T-34s at a rate of 1,200 a month. The Germans were at the end of their strength and had to depend on highly unreliable Italian, Hungarian and Rumanian troops to make up their numbers in the field. Hitler refused to listen to warnings on these figures, declaring them to be 'twaddle'.
10. *Command and Staff of the Soviet Air Force,* op. cit.
11. See Merono, Fransisko, *I snova v boi*, Moscow, 1977.
12. Ibid.
13. See Chapter Eight.
14. See *Pikirovshchiki*; Notes by L.N. Dubrovin, Moscow, 1986.
15. Ibid.
16. Dubrovin claims that six months in an army penal battalion was considered the equivalent of eight *years* in a Gulag!

8. New Tactics, New Defences, New Confidence

1. Andrei Alexandrov to the Author, 17 September 1999.
2. The Russian equivalent of 'Bombs Away' was *Poshel* (or *Poshyol*, pronounced 'Posh-Yole').
3. Based on information from George Mellinger to the author 25 May 2000. The two-volume *Geroi Sovetskogo Soyuza* seems to be based on the original *nagradnie listy* (awards nominations), and combat sortie totals were often drawn up en masse at the end of the war.
4. For the complete story of this convoy see: Smith, Peter C., *Arctic Victory: the story of convoy PQ18*, Crecy Publishing, Bristol, 1994.

9. Tilting the Scales – Stalingrad to the Donets

1. Fedorov can also be transliterated and is pronounced Fyodorov.
2. See Aleksei Fedorov, *V Nebe Pikirovshchiki,*
3. See *Biographical Directory of Heroes of the Soviet Union*, 2 Vols. Translated by George Mellinger.
4. *Command and Staff of the Soviet Army Air Force,* op. cit.
5. Colonel I.V. Timokhovich, *Operativnoe iskusstvo Sovetskikh VVS v Velikoi Otechestvennoi voine* (*Soviet Air Forces Tactical Skill during the Great Patriotic War*), Military Publishing House, Moscow, 1976.
6. See Dariusz Tyminski, *Piotr Kozachenko – F.J. Beerenbrock's defeater (?),* in *WWI Ace Stories,* 2001.
7. See Czeslaw Krzeminski, *Walczyli I polegli za Polske*, KAW RSW, Warsaw, 1977, pp.143-8.

10. Heroines of the Skies

1. See Madelin Blitzstein, *How Women Flyers fight Russia's Air War*, article in *Aviation* Magazine, July 1944.
2. See Peter C. Smith, *Dive-Bombers in Action*, Blandfold Press, London, 1985. For the latest in a long line of histories of Soviet female flyers, see Dr Reina Pennington, *Wings, Women and War: Soviet Airwomen in World War II Combat*. Pennington has excellent qualifications as an Intelligence Officer and Russia specialist with the USAF and DIA, including time at 'Top Gun'. Her research and interviews are outstanding but, regrettably, the unrelenting feminist overtones, seem quite unnecessary.
3. See Peter C. Smith, *The Junkers Ju.87 Stuka*, Crowood Aviation Series, 1998.
4. See L. Zabavskaya, *Women Fighter Pilots*, article *Soviet Military Review*, March, 1977 edition. It is indicative of the almost pathological aversion held in the west to any aspect of dive-bombers and dive-bombing that only the book by Bruce Myles, *Night Witches: The Untold Story of Soviet Women in Combat*, Edinburgh, 1981, based upon R.E. Aronova's *Nochnve ved'my, Rossilia*, 1969, and M.P. Chechneva's *Samolety ukhodiat v noch'* (The history of 46th Night Bomber Regiment), Moscow, 1962) and which concentrates on only the work of the Po-2 units. This book, of course, *totally* ignores the much more widespread Pe-2 operations.
5. Recommended works include M.P. Chechneva, *Letali devchata v gvadeiskom* (The Taman Aviation Regiment during the Second World War) Cheboksary, 1968; Soviet Official, *Geroni voiny*, (Women war heroes who became Hero of the Soviet Union) Moscow, 1963; and Mol Gvadiia, *V nebe frontovom*, (Distinguished women pilots), Moscow, 1962.
6. See Frontispiece.
7. See – Fedutenko, Nadezhda Nikiforovna (Obituary) *Kratkiy biograficheskiy slovar*, Moscow, 1988; Andreyev, S.A. *Sovershennoye imi bessmertno*, Moscow, 1986; Shamyakin, I.P., Ed. *Navechno v serdtse narodnom*, Minsk, 1984. Also in English: Peter C. Smith, *Dive-bombers in Action*, London, 1980; Kazimiera Janina Cottam, *Women in War and Resistance: Selected Biographies of Soviet Women Soldiers*; New Military Publishing, Nepean, Canada, 2000; Annie Noggle, *A Dance with Death, Interviews with Soviet women combat pilots*.
8. This is largely based on George Mellinger's *critique* of Reina Pennington's book, *Wings, Women & War: Soviet Airwomen in World War II Combat*, University Press of Kansas, 2001. It is noteworthy, also, that Pennington totally ignores my own unstinted praise of Soviet female Pe-2 pilots written a quarter-of-a-century earlier in books like *Dive-Bombers in Action, op. cit.*
9. See Mariya Dolin, *Pryzhok iz plameni*, M.A. Kazarinova Ed. *V nebr frontovom*, Moscow, 1971; G.I. Dzhunkovskaya-Markova, *Vzlet. O Geroye Sovetskogo Soyuza M.M. Raskovoy*, Moscow, 1986; Dzhunkovskaya-Markova G.I. *Komesk*,

NOTES

M.A. Kazarinova Ed. *V nebe frontovom*, Moscow, 1971; L.I. Stishova. Ed. *V tylu in na fronte*, Moscow, 1984.

11. The Fighting Finns

1. There are also claims by some that captured Pe-2s were used by KG.200 on clandestine missions.
2. The unprovoked Soviet attack on Finland, known as the 'Winter War', had taken place between 30 November 1939 and 2 March 1940. The tiny Finnish army initially had given the Soviet hordes a bloody nose. Eventually, sheer weight of numbers told and the Finns were forced to cede huge chunks of the vital defensive territory of Viipuri to Moscow. Not unnaturally, they were keen supporters of Hitler's attack on Russia in June 1941, if only to get their own territory back! Thus, they considered this a 'parallel' war, with the Axis against the Soviets, rather than of the Axis (even though they joined it in 1941) against the rest of the Allied powers, and so it was as a continuation of the 'Winter War' that the Finns saw it.
3. See Chapter Three. These notes are based mainly on information supplied to the Author by Hannu Valtonen, Director *of Keski-Suomen Ilmailumuseo* (Finnish Air Force Museum), 22 June 1999; also K. Keskinen, K. Stenmaa and K. Nilsen, *Finnish Air Force History, Volume 9, Russian bombers of the FAF*, English translation, and an article by Jukka Rainio for *Ilmailu* magazine, 1990, which was translated by Jukka Juutinen. Copy made available to the Author by Jukka Juutinen, 30 June 1999.
4. PE does not derive from Petlyakov but from the Finnish word *Pääeskiunta* (General Staff).

12. Production Line Progression

1. Il-2 production far exceeded these figures of course, being 39,000+, but she was a ground support aircraft, and *not* a light bomber.
2. With the end of production in the winter of 1945/46, the story quickly changed and the Tupolev very quickly replaced the Pe-2, which was phased out rapidly.
3. The most notorious example is the Pe-2-FT from the 110th series, which introduced the new Type FZ gun turret and other improvements with heavier armour protection, dive brakes were omitted and portable ShKAS side guns added. This had been repeatedly referred to as the Pe-2FT, in both Soviet and western history books, but there was *never* such a designation officially.
4. Kotel'nikov and Leyko, *Pe-2 evolution,* op. cit.
5. Ibid.

6. Sharov, Vol. 2, op. cit.
7. See Selyakov, Leonid, *Front-line demand*, article in *Kryl'ya Rodiny*, May 1995.
8. Ibid.
9. Ibid.
10. Ibid.
11. See Kotel'nikov & Leyko, *Pe-2 evolution,* op. cit.
12. Ibid.
13. Sharov, Vol. 2, op. cit.

13. The Great Offensive – June 1944

1. See *The Command and Staff of the Soviet Air Force,* op. cit.
2. See *16-ya Vozdushnaya Armiya (The 16 Air Army),* Moscow, pp.141-2.
3. See *The Command and Staff of the Soviet Air Force,* op. cit.
4. Ibid.
5. Ibid.
6. However, this claim was unsubstantiated, for the *Niobe* (built in 1899 for the German Navy, sold to Yugoslavia as the *Dalmacija* in 1925, taken over by the Italians as the *Cottaro* in 1941 and again by the Germans in 1943, reverting to her original name), ran aground on the island of Silba in the Adriatic and was there torpedoed and put out of commission by Royal Navy *MTB-298* on 22 December 1943.

14. On to Berlin!

1. The *Soviet Air Force in World War II,* op. cit.
2. Ibid.
3. See *9 maya 1945 goda*, Moscow, 1970.
4. See *The Command and Staff of the Soviet Army Air Force*, op. cit.
5. The Germans were the most advanced in this field at the outbreak of the Second World War; they had already equipped their Ju.87s and Ju.88s with such devices. See Squadron Leader D. Lapraik, Report – *The German BZA-1 Dive-Bombsight,* dated 12 September, 1941, AIR 40/36, and Royal Aircraft Establishment, Farnborough, *Report on comparisons between actual German and proposed British dive-bombing sight,* dated 1 February, 1940, National Archives, London. Despite constant pleading from the Royal Navy from 1934 onward, the Air Ministry steadfastly refused to develop such a bomb-sight for the naval dive bombers like the Blackburn Skua, see Admiralty, *Meeting of Bombing Sub-Committee on proposed dive-bombers and proposed dive-bombing sight*; AIR 20/14155, National Archives, London; Smith's Industries were later put to work on developing such a sight but nothing much came of it. In the United States, the US Navy's Bureau of Ordnance expended much time and energy on developing such a dive-bombing sight, and were ultimately successful. However, US Navy pilots scorned it, preferring to use eye-sighting

NOTES

to the last, see US Navy- *Aviation Ordnance Development*, US Navy Bureau of Ordnance, Washington, DC, 1949. Much detailed work was done in Sweden by Doctor of Technology Erick A. Wilkenson which ultimately resulted in an excellent dive-bombing sight, which aroused interest in both the United States and Britain and which was fitted to the *Flygvapnet's* dive-bombers post-war, see Dr Erick A. Wilkenson, *Dive Bombing – A Theoretical Study*, Norrkopings Tidningars Akiebolag, 1947.

6. See Peter C. Smith, *The Junkers Ju. 87 Stuka*, Crécy, 2011.
7. See Peter C. Smith, *The Aichi D3A1/2 Val*, Crowood Aviation Series, Ramsbury, 1999.
8. This section is based on a much fuller account of Polbin's life contained in Peter C. Smith, *Into the Assault – Famous Dive-Bomber Aces of the Second World War*, London & Washington DC, 1985.
9. See Soviet Official Series, *Dvazdy Geroi Sovetskogo Soyuza (Twice Heroes of the Soviet Union), I.S. Polbin*, Moscow, 1968; also *Krylatyye Syny Rodiny (Winged Sons of the Motherland)*, Moscow, 1975.
10. See Kozhevnikov, M.N., Komandovaniye *I Shtab VVS Sovetskoy Armii v Velikoy Otechestvennoy voyne 1941-1945 gg* (*Command and Staff of the Soviet Army Air Force in the Great Patriotic War 1941-1945*), Moscow, 1977.
11. Ibid.
12. *The Soviet Air Force in World War II,* op. cit.

15. Action in the Far East

1. See *Voyenno-istoricheskiy zhurnal,* No 8, Moscow, 1975, p.66.
2. M N Kozhevnikov, *The Command and Staff of the Soviet Army Air Force in the Great Patriotic War 1941-1945*, Moscow, 1977.
3. Information supplied to the Author by George Mellinger, 6 March 2002.

16. Variations on a Theme

1. See Markovsky, Viktor and Medvyed, Alexander, *Not so successful 'Peshka'*, article in *AviaMaster,* April/May 1997, translated by the Russian Aviation Trust and made available to the author.
2. See Markovsky and Medvyed, op. cit.
3. On Production Pe-2s the number of tanks had been reduced from eleven to nine, commencing with Batch No. 64.
4. See Markovsky and Medvyed, op. cit.
5. See Markovsky and Medvyed, op. cit.
6. Putilov was transferred to the TsAGI's future projects department, working on, among other things, the delta wing, until 1948. Concurrently he continued to work in education at VVIA's department of aircraft design (V.F. Bolkhovitinov) in test-bed development. Sharov, Vol.2*,* op. cit.
7. See *The successors of the legendary 'Peshka'*, article dated November 1999.

8. It was at this time that the term Pe-2D *first* began to be used in connection with this aircraft, in correspondence between OKO 22 and the UVVS RKKA.
9. In addition, a Pe-8 designation was mentioned in association with the TB-7 in September 1942.
10. See Markovsky and Medvyed, op. cit.
11. GAZ 22 was producing the *Peshka* in batches of ten-to-twelve machines at a time, at the monthly rate of 200-240 aircraft, and these planes had nowhere else to be stockpiled pending flying conditions improving.
12. See Markovsky and Medvyed, op. cit.
13. Types which thus experimentally installed the AM-82 included the Il-2, Il-4, LaGG-3, MiG-9, Pe-8 and Yak-7.
14. Based on the article *Pe-2 with radial engines* by Vladimir Kotyel'nikov, Alexander Medvyed' and Dmitri Khazanov, *Kryl'ya Rodiny,* July 1994, translated and made available by The Russian Aviation Trust.
15. Such problems were quite common, even in the USA. For a typical example see the similar difficulties encountered repeatedly by the American-built A-31/A-35 Vultee Vengeance dive-bomber at this same time, which led to its delayed entry into service, aided its rejection by the USAAF and caused numerous operational problems when operationally employed by the RAF, Free French and Brazilian air forces. Peter C. Smith, 'Trouble with the Vultee', articles in *The Army Quarterly and Defence Journal,* Tiverton, UK, Vols. 123, No.3, July 1993 & No.4, October 1993.
16. See Markovsky and Medvyed, op. cit.
17. This terminology may possibly have been the *intended* designation for the Pe-2/M082F should it have been successful, but, in the event, was *never* officially adopted or used outside these reports.
18. Sharov, Vol. 2, op. cit, states that a Pe-2 2 ASh-82FN with air-cooled radial engines with direct fuel injection obtained a maximum speed of 547km/h at 6,000m, had a ceiling of 9,100m and a limited batch resulted. One of the latter was fitted with a revised airflow section wing, which reduced approach speed from 240km/h to 200km/h. The wing profile was experimentally changed on one aircraft, which lowered the ground approach speed from 240 to 200km/h.
19. A. Yak. Shcherbakov graduated from the Kharkov Institute of Aviation and specialised in the designing pressurised cabins for high-altitude aircraft. He later designed the military transport TS-1 (Shche-2).
20. Sharov, Vol. 2, op. cit.
21. Ibid.
22. *Results of State testing of Pe-2 airplane with two VK-105PF engines, VISh-105APV airscrews, diameter D=3.1m, with modified wing.* Scientific Research Institute of Red Army Air Force (Nll VVS), Classified, Copy No. 2, Chief Engineer of Red Army Air Force General Colonel of Engineering Aviation Service, A. Replin, dated 24 June 1944. Translated by Guennadi Sloutski for the author, 6 December 1999.
23. Copies of this report were set out as follows: Copy No. 1, original, store in files of Department No 3 of Red Army Nll VVS; Copy No. 2 – to Comrade A.I. Shakhurin, People's Commissar of Aviation Industry of USSR; Copy

No. 3 – to Control Commissariat of the Central Committee of All-Union Communist party (Bolsheviks), Comrade N.S. Shimanov, Colonel General of Engineering-Aviation Service; Copy No. 4 – to Comrade A.K. Repin, Chief Engineer of Red Army Air Force, Colonel General of Engineering-Aviation Service; Copy No. 5 – to Comrade Selezniev, Head of Acquisition Department of Red Army Air Force, Lieutenant General of Engineering-Aviation Service; Copy No. 6 – to Director and Chief Designer of Factory No. 22; Copy No. 7 – to Chief Military representative at Factory No. 22. 18 June 1944.

24. Sharov, Vol. 2, op. cit.
25. Ibid.
26. See Astashenkov, P.T. *Pervye reaktivynye ustanovki na samolyotakh*, article in *Aviatsiya I Kosmonavtika,* Moscow, January 1971.
27. Based on 'Pe-2 with rocket engine', by *Ing*. K. Kosminkov, and 'RD-1 powered Pe-2' by P. Astashenkov, articles in *Krilya Rodiny*, translated and made available to the author by the Russian Aviation ResearchTrust.

17. Pe-2 Colour Schemes

1. Marcus Wendel, 2001, op cit.
2. *I-153* by Mikhail Maslov, Tekhnika-Molodezh, Moscow, 2001, pp.63-5, translated by George M. Mellinger.
3. Parts I, II, III, IV, V, VI and VII.
4. Erik Pilawski to the author, 28 November 2001.
5. Vakhlamov & Orlov, Part IV.
6. Quoted by Vakhlamaov & Orlov, Part VII.
7. See for example – V. Voronin & P. Kolesnikov, 'Sovetskie istrebitreli Velikoi Otechestvennoi voiny' (Soviet Aircraft of the Great Patriotic War) and I. Khormat, articles in *Letectvi a Kosmovautika*, Nos. 11 & 12, Moscow, 1989.
8. This series of photographs was once mounted on the wall of the old *Gosudarstvenni Musee Aviatsii*, in St Petersburg, but the collection has been dissolved.
9. Ulf Audun Larsstuvold to the author, 29 September 2003.
10. Erik Pilawski to the author, 28 November 2001.

18. The Final Developments

1. Medvyed, Alexander, 'Super-*Peshka*', article in *Avia-Master,* Vol. 2., Moscow, March 1998.
2. This author's emphasis.
3. 'Brief principles of the Pe-2I combat scheme', quoted in Medvyed, op. cit. Myasishchev's team was not alone in having to accept this fact; Tupolev had to make the same concessions.
4. And not just in the West, Selyakov recorded that after the NII VVS had evaluated the de Havilland Mosquito 'Myasishchev invited me, suggesting

developing a Pe-2 modification, to create its Soviet equivalent'. Translated and made available to the author by The Russian Aviation Research Trust.
5. Shavrov, Vol. 2, op. cit. Medvyed, op. cit, states 1,500hp.
6. Medvyed, op. cit.
7. Sharov, Vol. 2, op. cit., claims that this was designated as the Pe-2FZ .
8. Medvyed, op. cit.
9. Selyakov, Leonid, *Front-line demand,* op. cit.
10. Medvyed, op. cit.
11. Shavrov, Vol. 2, op. cit
12. Myasishchev had written direct to Stalin on 4 January 1944, telling him that 'The analysis of the series production Pe-2 at No. 22 GAZ, indicate that, given certain modifications, combined with VK-107A installation, development of a new fast day bomber, capable of 640km/h maximum speed with a 3,240km range, able to carry its entire bomb load up to 1,000kg, is viable.' So Stalin was directly in the picture long before this. Myasishchev had added in the same letter: 'The projected aircraft, with its potentially very high performance parameters, could also be utilised as a long-range or patrol fighter; such an aircraft could carry heavy firepower, including 45mm cannon. The conversion from the bomber into the fighter variant could be conducted at unit level by service technicians in field condition.' This statement was the origin of the I (*Istrebitel* or Fighter) suffix for this design.
13. Medvyed, op. cit.
14. Kosminkov, *From 'Sotka' to 'Peshka',* op. cit.
15. Medvyed, op. cit.
16. Ibid.
17. The death knell of the *Peshka* was heralded by the decision taken in July 1945, that GAZ 22 should switch to Tu-2 series production (as the B-4). I.F. Nyezval' took over the 22 OKB with A.N. Tupolev as chief designer.
18. Shavrov, Vol. 2, op. cit.
19. Medvyed, op. cit.
20. Myasishchev to P.V. Dement'yev, deputy head of NKAP, 19 January 1945.
21. All hope of mounting the DEU barbette was apparently abandoned by this time, as its faults appeared without hope of rectification without further technical advances. This was to be gleaned from captured Luftwaffe aircraft and study of the American Boeing B-29, but too late to affect the DB-108.
22. Shavrov, Vol. 2, op. cit.
23. Myasischev to Shakhurin 2 June 1945.
24. One post-war Western critic, Robert Jackson, claims that the Pe-2 night-fighters sent to protect American B-17s during the massacre at Poltava on 22 June 1944 lacked any form of AI radar and thus failed to make contact with the attacking bomber force. See Jackson, Robert, *The Red Falcons: the Soviet Air Force in action 1919-1969*, Clifton Books, 1970.
25. Medvyed, op. cit.
26. Shavrov, Vol. 2, op. cit.
27. Shavrov, Vol. 2, op. cit.

NOTES

28. NKAP Oder no. 271 which followed, confirmed Myasishchev as design support and supervisor for the servicing of the existing VVS Pe-2 fleet, with a team led by Yu.T. Shatalov with fifteen specialists, transferring to GAZ 482 for this purpose. This order was issued a week after the decision to halt Pe-2/VK-107A production at GAZ 22 and appoint A.N. Tupolev as chief designer for B-4 production there.
29. Medvyed, op. cit.
30. Among those who remained were N. Zyrin, Yu.T. Shatalov, M.K. Yangel' and P. Smirnov.
31. As a poignant footnote to the history of the *Peshka*, on 5 March 1947, the Commander-in-Chief of the VVS wrote to M.V. Khrunichev, informing him that the VB-108 with pressurised cabin had not passed the State Acceptance evaluation programme. Myasishchev was *not* so informed.
32. See G.P. Svischev (Chief Editor), *Great Russian Encyclopedia, Aviation Encyclopedia*, Moscow, 1994.
33. See V.B. Shavrov, *History of aircraft construction in the USSR,* Vol. 2, op. cit., pp.154-65. Also A.S. Yakovlev, *Fifty Years of Soviet Aviation History,* op. cit.
34. For a detailed description of the M-50 and her failure see Roy M. Braybrook, B. Sc., AFRAe.S, 'A Mighty Failure – the Bounder', article in *Flying Review International*, Vol. 20, No 3, November 1964 edition, pp.32-4.
35. See Alexander Boyd, *The Soviet Air Force since 1918,* op. cit.

19. The *Peshka* in Foreign Service

1. The author gratefully acknowledges the detailed information provided to him for this book by Robert Michulec, which proved invaluable.
2. Medved, Aleksandr, *Pol'skie aviatisonnye formirovaniiav SSSR v gody Velikoi Otechestvennoi voiny*, Istorija Aviatsii, Np. 4/2001, pp.26-9.
3. The 2 Krakow Night-Bomber Regiment, equipped with Pe-2s, was a Polish unit which Robert Jackson claims began to operate in the front line in July 1944, as part of 1st Polish Composite Air Division, see *The Red Falcons,* op. cit. Polish sources do not support this, however. The same author also claims Soviet Pe-2 night-fighters attacked RAF, USAAF and SAAF aircraft flying supplies into Warsaw during August-October 1944.
4. Sources vary on the exact date the 25th was officially formed; 9 May has been cited by some references, but 1 May 1946 is the most likely date. Information to the author from Martin Ferkl 28 October 2000.
5. The other half comprised 24th Bomber Regiment 'Atlantic' flying de Havilland Mosquito FB.VIs.
6. Information to the author from Martin Ferkl, 8 February 2001.
7. Information to the author from Martin Ferkl, 28 October 2000.
8. Information to the author from Stanislav Štěpánek, 9 July 2000.
9. See *Aeromagazine,* nos. 2 & 3, 1990, translated for the author by M. Bosanac, 2 March 2002.

10. There were *two* places of that name in the old Soviet Union, one in the Ukraine and another in the Altai Mountain region in the Far East.
11. Information to the author from Dr Zvonimir Freivogel, 3 February 2001.
12. Information to the author from George Mellinger, 13 July 2000.
13. This claim, first made in Robert Jackson's book, The *Red Falcons,* op. cit., and later repeated in *Petlyakov Pe-2 and Variants* by Malcolm Passingham and Waclaw Klepacki, Profile Publications, Windsor, is still being repeated; see for example, Przemyslaw Skuiski, *Petlyakov Pe-2 Peshka*, article in *Scale Aviation Modeller International,* Vol. 6, Issue 1, January 2001, pp.54-9, but still with no cited sources.

20. The Survivors

1. Information to the author from Dr Mikhail Souproun, 2 February 2001.
2. Information to the author from Ulf Larsstuvold, 1 October 2001.

Appendix 3

1. *Boevye zvedy Kievlyan*, pp. 100-2.
2. *Boevye zvedy Kievlyan*, pp.97-9.
3. *Boevye zvedy Kievlyan*, pp.226-8.
4. *Boevye zvedy Kievlyan*, pp.278-81.
5. Mikhailov, Lydia, 'Su-2 v boiu', *Kryl'ya Rodiny*, 7.99, pp.16-17.
6. Bubin, B. A., p. 11; Ratkin, Vladimir, 'Geroi Sovetskogo Soiuza Anatolii Ivanovich Pushkin', *Mir Aviatsii*, No.2 (19), 1999, Moscow, pp.5-8.
7. Tsupko, p.151, ff.
8. *Boevye zvedy Kievlyan*, pp.395-6.
9. Gordon, Khazanov & Medved, p.33.
10. Shinkarenko, pp.42-3.
11. Tsupko, P.I., passim.
12. Gubin, p.10.